# The Bible

# According to Einstein

A Scientific Complement to the Holy Bible

for the Third Millennium

Jupiter Scientific Publishing Company
New York, NY

# The Bible According to Einstein

Published by:
Jupiter Scientific Publishing Company
Columbia University Post Office
P. O. Box 250586
New York, NY 10025 USA

Disclaimer: In no way should *The Bible According to Einstein* be construed to be written by Albert Einstein. On the other hand, the true contributors of this book are the many men and women of science who, during centuries of work, have discovered the laws of Nature. Without their contributions, this book would not be possible. Likewise, the word "bible" in the title does not refer to the Holy Bible. Rather, it indicates the ancient meaning of the word, namely, "a collection of books."

**Publisher's Cataloging-in-Publication Data**
The bible according to Einstein : a scientific complement to the
    Holy Bible for the Third Millennium. – first edition
        p. cm.
        Includes index.
        Preassigned LCCN: 97-71753
        ISBN: 0-9655176-9-1
        1. Science. 2. Cosmology. 3. Physics.
Q175.B53 1997                 501
                              QBI97-40531

 Jupiter Scientific Publishing Company

# Table of Contents

# Introduction

The Holy Bible is one of the greatest books ever to appear. It is the holy doctrine and basis of the Christian and Judaic religions. It emerged thousands of years ago and remains widely read today.

In an art gallery in Europe, there is a medieval painting of a bearded elderly man, reading at a desk in a dark room. A candle lights a book, the man's face, and a small portion of the desk. The man through wire-rimmed glasses stares at the text. The book is the Holy Bible.

Throughout history, devout men and women, like the man in the painting, have studied and restudied the Holy Bible in search of moral truth. The Holy Bible has been a dominant force for many people for many years. It represents the word of God. For quite a few people, it says what is right and what is wrong. For example, the most basic moral principles are enumerated in the Ten Commandments:

(1) Thou shalt have only one God.

(2) Thou shalt not make any graven image of anything that is in heaven above or in earth below.

(3) Thou shalt not take the name of the Lord thy God in vain.

(4) Thou shalt labor six days and do all thy work, and thou shalt rest on the seventh day. Keep the seventh day, the Sabbath day, holy.

(5) Honor thy father and thy mother.

(6) Thou shalt not kill.

(7) Thou shalt not commit adultery.

(8) Thou shalt not steal.

(9) Thou shalt not bear false witness against thy neighbor.

(10) Thou shalt not covet thy neighbor's house, nor his wife, nor his servants, nor his ox, nor his ass, nor anything that is thy neighbor's.

These and other biblical statements provide to a large extent the moral foundation for Western societies. These moral truths are indoctrinated into the laws of modern democratic societies. Today we live in a world where one must not steal, lie or kill. One is obliged to respect one's father, one's mother and fellow mankind. Democracies operate under the assumption that people believe in such moral doctrines.

For some people, the moral truths follow from one principle, the Golden Rule: "Do unto others as you would have them do unto you." The Golden Rule is perhaps the greatest moral doctrine of all.

Hence, the moral beliefs of today virtually coincide with the moral beliefs at the time when the Holy Bible first came into being. Other holy books, such as the Koran, the Veda and the Upanishads, contain similar moral principles. It appears that the fundamental moral truths were discovered and written down in holy texts thousands of years ago. These truths are as valid today as they were then. What was right and wrong 3000 years ago is, to a close approximation, what is right and wrong today. The lack of evolution of moral doctrine is surprising. Almost every other aspect of human life has changed enormously during this period. This suggests that moral doctrine might be universal and absolute. Since the laws of morality and conduct are known, the main problem facing modern society is their implementation.

.   .   .   .   .   .

We live on a tiny planet in a vast Universe. Human beings on Earth are like ants on a leaf floating in the Pacific Ocean. The ants may construct colonies, they may crawl frantically around in search of food and materials, they may fight some foreign insect to survive, but if the leaf were to sink, the effect on the Pacific Ocean would be negligible. What happens on Earth has little effect on the Universe and the billions and billions of stars and astrophysical objects elsewhere. However, within our tiny world, there is a sense of purpose and morality which appears to be universal.

If life as intelligent as man exists elsewhere in the Universe,[1] do those beings follow a law and order similar to ours? The answer could be yes. Violation of the above-mentioned moral doctrine leads to a less stable society and a higher chance for self-destruction. One Hitler-like leader, who possesses a large nuclear arsenal, is capable of destroying all human life with the press of a button. If moral truths and other survival principles are not obeyed, the human race may suffer greatly or even cease to exist. Moral truths have been largely obeyed because they provide a more stable way to live, both for individuals and for societies. In short, moral laws do not have to be obeyed, but it is advantageous for us to do so.

Unlike moral principles, which were discovered thousands of years ago and have remained essentially unchanged, physics laws are *continually* being discovered and refined. These laws determine how Nature behaves. A ball falls to the ground according to Newton's law of gravity. This law describes precisely how the ball moves at the surface of the Earth. Newton discovered the law in the seventeenth century. In some instances, proposed physical laws turned out to be incorrect. For example, until the Copernican revolution, it was believed that the Sun and planets revolved around the Earth. Analysis of planetary orbits allowed seventeenth century astronomers to demonstrate that the planets, including the Earth, revolve around the Sun. Of course, in the vast

---

[1]Given the thousand-billion-billion other stars, there surely exist many other planetary systems. In fact, recently other planetary systems *have* been discovered – the first of these is known as Pegasi 51. Given the presumably billions of billions of other planetary systems, there must be millions of billions of planets with Earth-like environments. Given the millions of billions of Earth-like planets, life elsewhere in the Universe is *very likely* to exist. In the vastness of the Universe we are not alone, yet in the vastness of the Universe we are so alone. The unknown question is whether such extraterrestrial life forms are "intelligent." It has taken about one-fifth of the age of the Universe for intelligent life to develop on Earth, and this development has been quite recent, corresponding to "a few minutes" of cosmological time. Hence, extraterrestrial life forms may not have had enough time to evolve to the sophisticated level that humans have obtained.

Universe, the Sun moves in an orbit in our galaxy, our galaxy is moving towards other galaxies in our local galactic cluster, and this cluster is moving away from other clusters as the Universe expands, so that our motion is much more complicated than a circle around the Sun because the Sun, too, is moving. Earth is just a tiny leaf being tossed about by giant waves in the vastness of the Universe.

The smallness of our role in the Universe and *presumably* our restricted physical and intellectual capabilities have prevented us from discovering all scientific laws. We probably understand Nature in a limited way and on a limited scale. We have discovered many physical laws, but we do not know how much more there is to discover. It is possible that we have uncovered only a tiny fraction of Nature's laws. If this is so, there remains a lot of work for science to do.

In summary, the main differences between scientific and religious laws are as follows. Physical laws are continually being discovered and modified. Moral laws were essentially determined thousands of years ago and have changed little. Physical laws must be obeyed. Moral laws are often broken by individuals, institutions and governments. Implementation of moral doctrine is the main goal of societies. Discovery of the fundamental laws of Nature is the goal of science.

.        .        .        .        .        .

Given that many scientific discoveries have been made over the last several thousand years, some biblical descriptions about physical laws are outdated.[2] This is in contrast to moral, historical and literary aspects of the Holy Bible, which have survived the passage of time. The purpose of *The Bible According to Einstein* is to present Nature's laws, as currently best understood, in a style and format that is similar to the Holy Bible. Undoubtedly, *The Bible According to Einstein* will, after a number of years, need to be updated. However, for the present, it is hoped that this book will serve as a means for people to understand the laws of Nature. The text is written in a manner that tries to imitate the way the Holy Bible might have been written had it been written in the twentieth century. Descriptions of the Universe earlier than one-ten-billionth of a second after the Big Bang are conjectures based on modern speculative theories. Certain other aspects of the text, such as the conception of life, also involve educated guesses. However, the text is based on established scientific thought, although it is not writ-

---

[2] One should imagine the situation when the Holy Bible was written. At that time, people saw clouds slowly marching across the sky. And they must have asked themselves, "What makes the clouds?" and "What makes clouds move?" The clouds to them must have been mysterious. And they must have responded to their questions with answers such as "Someone must make the clouds" and "Someone must make the clouds move." And for them that someone was God. In ancient times, God was in part an explanation of all things. Chapters 36-39 of the Book of Job of the Holy Bible exemplify this. Today there are many natural phenomena that we still do not understand. But there are things that we do know. And today we know what makes the clouds and what makes them move.

ten in a way that scientists write. In particular, much of the text is
written to be read aloud.

The reader should be aware that narrative, poetic, literary and
expository styles are used and intermingled in *The Bible According to
Einstein*. It is not often that such divergent structures and modes of ex-
pression are combined. It is like rock. Sedimentary rock is fragile, thin
and is found only near the surface of the Earth. In its layers, sedimentary rock contains concentrated geological information. It is highly varied and beautiful. It is in some sense like poetry. Igneous rock, on the
other hand, is strong, omnipresent and makes up the mantle. Although
igneous rock is more abundant, it is difficult to extract information from
it. It is almost immutable and bold. Igneous rock is in a rough sense
like prose. In *The Bible According to Einstein*, poetry and prose are
mixed. In *The Bible According to Einstein*, rhythm, rhyme and reason
are intermingled. Some metamorphic magic is performed. The most
beautiful rock of all is perhaps metamorphic rock – it is made from igneous *and* sedimentary rock.

Religion and science do not mix. They are like oil and vinegar.
But if oil and vinegar are thoroughly stirred and appropriate spices are
added, then something neither so bitter nor so oily is produced. May
palatable concoctions be conceived.

Black is beautiful. White is also beautiful. Gray is dull. But black
and white patterns are perhaps the most beautiful of all. They constitute, for example, printed text. May one's vision not be blurred.

.     .     .     .     .     .

Although it is usually thought that science and religion are very
different, in fact, they have some things in common. Both attempt, at
least in part, to explain phenomena in Nature. The first chapter of
Genesis in the Holy Bible describes Creation. Modern cosmology also
provides a picture of Creation, the so-called Big Bang. Although the
Holy Bible is concerned with moral issues, some parts of the Holy Bible
deal with natural laws. Although science mostly deals with the laws of
Nature, moral issues sometimes arise. Both science and religion try to
describe the ultimate fate of the Universe. According to the Holy Bible,
the world ends on Judgement Day. According to modern cosmology, the
Universe has three possible fates: (i) it may go on expanding forever, (ii)
it may cease its expansion, contract, collapse and undergo the Big
Crunch, which is the opposite of the Big Bang, or (iii) it may choose a
path between the two by expanding at slower and slower rates so that
in the infinite future it virtually ceases its expansion.

Both science and religion have a set of dogmas. Religious dogmas
are moral laws such as the Ten Commandments. Scientific dogmas are
physics laws. Both science and religion search for truth. Religion seeks
to find *moral truth*, while science seeks to find *natural truth*. Often scientists think they understand a particular law of Nature, only to find
out later it was wrong or somewhat inaccurate or only valid in a certain

regime. Likewise, people sometimes misunderstand moral truths. With the passage of time, a more precise understanding of moral truths seems to have been achieved.

Ancient people built the Tower of Babel as an attempt to reach the heavens and the Supreme Being. Scientists have made microscopes and telescopes to see the near and far. They have built high-energy particle accelerators and constructed spacecraft full of sophisticated equipment to further probe the small and large. The quest of scientists is not so different from that of clergymen. The latter are in search of holy and moral doctrines; the former are in search of Nature's laws. Both are trying to understand better what is already known and both are trying to discover what is now unknown. To see what no man has seen before, to sense what seems to be senseless, to give meaning to what seems meaningless – these are the goals of religion and of science.

Religion often involves a striving for salvation. In many religions, salvation is achieved by pursuing a good life on Earth. Salvation is ultimately obtained by going to Heaven. Science, on the other hand, is driven by the quest for a better understanding of Nature. Such understanding generally brings great technological and practical benefits. The premise has been that new scientific knowledge leads to a better life. Although this was probably not its intention, science has played a role in taking care of mankind. It is also possible that science one day will save humanity from extinction. Someday, a sizeable asteroid will strike Earth. If man is still present at that time, the impact will threaten to kill off the human race. In such a circumstance, it might be possible to take precautions to save all or some people. As another example, new deadly diseases will arise. Among them might be one capable of spreading to all individuals, thereby threatening to wipe out humanity. It would then be the task of biologists and medical researchers to find a cure. Finally, far in the future, the Sun will explode, engulf the Earth and destroy all life. The only possible salvation from this fate is for life forms on Earth to escape to the outer planets or to a nearby planetary system.

Revelation, the act of disclosing divine reality and sacred purpose to an individual, has an analog in science. It is scientific discovery. Revelation in religion often occurs through spiritual experiences, through historical events, through religious study or through mystical insight. Scientific discoveries often arise through experiments or through pure thought based on esthetics and fundamental principles. Sometimes the discovery occurs by accident. In many cases, the process of discovery seems almost mystical.

Enlightenment occurs both in religion and in science. When a person, for the first time, suddenly understands a new religious truth, it is a moment of wonder and excitement. There is a feeling of elation. The same excitement happens when a scientist makes a discovery.

Both science and religion make predictions.[3] The Holy Bible contains predictions of catastrophes and of many other events, such as the Old Testament prophecy of the appearance of a messiah. Science attempts to predict the future motion of inanimate objects such as balls, trains, planes, waves, planets, missiles, molecules and electrons. The laws of Nature are used to make these predictions. When a new law is uncovered, the predictions can seem highly counterintuitive, almost mystical. The recent predictions of quantum mechanics and relativity are often viewed this way by non-scientists. It is only with the passage of time that one becomes familiar with such new phenomena and accepts them as natural.

Perhaps few realize it, but science operates to a large extent on faith. The simplest example of this occurs in schools and universities. Students read textbooks and are told the scientific truths and results. Students usually accept what they read or what they are told, independent of whether experiments are conducted to convince the students. Scientific research is conducted similarly. Individuals carry out experiments, perform computations and present results in journals. Other scientists read the journals and usually accept what they read without further verification. Sometimes one or more groups do verify an experiment – even in such a case, most of the scientific community still accepts the results without performing the research explicitly. Scientists accept the work and conclusions of others on the basis of trust. Scientists have faith in one another.[4]

Speculations about the Universe at the earliest times and about physics at scales smaller than a billionth of a billionth of a meter are based on the idea that there might be a single fundamental law of Nature that encompasses all laws. The fundamental forces and perhaps other undiscovered forces would follow from such a Uni-Law. The term "Uni-Law" is not used by physicists. However, the concept exists in Grand Unified Theories, Superstring Theory, M-theory and "Theories-of-Everything." For physicists, the Uni-Law is perhaps the analog of the Golden Rule.

Like religion, science has its "priests." These are the ordinary scientists and science teachers who expound their knowledge. Students in science classes are told what to believe, and most students believe what they are told. As in religion, science has its saints. These are the giant figures who have made great scientific contributions. Often Nobel Prize winners are "revered" by devotees of science. Books, biographies and histories are written about the famous men and women of science and their achievements. And indeed, Newton, Einstein, Darwin and

---

[3] The character of the predictions, however, is very different. Also, non-believers in religion usually view religious predictions with skepticism.

[4] Faith in science is different from religious faith, because in principle one can repeat the experiments and calculations to verify the results.

others were truly great scientists and deserve to have their names etched in monuments paying tribute to them.

Science exists *because it works*. In medieval times, there was little difference between alchemy and chemistry. Alchemy, which was unsuccessful, died out as a science. Chemistry, which was successful, remained. Religion exists because it gives meaning to life and life-after-death. It provides moral fortitude, comfort, guidelines for daily conduct and emotional support. Even *those who do not believe in religion* must admit that it can have some psychological benefit for individuals.

Science works because Nature appears to follow a set of universal laws. When a scientist completes an experiment and confirms an expected result, the scientist is gratified to see that Nature obeys its laws. Technological devices work because the science behind them works and because Nature does indeed obey Nature's laws.

Today science is so pervasive in our lives that we accept its achievements as routine. We often forget that even something as simple as a light bulb is a product of science. Many of us cannot live without a television set, a car, or a computer. Modern medicine has dramatically improved the quality of our lives. Today science permeates our world, much the same way that religion did in medieval times and earlier.

Given the similarities between science and religion, perhaps science should be considered as a kind of religion, at least in a liberal sense of the word. For some, science functions as a framework for understanding Nature and for determining, in part, one's actions and decisions. Science can assist in the conduct of our lives.

As an example of how science would deal with an issue, consider life-after-death. According to physics, chemistry and biology, once a person dies, biological processes begin to terminate. Decay sets in. Eventually the body decomposes and molecules are dispersed. In such a state, a person is not alive. There is no "life-after-death." For the dead person, there is nothing: No thought, no consciousness, no fear, no sadness, simply nothingness. There is, however, "existence-after-death." One still "exists" as a decomposed body. The body might be the host of other life forms such as bacteria. It might even become the food of an animal or the fertilizer for a plant. Eventually, one exists not as a coherent unit but as molecules and atoms dispersed throughout the Universe. This is what science would say about life-after-death.[5]

In science, what plays the role of God? One possibility is Nature. Nature is an abstraction of everything that exists. Nature is omnipresent and powerful. Nature through chance and time created life. The domain of Nature is the Universe, which is all. If the word "God" is replaced by "Nature," then Genesis I of the Holy Bible more or less

---

[5] It does not, however, say that all scientists do not believe in life-after-death. What science says and what scientists believe can be different. As individuals, scientists believe in different things.

makes scientific sense. In a similar way, a reader might find that, by replacing "Nature" by "God" and "natural" by "holy," parts of *The Bible According to Einstein* make meaningful spiritual sense.

.     .     .     .     .     .

Like the Holy Bible, *The Bible According to Einstein* is divided into two parts: an Old Testament and a New Testament. The Old Testament is historical. It discusses the creation of the Universe, the emergence of galaxies and the solar system. It narrates the evolution of Earth and the development of life. A few sections are included for completeness because the purpose is to tell the whole history from the beginning to the end. Although the New Testament covers some recent history, it is mainly concerned about man and his scientific knowledge. The laws of physics, the rules of chemistry and the basic principles of biology are presented. The information about the world, as currently understood by scientists, is compiled. The fundamental building blocks of matter are unveiled.

For reasons of completeness, *The Bible According to Einstein* in a couple of places enumerates facts. This is not so different, for example, from the Book of Numbers in the Holy Bible, where the children of Israel are listed. A reader can simply glance over such enumerations, unless a specific listing or definition is sought.

In *The Bible According to Einstein*, metaphors sometimes replace complicated physics concepts; it might be criticized on this basis. But perhaps it is better to speak in metaphors in a way that can be understood than to speak in precise scientific jargon in a way that cannot be understood.

In relating the history of the Universe, one is faced with the problem of describing things that currently do not exist. Among these are some which resemble present-day objects. In this context, a useful device can be employed. The prefix "proto," which means "that which existed before and led to," can be attached to a word. This prefix indicates a primitive state of formation. A proto-object is what existed before the object. It is the progenitor, the predecessor. Here are some examples. A proto-star is a dense concentration of gas in which nuclear fuels will ignite in millions of years and produce light. When a proto-star produces light, it becomes a star. Proto-Africa is the land mass that existed hundreds of millions of years ago and which eventually turned into Africa. A proto-homo-sapien is an ape-man or a monkey. In principle, the prefix "proto" can precede almost any noun.

In the discussions of biology, physics and chemistry, chemical compounds, such as oxygen gas, water vapor and methane, are mentioned. Their composition is given near the end of the New Testament Book of *Chemistry*. An index-glossary of scientifically related words is provided in the back of the book. Words in the index-glossary are defined in context in the body of the book, where they are italicized. Italicization is also used for emphasis in the same manner as the King

James version of the Holy Bible. The text in script at the beginning of a section is a quotation, often from the Holy Bible and usually paraphrased. *The Bible According to Einstein* usually uses the name of a species as an individual member rather than as the animal class. Although they are capitalized and italicized in normal scientific writing, the names of species and life forms are written in lower case and are not italicized – this helps to emphasize that one is referring to an individual and not to a species class.[6] The word "man" almost always refers to the human race and not simply to the male population. The Sun, Moon and planets are all capitalized. Thus "Earth" refers to the third planet from the Sun, and "earth" refers to dirt.

*The Bible According to Einstein* should be read more than once: The more one reads, the more one will discover. The knowledge in its New Testament provides the understanding for the "Genesis" of its Old Testament. *The Bible According to Einstein* is a great opportunity for a reader to learn about a vast array of scientific subjects. The reader who studies this book will learn a great deal.

The Old and New Testaments are related. An understanding of the past helps one better understand the present – history contains lessons for the present. Likewise, an understanding of the present helps one better understand the past. In fact, the geological past is mostly deduced from studying the relics and fossils found today. As another example, insight into cosmology is achieved by modern scientists using present-day theory and experiment. Knowledge gained in the twentieth century concerning fundamental physics has led to a better understanding of the events that took place just after the Big Bang.

The reconstruction of natural history is similar to a criminal investigation. Evidence is available. It must be meticulously gathered and examined. From the evidence, one draws conclusions. The inspectors, detectives, coroners and investigators are called geologists, paleontologists, archaeologists and cosmologists. Consider, for example, the evolution of the Earth and life. The evidence is located in sedimentary rocks. Fossils are like fingerprints. Footprints of ancient animals, like crime-scene footprints, indicate how individuals moved about. A piece of shell determines the age of a layer of sedimentary rock – just like a broken watch fixes the time of a modern crime. Carbon-dating and the analysis of radioactive elements tell how long a prehistoric sample has existed. An autopsy on the body of a murder victim reveals his time of death and his means of death. Likewise, the dissection of preserved soft parts of extinct creatures reveals much information. DNA, now a tool of criminal investigations, is being used to determine the evolutionary tree of life. Through DNA analysis, one is able to decide how species evolve from one another. By these means for example, it was

---

[6] For example, "A homo sapien picked up a stone." would be expressed in standard scientific writing as "A member of *Homo sapiens* picked up a stone."

determined that an African ape, and not an Asian ape, was the ances-
tor of the homo sapiens.

.     .     .     .     .     .

In the scientific literature, the creation of our world has been told
in pieces. In *The Bible According to Einstein*, the whole story is told,
from start to finish. It was easy to write the history that is about to
unfold. The story line did not have to be invented. One simply had to
look and listen and to see and hear what the Universe had narrated.
One had to "feel" the atom and the nucleus. One had to examine the
cells of life. One had to read the rock. One had to see the information in
the stars. Thus the story was written in the micro-world of the molecule. Thus the story was written in the Earth. Thus the story was written in the heavens.

May you too feel the atom, touch the rock and hear the heavens.
May you read and understand.

## Important Advice to The Reader

The manner in which one reads *The Bible According to Einstein* depends on one's background and purpose. Just as most people would not read the Holy Bible from beginning to end, one need not do so with *The Bible According to Einstein*. The books can be read in any order. More specifically, readers can focus on those subjects in which they are most interested. Like the Holy Bible, each book can be read alone and still serve a purpose – each functions as a unit. Of course, relations exist between different parts, and these provide some of the power of *The Bible According to Einstein*. However, it is *strongly recommended* that the reader without a scientific background *not* begin with *Genesis I: The Planck Epoch*. Those initial moments of creation are very foreign from the world of today – the "Beginning," being the most remote moment in the past, is perhaps the most difficult to understand without the knowledge of the New Testament. The *non-scientifically oriented reader should begin with Homogenesis*, which is the first book of the New Testament.[7] Such a reader can continue to the *Ten Commandments of Science*, skipping over the histories of electromagnetism, elementary particles and modern science and coming back to them later. Then some of the Books of Physics can be read. At this point, many options are available: The reader intrigued by life can skip to *Biogenesis* or *Biology* and later skim the sections on evolution in the Old Testament's *The Archean Eon II, The Proterozoic Eon, The Paleozoic Era, The Mesozoic Era* and *The Cenozoic Era*. The reader who wants to know about geology, Earth and planets can skip to The Books of the Solar System and then skim *Exodus XII: Geogenesis I* through *The Cenozoic Era*. The reader interested in the cosmos and its contents can skip to the Old Testament books of *Exodus IV: Recombination* through *Exodus X: Nucleogenesis*. The reader who wishes to know what the future has in store can consult the New Testament Book of *Prophets*. Finally, the reader who is driven by the desire to know *how it all began*, that is, the Universe's birth, can read the account of the first three minutes, which are contained in *Genesis I: The Planck Epoch* through *Deuteronomy*. The scientific expert may want to begin with *Genesis I: The Planck Epoch* and continue through to *Exodus VII: Stellar Birth*, at which point such an expert can skip to topics he or she finds most interesting. All readers should read *The Last Commandment* – it is thy commandment.

*Ye who see the light will know the light.*
*Ye who know the light will understand the light.*

---

[7] To encourage readers to begin with *Homogenesis*, this version of *The Bible According to Einstein* has changed the ordering of books from the original format. In a later version, the natural order, in which the Old Testament appears first, will be restored.

# The
# New
# Testament

*The twenty-second book of Creation*
*and the first book of the New Testament, called*

# Homogenesis

*And a line in time was drawn.*

## Chapter I: Australopithecus

*And man was separated from the ape*
*and made to rule over flocks of sheep.*

It was five-million years ago. The jungles of Africa were *thick with vegetation* – trees strove to grow to be the highest trees; vines wrapped around their trunks; bushes stood in each other's way; tall grasses grew wherever grass could grow. And the jungles were *full of life*, from the colonies of tiny ants dwelling in small mounds of earth, to the herds of giant elephants swinging long trunks as they strode forth. And Earth's animals were *free* – they were free to climb the trees, free to feed wherever food was found, free to roam the land. And birds of exotic colors flew from limb to limb. And giraffes did stretch their necks to reach for leaves. And crocodiles were on the lookout in the swamps. And screeching monkeys jumped chaotically in trees, while lonely lions roamed the wild.

And *it came to pass* that a thunderstorm swept over eastern central Africa. And rain streamed down in lines from clouds above and pelted trees and earth below. And it rained until the evening and then stopped. Now the next day when the Sun rose up, the last few clouds had fled. And heat began to bake the land. And *vapors rose up* everywhere and curled about Earth's vegetation. And in the shade of jungle trees, mist condensed and did get thick. And *a soft wind* blew the mist about, making it turn as in a whirlpool. And the movement of the mist did seem to have a purpose, *as if* someone with a finger stirred it. And out of the steamy jungle and into an open field emerged an ape-like creature – it was a female proto-hominid.[1] And as she stretched her arms apart and *received the rays* of morning sun, the fur on her wide chest was warmed. Then she turned and disappeared into the jungle and was gone.

And the morning Sun inched up the sky. And mist did lift and earth did dry. The air was clear and fresh.

Now this female proto-hominid was *different* from the proto-hominids of the middle-Miocene, for she spent more time on land than in the trees. And when she ran, she ran on all four limbs – she galloped awkwardly and slowly. But when she walked, it was with *just her two hind limbs*. And that left her two forelimbs thus dangling by her sides.

---

[1] *Hominid* means "man-like."

And that night, she slept in the *safety* of a sturdy bough. And a cosmic ray *was sent* from outer space. And the ray descended through the clouds to Earth and struck a piece of DNA[2] within an egg-cell in her womb. And when the DNA did duplicate, it duplicated in a *different* way. And some changes in some genes were made.[3]

And *many months* went by. And it came to pass that the female proto-hominid gave birth. She held the newborn in her arms and nurtured him.

And *many years* went by. And the newborn grew into a healthy adolescent. But he was *slightly different* from his mother proto-hominid. Now he had long arms and short legs *like her*. But his mouth and chin were well forward while his forehead was receded. He had the body of an ape. And his face *was as* the face of *a large chimpanzee*. His teeth and skull were bigger than his mother's. He was a beast that was more human-like. And these things would be true of his descendants.

And so it came to pass in Kenya that the proto-hominid evolved into the hominid. And *this first hominid* was provided with a name. And the name was australopithecus, which means the "southern ape." But australopithecus was *not* an ape – *australopithecus* was an ape-man; he was part ape, part man. And this first australopithecus was more *like* an ape than like a man.

And australopithecines increased their *numbers*. But still, at this time in geo-history almost five-million years ago, the australopithecines did number few.

Now male australopithecines weighed roughly forty kilograms[4] and they were somewhat taller than a meter,[5] while female australopithecines were smaller – one-fourth to one-half less. And these ape-women and ape-men had brains only slightly larger than an ape's.

And in a jungle in East Africa, an ape-man *reached up with his arms* and grasped a tree-branch with his hands. And with one movement did he break it off. Then he stripped the short branch of its leaves and *it* became a stick. And *he knelt down* on earth. And the ape-man lowered his hands, which were interlocked about the stick. And he dug the dirt around a plant, grabbed the plant and pulled it up. And the plant possessed a dirty root. And the ape-man rubbed clean the root and *ate of it*.

And elsewhere in an open field, an ape-man placed a nut upon a large flat rock. And he grabbed a *round stone* in his right hand *and* he slammed it down. And the round stone struck the nut with force. And the nutshell broke in pieces.

---

[2] For the definitions of words such as DNA, see the Index/Glossary.

[3] Genetic changes from cosmic rays are rare occurrences. More commonly are genetic changes created by other reasons: exposure to ultraviolet light, environmental poisoning, contact with certain chemicals, random errors in reproduction of DNA, et cetera.

[4] Ninety pounds.

[5] Thirty-nine inches.

And a female australopithecus walked around while looking at the ground. And she spied a small sharp rock, picked it up and *grabbed* it *with* one hand. And grasping a *sweet fruit* in her other hand, she moved the sharp rock back and forth across the sweet fruit's rind. And so the rind was grooved with several slits. Then she peeled away the rind and ate the juicy fruit inside.

And tens of thousands of years went by. And australopithecines did *naturally* evolve: Their teeth got stronger, for they spent much time in chewing hard fruits, tubers, nuts and roots. When walking, they leaned back a little more. The big toe on the foot moved closer to the other four. And when they ran, they ran on *two* legs, not on four. Thus their hands were free for doing other things. And so in moving forward and about, australopithecines looked a *little different* from before.

And they used their hands in *many* ways – climbing trees, digging roots, grabbing nuts, peeling fruits, stripping trees of leaves, throwing rocks, holding food, and holding hands. And such daily tasks did lead to fingers with a greater flexibility and skill. And thumbs got stronger and more versatile.

And australopithecines walked through woods in search of nuts, pods, berries, vegetables and seeds. But their favorite food was *fruit*. And they often climbed the trees to pick bananas.

Now it happened that an ape-woman and ape-man were walking through the jungle. And nearby a lion crouched behind a bush. And by chance, the ape-man turned his head and *spied* the lion's mane. The ape-man uttered a low sound and pointed with his finger. The ape-woman scampered to the nearest tree. The lion leaped. The ape-man's mouth *in a split instant* opened wide; the lips curled back, displaying large white teeth. His vocal cords let loose a savage howl. The *startled* lion stopped. The ape-woman quickly climbed the tree. Then the ape-man turned and ran. The lion sprang again. The ape-man scrambled *up* the tree. The lion leaped and swung its paw. But the ape-man was well up the trunk and out of reach.

Thus *it came to be* that australopithecines used their brains to solve problems of defense and food.

Now ape-men *shared* the woodlands with the apes. And apes numbered *more* than ape-men. And although the body features and the faces of these two creatures *looked* about the same, the apes hunched over, using arms and knuckles like crutches when they hopped about, while ape-men walked more upright *on two legs*.

And those australopithecines, which had slightly larger brains, made better use of sticks and stones, invented different tricks for finding food, and learned resourceful ways to avoid hyenas, lions, leopards, jackals, wild dogs and cheetahs. And australopithecines with bigger brains lived *longer* lives and mated *more*. And *they* became more numerous. And the australopithecines with smaller brains fell victim to predators, went hungry *and* they mated *less*. And *they* became less numerous. And during hundreds of thousands of years, the brains of australopithecines got slightly larger.

And those australopithecines that were a little stronger fared *better* too. And when food was scarce, they overwhelmed the others for the food. And they could better defend themselves against Earth's predators. And so the stronger australopithecines became *more* numerous. And with time, the smaller weaker australopithecines did number *less*.

Thus began the battle to be smarter, stronger, bigger.

And half-a-million years went by. And australopithecines had *spread* from Kenya into Ethiopia and Tanzania. And among the habitants of Ethiopia was one named *"Lucy."* Now Lucy lived for forty years. And when she died, her bones got buried in the ground. And luck would have it that the skull and bones of Lucy *would* survive *unto this day*. And in the year one-thousand-nine-hundred-seventy-four AD, her remains would be *discovered* in digs by paleontologists in Ethiopia. And from the bones, it would be known how Lucy looked. And at a site *nearby*, the remains of thirteen others like her *also* would be found. And because they lived together, *they* would *be* called *"the first family."*

And time passed and disappeared – it was three-million years ago. Australopithecines *had migrated* to the southern part of Africa. Now they had a more spherical and larger head; inside the head was, compared with the first australopithecus, one-tenth more brain – four-hundred-and-fifty cc's[6] of brain. And the neck was thinner and the nose was smaller, but *still* the nose was fairly large. And the teeth were more like human teeth. But the mouth and lower jaw *still* protruded like an ape's.

And half-a-million years went by. And in eastern and in southern Africa, australopithecines progressed – the struggle to survive had made them larger and more muscular. But in relation to their size, their brains were *not* much bigger. And when they walked, they were *nearly* upright. But they stuck to primitive ways – rummaging for small dead animals to eat, digging with sticks, and hammering hard nuts with stones. And in a million years or so, this race would die. And *nothing* would remain of them or of their relatives but bones.[7]

---

[6] The abbreviation cc's, pronounced "see-sees," stands for cubic centimeters.

[7] The demise of australopithecus is understandable: australopithecus had been stronger but not significantly smarter. In the Pleistocene, "big was better but smart was best."

## Chapter II: Homo Habilis

*Let there be man.*
*And let him have dominion over the fish of the sea,*
*and over the fowl of the air,*
*and over the beasts of the Earth,*
*and over every creeping thing that creepeth on the Earth.*
*And it was so.*
*And this happened on the sixth day*
*of the first month of a long lost year.*

It was about two-million years ago. And it had come about that the craniums of some australopithecines in Kenya and in Tanzania had *increased* in size — their skulls contained six-hundred-and-fifty cc's of brain. And the "smarter australopithecus" was *given* a new name. And the name was *homo habilis*, which means "handy man."

Now the neck muscles of homo habilis *were as* the powerful neck muscles of the ape. And as for homo habilis, his forehead was receded. And he had bony cheeks, bushy eyebrows and a hairy face. But this ape-man *was* more man than ape. And compared with australopithecus, his jaw did not protrude as much. And his front teeth were smaller, thinner as well as sharper, and so for cutting and for tearing, *they* were better. And his *hands* were more adept.

And homo habilines lived in secluded habitats on land. And they rarely climbed up trees. They sometimes searched the countryside for animals that had been killed by predators. And they took the bones of recent kills and broke them open with a stone. And then ate they the marrow of the bones.

And fifty-thousand years went by and disappeared.

And with two strong hands, a homo habilis lifted up a *heavy* stone above his head. And he eased it forward and he let it go. And it landed on a large flat rock embedded in the earth. And the heavy stone *broke* into fragments. And among the fragments, *one* had one sharp edge. And he took this piece and *kept* it as a tool. Homo habilis had *made* a tool from stone — this moment marked the start of *the* Stone Age.

## Chapter III: Homo Erectus[8]

*Out of Africa they exited,*
*and into other lands they passed.*
*And they wandered in the deserts, in the mountains,*
*in the dens and in the caves of Earth.*

It was one-million-and-six-hundred-thousand years ago. In East Africa, it came to pass that homo habilis leaned back and walked completely upright. And homo habilis was *given* a new name. And the name was *homo erectus*, which means the "upright man."

Now homo erectus was the smartest creature *at* that time on Earth – his brain was twice the size of that of the australopithecus. And homo erectus had a smaller head, like modern man. And compared to apes, his face protruded less: the profile was the half-arc of an oval – the line between the eyebrows and the lips was *even* vertical. And his teeth in back were *smaller*, as in modern man. But his lips were fat, his mouth stuck out somewhat, his nose was wide and flat, his forehead still was little and drawn back a bit, his eyebrow bones were big, and from head to toe there was dark brown hair. This creature was a man-ape.

And homo erectuses *ate of* eggs, birds and turtles; vegetables; small animals including rats; the dead remains of mammals; insects such as centipedes and locust; and fruits, fish, berries, nuts and roots.

And one-hundred-thousand years went by. And one day, a homo erectus broke several sizeable branches *off* a tree and placed them in a pile. And from the pile, another homo erectus took one such branch and cut away the stems and leaves – the branch became a *pole* three meters long. And a third man-ape with stone in hand rubbed *smooth* the pole. Now the homo erectuses worked throughout the morning. And by midday, they had a pile of bushy branches and four poles. And gathering up the branches and the poles, they headed off into the jungle.

Now the three homo erectuses arrived at a cave where four females and five children *waited*. And the bushy branches and the poles were placed beside a pile of round and fist-sized stones.

And in the early afternoon, the man-apes gathered up the tools: Three males picked up the poles *and* several stones. And two females gathered up as many bushy branches as *they* could *hold*. And the three males and two females *left* the cave.

And in the jungle, they walked all afternoon. And just before the Sun had set, they spied a cheetah, which had killed a sheep. Now the sheep was *bleeding* at the throat. And the cheetah was *biting* at the neck. And two males put down the round stones on the ground. And hiding behind the bushy branches, the females took positions in the

---

[8] Other species of the "homo family" also appeared during the last two million years. For example, homo rudolphensis dwelt on Earth around one-million-and-eight-hundred-thousand years ago, and homo ergaster arose around the same time as homo erectus.

front. And standing *behind* the females, two males held the four poles forward so that the four poles protruded through the branches. And holding fist-sized stones, the third male waited in the rear.

And the five *advanced* in little steps. The females shook the branches and the males hollered loudly. The cheetah raised its head and watched with curiosity. Then the male in the rear did heave a stone, which almost hit the animal. The startled cheetah *leaped* back a little. The branches and the poles advanced. A second stone was thrown and hit the cheetah on the paw. The cheetah roared, *displaying* its sharp teeth. The male in the rear grabbed pebbles on the ground and threw them *at* the wild cat. The females *shook the branches* even more; the males yelled ferociously, and back and forth they *thrust* the poles. The cheetah clawed the ground and took two steps forth as *if* it would attack. Another stone was thrown and hit the cheetah in its side. The cheetah moaned and then ran off.

And the slain sheep was carried to the cave. And just outside the cave, using a sharp-edged stone, one homo erectus sliced the animal. Blood dripped to the ground. And during the next three days, the man-apes ate the raw sheep meat – it *was* not often they ate meat.

And a homo erectus took the woolly sheepskin to a nearby stream and *washed* it *clean*. And he came back and laid it next to other skins, *which* were lying in the cave.

And night did come. And the homo erectuses retreated to the cave. And the females gathered all the bushy branches, and in a heap they placed them at the entrance – the cave was *almost* sealed. And skins of antelope and sheep were spread out *on* the ground. And all the homo erectuses lay down and went to sleep.

And two-hundred-thousand years went by. And it happened that six homo-erectus males set off into the jungle carrying several wooden clubs and two large stones. And through thick vegetation *did* they hike for half-an-hour. And it came about that one of them beheld a boar. And he touched the others on the shoulders and pointed *with* his finger. And the six males tiptoed cautiously about and formed a ring around the unsuspecting boar. And the leader raised his hand and *signalled*. The *six* charged *at* the animal. The boar ran quickly in a *random path*. A club came flying down and struck the creature on its head. The boar let loose a shrill. A second blow did strike the boar below its neck. Stunned, it tried to run. And when still another club was shoved into its belly, the boar rolled over. And before the boar regained its feet, another male did raise a stone above his head with *his* two hands and heaved it down. It hit the creature on its crown. The boar was dead.

Now it was rare that homo erectuses hunted animals for meat – most small mammals simply *ran too fast*; others such as elephants, hippopotamuses and rhinoceroses *were too big*. And still others such as monkeys, apes and squirrels *could escape* by climbing trees.

. . . . . . .

Now it *happened* that a tribe of twenty-five homo erectuses was living by a cave. Each night, to determine who would sleep inside the cave, they grunted at each other, pushed each other, and even sometimes hit each other. And usually, the *strongest* dozen slept inside, while the others had to sleep outside. And one day, a male returned from a two-day journey through the jungle. And he jumped up and down and grunted *at* the others. Now the next day at dawn, ten males left the site with several poles and many heavy stones. And at dusk they came upon a hill. And there, they stooped down, *crouching* to the ground. Below, there was a cave, in front of which australopithecines were walking, standing, sitting and/or eating. Now the ten males *waited* until darkness came. Then they tiptoed down the hill and to the entrance of the cave. And *quietly* they went inside. Now seven australopithecines were snoring in the cave. And seven of the ten homo erectuses assumed positions next to the australopithecines. And with two hands, each raised a heavy stone above his head – the other three held poles. *Then* the leader gave a nod. The stones came crashing down upon the heads. In their dreams, australopithecines did scream. And in their wakened state, they screamed. Repeatedly, stones *struck* the heads. Poles were *thrust* into the abdomens. Blood trickled from the heads of several dead. Blood spurted out of the abdomen of one of them. The poles were thrust repeatedly.

And four days later, the other fifteen homo erectuses arrived. And they had a feast, for the meat of the australopithecus was good to eat. And a dozen homo erectuses moved to the cave of the australopithecines and stayed – the *tribe* was *split* in two.

And some homo erectuses went to a brook, naked without *any* clothes. And they bent over, cupped the clear brook water in their hands and threw it in the air. And *droplets* sparkled in Sun's light. Then they threw the water on themselves to wash with *this* brook's water, which *was* the purest of *all* waters.

Now elsewhere in East Africa, homo erectuses hunted animals. And elsewhere in East Africa, australopithecines fell *victim* to the poles and stones of homo erectuses. And although some australopithecines had stronger muscles than the homo erectuses, the australopithecines had no weapons. And these australopithecines did *not* run very fast, *nor* were they very big, *nor* could they climb the trees. And caves that had belonged to australopithecus became caves which homo erectus conquered *and* then occupied. And in fifty-thousand years, many East African australopithecines did disappear.

And elsewhere the australopithecines' numbers did decline. And with diminishing numbers, australopithecus eventually died out and disappeared.

*A link between the man and ape was gone.*
*In the battle of the brain and brawn,*
*the brain had won.*

And during the rest of the Pleistocene, the brain would go on winning.

.     .     .     .     .     .

And homo erectus greatly did increase his numbers. And homo erectuses began to *move* about. From East Africa, they *headed* south to southern Africa and *proceeded* north to northern Africa. And during one-hundred-thousand, they *wandered* to the Middle East. And during another hundred-thousand years, they *ventured* into southeast Asia. And in one-million years BC, *they* arrived in Java.

## Chapter IV: Tools

*Thus Nature left in earth*
*the signs of ancient past activities.*

And a homo erectus *placed* upon the ground a strong flat stone. And he grabbed a rock of *quartzite* and smashed it down against the flat strong stone. And the quartzite broke in pieces, among which there were *ones* that had sharp edges. And he selected *those*.[9]

It was a million years ago. And a homo erectus grabbed one stone in his left hand and one stone in his right. And the right stone did he bang into the left. *And* a piece broke *off*. And on *one side*, the piece was blunt, while on the *other*, it was somewhat sharp. This homo erectus was among the first to manufacture tools.

And several hundred-thousand years went by. And a homo erectus picked *up* a leg bone from a dead gazelle. And with a sharp stone did *he* reshape the bone. And after the end of the bone was *worn* down to a point, he placed it in a pile with other whittled bones. Next he picked up two *chert* rocks. And with one quick stoke, he struck one rock against the other. And a *flat large flake* broke off. And on one side, it was sharp. And on the other, it was smooth. And the flake fit snugly in his hand. And next to him were *several* piles of tools: Some tools were made from stones, and some were made of wood, and some were made from bones.

And there were pebble choppers, quartz flake cutters, block-like rocks for grinding, concave scrapers, pointed wooden sticks, and bones with two-pronged ends. And as for making tools, he was the master of his peers, for he *had* perfected it – he had *even* made some tools for making tools; he *was* the *first* tool engineer.

And the primitive tool trade evolved – the manufacturing of stone artifacts became a "valued art."

And as two-hundred-thousand years passed by, the making of *domestic tools* progressed. And many tools were more refined and smaller. And homo erectuses made *well-shaped* cutters, choppers and hand scrapers out of flint and wood. And they had many tools to manu-

---

[9] A million years earlier, homo habilis had made tools in a similar manner. Now the "homo lineage" was selecting special stones like quartzite.

facture tools. And homo erectuses carved out hollow regions in large stones – such crude bowls were used for holding things. And from animals, they made tools from skins and bones.

And the making of *hunting tools* progressed. And a stone was shaped with two sharp sides – it was an axe.[10] Now it would not be long before a short stem of stone *was* included in the axe. And *this* would be the handle. And such axes would be used for cutting, scratching, hunting and for many other tasks. And with time, wooden poles were made straighter and more pointed – such spears *could* be either thrown or thrust.

Now it happened that a homo erectus, while hunting in the woods, spotted a large rodent. And he raised an axe above his shoulder. And with *one* flip of his wrist, he sent the axe forth spinning. But the axe disappeared into a bush beyond the rodent. And the startled creature jumped and then ran off. And for this homo erectus, it *was* bad luck – sometimes the axe went by its target; sometimes it struck.

## Chapter V: Homo Erectus Becomes Smarter

And from the Middle East, homo erectus *ventured* into Europe. And at the same time from southern Asia, homo erectus *wandered* into northern China. And in that land, *he* was called the Peking man.

Now the brain capacity of homo erectus had expanded – elevenhundred cc's of volume was his brain. And homo-erectus children often played nonsense yelling games. Little did they know these games would train their brains.

.    .    .    .    .    .

And one day in China, a thunder storm swept up the coast. And lightning *struck* a tree. And the tree went up in flames. And when the rain subsided, the trunk was *still* on fire. And a homo erectus took some leaves and made of *them* a heap. And then he broke a small branch off a tree and poked one end into the fire. And the branch began to *burn*. And to the heap of leaves he brought the flaming branch. And when he placed the flaming branch on top, the leaves below began to burn. And he watched with curiosity as the pile created red and yellow flames. Five minutes *passed*. The fire almost had consumed the leaves. And he went and collected other fallen leaves and *placed* them on the burning pile. And the flames sprung up before his eyes. And in some *strange* way he felt *good*. And in some rudimentary way he understood. And what he sensed was that fire was like homo erectus. And just as he and his companions had to eat, a fire had to eat. But the food that homo erectus ate was *different* from the food that fire ate – fire ate plants and leaves and wood.

---

[10] The definition of an *axe* is a triangular bifacial cutter. In prehistoric times, axes were often quite small.

Now he had *made* a "theory." His theory was that fire needed food and must be fed to stay alive. And his idea explained why fires lived and died. But his theory was *not* completely true, for fire (as man would later learn) was *not* alive. And so he was a proto-scientist – *he was the first scientist.*

Thus it came to be that homo erectus mastered fire. And with the passage of time, other tribes acquired fire.

Now some tribes lived in open camps along the banks of streams and shores of lakes. And *always* had they several fires burning; the females and the children constantly collected leaves, plants and wood to feed the fires. For the homo erectuses, *fire*, with its flickering hypnotic flames, was *mystical.* At night they sat around with light reflecting off their faces. The fires seemed to keep the predators away. And if a particularly aggressive wild cat moved in to try to make a kill among the young, a male would set a branch ablaze and wave the flames. And screams and a few well-directed well-thrown stones would always scare such predators away. With fire, homo erectuses were *safe* from wild dogs and wild cats. With fire, they no longer had to stay in caves and in secluded habitats. With fire, they *were* no longer cold in winter. With fire, they could move to habitats in slightly colder climates.

At times, they *danced* around the fire and made grunts. At times, they fed the fire with an animal instead of wood. Since meat was good for them to eat, meat should be good for fire to eat. They *seemed* to worship fire. For them, a fire was a god.

. . . . . . .

Now it happened that a homo erectus had the urge to eat. And he came upon an abandoned campsite, in which a fire *still* was smoldering. And a burnt animal was in the fire. And with a stick he pushed the animal aside and then picked up the carcass. But it was hot – he let it drop and shook his hand. And he waited several minutes, for he *knew* that the food that fed a dying fire, such as wood, eventually cooled off. And when he lifted up the carcass for a second time, the carcass was not hot. And he ate the meat and it was *very* good. And later, this homo erectus deliberately put carcasses in fire, for, to him, meat *tasted* better cooked.

And soon[11] other homo erectuses discovered that certain foods were better cooked. And they roasted seeds and sometimes roasted nuts. Thus it came to pass that although they mostly ate of vegetables and fruit, *cooked meat* tasted best to them. And they began to hunt more frequently.

And so fire *was given* to homo erectus. And he could warm his hands if *they be cold.* And fire could be added to a stick to make a torch. And such a torch *could* be waved about in order to put *fear* into the eyes of beasts and keep such beasts away.

---

[11] Here, "soon" means thousands of years.

## Chapter VI: Homo Sapiens

*The first man is of the earth.*

And it was *as if* a mysterious and vaporous hand passed over Earth. The struggle to survive and evolution brought about a *change*. And so it happened that the body of the homo erectus changed: The skeletal structure of his head became *lighter* and more delicate – the jaw bones were less heavy and more intricate; the bony eyebrows disappeared; the head was rounder and more fragile; and the teeth were smaller and more specialized. And the brain case was more spherical and *more* voluminous.[12] And although the cranium contained more brain, the cranium itself was thin and light.

Now there were other changes too. The forehead and the chin were forward; the facial profile essentially was vertical; and the nose was less flat, more pointed and refined, and it stuck out. And since the head was lighter, the neck muscles had *shrunk* in size. And since, during the last several hundred-thousand years, homo erectuses had been chewing less – for they used tools instead of teeth to do their chores – the jaw muscles, although still fairly strong, were smaller.

And the fingers were exceptionally *skillful* – they could hold a twig in the position of a pen, manipulating it at will. And with such fingers and such hands could *finer* tools be made.

Slow and steady evolution had made homo erectus a "new man." And since homo erectus was smarter, he was *given* a new name. And the name was *homo sapien*, which means "wise man." It was four-hundred-thousand years ago. And man was man.[13]

*And to celebrate the new creation,*
*somewhere, voices sang.*

And there in the jungle stood *the first couple*. And this archaic male homo sapien *was* provided with a name – his name was *Adam*. And this archaic female homo sapien *also* was provided with a name – her name was *Eve*. And Eve was so named Eve, for she was the mother of all men. And nearby, a snake crawled among the branches of a tree of fruit.

And it came to pass that Eve and Adam had many sons and daughters. And *they* were *the first generation*. And in those days, men and women were naked *and* were *not* ashamed.

And these archaic homo sapiens heard the call of Nature, "Go into the *wilderness* and make thy seed a *hundred-fold*." And archaic homo sapiens *did* just so.

And as one-hundred-thousand years went by, the art of making tools progressed. And one sunlit day, an archaic homo sapien placed

---

[12] The brain-case volume was almost fifteen-hundred cubic centimeters.

[13] "Man" used in the general sense, here and below, indicates the human race of *both* males and females.

upon the ground a strong flat rock – it *was* an anvil-stone. And he picked up a strong rectangular stone in his right hand – it *was* a hammer-stone. And he grabbed a piece of *flint* in his left hand and placed it on the anvil-stone. And using vertical blows with the hammer-stone, he struck the flint. And *flakes* broke off. And he selected *one* large flake that *he* liked best. Then he set aside the hammer-stone and grabbed a rock, which was V-shaped at one end – it *was* a chisel-rock. And striking the large flake repeatedly with this tool, he *chipped* off tiny bits. And finally, he took a fine-pointed stone and made some indentations. *And* when he was done, the flint flake was a well-sculptured axe. And it was *very sharp*.

And in several hundred-thousand years, wood and stone would *be* combined. And there would be spears with axes on one end. And there would be hammers with granite heads and wooden handles. Now *eventually*, modern man would supplement the wood and stone with metals. And *eventually*, bows and arrows would appear. And for a while, such weapons *would* control the world. But in the Holocene, more sophisticated *weapons* would appear. And *they* would rule the world.

And at a campsite, it happened that a *fire* was getting low – all that remained were glowing coals. And an archaic homo sapien made a *heap* of leaves and wood nearby this dying fire. And he picked up two short leafy branches and cradled them to form a shovel-branch. And with this shovel-branch, he shovelled up some coals. And carried he the coals to the heap of leaves and wood. And *there* he placed the coals. And kneeling down he blew the *coals*, and *they* glowed red. And soon the leaves began to flame. Thus at the campsite, *a new fire* blazed.

## Chapter VII: The Word

*In the beginning was the word.*

It was a cloudless day in the Pleistocene. The women and the children of a tribe of homo sapiens sat in the sun outside their caves. And a baby *crawled* to where the woods began. And her mother stood up and yelled out, "na, na, na." And back and forth she *waved* her hand. But the child crawled behind a bush. And the mother hurried over to the baby and did bring him back.

Thus it came to pass that archaic homo sapiens seemed to learn to give *meaning* to the grunts and sounds they made.

And it was only a question of time – sound *would* turn into signals. And sound signals *would* turn into words: "ya" would mean acceptance, "na" would mean refusal, and "aahh" would indicate a pain. And "mama" *would* mean mother. And "dada" *would* mean father. And so on. And eventually, words would be combined to make sentences and speech. And homo sapiens *would* communicate through sound. Now writing would come later – formal written language would not appear until the Holocene. And it would begin with one man making *marks* in dirt with sticks; at first, the marks would look like pictures of the objects they depicted. But these first pictographs would be a giant step in word-to-word communication, for later, abstract concepts would be represented. And eventually would *come* the written *word.*[14]

## Chapter VIII: The World-Wide Man

*Thou shalt spread abroad to the west, and to the east,*
*and to the north, and to the south.*
*Thy seed shall be as the dust of Earth.*

And archaic homo sapiens continued to evolve at different times in different *places* in the world. And in four-hundred-thousand years BC dwelt Vértesszollos men in Hungary and Swanscombe men in England. And from four-hundred-thousand years BC to seventy-thousand years BC, the Omo homo sapiens and others in East Africa did live. And archaic homo sapiens *progressed*: From one-hundred-seventy-thousand years BC to forty-thousand years BC, the Neanderthals occupied Europe, western Asia and the Middle East. And the strong and muscular *Neanderthals* learned to live in the cold and varying conditions of the Pleistocene by using fire in their caves.

Then around eighty-thousand years BC in Africa, some archaic homo sapiens *became* less muscular, *and* their bones grew lighter. And the modern homo sapien was born. And he was called the *homo sapien sapien* or "wise wise man."[15] And homo sapien sapiens *multiplied*, *spread* and *populated* all of Africa. And they moved into the Middle East. From there, they went off to the west, which was *one* of the *four* directions from which humans had divided *all* directions. And so, in forty-five-thousand years BC they entered Europe, where they were called Cro-Magnons. And the "cultural revolution" *came* to pass: Cro-Magnons made sculptures, created carvings and painted animals on walls of caves. And Earth had *its first art*. And Cro-Magnons practiced mysticism and performed religious rituals. And deliberately buried *they* their dead, sometimes placing flowers by the graves. And Earth had its *first religious race*. And from the Middle East, homo sapien sapiens did wander into Asia. And to all the corners of Eurasia did they spread. And they crossed a cold and frozen Bering Strait to northern North America. From there, they headed south and filled the land of North America. And they continued moving south through Central America and then to South America. And from mountain to towering mountain, from stream to winding stream, from plain to windy plain, everywhere was man – man was *everywhere* on Earth.

---

[14] From such a beginning, man would one day go on to write plays, novels, poetry and songs. He would create drawings, paintings, sculptures and great works of art. And he would record sacred and religious experiences in books.

[15] With a lack of modesty, modern man designated himself to be "the smartest."

*The second book of the New Testament, called*

# The Evolution of Intelligence

*Give me wisdom and knowledge.*

## Chapter I: Reflex, Instinct and Intelligence

*And wisdom and knowledge was he given.*

*I*n *the beginning*[16] was the reflex. And primitive life forms had no choice – the external stimulus produced a determined chain of chemical reactions which, in turn, produced a definite response. In the beginning, a given external input caused a fixed internal output. This was *reflex* – it was the neural network in *its* most elementary form.

Then came the instinctive varying response. And still, ancient life forms had *no choice*, but the outcome was *not certain*. The external stimulus produced a certain chain of chemical reactions which, in turn, *sometimes* generated one response but *sometimes* caused another. And it seemed *as if* Earth's life forms *made* decisions. But *this* was an illusion. Although a given external input did not cause a fixed internal output, possible outputs were *probabilistically* determined. This was *instinct*. And in effect, evolution chose the probabilities with "wisdom." Thus instinct invoked "intelligent" reaction.

Then after hundreds of millions of years came the *truly intelligent response*. Now intelligent response was absent from all animals at birth, for, by definition, animals at birth had instinct only. Intelligence was based on *two* important processes. The *first* was memory: During an animal's existence, past events were stored for later use. And in particular, past responses to stimuli were *stored*. Now learning was the *second* crucial process. Learning was the changing of response-probabilities to optimize *desired* response-outcomes. As a creature lived, it learned. Thus once a creature put a finger in a flame and knew the pain, the finger would not touch a flame again. And so when a stimulus occurred, a certain response would ensue. This was called *decision*. But in fact, a fixed response *was* not guaranteed – it was simply favored: decision-type reaction was probabilistically determined. Now most of the time, intelligent creatures reacted in a "sensible," "intelligent" way. But once in a while, they responded in a "foolish" way. And why? The answer was by *chance* – the communication networks, that is, the nervous and hormonal systems, *picked a path* that actuated a low-probability response. And a "poor" result ensued.[17]

And what were the driving forces involved in molding response-probabilities? They were mainly *pain* and *pleasure* and their derivative

---

[16] The evolution of intelligence began when life on Earth first appeared, more than three-billion years ago.

[17] In short, *learning* was the training of the response system; intelligence was the adaptable response system.

emotions such as fear, desire, greed and lust. These driving forces were instilled in animals by Nature and by evolution.

But in a man, emotions would obtain a higher state. And so there would be feelings such as *faith* and *hope*.

## Chapter II: Man, the Intellectual Miracle

*The eyes of the blind shall be opened.*

And man took learning to a higher level: he learned to learn. And he came to *understand* the learning processes *themselves*. Thus human beings learned to *teach*. And this is typified by textbooks. Thus human beings learned to *train* the mind. And this is typified by the use of practice, drills and repetition – self-training by self-motivated actions. And human beings learned to more or less *adjust* the response-probabilities without direct involvement – they learned to train the neural net without engaging in direct experiences. And this is typified by reading, abstract thinking and deduction. Finally *true* decision making was acquired – human beings found a way in which they could *delay* response-reaction. And this gave them *time* to think and analyze *before* responding and reacting. Thus human beings learned the secret of the "vital force" of thought. And this gave them motivation and a certain level of free will.

Now the development of intelligence was like the growth of the homo-sapien tool trade. First objects were picked up off the ground at *random* to be used as tools. Then tools were *made*. And finally, tools were made which could make tools. And it was this last level of sophistication that was crucial.

Thus learning to learn and to control the learning was the key to true intelligent behavior and true thought. And it was *that* which gave a human being freedom.

And so it came to be that life defeated *absolute* determinism. Now this was not a consequence of quantum mechanical uncertainty – it was a feature of a *special* complex system.[18] Chaos overcame determinism. Animals and human beings found a way to "tilt the odds." *Order* out of chaos was achieved. And out of randomness there came free will.

Thus it came to be that human beings could decide what not to do and what to do. A human being was a rare self-organizing system, which could control in part its destiny.[19]

Now man would use his brain to learn *great things*. And he would discover scientific truths. And he would *write* them down and *teach* them to his fellow men. And he would learn to *understand* the Universe. And he would try to understand *Creation*.

---

[18] This is not to say that quantum mechanics does not play a role; if quantum mechanics *does* play a role, it is a relatively minor one.

[19] It was *as though* man were part god.

## Chapter III: The Effect of Intelligence on Evolution

Now learning to learn and learning to teach accelerated human evolution, for hitherto, in order to evolve, a species had to *wait* for positive environmental pressures and genetic changes. Such processes were *slow* and often were not implemented in all members of a species. But with the human intellect, humans could evolve *without* direct genetic change. Thus when one man uncovered a discovery, such as a new way to make a tool, or a better way to master fire, or a new hunting method, or how to use a mammal skin to keep one warm, or how to make new metals, or how to write, or how to domesticate an animal, or how to build a boat, or how to build a house from wood, or how to cross breed animals, or how to heal a wound, or how to cure the sick, or how to predict the motion of a ball with Nature's laws, or how to control a chemical reaction – thus when one man made such a discovery, he *could* teach it to others, and instantly would others *know*. Thus for example, if exercising made one strong, then man could exercise, and *stronger* would he be. Thus for example, if study made one wise, then man could study, and *wiser* would he be. And so on. And in this way, man began to influence and shape his evolution.

Thus man used his *mind* and *intellect* to his advantage. And unto this day has man done so. And hereafter will man use his mind and intellect for his advancement.[20]

## Chapter IV: Man's Imitating Nature

And man would build *machines* to imitate the animals. He would see birds: planes would be built. He would see water fowl: boats would be built. And so on. And man would conceive computers to imitate the computations of the brain. And man would play biology: there were would be artificial hearts and limbs and body parts.

And Nature and its evolution would be imitated *almost* as if by accident by man. Thus in medieval times, knights would wear a coat of metal plates. And *this* would *be* called armor. And shields would be used to fend off swords. Would a shield not be so different from a shell? Would knights not be like placoderms, the Devonian fish that were encased in bony plates? And twentieth century soldiers would wear a metal helmet. Would such a soldier not resemble pteraspis, the ancient jawless fish that wore a dome-shaped shield upon its head? And modern man would *build* balloons, blimps, gliders, planes and jets. And man would fly. In the beginning, the contraptions would be primitive and mostly *glide* instead of fly. And would this not be like pterosaur,

---

[20] Man can already modify genes directly for his benefit. Such modifications will first be employed to aid patients with genetic diseases. Eventually, they might be used to enhanced desired human features. In such a case, the pace of evolution will dramatically accelerate. Man will twiddle with basic, vital microscopic aspects of life almost like a god.

the first reptile to invade the sky? And man would use air tanks to swim below the surface of the sea. And he would put flippers on his feet to better swim. And would flippers not be just like the tail fins of fish? And to explore the deeper sea, man would manufacture submarines. And submarines would use a tank for buoyancy and movement up and down. Would submarines be not like nautiloids, the swimming chambered shells? And man would venture *where* no man had been before. Thus in the late twentieth century, man would put his feet on the dust-ridden rocky surface of the Moon. And would this not be like ichthyostega, when it first *left* the oceans *and* stepped onto land?

Thus by accident or by intent, *man* would reinvent what Nature had created. And this would be natural, for that which does appear in Nature is normal, evident and practical.

## Chapter V: Weapon Evolution

Now the development of weaponry would have a lengthy history. Thus in the beginning, behind trees and bushes ape-men *hid*. In modern times, infantry would wear green-brown colored uniforms and helmets.

Thus in the beginning did ape-man use flint tools for cutting. Later, man would melt *metal* to make knives. Still later would emerge the sword. And knives and swords would slay for centuries.

Thus in the beginning did ape-man throw handfuls of pebbles at lizards, birds and animals. Later, modern man would find *faster* ways to launch the pellets: And pellets would turn into bullets, and guns would be. And *eventually* would come the rapid-fire gun.

Thus in the beginning, spears did ape-man thrust and throw to kill. Later, man would make thinner, more-refined projectiles. And the poisoned dart and bow-and-arrow would emerge. And in modern times, there *would* be poison-gas and missiles.

Thus in the beginning, ape-man did heave stones to kill large animals. Later, modern man would make exploding spheres. And these would *be* the hand grenades. And they would evolve into more *powerful* explosives – there *would* be bombs. And finally would come atomic bombs.[21]

## Chapter VI: To Be the Mighty Master

*And He created man in His own image.*

And man would use his intelligence to *control* a part of Nature in a tiny way. And in the twentieth century, man would effect great change – he would *reshape* the land of Earth; he would construct skyscrapers *and* build roads; he would sometimes seed a cloud and make

---

[21] With these modern weapons of destruction, man would be able to wage twentieth-century war.

it rain; and he would learn to swim with boats and fly with planes. And in the beginning, man would build *aqueducts* and *wells*. And he would *divert* the waters of some rivers with his dams. And with this water would he work the land. And man would also learn the rudiments of *life* and of *biology*: He would breed the animals for *his* own benefit. And *he* would learn genetic engineering. And man would begin by the third millennium AD to *manipulate* life forms and evolution. And man would start to try to play one role of God.

# The Books Containing
# the Chronicles

## Introduction to the First Four Books

*And man was formed out of the dust of the Earth.*
*And man breathed into his nostrils the breath of life.*
*And man became a living soul.*
*And this happened on the seventh day*
*of the first month of a long lost year.*

Now man would develop in spirit as well as wit. And spiritual leaders and holy teachers would educate their fellow men about the soul. And they would bring to Earth a light *different* from the physical light of flames, stars and lamps – they would bring to Earth *religious* light.

Now mark these words: there is a difference between scientific light and holy light, for science enriches the *mind* but only religion can stir the *soul*.[22] And those who confuse the two will have tormented lives.

As for religion, it began and then evolved quite *naturally*. In the beginning, fire was a *mystery* for man. And so eventually man assigned a spiritual *significance* to fire. And thus was born the *god of fire*. And the rising and the setting of the Sun also was a *mystery* for man. And so eventually man assigned to Sun a spiritual significance. And thus was born the *god of Sun*. And likewise did it happen for the Moon. And man employed and needed deities to explain the *movement* of the clouds and the *stirring* of the wind. And soon were gods of many kinds.

And eventually churches, temples, mosques and synagogues were built so that man would have a house of worship, where *anyone* could pray.

Now there appeared upon the land called Earth four *great* religious leaders.[23] They were Moses, Buddha, Jesus and Muhammad. Here are the stories of these holy ones.

---

[22] This is the Declaration of the Separation of Church and Science.

[23] The fifth major world religion, Hinduism, has no founder.

*The first book of Chronicles, called*

# Moses

*He led his people out of slavery
and brought them to the Promised Land.*

This is the story[24] of Moses, one of the greatest moral prophets.

## Chapter I: A Hebrew Son Is Born

It was three-and-half-thousand years ago. Egypt was a powerful nation. The Pharaoh ruled North Africa and part of the Middle East. Egypt had made slaves of many peoples. Under forced labor, slaves built great structures and treasured cities. Among the slaves were the Children of Israel, the Hebrews. The slaves *suffered* under the burden of their labors.

But the Hebrews continued to live their lives. And they *multiplied* their numbers. And when the Pharaoh saw that the Hebrew population was increasing rapidly, he became worried that they might number too many and might revolt. And the Pharaoh ordered the death of all newborn Hebrew males.

And it came to pass that a certain Hebrew woman bore a son. And *goodness* did she see in the face of her newborn. And knowing that the Pharoah's men would come, she collected reeds and wove them into a basket and placed her infant in the basket. And a teardrop from her eye baptized the baby. Then set *she* afloat the basket in the Nile.

And the basket drifted in a *random and mysterious way* and came to settle on a sandy bank.

Now it happened that the daughter of the Pharaoh went to the Nile to wash. And she spied a basket half on sand and half in water. And inside the basket was a newborn child. And she knew that he was a Hebrew son. And *goodness* did she see in the face of the baby. And she wept. And she instructed her maid to take the child away and nurse it.

And the child was given a name. And the name was Moses, which means "is born."

## Chapter II: Moses in His Youth

And Moses grew up in the palace of the Pharaoh. And to Moses gave the servants education – he was trained in *science* and was taught of *natural phenomena*. And so Moses *understood* what Nature was about. And most importantly, his servants *revealed to him* the moral truths. And Moses also studied magic and amused himself and others with his magic. And he learned the rudiments of military warfare; with

---

[24] A scientifically plausible *rendition* of Moses' story is given here.

a sword did Moses drill with others. And through frequent wrestling matches, Moses became a burly warrior. And compared with others of his age, he was superior, save one handicap – he stuttered. And although his tongue did falter, his body was full of strength, and his mind was full of *wisdom*.

And it came to pass that a woman among those who had reared Moses revealed to Moses his identity – he was a Hebrew. And *with this secret* lived Moses as a prince among Egyptian rulers.

And one day Moses spied an Egyptian taskmaster whipping a Hebrew slave. And emotions inside Moses *moved* him. How could such injustice be inflicted unto one who *was* of his own blood! And rage flowed through the veins of Moses. And Moses slew the taskmaster and buried him in sand.

Now the next day did Moses see two Hebrews fighting. And Moses stopped the fight and *asked* why two of the same blood should fight. And one of the two Hebrews replied, "Who made you a prince to rule over us. Do you intend to kill me as you killed the Egyptian?"

Thus the word of his act spread among the Hebrews. And fearing that the Pharaoh might find out, Moses *fled* to Midian in northwest Arabia. And there did Moses live for many years.

## Chapter III: Moses in Exile

And one day sat Moses in the shade by a well. And *seven daughters* of a priest came to draw water from the well for their flock. And while the daughters were drawing water, shepherds came to draw water too. And the shepherds drove away the daughters so that the daughters could not drink nor draw water for their flock. And Moses saw *goodness* in the faces of the daughters. And he was angered by the shepherds' act. And he fought the shepherds, driving them away. And the daughters drew *water* for their flock.

Now the daughters returned to their father and did tell him what had happened – how an Egyptian had delivered them from danger. And the priest *called* for this Egyptian.

And Moses came to the priest, who gave him bread and wine. And Moses ate the *bread* and drank the *wine*. And the priest presented a daughter to Moses to be his wife. And took *Moses* responsibility for the flock: Moses led the flock and roamed the wilderness in search of green pastures.

## Chapter IV: Moses Returns to the Egyptian Capital

And many years went by. The Pharaoh died. A new Pharaoh ruled the Egyptian empire. And this new Pharaoh *desired* great buildings: He forced the slaves to harder work. And the Children of Israel cried out unto God *by reason of* the bondage. And sound of their cries filled the air and created a *disturbance* in the atmosphere.

Now Moses was tending his flock in a green pasture in a desert. And on the grass lay Moses, relaxed, calm and at peace with Nature. And suddenly *a strange wind* blew the dust in swirls. And tumbling over sand was a *bush on fire*. But the flames did *not* consume the bush. And Moses stood up, ran toward the bush and stopped – he was mesmerized by it, for although the bush continued to tumble and to flame, it did not burn. And suddenly did Moses realize his purpose: In a vision, he saw slaves laboring in Egypt. They, with sunburnt backs and sweaty arms, *suffered* as they toiled. And then he realized they were of his own blood – "his brothers." And emotions filled the blood of Moses. The tear drops which wet the sand soon dried.

And Moses returned to his father-in-law. And the priest saw *purpose* in the eyes of Moses. And the priest said, "I know your calling has come. Go in peace." And Moses set out for Egypt. Now along the way Moses met a man named Aaron, and the two became like brothers. Henceforth, Moses stuttered into Aaron's ear, and Aaron spoke for Moses.

And Moses and Aaron arrived in the ruling city of Egypt and went to the Pharaoh. And Moses *whispered* into Aaron's ear. And Aaron said to the Pharaoh, "He has spoken and his words are 'Let my people go'." And the Pharaoh shouted, "Who is he whose voice I should obey. I know him not, neither will I let the Hebrews go. Out! Out!"

## Chapter V: Moses Uses Magic

And the Pharaoh doubled the work load of the slaves. And the Children of Israel cried out to God *by reason of* their bondage. And the sound of their cries filled the air and created a *disturbance* in the atmosphere.

Now Moses sat upon the sand beneath a palm, because the *shadow* there was *good*. And the palm leaves began to flutter in the *wind*. And Moses pondered deeply. And his inner voice did say to him, "Ye must persuade the Pharaoh by any means – by magic, trick, deceit or through thy use of knowledge of the natural world."

Moses and Aaron returned to the palace. And Moses took a magic rod in hand. Aaron spoke, "He is of great powers. Behold the rod." And with a sleight of hand the rod was cast down and a giant snake appeared *and* crawled on the marble floor. And the Pharaoh called for his magicians. And they too had *magic rods*. And when they threw *them* down, small snakes crawled among themselves *like* a nest of worms. Now the giant snake had not been fed for several days and when it spied the swarming pile, it lashed out and ate the smaller snakes. And the Pharaoh spoke, "Your snake may eat my snakes, but your magic is matched by my magicians' magic."

## Chapter VI: The Nile Turns Blood Red

Frustrated, Moses left and walked two days along the Nile. Then did suddenly Moses smell a *foul* odor. And he saw that the Nile was red with mud and rotting fish. And he knew that a *natural* mud slide of carmine-red soil had dirtied the waters of the Nile and that red organisms had flourished in the muddy water, making *it* blood red. And Moses saw the red waters drifting downstream toward the Egyptian capital. And then decided Moses to use Nature to instill *fear* into the Pharaoh's mind. Moses ran, found Aaron, and the two hurried to the Pharaoh. And said Aaron to the Pharaoh, "He is disappointed that you will not free the Hebrews. The waters of the Nile *shall* turn red."

Now the next day the muddy waters, with rotten fish and blood-red algae, entered the Egyptian city. And the water could *not* be drunk; *air* smelled foul; and flies flew everywhere. And for seven days could the Egyptians not drink the waters of the Nile. But the Pharaoh did not let the Hebrews go.

## Chapter VII: The Plague of Frogs

Moses and Aaron sat along the bank of the Nile. And suddenly saw they *thousands* of frogs leaving the waters of the river. And Moses knew that the mud flow had disrupted their habitats. And the two ran to the Pharaoh. And Aaron spoke, "If you do not let the Hebrews go, frogs will invade your city." The Pharaoh shook his head, "I am a great man. How dare you threaten me with frogs." And Aaron said, "We do not threaten you. It is a *natural* force that shall bring disaster to you and to your people." To which the Pharaoh said, "Natural force? I do not understand these words."

Hours later, the frogs reached the city. In all the streets they hopped. Some slipped into the homes of people. Entered frogs in *all places* of the city. And the Pharaoh was enraged that frogs should occupy his palace. And in a fit without thought, he said, "Take the frogs away and I will let your people go." And after several days of being away from their natural water habitats, the frogs in the hot dry heat began to die. Dead frogs were everywhere. The city stank.

And when the Pharaoh saw that the plague of frogs had passed, his heart *hardened. And* he did not let the Hebrews go.

## Chapter VIII: The Sun Turns Black

Moses and Aaron sat under a palm wondering what to do. And Moses said to Aaron, "We must wait until more natural disasters come and convince the Pharaoh that their reason *be* the slavery of our people. In the meantime, go and find fellow Hebrews who will help our cause." And Aaron gathered a group of faithful ones. And they became Moses' disciples, followers and helpers.

And several months went by. Now Moses knew that, on the Monday of the following week, the moon would *eclipse* the Sun at noon. Moses and Aaron went to the Pharaoh and did tell him, "You must free the Hebrews lest the Sun on Monday noon turn black." But the Pharaoh turned his head away. And at Monday noon, the Moon *eclipsed* the Sun. And the Pharaoh, who had never seen an eclipse, was *filled* with fear. And he said, "I shall let the Hebrews go. Please give brightness to the Sun." And Aaron, speaking for Moses, said, "It is Nature who makes your Sun grow black. But your promise to release the Hebrews will bring forth light." And a dozen minutes later, the first rays from a crescent Sun shone forth. And in several hours, again the Sun was fully bright.

But the next day, the heart of the Pharaoh *hardened* and he did not let the Children of Israel leave.

And months went by. And chained by foot and hand, the Hebrews labored under a hot Sun.

## Chapter IX: The Plague of Locusts

And one day Moses saw a *dark cloud* in the distance. And he sent a disciple to investigate. And the disciple returned, saying, "The cloud is not a cloud. It is a swarm of locusts."

And Moses saw that the cloud was approaching the Egyptian city. And he and Aaron went to the Pharaoh. "A natural disaster is coming, if you do not free the Hebrews. Locusts will come and eat your crops." But the Pharaoh refused to free even a *single* slave. And by end of day, locusts covered the face of Egypt. They invaded the land and ate the crops. They covered *every stone* in every street. They infested homes. And the people could not go outside, lest locusts cover all their body. And the Pharaoh wanted this man called Moses killed. He called unto his *wise* men to consult. And his wise men said, "Do not kill this Moses, lest the locusts never go." And the Pharaoh sent for Moses and said, "End this plague of locusts and I shall set the Hebrews free." And Moses answered, "You must be patient. In two days will the locusts leave."

And in two days, the locusts left. But shortly thereafter, the heart of the Pharaoh *hardened*, and he did not let the Hebrews go.

## Chapter X: The Plague of Hail

And many months went by. And it came to pass that Moses saw *dark* clouds and lightning in the distance. And he sent a disciple to investigate. And the disciple rode *swiftly* across the desert on the back of a camel. And when he arrived below the clouds of the thunderstorm, he saw great balls of hail *falling* from the sky. And he returned to Moses and told him of his findings. And Moses observed that the clouds had almost arrived at the Egyptian city. And Moses and Aaron went to the Pharaoh, saying, "You must let the Hebrews go, else balls of ice will fall from the sky and destroy your crops." And the Pharaoh *ignored* these words. And thirty minutes later, the storm arrived. Hail fell everywhere – upon the roofs of houses, in the streets and in the fields. People took shelter in their houses. Limbs broke off trees. Lightning flashed and set fire to bushes and to grass. Damage was done to roofs of houses when the pellets fell from heaven. As hail struck the flax and barley, crops were crushed. And the Pharaoh called Moses and *begged* him to stop the rain of ice. And on behalf of Moses, Aaron spoke, *saying*, "It is not I who creates disaster. It is your stubbornness which has disturbed Nature. Nature is outraged with you, for you will not let the Hebrews go." And the Pharaoh said, "Enough. I shall let your people go."

And after six hours, the storm subsided and the hail ceased. But the next day, the heart of the Pharaoh *hardened* and he did not let the Children of Israel leave.

## Chapter XI: The Plague of Darkness

And many months went by. It was a beautiful cloudless summer day. And Moses saw a *blackness* on the horizon in the East. And he thought this *strange*, for his knowledge of weather told him that fair skies should prevail for at least another day. And Moses took a camel and trotted off toward the cloud of black. And four hours did he travelled. And as he approached the cloud, a dirty fog appeared. The air was full of soot and ash. And Moses *knew* that an enormous volcanic eruption had taken place – he had been told of such things as a youth. And he knew that it would take several days to clear. And Moses returned to the city of the Pharaoh. And Aaron spoke for Moses, "Pharaoh, a disaster is about to happen. You must let the Hebrews go, lest darkness will be upon the face of Egypt." And the Pharaoh *thought* this funny and he laughed.

And an east wind arose and *blew in the heavens*. And that evening, the cloud of soot and ash engulfed the city. The next morning *all* was black – it was day but it was night, for the Sun shone not and blackness was upon the face of Egypt. It was a darkness *which could be felt*, for soot was in the air. And the Pharaoh was terrified. He summoned Moses. He *begged* forgiveness. And Moses thought that *this time* the Hebrews *would* be freed. And the Pharaoh heard the words, "Let the Hebrews go and the darkness will be gone in three days' time." And the Pharaoh said, "Be it so."

But the Hebrews could not travel, for darkness was upon the face of Egypt and the air was full of soot. And so the Hebrews waited for the sky to clear. And the Pharaoh spoke to his head taskmasters, telling them that the Hebrew slaves had been released. And one head taskmaster said, "If you let the Hebrews go, the other slaves will revolt, discipline among the workers will be lost, and buildings will *not* be built." And the Pharaoh realized *this* was true. And he gave the command not to release the Hebrew slaves. And on the fourth day, the air cleared. But the Hebrews found themselves again with chains around their arms and fetters on their feet.

## Chapter XII: The Plague of Lice

And Moses and his followers met in a *secret place*. And Moses spoke to them, saying, "We cannot continue to wait for natural disasters. We must make trouble for the Pharaoh. We must *do* what Nature does."

And he *sent* his disciples to find rat lice, for rat lice are the fastest breeding lice of all. And his disciples travelled several weeks to a forest where rats lived. And they collected lice in containers and brought them back to the Egyptian capital. And at night, they tossed the lice through windows into homes.

Then did go Moses and Aaron to the Pharaoh and say, "If you do not let my people go, lice will invade your city in three days." But the Pharaoh had Moses and Aaron thrown out of the palace. And in three days' time did the lice multiply a *hundredfold*. And the people of the city found lice in the hairy parts of their bodies. And the people, being superstitious, *thought* that an evil spirit had invaded them. And the Pharaoh sent for Moses and said, "End this plague of lice and I shall set the Hebrews free." And although Moses knew a formula for a potion that would kill the lice, he told the Pharaoh, "Your bad faith *is* beyond reprieve. It is natural that lice invade your homes and breed. The *anger of Nature* cannot be stopped unless you free the Hebrews. If you do not break the chains, sickness will strike and kill your cattle." But the Pharaoh did not set the Hebrews free, for the Pharaoh *remembered* the words of the head taskmaster.

## Chapter XIII: Moses Multiplies His Attacks

And Moses had his disciples travel to a far away town and buy poison. And when they returned, they *spread* poison in the fields where cattle grazed. And several days later, cattle lay upon their sides in pastures. And several days after that, the cattle died. But the cattle of the Hebrews did not die, for they grazed on *different* pastures.

And Moses sent some of his followers to find sick souls with diseases similar to small pox. And he *instructed* his followers to wear thick cloth over their mouths and to keep a distance from the sick. "Tell the sick that I am one who can cure their ills." And in several months, many sick were brought to Moses. And Moses, through the voice of Aaron, spoke to the sick, *saying*, "To cure your sickness, you must spit on the ground and cough through the windows of the houses in this city."

And Moses and Aaron went to the Pharaoh. "You must free the Hebrews, lest in a week your people have sores on their skin." But the Pharaoh did *refuse*. And the people of the Egyptian capital fell sick. Sores did appear upon their skin. Spots could be seen upon their hands and faces. And the people were fearful of the *evil* that had permeated their Egyptian city. And pestilence *was* upon the people. Some elderly did die. Some children died. And among the dead *was* the Pharaoh's son. And the Egyptians rose up in *protest* against the Pharaoh. And they *blamed* him for their miseries. And the Pharaoh saw his city ruined. He summoned Moses and Aaron, and he said, "I shall let the Hebrews go, but you must promise to stop the plague of sickness on the people. Take your flocks and herds, and gone be you." And Aaron spoke, saying, "In three days shall the plague be gone."

The chains were unlocked. The Hebrews *threw down* the iron that had held them so. And they joined Moses and headed off toward the Sinai. And they did not stop to sleep at night, for Moses *knew* that only Nature and not he could stop the plague.

## Chapter XIV: The Pharaoh Pursues the Israelites

And after three days, more people in the Egyptian capital fell sick and died. And the Pharaoh was *enraged* because Moses had not kept his promise. The Pharaoh told his chief military leader, "Gather the most able soldiers *and* pursue the Hebrews. Bring them back. Bring this evil Moses to me." And *six-hundred* chariots exited the city and sped off into the desert.

## Chapter XV: Moses Prepares His Escape

Now Moses *knew* the route to the Sinai. And he *knew* that he and his people would have to cross the Sea of Reeds. And he *knew* that the Pharaoh's army would arrive in a few days. The escape had he well prepared.

The strongest Hebrew men went upstream where the Sea of Reeds narrowed between two large rocks. And they cut down trees and threw them in the water between the two large rocks. And some trees floated away but *some* trees stuck. And they gathered bushes and threw them into the water where lay the trees. And they rolled large boulders forth into the river. And the labor was hard but it was a *labor* they well knew. Pleased were the Hebrews to do such work when freedom was the goal. And with much effect, they *diverted* the waters of the Sea of Reeds.

## Chapter XVI: The Hebrews Cross the Sea of Reeds

Downstream, the Sea of Reeds became a trickle. Moses announced, "We have turned a sea into a stream. *Let* us pass." And the Children of Israel crossed the shallow waters and entered a new land.

Thus they did succeed in passing to the river's other side. And river's *other* side became river's *nearer* side. And after everyone had passed, the strongest Hebrew males returned to the site of the two large rocks. And they stood on the eastern bank and thrust logs and threw *large* stones at the dam. And broke there finally a hole. And the *waters* of the Sea of Reeds rushed through. And soon other pieces of the dam gave way. And a *giant* wave sped forward down a hill.

## Chapter XVII: The Hebrews Escape to Freedom

Now downstream, Moses and his people spied chariots. And fear *filled* the Hebrews' hearts. Chariots entered the *shallow* waters. One chariot reached the other side – Hebrews attacked the chariot and made it overturn. Then in the bed of the Sea of Reeds came a *giant* wave of water – it struck the army like a giant fist. Chariots toppled over and were washed away. Horses showed their teeth as they neighed and were propelled downstream. Soldiers full of fear bobbed helplessly in the white foaming waters *and* were swept away.

Thus Moses led his people out of the land of Egypt. Thus Moses led his people out of slavery and to freedom.

And the Hebrews made Moses their leader. And Moses would command the Hebrews *until* his death.

## Chapter XVIII: Moses Forms a Society and Religion

Now during the rest of his lifetime, Moses taught his people all his *knowledge*. He showed them maps and instructed them in geography. He *explained* how volcanos, mountains, plains, lakes and streams formed. He taught them about disease. He provided formulas for medicines. He explained the clouds and weather. He taught the Hebrews about plants, mammals, reptiles, birds, amphibians and all life. He had them *understand* the stars in heaven. In short, he explained how *Nature* worked. And the Hebrews became the wisest people anywhere.

And Moses laid down the rules for daily life. Issues of cleanliness and the proper preparation of food were explained. And Moses *preached* the laws for daily conduct. Rules concerning marriage and family affairs were written down. Laws of inheritance were issued, civil liberties and regulations were announced, and the penalties for violation of laws were posted. And Moses selected and trained judges to decide disputes. And when conflicts were unresolved, he presided over *them* and *they* were solved.

And Moses founded a religion: "There shall be one God and *only* one. Six days shall man labor. And on the seventh must man pray." And other religious rules were then established. Ceremony, atonement, worship and sacrifice were so explained. Holy garments were woven and priests were consecrated. *And so on.*

Hence Moses was a leader, teacher, scientist, priest and judge.

But the most important teachings of Moses were his *moral* teachings. He explained what was *right* and what was *wrong*. He wrote down in stone the commandments of moral conduct: Thou shall honor thy father and thy mother. Thou shall not steal. Thou shall not lie. Thou shall not kill. *And so on.*

## Chapter XIX: The Land of Promise Is Found

A nd so the Hebrews did escape the land of bondage. And they *came* unto a desert. And for forty years the Hebrews wandered in the deserts of the Middle East. Then *they* did make it to the *other* side. And they went in search for *a just land* for their people and religion. And one day when Moses was very old, the Hebrews arrived on top of Mount Pisgah, which overlooked a splendid land of pastures – it was a land of milk and honey. And Moses spoke, "This is the land of promise. This is *our Promised Land.*"

Moses had delivered his people. His mission was completed. And tears filled the eyes of Moses, for so happy was he so. And Moses died there on the hill with his teary eyes still open, still staring at the land of promise. And the spirit of Moses rose up and was *placed* among the holy ones.

*The second book of Chronicles, called*

# Buddha

*Evam me sutam.*[25]

This is the story of Buddha, an ancient pious Asian leader.

## Chapter I: The Buddha's Early Life

And in the sixth century BC in the Sakyas,[26] there were a wealthy king and queen whose names were Suddhodana and Mahamaya. Now these were ancient times when *reincarnation* was accepted dogma: No one really died – at death there was rebirth.

And Mahamaya had a dream: She saw an elephant so beautiful and white. And her body opened up a hole, and through her *side* the elephant did enter.

Now the next day, she asked her priests, "What does this vision mean?" And to her they said, "*Thou* shalt have a son. And thy son will be presented with two paths – either he *will* become an emperor or he *will* become a universal teacher. Like a fork in a road, these two destinies will lie before him. *Four signs* will indicate to him which way to go."

And nine months later, on the full-moon day of the month of May, in five-hundred-sixty-three BC, and in the shelter and the shade of a green park, Mahamaya did give birth – she *gave* the world a son.

Now Asita, the king's oldest wisest spiritual advisor, went to see the newborn boy. And Asita scrutinized the newborn's skin for *telltale* signs. And suddenly did Asita's face light up. And he was overjoyed and overwhelmed, for the patterns on the skin foretold this boy would *be* a buddha.[27] But then a darkness filled Asita's countenance. And he did so weep, for he knew his *own* death would come before the instant when this prince became a buddha.

And Asita told the king his findings. And Asita and the king knelt down before the child and prayed.

Five days later, priests were summoned to give the child a name. And the child became Siddhattha, which means "One-Whose-Aim-Shall-Be-Accomplished." And Gotama was his family name. And among the priests were eight *specialists* at reading body marks. And the eight men scrutinized the young one's skin. And seven out of eight predicted two possibilities for Siddhattha's fate – *if* he remained at home, he would become a universal ruler, but *if* he left the palace he would become a buddha. But the eighth priest, whose name was Kondanna, said Siddhattha *would* without a doubt become a buddha.

---

[25] Thus I have heard.
[26] This is a region near the border of Nepal and India.
[27] The term buddha means "Enlightened-One."

And two days later did Siddhattha's mother die – his sister would become his mother.

And several years went by. And it came to pass that the yearly agriculture festival took place. And King Suddhodana and his ministers and farmers went to the *countryside* to celebrate. And the little prince Siddhattha came along. And his nurses took care of him *inside* a tent. Now outside, the nurses heard the singing, cheering, and the laughing. And all the nurses *went* outside to join the fun. And their hearts and minds were occupied with earthly pleasures. And they too sang and danced and laughed. Then one of them remembered that their duty was the care of Suddhodana's son. And they rushed back to the tent and found the prince there *sitting*, cross-legged with hands on knees and in a *trance*. How *strange* it was to see Siddhattha in a trace! And someone summoned Suddhodana. And the king saw his son there like a yogi meditating. And for a second time, the king knelt down before the child and prayed.

Now Siddhattha grew into a strong and charming lad. And he was divinely handsome – he possessed a beauty that transcended even a woman's beauty.

Now Suddhodana did not want the prince to leave the palace – he could not bear to see his son, the prince, a wandering shaved-head ascetic, as some *priests* had *so* predicted. And so Suddhodana was determined to have his son become an emperor. And the child was *shielded against* the outside world – the prince was prevented from seeing anything that might make him *want* to be a priest.

And lotus ponds were constructed for the prince. In one pond, the lotuses were *red*; in another were they *blue*; and in still another were they *white*. Siddhattha was clad in clothes of finest cloth. His servants dressed him in the morning and took off the clothes at night. Siddhattha ate the *finest* food, while female musicians played and sung and *filled* his ears with melodies and songs. Three palaces were built for him – one for winter, one for summer and one for the two *other* rainy seasons.

And so Siddhattha spent his youth in luxury. He did not see the misery of peasants living in the villages and countryside.

And among his cousins there was one, who was a lovely *beauty* to behold. Her name was Yasodhara. And when she was sixteen years old, the king announced a contest of skill and strength in which the winner would *win* her as his wife. And Siddhattha, who was sixteen too, engaged in battles with the others. But no one was a match for him. And Siddhattha married Yasodhara.

## Chapter II: The Four Signs

And for many years did Siddhattha live in *luxury*. He had a lovely wife, money, and good health; he possessed a thousand personal belongings; he had beauty, charm and personality; and he was adept at everything. He had what most would say was *everything*. And in his palaces Siddhattha lived a happy easy life.

Yet there was something *missing*. And Siddhattha started studying religion.

And at the age of twenty-nine, the prince began to wonder of the outside world. And so one day, he *summoned* his servant-driver, and the two went riding in a chariot. And lo, they came upon an agèd man whose *back* was badly *bent*, who used a *staff* to walk. And Siddhattha asked, "What has happened to that man?" And his servant-driver said, "That man is old. All men eventually turn old." And the prince, who had never seen anything but pleasant sights, was inside *disturbed*.

And some time later, Siddhattha went riding in his chariot again. And it came to pass that he came upon a man *lying* in the road – the man was very ill and *suffering*. And one could smell the stench of sweat and urine. And Siddhattha was perturbed, "What has happened to that man?" asked he. And his driver said, "That man is sick. All men at some time get sick."

And on still another trip, Siddhattha and his driver came upon a corpse. And Siddhattha asked, "What has happened to that man?" And his driver said, "That man is dead. In the end, *all* men end up dead."

And on a fourth trip, Siddhattha and his driver met a shaven-headed man, draped in a yellow robe. How *peaceful* was his face! And Siddhattha was perplexed – *how* could such a man be so serene in the midst of misery. And Siddhattha vowed to solve the riddle of serenity and misery.

And Siddhattha saw a little light. And in a small way was he enlightened – he *realized* the first three signs were signs of human suffering. Now this was particularly disturbing, for suffering was indeed an awful thing, but to be reborn after death into a life of suffering again and then again and so on was a horror too horrible for any mortal mind to bear.

And Siddhattha asked himself, "How could one *escape* the endless cycle of birth and suffering, of suffering and death, of rebirth and further suffering, and so on to the end of time?" Now Siddhattha did not know the answer, but he knew that the robed ascetic knew the way.

And upon arriving at the palace, the prince was greeted with good news – his wife had given them a son. The son was named Rahula, which means "fetters." And this was indeed ironic, for *soon* the prince would break his family bonds.

## Chapter III: The Great Renunciation

And Siddhattha's mind and soul became perturbed. He was disturbed by human suffering. So much did he *want* to find a way to end all suffering. His family life no longer brought him pleasure, and he

tossed and turned at night in bed. He was one who had everything it
seemed, and yet, *he* inside was suffering.

And one night quite late, from his bed the prince arose. And quietly he dressed himself and headed *out* the room. At the door he looked
back at his wife and son. This would be one of two times that he *would*
look back.

And while all others were asleep, he mounted Kanthaka, his favorite horse. And *left* the prince his palace and his home. And it was
*strange*, but the hoofs of Kanthaka against the ground did make no
sound. Behind him was the city of his youth and the capital of Suddhodana's kingdom.

And just before the Sun rose, he arrived at *a great river*. And he
turned around and saw his father's city far away. That would be the
*last* time he looked back. And he dismounted, discarded his princely
clothes, and donned the habit of a monk. And after remounting Kanthaka, he stood momentarily upon the bridge, watching the waters, the
steady current, and the peace that passèd there beneath. Then he
crossed the flowing river's waters – this would be the first of *many*
mighty rivers he would cross. He shook the reins with vigor and rode
off.

And Siddhattha headed *south*. And *there* he met a king. And
King Bimbisara was struck by Siddhattha's beauty and serenity. And
on discovering that this ascetic *was* a prince, the king offered to the
prince regal comforts and a place to stay. But Siddhattha said, "Of
these pleasures do I know. I am in search of *truth*. So I must go." And
*said* the king, "When thou find the truth, I pray thee, return to here
and tell me of the truth." Siddhattha so agreed.

## Chapter IV: The Noble Quest: The Search for Truth

And Siddhattha left the king and *sought* out holy teachers of the
truth. And he studied under one such priestly master, practicing
self-discipline and meditation. And one day, he fell into a trance. And
of his self and soul did he forget – he had reached a low-level transcendental state. *It* would *be* the first step to the higher meditation states.

And so through meditation, thought and learning did the prince
attain a state of "No-Thing." And Siddhattha said, "Master, *teach* me
more." But his master said, "Thou hast obtained the highest state of
mind and mediation that I know – I *cannot* teach thee more."

And although few men attain the state of "No-Thing," Siddhattha
was not satisfied. And so he left his master in *quest* of deeper universal
truths.

Thus began the search for *high enlightenment*. Thus began the
journey to escape the everlasting and unchanging suffering of man.

And Siddhattha went to a famous meditation master. And
Siddhattha studied all the master's wisdom. And one day, the prince,
while in a trance, forgot his self and soul. Oblivious was he to *all*

around him, for he had reached the higher state of "No-Perception – No-Nonperception." And this indeed was something that *few* monks attained. But *still* the prince was not content. And he left the meditation master to seek out even higher states.

And Siddhattha travelled to the countryside and *wandered* in the forest. And there found he a quiet *natural* setting – it was a land of beauty, with lovely trees, green pastures and a flowing stream of clear blue water. And *there* he lived a hermit's life. And *there* he learned new meditation methods – his self-discipline was developed to a deeper level. But this was *not* enough, for although Siddhattha's soul was suffering a little less, it *was* still suffering.

Then it happened that he met a group of five ascetics. And behold, among the five was Kondanna, the priest who had predicted that the prince would one day be a buddha. And Siddhattha joined the five and practiced *their* ascetic way. Self-mortification, self-denial and meditation *were* their way.

And with little nourishment did he grow thin – his joints *withered* into smallish knots; his back-bone protruded, looking *like unto* a chain of balls; his ribs pushed through the flesh; the sockets of his eyes became large cavities; his belly bulged like a woman pregnant with a child. And so badly wanted *he* to give up and give in. But *he* resisted so. And for six years he lived an austere life of self-directed, self-induced denial.

And one day, he *lost* all *consciousness*. And those around him thought he'd passed away. Indeed, he passed quite near death's path. When he awoke, he had a revelation: He *realized* he had strayed – the path to Nirvana did not pass through the land of the ascetic. He, by chance, had walked into a "*desert* land." And he had somehow gone astray. Beneath his feet was not an earth but "sand." And so he did retreat.

And the prince gave up asceticism. In a normal fashion did he eat. He exercised his body so that he could better exercise his *mind*.

And his five ascetic friends, *saddened* by his change, departed disappointed. And they left the land of the flowing stream and lovely trees and continued on the path of self-induced denial.

## Chapter V: Enlightenment at Last

*As the Sun sets each day,*
*so go the dead.*
*And in the morning when the Sun rises,*
*then men are born again.*

And it came to pass that when Siddhattha, the bodhisattva,[28] was thirty-five years old, he *sat* himself beneath a bo fig tree.[29] And he

---

[28] The word bodhisattva means "Buddha-To-Be."

[29] Known in botany as *Ficus religiosa*.

vowed *not* to leave until he solved the riddle of eternal suffering. And there he sat cross-legged, thump to finger, palms pointing to the heavens, and eyelids closed. And without food, he contemplated for nine and forty days.

And Mara, *the evil being*, came. And Mara tempted him to stray by trying many things to try to *break* Siddhattha's trance. *First* created Mara whirlwinds, which swept leaves and dust about. And Siddhattha swayed back and forth but *stayed* steadfast. Then came a flood from nowhere. And the gushing water reached Siddhattha's chin. And *still* he did not flinch. *Next* did shake the earth. And the shaking earth did shake the bodhisattva's body, but his mind still *did* not budge. Then came three gorgeous women in transparent garb. And seductively they danced around. And they introduced themselves – their names were Passion, Pleasure and Desire. And although they danced before the bodhisattva's eyes, none of their images did enter *his* mind's eye.

And he defended himself with the ten Great-Virtues:[30] wisdom, effort, patience, truth, determination, charity, renunciation, love, morality, and equanimity.

And Siddhattha heard inside himself the words "Look *at* thyself. *Thou* be emaciated, pale, near death. *Thou* must live. Surely life is better than *excruciating* pain. Why try to strive for things which *thou* can't hope to so obtain? *Break* thy trance and live!" And these were Mara's words. And the bodhisattva spoke to the inner voice, "Lust be thy first army, dislike for pious life be thy second force, the third be thirst and hunger, thy fourth force be of craving, the fifth be idleness and laziness, the sixth be fear and cowardice, the seventh army uses doubt, the eighth employs hypocrisy and stubbornness, while the ninth consists of want of praise, honor and false glory, and thy last army, the tenth, be the disdain of others and the exaltation of one's self. No feeble man can conquer your invading forces, yet only by destroying them can a bodhisattva reach Nirvana. *Shame* on me if I retreat. Better to die in battle than to live a life consisting of defeat." And the bodhisattva's thoughts went out like *countless shooting arrows.*

And so the Buddha-To-Be resisted all temptations. And he *turned* back all attacks. And on the last of the nine and forty days, Mara *beseeched* the bodhisattva for evidence of his benevolence. And with a *fist* did the bodhisattva *pound* the ground. And there the earth did *shake* and rumble like a thunder. And out of the thundering ground did *sound* the words: "*I am his witness.*"

And Mara fled.

And deep meditation descended on the bodhisattva, *as if* it had come from Heaven. And he had a thousand dreams it seemed. In each dream he saw the *story* of a different man. But each man was he. And

---

[30] In the sacred Pali language these are called the Paramitas.

in this manner, he acquired all knowledge that he had already in past lives acquired. And so he gained the experiences of *past* existences.

And in his trance he had a vision. And in the vision were so many *ghosts* of human dead. The corpses drifted to a *mighty river* where there stood a bridge. The multitudes – a million screaming "Munchs" – just *streamed* toward the bridge. Like water did they flow. Non-intermittent *was* the flow. And through an iron gate, the ghostly corpses passed. So many seemed to go. At the first bridge post, their *skin* dissolved away. At the second post, *they* were bloody inner *flesh*. At the third bridge post, all flesh did melt and vaporize. At the next post, they were but *bones* – but inside each one's rib-cage was a *glow*. At the fifth and last bridge post, gone *even* were the bones. On river's *other* side were only glowing spheres. To the bodhisattva's eyes, the stream of glows was a scene of beauty to behold; they were like moving blurry candle flames. And along river's other bank did stream the glowing spheres. And they drifted to another bridge, and over it they passed. And in doing so they moved from river's *other* side to river's *nearer* side. And as each re-crossed the river, each glowing sphere did shrink. And at another iron gate, each *glow* became egg-like and miniscule. And upon arriving on river's near-side bank, the objects radiated out in *all* directions.

And so the bodhisattva gained the superhuman eye, the power to see the passing and rebirth of human beings.

And the bodhisattva saw imperfections in his mind and body. And he *cleansed* his mind and body of all flaws.

And the bodhisattva saw Four Noble Truths. Now the First Noble Truth was that of *suffering*. Suffering was inherent in all life. It began at birth, it continued in times of sickness and old age, and it came in death. It arose in contact with unpleasant things. But it also came in separation from the pleasant. And it arose in failing to obtain one's goals or one's desires.

Now the Second Noble Truth concerned the *source* of suffering. And this source was human craving. "When there is delight and passion, one *thinks* that one is happy. But when delight and passion go away, the desire of them *leads* to suffering. The thirst one has today can be satisfied by a glass of wine, but tomorrow will the thirst return. Hunger may be appeased one day by the eating of some bread, but the next day will the hunger come again. The lust for pleasant things can only *momentarily* be satisfied." These were the thoughts the bodhisattva *realized*. Thus life was an endless cycle of hunger, thirst and lust; hunger, thirst and lust. And the instinct *to want to live* was the source of man's rebirth. And then at rebirth *would* the craving once again begin.

Now the Third Noble Truth concerned *cessation* of the suffering. "By giving up desire shall ye overcome thy craving. And having overcome thy craving *shall* ye then be free." These were the bodhisattva's thoughts.

Now the Fourth Noble Truth described the path leading to elimination of *the craving wants*. And this path was the Eightfold Path of Proper-Things: right action, right view, right thought, right speech, right livelihood, right mindfulness, right effort and right concentration. And by following the Eightfold Path shall *craving* be extinguished. And once it is extinguished, *deliverance* from suffering shall be obtained.

And the bodhisattva saw the light. And this time he saw *all* the light. He had *solved* the riddle of eternal suffering. He *knew* what path to choose to rid oneself of suffering. And with this revelation came Enlightenment. And *he* became The Buddha.

Now to rid himself of suffering, Gotama the Buddha mediated more. And through mediation did he journey on the *path of Proper-Things*.

And after another nine and forty days, with legs folded open *and* with wrists on knees, The Buddha did breathe *deeply* in and out. And a deep relaxation *passed* through Buddha's body. And he had another transcendental trance. His skin, a barrier, *dissolved* – he could *feel* his surroundings. And in some sense his surroundings *were* his skin. Then his flesh dissolved. His body and surroundings melted into one. He and Nature were united – *they* were *one*. The region of his presence grew. It expanded exponentially. His mind expanded astronomically. He *sensed* the outer reaches of the Universe. The Universe and he were *one*.

Then the entire history of the Universe passed *through* his mind. Ignorance was *cast* away. Science and knowledge were obtained. Darkness vanished, and light arose. His *mind* attained emancipation.

And when he descended from his trance, there was a total and eternal *peace* of mind and soul. *He* was in a *perfect* state of calm insight. *He* was passionless and wise. He *had* achieved Nirvana.

Thus after two times nine and forty days, on the full-moon day of the month of May and beneath a bodhi tree, did Gotama the Buddha so attain a transcendental freedom. And no longer *would* he be subjected to the sorrows of existence and rebirth.

*(And a voice spake, saying,*
*"May ye achieve a state of spiritual perfection.*
*May ye follow in the footsteps of a buddha*
*and Nirvana find.")*

## Chapter VI: Dissemination of the Truth

And Gotama the Buddha saw the Universe as no other had before. *All* was relative and interdependent. There was no eternal, everlasting, unchanging thing. Not even *soul* was permanent.

And The Buddha sat himself beneath a banyan fig tree and announced, "I have discovered A-Great-Truth, which is *deep* and difficult to understand. And those with passion cannot see this truth. Such men can only see the *darkness* that surrounds this deep and subtle truth."

And because the *truth* was *so* profound, The Buddha did hesitate to tell *it* to the holy priests before him. "*How* can others understand what I have understood," he thought. "This truth is too profound." But one wise priest then spoke, "In a lotus pond are lotuses. And some lotuses sit *beneath* the water. And some lotuses float *in* the water. And still other lotuses hold their petals *above* the water. As *be* the lotuses, so *be* the minds of men." And then The Buddha realized that, among those in front of him, *some* would understand at least in part. And The Buddha decided to disseminate the truth. The Buddha had the priests before him put aside their feelings. And into a tranquil state he put their minds and souls. And he explained to them the *truth* that he had just discovered. Thus began The Buddha's role as a great religious teacher.

And The Buddha sought out others who might understand, for having understood, they *too* could spread the truth. And he returned to the five ascetics of his past. And he announced, "I am A-Perfect-One, I am An-Awakened-One, and I am one who will transcend the earthly world. I have come to teach The-Law."[31] And they did not believe his words, *for* they thought the way to perfectness lay in asceticism. How could Gotama, who had abandoned their path to perfection, be *now* "A-Perfect-One?" And Gotama replied, "Do ye not see before thee *one* who is so changed? Did I speak to thee in words like these before?" And indeed he spoke in an astonishingly open manner and with an *awe of wisdom* they have never heard before.

And then Gotama the Buddha gave a sermon. And he spoke of one who left a home of luxury to live a life of self-denial. And only later did this man learn that the *path* to "One-Who-Has-Attained"[32] lay in the *middle* road. And the middle road, the Noble Eightfold Way, contained the path to awakening, truth, vision, calmness, knowledge and Nirvana. And the Noble Eightfold Path consisted of eight Proper-Things. And he *explained* the eight correct and Proper-Things. Then spoke The Buddha of Four Noble Truths. "First know that man's existence is full of sorrow, conflict, pain and suffering. And this is the First Noble Truth – it is *the truth of misery*. Next know that all this be caused by man's desire – the never-ending hunger, the unrelenting thirst, the craving for the earthly things, the lust for pleasure and the drive to be. Even Wanting-Not-To-Be is a type of craving. And this is the Second Noble Truth – *the truth of great desire*. Next know that liberation from all this, for human beings, does exist; this is called Nirvana. Know that desire too can be dispelled. And this is the Third Noble Truth – *the existence of a path to transcendental freedom*. Lastly know that this path be the Noble Eightfold Path. And this is the Fourth Noble Truth – *thou shalt pursue the Eightfold Path*."

---

[31] In the sacred Pali language, "A-Perfect-One" is called an Arahant, "An-Awakened-One" is called a Sammasambuddha, and "The-Law" is known as the Dhamma.
[32] "One-Who-Has-Attained" is called Tathagata in Pali.

And the five ascetics were *enlightened* with the sutta. And they bowed down, saying "Lord Gotama the Buddha." And the five became the *first* five Buddhist monks.

And the sermon was so named: "To-Set-the-Wheel-of-Truth-in-Motion." And so the wheel of truth was set in motion.

And a few days later, Gotama the Buddha spoke again. This time the subject of the sermon was No-Self. "To go from Atman to Anatman, to go from Self to No-Self, *this* shall be thy goal. Know ye The-Law-of-Karma, that every *karma* has its consequence, that every *act* shall have effects." And the five Buddhist monks did understand. And they became Perfected-Ones. And they *left* the land where they had lived in self-denial. And they themselves went out to spread the truth.

And so, The Buddha became, as prophesied, The-Great-Religious-Teacher. And he *ventured* through the lands and gave religious sermons. Priests were enlightened and converted. And they too went out to spread The-Law. And soon *many* monks became disciples of The Buddha. And so began Buddhism.

And The Buddha spoke of compassion, peace and wisdom: "I, Gotama the Buddha, am free of *chains* – the human earthly chains, and the divine and holy chains. So too shall *ye* be freed from divine and human chains. And when ye *be* free, go forth and wander so and spread The-Law. For the *good* of the many, for the *blissfulness* of mind, for *compassion* for the world, go teach The-Law, for The-Law *be* good at the *beginning*, for The-Law *be* good in the *middle*, for The-Law *be* good at the *end*."

And sixty disciples heard his words and they were freed, for *they* were Perfect-Ones. And they went out to spread The-Law. And no two Perfect-Ones took the same road – they went out toward *sixty* different compass points.

And The Buddha came upon three matted-hair ascetics. And he spoke to them, "There is the *fire* of lust. There is the *fire* of hate. There is the *fire* of delusion. All man's existence is in the *burning* of these fires. One feels such fires must be fed. But *they* are like desires. Ye must kill these fires." And his followers named this sutta the "Fire Sermon" of The Buddha.

*To no longer be enflamed.*

And The-Great-Teacher spoke, "Know that inherent is the chain of human suffering, for it is natural to want to be an individual. But individuality leads to limitation. And limitation *gives* rise to desire. And then desire *causes* suffering, for the thing that is craved is ever-changing and the thing that is craved can never last – it comes, passes and perishes.

"Thus the first step is to rid oneself of Self. To attain No-Self is to *break* the bond with mundane things."

And he continued, "Good deeds shall *bring forth* good deeds. And bad deeds shall *bring forth* bad deeds. Each act shall be connected in a chain. *This* shall be The-Law-of-Karma."

And the more he preached, the more disciples did he gain. And the wisdom of his words spread out like *winds* throughout the land. Communities of monks were organized; monasteries were built where one could meditate and find The-Way; and his knowledge and techniques were *taught*. And his disciples learned self-discipline. And they sought the path to freedom from eternal suffering – they tried to find Nirvana.

And through *respect and love* did Gotama the Buddha *maintain* an order and a discipline among the members of the Buddhist Order.

Some said his acts were miracles.

And The Buddha preached not only to the holy priests, but also to *the common people*. And he instructed laymen on ethical behavior, proper conduct, and *right living*. And Gotama the Buddha travelled through the *Ganges Plain*, preaching the new doctrine and The-Law. *There*, The-One-With-Great-Kindness spoke, "Spiritual perfection shall come through generosity, humility, non-violence, compassion, and above all, self-control."

*To pick the just path among all paths.*

And he went visiting the sick in monastery wards. And one fellow monk dared say, "How can Buddha waste time with the sick?" To which The Buddha so replied, "He who looks after the sick looks after me."

And as promised, Gotama returned to King Bimbisara. And he told him of The-Law and truth. "To escape the cycle of birth and death and then rebirth – that *is* the goal. *Woe* be they who die and *still* be born again." And King Bimbisara was converted to a Buddhist.

And everywhere the people *bowed* to Buddha. They called him by such titles as The-Sage-of-the-Shakya-Tribe, He-Who-Has-Attained, The-Great-One, and The-Lord.

And The-Great-Sage spoke, "And how does one know that there *be* a state of Non-Existence? The answer is as so: From the unborn comes the born. If there be Being, there *be* Not-Being."

And more monasteries were built for Buddhists in the valley of the Ganges. And Buddha's followers increased *enormously*.

And to the masses did he preach, "To obtain that *blissful state* of insight, to have *oneness* with the Universe, *to be released* from suffering and from desires, to achieve a state of spiritual perfection – all these come when one obtains Nirvana."

*In the cool cave burn no fires.*

And Gotama the Buddha went back to the city of his childhood. And he went from door to door and *begged* for food. And his father, the king, was upset and grieved when he heard this. He summoned forth his son. To his father, Gotama replied, "Do *thou* not know? All buddhas go from house to house and beg – it is a blessing to be begged by a buddha, by A-Blessèd-One."

And Buddha went to see his wife, the wife he had not seen in many years. And she threw herself before him, clasped his ankles with her hands, and put her head upon his feet. And all the family members of The Buddha become members of the Buddhist Order.

## Chapter VII: The Buddha's Death

*Death is Nirvana,*
*the great release,*
*the ultimate tranquillity,*
*the final peace.*

And Gotama the Buddha *for all his living days* did preach The-Law, the Eightfold Path, the Noble Truths, Nirvana and Enlightenment. And *as* he grew in years, so grew the reverence for him from his disciples and his followers.

Now one of Buddha's cousins, Devadatta, *desired* to succeed the aging Buddha. And *he* asked Gotama to pass to *him* the Buddhist leadership. But The Buddha said, "There is *no one* who can lead the way. *Together*, all the Perfect-Ones will have to lead the way." And Gotama the Buddha then announced the rules for future Buddhist rule.

Now Devadatta *was* not satisfied. And he vowed *vengeance* on The Buddha. And Devadatta sent a mad elephant running in The Buddha's way. But when The Buddha saw the elephant, he waved his arms and he created in the air a holy gentleness. And behold, the elephant knelt *down* before The Buddha. And one witness said, "Even a mad elephant cannot move The Buddha from his path." Now twice more did *Devadatta* try to kill The Buddha. And twice *more* did *he* so fail. And with anger did he leave the Buddhist Order. And he began his own community of followers. But Devadatta soon fell sick – a high fever struck him like a *desert heat*. And for nine months did *he* so suffer. Then *he*, and not The Buddha, died.

And at the age of eighty years did Buddha set forth north. And a mighty line of followers did follow him. And then Gotama announced, "In three months *shall* I die." And soon The Buddha fell severely ill. But with determination did he push aside the pain. And although his inner body did decay, his face maintained *a calm*. But when he walked about, he *did* not seem the same.

And one among his Perfect-Ones asked him for instructions for the Buddhist Order. And Buddha so responded, "Thou need *no* such instructions, for thou hast The-Law. The-Law shall *be* thy teacher."

And three months went by. And The Buddha summoned his devoted monks for one last meal. And one among them, Cunda, cooked many delicacies and dishes. Now The Buddha asked Cunda to prepare for him a *special* food of pork. And he told Cunda, "Only I may eat this food. And of the food that shall be left, thou in a hole must bury it."

And it came to pass that after dinner did The Buddha come down sick. And there was *inside* much *pain*, but there was *outside* a *tranquil* face. And Gotama said in private to one of his most devoted monks, "There will be *those* who say that The-One-Who-Has-Attained has died from Cunda's food. Tell Cunda *not* to have remorse. Tell Cunda that there are *two* great offerings of food in life. And of equal fruit and profit shall they be. And the *first* great offering of food is the one before Enlightenment. And the *second* great offering of food is the one before the *passing* of A-Perfect-One." And Gotama then said, "I *soon* shall pass away." And the monk broke into tears, saying "Master, who be so kind to me, I pray thee not leave me." And The Buddha said, "Weep not. I have told thee many times of the separation of the near and dear – inevitable be it. Whatever be produced must also be dissolved. So *thus* be it."

And after many minutes, asked the monk, "What should we priests do with *thy* remains?" And The Buddha said, "Do not occupy thyselves with my remains. Let the common followers handle them. Ye *must* forget such things and *strive* for spiritual perfection. When I am gone, *still* have ye The-Law. The-Law shall be thy teacher."

And on the full-moon day of the month of May, Gotama the Buddha sat himself between two trees, two sal evergreens – he was *delighted* with this natural setting. And he crossed his legs and set his palms *pointing* to the *heavens*. And *there* he died. And his soul escaped to a natural place of everlasting calm and peace. And for The Buddha, his death this time was a tranquil *final* death.

> *And The Buddha's spirit passed to river's other side,*
> and *did* not *return.*

# The Gospel According to the Gospels

*And He was baptized not with water
but with the Holy Ghost.*

## Chapter I: Introduction

For the Universe, there was only one day and one night. And that one day lasted for the first three-hundred-thousand years. And it has been night *ever since*. It has been night for the last fifteen-billion years or so. And do not be confused by the *illusion* of the Sun. Even now there is only night for the Universe. The day ye see each day is a day created by the Earth's rotation. When thy part of the Earth *faces* the Sun, ye see the Sun and ye have day. And when thy part of the Earth turns *away from* the Sun, ye have night and ye see the Universe *as it is*. And it is *dark* and *black*. Thus the dark and black of night is the dark and black of the Universe.

And to light the night a star was made. But the Universe was vast and very black. And the star only lit a very very tiny part of the *gigantic* Universe. And so stars *were made* in great numbers and assembled in huge galaxies. But the Universe was still vast and very black. And each galaxy only lit a very tiny part of the Universe. Thus galaxies were made in great numbers. And the galaxies *lit* the Universe but *dimly*.

And the Universe, which is vast and dark and black, was, is and shall be dimly lit by the stars and galaxies which Nature made.

## Chapter II: The Genealogy of Jesus

And a *Holy* leader and religious prophet was *presented* to the peoples of the Earth. And wherever He walked, there was cast among the shadows a *spirit* and a *light*. And that prophet's name was Jesus – He was of the ninety-second generation of mankind:

Adam and Eve had several sons among whom one was Sheth. And Sheth married and had Enosh. And Enosh married and had Kenan. And Kenan[33] married and had Mahalaleel. And Mahalaleel married and had Jared. And Jared married and had Henoch. And Henoch married and had Methuselah. And Methuselah married and had Lamech. And Lamech married and had Noah. And Noah married and had Shem. And Shem married and had Arphaxad. And Arphaxad married and had Shelah. And Shelah married and had Eber. And Eber married and had Peleg. And Peleg married and had Reu. And Reu married and had Serug. And Serug married and had Nahor. And Nahor married and had Terah. And Terah married and had Abram, which

---

[33] Also spelled Cainan. Some of the other names appearing here have alternative spellings.

was short for Abraham. And Abram married and had Isaac. And Isaac married and had Jacob, who was also known as Israel. And Jacob married and had Judah. And Judah married and had Pharez. And Pharez married and had Hezron. And Hezron married and had Ram. And Ram married and had Amminadab. And Amminadab married and had Nashon. And Nashon married and had Salmon. And Salmon married and had Boaz. And Boaz married and had Obed. And Obed married and had Jesse. And Jesse married and had David. And David married and had Solomon. And Solomon married and had Rehoboam. And Rehoboam married and had Abia. And Abia married and had Asa. And Asa married and had Jehoshaphat. And Jehoshaphat married and had Joram. And Joram married and had Ahaziah. And Ahaziah married and had Joash. And Joash married and had Amaziah. And Amaziah married and had Araziah. And Araziah married and had Jotham. And Jotham married and had Ahaz. And Ahaz married and had Hezekiah. And Hezekiah married and had Manasseh. And Manasseh married and had Amon. And Amon married and had Josiah. And Josiah married and had Jehoiakim. And Jehoiakim married and had Jeconiah. And Jeconiah married and had Salathiel. And Salathiel married and had Zorobabel. And Zorobabel married and had Abiud. And Abiud married and had Eliakim. And Eliakim married and had Azor. And Azor married and had Sadoc. And Sadoc married and had Achim. And Achim married and had Eliud. And Eliud married and had Eleazor. And Eleazor married and had Matthat. And Matthat married and had Jorim. And Jorim married and had Eliezer. And Eliezer married and had Jose. And Jose married and had Er. And Er married and had Elmodam. And Elmodam married and had Cosam. And Cosam married and had Addi. And Addi married and had Melchi. And Melchi married and had Neri. And Neri married and had Salathiel. And Salathiel married and had Zorobabel. And Zorobabel married and had Rhesa. And Rhesa married and had Joanna. And Joanna married and had Judah. And Judah married and had Joseph. And Joseph married and had Semei. And Semei married and had Mattathias. And Mattathias married and had Maath. And Maath married and had Nagge. And Nagge married and had Esli. And Esli married and had Naum. And Naum married and had Amos. And Amos married and had Mattathias. And Mattathias married and had Joseph. And Joseph married and had Janna. And Janna married and had Melchi. And Melchi married and had Levi. And Levi married and had Matthat. And Matthat married and had Heli. And Heli married and had Joseph. And Joseph married Mary and had Jesus.

And these early generations did form the basic human elements – they were like Nature's elements. And upon these first ninety-two would future generations so be built.

*Adam was like unto an atom. So was Eve.*

And later, eleven apostles would continue the legacy of Jesus. And they would be Simon Peter; Andrew, his brother; James, the son of Zebedee; John, his brother; Philip; Bartholomew; Matthew; Thomas; James, the son of Alphæus; Simon Zelotes; and Judas, the brother of James, who was also known as Jude and as Lebbæus Thaddæus. And these eleven apostles would also *serve* as human elements.

And the twelfth apostle, Judas Iscariot, who would become a traitor, would not survive. And later on, additional disciples, such as Paul and Barnabas, would join the original twelve apostles and continue the Holy Bible's teachings and traditions.

. . . . . . .

What follows *is written in the Holy Bible*. Here is but a brief account, a simple summary. The Gospels of the Holy Bible give the details.[34]

## Chapter III: The Birth of Jesus

And in the year seven BC, Jesus, the embodiment of David and the spirit of God was *embedded* in the womb of Mary. And shortly thereafter, below a brilliant star, between an ox and ass, a babe was born in Bethlehem. It would be a *remarkable* event.

*The Universe, which had been dark, was given light.*
*The Earth, which had been dead, was given life.*

*In the Beginning was the* Word.
*And the Word was with God.*
*And the Word was God.*
*And the Word was made flesh*
*and dwelt among the people.*
*But the Word* was *not always heard.*

And the newborn was given a name. And the name was Jesus of Nazareth, for "Jesus" means "Yahweh saves." Jesus was the prophet that the prophets had predicted. He was the Messiah, the Son of David, the Son of Man, the Son of God and the Lord. And later, He would become the Holy Spirit.

## Chapter IV: Herod Tries to Kill the Babe Jesus

And Herod the Great, hearing of the birth, was *troubled*. And he commanded wise men from Jerusalem to go as *scouts* to Bethlehem. They were instructed to bring back information on "this King of Jews." The bright star in the heavens *led them* across the desert sand,

---

[34] Some will say

*"What follows is susceptible to logical contention."*

And they will ask

*"Is there a scientific reconciliation?*
*Is this history not subject to some speculation?"*

but when the wise men came to Bethlehem and beheld the infant Jesus, they saw a *deeper* light. And they did *not* return to Herod but headed to an unknown land.

And fear of Herod made Mary, Joseph and Jesus flee to Egypt.

*The Voice spoke,*
*but Herod did not hear it:*
*"That which is born of flesh is flesh.*
*That which is born of spirit is spirit."*

And Herod killed *all* the babes in Bethlehem. But Jesus was in Egypt.

## Chapter V: The Spirit of Jesus Develops

And Mary, Joseph and Jesus dwelt in Egypt and they waited. Then, Herod died in four BC. And when he died, a *winged creature* led Mary, Joseph and Jesus back into the promised land of Israel. There, Jesus was baptized by John with the waters of the Holy Ghost *and* with fire.

And it came to pass that Jesus ventured into the *wilderness*. And Jesus began a fast of forty days and forty nights. A *horned creature* from beneath the earth did offer him some stones as bread. But Jesus did not touch the food – He was *faithful* to the fast. And He grew in wisdom and in spirit fast.

And He began to preach,

*"Build thy house upon a rock.*
*Protect it with a wall,*
*for when the rains descend*
*and the floods flow*
*and the winds blow*
*and all beat against thy house,*
*it will not fall.*

*"The messenger of God has so been sent.*
*Let it be here and elsewhere heard.*
*Ye, who have sinned, repent.*
*Now and forever believe thee in the Word."*

And some listened to His speeches. And some listened to His teachings. But *others* turned a *deaf ear* on His wisdom and closed the door to his Father's Kingdom.

And then He gathered His disciples. They numbered twelve. They were fishermen, peasants, craftsmen, a tax collector and several Zealot priests. The fishermen became fishers *not* of fish but men.

And He walked along the Sea of Galilee. He raised moral questions, taught *righteousness* and preached the Word. His sentences were full of *religious insight*. He began to weave a moral truth. His followers began to see the *light*.

And then in Cana, in Galilee, did He turn water into wedding wine – this marked the beginning of the miracles.

## Chapter VI: The Sermon on the Mount

And He climbed a mount and spoke,

> *"Whoever drinketh the water of the well*
> *shall thirst again.*
> *Whoever drinketh the water I give*
> *shall never thirst.*
>
> *"The first shall be the last.*
> *The last shall be the first.*
>
> *"Blessed be those who do no wrong,*
> *for they shall have eternal peace.*
> *Blessed be the humble who kneel down and nod,*
> *for they shall have a spirit strong.*
> *Blessed be the pure in heart,*
> *for they shall see the Lord our God.*
>
> *"Love thy enemies.*
> *Do good to those who hate thee.*
> *Bless those who curse thee.*
> *Pray for those who persecute thee.*
>
> *"Others cannot execute ye,*
> *neither with the tongue nor with a sword.*
> *Others cannot judge ye.*
> *These powers lay with God our Lord."*

The wisdom of the words left many people full of awe. Now sometimes He spoke in sentences that could not be:

> *"The deaf shall hear.*
> *The lame shall walk.*
> *The mute shall speak.*
> *The dead shall live.*
> *The blind shall see."*

His words, like the stars in heaven, which appear soon after dusk, *brought forth light* against a background black.

## Chapter VII: Jesus Preaches in the Country

And Jesus taught in temples, along the shores of lakes, in the mountains and the valleys, and by country roads:

*"Venture into the wilderness.*
*Seek truth.*
Nod down *thy head and pray.*
Lift up *thy eyes to heaven.*
*The Kingdom of the Lord* is *above thy roof.*

*"Ask and ye shall receive.*
*Seek and ye shall find.*
*Knock and it shall be opened.*
*For he who asketh* receiveth.
*For he who seeketh* findeth.
*For he who knocketh, it shall be opened."*

Such were examples of the words *that* were spoken.

## Chapter VIII: Jesus Heals the Sick

And Jesus travelled on foot throughout the Holy lands. And He *healed* the sick who believed the Faith.

*By a road, in a village, beneath a tree,*
*the insane were given reason,*
*the lame were made to walk,*
*the foolish ones were given wisdom,*
*the maimed were given limbs,*
*the blind were made to see.*

*Yet some who saw were blind.*

*The truth shall set you free.*

And great multitudes of people heard His sentences and *did* believe. And they became His followers. He made evil spirits *flee* the bodies of those possessed by *wicked* thoughts and spirits.

His movement soon gained great momentum. His ideas were *widely* heard. Twelve disciples were sent out throughout the Holy world to spread the Word.

## Chapter IX: The Pharisees Are Reproved

And the Pharisees, the self-righteous hypocrites, saw Jesus and His followers pluck ears of corn *on the Sabbath day.* And one Pharisee spoke out, "Do you not know that it is unlawful to eat today?" And Jesus retorted,

*"The Son of Man is Lord* even *on the Sabbath day."*

And Jesus healed a man whose hand had withered. And one Pharisee spoke out, "Do you not know that it is unlawful to heal on the Sabbath day?" And Jesus retorted,

*"The Son of Man must labor* even *on the Sabbath day."*

And Jesus turned, saying of the Pharisees,

*"They have eyes but they see not.*
*They have hands but they touch not.*
*They have ears but they hear not."*

And behind Jesus, *thousands* walked.

And the Pharisees met and talked. And among them, there were *some* who wanted Him dead. But no man laid a hand on Him, for His hour had not come.

## Chapter X: Parables

And Jesus preached in parables: "Seed thrown in the road shall be *devoured* by the fowls. Seed thrown in stony places shall *not* take root. Seed thrown among the thorns of thick bushes shall be *choked*. But seed thrown into *good earth* shall bring forth a multitude of fruit.

"In a plantation, a good seed was sowed. But one night, an *enemy* came and planted *tares* among the wheat. And the servants asked, 'Shall we go and pull *up* the tares?' And the plantation owner said, 'No. If you pull up the tares you will also *uproot* the wheat. Let both grow on the land until the harvest. Then at harvest, gather *first* the tares, and have them bound and *burned*. Then collect the wheat and put it in the barn.'"

## Chapter XI: Dead Are Brought Back to Life

And an old man came to Jesus telling of his dying daughter. And when the daughter died, the old man wept. "Weep not," said Jesus, "She is not dead but just *asleep*." And He took her by the hand. "Ascend," He said. And *then* she rose. It seemed that she had risen from the dead.

And wherever Jesus walked, *evil and unclean spirits* fled – to the netherlands were *they* so driven.

And elsewhere, with a single touch, the sick were cured, the blind saw, the lame walked, the deaf heard. And the young and old were blessed. And sinners were forgiven.

## Chapter XII: John Is Beheaded

*Beware of the woman*
*whose beauty melts a man.*

In a palace room decorated with gold and flowers, Herod Antipas, the ruling son of Herod the Great, was *hypnotized* by the dance and *beauty* of a women. Her perfume *overwhelmed* his senses. "Ask and I will give," he said to her, "It can be *any* matter." And her deathly gift was granted.

The executioner performed the order. In the next room, a maidservant gave a shrill, which sounded almost like a laughter. Then a male servant entered with a tray. And the head of John the Baptist was presented to the women on a platter.

## Chapter XIII: The Feeding of Five-Thousand

And hearing of John's death and *sensing danger*, Jesus and His disciples fled to an unpopulated place. There, with five loaves of bread and two fish, Jesus fed *five-thousand*.

*"Remember,*
*He that eateth this bread shall never hunger.*
*He that eateth this bread shall live forever.*

*"I come not to judge the world but to save the world.*
*He that seeth me seeth Him that sent me.*

*"If a man has hands, let him touch.*
*If a man has ears, let him hear.*
*If a man has eyes, let him see.*

*"Give to every man who asks of thee.*

*"Judge not and ye shall not be judged.*
*Condemn not and ye shall not be condemned.*
*Forgive and ye shall be forgiven.*
*Give and unto ye it shall be given.*

*"Beware of false prophets in sheep's clothing."*

## Chapter XIV: Jesus Walks on Water

And Jesus took a ship and followers. And Jesus fell *asleep*. And the *unguided* vessel went *astray*. A raging storm arose. Giant waves beat upon the deck. His followers *were* indeed *afraid*. And Jesus woke, rose and walked upon the waters. His footsteps *calmed* the raging ocean waves. He spoke. His followers heard His words: "Why ye be of so little faith?" And passing His hand above His head, the blackish clouds turned white and parted. A balmy blue appeared.

*Who was this man*
*who could command*
*the winds and waters with his hand?*
*Some ran away, while others stayed.*
*Some heard His voice,*
*"Tis I. Be not afraid."*

Yet there were skeptics who debated *His origin*. "Who is He, He who, when *it* be needed, walks upon the sea?"

## Chapter XV: Wise Sayings

And Jesus preached,

*"Do not hold judgement of others,*
*for you do not have the power to judge.*
*To laugh at another*
*is to have others laugh at you.*

*"Knowledge and religious truth is the* highest *wealth.*

*"The tongue, when razor sharp,*
*shall not slay thy enemy*
*but thy mouth and thus thyself.*

*"Have compassion for the meek and feeble.*

*"Woe to you who be rich.*
*For it is easier for a camel*
*to pass through the eye of a needle*
*than for a rich man to enter in God's kingdom.*

*"New wine must be put in a new bottle,*
*else the bottle break and* both *be waste.*

*"He who is humble shall be exalted.*
*He who exalts himself shall be abased."*

## Chapter XVI: The Transfiguration

And on a mountain, in a cloud, Jesus met with Moses, Elias and God. Three tabernacles were constructed. The *covenant* was accepted. And when the cloud departed, *gone* were Moses, Elias and God.

## Chapter XVII: The Word

And Jesus sent out more disciples to spread the Word. He drew His people into *oneness* with the Lord. He taught them how to pray.

*"Our Father,*
*Who art in Heaven,*
*hallowed be Thy name.*
*Thy kingdom come.*
*Thy will be done,*
*as in Heaven, so on Earth.*
*Give us this day our daily bread.*
*And forgive us our debts,*
*as we forgive those who trespass against us.*
*And lead us not into temptation,*
*but deliver us from evil.*
*For Thine is the kingdom,*

*and the power,*
*and the glory,*
*For ever and ever.*
*Amen."*

And Jesus explained the Law, the *Moral Law*. And some people heard. And some people listened. And some people *saw*.

And Jesus spoke,

*"I am the bread of* everlasting life.
*He, who eateth my flesh*
*and drinketh my blood*
*and dwelleth in me, shall have* eternal life."
*And then he put his hands together*
*as if to form a cup and He continued,*
*"And on the last day,*
*he who hath embodied me will so rise up."*

## Chapter XVIII: Jesus Foresees His Death

And He told His disciples. "The Son of Man shall be delivered into the hands of *certain men*. And they shall kill the Son of Man. And on the *third day* after His death, He *shall* rise up." But His disciples did not understand.

## Chapter XIX: Christ and the Children

And He *baptized* babies with the Holy Ghost. And the children of the world became *His* children.

## Chapter XX: Diverse Opinions of Jesus

And there were *those* who did not believe His words. And *some* threw stones.

*And He said,*
*"He who believeth in me, though he be dead, shall* live.
*And he who believeth not, though he be living,* shall *be dead.*

*"He who seeks to save his life shall lose it.*
*He who loses his life shall save it."*

## Chapter XXI: The Resurrection of Lazarus

And Lazarus, the beggar, who had been a friend and a believer, died. And Jesus came. "Come forth, Lazarus," He said. And as soon as the words were spoken, the eyes of Lazarus did open.

## Chapter XXII: Priests Take Counsel

Now as word about Jesus and His miracles spread throughout the Holy lands, more and more *believed* and followed Him. And the Pharisees thought this *dangerous*. And they and chief priests discussed what should be done "about this so-called Son of Man." And among them, there were *some* who wanted Him dead. But no man laid a hand on Him, for His hour had not come.

## Chapter XXIII: Christ's Good Deeds

*He led those away who had strayed near the purgatory gate.*
*And those with bent backs were made to stand up straight.*

*He gave* shelter *to those who had no shelter.*
*He gave* bread *to those who had no bread.*
*He instilled* faith *into those who had no faith.*
*And everywhere He walked, evil spirits fled.*

And Jesus went to Jordan. And Jesus went to Jericho.

## Chapter XXIV: Jesus Rides into Jerusalem

And Jesus went to Jerusalem – He came there to explain good and evil, to show how to be *a child of God*. He had come to fulfill a *promise* and a *destiny*. He entered riding on a colt. And people poured into the street to meet Him. The *multitudes* were moved.

*He led His people like a shepherd leads his sheep.*
*Lost sheep were found and saved.*

*But a few non-believers* turned *their heads and fell asleep.*
*"Woe unto you that are full,*
*for ye shall hunger.*
*Woe unto you that laugh now,*
*for ye shall mourn and weep."*

And to his followers He said,

*"Beware of foxes wearing the wool of sheep."*

And Jesus went into the temple. And some were *selling* trinkets, doves and wares. And He *overturned* the tables and He *threw away* the chairs. And the moneychangers *fled* the church in droves.

*"He who is rich shall be poor.*
*And the poor*
*shall pass through a needle*
*and be rich.*

*"Can the blind really lead the blind?*
*Shall they not* both *fall in a ditch?"*

And then He said,

*"Let the dead be buried by the dead."*

## Chapter XXV: Tribute to Caesar

And Jesus spoke of the king and of his kingdom. And some Pharisees tried to trick Jesus with *His* own words saying, "Is it lawful to give tribute to Caesar, or not?" And Jesus spoke, "Render to Caesar that which is Caesar's. And render to God that which is God's."[35] And many of these Pharisees *marvelled* at His words. Some even understood what Jesus preached and taught. And they soon followed Him. But others continued to try to trick Him with His words *but* could not.

*He was subjected sometimes to misinterpretation.*
*It would lead to His bodily destruction and His crucifixion.*

## Chapter XXVI: Jesus Preaches to the People

And Jesus taught in the streets of Jerusalem. He preached the Old Testament tradition, but He provided a *new* interpretation. And the masses learned the evils of corruption, the basics of confession, and the meaning of redemption.

He modified the Ten Commandments. He glorified two principles:

*"Thou shalt love the Lord thy God*
*with all thy heart, with all thy soul,*
*with all thy strength, with all thy mind.*

*"And thou shalt love thy neighbor as thyself."*

## Chapter XXVII: Calamities Are Foretold

And He foretold the ruin of the temple and more: "Someday the Sun shall *darken*. And the moon shall *not reflect* its light. And someday shall the stars in heaven fall. And the Universe shall be destroyed. And there shall be nothing, *nothing* shall be all."

*"Watchman, what of the night?*
*The morning cometh, and also cometh night."*

*The Second Coming will be coming.*

*"He that believeth shall be saved.*
*He that believeth* not *shall be condemned.*

*"Do not be a virgin of the night*
*without the oil to light the oil-lamp light."*

---

[35] This was the Declaration of the Separation of Church and State.

## Chapter XXVIII: Jesus Foretells His Death

And among the masses, there were *some* who wanted Him dead. This time, His hour *was* about to come.

*"My tears will be thy drink.*
*My body will be thy bread,"*
*He said.*

*With vision,*
*He foresaw His crucifixion*
*and His resurrection.*
*His death was an anticipation.*
*His death would be emancipation.*

## Chapter XXIX: Judas Sells Jesus

And Judas Iscariot, one of the twelve disciples, went and *met* with the chief priests. And they spoke in *soft voices* – soft voices *always* speak in secret. Judas *would* deliver. He departed with *thirty* coins of silver.

## Chapter XXX: The Last Supper

And the twelve disciples and Jesus sat around a table and did dine. For Jesus, it would be *the* last meal of bread and wine. And Jesus spoke, "The Son of Man goeth *as is written*. Woe unto the man among you who *has* betrayed the Son of Man." The others did not understand.

And Jesus took the bread, blessed it, divided it, and gave it to His disciples, saying, "Take, eat; this is my body." Then He took up a cup of wine and said, "Take, drink; this is my blood." And the cup was passed among them.

And the wine was *the blood* of the new testament. It was the blood that would be shed for *many*.

And Jesus poured water into a basin. And He said to His disciples "Ye are not all clean." And He bent down and washed their feet with water.

He gave the *last* commandment,

*"Love one another, as I love you."*

And they went to sing a hymn. And they did not realize that they were singing it for Him.

## Chapter XXXI: Peter's Denial Is Foretold

And Jesus turned to Peter, "Before the cock crows twice, thou shalt deny me thrice." And Peter replied, "Oh no, master. I will not."

## Chapter XXXII: Agony in the Garden

Then they went to Gethsemane and they prayed. And in a separate chamber Jesus met with Peter, James and John. And *they* were somber.

## Chapter XXXIII: Jesus Is Taken Away

And Judas came with others who carried *swords* and *staves*. And Judas stepped forward to *kiss* his Master's foot. Now, there is the kiss of love and there is the kiss of treason. And this kiss was the kiss of treason and the kiss of death.

The band of officers led Jesus off. They brought Him to a palace where Caiaphas, the high priest, reigned. And Peter *followed* Jesus and the officers.

Jesus was blindfolded and interrogated. False witnesses *were* called in. Silence was His first defense.

And then the high priest asked, "Art thou the Christ, the Son of God?" And Jesus broke His silence, saying, "Ye say it." And He added, "Someday ye shall see the Son of Man sitting in the right hand of the power beyond the clouds in heaven."

"All ye have heard this blasphemy. He is guilty. His punishment is death," someone cried out.

A maid spied Peter in the palace and she asked, "Art thou with Jesus of Nazareth?" And *fearful*, Peter said, "I am not." Others came. Peter had been caught. Another man asked him, "Know thou this man?" And Peter said, "*I* do not." And still another asked, "Art thou among His lot." And Peter said, "I am *not*." Then Peter heard the crowing of a cock.

## Chapter XXXIV: Jesus Before Pilate

And Jesus was taken to Pontius Pilate, the governor. Pilate listened to the pleas of priests. The governor questioned Jesus. And Jesus defended Himself with silence and with seemingly meaningless sentences.

*"My kingdom is not of this world."*

Pilate found *no cause* for condemnation. Then *came* the *outcry* of the priests. "Crucify Him! Crucify Him!" And Pilate yielded to the pressure.

*Thereafter, Judas realized what was at stake.*
*He had committed a grave mistake.*
*His downfall had been the greed for wealth.*
*And Judas confessed his sins and hung himself.*

Jesus had educated the populace. He had *healed* the sick, *cured* the incurable, and made sane those who had lost their wits. He had *built* the kingdom of Christianity and God. He had not denied. He had not lied. He had merely spoken words of *truth* and *wisdom*. For *this* He would be crucified?!

## Chapter XXXV: Christ Is Crucified

*And they did shake – the main two pillars*
*on which the temple stood.*
*And when the two did break,*
*the temple tumbled to a rubble.*

And on that Friday, Jesus was released to a raucous crowd. They *stripped* Him of His clothes. The made a *mockery* of Him. They spit into His face. They struck Him on the head. They carried Him to Golgotha, the place of skulls. And *followers* came from *everywhere* and *wept* for Him. And He said, "Weep not for me. Weep for thyselves and for thy children." He was given *vinegar* to drink. The members of the mob drove *nails* through His hands and pinned Him to a cross. They parted with His garments, casting lots for different parts. And there He hung between two others being hung – two thieves.

At the sixth hour, *darkness* fell upon the land. At the ninth hour, He cried out. A soldier drove a sword into His side. Blood and water did pour out. The Earth trembled. The temple cleaved in two. The graves of saints *were opened*. Dust, like living spirits, rose into the air.

He had preached religious doctrine and clarified the moral law. And *for all this*, He was nailed to a cross and crucified?! He had given mercy, pity and love to the suffering, the guilty and the outcast. And *for all this*, He was nailed to a cross and crucified?! He had taught men to love their neighbors and their enemies. And *for all this*, He was nailed to a cross and crucified?! And He had taught the Word of God. And He had taught the love of man and God. And *for all this*, He was nailed to a cross and crucified?! In His thirties, He had died.

## Chapter XXXVI: Christ's Burial

And the body of Jesus was wrapped in cloth and buried. And chiselled in a slab of slate were the words

*Jesus Christ,*
*son of Abraham,*
*child of the Holy Ghost,*
*King of the Jews,*
*the Lamb of God.*
*Christ, the Messiah*
*and the Savior of the World.*

Then several robust men rolled a great stone forth and *sealed* the tomb. And soldiers soon were sent to *guard* the stone.

## Chapter XXXVII: Christ After Death

On Monday, struck an earthquake aftershock. The giant stone rolled back. There lay an *empty* tomb. The body of the Son of God *was gone.*[36]

*Peace be unto you.*

And it was written in the Holy Gospels that His spirit had so *risen* from the dead, that this was the Resurrection and the Ascension, that the Son of God assumed a *final* elevation, that He had achieved a position of restoration and that He sat in the right hand of the Lord.

*So is it written.*

## Chapter XXXVIII: The Legacy Lives On

*He tried to create a world*
*in which the lion and the lamb could live together.*

This was the life of Jesus of Nazareth: from incarnation to humiliation, from resurrection to glorification – Jesus the Great Creator of religious spirit.

For centuries thereafter, Christians would retell the story. Jesus would achieve a godly reputation. Christians would say He was the Father, the Son and the Holy Ghost.

And still the question shall be raised by some: Magician, man, or Son of God? For the nonbeliever, the story of His life shall seem to be a mystery.

---

[36] Some will raise the question – magic, theft or Resurrection?

*The fourth book of Chronicles, called*

# Muhammad

*Lâ ilâha ill-Allâh,*[37]
*there is no god but Allah.*

This is the story of Muhammad, Allah's Arab prophet.

## Chapter I: Ancient Mecca

Now in Arabia in ancient but post-Christian times, there was a holy city. And *Mecca* was that city. And Mecca was a holy place, for it possessed the sanctuary of the Kaaba.

Now Mecca had no nearby oasis – this was *unlike* most desert towns. It had sufficient water for its people and its camels but not enough for growing crops. The water came from wells. Now Mecca was favorably located on caravan trade routes: Camels carried goods between Mediterranean countries and Syria on one hand and Ethiopia and Yemen on the other hand. And even goods from India sometimes passed by Mecca. Now in the desert, nomadic tribes often *raided* caravans – these were times of *lawlessness* in which the raiding of one group by another was a way of life. But as a civil and well-organized commercial city, Mecca was a *safe sanctuary* for the traders. And so Mecca was a wealthy center of exchange. But the wealth of Mecca resided in *few* hands, the hands of leaders and of merchants. And that left most people poor.

And although the influence of Mecca radiated outward, Arabia was well *divided* into separate competing regions and communities – there was no Arab unity. And there was no unique religion in the region. But one man would come and *change* all this.

## Chapter II: Muhammad Makes His Earthly Presence Known

And in the year of five-hundred-seventy AD, a boy was born. And Abu al-Qasim Muhammad ibn Abd Allah ibn Abd al-Muttalib ibn Hashim was his name. And this boy, who would someday *be* a man and *more*, was called, for short, Muhammad. Now Muhammad's father died before Muhammad's birth. And so his grandfather *filled* the role of father.

Now Muhammad was a member of a ruling Meccan clan. And this was not surprising, for Mecca had several ruling clans.

---

[37] The approximate anglicized pronunciation of this phrase is LA-il-LA-hah ILL-LALL-LA. The holy Muslim Arabic cannot be translated into foreign languages. The reader should bear this in mind while reading this Book of *Muhammad*. As a consequence, something is lost in the translation of "lâ ilâha ill-Allâh" into "There is no god but Allah." It could, for example, be translated as "None has the right to be worshipped but Allah."

And Muhammad's mother died when he was six. And his grand-father died when he was eight. Thus at eight Muhammad was an *orphan*. His uncle, who was a leader of a Meccan clan, would bring him up.

And at twenty-five, Muhammad married a rich and older woman, who was almost forty. Not only did her wealth *provide* Muhammad with financial freedom, but her kind heart *took* good care of him. And in the coming years, they produced four daughters and two sons.

## Chapter III: Muhammad Has a Vision

And in six-hundred-ten AD, on the ninth month of the Arab year, Muhammad went into a *trance*. He saw a *wingèd figure* descending from the heavens.[38] Then a *voice* spoke to his barely conscious mind, "Recite ye: In the name of Allah,[39] the God of mercy and compassion." And in Muhammad's barely conscious mind, his inner voice repeated Allah's words. And Muhammad heard, "Recite ye: Allah is most generous. He teaches by the *word*. He teaches man what man knows not." And Muhammad in his inner voice *repeated* Allah's words.

After the trance, Muhammad could *hear* the sentences in his fully conscious mind. Now Muhammad was *perturbed* by what had happened. And he told his wife, "It felt as if a great mountain was pressing on my chest." His wife allayed his fears.

And several weeks went by. And Muhammad went into *another* trance. This time he saw no vision but he heard a *noise*, a kind of bell. And although it was a cold night, he sweated uncontrollably. Then spoke a voice, saying, "Thou *art* the messenger of God." And Muhammad realized that *verily* the words he heard were God's.

Now these would be the first of *many* revelations, for Allah's messages would often come to him throughout his life. And there usually would be no voice nor vision – simply a message would be left in Muhammad's conscious mind.

And friends soon witnessed Muhammad in a revelation-trance. And Muhammad *told* to them what God had said to him. And Muhammad's friends were sure that these were Allah's words. And they were also *sure* Muhammad was a prophet.

And so his friends joined him, the Prophet. And they worshipped and they prayed, as they *turned toward* Jerusalem and touched their foreheads to the sand. And soon, friends of friends did join Muhammad's group.

---

[38] Later he would learn that the wingèd figure was the angel Gabriel.

[39] "Allah" is the Arabic word for God.

And when Muhammad had his revelations, he repeated them aloud, "Recite ye: God is good. Allah is all powerful." And the words were *written down* or memorized by those around him.[40]

## Chapter IV: Muhammad Preaches to the Public

And three years passed. And Muhammad heard the words, "Thou art *ready* now. Speaketh of the *word* of Allah to all of those around thee." And near the Kaaba, the holy shrine of Mecca, Muhammad preached *openly* in public: "Allah is everywhere – Allah is *all*. He is the High God, the Supreme Being and the Originator of all things." And he continued, "Do *good* and ye shall be *rewarded*; do *bad* and *punishment* shall be thy recompense, for Allah has spoken of the Day of Reckoning, the Judgement Day, when the Sun is folded up and the stars are cast away, when mountains are removed, when the she-camels, ten months pregnant with their young, shall be neglected, when the seas surge up and the skies fall down, and when souls shall be reunited with their bodies. And *judgement* shall be cast upon all souls. Great *joys* shall be awarded to the faithful. But the *wicked* shall burn in an eternal fire, a *fire* just reserved for *them*."

Now some Meccans heard him and thought he was *one* of the religious oral poets.[41] But some around him were in *awe*. And they became his *followers* – many were the sons of rich men. And often to the Kaaba, Muhammad and his followers did go to kneel and pray.

Now at this time, most Meccans worshipped *many* gods. And some merchants worshipped *none* – they felt that wealth and proper human planning could accomplish all. And pagan Meccans believed in fate, a fate over which a man had no control. They often bowed to idols. And some clan leaders as well as tribal priests engaged in *self-idolatry* – they claimed to be like gods. They used soothsayers, poets, fake prophets and magicians to spread sorcery and superstition. Now Muhammad knew the *word* of Allah. And Muhammad knew that Meccans were *practicing* religious nonsense. And he was upset by the religious ways of all, including his own tribe. And he denounced the ancient paganism and the use of idols. And he openly criticized the Meccan tribal leaders by announcing that Allah was full of *wrath* at the ungodly conduct of the people. And of "many gods," this is what he had to say: "Allah has no equal. Allah has no partner. Allah has no daugh-

---

[40] These revelations were the Koran, or *al-qur'an* in Arabic, which means "to recite." Hence at this point in time, the Koran was not a book but a collection of recitations. After Muhammad's death, from those who memorized the sayings and from the writings that had been written down, the recitations were assembled in a book. That book became the Koran. Hence the Koran was written to be recited. It was Allah's voice, expressed in the purest Arabic. It contained many of the Holy Bible's writings – even The Lord's Prayer was there. It had a certain captivating power. The Islamic followers learned to read Arabic by reading it.

[41] In these times, such poets were common. Leaders used them, as well as magicians, to advance their purposes.

ters. Allah did not walk the Earth in the body of a man. There is no *holy spirit*, for Allah is alone. And Allah *be*. He is the Greater God. There is no God but Allah."

And Meccan leaders tried to appease Muhammad by *offering* him a greater stake in trade and profits and by offering a marriage into a wealthy family. But Muhammad rejected these *ungodly* things – to him they were but sacrilegious bribes.

And he *invited* Jews and Christians to submit to him. But the Christians and the Jews resisted – they already had their prophet-leaders, such as Moses, Abraham and Jesus. "Such people, be they Arabs, Jews, or Christians, are corrupted ones," Muhammad said, "if they do not *surrender* to the *word* of Allah."

## Chapter V: Muhammad Meets Resistance

And in the year six-hundred-and-fifteen AD, outright opposition to Muhammad did emerge, for some leaders feared the power which Muhammad was amassing – for he might overthrow *their* rule. And so tribal leaders and rich merchants *criticized* Muhammad's revelations. And in such attacks on the Koran, his followers responded with the phrase, "There is no God but Allah. And Muhammad is His prophet."

And economic pressure was brought to bear on his supporters. And mild persecution soon did follow. And a boycott was ordered on Muhammad's family clan. But since few members of *that* clan were members of Muhammad's group, *they* had *no control* on him – they viewed him as a wild one who was somewhat deranged. And so the boycott failed to halt Muhammad's preaching and his revelations. How *could* it halt his revelations? They were not originating from Muhammad – from Heaven there were coming!

And for three years, Muhammad prayed and preached but under adverse circumstances.

And his followers did follow him around, waiting for each recitation-trance. And if it happened in a *street*, or in a *market*, or by a *shrine*, Muhammad recited *there* what Allah said to him.

And it happened that, in a courtyard, Muhammad went into a revelation-trance, "Recite ye: Allah is knowing and is wise. Allah is the *sole* creator and sustainer of the Universe. Out of His great mercy has the unity and order of the World been made. Bow down and pray to Allah. Allah has mercy on those who do *submit* to Him. Ye who *believe* in Allah will bring Him to thy blood – Allah will be no farther than thy very flesh. Through Allah shall ye find the right way, the straight path." And his followers chanted *Allahu akbar*, meaning "Allah is the greatest." And with his eyes squeezed shut, one man nearby repeated the sentences several dozen times so as to *fix* them in his memory. And he did this so that the lines could be *repeated* later.

And in the year six-hundred-and-nineteen AD, both Muhammad's wife and uncle died – for Muhammad *this* was devastating. And the

leadership of his family clan was passed to another. – he was a rich uncle of Muhammad who had little sympathy for this "so-called prophet."
And Muhammad was *rejected* by his family clan. Now without the protection of the clan, Muhammad was an easy *target* of attack. Henceforth, he often had to hide. And by hiding, he had no means to preach
in public – Muhammad and his religion were *in trouble*.

Up to now, Muhammad had had but *just* one wife. But during
the coming years, he would marry several times. Thus Muhammad,
like many men of these old Arab times, would maintain a multiple of
wives. And the marriages would serve a purpose *more than love* – they
would help him to establish political blood ties, for he would marry
daughters of influential Arabs.

And as Muhammad gained a larger following through his preaching, the Meccan leaders *very much* felt threatened. And leaders scorned
his words and speeches.

And for a short time, Muhammad left Mecca and attempted to
spread Allah's message in a nearby town. But the people there were
*unprepared* for Muhammad and his message – they thought, "Who is
this self-proclaiming prophet?"

Now Muhammad used the little influence he had in Mecca to persuade a non-family clan to provide him with *protection*. And so it came
to pass that Muhammad did return to Mecca. But the *persecution* of
Muhammad and his members so continued – there were name-callings,
public humiliations, and at times some shoving. And one day,
Muhammad came home late to find a pile of dung at the doorstep of
his house.

## Chapter VI: Muhammad's Emigration to Medina

The year was six-hundred-twenty-one. And during the annual summer pilgrimage to Kaaba, Muhammad preached nearby the holy
shrine, "God, the *merciful* and *compassionate*, is robed in *righteousness*.
Allah is the *ruler* of the world and of the Universe. Allah is *everywhere*
in time and space. After death, the soul of every man shall be suspended, waiting for the Retribution-Resurrection Day, when *Allah's
judgement* so shall be proclaimed." And Muhammad then continued,
"Ye shall submit to Allah's power – this is islam. And ye who listen
and surrender to the *word* of Allah shall be Allah's Muslims."[42] And
among the listeners were twelve from nearby Medina. And they surrendered to the will of God and were converted into Muslims. And
Muhammad instructed them to go back to Medina and spread the
*word* of Allah there. And they did *so*.

---

[42] The word *islam* is Arabic for "surrendering." In the context of Muhammad's recitations, it meant to surrender to the will of God. The Arabic word *muslim* means one who
had surrendered.

Thus Muhammad's followers became the Muslims. Muslims were believers in the *word* of Allah, as spoken through Muhammad, Allah's prophet.

And one year went by. And seventy-five Muslim converts from Medina came to Mecca for the summer pilgrimage. And they swore allegiance to Muhammad – they would defend him and *the religion* as *their* own children. Now Muhammad instructed them to go back to Medina and prepare the people there for him, for Muhammad would make Medina his new home.

And one Meccan merchant, realizing the *intentions* of Muhammad, told his fellow merchants and his tribal leaders that Muhammad *must* be killed before he reached Medina. And a leader named Omar set out to slay the "so-called prophet." And when he found Muhammad, Muhammad was in a trance and was an *easy prey*. And Muhammad was reciting words of wisdom. And Omar heard the words, was amazed and thought, "Such *awe and wisdom* do these holy words evoke – these surely *are* the words of Allah." And Omar let his sword drop to the ground. And *he* knelt down and prayed.

Now Omar was an influential person at the time. And his conversion to Islam swayed *others* to convert and join the Muslim movement.[43]

Now Muhammad, sensing the danger and the threat in Mecca, quickly left the city. And he used *unused paths* to cross the *desert*. And on the twenty-fourth day of the ninth month of the year six-hundred-twenty-two,[44] Muhammad made it to Medina. And some Muslims went there with him, while others stayed behind in Mecca.

## Chapter VII: Muhammad in Medina

Now Medina was a town on an *oasis*, where date palms and grains were grown. And the best lands were in the hands of several Jewish clans. Now there were eight main Arab clans, which had been feuding; people even had been killed. And when Muhammad arrived in Medina, a peace had not been fully put in place. And so the Arabs of Medina *welcomed* the arrival of Muhammad – they had heard of him and *hoped* he could negotiate a peace.

And so Muhammad acted as an arbitrator. And he arranged a great agreement – there would be nine Arab groups, eight clans from Medina and one new clan of Meccan Muslims. Now Muhammad was given no special ruling powers in the document of the *Constitution of Medina*, but in the preamble it was written, "Muhammad is our prophet." And Muhammad was appointed arbitrator of any further feuds.

---

[43] Two years after Muhammad's death, Omar would help maintain the Muslim state.

[44] Later, this year would mark the beginning of the Islamic calendar.

Now the Jews had been *invited* to negotiate. But they did not participate, for they *refused* to recognize Muhammad as a prophet. And so there was no Jewish clan – instead, the Jews were arbitrarily assigned to certain Arab clans.

Now Muhammad was presented with a piece of land, on which Muhammad *built* a house.[45] And Muhammad's house contained a courtyard around which were many small apartments for his wives. And Muslims *often* came to Muhammad's home to *pray*.

Now Muhammad *preferred* to spread his message *without* the use of military might. But if he was forced to do so, he *would* use military force.

And in Medina, Muhammad spoke the Koran recitations: "Say ye: God is forgiving and compassionate. He is the *Guardian* of the flock, the *Protector* of the people, the *Defender* of invading forces, the *Sender* of the heaven's rains, the *Judge* of all disputes. Recite ye: Allah is *everlasting*. He begets no one and He has never been begotten. Nor is there anyone like Him. He is God alone." And one of Muhammad's followers did say, "Allah is speaking – we must write down the words." And they took a *palm leaf* and inked the words on *it*.

And when they did not have a leaf, they etched the words in *stone*. And when they had neither leaf nor stone, they grabbed a piece of *leather* and they rubbed the words in *it*. And when they had neither leaf nor stone nor leather, a man would take off his shirt and write the words in his own *skin*.

And later, these writings would be *assembled* in a book. And that book would be Muhammad's revelations. And this set of recitations would constitute the holy book of Allah, the *Koran*.

And Muhammad described how, in the beginning, Allah had made two creatures endowed with reason and responsibility. And they were man and *jinn*.[46] And man was made from clay, while *jinn* was made from fire. And when Adam ate the apple, Allah was merciful, forgiving Adam for his sin. And Muhammad told of Noah and the Flood. And Muhammad recounted the story of Joseph and his brothers. And the descriptions were *similar* to ones in the Holy Bible, but there were differences. And when asked why there were such differences, Muhammad so responded, "To communicate His will, Allah has sent messengers. These messengers are the prophets, the great ones such as Adam, Noah, David, Moses, Abraham and Jesus. The prophets for their faith and courage have been *rewarded* so: Abraham was *saved* from fire, Noah was *rescued* from the Flood, Moses and his people were *liberated* from the Pharaoh, Jesus was *resurrected* from the cross – these were *acts of Allah*. And of Moses, Abraham and Jesus, they preached the *word* of islam. Now the Christians and the Jews have

---

[45] After Muhammad's death, his home was made into the mosque of Medina.
[46] The *jinn* is a spirit being.

written the words of Allah in the Torah and the Holy Bible. And indeed these books are sacred books. But those who wrote these books have *distorted* Allah's words. Now I too am Allah's messenger. I am *the* last prophet. When I speak, Allah speaks – the words are pure, coming directly from the mouth of Allah."

And his followers responded, *speaking* what Muhammad had just spoken and then saying, "The angel Gabriel has brought from Heaven *the Koran*. Thank Gabriel and God for *the Koran*."

And once *again*, Muhammad invited Jews and Christians to join the Muslim movement. But once *again*, the Christians and the Jews *refused*. And Muhammad, annoyed at their intransigence, declared *his* religion to be a religion *specifically* for Arabs. "We must *turn away* from Jews," he said. And the Sabbath day, the holy day, became Friday instead of Saturday. And in prayer sessions, he had the Muslims turn to Mecca – no longer would Jerusalem be the direction praying Muslims faced. Instead, Kaaba in Mecca became the *object* of the Muslim's prayers. And Muhammad then announced that Allah's religion shall be *distinct* from other faiths. And Muhammad gave a name to his religion. And *Islam* was its name. And so a new religion was proclaimed. And Arabic was declared to be its holy tongue.

And upon being asked why Mecca should be the *chosen* sacred city, Muhammad so replied, "Mecca is the navel of the Earth, attached like an umbilical cord to Heaven. Now Kaaba was built in ancient times by *angels*. The first man, Adam, *did* dwell there. And after the Great Flood, while Abraham and Ishmael were restoring Mecca, Allah sent a stone from Heaven. And *that Black Stone* lodged itself in the southeast corner of the shrine. Thus Kaaba is a sacred place, a spot where Heaven and the Earth do *touch*."

## Chapter VIII: A Time of Conflict

And to gain money for the brotherhood of Muslims, Muhammad ordered *raids* on caravans passing near Medina en route to Syria from Mecca. Now most such raids did not at first succeed. But in January of the year six-hundred-twenty-four, Muhammad's men attacked a caravan from Yemen. And a lot of goods and gold were gained. And so it came to pass that the Meccan merchants, traders and leaders were *directly* threatened by Muhammad and the Muslims. And in March of the same year, Muhammad and three-hundred of his men attacked a wealthy Meccan caravan, but the Meccans did escape with all their goods. And a force of eight-hundred Meccans was sent to *teach* Muhammad *a military lesson*. At Badr did the two forces clash. And fifty Meccans died, including the leader of the force, and seventy Meccan men were captured. The Meccan force *retreated* in defeat. Now the death toll for the Muslims numbered *only* fourteen men. And Muhammad so declared, "It is *Allah* who has helped our smaller force defeat the Meccans." And in Medina many joined the Muslim movement, for they believed in Allah's intervention.

And Muhammad spoke, saying, "Allah has commanded me to wage the war of Islam. I *shall* defeat my enemies and *purge* the pagan idolaters. Allah's religion shall be *restored* throughout the land. Now Muslims, hearken to my words. We are brothers unto one another. Our brotherhood *is* the good community. We must foster *goodness* and forbid all evilness, using cooperation as the basis of our brotherhood. Coordination of our efforts *must* be made, so that the opponents of our movement can be destroyed with force." And he continued, "Ye have walked separately *the well-trodden path*.[47] Now we shall walk *the path* together."

And in Medina, Muhammad exerted force – he put to death those who had ridiculed the words of the Koran. The threat of death at the sword's blade *weakened* his opponents. He drove out some members of the Jewish clan. And so he turned *victory* and military prowess into political successes, gains and *profits*. And he had his daughters marry into other clans – this helped advance his influence and power. And Muhammad entered into agreements of nonaggression with certain nomadic tribes, so as to establish alliances in other Arab lands. Later, many nomads *would* convert to Islam. And Muhammad continued raiding caravans. And both his wealth and others' fear of him increased.

And in March of six-hundred-twenty-five AD, a Meccan force of *three-thousand* men entered the outskirts of the oasis of Medina. Again their target was Muhammad. And one-thousand Muslims and Muhammad went out to *defend* Medina and the crops about to harvest. And at the hill of Uhud, Muhammad drove the Meccans back, as many Meccans died. And two days went by, as Muhammad's men lay waiting. Now the thrust forward had left his forces *vulnerable* to flank attack. And the Meccans took advantage of this fact. And Meccan cavalry shot arrows into "Muslims' sides." And pandemonium prevailed. Some Muslims fought the flank attack, while Muhammad and others retreated to a *safer* spot. A *bloody* battle did take place in which *neither* side did win. And the next day had the Meccans disappeared, heading home, for they did not want to lose more men. Muhammad attempted to pursue them, but *already* were they far away. Now seventy Meccan men had Muhammad's forces killed. But since Muhammad's losses were about the *same*, he could not claim a victory. And although he *had* not been defeated, the confidence of some in him declined: "*How* could Allah intervene at Badr and *not* at Uhud," they *asked* themselves. But others saw things differently: "Had not Muhammad defended Medina, thereby saving it?" they said.

---

[47] In Arabic, this is called the *sunnah*.

And diligently worked Muhammad to *restore* the faith. And his struggle turned from fighting in the battlegrounds to preaching to the people in the streets.

And Muhammad once again reminded Muslims of the Judgement Day: "Verily the day of decision is an *appointed time* – on that day shall sound a trumpet. The dead shall come in troops, and the *heavens* shall be *opened*. And the dead shall be questioned by two angels. And Allah, who is all-powerful, shall bring the dead ones back to life. A *judgement* shall be made. Souls shall go in one of two directions – to Heaven or to Hell. Verily the good ones, *those* with faith, shall be reborn. And they shall go to Heaven and be rewarded blissfully. Thus for the Allah-fearing ones, there shall be a *final* place of *happiness* – a garden with vineyards and with girls of swelling breasts. These faithful ones shall verily abide with Allah, who shall sit in a throne on waters in the highest realm. Angels shall surround Him, and *all* shall worship Him. Verily the *evil spirits*, on the other hand, will be *destroyed*. The pagan ones shall go to Hell and suffer for eternity. The foolish and outrageous souls shall dwell *forever* in a flaming Hell. Their bodies shall burn continuously. And their lungs shall want a cool moist air – but only hot and fumy gas shall they breathe in. And they shall thirst and have no drink. *Forever* shall *they* regret their sin.

"Recite ye: Allah has created all. To everything which Allah has created, there *is* a purpose." And all the people did recite. "Recite ye: The Universe's parts fall in a *pattern*, which makes the Universe a *whole*. And the Universe is self-contained through its own inherent laws, the laws which *Allah* has provided.[48] Through such laws the behavior of everything is limited. Thus *all depends on God* and God alone." And the Muslims recited all, bowing as they spoke.

And then Muhammad modestly continued, "Like all prophets, I am human. I am not divine – only Allah is divine. I am a mere messenger, a *voice* through which Allah's angels speak.

"Recite ye: Three times[49] a day shall ye to Allah pray: morning, evening and in the middle of the afternoon. Recite ye: Before ye pray, ye shall wash thy hands, thy face and feet. And ye shall sit upon thy calves. Recite ye: Ye shall bow up and down, saying *'God is great'*."

And gradually Muhammad gained more followers.

Now both Meccan and Islamic sides began preparing for a war. And Muslims attacked the caravans *not* for goods or silver coins but to

---

[48] Because there is no separation of science and religion in Islam, modern scientific discoveries seem to suggest contradictions in places in the text of the Koran. In recent times, some accommodation has been attempted. For example, "the *jinns* that cause disease" have been interpreted as viruses. Likewise, interpretations of the Koran consistent with Darwinism have been evoked. It should be noted, however, that for the Muslim, the Koran is without flaw. It is decisive, unmistakable and clear. Thus for example, Allah's creation of the Universe cannot be questioned.

[49] Later, the prayer schedule would be changed to five times a day.

disrupt the Meccan military preparations and to intimidate the Arab clans.

Now a couple of clans in Medina *still* opposed Muhammad. And Muhammad had a showdown with their leaders. And in Muhammad did the people of Medina *voice* their confidence and their support. And the opposing leaders *submitted* to Muhammad's power.

And in April of that year, a force of *ten-thousand* men left Mecca for Medina. Now Muhammad's *spies* foretold him of the coming threat. Thus Muhammad ordered crops to be harvested as best they could and *had* a trench dug in the farmlands all around Medina. And when the Meccans struck with all the force they had, Muhammad's men were *very ready* for a fight. *In the name of Allah* did the Muslims fight. Medina was under siege for two straight weeks. But Meccan supplies began to dwindle, and rainy weather made things worse for them. The Muslims *knew* that it was *Allah* who had brought the rains. And no matter what they tried, the Meccans could not penetrate the trenches. And in the end, they gave up and headed home.

Against a great Meccan force, Muhammad had *defended the oasis* of Medina. Muhammad was a hero.

Now the Medinan Jews had not helped Muhammad and the others in the war. And Muhammad had heard *rumors* that a few Jews even wanted to assassinate him. And Muhammad's forces raided the Jewish quarters of Medina. And *all* the Jewish men were killed, while the women and the children *were* sold off as slaves.

Now many nomadic desert tribes were loyal to Muhammad. But among large tribes, a hostile one remained. And Muhammad led an army to destroy this hostile tribe. At Hunayn a *great battle* with fierce fighting did take place. And in the beginning, it *seemed* that there would *be* no winner. But in the end, the nomads *were* defeated. The Muslims took the wives and children as their own wives and servants. The nomads' belongings were *divided* up as booty. And when Muhammad returned to Medina, he gave some of the "winnings" to the poor.

And Muhammad preached to his followers, "*Never* must ye raise thy arm against a member of our brotherhood. A Muslim must *never* kill a Muslim, for we are Allah's people, and to kill one of Allah's people is to kill a piece of Allah."

## Chapter IX: Muhammad Marches into Mecca

And Muhammad had a *dream*. And in the dream he saw himself. And behind him was a *crowd of countless* people. And he and they were *marching* to the shrine of Kaaba. And at the shrine of Kaaba, the masses *knelt down and prayed*.

And in the year six-hundred-twenty-eight, Muhammad tried to *make* the dream come true. He summoned the Muslims of Medina. He told them of a journey with Mecca as the *destination*. And in March of the same year, sixteen-hundred Muslims left Medina with Muhammad to make the pilgrimage to Kaaba. And although sixteen-hundred men were many, there were *not* as many as in Muhammad's dream.

Now since Meccan leaders did not want Muhammad making such a pilgrimage, the Muslims were prevented from *crossing* the frontier. And Muhammad began negotiating with officials there. And after several days, a pact was signed – Muhammad could enter Mecca the next year, if Muhammad *ceased* the raiding of the caravans.

And in March of the year of six-hundred-twenty-nine AD, Muhammad led his people into Mecca. And Muslims prayed at Kaaba. And while kneeling did they touch their foreheads to the Meccan ground. And Muhammad left Mecca without incurring any difficulties. And people were *amazed* that a man could enter *the land of his enemy* and *pray in peace*: "Verily is he Allah's prophet," many thought. And more Arabs were converted into Muslims.

And at this time, Muhammad married several Meccan leader's daughters. And in this way, Muhammad established links with certain Meccan leaders.

And Muhammad spoke out *against* the Christians and the Jews, saying, "They have erred. They have *falsified* the holy scriptures." And the Arabs *knew* that this was true, for Muhammad was the original true *voice* of God, the uncorrupted, preserved and unchanged *voice*.

And Muhammad *led* his most faithful followers north to a Jewish settlement. And there he besieged the town. And in the beginning, the Jews resisted well, but in the end they had to give up and give in. Now Muhammad said the Jews *could stay* as long as one-half their crop of dates was sent to him. And so the Jews remained and paid Muhammad's yearly ransom.

And elsewhere, Muhammad took payments from Christians and from Jews in *exchange* for Mussulman protection.

And Muhammad's military, political and economic successes led to many converts to Islam, not just in Medina but in *many* Arab towns – his movement gained a great momentum.

And meanwhile, business was bad in Mecca – some Meccan merchants had even emigrated to Medina and were trading there. And Meccan leaders fought among themselves. Even the peasants were upset – their gods were *not rewarding* them.

And in November of six-hundred-twenty-nine, Meccan allies attacked some allies of Muhammad. And Muhammad angrily announced, "Our pact with the Meccans is annulled," as he declared a *holy war* on Mecca. And in January of the next year, he led *ten-thousand* men to Mecca. Now because the Meccan leaders feared the destruction of their city, they went to the outskirts of Mecca to *negotiate* a peace. And they agreed to surrender to Muhammad if Muhammad granted amnesty to everyone. And so with almost no resistance, Muhammad entered Mecca. And as he entered, he addressed non-Muslim Meccans, saying "What ye practice is corrupted. It is *not* too late. *Repent* and *submit* thyselves to God. The human soul itself reflects the unity and grace of God." And the next day, there was another recitation: "Man has been negligent in his faith to God. Man's will is frail – he often goes astray. Thus ye must listen to the word of Allah so as to know the way." And the masses recited all, bowing *as* Muhammad spoke.

And Muhammad set up a ruling order. And Muhammad had the idols in Kaaba and other holy shrines destroyed.

And Allah spoke through Muhammad, "Recite ye: Ye must be *generous*. To the poor must ye give alms. Help ye the needy. *Alleviate* the suffering of those who suffer so. But Satan shall try to prevent thy giving-acts by placing greedy thoughts in thy mind's eye. Ye must resist such thoughts. Thank Allah by giving to the poor."

And Muhammad demanded that the richest men in Mecca give a percentage to the poor. And they did *so*. And the poor in Mecca saw Muhammad as a great one – he was indeed *their* prophet. And almost all poor people joined Islam.

And Muhammad preached in the Meccan land, *"There is no God but Allah*. Allah is all. He is great. And I am Allah's prophet. Through me does Allah speak." And on their knees, the Muslims waved up and down their outstretched arms before Muhammad. And many of Muhammad's former Meccan enemies heard his words and were converted into Muslims.

## Chapter X: Muhammad Establishes the Islamic State

And Muhammad set up a legal system. And *ordinances* concerning institutions were *established*. And rules for daily living and for family were written down. And regulations on sex, on marriage and divorce, and on inheritance were issued. And *laws* governing business, trade and commerce were also *instituted*. And taxes were established, when Allah, through Muhammad, spoke, "Recite ye: Each year to Islam shall ye pay a gift. And on land watered by the rains, it shall be one-tenth of the harvest's fruits and grains. And on land watered by hand by man, it shall be half of this. And of cash and precious metals, another factor of one-half *shall* be factored in."[50] And because of the decrees, the practice of killing female babies at birth *was* no longer possible. And the low social status of women, slaves, the poor and orphans *was* raised up.[51] Thus for example, slaves were given legal rights – their freedom *could* be bought.

And rules for war were spoken: "Recite ye: In the name of Allah shall ye wage war but never in the name of glory, wealth or power."

Now in all of Arabia, Muhammad was *politically* the strongest man. He was *admired* for his religious fortitude and unwavering convic-

---

[50] This made the tax one-fortieth of cash, or 2.5%.

[51] However, the equality of women with men was never attained under Islam – women were considered different and were treated differently.

tion and for being courageous, resolute and generous. And he preached to the masses of Arabia to surrender to Islam and Allah. His *message* was *distributed* to the Arabs of towns and villages and to the nomads of the desert. And a large region of Arabia became essentially Islamic.

Now it had happened that the Persian Empire had been defeated by the Byzantines in six-hundred-twenty-eight AD. Now many places in the Middle East had been dependent on the Persians for support. Thus with a weakened Persia, *vulnerable* were many countries to attack.

Now in all of Arabia, Muhammad was *militarily* the strongest man. And in a bold move, he led *thirty-thousand* soldiers to the Syrian border. From there he orchestrated the conquering of Syria – in some places, resisting forces were attacked and eventually destroyed; in most places, conquest was achieved through negotiated settlements.

Now there were many Christians living in the Syrian towns. And they were outraged by Muhammad's use of force to wrest their freedom from their hands. And in the next two years, Christians organized two great attacks on Islam. But by then, Islam was quite powerful and the attacks did *little* harm.

And so Islam became established, not just as a religion, but also as a state[52] of Arab states – it was a brotherhood of Muslims, bounded by a common faith.

And Muhammad decided that neither race, nor spoken tongue, nor political or economic stature, nor sex, nor color of the skin should play a role in the *ability to submit* oneself to Allah: "Recite ye: All men are Adam's children. Therefore all men are *equal*. And the best be those whose faith is strong. And the worst be those whose faith is weak. And all this is independent of one's wealth or social caste."

Thus Islam was opened up to *anyone* who submitted to Allah and who *believed* that Muhammad was his prophet, that the Koran recitations were but Allah's words, and that the Judgement Day would come when Allah's judgement would be final.

And in his later years, Muhammad *continued* to deliver Allah's recitations: "Say ye: We[53] have revealed to thee the Arabic Koran. May ye happily recite and understand." "Recite ye: Man is susceptible to mischief. As for his actions, man must take responsibility. And through Allah shall man know *the path*. Man shall serve Allah and submit to *Allah's will*." "Recite ye: Above all, *arrogance* is sin. Beware of Satan, the most arrogant of all, who shall try to make thee err and sin. Happily his destruction will be consummated on the Judgement Day."

---

[52] Because Islam is a political entity as well as a religion, there is no separation of church and state – Muslims consider themselves united under Islam independent of geographical boundaries. The lack of separation of church and state leads to the *jihad* or holy war. Under certain circumstances, a *jihad* can be declared. Then Muslims are to wage war in the name of Allah.

[53] Often, Allah spoke through Muhammad using the first person plural, "we," instead of "I" or "I, Allah." For reasons of clarity, this Book of *Muhammad* has avoided doing this.

And the *masses* throughout the Arab lands recited Allah's recitations. And they spoke of Muhammad, saying, "He is the last of Allah's prophets – he has *sealed the Faith*. Allah has chosen him to reveal to man His word. *Muhammad is our prophet.*"

And the rules for religious practice were set up. There would be five affirmations. And they were that Allah is unique and great, that the Day of Reckoning shall come, that Muhammad is the last of Allah's prophets, that the Koran is the bible of Islam, and that those who do believe in Allah are part of the brotherhood of Muslims.

And Islam would have no priests to preach the word of God – only *the Koran* would speak the word of God.

And Muslims had five duties – they were the five *pillars* of Islam. The first was the *reciting* of the creed, "There is no God but *Allah*. And Muhammad is His messenger." The second was that of *worship* and of prayer – five times daily would the Muslims pray: when the Sun rose at daybreak, when the Sun was overhead at noon, when *came* late afternoon, when the Sun did set, and when a Muslim went to bed. And on Fridays would the Muslims pray in mosques. But if one *were* sick, one was to pray in bed. The third pillar was the *fast* of Ramadan – on that month, Muslims would abstain from food and drink and sex from dawn to dusk. The fourth was *charity*, the giving to the poor of alms. And the fifth was the *pilgrimage* to Mecca – Muslims would go to Mecca at least once before they died.

And of the fast of Ramadan, it was said: "*Righteousness* is the path that ye must follow. And on the ninth month of the Muslim lunar year, *ye* shall fast. And from sunrise to sunset ye *shall* not eat nor drink nor smoke, for, on the ninth month, was the Koran of Allah first revealed."

And of the fifth pillar, it was said: "And once during thy lifetime, during the last month of the Muslim lunar year, *shall* ye make a pilgrimage to Mecca. Ye *shall* not cut thy hair. Neither shall ye trim thy nails. Ye shall shed thy shoes and wear a seamless garb. Seven times shall ye walk around the Kaaba sanctuary. Of the Black Stone, ye shall touch it with thy lips. Of the waters of the holy well *shall* ye drink. And ye shall recite the prayers that the Prophet has so taught. And seven times shall ye run between Mount Safa and Mount Marwah. Then ye shall go to Mount Ararat and listen to a sermon. And ye shall *witness* the feast of sacrifice." And so the people were *provided* with a faith and a religion.

And so it came to pass that Islam occupied almost all of the Arabian Plain between the Red Sea and the Persian Gulf. And Islam would spread *elsewhere* in the Middle East. And eventually it would reach North Africa, eastern and southern Asia, and many places in the world.

And it came to pass that the accomplishments of Muhammad surpassed those of *any* other man.

And in March of six-hundred-thirty-two, Muhammad led an enormous pilgrimage to Mecca – it was a pilgrimage *beyond* his expectations and *equal* to his dream. And faithfully his followers did follow him, for Muhammad was *their prophet*.

And having achieved his goal, the defeat of paganism, the establishment of a new religion and a new state, Muhammad was content. And on the eighth day in June of the year six-hundred-thirty-two, Muhammad died.[54] And Muhammad's soul was *sent* to the rock sticking in the top of King Solomon's great temple in Jerusalem, the same spot where Abraham had offered as sacrifice his son. And there Muhammad's soul *ascended* on a wingèd horse to Heaven. And although Muhammad's body was laid to rest in Medina, his Islam and his legacy lived on.[55]

---

[54] Henceforth, whenever Muslims mentioned the name Muhammad, they would recite, "God bless him and grant him peace."

[55] Soon after Muhammad's death, the Muslims defeated the Byzantines and Persians. The Islamic religion was extended into northern Africa and southern Asia, and a great Islamic empire was built.

*The fifth book of Chronicles, called*

# Catastrophes[56]

*For nation shall rise against nation,
and kingdom against kingdom,
and there shall be famines and pestilences
and earthquakes in diverse places.
And all these are the beginning of sorrows.*

*– The Holy Bible*

## Chapter I: Nature Speaks

*Dost thou fear Nature for nought?*

And Nature will behave as Nature must behave, for She is driven by *the laws of physics*, which govern all. And man is powerful but often not powerful enough for Nature's power.

And when Nature speaks it can be terrifying. She can be like the wizard in the Wizard of Oz. Thou enterest a room with certain hopes. Thou expectest to meet a friendly wizard who will resolve thy difficulties. Instead the room is frightening and full of fire and fear. And no wizard is to be seen. Instead, a deep and disturbing voice shouts out. And the voice chastises thee for disrupting the peace. Thou art terrified and thou shakest.

And only later dost thou realize that behind the curtain is a timid, cowardly figure of a wizard. And the room is just a ploy.

*(And a voice spake, saying
"She is Nature and does not listen to thy prayers.")*

What follows are examples of Nature, when Nature is upset.

## Chapter II: Mount Vesuvius

*And the mountain burned with fire unto the midst of Heaven,
with darkness, clouds, and thick darkness.*

*Then the Earth shook and trembled;
the foundations of heaven moved and shook,
because He was wroth.
There went up a smoke out of His nostrils,
and fire out of His mouth devoured:
coals were kindled by it.
He bowed the heavens also, and came down;
and darkness was under His feet.
And He rode upon a cherub, and did fly:
and He was seen upon the wings of the wind.*

---

[56] To Job be this book so dedicated.

*And He made darkness pavilions round Him,*
*dark waters,* and *thick clouds of the skies.*
*Through the brightness before Him were coals of fire kindled.*
*He thundered from heaven,*
*and the most high uttered His voice.*
*And He sent out arrows and scattered them,*
*lightning and discomforted them.*
*And the channels of the sea appeared,*
*the foundations of the world were discovered,*
*at the rebuking of Him,*
*at the blast of the breath of His nostrils.*

*– The Holy Bible*

On the fifth day of the second month of the year sixty-two AD, did an earthquake *shake* the regions southeast of Naples. During the next seventeen years, there would be *many* quakes in this green and otherwise tranquil land. The Romans there would get used to the periodic tremors *and* not worry. They would go on growing grapes in the ash-rich soil of the vineyards around the mountain of Vesuvius. The farmers and townspeople did not know that Vesuvius, with its gently sloping green and fertile shoulders, was not just a mountain. And they did not understand *the voice of Nature,* which, through the tremors, was trying to tell them something. They did not know that Vesuvian tremors should instill the fear of God in them and *warn* them of forthcoming doom.

Sometimes did an earthquake put a *crack* in a Roman wall, or break a column or even make a dwelling topple. At one time, the Temple in Pompeii was damaged. In these cases, the Romans *rebuilt* the dwelling or *fixed* the column or *repaired* the wall. They toasted the reconstruction of the Temple by sipping wine. After such repairs, the citizens went on with daily life. At sunrise did they walk the *peaceful* countryside. At evening did they watch the Sun set in the Bay of Naples. At night slept they in comfort. They were enjoying the prosperity of the Roman Empire at its height.

But in the year seventy-nine AD, there came about a *change.* The tremors shook more frequently. The Romans walked around in white robes, complaining about the bad behavior of servants, maids and slaves.

Then at noon on the twenty-fourth day of the eighth month, a *mysterious* cloud appeared above Vesuvius in what had been a sunny day. And the cloud grew rapidly and spread its arms until it resembled a Mediterranean pine tree with a bare trunk and a crown of branches branching out. And the cloud expanded vertically – the *highest* point got *higher* and the *lowest* point got *lower.* And the lowest point touched the mountainside. And it started snowing on Vesuvius. But white ash was coming down, not snow. Like a Roman, Mount Vesuvius put on a robe of white.

And Vulcan, the Roman god of fire, lashed out his flaming tongue – Vesuvius erupted. Vulcan would lose his temper for two days.

And the cloud got darker, larger, and engulfed the summit. And *dark shadows* were cast upon the green and tranquil countryside. And the cloud got bigger, blacker, and sank lower. Then flames shot out of Vesuvius. Behold, Vesuvius was a fountain *full* of flames. Farmers in the vineyards fled.

Then the heart of Vesuvius exploded. And lava flowed down its slopes. And a column of smoke, steam and ash streamed out and up – it rose for ten kilometers.[57] And it drifted to the south and east. And *darkness* did descend upon surrounding land.

And the cloud let loose its contents, but the contents were not rain or water, but ash and chunks of pumice. And glowing coals were falling from the heavens – it was raining fire. And so the *fire of Nature* fell from heaven.

And white ash settled on the nearby towns of Pompeii and Herculaneum. *Some* townspeople grabbed their most precious possessions, gold and jewelry, and *fled*. Wealthy Romans left in horse-drawn chariots, while poorer people walked. It was *like unto* a line of refugees. They arrived at the Bay of Naples, got in boats, and sailed off.

But most Romans did remain, for they did *not believe* the wrath of Nature could or would be harsh. And they went inside their homes to *wait* until the fallout from the sky subsided. And ash and pumice accumulated in the streets outside and on the roofs.

And in the countryside, *glowing* flakes did fall from the sky and set the plants and trees ablaze.

And like snow, pumice piled up in Pompeii a meter high. And roofs of houses sagged. And tremors shook the houses and *those* who hid inside – *this* time *they* were scared. And more Romans left their houses and headed out of town.

It was five-thirty in the afternoon, but *already* was it dark. Lightning flashed around the summit of Vesuvius – it was *like unto* a thunderstorm with ash instead of rain.

In Pompeii, the weight of pumice blocks became too great, and roofs started caving in. Multitudes of citizens were crushed and died. Some of those alive grabbed pillows, went outside, and started plodding through the ash. *They* were met with darkness, *though it be day*; they groped about *as if it be* the night. Those with torches tried to light the way. Those with pillows put the pillows on their heads. But bits of pumice coming from the heavens struck the pillows and their arms. They waded through the ash, while more black flakes rained down on

---

[57] A kilometer is about 0.6 miles, so that ten kilometers is about six miles.

them. Soon *they* were painted black. The procession through the streets was like unto a *procession* of dead souls.

And some groped in the dark without light, staggering like drunken men and shaken by frequent strong earthquakes. Sulfurous fumes did make them choke. The water in their mouths became acidic. And they *thirsted* for a cup of water to cool their burning throats.

The voice of thunder *sounded* in the heavens. In flashes did lightning light the land. And the earth did tremble and did shake.

And midnight came. And once more Vesuvius *exploded* fiercely. And a column of debris shot high into the sky. It peaked then fell. And hot ash and lumps of pumice dropped into the Bay of Naples ten kilometers away. Debris in the column also fell and struck the summit of Vesuvius. And a wave of *incandescent* ash and dust sped down the slopes and outward from Vesuvius. And low to the ground did move the *wave*; left in its wake were toppled trees.

And the ground-hugging wave, speeding outward at one-hundred kilometers per hour, struck Herculaneum six minutes later. And people, dogs and horses flew *through* the air. Houses were like paper blown away. *Everyone* within the town was dead.

At 6:15 a.m.[58] on the twenty-fifth day of the eighth month, Vesuvius *exploded* with a force that could not be imagined. Again a column of debris *rose* into the sky, peaked, fell and sent a hot *wave* of incandescent ash outward at one-hundred kilometers per hour. But this time the hot wave travelled *southward* all the way to Pompeii. In that town, hot gas, dust and winds *blew off* the tops of roofs. Each Roman who had stayed gave one last contorted struggle and then his *vital force* was lost. As the wood of homes went up in flames, human flesh was cooked. This was Vesuvius's holocaust. And by the breath of its nostrils were *people* so consumed.

At 8:00 a.m., an even stronger surge of hot wind and ash struck "poor Pompeii," levelling everything above the two-meter layer of ash. Pompeii had been beheaded – its people executed.

And while waiting for boats, Romans on the beach *suddenly* did see the sea recede, leaving fish and shells stranded on the sands. And a giant wave, a tsunami, came surging back. The *wave* washed up the shore. The *hand of death* reached out and grabbed the Romans, as thousands *were* pulled out to sea. And as water filled their lungs, they died. And the *vital spirits* in them *fled*.

Now the next day *was* not day – it was *like unto* a moonless night. And the *only light* was frequent *lightning flashes*. And in between the flashes was it as black as in a room without a light at night. It was a land of darkness as darkness *itself* and like the shadow of death, without any order and where the *light* was as *darkness*.

---

[58] From records, the time of the eruption is known within minutes.

And a cloud let loose a heavy rain. This time it was *real rain* – the drops were water. And the rain beat down upon the land, mixing with ash and earth, as mud was made. This mud slid down the mountainside and met mud in the countryside. And a great mud-flow *surged* toward the Bay of Naples. Now Herculaneum was in its way. And in minutes, Herculaneum was *overwhelmed*, buried under twenty meters of black mud.

In several days, winds *cleared* the air. The Sun pierced through the haze. And Vesuvius became visible, but its top was *gone*. And in its place was a crater two-kilometers in width. Behold, Vesuvius had lost its head and gained a hollow cone instead. And the buildings of Pompeii had *disappeared* – the town was in a three-foot[59] layer of ash. Now mud and ash would eventually cast the bodies of the dead in molds. And these bodies would dissolve away.

And the woodlands, vineyards and greenery around Vesuvius were laid waste – the region was an uninhabitable brown-gray land of ash and mud.

.   .   .   .   .   .   .

And many years went by. And it came to pass that molten rock pushed upward from beneath the earth. And a new cone appeared in the crater of Vesuvius. And so Nature *rebuilt* the peak of Mount Vesuvius. Vesuvius was *resurrected*.

And in the year of one-thousand-seven-hundred-thirty-eight AD, excavations uncovered Herculaneum. And ten years later, excavations uncovered the lost Pompeii.

And in modern times, archaeologists removed the ash and found the *empty chambers* where corpses had decayed. And they filled the chambers with a plaster and reconstructed bodies – it *was* like turning ghosts to stone. And detailed sculptures of the Romans were obtained. The sculptures showed human bodies in contorted positions about to die. The sculptures showed the grimaces of human faces of those about to die.

## Chapter III: The Black Death

*And a mysterious and invisible shadow*
*passed over the face of Earth.*

It was a *moonless* night in thirteen-hundred-thirty-eight AD. And a *ship* there in a port was rocked by waves – the next day would *it* set sail. And it came to pass that a rat ran up the boarding platform – it was a rat that had the devil in it; it was a rat that had the plague in it. And the rat hid in the galleys of the ship and waited so. And in the morning, the sailors got on board. And they were joking and quite cheery – they were *happy* to head home to Italy. And so the ship *left* the Middle East. And off into the Mediterranean Sea it sailed.

---

[59] One meter.

And when the ship arrived in eastern Italy late one afternoon, all sailors went ashore. But the rat *stayed* in the galley and waited so. When night did come, the rat with evil in it ran down the platform onto land. Along the gutter of a moonlit street the rat did go. And it headed to a grain shop, and there it *hid* among the bags of wheat and waited so.

At dawn the shopkeeper, who was not married, unlocked the door *and* prepared for business. Now in the fur of the rat, a rat flea lived. And out of the fur, it flew. And it landed on the sock of the owner of the shop. A hand came sweeping down and swatted at the sock – but *already* was the rat flea gone.

And five days went by. And in the middle of the afternoon, *suddenly* the owner of the shop felt sick. He started shivering. And he closed up business early and went home. Now the next day, he woke up with a bubo[60] near his groin. And he stayed in bed that day. And in the afternoon a *fever* came. And this was followed by a headache which, like a knife, seemed to *cut* his head in two. And his tongue was coated white.

That evening *badly* did he sleep. And he had chills. And in the morning did he vomit. And he had buboes in his armpit and on his neck, but on the left side of his body *only*. Scared, he got out of bed, staggered out the house, headed to the house of a physician. And although it was a cloudy day, the light did make him close his eyes. "Why *was* the light so *bright*?" he thought. A dizziness *sank* into his brain. And as he walked, he wavered back and forth. And nearby peasants thought him drunk.

. . . . . . .

When he awoke, he found himself in the gutter of a street. And there was pain in both his legs and arms and in his back. And his eyes were sore – they were *inflamed* and red – there seemed to be a *fire* in his eyes. And his tongue and mouth were dry. His mind could not think straight – he was *delirious*. Now the chills he had the day before were gone – instead he had a fever so severe that he felt his head would burst. And the color of his tongue had *changed* from white to yellow.

And a passerby helped him to his feet and back into his house. And upon his abdomen, he lay in bed. And one bubo opened up and pus came out. And on his stomach were red spots.

And the next day the passerby came back to see how he was doing. But the gray arms and legs and face were *evidence* enough – the man was dead.

And one week later, another in that town did die. And then another, and another. Soon dozens of citizens fell sick. And half of them did die.

---

[60] A bubo is a swelling of a lymph node associated with the bubonic plague.

At night the rats came out. And they *crawled* along the gutters of the street. They *hid* in cellars and in sheds. Like a shadow of death, throughout the town they spread.

.    .    .    .    .    .    .

Nine years went by – it was thirteen-hundred-forty-seven. And the black death was *everywhere* in Italy and Greece: Sick were two-thirds of the dwellers of the towns and cities. And more than half the sick did die – death came when the plague bacilli infiltrated the liver, spleen, bone marrow and lymph nodes.

And in one town, a man in ragged clothes whipped a horse to make it move a cart. And every now and then, he stopped, got off, *lifted up* a body in the street and heaved it on the cart. And after several hours, on the cart were dead ones in a heap. And the man drove to the outskirts of the town. There he tossed the dead ones, one by one, into a trench. And nearby were other pits *full* of blue-gray bodies of the dead. The bodies there produced a stench.

And one year went by. And the black death passed over Europe like the *darkness* underneath a group of clouds. And France and Spain were decimated. Later in that year, the *shadow* passed to England. And half the Londoners did die. At the University of Oxford, two-thirds of the students perished. At schools and universities, classrooms were half full. And the teacher who began a course sometimes did not finish it: Substitutes were ushered in to teach what dead teachers would have taught. The curriculum contracted, as there were few professors still alive to instruct in subjects such as geometry and Latin.

And in Marseilles, late in the evening, a dock worker spied a ship offshore, *drifting* to the port. It seemed *strange* that no sailors were standing at the bow. There was no motion on the ship, save the flapping of gray sails with holes. And when the wind *blew* the ship to shore, the dock worker stepped on board and looked. And what he saw was *death* – the blue-gray faces, arms and ankles of the dead – it was a ship of death.

And soon, there *were* more boats of "ghosts," for people knew not what to do with the infected ones. And so, in seashore towns, the sick were often loaded onto boats and left to drift and die.

And one year when by. And *the black cloud* headed north and east and passed over central and eastern Europe, Scandinavia and Russia. And by the end of the year thirteen-hundred-fifty-one AD, two-thirds of Europeans had contracted the disease.

And in the cities, it was difficult for horse-drawn carriages to pass, as sick were *lying* in the streets. And in the country, farms grew weeds, as there were *few* on hand to work the land. An economic disaster struck all of Europe: The production of commodities went down, the supplies of food and clothing shrank, and the price of goods went up.

And Nature's plague struck indiscriminately – the houses of the rich, along with the huts of peasants, were uninhabited except for *bod-*

*ies* left in bed. As paint chipped off and shingles dropped and curtains fell, many homes turned into "haunted houses."

And *everywhere* were dead.

Some people looked up to the skies for help. Others cursed the Vatican. Some even blamed the government.

And in a Germanic town, two men in a central square took turns whipping one another. And others thought this *strange* and stared. And when asked, the two men said, "Man's plight is due to *sin*. As men, have we have committed *sin*. Our punishment is by the whip. Only by whipping one another can we obtain *forgiveness*." And selectively in Europe, men in public places whipped each other. But elsewhere, peasants gathered into groups, fell to their knees, and chanted words of mysticism, while others in the streets hopped from leg to leg in dances resembling those of primitive societies.

And new religions did arise. And one was based on worship of the *clouds*. And people prayed to spirits and to devils. And others worshipped idols.

And everywhere the rate of theft increased, for the economic depression *was* widespread. But it also increased because *many* people lost their *faith*. "If the world is evil, then why not steal?" is what they said.

And the plague moved as the *wind* moved. And it arrived in Asia. And there, *fifteen-million* Chinese perished. And countless other Asians from other countries also died.

Now this was just the beginning – the plague would rage for decades.[61] And relatively minor outbursts would continue for the next three centuries.

Now this *had* not been the first such plague – one had struck eight-hundred years before, and in Europe it had lasted fifty years. In biblical times, plagues had struck the world as well. Nor *would* this be the last such plague. Six-hundred years later in the second half of the nineteenth century, the plague would strike again – mainly on the Asian continent. And in India alone, twelve-million habitants would die.

And as sure as the Sun rises, *sickness* shall strike mankind again. And great diseases shall spread across the Earth again. And then man shall face the face of *death* again.

---

[61] More than twenty-five-million Europeans died from the bubonic plague – one-fourth of the European population. The fourteenth century is the only period in recorded history when the world's population decreased. It dropped from about four-hundred-million people to somewhat more than three-hundred-million people, a decrease of about 20%.

## Chapter IV: The Quake for All Saints

*And the Earth opened up and swallowed Dathan,
and covered the company of Abiram.*

And on the first day of the eleventh month of the year one-thousand-seven-hundred-fifty-five AD, the *faithful ones* in Lisbon, Portugal were in church celebrating All Saints' Day. And it came to pass that at 9:45 a.m., there was a low, almost silent rumble. And people in the cathedrals looked up high to the light *streaming* through the windows. Then the ground shook uncontrollably – all over Europe *was* this earthquake felt. And for six minutes did it shake, while collapsing Lisbon churches *crushed* all the praying ones inside. And the *vital spirits* of those dead so fled. Outside and all around, several thousand houses tumbled to the ground. And fires soon broke out, *fueled* by wooden rubble and fanned by *strong* high winds. And the fires burned the houses. And seventeen-thousand homes were thus destroyed, leaving only several thousand standing. Meanwhile, to escape the *spreading* flames survivors in a panic ran to the quay. And to the beach fled others. And forty minutes passed. A second *shock* did open up a mighty fissure just along the quay. And the quay and all the people on it were swallowed up *as like* the sinners on God's Judgement Day. Then suddenly the ocean dropped *as if* it were low-tide. And three tsunamis, each fifteen meters high, from the Atlantic Ocean did *sweep* in. And the giant waves crashed *on* the beach, flowing inland for several hundred meters. The sea *overwhelmed* those standing on the shore – the *vital spirits* in them fled. And *fires* did burn Lisbon for five days. Nature in three of its four forms – water, earth and fire – destroyed Lisbon and its citizens. And in the end were more than fifty-thousand dead.

*The wrath of Nature did not distinguish
the believers from the non-believers.*

## Chapter V: The Laki Fissure

*And dragons shall breathe fire into Earth.*

And twenty-five years went by after the great All-Saints Lisbon quake. In the North Atlantic Ocean was a land of white majestic mountains, of green and peaceful valleys, of brown and tranquil plains, and of hot and steamy springs – it was Iceland. And a serenity was *upon the face* of this relatively isolated land. But a *danger* lurked beneath the earth.

And it came to be that the year was one-thousand-seven-hundred-eighty-three AD. And during the first few days of the sixth month of that year, earthquakes shook south-central Iceland. And on the eighth day of that month, Mount Hekla did erupt. And nearby the mount, the ground cracked *open*: Suddenly the Earth had a new twenty-kilometer-long fissure. And lava did pour forth into the adjacent

Skapta Valley and *filled* the valley *to the brim* – in places was the liquid rock two-hundred meters deep. And *glowing* liquid rock flowed over and upon a lowland region, *destroying* fields and farms. Bits of molten rock were ejected from the fissure in a line of fire. A sixty-five-kilometer-long stream, not of water but of lava, flowed into a second valley. And ash flakes fell on southern Iceland and *fires* burned the crops.

And the strong flow of liquid rock *continued* for five weeks. And five-hundred square kilometers of land were covered in an *ash*. And twenty villages were obliterated by the lava and the ash.[62] And toxic fumes killed people, as well as cows, cattle, pigs and other animals.

For several months thereafter, dust, fog and haze did fill the skies of Europe. Deterioration of the climate and the acid gas in *Iceland* killed three-quarters of the livestock *there*. And so *did* a famine follow, as one-forth of Iceland's thirty-six-thousand people from starvation died.

And the fissure was provided with a name – the name was *Laki fissure*.

## Chapter VI: Mysterious Footprints

And in the year one-thousand-and-eight-hundred-two AD, it *happened* that a farm boy discovered birdlike footprints in sandstone slabs along the Connecticut River near South Hadley, Massachusetts. And the boy showed the footprints to his father and *asked* him what they were. And the father said, "I do not know." And the boy's father called upon a priest and brought him to the site. And the father *asked* the priest what marks they were. And the priest replied, "These are the footsteps of the raven that entered Noah's ark three-thousand years ago or so." And there was a panic; *people* in the community were terrified, for *they* feared God. "Surely Judgement Day is near," they thought.

But the priest had been mistaken. And twenty-two years later, a giant jawbone was discovered. And from this piece of evidence and others like it, extinct "monster reptiles" were proposed. And during many subsequent years of study, scientists turned footprints, bones and fossils into *images of dinosaurs*.

---

[62] In all, twelve cubic kilometers of lava spilled onto the land. In all, two cubic kilometers of molten rock were ejected in the air.

## Chapter VII: Krakatau

*And with the blast of thy nostrils,*
*the waters were gathered together,*
*floods stoop upright as in a heap,*
*and the depths were congealed in the heart of the sea.*

And on the nineteenth day of the fifth month of the year one-thousand-and-eight-hundred-eighty-three AD, all was *peaceful* in Krakatau. Now Krakatau was a small island between Java and Sumatra in the Sunda Straits – four volcanic peaks made up the island. Yet most of the body of these four volcanos lay *unseen* below the sea, although some peaks poked up and formed a group of tiny islands nearby Krakatau.

Now on the next day, explosions rumbled in the "abdomen" of Krakatau. And each *explosion* made a sound, which from afar, seemed like a gunshot fire. The rumbles could be heard one-hundred kilometers away. And explosions in the earth created pressure waves, which propagated in the body of the Earth. In Java and Sumatra, windows rattled, lamps shook and walls of buildings quivered. And there the villagers *thought* it was an earthquake.

And behold, a great column of steam rose out of the mouth of Krakatau, ascending ten kilometers. And *glowing* ash descended on the lands – within five-hundred kilometers of Krakatau, ash was falling *from the sky.*

And *for many days* continued the eruptions. And the abdomen of Krakatau made sounds so great they would have left a human deaf – bang-bang-boom, din-din-pang, et cetera. At one kilometer from the island, it was *like unto* having guns shot off at inches from one's ears. And *these* were Nature's *warning* sounds.

And it came to pass that every dozen minutes, a *burst* shot ash two-thousand meters high. And these were natural but violent fireworks. From time to time, stronger blasts sent up streams of steam, each one being *like unto* a geyser, save that the gases rose much higher – *three kilometers* into the sky. And on the north part of the island, *strong* winds stripped the trees of leaves.

A fine white *ash* covered the island like a *snow.*

And in the crater of the northernmost volcano, black molten rock sometimes cracked open, giving off a reddish glow.

And in the early days of June, Krakatau convulsed. The head of the northernmost volcano did blow off. A column of steam and ash rose so high that it *seemed* to disappear into the heavens – it was Nature's Jacob's ladder. And multiple *explosions* followed. And *they* got stronger and got louder.

And a month did pass. And the *disturbances* of Earth became more violent: Blasts blew away the vegetation on the island. Only thick

tree trunks stuck in layers of ash. And earthquakes *shook* the region –
it seemed *as if* the Earth would come apart.

And another month did pass. And there appeared three giant
columns formed of steam and ash.[63] And behold, the island had a
dozen other holes, which threw out steam and ash in small explosive
bursts.

And on the twenty-sixth day of the eighth month at two p.m.,
Krakatau spewed its guts: A black cloud mushroomed twenty-five
kilometers into the sky. *Unimaginable* blasts exploded every dozen
minutes. The "bang-din-bang-boom" sounds were heard two-hundred-
ten kilometers away.

And at five p.m., windows *rattled* in the coastal towns of Java
and Sumatra. Pictures fell off walls, and hanging lamps swayed back
and forth. From these coastal towns, the "bang-din-bang-boom" sounds
*were as* the sounds of cannons at close range – townspeople *thought* a
war had broken out.

Pumice in large pieces *fell from heaven* in the Sunda Straits.
Fierce lightning *flashes* did light up the sky. And the cloud above
Krakatau *was as* a giant pine tree with many stems and branches.
And behold, lightning flashed between the branches.

When night came, ash rained *down* upon the region. And fumes
of sulfurous gases filled the air. And lightning struck all pointed objects
on the land and *lit* them up – trees looked like *glowing* human skeletons.

Then a respite came. And in the early morning of August twenty-
seven, the eruption did "cool down" a bit. But *not* long did the respite
last, for at ten a.m., a giant blast ripped Krakatau apart – it was the
final cataclysmic burst. Pumice chunks were *launched* like missiles five
kilometers into the air. Outpouring gas blew ash *forty* kilometers into
the atmosphere. And sleeping souls three-thousand kilometers away
were woken up. And lo, the explosion was *even* heard in Sri Lanka,
five-thousand kilometers away. And a pressure wave travelled several
times around the Earth and made the needles of barometers deflect.

And a collapsing tower of debris sent hot gas and ash *crawling* on
the sea. And the hot surge struck the nearby coasts. As it blew upward
through the baseboards in the homes, furniture and people burned.
And behold, one-hundred kilometers away, the blast blew windows
out, and it put cracks in walls.

And the sea rose up and the sea sank down and a series of tsunamis sped out into the Indian and Pacific oceans.

Then a column of smoke, dust, water vapor and gas rose *eighty*
kilometers into the stratosphere. And pumpkin-size pumice peppered
Earth for dozens of kilometers. And within one-thousand kilometers

---

[63] Witnesses say that, at this point, Krakatau looked like a factory with three smoke
stacks.

did *ash* rain down, with some ash even landing on the Coco Islands.[64] And in the Sunda Straits were sailors shaking sails and rigs to rid them of the ash. The ash accumulated on the deck like snow – in each minute, half a centimeter did it rise. And sailors shovelled it and pushed it overboard.

Out of the volcanos lava poured.[65] And it *flowed* into surrounding seas. And on the surface of the water, the lighter lava crawled! The upper waters of the sea were *vaporized*. And the heavy lava sank, sliding down the underwater slopes of Krakatau.

And all around, three-foot rafts of pumice floated on the sea.

At one-half hour after noon, the summit of mount Krakatau collapsed. And the downward falling mass did *strike* the ocean floor. Forty-meter-tall sea waves emerged; and tsunamis sped out and struck surrounding islands. Entire towns were *overwhelmed* by water. Anger, the nearest port in Java, was *washed* away. Parts of wooden buildings floated in the sea. Then water flowed up and over the smallest nearby islands and swept the coasts of Java and Sumatra, drowning humans in its path. And six-and-thirty thousand people died. And giant waves sped across the Indian and Pacific oceans and then crossed the South Atlantic Ocean.

And ash, pumice and thick darkness descended on the nearby region. It was a darkness which *could* be felt. And it was night for two straight days.

And on the twenty-eighth day of the eighth month of the year one-thousand-and-eight-hundred-eighty-three, the last explosion sputtered. And there was a mild rumble. Then the soul of Krakatau was *silent* – Krakatau was dead. And behold, of the island, two-thirds had *disappeared*. And the remaining third soon sank. And all that remained of Krakatau was a great crater underneath the sea.

Now a forty-meter layer of pumice lay at the bottom of the sea. And two small new islands, Steers and Calmeyer, had *appeared* – debris and fallout had *created* them, for they were made from piles of pumice. And the nearby islands of Lang and Verlaten were larger than before – volcanic ash had *added* to their mass.

And the Sunda Straits were littered with debris. But *all* was *calm*.

And in September, dust in the atmosphere circled round the globe and blocked in part the rays of sun. And the average temperature in Celsius of Earth did *drop* a half degree. And golden sunsets were observed worldwide for months.

.     .     .     .     .     .     .

And many years later, in the year one-thousand-and-nine-hundred-twenty-seven, molten earth pushed upward in the Krakatau

---

[64] These islands were one-thousand-and-eight-hundred kilometers away from Krakatau.
[65] A total of eighteen cubic kilometers of lava poured out.

caldera.[66] And the submerged seamount rose until a *new* basaltic cone was made. And a peak appeared above the sea in the first month of the next year – Nature had *resurrected* Krakatau. And Krakatau was *given* a new name. And the name was Anak Krakatau, which means the "child of Krakatau."

## Chapter VIII: Tambora

*And I will make thee a burning mountain.*

And it came to pass that in the year one-thousand-and-eight-hundred-twelve AD, a mysterious black cloud appeared above the island of Sumbawa.[67] And the cloud expanded upward and curled over *like unto* a mushroom. Now the problem *was not in the sky above*, for moisture had not made the large black cloud; the source was smoke coming from the earth *below*.

And during the next three years, pressure in the earth beneath Sumbawa slowly was *built up*. Then, on the fifth day of the fourth month in the year one-thousand-and-eight-hundred-and-fifteen, Tambora, a four-thousand-kilometer-tall volcano on Sumbawa, blew its top in a horrific blast.[68] And nearby, *whirlwinds* sucked in men and animals as *if* they were of straw. And twelve-thousand human beings instantly were killed by the "volcanic bomb." And the sea rose up. And the sea sank down. And tsunamis flooded nearby lands.

In the week that followed, *enormous* quantities of ash and dust and rocky matter were ejected in the air.[69] And great tongues of lava *did* pour out.[70] And for half a week and within three-hundred kilometers of Tambora, *pure darkness* was upon the face of earth. And as volcanic fallout *rained* upon the lands nearby, crops were buried or were burned, and livestock died.[71] And when the skies did clear, the upper third of Tambora was gone.[72]

---

[66] A *caldera* is a large crater left in a volcano after an eruption.

[67] Sumbawa is located four-hundred kilometers east of Java.

[68] The eruption was so loud that it was heard one-thousand-and-five-hundred kilometers away.

[69] The total quantity was one-hundred cubic kilometers.

[70] The total output of lava was fifty cubic kilometers.

[71] During the next few months, eighty-thousand people died from starvation and from sickness.

[72] The eruption of Tambora was the most powerful volcanic eruption in the Christian era. The estimated energy output was one-hundred-fifty-billion-billion joules, three times the equivalent energy of the 1980 world's stockpile of nuclear weapons. The dust that entered the atmosphere produced "a year without a summer." In New England, it snowed in June, and some mornings with below freezing temperatures were reported in July and August. Crop failures occurred in North America and Europe.

## Chapter IX: Mont Pelée

On the twenty-fourth day of the fourth month of the year one-thousand-and-nine-hundred-two AD, Mont Pelée, a volcano on the island Martinique, spewed ash into the air. And *this* was *the* first sign. And a dozen days went by. And on the fourth day of the fifth month, the crater in the dome did glow. And the *second* sign was *this*. And sulfurous gases from the summit gave the air a foul smell. And *this* was *the* third sign.

Now in the nearby seaport of Saint Pierre, the people *felt* the ash and *saw* the glow and *smelled* the gas. And they were scared. But the local authorities persuaded citizens to stay in town – the authorities did not want to call off town elections, scheduled for the soon-to-come eleventh day of May.

Now on May eighth, which was Ascension Day, out *of* Pelée did very-liquid lava pour. And then began an avalanche, *not* of snow but lava, hot rocks, ash and gas. And a dense, violet and Hellish cloud emerged around the hot volcanic substances – the cloud was a *nuée*. At one-hundred-and-fifty kilometers per hour, the nuée surged down Mont Pelée; *it was as* a scorching hurricane. And the hot avalanche zoomed into a valley, five kilometers away. And some hot ash and gas did reach a nearby bay. And there, the gas and ash flowed over water, as fire *walked* on water. And ships and boats were set ablaze. Now at 7:50 a.m. on that same day, an arm of the hot avalanche spilled over a steep ridge onto the town of Saint Pierre. Masonry walls a meter thick could not contain the heat and *shattered* into pieces. Likewise, casks of rum in cellars *exploded*. And buildings burned and *vaporized*. In just two minutes, complete destruction was achieved – Saint Pierre was instantly incinerated in a heat of Hell. And cremated were *all* but one of Saint Pierre's thirty-thousand citizens – the *sole* survivor was a Negro prisoner, discovered badly burned but still alive below the ground inside a dungeon cell.

On the twenty-first of May, a dome in Pelée's crater pushed up like a mushroom. In the beginning, it seemed like an igloo which was grey. As the weeks went by, it *grew*. And it became one-hundred meters big. And several months went by. And in September, it happened that a crack appeared. And out of the crack did viscous lava ooze like toothpaste out a tube. And contact with the air solidified the lava into rock. And as the lava flowed, so grew the rock into a spike. And in one month, the spike became a giant spine, sticking out of the dome *as if* it were a tombstone for the town of Saint Pierre. And as the next nine months went by, the spine continued to push up *toward the sky*, until it was three-hundred meters long: Mont Pelée looked *like unto* a unicorn. Then came rumbles and explosions in the earth which *shook* Pelée and caused the spine to break apart. But the dome continued to balloon. And in September of one-thousand-and-nine-hundred-three AD, the three-hundred-meter dome contained igneous rock and liquid

earth with a volume of *one-hundred-twenty-million cubic meters* – Mont
Pelée *was as* a pregnant woman. But it would be many years before
the next eruption, when Pelée would labor and deliver magma rock.

## Chapter X: Three Quakes

*And when there is unrest,*
*Earth shall shake itself.*

And by the year one-thousand-and-nine-hundred-five AD, a *tension*
in Earth's earth had been built up in central India. And on the
fourth day of the fourth month of that year, the tension was *released*.
And an earthquake shook the heart of India, as one-million-and-five-
hundred-thousand square kilometers of land did shake. And walls of
homes fell in *upon* inhabitants. And of four villages, there was *nothing*,
save a heap of broken rock and rubble. And in other towns had houses
everywhere collapsed. And more than three-hundred-fifty-thousand
people died.

. . . . . . .

And one year later, at 5:12 a.m. on the eighteenth day of the
fourth month, the Pacific tectonic plate slipped past the North American tectonic plate along a four-hundred-ten-kilometer-long segment of
the San Andreas fault near San Francisco. And an earthquake and two
after-shocks did tumble buildings and some houses there. And when
moving earth *ruptured* gas and water mains in San Francisco, fires
broke out everywhere. And in *droves* did people *flee* the burning city.
Now fire hydrants almost everywhere produced no water, for the pipes
beneath the ground were snapped in pieces. And superheated air
sucked in Pacific winds, which further fanned the fires. And for three
straight days did ten square kilometers of San Francisco burn in a re-
lentless holocaust.[73]

. . . . . . .

And two-and-a-half years later, on the twenty-eighth day of the
twelfth month of the year one-thousand-and-nine-hundred-eight, a section of the African tectonic plate inched north. And an earthquake
struck Sicily and southern Italy. And the city of Messina was destroyed. And rubble fell on dwellers. Victims bit their lips and *took*
*their flesh in their own teeth*. And the pressure on their heads was
great, the burden on their chests was overwhelming, and with crushed
legs and broken bones, one-hundred-fifty-thousand souls *gave up the*
*ghost*.

---

[73] Two out of three of San Francisco's three-hundred-and-fifty-thousand citizens were
left homeless.

## Chapter XI: Threats from the Heavens

*Behold, there came fire down from Heaven.*

And on the last day of the sixth month of the year one-thousand-and-nine-hundred-eight, a small asteroid was *drawn* to Earth by Nature's force of gravity. And when it *struck* the atmosphere of Earth, friction made it *glow*. And it glowed as *brightly* as a daytime Sun. Now as it neared the Earth, it *exploded* a few kilometers above a forest in Central Siberia near the Tunguska River. And the enormous blast delivered there was like ten megatons of TNT. And the blast, radiating outward, flattened and/or scorched two-thousand square kilometers of pines. And behold, there came *a great wind* from the wilderness. And far away, people were knocked to the ground by *strange*, strong winds. And within a thirty kilometer radius, fallen trees did form a hedge-hog pattern – the trunks of pines pointed outward from the impact point.[74]

.    .    .    .    .    .    .

On the twelfth day of the eighth month of the year one-thousand-and-nine-hundred-thirty, the Perseid meteor shower *flashed streaks of light* across the sky at night as it had done in August every year. And early the next morning, a large meteor of rock and ice was *sent* piercing through the atmosphere of Earth, high over Mexico. And it streaked southward until just above the jungles of northwest Brazil, it burst in three. And shrilling sirens sent birds flying from the trees. And from the skies fell balls of fire. *Thrice* did half-a-megaton explosions boom. *Thrice* did shake the Earth in little quakes. And a curtain of red ash *descended* from the sky, and the yellow early morning Sun turned red.

And natives in the jungle-forest dropped *to their knees* and prayed to God – for them this was God's Judgement Day, at least that was what they *thought*. And terrified children ran to hug their mothers. And fear was everywhere, as ash continued to rain down until midday.

Now the next day the natives made a vat of poison – they would *rather* die from poison than from the wrath of God. And they were about to drink the poison when "fate" would have it that a Catholic monk named Fidele d'Alviano ventured to the tribesmen's town. Now Fidele was a missionary and his mission was to *uphold and spread the faith*. But, as Father Fidele listened to the natives who told to him what they had seen and heard, he realized that the thunderbolt-like balls of fire were *not* an act of God but some strange act of Nature; Fidele, though well-versed in godly matters, had *also* studied science. And with some effort, Fidele persuaded the natives not to drink.[75]

.    .    .    .    .    .    .

---

[74] At the impact site no crater was found. Apparently, the bolide, as it is called, exploded above the ground.

[75] The incident was subsequently reported to the Vatican by Fidele.

And these events, although destructive, were not so catastrophic for humanity – just a *warning* from the heavens that, from time to time, asteroids and comets will strike Earth.

## Chapter XII: Ten-Thousand Smokes

*And strange vapors rose up from the underworld.*

And in the year one-thousand-and-nine-hundred-twelve, heat accumulated in the earth beneath Mount Katmai, in Alaska. And on the sixth month of that year, Mount Katmai did erupt for several weeks. And ash was thrown kilometers into the sky. And the ash descended from the heavens high above and landed in a fifteen-kilometer-long valley in the earth below. And in this "ash-valley," cracks appeared *in countless places* and gave off smoke and gas. And when water came in contact with the ash and with hot underground terrain, the water *turned* to steam. And fissures spewed out gas and steam. These fuming cracks were *fumaroles*. Thus in the valley near Mount Katmai, which *seemed like* the land of the shadow of death, quivering poles of smoke and vapors hung above the cracks for many years. And a name was given to this land. And the name was *Valley of Ten-Thousand Smokes*.

*It was like unto an* ancient *resting ground,*
*where* dead spirits *were made* visible
*in their exit from the Earth.*

## Chapter XIII: Earthquake in Tokyo

*And Samson pushed the pillars*
*with all his mighty strength and faith.*
*And walls came tumbling down.*

And in the last week of the eighth month of the year one-thousand-and-nine-hundred-twenty-three, Frank Lloyd Wright completed the Imperial Hotel in Tokyo. And *knowing* that the earth below did sometimes shake, he had the H-shaped building constructed on concrete pontoons specifically designed to move with Earth, if it should quiver in a quake.

And it was *as if* Nature wanted to test the new construction, for just a few days later, on the first day of the ninth month of that year, an earthquake struck the region. And the Imperial Hotel swayed back and forth *like a ship in a strong storm*. And around the hotel and elsewhere in Tokyo, the houses and the buildings so collapsed. And the city of Yokohama was *also* struck. And fires broke out and burned both cities. Out of *fear* of fire, multitudes fled Tokyo and headed for an army clothing depot near the Sumida River. There they waited, thinking that they were in *a safe haven*. But flames raged and spread, and they eventually engulfed the army depot: Five-and-thirty thousand souls inside were burned to death. Elsewhere *two-hundred-thousand* people perished, and more than a million were left injured. And *razed* were all of Yokohama's seventy-five-thousand houses, while in Tokyo, *three-hundred-thousand* houses were destroyed. But the Imperial Hotel in Tokyo survived *unscratched* – it stood there like a temple mid the rubble.

## Chapter XIV: Earth's Sea Monster

*And a beast rose up out of the sea,*
*having seven heads and ten horns.*

And in the year one-thousand-and-nine-hundred-sixty-three, the Atlantic waters southwest of Iceland started *mysteriously* to bubble. And steam *rose* into the air. And the waters foamed and sizzled. And behold, a blast of gas and water shot into the air – it seemed *as if* a whale were sounding off. But then a giant red-brown form, too big to be a whale, *emerged* above the sea – it was thought to be a monster of the deep. But when lava started spurting up like water from a fountain, people realized *it* was *not* alive. And suddenly, where water once had been, a land there was, for a volcanic island had been made. And this new island was provided with a name. And *Surtsey* was its name. And Surtsey was then added to the list of islands belonging to the Westmann Islands.

## Chapter XV: Two Great China Quakes

*The people did not heed the sacred words.*
*Upon loose rock did they construct their homes.*
*Such "trees" do not stand up forever.*
*Such structures shelter from above but not below.*
*The temples built were temples of impending doom.*
*Walls were not straight but leaned over.*
*The cracks of old age were left to grow.*
*Then Nature struck and there was gloom.*

Now in Tang-shan,[76] miners, wives and children *dwelt* in houses made of clay with foundations *in the dust*. Originally, workers had daubed the houses with untempered *mortar*.

Then, at night on the twenty-eighth day of the sixth month of the year one-thousand-nine-hundred-seventy-six, an earthquake *moved* the earth beneath Tang-shan. And the walls of buildings wobbled, for with *no* foundation was there *no* support. And so the walls came tumbling down. What could the walls with little mortar do but fall? Among the rubble, there was *one* who winced with pain – the muscles in his face did bulge; his hands were two solid fists about to break. Then the

---

[76] Tang-shan is a coal-mining and industrial city one-hundred kilometers east of Beijing.

mouth opened, the skin upon his face was smooth again, *and* his arms hung loose. And that day there were two-hundred-and-forty-thousand citizens like *he* who in their sleep *gave up the ghost*. But the unlucky ones were those who did survive. Beneath the heavy rubble were five-hundred-thousand who *squirmed in pain* but were alive.

. . . . . . .

But the Tang-shan quake was not the most deadly Chinese quake – there was another for whom the bells tolled worse. And it happened in the year one-thousand-five-hundred-fifty-two, when in Shensi Province, the crust of Earth slipped along a line of faults. First the ground shook terribly *up and down*. Then the ground *shook* terribly *from side to side*. Trees were *instantly* uprooted, while soil and rocks slid down the sides of hills. And cracks appeared in earth. And wells and walls collapsed. And when houses tumbled to the ground, peasants in their homes were crushed – their faces stricken. And dead were eight-hundred-thousand people.

## Chapter XVI: Mount Saint Helens

And on the eighteenth day of the fifth month of the year one-thousand-and-nine-hundred-eighty, Mount Saint Helens, in the state of Washington, blew up.[77] And three cubic kilometers of rock and ice were *blasted* from the north side of the summit. For hours did eruptions detonate – it was like setting off Hiroshima-sized atomic bombs at one per second for eight hours. And the explosions *devastated* trees – some snapped like match-sticks, others burned to crisp, still others were uprooted, and some were stripped completely bare.[78] In the end, five-hundred square kilometers of forests were obliterated, and ten-million trees were killed.

And although a billion dollars worth of damage had been done, the blast was mild when compared with the great ones of the past: the eruption of Krakatau had been thirty times more powerful; the eruption of Tambora had been one-hundred times more powerful.

## Chapter XVII: A Close Encounter

### *The Earth saw and trembled.*

And on the fifth month in the year one-thousand-and-nine-hundred-ninety-six, asteroid 1996JA1 from the black of outer space *headed* at the Earth. And again, Earth was *threatened* by an extraterrestrial invader. But the asteroid *did* not strike its mark. Instead, at four-hundred-and-fifty-thousand kilometers from Earth – just beyond the distance to the Moon, it sped past Earth, continuing on its journey in

---

[77] The importance of this eruption is that it would be the most highly studied by geologists in modern times – sensors in the mountain would relay a wealth of geo-information. Field trips and overhead flights would also provide much valuable data.

[78] These trees looked like telephone poles.

the wilderness of outer space. Now this was a close encounter of the disastrous kind, for had the orbit of the asteroid been slightly different, a cosmic catastrophe *might* have taken place.

## Chapter XVIII: Shoemaker-Levy Strikes

And in the year one-thousand-and-nine-hundred-ninety-two, a comet passed by Jupiter. And Jupiter's strong gravity did cause the comet to break up into parts: twenty-one pieces zoomed through out the solar system *as a group*. Now two years later, in the seventh month of the year one-thousand-and-nine-hundred-ninety-four, the natural multiple warhead headed directly at a planet. And one by one, the pieces *crashed* into the planet: On July 16, fragment A struck and, like a thermonuclear bomb, exploded. A plume two-kilometers in diameter rose up one-thousand kilometers into the atmosphere. And a dark spot appeared upon the planet's face. Now fortunately for ye on the Earth, the *target planet* was not Earth – *it* was Jupiter.[79] Now astronomers turned their telescopes and saw. On the next day, the larger fragment G impacted, delivering a blast equivalent to a million megatons of TNT. And astronomers *observed* in awe. And behold, three-thousand kilometers high did rise debris, and a dark cloud *twice the size of Earth* appeared. A ring expanded from the impact site – it was a pressure wave, which rippled through the atmosphere. Now during the week, one fragment after another struck and created blasts *of* enormous energy. But Jupiter, being a giant planet – three-hundred times the mass of Earth – *survived*.

Now a few years later another object from outer space would strike the planet Jupiter – it would be Galileo, the man-made probe from Earth. And Galileo would pass through a cloud-break in the atmosphere and beam back information to the Earth. Then the probe would hit the liquid surface of the planet. And *hardly* would there be a splash.

## Chapter XIX: The Voice of Nature Shall Be Heard

*Oh my Nature.*

And in the future, Nature will continue to frighten and sometimes terrify the world,[80] for the conduct of Nature is often unpredictable. But behind the scenes, She is basically neutral – neither good nor bad – neither destructive nor constructive. Nature does not plan disasters –

---

[79] After passing by Jupiter in 1992, the comet fragments had orbited the giant planet, only to return to it in 1994.

[80] Besides the above-mentioned catastrophes, Earth has been struck by floods, droughts, fires, famines, hurricanes and tornadoes. Some examples are as follows. In 1666, the Great Fire of London burned the city for five days, destroying 90 churches and leaving 80,000 people homeless. In 1881, 300,000 people died when a typhoon hit Haiphong, Vietnam. In 1959, typhoon Vera left 1,500,000 people homeless in Japan.

She simply follows her own laws. And the problem is that Nature is, at times, too powerful.

The voice of the wizard is at times *terrifying* and at times quite *shy*.

*Nature has given the world great things.*
*And Nature will at random take great things away.*

*The sixth book of Chronicles, called*

# Atom

*Blessèd be the atom.*

## Chapter I: The Atom Was Conceived By Man[81]

And in the fifth century BC, the Greek philosopher Leucippus of Miletus created the concept of a tiny basic building block of matter. And in the year four-hundred-thirty-one BC, his disciple, Democritus of Abdera, named it *atomos*, which means "indivisible."

And twenty-two-hundred years thereafter, in the early nineteenth century, did Joseph-Louis Proust, John Dalton, Amedeo Avogadro, Joseph-Louis Gay-Lussac and others sense the presence of the atom. And through them, the scientific basis of the atom was established.

And one-hundred-fifty years thereafter, in the late twentieth century, man saw the atom with electron microscopes. And the "invisible" was seen – it seemed to be a *miracle*.

---

[81] Man conceived the atom, but it, of course, *always* existed.

*The seventh book of Chronicles, called*

# Newton

*Father, speak to me.*

Now it came to pass that, in the year 1609, Johannes Kepler wrote down the three laws of planetary motion.[82] And suddenly did planetary motion have a *mathematical description*. And soon thereafter did Galileo Galilei observe and measure falling bodies. And suddenly he *understood* the falling motion of a falling body. And he realized *all* bodies fall the same. And he understood the projectile motion of a cannon ball.

And so the seeds of classical mechanics were tossed into a *fertile* ground; in such soil would one man cultivate great things.

And it came to pass that Galileo Galilei died in 1642.[83] And like the transcendental passing of a Dalai Lama, the scientific spirit of Galileo Galilei *passed into* the body of a newborn child. And that newborn's name was Isaac Newton.

Now in his youth, Newton studied the work of Aristotle, Descartes, and others. And Newton spoke:

> *"Amicus Plato,*
> *amicus Aristoteles,*
> *magis amica vertas."*

which means

> *"Plato is my friend,*
> *Aristotle is my friend,*
> *but my best friend is truth."*

---

[82] See the New Testament Book of *Classical Physics*. The other physics terminology and laws of this Book of *Newton* are also explained in *Classical Physics*.

[83] During his life, Galileo made important astronomical observations, some of which supported the Copernican idea that planets revolve around the Sun. When Galileo turned his telescope toward the *heavens*, he saw *them* as they really were: The Moon was not a flat object painted on the celestial dome, as many had supposed; indeed there were shadows on the Moon cast by craters and small mountains. And Galileo saw four spots of light going around Jupiter and *not* the Earth. And by observing the position and the phases of the planet Venus, he could deduce that Venus was orbiting the Sun. The heavens were telling him that heliocentric theory was correct. And when Galileo announced his findings, there was an outrage, particularly from Aristotelian professors. He was denounced for blasphemous utterances. In 1616, Catholic authorities in Rome declared Copernicanism to be false and told Galileo that, although he made discuss the theory, he could neither defend nor hold its doctrines. Sixteen years later, in 1632, Galileo's *Dialogo* appeared. In this book, which was understandable to the common person, a debate occurs among three characters over solar system motions. In 1633, Galileo stood trial in Rome and was found guilty. Bowing to pressure, he recanted his heliocentric beliefs. Although he should have gone to jail, the Pope commuted his sentence to house arrest. Galileo spent the last eight years of his life in isolation.

In 1992, the Catholic Church reopened the case, issuing a retroactive sentence of not guilty and saying that the original judges *had not properly separated issues of faith from facts of science.*

Now in the year of 1687, Newton wrote a book: *Philosophiae Naturalis Principia Mathematica* – it would come to be a part of the old testament of physics. And it *explained* the movement of the planets. And it explained the movement of the Moon. And *suddenly* were Kepler's laws derived from fundamental principles. And the *universal law* of gravity was understood: The Earth had always been attracted to the Sun; the Moon had always been attracted to the Earth; rain had always fallen from the sky. Now man knew why. Suddenly, like a revelation, the motions of the heavens were quantified. The three fundamental laws of classical mechanics were written down for good. Circular motion, harmonic motion, projectile motion, essentially all macroscopic motions were understood. Like magic, Newton *could predict* the positions of planets with geometry and calculus. And so when *Principia* was published, the foundations of mechanics were established.

Now universality of gravity was like a *miracle* – it was as if Nature had somehow waved a magic rod. Of this, Newton wrote, "This most beautiful system of the Sun, Planets and Comets could only proceed from the counsel and dominion of an intelligent and powerful being, a God." To Newton, laws of Nature seemed like laws of God.

Next Newton studied light. And *light* did Newton see. And light turned into words, as *Opticks*, another book of the old testament, appeared. And so in the year of 1704, there was *another revelation* – it was another physics revolution, for finally *light* was understood. And lenses, mirrors, diffraction and refraction were explained. And this was good. And when white light was separated into components with a prism, the rainbow was clarified and understood. Then Newton placed curved mirrors in a tube – the first reflecting telescope did he construct. And so the heavens were seen *a little closer*. Now some people said that light was made of waves. However, Newton said that light was made of corpuscles. Later, one would learn that light was *both and neither*. But for Newton, light was microscopic particles moving in an ether.[84]

And in the year of 1705, Queen Anne knighted Newton – the sword that touched the shoulder *flashed* a beam of light.

And so in five-and-eighty years did Sir Isaac Newton write the gospel texts of classical mechanics and of gravity. And in *Principia* and *Opticks* did Newton deliver the laws of physics not in two books but on two slab blocks – not on paper but in stone.

And on March 20, 1727, Newton died. And his body was placed in a tomb in Westminster Abbey. And there the body lay but not the spirit, for the spirit and intelligence of Newton *escaped the tomb*, rose up and were placed among the stars.[85]

---

[84] Ether was a hypothesized medium through which light could travel. Starting at the end of the nineteenth century, it was gradually realized that such an ether does not exist.

[85] The writings of Newton would not immediately affect the common man – eighteenth century man would not care if one could compute the position of the Moon among the stars. But a century later that would change, for the work of Newton and the work of oth-

*The eighth book of Chronicles, called*

# History of Electromagnetism[86]

*Let there be light.*
*And there was light and more.*

## Chapter I: Ancient History

Now man has known about magnetism and electric forces since antiquity, but before the last four centuries of the second millennium, man regarded them *as* a kind of natural mysticism.

## Chapter II: The Seventeenth Century

Now in the middle of the seventeenth century did scientists *play with light* in many ways. To determine "how light acted," scientists performed experiments. And through such experiments, interference and diffraction were observed. Thus in the year 1665 did Robert Hooke propose that light was made of waves, for waves can interfere and can diffract.

And it came to pass that, in the year 1676, the eye of an astronomer peered at Io through a telescope. And he saw Io orbiting around the planet Jupiter as it had always done. And with a watch in his left palm and a pen in his right hand, the astronomer wrote down the times at which Io *disappeared behind* the planet Jupiter. And for many months did he do *this*. Now when Jupiter moved *away* from Earth, the orbital times were *longer* by a tiny bit. And when Jupiter moved *toward* the Earth, the orbital times were *shorter* by a tiny bit. And the astronomer went into deep contemplation. And from deep thought emerged a *revelation* – the answer to the puzzle was an "optical illusion" – not a mystical but a *physical* optical illusion. And the astronomer concluded that the *speed of light was finite*, for *if* its speed were finite and *if* Jupiter were moving *away* from Earth, then *extra* time would be needed for light to reach the Earth from successive disappearances of Io. And *if* the speed of light were finite and *if* Jupiter were moving *toward* the Earth, then *less* time would be needed for the light to reach the Earth from successive disappearances of Io. And from solar system information, the speed of light was crudely measured. And for the first time was it *realized* that light did not go instantly from here to there. And so by observing Io and Jupiter at night, man became *enlightened* about the speed of light.

---

ers would produce a non-scientific revolution. That revolution would be the industrial revolution. The understanding of classical mechanics would pave the way from simple tools such as pulleys and levers to modern marvels such as rockets and robotic automation.

[86] For an understanding of electromagnetism, see the New Testament Book of *Classical Physics*, Chapters XI-XIII.

## Chapter III: The Eighteenth Century

Now at the beginning of the eighteenth century did Newton, the mighty scientific prophet, propose that light might be made of particles. But others disagreed. And a *battle* between those who *thought* that light *be* particles and those who *thought* that light *be* waves. This battle over light would last two hundred years.

Now in the year 1729, electricity was shown to flow. And so, electricity was *thought* to be a fluid. And in 1745, electric sparks were captured in a Leyden jar: Apparently, the "fluid" could be stored. At that time, electricity seemed like a *mystery*.

Then in the year 1752 did Benjamin Franklin go out into a thunderstorm with kite and key beneath his arm. And he set the kite aloft, and to the string he tied the key. And when lightning struck the kite, the key lit up. From this, Franklin concluded that lightning was electricity in air. So lightning *in part* enlightened man.

Then some years later, Franklin *hypothesized* two kinds of charge – positive and negative. And furthermore, he guessed that electricity *was* the flow of negative-type charge. Next he proposed a *fundamental* law – the conservation of electric charge. Someday his hypotheses and proposals would *become* accepted truths. And for his insights and his thoughts, he became the father of electricity.

And it came to pass that, in the year 1767, the electric force was quantified – experiments showed that the electric force weakened with distance as the distance squared.[87] And by 1785, *another law of Nature* was uncovered – it was Coulomb's law, the law that governed force between electric static charge.

## Chapter IV: The Early Nineteenth Century

And in the year 1800, scientists placed certain *chemicals* in jars, which reacted and produced electric flow. Thus chemical energy was converted into electricity – the battery came into being. The moment marked the beginning of electrochemistry. And scientists began "to play" with electricity and chemicals in many ways. And *some* ways *seemed* mysterious. And for example, when electric currents ran through water, water was divided into hydrogen and oxygen *in* the form of gas. Thus man began to *split* the molecule by using sparks.

And in the year 1801, infrared and ultraviolet radiations[88] were discovered in the Sun. And in 1813, Siméon-Denis Poisson summarized the laws of electrostatics using two equations. Then in the early nineteenth century, the *laws* describing static magnetic forces were established, and Michael Faraday experimentally *confirmed* the conservation of electric charge.

---

[87] This is called the inverse square law. See the Book of *Classical Physics*, Chapter XI.
[88] These radiations are discussed in the Book of *Electromagnetic Waves*, Chapter V.

## Chapter V: The Unification of Electricity and Magnetism

And in the year of 1820, Hans Christian Ørsted *announced* that electric current flows produced a magnetism – the mechanism of magnets seemed like mysticism. Then André-Marie Ampère turned wires carrying currents into magnets: Parallel wires with currents flowing in the *same* direction were *attracted* to each other, while parallel wires with currents flowing in the *opposite* direction *repelled*. And it was hypothesized that magnets were created by microscopic currents – the hypothesis would someday be *accepted as* a truth. And the difference between electricity and magnetism *thus* began to blur.

And it came to pass in the year of 1827 that Georg Simon Ohm quantified electric flow; he showed that current flowing in a wire increased with increasing voltage: When *doubled* he the voltage, the rate of flow of charge so *doubled*. And he showed that current-flow decreased with an increase of resistance of a wire: when he *doubled* the resistance, the rate of flow of charge so *dropped* in half. And this new law of physics was entered in the scientific testament. And *Ohm's law* was its name.

And in the year of 1831 did Faraday in England and Joseph Henry in America separately announce that changing magnetic forces made electric currents flow. And the *difference* between electricity and magnetism once again *diminished*. But even scientists considered the connection between electricity and magnetism as mysterious as ever. But from 1831 and on, man would be well aware that magnets could *create* electric force.

And years went by. And it came to pass that Faraday proposed the concept of magnetic and electric fields and lines of force. Now the *electric field* was defined to be the electric force per unit of electric charge. And the *magnetic field* was similarly defined. And it was hard for common man to understand how lines of force, like wind-blown hair, could flow through *empty space*.[89]

And in the year of 1865, *a great synthesis* occurred – James Clerk Maxwell unified the laws of electricity and magnetism. And the new laws were given a new name – *Maxwell's equations* were *they* so named. Finally, *electromagnetism* was established. And as a consequence of these equations, Maxwell *predicted* the opposite of Faraday induction, that changing electric fields *would create* magnetic fields. Furthermore, thought he, if changing magnetic fields produce changing electric fields and if changing electric fields produce changing magnetic fields, then "perpetual motion" of these fields should so persist! Now such fields should travel at a certain calculable speed. And Maxwell calculated the *speed* from his equations. And behold, it was the speed of light! And so Maxwell *concluded* that light was the "perpetual mo-

---

[89] Electric and magnetic fields are discussed in Chapters XI and XII of the Book of *Classical Physics*.

tion" of a wave, an electromagnetic wave. For *him* all seemed to fit, but his theory was formulated in a complicated way, *and* few physicists accepted it.

And in the year of 1884, it came to *pass* that Heinrich Hertz reformulated Maxwell's four equations in their modern form. And the *fundamental symmetry* between magnetic and electric forces was made manifest at last.

And four years later, Hertz observed that certain non-light waves *also* travelled at the speed of light – these waves were radio waves. This discovery was the confirmation of a *prediction* Maxwell previously had made. And the *non-believers* of electromagnetism suddenly became *believers*. And so scientists accepted Maxwell's theory.[90]

## Chapter VI: QED

Now in the year of 1887, Hertz by accident discovered the photoelectric effect, in which electricity is generated from the surface of a solid by striking it with ultraviolet radiation.[91] And further observations produced a pair of *puzzles*. And the *first* was this: If the frequency of ultraviolet light was low, no current from the surface flowed. And this was true even if the ultraviolet-light intensity was *substantially* increased. Now the *second* puzzle appeared much later, after the discovery of the electron. And *it* was this: The energy of charged electrons emitted from the solid depended *only* on the frequency of ultraviolet light and *not* on its intensity – intensity controlled instead the number of emitted charges.[92]

And in the year of 1895, electric currents *were forced* to flow between two metal wires in a bottle *void* of air. And behold, the electricity flowed in the *bottle*, though *it be void of air* – the *cathode tube*[93] had come about. Now since the rays were so mysterious, they were named *X-rays*; these were the first such man-made rays. And it *happened* that X-rays, escaping from a bottle, were recorded on a photographic plate. And by chance, the rays passed through an outstretched hand. And bones were seen upon the photographic screen. Then scientists "turned into doctors" and photographed the skeletons of people.

And in the year of 1897, with a cathode tube in hand, Sir J. J. Thompson demonstrated that electric currents were the flow of *micro-*

---

[90] Thus the principle fathers of classical electromagnetism were Maxwell, Faraday and Hertz. Many units of measurement are named after scientists: amps after Ampère, ohms after Ohm, hertz after Hertz, etc.. See the New Testament Book of *Basic Units*.

[91] Since electricity is the flow of electrons, the *photoelectric effect* is the ejection of electrons out of a solid by striking them with electromagnetic radiation.

[92] Increasing the intensity of ultraviolet light simply means shining more ultraviolet light; in other words, the ultraviolet light is brighter. Changing the frequency of ultraviolet light corresponds to changing the rate at which its waves oscillate; for visible light, changing its frequency changes its color.

[93] The cathode tube is the basis for most electronic screens such as computer monitors and television sets.

*scopic* particles of *tiny* charge and mass. Although smaller than an atom, these particles, named *electrons, had* been "indirectly seen" and thus discovered. And so one principal *source* of electromagnetism was uncovered.

Then in the year 1905, Albert Einstein *proposed* that electromagnetic radiation was composed of *packets* of fixed energy – each packet was a *photon.* Now this idea *resolved* the two photoelectric puzzles: When the frequency of *ultraviolet light* was low, then the energy of *its* photons, too, was low; and such photons had too little energy to knock electrons out of atoms in a solid. But when the frequency of *ultraviolet light* was high, then the energy of *its* photons, too, was high; and such photons had sufficient energy to knock electrons out of atoms. And as for the second puzzle, it was resolved as follows. When *ultraviolet light* was of higher intensity, *it* contained more photons available to strike electrons. Hence higher-intense ultraviolet radiation produced a higher current.

And in the year of 1922, it happened that Arthur Holly Compton scattered X-rays off electrons. And the X-rays deflected just like microscopic particles. And so the *question*, which was *posed* two centuries before, arose again: How could light be both a particle and wave? In quantum theory, the answer lay.

And in the decade of the 1920's, there was a *scientific revolution –* it was the quantum-mechanic revolution. Now quantum mechanics explained the nature of the atom and the small. And Niels Bohr, Louis-Victor de Broglie, Erwin Schrödinger, Werner Heisenberg, Max Born and others *etched in texts* the theoretical foundation. And subsequently, Paul A. M. Dirac, Wolfgang Pauli, Heisenberg and others made quantum theory compatible with special relativity – the result was relativistic quantum theory.[94]

And in the decade of the 1940's, Freeman Dyson, Richard P. Feynman, Julian S. Schwinger, S. Tomonaga and others constructed a consistent quantum version of electromagnetism. And it was *provided* with a name: *quantum electrodynamics*, or *QED.* And it explained the interaction[95] between photons, protons and electrons. And the basic notion was that electric and magnetic forces arose from the exchange of photons.[96]

---

[94] For an explanation of quantum theory, see the Book of *Quantum Mechanics.*

[95] The word "interaction" is synonymous to "force."

[96] In QED, the answer to the question "Is light a particle or a wave?" is simple: The microscopic world is vastly *different* from the macroscopic world of man. Man thinks in terms of things he sees. Man attends a sports event – he sees a ball. Man observes the sea – he thinks of waves. But why should balls and waves exist in the microscopic world? Words like "ball" and "wave" can, at best, be *metaphors* for the dominion of the small. Energetic electromagnetic radiation is *like* a bullet or a ball. Low-energy electromagnetic radiation is *like* a wave. Thus light behaves *like* a bullet and *like* a wave. But light is neither particle nor wave. Light is what it is. Light is light.

## Chapter VII: Electroweak Unification

It was the decade of the 1960's. It was a time of revolution. And it came to *pass* that Steven Weinberg, Abdus Salam and Sheldon Glashow unified QED with *the* weak force.[97] And the *electroweak theory* thus was born at last. Now the theory *predicted* the existence of three heavy particles, the W-plus, W-minus *and* the Z. Now for some physicists, it was a prophecy, which although incredible, just had to be. And fourteen years later in the year of 1983, an accelerator near Geneva, Switzerland, produced the predicted heavy W-plus, W-minus *and* the Z.

Now in the decade of the 1980's was the *internal magnetism* of the electron measured. And *it* agreed with theoretical predictions from QED to one part in ten-billion. Then in the last two decades of the twentieth century, accelerators near Geneva measured quantum electroweak effects. And measurements agreed perfectly with theory. And so it seemed the theory had no defects.

## Chapter VIII: Electromagnetic Technology[98]

Now what were the twentieth-century technological wonders generated from electric and magnetic science? Water flowing through dams could be converted into currents flowing in a wire. Energy could be obtained by inserting a pronged object in a pair of holes in household walls. Filaments encased in glass could give off light sufficiently bright to light rooms and roads at night. Humans thousands of kilometers apart could talk with one another by speaking into hand-held devices. A crate could keep a chamber cold enough to maintain food. Another kitchen apparatus could cook food on a surface coil or in a cubic cavity. An even smaller box could heat food by striking it with microwaves. Humans could listen to beautiful sounds on disks by placing them in a seemingly mysterious device. Or they could go to auditoriums with rows of seats to watch screens with images and voices. Humans could be transported in *apparatuses* with wheels simply by pouring liquid in a hole and turning keys to make *them* start. Bird-like structures with several hundred passengers inside could be made to fly through clouds. Messages, on the backs of unseen waves and emitted from tall towers far away, could pass through buildings, air and walls and be detected with a box inside a home to yield images and sound. And arti-

---

[97] For more on particle forces as well as the W and Z, see the Book of *Subnuclear Physics*.

[98] During the twentieth century, electromagnetism passed from science to technology. It passed from the laboratory to the home. The electronics revolution changed the world. In the beginning, the electric motor was the workhorse behind household appliances and industrial equipment. The transistor, invented in 1947, led to modern electronic marvels. Though priced in terms of pennies, transistors were for man collectively more valuable than gold. The transition from the vacuum tube to the transistor to the chip shrank the sizes of electrical devices many-fold.

ficial arms could maneuver to assemble cars in factories.[99] *To ancient man*, these inventions would have seemed like mysteries.

And the twentieth century held more marvels.[100] Children played with toys that floated, flew, walked or talked. Boxes containing microscopic chips and tiny wires were used to calculate and think. Probes were propelled to outer space to spy on the Moon and distant planets. Images of inner bones were made by passing unseen rays through human bodies. Likewise, with magnets, pictures of organs or the flow of blood in the body or the brain were made. Artificial human parts were implanted and made to function like their real counterparts. A person with a faulty heart had a device inserted in the chest to help him keep the beat. Another module in the ear made the hard-of-hearing hear. Electric shocks sometimes restarted hearts which had, for several minutes, stopped.

*To ancient man, these would have seemed absurd.*

The hard-of-hearing were made to hear. The dying were given longer lives. Among the stars of night were man-made spots of moving light. The invisible was made, in certain cases, visible. That which produced no sound was heard. The non-living were made to move and think.

*Were these not miracles?*

-------------------------------------------------------------------

[99] Electromagnetism and mechanics have been given to man for his benefit or his destruction. The satellite is used to communicate *or* spy. For the radio, there is the radar dish. For the truck, there is the tank. For the plane, there is the bomber. For the rocket, there is the missile. For the nuclear power plant, there is the atomic bomb.

[100] To us, these things may seem commonplace; we have become use to them. One should try to imagine how a person of the eighteenth century or earlier would have viewed them.

*The ninth book of Chronicles, called*

# Darwin

*The strongest shall survive and multiply.*
*The weak shall die.*
*And the clever meek, if they survive,*
*will have to hide or put on a disguise.*
*And these became the laws*
*of the survival of the fittest.*

## Chapter I: Darwin's Early Life

And in the year 1809, Chevalier de Lamarck published *Philosophie Zoologique*, in which he proclaimed that organic evolution was a *universal* principle of Nature. And although the idea was immediately *rejected* by all scholars at the time, the spirit of the idea did rise up and enter the mind's eye of one newborn boy. And family members gathered to give that boy a name. And that name was Charles. And so it came to pass that Charles Darwin was born in England on the twelfth day of the second month of that year.

Now it *happened* that Charles Darwin had "biological blood" in his own blood: His grandfather, Erasmus Darwin, was a physician, botanist, philosopher and poet.[101] His father, Robert Darwin, was a doctor with a large and profitable practice.

And Darwin enjoyed an ideal childhood with few concerns. Money from his father would throughout his life alleviate him of financial worries. But at the age of eight, his mother died. Now as a young man he studied chemistry – he found it fun to mix the chemicals to see what would result. And he spent endless hours collecting shells, birds' eggs, butterflies and beetles – insects and *creeping* creatures interested him. Now it would turn out that Darwin would have to choose between one of *two paths* for his career: science or religion.

And at sixteen years of age, entered he the University of Edinburgh. And there he studied medicine. But he did not take a liking to the lectures and the books – he was an undistinguished student. Instead, he spent much time talking to zoologists and to geologists – *Nature's animals* and *Earth's structures* seemed to interest him. Then one day, the students of his class went to see an operation. Now in the early 1800's, there was no anesthesia. And right before the students' eyes, the doctors cut open a sick-one's flesh, who *gave out a cry* of anguish and of pain. And Darwin had to leave the room – he could not stand to see this sight of *suffering*. Soon thereafter, Darwin left the University – he had no desire to become a doctor.

---

[101] In 1794, Erasmus Darwin published a treatise on the theory of evolution called *Zoonomia*. Just before he died in 1802, he wrote the book *The Temple of Nature*.

## Chapter II: Career Decision

And so Darwin had to find a new vocation. Now at this time Darwin, like most Englishmen, was a *firm believer* in the doctrines of the Church. And in the year of 1827, Darwin entered Christ's College, at the University of Cambridge. There he studied divinity and the word of God. And so Darwin prepared himself to be a minister. But Darwin spent much time hunting animals and shooting birds. And he went riding and socializing with his friends.

Now Darwin wanted to also learn about the *natural* things – living creatures and geology. But Cambridge at that time had no degree in natural sciences. Nonetheless Darwin met a distinguished group of scientists at Cambridge. And among them was a clergyman and botanist whose name was Henslow. Darwin spent endless time walking with Henslow and learning of the animals and plants. And Darwin became excited about the *scientific world*. And correspondingly his studies of divinity declined – the religious path was *not* for him. And Darwin abandoned the University of Cambridge in 1831 – this year would be a turning point for his career.

And Darwin decided to go on a scientific trip to the Canary Islands. As preparation, he read some of Humboldt's works on Humboldt's scientific trips to northern South America. And Henslow suggested that Darwin visit Wales to gain experience in geologic fieldwork. And so Darwin went to Wales. There Darwin studied *earth*.

Then in August 1831, Henslow recommended that Darwin be an unpaid naturalist on the *HMS Beagle* – the *Beagle* was a naval vessel with two main masts.[102] Now Darwin's father objected to the trip – he felt a lengthy voyage to such faraway places as South America and the Pacific Ocean would be a waste of time and would do little to contribute to Charles' floundering career. But pressure from Robert's brother-in-law made Robert finally give in. And on December 27, Charles Darwin, at the age of twenty-two, sailed out of Plymouth, England, and into the Atlantic. And so Charles Darwin *left* his family – he left behind his father, brother, sisters and other relatives. Now the voyage, whose purpose was to survey the South American west coast and to set up chronometric stations in the Pacific Ocean, was *expected* just to last for two short years. But expectations and reality do not always coincide: Five years the trip would last.

## Chapter III: The Voyage of the *Beagle*

*In the name of Nature, the compassionate, the merciful.*

And the *Beagle* headed south. And while waiting to reach the volcanic island of Tenerife of the Canary Islands, Darwin read about

---

[102] A third smaller mast was at the stern, and there was a bowsprit.

the latest theory of geology.[103] Now this *new theory* spoke of how the face of Earth had changed *slowly* over periods of time – volcanic eruptions, earthquakes, erosion by wind and water, the re-distribution of sand, earth and sediments by streams and rivers – all these *natural forces* affected landscape shape. Thus the surface of the Earth was susceptible to *change*, a change that was continual and *gradual*. And this new view was *different* from earlier ideas, which said that God-like and dramatic short-lived events had raised mountains, sunk land or created world-wide floods like Noah's flood. Now *few* people, including scientists and religious thinkers, believed in the new view. And likewise Darwin was *disturbed* by it, for he had read the *Holy Bible* and knew what *it* had said.

And in Tenerife, Darwin studied Earth and its terrain – he was *searching* for an answer *in the earth*, but he found no answer *there*. Rather, he saw some natural wonders like the bluebird and the dragontree.[104] And then the *Beagle* headed south again. And this time it came upon São Tiago, a member of the Cape Verde Archipelago and the *driest* island in the world. And Darwin continued there his quest for *truth*. And Darwin saw a cliff in which there was a white band containing many shells. Now the shells were the same kinds that could be found on São Tiago beaches. And Darwin *realized* that the structure had been formed by *two* events – first lava must have flowed on top of a seabed containing shells, and then the seabed must have been heaved up to form the cliff. Next Darwin studied the island's land in detail. And he saw giant "tongues" of lava lapping over one another. And he reasoned that *many* lava flows were needed for such structures. And he concluded that the surface of the island had been built by *many* lava flows. And what he saw before him was the *truth* about the Earth.

And a great ocean, the Atlantic Ocean, did the *Beagle* cross. There Darwin saw porcupine fish, dolphins, sperm whales and many other swimming creatures *which* did swim the seas. And a wind with purpose *blew* the sails of the Beagle, and down the east coast of Brazil, Uruguay and Argentina did the *Beagle* go. And Darwin saw brown boobies,[105] flamingos, morpho butterflies and many other flying creatures *which* did fly the skies. These exotic lands delighted him. And he went wild like a wild cowboy when he went riding with the gauchos in the vast pampas-plains of Argentina. His spirit, which had been *unkindled* in his studies at universities, burned like a towering *flame* – he had been transformed into a naturalist.

---

[103] An important book, which had considerable influence on Darwin, was the *Principles of Geology* by Charles Lycell, published in 1830.

[104] The dragon-tree, a member of the lily family, is a plant that looks like a tree. It has pointed leaves and hidelike bark.

[105] The boobies fly high above oceans then plunge hard into the water to catch their prey. They are tame and have no fear of humans. Early sailors, who easily killed the birds, named them boobies due to what seemed to be a lack of intelligence.

And the *Beagle* visited the archipelago of Tierra del Fuego[106] off the southern tip of South America. And Darwin *saw* the forests of snow-tipped mountains rising out of the Magellan Strait. And near the seas and among the trees were Yahgan Indians, who were, in Darwin's words, poor and naked natives who fished and gathered shells in leaky boats in order to maintain a miserable existence.[107]

And up the western coast of Chile did the *Beagle* go. And Darwin ventured inland where he *saw* the Andes Mountains. "How *majestic,* giant and magnificent they be," he thought. "The world before me holds great truths." And *at four-thousand meters high,* he found some truth within the rugged mountains – he *discovered* fossil-shells. "What were seashells doing there?" he asked himself. And in notebooks, he wrote down his geologic observations. And he collected rocks for further study and for later use.

Now the South American tropics were a *paradise* for him. He explored the hot and humid jungles where hid exotic plants and animals. And although there were dangers in the *wild* jungles, curiosity was a force in Darwin that made danger fall aside. He examined lizards, beetles, frogs and other tiny creeping creatures *which* did creep in earth. And he studied deer, rheas,[108] jaguars, armadillos, llamas and other crawling creatures *which* did crawl on earth. And he discovered a fossil of giant-ground-sloth and a fossil of the predecessor of the tuco-tuco.[109] And these were indeed discoveries, for later he would learn that no such fossils of these creatures had been seen by man before.

And when he did find *fossils,* he brought *them* aboard the *Beagle.* And these fossils would turn out to be like *natural scriptures,* for in them would be written truths about the ancient world of living things.

And it came to pass that an earthquake struck in Chile. And he saw the land rise up a couple of meters *right* before his eyes. And as the ground shook terribly, it shook Darwin physically, mentally and emotionally. And when the ground quivered, it *seemed* to speak to him. And Darwin understood, for there was "wisdom" in the rumblings of

---

[106] In Spanish, this name means "island of fire." The name was provided by Magellan – when he "discovered" the island at night, Indian bonfires were seen everywhere.

[107] Two years before Darwin's voyage, the *Beagle* had passed by Tierra del Fuego and British sailors had seen the unfortunate life of the Yaghans. As a "favor" to these "savages," the sailors brought three young Yaghans aboard. The three were given the names York Minster, Fuegia Basket and Jeremy Button and brought back to England. There, they were taught English, converted to Christianity and educated as Englishmen. The three reboarded the *Beagle* along with Darwin in 1831. When the Beagle passed by Tierra del Fuego, the three "educated" natives were dropped off so that they could civilize their former native compatriots. The "civilization" of the Yaghans was unsuccessful. Nonetheless, civilization eventually did come to the area. But European diseases also came and took their toll among the natives. In the middle of the twentieth century, the Yaghans numbered only nine. Another group of natives, the Chonos, whom Darwin had observed and who were also shellfish gatherers, went extinct.

[108] The rhea is a flightless bird similar to the ostrich.

[109] The tuco-tuco is a small burrowing rodent, which resembles a gopher.

the Earth. Thus this earthquake, the first that Darwin had experienced, provided him with insight.

And by the time the *Beagle* left the west coast of the northern part of Chile, Darwin, from his geologic observations, had become convinced that the new theory of geology was right: In the Americas, he had seen new landscapes on majestic scales. He had come to know how truly great the Earth and Nature were.

### And Darwin saw a little light.

Now everywhere he went, he collected specimens. And all the time in notebooks did he ink in words his findings. And months of observation sharpened his *sense* of seeing. And months of writing sharpened his hand at writing. And through all of this activity, his ability to gather facts advanced.

And in the year of 1835, it came to pass that the *Beagle* landed in the Galápagos[110] Archipelago. These islands were a *paradise* of life. And Darwin was in awe of the *natural* magnificence and was fascinated by the variety of faunal forms, virtually none of which *had* he seen in any other land. And he paced beside a great land tortoise to judge its crawling pace. And later, he would learn that these giant tortoises were indigenous *only* to Galápagos. And he was fascinated by unique marine iguanas, which fed on seaweed and covered coastal rocks in groups of several hundred. And he was particularly intrigued by the great variety of finches and their beaks. And he took detailed notes about the fourteen kinds of finches living on these isolated islands. Now among the finches, two used cactus spines to dislodge insects in tree-bark.[111] And *strangely*, on these warm tropical islands were Antarctic-like fur seals and penguins. And Darwin also saw cormorants – these birds could not fly but *swam* like dolphins after fish.

And by this time, he was *fascinated* by the Earth and Nature. And he experienced a kind of bewilderment and underwent a certain enlightenment about the natural world.

And the *Beagle* set out west. There in the Pacific Ocean was the Beagle, *like* a leaf with purpose. And it sailed to Tahiti of the Îles du Vent.[112] And along the way, Darwin spotted frigate birds and albatrosses with wing-spans of two meters. And amazingly these birds glided endlessly for hours without the flapping of a wing.

Now Tahiti was a scenic and seductive island with jagged mountains – on two eroded volcanic cones had Tahiti long ago been built. And Darwin saw how *swift streams* drained the waters, when heavy rains did fall. How exotic was Tahiti! It was full of tropical fruit trees, and was fringed by coral reefs and large lagoons. And Darwin saw

---

[110] The word *galápagos* is an old Spanish word for giant land tortoise. This tortoise is thought to have the longest life-span of any creature on Earth.

[111] These are the only birds known to use a tool for feeding.

[112] In French, this means the "islands of the wind."

beautiful bare-breasted women. Now the natives were organized in large families headed by a tribal chief who used magic, enforced taboos, engaged in rituals and worshipped *many* gods. And in the warm attractive climate, Darwin ate sweet fruits and coconuts. And Tahiti's seductive charm tempted him to stay. But Darwin did not stay. Instead he continued with the *Beagle* to other South Sea Islands. And Darwin saw exotic fish such as the trigger fish[113] and trunkfish.[114] And while travelling the Pacific, the British sailors left in stations clocks to keep the time. But Darwin had on board time-pieces of a *different kind* – fossils, broken clocks of ancient times.

And Darwin studied the topography of islands and surrounding waters. And he realized that long ago volcanos had caused the seafloor to *rise up*, and that subsequently it had *slowly sunk* – and this gave further credence to the notion of large vertical motions of Earth's crust. Later, this vast region of the southwest Pacific would be named *The Darwin Rise*.

Now on the islands of the South Pacific and in the Americas, Darwin had observed strange tribes of different races. And to himself he thought, "The tribes of different natives – how different be their cultures, languages and lives! How different are their statures, skin and faces!"

And all this time, *Nature* was providing him with hints and signs.

And in New Zealand, he saw how glaciers had cut deep U-shaped valleys in the sides of majestic snow-capped mountains. And in the *vast* forests, which contained dozens of different types of trees, he *saw* birds that could not fly such as notornises[115] and kiwis.[116] And on the southeast coast of Australia, he found the duck-billed platypus, the rat kangaroo[117] and other non-European animals. And there were birds of beautiful colors such as the crimson rosella[118] and the pink cockatoo. And the *Beagle* ventured to Tasmania, where the tasmanian wolf and the tasmanian devil[119] live.

Next Darwin and the *Beagle* headed to the third of Earth's great oceans, the Indian Ocean. And vertically flat butterfly fish and surgeon fish, as well as flying fish – which could for short-distances glide through the air – were seen swimming in the sea. And Darwin saw

---

[113] The triggerfish, which is a tropical marine fish found near reefs, is named as such because it possesses a fin spine which can be locked into place and only released by a second fin spine.

[114] Trunk-fish are colorful shallow-water tropical fish encased in a rigid box-like trunk.

[115] A notornis is rare bird beautifully colored partly in blue and partly in green with a large red beak.

[116] A kiwi is a chicken-sized brownish bird with small eyes and a long bill.

[117] A rat kangaroo is a rabbit-sized marsupial.

[118] The crimson rosella is a type of parakeet.

[119] The tasmanian devil is a fierce skunk-sized marsupial.

and studied *them*. And cape pigeons, fairy terns and gannets were flying through the ocean air. And Darwin saw and studied *them*. And during the quiet moments of the voyage, when he was being rocked by ocean waves, he thought and theorized about the *things* that he had seen.

And a wind with purpose *blew* the sails of the Beagle in the Indian Ocean.[120] And in the year of 1836, it came to pass that the *Beagle* landed on the Keeling Islands, small coral islands covered with coconut trees and palms. There and elsewhere, Darwin *collected* shells. And in this region, he observed the hermit crab and studied coral structures in detail. Now Darwin had observed many reefs and atolls in the Pacific and the Indian oceans. And Darwin came to *realize* that coral reefs were built up by a *gradual* process – the coral, which only grew in shallow water, built up the seafloor as *it* built up itself. Now previously, atolls were thought to be an *accident* – the consequence of a volcano whose cone and rim were at the level of the sea. But Darwin realized the true way in which the atolls formed: First, coral built *up* the seabed round an island. Now if the island sunk sufficiently slowly, then coral growth could be maintained.[121] Then if the island dipped below the sea, *what would remain* would be a ring around the former island. Thus through observation, Darwin did discover how the Earth and Nature worked.

And Darwin saw Nature as no *other* had before. Thus Darwin obtained a certain "oneness" with the natural world.

And the *Beagle* went around the southern tip of Africa and crossed the Atlantic Ocean for a second time. And after one stop in the western part of South America, the *Beagle* headed home.

Darwin had been around the World. Thus Darwin *had seen* the *World* and witnessed *Nature* as it *was*.

After five years of travelling, he arrived in England on October 2, 1836. Verily had he become an adventurer of natural phenomena.

## Chapter IV: Darwin's Renaissance: His Search for Truth

Now Darwin handed over much of his collections to experts who could conduct analyses in further detail. And it had *happened* that Darwin had in South America discovered new forms of life, such as a new lizard, a new tanager,[122] new finches, a new frog and a new rhea. And eventually these new species became known as Darwin's lizard,

---

[120] But there was another wind in the air, invisible and impalpable. *Against this other wind*, the *Beagle* sailed.

[121] Coral only grows in calm shallow waters so that if the seafloor sunk too fast, the coral would die. Also, small islands tend to sink under their weight, so the sinking of an island is a relatively common phenomenon.

[122] A tanager is a small colorful songbird that feeds mainly on berries, insects and nectar.

Darwin's tanager, Darwin's finches, Darwin's frog[123] and Darwin's rhea.

And he was told that thirteen of the finches he had seen in Galápagos were not merely different *types* but actually were *different species*. Likewise, the mockingbirds that he had seen were also of three *different species*. And among the land tortoises of the Galápagos, two were indigenous to the archipelago but not to *any continent*. Now Darwin thought these things *strange*, for the current dogma, which almost everyone believed, was that each species had been brought into the world at its own separate and special creation-moment and that life forms had remained the same since the beginning of the World.

And among his fossils was one that happened to be an *extinct* armadillo. And the fossilized armadillo was different from *any* living armadillo. And Darwin thought this *strange*.

Now the expedition had provided him with deep knowledge of Earth's fauna, flora and geology. And at the archipelagos that he had visited, Darwin had had a chance to observe the development of life in isolation.

In England, *publicly* Darwin worked and lectured on the geology and natural history of the places he had visited. But *privately* he was puzzled by what he called "the species problem." This problem was the *origin* of creatures. And he scrutinized his notes and specimens for *hints* to its solution. Now Darwin noted a geographical difference between the faunal species: In one part of Argentina were giant rheas, but in another part they were much smaller. And both of these were different from the ostriches in Africa. And the animals of the Galápagos were in general *different* from the animals of South America. But curiously, the sea birds and sea turtles were the *same*. And Darwin found this *strange*. Likewise other islands had their own species, which resembled the species of nearby continents, but nonetheless were *not* the same.

And in the year of 1837, Darwin began a notebook in which he wrote down information bearing on the question of Earth's species.

Now he discussed the issue with zookeepers, breeders, naturalists and botanists. He read everything there was to read related to the subject. Clandestinely did he proceed. And there was *good reason* why he kept his studies secret – he knew that the issue of species creation was *religiously* highly controversial: England at this time was intensely evangelical; Darwin knew he *could* be hanged for the thoughts that he was having. And he was very much afraid, for he knew about the persecutions of the Renaissance astronomers.

As for his public life, he proceeded more conservatively: From his expedition notes, he wrote three books on the geology of South America.

---

[123] Darwin's frog has the curious behavior that the males pick up eggs just before they are to hatch and carry the developing young in an expandable throat pouch until the young frogs are able to take care of themselves.

And these works brought him instant scientific fame: He was made a member of Geological Society of London. And three years later he was elected to the Royal Society of London for Promoting Natural Knowledge. And within the British scientific circle, *Charles Darwin* was a well-known name.

And in the year of 1839, he married a wealthy woman, who was a devout Christian and who would soon become a devoted mother and an excellent housekeeper. And a house in the English town of Downe became their home. And they acquired many animals as pets; a dozen cats and dogs went running wildly in the yard. And as he observed the animals' behavior, his home became a place of study. And, in some sense, Darwin's house would one day be a temple.

## Chapter V: Enlightenment

And it came to pass that Darwin had a *revelation*. He realized why the terrestrial life of isolated islands such as the Galápagos was different from the life on nearby continents, while the amphibians and sea birds were essentially the same. And the reason was that life *evolved*, for if life did evolve, then life in geologically distinct regions would develop different features. And so terrestrial life on the Galápagos Archipelago was different from the terrestrial life of South America. But amphibians and sea birds, which could "bridge" the seas between the *islands* and the *continent*, would populate them *both*. And *that* was why these life forms were the same. And so it came to pass that Darwin did develop evidence for evolution. And the *more* he scrutinized his data and his notes, the *more* convinced did he become in evolution – the kingdom of the animal was not immutable; it *changed*.

Now Darwin wanted to understand why different finches had such different beaks. And it came to pass that Darwin realized the beaks had been *adjusted* for the finches' eating habits. Now the seed-eating finch had a powerful and wide beak so that it could hold and crack hard seeds, while the woodpecker-like finch had a short sharp beak so that it could chisel bark and eat the insects living there. Still another finch had a long delicate and downward-curving beak – and *nectar* did it drink. And since the finches had evolved in isolation on the Galápagos Archipelago, Darwin hypothesized that all the island's finches had originated from a *single* species and that evolution had shaped the beaks and bodies for the finches' purposes. Thus the features of the finches had adjusted to their habitats and the environment. And this was *natural adaptation*.

And so Darwin *realized* that, like the face of Earth, life also *was* susceptible to *change*. And Darwin was enlightened.

*This time Darwin saw a greater light.*

And it came to pass that Darwin thought of God. And he reread the Holy Bible's Book of Genesis. And he was verily disturbed, for, although his mind supported evolution, evolution was, for him, an *invasion* of his Faith. And during such moments, when Darwin thought of God and evolution, it seemed to him as though a knife thrust through his heart. And it came to pass that a *certain* sickness fell upon Charles Darwin. All over did he feel a body weakness. And this illness would remain in Darwin almost to the end of Darwin's life.

Now it happened that he read a work by Thomas Malthus on population growth. And in the essay it was argued that populations exponentially increased. And a population would explode in number, save for the food supply, which was but limited. "Would this not create a certain competition even within a single species," thought Darwin, "for at some point there would be a struggle for the food." Thus each member of a species would *battle* others for the food. And those members that were stronger or better adapted at obtaining food would so survive. And those members that were weaker or not well adapted at obtaining food would die. And so was born the concept of the *struggle to survive.*

Now many scientists had previously observed the *brutality* of one species on *another* – the *lion* had always brutally attacked the *lamb.* But what Darwin realized was a different type of cruelty – in Nature's world, the members of a *single* species were up against each other. And those species with the fancier set of antlers, the more colorful attractive feather, the sharper beak, the stronger limb, the swifter leg, the longer claw and so on would have better chances to survive and reproduce. And this was *natural selection.* And if such traits were passed to succeeding generations then this would explain the changes in a species, which is evolution.

Now natural selection, argued he, was analogous to artificial selection done by breeders of domestic animals and plants. Such breeders had seen how traits were passed from one generation to the next – the passing of traits was common knowledge, an experimental fact. Now Darwin reasoned that in the competitive natural dominion, "good aspects" of a species should *naturally* be passed to future generations. But "bad aspects" should be *naturally* suppressed. And the passing of favorable aspects should create slow changes in a species. And such change would lead to evolution of a species. *Thus* creatures should evolve.

Thus bad traits will perpetuate themselves and be destroyed but good traits will be preserved. And this was Darwin's "law of karma."

And so he had discovered a great truth: *the survival of the fittest* – the basic principle of evolution. And when he discovered this, ecstatic was his mind. But his stomach felt upset. And for several days did Darwin lie in bed. He was suffering. It was a kind of suffering which would *last* for a long time.

Now theories of evolution had been around for many years: His grandfather had been one of the developers; the naturalist Larmark had speculated that evolution was even pertinent to man – Larmark had drawn a ladder with a human at the top and a protozoon at the bottom. But at that time few people, including biologists, believed in evolution – it was a speculation, a crazy thought with no foundation. Now Darwin provided two important things – *evidence* for evolution *and* a *mechanism* by which evolution could proceed. The evidence consisted of his specimens, his fossils and the data in his books. The mechanism was natural selection. And so was born a *theory* of evolution based on survival of the fittest.[124]

*Upon a strong rock did Darwin*
*begin to build a temple.*

He would spend the rest of his life placing pillars on strong rock.

Now Darwin's mind did *know* the truth, but his soul remained fast-faithful to the Church. And so his heart did bring him pain. And although ill, Darwin's *quest for truth* drove him forward in his thinking.

## Chapter VI: The Origin of Species

Thus Darwin solved the puzzle of the origin of species. And in the year of 1842, he wrote an abstract of his thesis. And in the year of 1844, he wrote a longer draft. And Darwin's health got worse: His heart had palpitations. And at times, he vomited. And he put aside the draft. Instead, he studied barnacles. And he spent the next decade collecting facts and organizing them into a treatise. Now in this work, he *wanted* to argue that different barnacles had been the product of a natural-selection process. But he was *afraid* that the public would denounce his work as heresy. And so he *only hinted* of the principle of natural selection.

Now he knew he had discovered a great truth. And he felt he *had* to tell the world. But he *withheld* the truth, for, it seemed to him, humanity *was not ready* for this truth.

And there raged a *struggle* inside Darwin. And *mind* and *soul* did battle. At times he was ecstatic. At times he was depressed. He often could not sleep at night. And he asked himself, "Should I or should I not reveal the principle of natural selection to the public?" And so his emotions and his scientific mind did battle. And it would be some time before these battles could be settled.

And several years went by. And it came to pass that more scientists began to talk about organic evolution. And *secretly* and *internally* Darwin thought about his revolutionary thesis.

And Darwin came to realize that the phylogeny of life was not a ladder but a branching tree, like the arborvitae,[125] and that branches

---

[124] The detailed mechanism of how one generation passes to the next its "good traits" was unknown to Darwin. Today one knows it is done through genes.

[125] Any one of several types of evergreen trees – the white cedar is an example.

were like candelabras – Darwin had discovered though observation and through thought *the tree of Life.*

And how he *longed* to tell the world. And how he *feared* to tell the world! And when his health was better, he sometimes edited his secret manuscript.

And several years went by. His manuscript was almost ready, but he *waited* – he was afraid that his friends and others would be offended by his theory; even his wife might say his thoughts were heresy.

And all this time, Darwin was still suffering inside.

And one day in 1858, a *terrible* storm struck England. And lightning flashed uncontrollably and violently, and thunder seemed to shake the Darwin home in Downe. And inside the protection of his house and by a *glowing* fireplace, Darwin read an abstract of a paper by another naturalist named Alfred Wallace. Now the abstract summarized the very thesis Darwin had developed during *twenty* years of work. And it was as though a priest had spoken out and beckoned Darwin to speak out.

Thus the abstract forced the hand of Darwin – he handed over his manuscript. Now the *word* would *soon* be out – the public would be *soon* presented with the truth. And in November 1859 was *On the Origin of Species by Natural Selection* published, and the public *was presented* with the truth.

## Chapter VII: Darwin's Later Years

*And so the flower shall bend its stem
and turn its face to face the light.*

And some scientists immediately *accepted* Darwin's work, for it was logical and based on Nature's evidence. But a *storm of protests* swept the world of the intellectual, the theologian, the philosopher and even common people.[126] Now clergymen *condemned* the book as heresy,

---

[126] It is clear why such storms of protest between science and religion arise at times. There is a *line* that exists between the domain of Nature and the domain of God. People long ago drew the boundary by accident *not* at the true line *but* in the land of science. Over the years through the discoveries about the Universe, mankind has realized that certain ancient religious issues are not of the holy domain but of the natural domain. Thus as time has progressed, the boundary, *which man has drawn*, has shifted toward the true line. Thus science has moved into areas once thought to be spiritual. The examples are many: the moments just after the creation of the Universe; the origin of the stars, the Sun and Earth; the origin of life; the development and evolution of plants and animals; the source of catastrophes; and how the Universe works through physics. But when science does advance over man's "misdrawn" boundary, people of strong religious belief construe this to be an attack. At such times a battle between science and religion generally occurs. Certain scientists are called heretics and certain scientific theories are called heresy. Unfortunately, some people of religious faith can become disillusioned if the evidence becomes so overwhelming as to convince them that one of their particular religious convictions is not true.* Such disillusionment was the source of Darwin's life-long illness. The disillusionment and battles between science and religion need not arise if one realizes the source of the problem: a "misdrawn" boundary. Thus science is the *complement* and not the opponent of religion. As argued in the Introduc-

for it was against the Biblical portrayal of creation. And theologians were unwilling to compromise and think of certain Biblical accounts as symbolism. And a great debate broke out among the naturalists, biologists and scientists.

Now after several months, most scientists supported *The Origin of Species*. But still a few opposed. And common people began to participate in the debates. Darwin was slowly gaining followers.

Now *Darwinism*, as it would come to be known eventually, was based on but *four truths*. The first truth was *variation*: the variation of life forms, the variation of species of a similar type and the variation within a species. And the second truth was *heredity* – traits and features in one generation were, to a certain extent, passed to the next. And the third truth was the *survival struggle*: Animals battled one another to survive: Different members *within* a species fought each other for food or mates. And all life forms were threatened by their surroundings – the environment had a hostile component in it. And the forth truth was *natural selection* – it was a consequence of the second and third truths and led to the first truth: In struggling to exist only the fittest would survive, and the fit would pass their traits to future generations, and this would lead to Nature's great floral and great faunal variations.

Now there were a few scientists who supported Darwin *so fervently* they proselytized, as if the concepts were the gospel truths. And Darwin was embarrassed by such idolaters of science.

And the public debate was great indeed – Englishmen and others engaged in arguments at work and in public places such as parks and pubs. Neighbors did the same – housewives, leaning over picket fences, gossiped on the evolutionary concepts.

And debates were held at distinguished universities, as professors engaged in intellectual duels. There was a great battle to decide *whether* Darwin's thesis was correct.

Now Darwin avoided the public eye as best he could. Instead he focused on gathering *more evidence* for his ideas on evolution. And he

---

tion, there are many similarities between science and religion. Perhaps science should be regarded as the "religion on the other side of the line." Someday man will draw the boundary where it *should* be drawn. And from that day onward, science and religion will walk hand in hand.

\* An extreme example of this is the life of Robert FitzRoy, a deeply religious man who was the captain of the *Beagle*. FitzRoy believed *every word* of the Holy Bible, but began to suffer from lingering doubts due to the knowledge gained of the World during the previous century. FitzRoy had hired Darwin as a naturalist with the hope of discovering the Garden of Eden. Finding this holy birthplace would fortify his faith and the faith of others in the Holy Bible. FitzRoy to alleviate the boredom of the Beagle in the high seas often talked with Darwin, and the two became friends. At times, the captain would argue that the specimens that Darwin had collected proved that the Holy Bible was correct.

In 1860, FitzRoy participated in the debate over *The Origin of Species*. At one point in a public gathering, he stood up waving a Holy Bible and shouted to the audience to "believe in God rather than in man." When Darwin's theory was generally accepted some years later, FitzRoy, depressed, killed himself.

studied the variations of animals and plants under man-made breeding and domestication.

And upon observing orchids, Darwin sensed their nectar had a *purpose*. Soon he realized that the purpose was to draw in bees. "Now why would orchids desire to attract the bees?" he asked. And one day, Darwin's trained eye spotted specks of pollen on a bee. Then he hypothesized that the reason for the nectar was to transfer orchid pollen. And by these means, orchids could *breed* the way that humans bred domesticated animals and plants. Thus the orchid used the bee instead of human hands to breed. Thus the plant and insect formed a symbiosis.

And as time went by, a larger fraction of the public did believe in evolution. And eventually Darwin's ideas were *generally* accepted. And no longer did scientists, philosophers and laymen see the world as fixed and as immutable. And questions arose as to whether there existed in the living world a *great design*. And as time went by, the controversy of the origin of species diminished and almost died. But the conflict between science and religion concerning evolution would continue throughout Darwin's life.

Then in the year 1871, Darwin's *The Descent of Man* appeared. And there was another outcry from the public, for it was argued that man was part of evolution. And it was proposed that the origin of man and all animals could be linked to an ancient primordial amoeba. And Darwin was ridiculed by *some* who called his hypothesis the "monkey theory." They said, "It is his ancient ancestors, the monkeys, which led him to such foolish thoughts." They made fun of Darwin – they asked him whether it was his mother or his father who had descended from the ape. But in the end, it would be neither humor nor ridicule that would prevail; it *would* be *facts* and *truth*.

Yet there were others who were more open-minded and said his theories brought *enlightenment*. And so controversy was rekindled each time Darwin wrote a book.

And throughout his later years, Darwin continued to publish works related to his findings. He argued that great apes and other "higher" mammals *had emotions* and perhaps they even had a psychological disposition – cats, dogs, monkeys, horses and in fact almost all the "higher" mammals moved facial muscles and emitted sounds indicative of feelings such as anxiety, despair, joy, devotion, fear and suffering. Hitherto, it *had* been thought that *only* humans had emotions. Such discoveries bought enlightenment to Darwin.

Next he pointed out the role of sex, how it created competition among males for females. And in the battles for the most attractive females, the stronger better males won out. And so the "better" males and females *passed* their traits to future generations. And he explained the beauty of the male peacock's tail, for in the peacock population was the role of sex reversed – females fought among themselves to mate with males that had the most attractive tails. And surprisingly, *few* scientists at the time agreed with the concept of the peacock sex-reversal, but after a century it would be almost universally *accepted*. And Darwin speculated that the intricate antlers of the male deer arose because of their defensive value and because females found them sexually attractive. Thus sex could play a role in evolution.

And with such arguments and evidence, Darwin *fortified* his temple.

And it came to pass that he engaged in artificial breeding – he did what Nature had been doing. And he viewed the *tree of Life* as an interconnected *wonderful* great structure, which held a *beauty* and a *truth* which far exceeded the old concept that each species was a separate act of birth-creation.

And finally, it came to pass that Darwin's illness, which had waned and waxed for many years, did go away. Darwin had internal peace – it was as though he underwent *nirvana of the scientific kind* – his suffering inside was gone.

And Darwin's life was full of joy and pleasure. And he became a great breeder, botanist and horticultural experimentalist – he was a *man of Nature*. And he noted that flowers that are pollinated by the wind have no nectar and are dull in color, but flowers that use insects have sweet nectars and display a range of colors. Thus flowers had evolved *according to* their reproductive needs. And he argued for natural selection within the floral kingdom: Some trees grew tall in the battle to obtain a better angle to the Sun; they would strive to grow to be the highest trees. Likewise, some vines spiralled to *achieve* a better heat and *light*. And to his surprise, he found that vines would not climb trees whose diameters were greater than a half a foot – it was as though vines *knew* such trees would be too tall to climb. And he investigated insectivorous plants, which could trap a fly with tentacles or glue-like substances. And so he discovered a power in the movement of the plants.

And so his principles were universal – they ruled all forms of life. And with these observations, his temple was complete.

Now Darwin's final work was a study of the habits of earthworms. He pointed out the role of worms in digesting fallen leaves to recirculate organic matter – this was natural ecology. And one black and moonless night, Darwin ventured outside with a candle. And he held the *candle* near a bunch of worms. And though eyeless, the earthworms moved away.

*They have no eyes but they see light.*

And it *cannot* be denied that Darwin's life's observations also shed some light.

And true joy did he attain, for by the late 1800's were his ideas on natural selection and on evolution *generally accepted* – he had *a great following*.

And on the nineteenth day of the fourth month of the year of eighteen-eighty-two, Darwin's mind and soul were laid to rest – he was buried in *Westminster Abbey*, but his spirit did not *there* remain, for it rose up and it was placed among the stars.

*The tenth book of Chronicles, called*

# History of Elementary Particles[127]

*They are tiny and invisible.*

## Chapter I: Quantum Mechanics History

And in 1900, it came to pass that Max Planck proposed a constant.[128] It *was* not then known that the quantum revolution had begun. It was not known *then* that the world would never be the same again.

And in 1911, Ernest Rutherford shot heliums[129] at thin gold foil. Now almost every helium did *pass* straight through. But one in twenty-thousand heliums were deflected greatly. And there was revelation in these events so precious and so few, for the heliums *must* have struck a tiny concentrated object in the foil – the *nucleus*, an atom's heart, had been discovered. And so a new understanding of the atom's inner structure was achieved.

And in 1913, the shell model of the atom *was* described by Niels Bohr. Ten years later, Louis-Victor de Broglie proposed that *particles*[130] behave *both* like particles and waves. And scientists began to understand the quantum world *a little more*. Then in 1926, Erwin Schrödinger introduced his quantum wave equation.[131] And the quantum revolution then was underway.

## Chapter II: The Early Particles

And it came to pass that in 1928 Paul A. M. Dirac wrote down the relativistic quantum wave equation to describe electron motion. Now the equation had a *mysterious consequence*, for it predicted the ex-

---

[127] This section assumes knowledge of elementary particles. For the basic concepts and definitions of scientific terms, see the Book of *Subnuclear Physics*.

[128] This constant would come to be known as the *Planck constant*. It controls the strength of quantum effects.

[129] More precisely, they were alpha particles, which are the nuclei of helium atoms.

[130] Particles are extremely tiny objects, smaller than an atom and invisible to the human eye, such as the alpha particles of Rutherford's gold foil experiment.

[131] This equation governs quantum mechanics. See Chapters VI-VIII of the Book of *Quantum Mechanics*.

istence of another particle like the electron but *positively* charged. Thus the theory prophesied an antiparticle, the *positron* – it was the "positive electron," a new state of matter, which was *antimatter*.

And in 1931, careful measurements were made on beta nuclear decay.[132] And behold, energy seemed *not* to be conserved in this unusual decay. And suddenly a fundamental law of Nature seemed invalid – would *then* one need to rewrite one commandment of the ten? Now among the physicists, there were those *who* no longer did believe and there were those who *still* believed in the conservation of energy. And Wolfgang Pauli was one of those who still believed. And so he postulated the existence of a light uncharged, seemingly invisible particle and called it a *neutrino*. And he proposed, in beta nuclear decay, that the neutrino *carried off* the "missing" energy.

And experiments conducted by Carl David Anderson in 1932 produced the positron. And so it came to be that the prediction of a "scientific prophet" *was* confirmed. [133]

And in that same year, it happened that James Chadwick made the nuclei of helium and of beryllium react. And a neutral particle with the mass of a proton was emitted – the *neutron* was discovered.

And in 1934, when Enrico Fermi formulated a theory of nuclear beta decay, the foundations of weak interactions *were* established. Now for a while, Fermi theory would be enormously successful. But flaws eventually would be uncovered: The first flaw *would* be found in 1957. And physicists *would* repair the defect by modifying the weak theory's laws. And for more than a decade, the theory would explain the weak-decay experimental data. But in the early 1970's, scientists would discover further flaws. And a new theory of weak interactions would be proposed with *very different* properties for processes involving highly energetic particles.

And in 1934, it came to pass that man made *the* first man-made fissions. Thus man did do what Nature sometimes does: Man *split* the atom.

And in 1935, Hideki Yukawa hypothesized that certain particles were the mediators and creators of strong force, which is the force holding nucleons together in a nucleus.[134] And he called these particles the pions. Now in 1936, a new particle was *discovered* in the cosmic rays streaming down to Earth from outer space. And it was *thought to be* the pion. But experimentalists had been misled and physicists *were wrong*. It would take some years for them to realize their mistake, for the muon[135] *had* been found instead.

---

[132] This process in which an electron is emitted by the nucleus is described in Chapter IV of the Book of *Nuclear Physics*.

[133] It took only four years for Dirac's prediction to be confirmed.

[134] A nucleon is a proton or a neutron. See Chapter II of the Book of *Nuclear Physics*.

[135] A muon is a heavier version of an electron. See Chapter IV of *Particle Physics*.

And it came to pass that in 1942 the first self-sustaining man-made chain reaction was achieved – nuclear power now was possible. And in 1945, the power verily was put to use – scientists in America produced the first atomic bomb. And the United States did drop "the bomb" on Hiroshima and on Nagasaki. The age of mass-destruction weapons had begun. And man was given in his hands *the power* to destroy himself on a large scale.

## Chapter III: The Post World War II Years

And in 1947, pions were discovered in the cosmic rays from outer space. And the prediction of existence of the pion was confirmed. *But* Yukawa's prediction at a *fundamental level* would be proven wrong, for gluons, not the pions, would turn out to be the microscopic mediators of the subatomic forces of the strong.

Then kaons were discovered in the cosmic rays. Now kaons *should have* decayed to pions relatively rapidly. But this was not the case. And scientists did think this *strange.* And so the kaon was assigned a property called "strange." Now *strangeness* explained why kaons did not readily decay to pions: Strangeness was like electric charge; it could neither be created nor destroyed at least in processes proceeding by nuclear strong forces. And since kaons carried strangeness and pions didn't, a kaon could not vanish into pions without violating conservation of strange charge. Now strangeness would, three decades later, be explained – it would come from the strange quark *which* the kaon would contain.[136]

And it came to pass that in 1948 the pion was produced by man in an accelerator. And this marked a monumental moment, for henceforth man would be a *particle creator.* Throughout the early 1950's, physicists would manufacture many particles with strangeness. And during the next fifty years, even more particles, both strange and not, would be detected and produced. Thus man began to make the particles that Nature made *during* the Big Bang and its aftermath.

Then in 1954, the *non-abelian gauge theory* was invented by R. L. Mills and C. N. Yang.[137] Now to most physicists, it seemed of little value, but for theorists it was cryptic and esthetic, possessing limitless amounts of symmetry.

And in 1956, for the first time did scientists detect directly the *neutrino* – some twenty-five years after *its* existence had been postulated. And the prediction of another prophet was confirmed. And the conservation of energy, the Sixth Commandment, thus was *saved.*

---

[136] A particle has *strangeness* if it contains a strange quark. Quarks are the components making up a large class of particles called hadrons. Protons, neutrons, pions and kaons are all examples of hadrons. See Chapter X of the Book of *Subnuclear Physics*.

[137] It was not known then that, a decade and a half later, non-abelian gauge theories would be the basis for the Standard Model of particle physics, for such theories would describe all subatomic interactions.

And in 1957, a particular weak-force decay of cobalt-sixty was observed, and yet the analogue decay, as would be in a mirror seen, did *not* occur. And scientists around the world pondered mirrors *and* become confused, for hitherto was it thought that mirror-imaged processes in Nature always could proceed. Suddenly, "Nature's mirrors" were seen as *broken* and precisely broken in *two pieces*, for the mirror-image of a fundamental process did not necessarily take place. Now for physicists, it was a moment of reflection and of revelation – a physics law, which had been tacitly and universally *assumed as true*, was wrong. The law was broken and badly broken, for the weak force was *maximally non-symmetric* under mirror-space reflection.[138] *So* it be – Nature did *not* possess this a priori fundamental symmetry. And theorists built a *new* weak-interaction theory which incorporated mirror-space-reflection violation.

And in 1962, the muon's neutrino was detected by the Brookhaven accelerator on Long Island. And the second of Nature's three neutrinos was observed – the elusive, almost "invisible" nu-mu was seen.

## Chapter IV: The Recent Developments

And it came to be that in 1963 constituents for protons and for neutrons were proposed. And the constituents were provided with a name. And the name was *quark*. Now quarks were predicted to have unusual properties such as possessing *fractional* electric charge. And quarks could be combined in threes to produce *eight* baryons – six possessing strangeness, plus the neutron and the proton. But quarks could also be combined in threes to produce a group of ten – but, as of 1963, only nine such baryons had been observed by man. And a name was given to the missing baryon. And the name was the *Omega*. And one year later, Omega was discovered with a mass *in remarkable agreement* with theoretical predictions. Now the quarks and antiquarks could also be combined to yield mesons. And such mesons *should* come in a set of *eight* – they were the three pions, the four kaons and the eta. And because there was a group of eight for mesons and a group of eight for baryons, the quark theory was nicknamed the *"Eightfold Way."*

And in the late sixties, electromagnetism and the weak force were united in a *single* theory. Soon thereafter, quantum chromodynamics and the unified electroweak theory became the basis of *the Standard Model* of the particles.[139] And the theory predicted the existence of some heavy particles, the Z and W, whose exchange led to the nuclear weak force.

---

[138] Mirror-space reflection is called *parity* by physicists.

[139] The Standard Model of particle physics would provide the basis for all the fundamental forces except gravity.

Now it happened that the Standard Model was inconsistent unless a new quark did exist. And in the year of 1970, theorists gave the hypothesized particle a name. And *it* was called the *charm quark*. And although theorists predicted its existence, they could *not* predict its mass. Now at this time, *this* quark was the fourth; the others were the up, the down and strange. And using accelerators, experimentalists began to *hunt* for charm.

And a few years later and some ten years after the conception of the quark and of the Eightfold Way, high-energy experiments *indirectly* sensed the quarks. And the electric charges of the quarks were measured. And they were fractions – in fact they were the fractions that the theorists *had predicted*. Again had scientific prophets spoken, and their truths had been *confirmed*. Now with the insights provided by experimental data, theorists constructed a theory of strong interactions. And the theory was assigned a name. And the name was *quantum chromodynamics*, or *QCD*. And it explained the underlying interactions of the quarks. It was a *simple* theory to write down. But the calculations from the quantum gauge equations were quite *difficult*,[140] and the consequences were not fully known.

And it happened that in 1974 the charm quark was produced. And the prediction of some scientific prophets was confirmed.

Then in 1975, experimentalists produced a new third lepton.[141] And *it* was called the *tau*. But the tau lepton was not light like the electron and the muon – the tau weighed more than a neutron or a proton.

And in the year 1977, it came to be that accelerators produced a fifth new quark, the *bottom quark*, which was also called the beauty quark. And experimentalists began to study forms of matter holding *beauty*.

Now the Standard Model with just a bottom quark was inconsistent, for quantum mechanics, it turns out, requires quarks to come in pairs. Up and down were paired. Strange and charm were paired. But bottom was unpaired. And so the presence of a fifth quark meant there had to be a sixth. And the *hypothesized* sixth quark was called the *top*. Now the *top quark* was also called the truth quark. And experimentalists began a search for *truth*.

And in 1983, CERN, a powerful accelerator near Geneva, Switzerland, produced the W and Z. And their masses were *precisely* the expected masses. Now fourteen years had passed since theorists had predicted the existence of the W and Z. Thus the mediators of the nu-

---

[140] Twenty years of subsequent theoretical analysis and numerical computation with the most powerful computers have yielded only partial insight into how quarks bind together in a proton and a neutron. However, the first concrete indication that quarks *might* be confined was uncovered by Kenneth G. Wilson in 1974. In 1982, he was awarded the Nobel Prize in physics for another contribution – a deeper understanding of phase transitions.

[141] The other two leptons are the electron and the muon.

clear weak force *had* been finally uncovered. And the predictions of some scientific prophets were confirmed.

And in Fermilab in Batavia, Illinois, the top quark was detected in 1995 – the partner of the bottom *did* indeed exist. And after eighteen years of searching, experimentalists had found the top. And the elusive search for this small bit of truth so ended – both the theorists and the experimentalists had *triumphed* and prevailed. And the top quark assumed its position in the lower left corner of the Table of the Fundamental Matter. And with the top quark in this place, the Standard Model was again consistent in a quantum way.[142]

---

[142] Discoveries in the second half of the twentieth century in particle physics concerning Nature at its most fundamental level led to Nobel Prizes in physics:

Chen Ning Yang and Tsung-Dao Lee in 1957 for their theoretical investigations into parity violation.

Emilio Gino Segre and Owen Chamberlain in 1959 for the discovery of the antiproton.

Sin-Itiro Tomonaga, Julian S. Schwinger and Richard P. Feynman in 1965 for contributions to the construction of the theory of quantum electrodynamics.

Murray Gell-Mann in 1969 for the classification of elementary particles based on quarks and the Eightfold Way.

Burton Richter and Samuel C. C. Ting in 1976 for the discovery of the charm quark.

James W. Cronin and Val Logsdon Fitch in 1978 for the discovery of violations of fundamental symmetries in the decay of kaons.

Sheldon L. Glashow, Abdus Salam and Steven Weinberg in 1979 for the unification of the weak and electromagnetic interactions.

Carlo Rubbia and Simon Van der Meer in 1984 for the discovery of the W and Z.

Leon M. Lederman, Melvin Schwartz and Jack Steinberger in 1988 for the discovery of the muon's neutrino.

Jerome I. Friedman, Henry W. Kendall, and Richard E. Taylor in 1990 for work on the experimental confirmation of quantum chromodynamics.

Marlin L. Perl in 1995 for the discovery of the tau lepton.

Frederick Reines in 1995 for the discovery of the neutrino.

*The eleventh book of Chronicles, called*

# Einstein

*Science without religion is lame;*
*religion without science is blind.*

*— Albert Einstein*

## Chapter I: Einstein's Life and Work

And on March 14, 1879, in Ulm, Germany, Albert Einstein, the scientific version of a prophet and a saint, was born. Now at the age of five, Albert was presented with a compass from his father. And Albert *turned the compass* in a circle. But the needle did not turn – the needle remained pointing to the north. And this had a profound effect on this young mind, for hitherto Albert had thought that *contact* was needed to make things move. And so Albert concluded that *something deeply hidden* had to lie behind the physics of the world. And in the case of a compass needle, that hidden, deep and mystical thing was magnetism.

And at the age of ten, Einstein engaged in self-taught education – he *read* Euclid and *learned* the rudiments and fine points of geometry; he *studied* books on science and developed scientific curiosity.

Now his father owned an electric factory in southern Germany. There, dynamos were manufactured to produce direct currents for consumption. And one day Einstein went out to tour the plant. And there, he saw moving conveyor belts, rotating wheels, turning gears and glowing bulbs. Thus he *observed electricity* in action and *magnetism* in the making. And in a tangible way did he learn what electromagnetism was about.

And at sixteen years of age, he began to ask himself deep physics questions. For example, he asked, "What would it be like *to ride a beam of light?*" But at this early age, he had no answers. Thus already in his youth did he devote himself to thinking of the *riddles* of the Universe. And later he would devote himself to *solving* them.

The year was 1905. And Einstein *postulated* that light consisted of particles called photons. And he *proposed* the theory of special relativity,[143] whose basic assumption was the constancy of the speed of light when measured by any constant-moving observer. And he *predicted* that mass could be converted into energy and vice versa. Thus the relation between mass and energy, $E=mc^2$, was established. And he had the answer to the question of riding on a light beam: *it could not be done*, for no one can move at or faster than the speed of light.

---

[143] Special relativity is a generalization of Newtonian mechanics. It predicts that objects travelling near the speed of light behave quite differently from slowly moving ones. It also unifies space and time into one entity. For more on this theory, see the New Testament Book of *Special Relativity*.

It was 1916. And Einstein published the general theory of relativity, in which it was postulated that gravitation was not a mechanical force but the consequence of the *curvature of spacetime* created by the presence of mass. And his theory explained for the first time an irregularity in the motion of the planet Mercury, namely that the ellipse, which Mercury follows in its orbit about the Sun, should rotate with time by an extra amount equal to forty-three seconds of arc per century. And his theory predicted that *light should bend* around massive bodies like the Sun. And it implied the existence of gravity waves and black holes. And it *predicted* that light moving away from surface of the Earth should lose energy and undergo a red-shift; its wavelength should get longer.[144] And this effect was called the *gravitational energy red-shift*. Likewise, the theory predicted that a clock near a very massive object such as a neutron star where gravity is strong, should *run slower* than a clock far from such a massive object where gravity is weak. And this was called the *gravitational red-shift time-dilation*.

Hence in the span of just eleven years, much of the "old testament" of physics was *rewritten*. Thus Albert Einstein rewrote the gospels of Sir Isaac Newton. They would become books of the new testament.

But Einstein did not embrace all the new developments of physics that were transpiring at the beginning of the twentieth century. And for example, he did *not accept* quantum mechanics and the probabilistic nature of the Universe,[145] "I cannot believe that God plays dice with the Universe," he said.

*God may not, but Nature does.*

And Einstein devoted the second half of his life in quest of a unified theory – he was searching for the Uni-Law. But the Uni-Law was *too subtle* even for the mind of Einstein.

And as Einstein aged, he became more philosophical. And he became a pacifist and public figure. And one day he said, "God is subtle, but *He* is not malicious."

*God may not be, but Nature sometimes is.*

And on April 18, 1955, did Einstein not wake up from a deep sleep. And the *spirit and intelligence* of Einstein escaped his body, rose up and was placed *among the stars*. And the ghosts of many other scientists rose with him – the fathers of electromagnetism, the discoverers of quantum theory, the physicists who had uncovered the fundamental subatomic interactions. And the ideas of Einstein and other scientific

---

144 When its wavelength is lengthened, light becomes redder. This is discussed in the fifth, sixth and eighth Books of Physics.
145 In the "quantum world," future events are not determined exactly; they proceed according to probabilities. See the New Testament Book of *Quantum Mechanics*.

prophets were written in the textbooks and *embedded* in the minds of men and women.

Somewhere it is written, "Einstein was a great scientific saint." Where it is written is between thy hands.

## Chapter II: The Prophecies of Einstein

*I spent my whole life trying to understand
the nature of electromagnetic light.*

*— Albert Einstein*

Now a few years had passed since the appearance of Einstein's paper on gravity – it was May 29, 1919. A solar eclipse was taking place. And astronomers *directed* their telescopes and waited. But it was a cloudy day. And the astronomers were quite dismayed until suddenly the *clouds broke open* and there was light. And moments later, the sky grew dark, and stars near the Sun were visible. And the *positions* of the stars were measured. Now the positions were *different* from those when the Sun was elsewhere in the sky – starlight was *being bent around the Sun*. Hence through gravity, a massive object, such as the Sun, *attracted light* just as it attracted a body with a mass. Furthermore, the measured bending of starlight *agreed* with calculations from Einstein's gravitation theory. And a prophecy of a prophet was confirmed.

It was 1932. And Abbé Georges Lemaître proposed that the Universe began as an explosion and was *still expanding*. And in fact, such an expansion of the Universe *was* a consequence of Einstein's gravitation theory. Now astronomers pointed their largest telescopes toward the distant galaxies and observed electromagnetic spectra.[146] And the spectra of such distant galaxies were *distorted in a systematic way*: Lines of blue appeared as yellow, lines of yellow appeared as red and so on. And this was a *velocity red shift*, a Doppler effect for light. And it meant that the galaxies were speeding away from Earth *and* away from one another. Thus the fabric of space *was* indeed expanding, and the expanding space was carrying the galaxies apart. And it was *as though* the Universe were a big balloon and galaxies were painted dots on the surface of this hypothetical balloon. And *someone or something* was blowing air in it and making it inflate. And as the balloon inflated, the dots did move apart. But *no one* was blowing into the Universe, for the expansion of the Universe was *natural*: Einstein's gravity theory had guaranteed it. Now the expansion rate was measured – in one year, five-billionth of a percent did space get stretched. The prophecy of a prophet was confirmed.

And the fractional rate at which the Universe expanded was assigned a name. The *Hubble constant* was that name. And the rate at

---

[146] Spectra are discussed in Chapter VI of the New Testament Book of *Atomic Physics*.

which the Universe had expanded in the past likewise was called the Hubble constant. But the Hubble constant *was not constant*, for earlier the Universe expanded percentage-wise more quickly. Each time the Universe's age has doubled, the expansion rate has dropped in half.

Now as astronomers made more measurements of distances and speeds of galaxies, they better understood the stretching of the Universe. And they extrapolated *back in time* the positions of the galaxies. And when they went back fifteen-billion years or so, they realized that all galaxies were concentrated *in a small region* of all space. Thus approximately fifteen-billion years ago, all matter was lumped together in a tiny place. And in the beginning, matter flew apart like debris in an explosion. But the Universe *did not actually explode* – all it did was to expand. And that initial moment, when matter was concentrated into tiny space, was provided with a name. And that name was the *Big Bang*.

It was 1939. The place was Copenhagen. And scientists split the uranium nucleus in two. The fission resulted in a *loss of mass*. Thus mass was *converted* into energy. And the loss in mass and the gain in energy were measured, and the relation between mass $m$ and energy $E$ was tested. And it *agreed* with the formula $E=mc^2$. And a prophecy of a prophet was confirmed.

Now during the first few seconds of the early Universe when matter annihilated antimatter, $E=mc^2$ was used *again and again*, although no one had yet written the equation. Indeed, at that time no living creature yet existed. Indeed, no cell existed then; nor any molecule; nor any atom; nor even any nucleus. Yet $E=mc^2$ was in effect, for $E=mc^2$ is a law. Man *does not make* the laws of Nature. Man merely writes them in a form that he can understand.

Although a few of the predictions of Einstein's general theory of relativity had been tested to be true, still some scientist had doubts about the new ideas. They were *non-believers*. But *other scientists* did believe and *they* were driven to experiment and to confirm the theory beyond *a shadow of a doubt*. Thus scientists continued their search for truth and confirmation.[147]

And in 1960, it came to pass that, in a laboratory, two scientists measured the wavelength of some laser light. And they directed the laser upward, measured the *wavelength* several meters up, and *it* was *longer* there. Now this meant that, *as the light rose up*, its energy decreased with height. This effect was the gravitational energy red-shift. And the difference in wavelength was measured and *did agree* with calculations from the Einstein theory. And a prophecy of a prophet was confirmed.

---

[147] Einstein's gravity theory is known as the general theory of relativity. It is discussed in the New Testament's sixth Book of Physics.

And similar measurements were made using extraterrestrial sources: Light that originated in the strong gravitational region at the surface of white-dwarf stars was carefully observed. And a gravitational energy red-shift was seen *once more*.

It was 1964. And scientists *waited* until Venus was about to pass behind the Sun. And they *directed* intense radar pulses toward the planet. And the radar pulses travelled from the Earth, went past the Sun, struck the Venusian surface and rebounded. And the *reflected radar pulses* headed back to Earth. And after passing by the Sun, *they* arrived on Earth. Now the time for the journey was measured by the scientists. And the time was *more* than when the Sun was not between the Earth and Venus. And the experiment was repeated with the planet Mercury, when Mercury passed near the Sun. Now the measured time delays *agreed* with calculations from general relativity. And the gravitational time-delay red-shift was verified. And the prophecy of a prophet was confirmed.

And an *extremely accurate* cesium atomic clock was placed in a modern jet. And a second cesium clock was kept on Earth. And the jet flew high above the Earth for fifteen hours and returned to Earth. Now Einstein's theories of special and general relativity *predicted* that the clock flown high above the Earth should run slower than the clock on Earth where gravity was stronger – the clock in the jet should be *forty-seven billionths* of a second slow. And at the end of the flight, the times of *the* two clocks were read. And compared to the Earth-based clock, the time of the airborne clock was *forty-seven billionths* of a second less. Thus the gravitational red-shift time-dilation was confirmed.

And in 1974, a new pulsar was detected by astronomers. It was in the constellation Aquila, fifteen-thousand light years from the Earth. Its name, 1913+16, told of its location: it was directed sixteen degrees above the equator and with a right ascension of nineteen hours and thirteen minutes. Now the pulsar beamed its radio *signal* seventeen times a second; in a regular manner did the beeps arrive. Hence, the pulsar signal functioned *as an astronomic clock*. But the clock told time with small inaccuracies. At times the clock was almost imperceptibly *slow*, while at other times it was almost imperceptibly *fast*. But the variations *were* perceptible and *were* detected by a thousand-foot radio dish in Puerto Rico. And from a detailed analysis of the variations in the signal, scientists deduced that the pulsar consisted of two neutron stars. And the variations in the signal allowed scientists *to see the orbit*.[148] Thus astronomers "saw with ears."

---

[148] From the signal information the following was deduced. The two neutron stars were separated by an average distance of two-million kilometers. They moved at several hundred kilometers per second in an ellipse. And they went around each other once every eight hours. In 1993, Russell A. Hulse and Joseph H. Taylor Jr. were awarded the Nobel Prize in physics for the discovery of 1913+16.

Now Einstein's gravity theory predicted that the binary pulsar system should undergo the analog of the Mercury irregularity.[149] But since the gravity in the binary pulsar system was much stronger, the effect should be much bigger. Calculations *predicted* that the ellipse should rotate four degrees per year. And astronomers listened to the pulsar and "saw" the ellipse rotate by four degrees per year. And a prophecy of a prophet was confirmed.

Now because the orbit was an ellipse, the *distance* between the neutron stars did *vary*. And because the distance varied, the force of gravity between the two repeatedly grew *stronger* and grew *weaker*. Thus there should be a gravitational red-shift time-variation. Now the general theory of relativity *predicted* that there should be four-thousandth-of-a-second *delays and advances* in the pulses. And listening to the pulsar with their radio dish, astronomers observed *lags and leads* of one four-thousandth of a second.

Now general relativity made an astonishing prediction: As the two neutron stars orbited each other, they should radiate *gravitation waves* and lose some energy. Hence the binary pulsar should act as a broadcast station which emits both radio-type waves and gravity-type waves. And as the two neutron stars lost energy, they should move toward each other and thereby *spiral in*. But since so little energy was lost in waves, they should approach each other very slowly – three-and-one-half meters in a year. And as they moved in closer, they should take *less time* to orbit one another. And listening carefully to the signal during many years, scientists did observe a decrease in the time to make one orbit. Thus *gravitation waves* were detected, although *indirectly*. Thus *their existence*, as predicted by the theory of general relativity, *was verily confirmed*. And from the observations, the decrease in the orbital time was measured. And from this time decrease, the loss in energy was so deduced. Thus the energy in waves of gravity emitted by the binary pulsar *was* by these means indirectly measured. And it *agreed* with relativistic calculations. And a prophecy of a prophet was confirmed.

It was 1979. A powerful telescope observed two quasars almost on top of one another. Never before had two quasars been seen *so close to one another*. And further observations showed that the two quasars were travelling at *the same speed*. And when the *spectral lines* of these two quasars were observed, *they* too were the *same*. Now such a coincidence *could not be* an accident. And scientists came to realize that the two quasars *were not two* – they were two images of *one*. And the situation *was as* a man who "crosses" his two eyes and sees in double. Now a telescope has *but* one "eye." How could a telescope *"cross"* its "eye?" Why was a double image seen? And a large array of radio dishes was directed at the strange exotic object. And it *too* revealed an extra

---

[149] See Chapter I of this book.

image. Apparently the doubling did occur for radio waves as well as light. Now Einstein's theory of gravity predicted that a very heavy object should act as a gravitation lens. *If* a massive galaxy existed between the quasar and the Earth, then the bending of electromagnetic waves by the galaxy *would make* a multiple of images. And astronomers directed their most sensitive telescopes to the region of the quasar. And one night when the atmosphere of Earth was calm and the sky was particularly clear, a faint galaxy between the quasar images *was observed.* And the distance to the galaxy was measured – the galaxy was halfway between the quasar and the Earth.

And other multiple-imaged quasars were subsequently seen. And scientists concluded that the Universe contained massive galaxies, which *caused spacetime to curve.* And curved spacetime acted *as unto* a lens.[150] And through the gravitational-lens effect, astronomers did see the curvature of space. Thus the basic principle behind general relativity was *verified.* And a prophecy of a prophet was confirmed.

Now according to Einstein's gravity theory, a *small dark massive* body also should bend light. But unlike a galaxy, which creates a multiple image, an object of the size of a large planet or small star should *focus* light. It should function as a magnifying glass, focusing rays of light into a brighter spot. Now in 1992, astronomers began to *monitor* millions of stars to see if any did get brighter. And the next year, several such events *were seen.* And after a short time, each such star dimmed, returning to its *normal brightness,* as the dark object finished passing by the star. Thus indeed there were *invisible* non-luminous objects which moved in front of stars and made them *brighten.* Hence, through gravitational lensing, astronomers saw what could not be seen with a telescope, radio dish or human eye. The *invisible* they saw. And these invisible bodies were assigned a name. And the name was *MACHO,* which means "massive compact halo object."

> *Spiritual prophets allow one to see the light.*
> *Einstein allowed mankind to see beyond the light.*

---

[150] This effect is called *gravitational lensing.*

*The twelfth book of Chronicles, called*

# Moments in Modern Science

*These are wondrous and marvelous things*
*beyond all comprehension.*

## Chapter I: Nuclear Alchemy

Now Nature made the elements in the Big Bang and in the stars. And the expansion of space[151] *dispersed* the light elements of hydrogen and helium and lithium throughout the Universe. And supernova explosions of stars *spread* the heavier elements throughout the Universe. And so the Universe was *filled* with diverse elements.

Now in modern times, man began to play with nuclei. And man, in a small way, began to do what Nature had already done – *make elements*. Thus man became an alchemist.

And so in 1940 scientists made *two new* elements: neptunium, named for the planet Neptune, and plutonium, named for the planet Pluto.[152] These two new elements were made by bombarding uranium with neutrons and deuterium.

Then from 1944 to 1952, scientists made *six new* elements: americium, curium, berkelium, californium, einsteinium and fermium.[153] And in 1955, miniscule amounts of mendelevium were made. Now mendelevium did not last long – it persisted for about an hour before *decaying* into lighter elements. And in 1958, nobelium was produced. And it lasted *just three seconds*. And in 1961, lawrencium was manufactured with a lifetime of *eight seconds*. And for several years, it would be the heaviest of man-made elements. But in the late twentieth century, scientists would create more massive nuclei.[154]

*And in the future, man,*
*the minor alchemist,*
*will go on making new and heavy elements,* if he can.

---

[151] In Einstein's theory of gravity, space is dynamic, like a cloth that can be stretched, deformed or bent.

[152] Later, these two elements would be produced in substantial quantities in nuclear power plants.

[153] In 1951, Edwin Mattison McMillan and Glenn Theodore Seaborg received the Nobel Prize in chemistry for their discoveries in the chemistry of transuranium elements.

[154] The elements in this paragraph are named after the Americas, Pierre and Marie Curie, Berkeley, California, Albert Einstein, Enrico Fermi, Dmitri Ivanovich Mendeleyev, Alfred Nobel and Ernest Orlando Lawrence. The husband and wife team Pierre and Marie Curie made important discoveries in radioactivity for which they received the Nobel Prize in physics in 1903; she became the first scientist to win two Nobel Prizes; the other prize came in chemistry in 1911. Fermi, the Nobel Prize winning physicist, developed the first theory of the weak interactions and made many contributions in particle physics. Mendeleyev was the Russian chemist who introduced the periodic table. Alfred Nobel invented dynamite and bequeathed the money for the Nobel Prize. Lawrence, inventor of the cyclotron, received the Nobel Prize in physics in 1939.

## Chapter II: The Cosmic Microwave Background Radiation

And in the year of 1965, two scientists, Arno A. Penzias and Robert W. Wilson, set out to build the modern version of the tower of Babel. But they *did* not build a tower – they built a "giant ear." Now it was not a normal ear – it was a *dish*, which could detect both radio waves and microwaves. Now the scientists had built their Babylonian structure *not to reach* the heavens but *to hear* the heavens, for this first radio telescope was constructed to listen to the Universe. And when the two scientists listened to the Universe, they heard some noise, *wondrous* noise. And the wondrous radiation coming from the heavens was provided with a name. And the name was *cosmic microwave background radiation* – it was the radiation that had been released as visible light during Recombination in the early Universe, some fifteen-billion years ago. Now the expansion of the Universe had red-shifted the recombination-light: With time, *the light* had stretched into the infrared. With more time, *it* had further stretched, so that now *it* was made of microwaves. And the temperature of the Universe was taken by taking the temperature of microwaves. And the temperature was three Kelvins – it was *very cold* – only three degrees above the coldest possible cold. And scientists counted the number of relic photons in the cosmic background radiation: There were four-hundred per cubic centimeter. Thus man, *for the first time*, heard the Universe *as it was* three-hundred-thousand years after the Big Bang, which marked the final moments of the Universe's first and only day.

## Chapter III: Man Ventures to Another Land

And in the year of 1969, a NASA spacecraft *left* planet Earth and sped through outer space. And the spacecraft approached and orbited Earth's Moon. And a module left the craft and *landed* on the Moon. And a hatch opened up, through which a man stepped out. Thus for the first time, *man* stepped *on* the Moon. And man looked up at Earth from the surface of the Moon and saw the Earth as *never* seen before. And Earth was beautiful, a seemingly tranquil sphere, a mix of blue and brown and white. And the colors swirled like in a modern painting – the Earth looked like a work of art. It was.[155]

## Chapter IV: Dark Matter

And in the late twentieth century, it came to pass that astronomers measured the speeds of stars in the Milky Way and other galaxies. And *surprisingly*, the speeds were faster than *expected* – apparently, the force pulling on the stars is *stronger* than the force of gravity generated by the mass of stars and gas. Now this discrepancy *can* be ex-

---

[155] Man would go to the Moon five more times. Then in 1972, twentieth-century moon missions would stop.

plained if non-luminous material is present in a galaxy – presumably, dark massive matter has collected in a galaxy. It is *as if* the galaxies are angels draped in unseen halos. Next, over a period of many years, astronomers observed the *motions* of the galaxies in clusters. And the motions of such galaxies were *not* as one expected – apparently, the gravity between the galaxies is *greater* than the gravity created by the galaxies themselves. And this can *also* be explained if even *more* unseen "dark matter" floats in outer space. And although astronomers knew not *what* it was, dark matter *had* been sensed – presumably, the Universe *is full of some unknown material*. Finally astrophysicists weighed the dark material using observation, the laws of physics, and gravity as weighing scales. And behold, it constitutes *nine-tenths* of cosmic mass – apparently, man is living in a World in which nine-tenths of its contents are not known to him. And this is a mystery – *the dark matter mystery*.[156]

## Chapter V: Superstring Speculation: Truth or Superstition?

And in the year of 1984, theorists showed through a "miracle of calculation" that superstrings were consistent mathematically.[157] Now *superstrings* were tiny Planck-sized filaments that had *enormous symmetry* – they had supersymmetry, which was boson–fermion-type symmetry, GUT-group symmetry and even *hidden* symmetries. And the theorists showed that the string's internal motions could potentially produce *all* the fundamental microscopic particles – the harmonic of a cord was such a particle. And strings produced gauge interactions by splitting, joining and combining. But most miraculous *was* that superstrings, naturally, among their interactions, yielded gravity[158] and that they were well-defined consistent quantum things. Thus one simple structure had the potential to explain *all* of Nature's laws. And some theorists were dazzled by the magic, miracles and beauty of the strings.

---

[156] Like a well-written mystery story, there are many possible suspects: If cosmic relic neutrinos have a small mass, they could be the missing mass. Another possibility is that dark matter is made of black holes. Still another speculation is that dark matter consists of some unknown particle.

The mystery will not be solved so easily. Scientists shall try by wit and by experiment to uncover the solution of this mystery which Nature has so well disguised. But sometime during the first century of the third millennium, the resolution *will* be known.

[157] Theorists often proceed using issues of consistency, simplicity, conciseness and esthetics, as well as symmetry principles, as guidance in constructing theories, particularly in domains where little experimental data is available. Unexpected results, which seem like magic to those performing the calculations, tend to make theorists believe that they are on a fruitful path.

[158] One of the greatest unsolved theoretical problems in physics is the quantization of gravity. Perhaps the biggest motivating factor for string theorists is that strings offer a potential solution to this problem.

And since the superstring could potentially explain all forces and all matter, string theorists nicknamed it "The Theory of Everything" – perhaps it is the Uni-Law.

But *obstacles* exist. First, superstring theory predicts that spacetime has ten dimensions instead of four! And, since time is one dimension, space should then have nine dimensions. Now the human world is three dimensions – what happens to the extra six? And theorists used *imagination*, suggesting, "Perhaps the extra six dimensions curl into a microscopic space, a space so small that *it's invisible*." And they argued by analogy: "When a two-dimensional flat piece of paper is rolled into a narrow straw, an ant crawling on it thinks its world is one-dimensional. Its world is like a wire. Perhaps humans, due to their bulky size, cannot sense the other six dimensions, for perhaps this hidden space simply is too small. *Perhaps a man is like an ant. Perhaps the Universe is like a straw.*"

*The story of the ant had been discovered.*

But it was *extremely difficult* for theorists to calculate in the theory of the superstring. And so theorists *could neither* prove nor disprove that the extra six dimensions did curl up to form a tiny space. Now another obstacle existed: Although the superstring *potentially* could generate the weak, strong and electromagnetic forces, theorists *could not prove* that these interactions were the only ones produced. And furthermore, although the superstring's internal motions yielded particles such as quarks, electrons, photons and neutrinos, theorists could not demonstrate that *all* these particles were there. Nor could they prove that *other particles* not seen in Nature but potentially present in the vibrations of the string *were not there*. And so superstrings became a subject of much speculation.

And theorists were *divided* in two groups: One, consisting of believers, *claimed* the superstring was Uni-Law. "The Theory of Everything" was what they thought to be the string. Now the other group was made of non-believers – they thought that strings were *nonsense*. For them, the Theory of Everything was a Theory of No Thing. And so there arose diverse opinions of the superstring.

*The superstring theory might or might not fail.*
*Its prophets wander in an unlit labyrinthine cave.*
*They grope in darkness and know not*
*whether there be a dead end or the Holy Grail.*

# Chapter VI: Supernova 1987A

*Thou shall never be a witness of the present,*
*for the speed of light is finite.*
*What thy eyes see is in the past.*

It was one-hundred-and-sixty-thousand years ago. And it came to pass that a star collapsed in the Large Magellanic Cloud.[159] And at the speed of light, neutrinos *streamed* out of the dying star. An hour later, a shock wave blew apart the star. And electromagnetic radiation flashed outward, also at the speed of light.

.    .    .    .    .    .

It was 7:36 a.m. universal time, February 23, 1987. A neutrino detector in a lead mine in Japan and a neutrino detector in a salt mine near Cleveland, Ohio, simultaneously began to spark – a neutrino burst was *passing through* the Earth.[160] And the blast lasted just a dozen seconds. A few hours later, an amateur astronomer in New Zealand saw a star in the black night sky *where* no star had been before – it was a supernova, *a gift from heaven*. And it was named SN1987A, for it was the first supernova to be seen by man that year.

And it came to pass that, each night, its *light* grew brighter in the sky, making it the brightest supernova in three-hundred-and-eighty-three years to be seen from Earth. And during the second millennium AD, it would *only* be the sixth such supernova visible to the unaided human eye.[161]

And for astronomers, SN1987A was a godsend – the opportunity of a lifetime. And around the world, astronomers *observed in awe* the supernova.[162]

And astronomers measured the distance to the supernova. And the distance was one-hundred-and-sixty-thousand light years – the object was the star in the Large Magellanic Cloud that had exploded one-hundred-and-sixty-thousand years ago. And it had taken that much time for the light and the neutrinos to travel from the Large Magellanic Cloud to Earth. Thus astronomers were looking *that much time* into the past.

---

[159] The Large Magellanic Cloud is an irregularly shaped galaxy near the Milky Way.

[160] Neutrinos are particles that are so weakly interacting that almost all of them pass through matter without any deflection.

[161] The first of these naked-eye supernovas was in 1006 AD and glowed half as brightly as the moon. In 1054 AD, a supernova left behind a giant cloud of exploding gas. That cloud became the Crab Nebula, and the supernova was thus named the Crab Nebula Supernova. The light from the third supernova arrived at Earth in 1101 AD. The fourth naked eye supernova was observed by Tycho Brahe in 1572, and it was called the Tycho Supernova. The fifth was called the Kepler Supernova after Johannes Kepler, who studied it in 1604.

[162] Astronomers aimed Earth-based optical and radio telescopes as well as X-ray, gamma ray, ultraviolet and infrared detectors in satellites at SN1987A. The astronomical observations produced a wealth of scientific information.

## Chapter VII: Nature's Ancient Relics

*And when they saw this faded light,*
*which was no longer light but microwaves,*
*they saw the face of the Universe*
*as it once was.*

And in November 1989, it came to pass that a satellite was launched. And inside the satellite was an instrument called *COBE*, the *COsmic Background Explorer*. Now COBE had the ability to sensitively measure microwaves. And during several years, COBE did detect the *relic photons* of the past.[163] And the microwave cosmic background radiation was *in glory detail* measured – it was *like* placing a thermometer *in* the "Universe's mouth." And when the thermometer was removed and read, it read in Kelvins 2.73 degrees – the Universe was like a *frigid* "microwave refrigerator." Now the temperature was *not* the same in all directions: There were tiny variations – *like unto* light and dark patches of an ancient faded charcoal sketch. And these variations *drew a picture* of the Universe as it had been *three-hundred-thousand years in age*. *The face of Nature* in its youth was seen.

Now the cosmic microwave background radiation is just one ancient fossil, for the Universe is *full* of relics of the past. From them, one constructs the story of the past.

*The grin of the Cheshire cat.*
*The shroud of Turin.*
*The trilobite fossil.*
*The relic photon.*

Now lithium-seven, much of deuterium, helium-three and helium-four were *forged* inside the Big Bang oven. And these elements survived fifteen-billion years of time and so remain *unto this day* – they tell a tale *of cosmic times*. In modern times, astronomers did measure the light-element abundances. And through them did they gain a picture of the Universe when it was *minutes old*.

Now some remnants of the past are *very* faint and feeble. And for example, the cosmic relic neutrinos, released when the Universe was *just a second old*, fill the spaces of the wilderness of outer space but interact *too weakly* to be sensed by modern man. And cosmic relic gravitons, which were produced when the Universe *was just a few Planck times old*, fill the spaces of the wilderness of outer space but interact *too weakly* to be felt by modern man. And so several hundred relic neutrinos and a dozen relic gravitons in *every* cubic centimeter of the Universe do form an unseen gas of particles that *permeates all space*. Verily, ghosts of the ancient past are they – *passing through everything* including the Earth, the Sun and Moon. They travel *through* the bodies of the living, such as man. But neither Earth, Sun, Moon nor man feel

---

[163] These are the same radiations discussed in Chapter II.

their presence, *for they touch not*. Alas, everywhere they're there, the invisible non-interacting relics of the past.

## Chapter VIII: The Mystery of Fundamental Mass

N ow the Standard Model, which explains all the microscopic forces between particles, consists of *several* parts. And *all* the parts have been experimentally tested and confirmed *but one*. And *that* part is the *Higgs sector*, the part which makes all mass. It provides the masses for the W and Z by breaking SU-two-cross-U-one to U-one.[164] Thus electroweak breaking is implemented via the Higgs part. And when the symmetry is broken, the quarks and leptons get mass too.

Now up to the year of 1997, experiments had not revealed this sector, leaving physicists to ponder on it nature: Some theorists thought perhaps it was a particle which created all the mass – if so, this particle was *to* be called the *Higgs*. Some surmised that certain interactions were the source of mass. Still others conjectured that the top quark managed to induce mass *both* for itself and for its brethren quarks. And a few physicists did even think that, perhaps, the mechanism of mass generation was beyond man's twentieth-century imagination – small can be the mind of man.

Now the problem of fundamental mass was *the last mystery* in the Standard Model of particle physics. And curiosity drove theorists to think and to create.

So man will go to build machines to find the answer. And someday will man know the mechanism that makes all mass. And on that day, man will understand at last.

*The fourteenth and last book of Chronicles, called*

# Now

*The moment – it is here and gone.*

T his is the book of Now. And Now *lasts* for a short time. That time is fifteen minutes, the lifetime of a neutron when it's outside a nucleus. *Fifteen minutes* of geo-time is like *two-thousand years* of real time, the time of two millenniums, the time from zero years AD to now.

---

[164] This symmetry breaking process occurred in the early Universe. See the seventh book of Creation, called *Exodus I*.

*The new testament book of*

# Psalms[165]

*These seven stars are the angels*
*of the seven churches.*

The time it takes to pray is half-a-minute. Half-a-minute of geological time is almost a lifetime. To pray, we only have our lifetime.

## Psalm I: The Lord Is My Shepherd

*The Lord is my shepherd.*
*I shall not want.*
*He maketh me to lie down in green pastures.*
*He leadeth me to still waters.*
*He restoreth my soul.*
*He showeth me the paths of righteousness*
*for His name's sake.*
*Though I walk through the valley of the shadow of death,*
*I will fear no evil*
*for Thou art with me.*
*Thy rod and Thy staff – they comfort me.*
*Thou preparest a table before me*
*in the presence of my enemies.*
*Thou anointest my head with oil.*
*My cup runneth over.*
*Goodness and mercy shall follow me*
*all the days of my life.*
*And I will dwell in Thy house*
*forever and ever.*
*Amen.*

*– The Holy Bible*

---

[165] As there be seven days, so *be* there seven psalms.

## Psalm II: The Earth Is Thy Keeper

*The Earth is thy keeper,*
*thy fortress and thy shield;*
*a shield of shining metal*
*and a fortress made of stone.*

*The Earth is thy safe haven,*
*thy refuge and salvation,*
*with a land of earth and seas below*
*and a sky of heaven and of stars above.*

*Build ye thy house on a strong rock*
*and next to it construct a tower,*
*a tower with a winding staircase*
*and a gaping window to the heavens.*
*Amen.*

## Psalm III: A Prayer of Thanks

*The wind is thy breath.*
*Thy lungs breathe.*
*The streams are thy drink.*
*Ye thirst not.*
*The lamb is thy meat.*
*Ye hunger not.*
*The stars are thy candles,*
*for they light the darkness.*
*Each day pray ye in verse*
*and thank the Great Creator,*
*the one who made the Universe.*
*Amen.*

## Psalm IV: A Time For Everything
### (adaptation from the Holy Bible)

*To every thing there be a season.*
*For every purpose under Heaven there be a time.*
*A time to be born*
*and a time to die,*
*a time to dance*
*and a time to mourn,*
*a time to throw a stone away*
*and a time to take stones in,*
*a time to pray*
*and a time to sin,*
*a time to cast it out*
*and a time to reel it in,*
*a time to throw away*
*and a time to keep,*
*a time to fight*
*and a time to play,*
*a time to hide one's face and weep*
*and a time to put the tears aside and laugh,*
*a time to wake*
*and a time to sleep,*
*a time for tenderness and love*
*and a time for anger and for hate,*
*a time for less*
*and a time for more,*
*a time to rend*
*and a time to sew,*
*a time to raise the knife and kill*
*and a time to shake one's hand and mend,*
*a time for war*
*and a time for peace,*
*a time for birth*
*and a time for death.*
*Amen*

And all come from one place. And *that place* is earth. Thus all are of the dust. And all shall go to one place. And *that place* is earth. Thus all shall be of dust again.

## Psalm V: What Be a Man

*What be a man who hath no knowledge?*
*He wandereth in the desert and knoweth not the way.*
*The Sun, a melting egg, beats down upon his head.*
*So hot is it at day; so cold be it at night –*
*thus* night *be dreaded; so* day *be dreaded too.*
*The land seems like a can-of-worms of paths.*
*He knoweth of no sound in such a desert –*
*just the droning of a wind.*
*And there* be *not even rocks,*
*for everywhere is sand.*
*He seeth all around saguaro cacti,*
*and thinketh he they be dead souls of men –*
*they are the hollow men, dead-pieces filled with stalks.*
*He crawleth in the sands and not knoweth why.*
*How dry the desert be;*
*parched throat, his hopeless thirst for rain.*
*What be a man who hath no knowledge?*
*A man whose every footstep be in vain.*

*The deep heat does blur his mind.*
*The bright light does blur his eyes.*
*And even during day there seems to him*
*to be the* darkness *of the night.*
*And shouldeth he speak out,*
*there be* no *one there to hear his cries.*
*Which way to go?*
*He headeth to the north; he headeth to the south.*
*And the west brings no peace; neither does the east.*
*And still he walketh there about.*
*And there seems to him no trodden path.*
*How lost he be! His mind has lost its wit.*
*Even the lizards seem to laugh –*
*their narrow tongues slip in and out.*
*Their jaws separate a bit – the teeth reflect no light.*
*No other motions seeth he, save a few ants crawling in the grains.*
*And then the dry wind folds the sand and* buries *all the small.*
*A land of sorrows. Pour soul, lost soul.*
*And to the heavens doth he raise his arms*
*and frozen standeth he like one of the saguaros.*

## Psalm VI: Give Thanks Unto Nature

*Give thanks unto Nature.*
*Make known her laws among all men.*
*Let the heart of them rejoice that see her truths.*
*Speak of Nature's wondrous works,*
*for great is her design.*
*And she is to be feared above all gods,*
*for the gods of people are just idols,*
*but Nature made the heavens.*
*She has given thee, who are the living,*
*the earth of Earth, the lot of thy inheritance.*
*The seeds of life, Earth's living creatures,*
*be they her children, the chosen ones.*
*Let be glad the heavens, let rejoice the Earth,*
*and let thy voice so sayeth, 'Nature reigneth.'*
*Let the sea roar; let the stalks of wheat bendeth beneath a wind.*
*Be ye mindful of her commandments,*
*which be unchanging and diverse.*
*Blessèd be her hand.*
*And of her marvellous works, be they remembered.*
*Her temple be the Universe.*
*Amen.*

## Psalm VII: The Lord's Prayer

*Our Father,*
*Who art in Heaven,*
*hallowed be Thy name.*
*Thy kingdom come.*
*Thy will be done*
*on Earth as it is in Heaven.*
*Give us this day our daily bread.*
*And forgive us our debts,*
*as we forgive those who trespass against us.*
*And lead us not into temptation,*
*but deliver us from evil.*
*For Thine is the kingdom,*
*and the power,*
*and the glory,*
*For ever and ever.*
*Amen.*

*– The Holy Bible*

*The new testament book of*

# The Ten Commandments of Science

*Ye shall keep my commandments.*

I. Thou *shalt* believe in one and only one law of Nature, the Uni-Law. Thou *shalt* follow its principles even in their broken state.

II. Thou *shalt* obey the force of gravity, for thou shalt move along the geodesics *in the natural geometry of spacetime.* Curved motion along geodesics shall constitute the force of gravity.

III. Thou *shalt* obey the force of electromagnetism. If thou art a charge, thou shalt be repelled by the charges of thyself and thou shalt be attracted to charges that are opposite of thyself. Magnetism shall be a consequence of the electric force and the motion of charges.

IV. Thou *shalt not* kill electric charge. Thus thou shalt neither destroy nor create electric charge.

V. Thou *shalt* obey the weak and strong forces, which govern the world of the nucleus and the subnuclear.

VI. Thou *shalt not* steal energy, momentum, or angular momentum. Thus thou shalt conserve these quantities. Energy *shall neither be created nor destroyed* but only changed from one form to another. Momentum in each of the three spatial directions *shall neither be created nor destroyed* but simply transformed among thee, thy brethren and thy neighbors. Angular momentum, which is the rotation of bodies and the spin of subatomic particles, *shall neither be created nor destroyed* but only be passed among thee, thy brethren and thy neighbors.

VII. Thou *shalt not* travel faster than the speed of light. The speed of light shall be the same whether thou art moving or thou art still.

VIII. Thou *shalt* be permitted to change mass into energy and energy into mass. Thus thou shalt treat mass as energy and energy as mass. Mass shall be converted into energy as the power of the speed of light squared.[166]

IX. Thou *shalt* obey the principles of quantum mechanics. Thou shalt not know whether microscopic states be particles or waves, for microscopic states shall sometimes be like particles and sometimes be like waves. Such states shall be determined by the *quantum wave equation.* Thou shalt not know with infinite precision the locations and momenta of objects. Thus thou shalt proceed *by uncertainty* and probability.

X. If thou art of half-integer spin then thou shalt be a fermion and obey the Pauli exclusion principle and thou *shalt not* occupy thy brother's state. And if thou art of integral spin then thou shalt be a boson and thou *shalt* be in perfect symmetry with thy brethren.

---

[166] In SI units, the speed of light squared is almost one-hundred-million-billion.

*The knowledge
of these ten commandments
shall be of intellectual and scientific wealth.
The Golden Rule of Science
shall be obedience
of the Uni-Law,
which shall encompass
the ten commandments
and itself.*

*The new testament book of*

# Numbers

*And a being stood up and provoked man
to count the numbers.*

## Chapter I: Basic Numbers

The principles of physics shall be made *precise* by using numbers. This is the book of numbers. Let us pray and count the numbers. Zero shall be *nothing* – it shall be emptiness. One shall be unity – it shall be *whole*. Thus zero and one shall be the Yin and Yang of numbers.

And let it be known *that* one plus one be two. Thus two shall be one more than one. And *that* two plus one be three. Thus three shall be one more than two. And *that* three plus one be four. Thus four shall be one more than three. And *that* four plus one be five. Thus five shall be one more than four. And *that* five plus one be six. Thus six shall be one more than five. And *that* six plus one be seven. Thus seven shall be one more than six. And *that* seven plus one be eight. Thus eight shall be one more than seven. And *that* eight plus one be nine. Thus nine shall be one more than eight. And *that* nine plus one be ten. Thus ten shall be one more than nine. And so on. And these numbers shall be *whole numbers*.

Now ten shall be the number of fingers on a human hand. And because primitive man began to count with hands, modern man shall think in terms of ten.

And two, three, five, seven, et cetera, shall be *sacred* numbers – each shall *only* be divisible by itself and one. These numbers shall be *prime*.

And ten times ten shall be a hundred. And a hundred shall be a big number. And ten times one hundred shall be a thousand. And a thousand shall be a large number. And a thousand times a thousand shall be a million. And a million shall be a very large number. And a thousand times a million shall be a *billion*. Thus a billion shall be a thousand-million. And a billion shall be *an* enormous number. And a thousand times a billion shall be a *trillion*. Thus a trillion shall also be a million-million, that is, a million times a million. And a trillion shall be a large enormous number. And the numbers of the Universe shall sometimes be enormously enormous. For example, a trillion-trillion shall be a trillion times a trillion. Thus a trillion-trillion shall be the same as a million-million-million-million, that is, a million times a million times a million times a million. Thus a trillion-trillion shall also be the same as a million-billion-billion, that is, a million times a billion times a billion. And to describe the Universe, even larger numbers sometimes shall be needed.

## Chapter II: Rational Numbers

And some numbers shall *not be whole*. And for example, *a half* is part of one. And two halves shall make a whole or one. And a tenth shall be one-tenth of one. Thus ten times one-tenth shall be one. And a hundredth shall be one-tenth of one-tenth. Thus ten times ten times a hundredth shall be one. Thus one-hundred times one-hundredth shall be one. And one-hundredth shall be a small number. And one-tenth of one-hundredth shall be one-thousandth. Thus one-thousand times one-thousandth shall be one. And one-thousandth shall *be* a tiny number. And a thousandth of a thousandth shall be a millionth. And a millionth shall be a miniscule number. And a thousandth of a millionth shall be a *billionth*. And a billionth shall be a tiny miniscule number. And a thousandth of a billionth shall be a *trillionth*. And a trillionth shall be an extremely tiny number. And the numbers of the Universe shall sometimes be extremely extremely tiny. For example, a trillionth of a trillionth shall be one-trillionth times one-trillionth. Thus a trillion-trillion times a trillionth of a trillionth shall be one. Thus a trillionth of a trillionth shall be the same as a millionth of a millionth of a millionth of a millionth. And so on. And to describe the Universe, even smaller numbers sometimes shall be needed.

And among those numbers, which are not whole, there shall be fractions. *Fractions* shall be parts. For each fraction, shall there be a whole number that makes the fraction whole – the fraction times this whole number *shall be whole*.

## Chapter III: Irrational Numbers

And those numbers that are not whole and are not fractions shall be *irrational*. And the square-root-of-two shall be an example – the square-root-of-two times the square-root-of-two shall be two. And the *golden ratio* shall also be irrational. It shall be one-half plus one-half times the square-root-of-five.[167] And a rectangle whose width to height

---

[167] $\dfrac{1}{2} + \dfrac{1}{2}\sqrt{5}$

is the golden ratio shall be esthetically pleasing to the eye. And irrational numbers shall be named as such because they are hard for man to understand.

And among the irrational numbers shall be special sacred numbers called *transcendental numbers*. And three of these shall be of special value – gamma, pi, and e. And *pi* shall be the ratio of the circumference of a circle to its diameter. And *e* shall be the natural exponent. And *gamma* shall be Euler's constant. And let it be known to thee and all around thee that these numbers can be written as pi= 3.141592653589793238..., e=2.718281828459045235... and gamma = 0.577215664901532861..., and these expansions never terminate. And *transcendental numbers* multiplied by themselves and added in combinations can never be made whole. Thus the square-root-of-two is not transcendental since by multiplying it by itself it *is* made whole.

Now *only* a few transcendental numbers, such as pi, which can be computed from a circle, can be *easily* understood by man. Thus most transcendental numbers are verily incomprehensible. And what is worse for man is that *most* numbers shall be transcendental.

Let us achieve a state of certain transcendental meditation. Let us repeat, pray, and engage in mathematical contemplation, knowing that most numbers shall be transcendental and be beyond the means of explanation.

*The new testament book of*

# Basic Units[168]

*Let us quantify the Universe.*

## Chapter I: Mass

Now man shall measure mass. And to have the means to measure mass, man shall have some units. A *kilogram*, which is the weight of water in a liter bottle, shall be a little more than two pounds. Since two thousand pounds shall be a *ton*, a ton shall be about nine-hundred kilograms. Seventy kilograms shall roughly be what weighs a man. Now a *gram* shall be one-thousandth of a kilogram. Thus a thousand grams shall be a kilogram. A paper clip shall roughly weigh a gram. The mass of the Sun shall be a *solar mass* – two-million-trillion-trillion kilograms.

## Chapter II: Temperature

Now man shall quantify the hot and cold. And to have the means to measure hot and cold, man shall have some systems, such as Kelvin, Celsius and Fahrenheit.

In *Celsius*, the freezing point of water shall be zero, while the boiling point shall be one-hundred. Twenty-one degrees shall be a typical room temperature. Thirty-seven Celsius shall the body of a human being be. The temperature of a hot kitchen oven shall be around two-hundred.

Now degrees in Fahrenheit shall be less useful, for water shall freeze at thirty-two and boil at two-hundred-twelve. Fahrenheit shall be archaic for purposes of physics.

Temperature in *Kelvins* shall be two-hundred-and-seventy-three more than the temperature in Celsius. Thus in Kelvins, at two-hundred-and-seventy-three degrees shall water freeze; at three-hundred-and-seventy-three shall water boil. Two-hundred-and-ninety-four Kelvins shall be a typical room temperature, while the body of a human shall be three-hundred-ten. A little less than five-hundred shall be *a hot kitchen oven*.

And let it be known to thee and all around thee that there is a lowest temperature – a coldest coldness. *No* object shall be colder; *no* temperature *shall* be lower. And this lowest temperature shall have a name. And *absolute zero* shall be its name. Thus absolute zero shall be the coldest that can be.

Absolute zero in Kelvins shall be zero. It shall be minus two-hundred-and-seventy-three degrees in Celsius.

---

[168] This book presents the definitions of physics units of measurement, such as kilograms, meters, joules, coulombs, Celsius, et cetera. It is included for completeness and for those readers who are unfamiliar with these terms.

Now temperature in Kelvins shall be most useful from a physics point of view, for temperature in Kelvins shall be *proportional to energy*. Thus it shall make sense to say that A is twice as hot as B if the temperatures of A and B *be* Kelvins, for this shall mean that A has twice the thermal energy of B. And temperature in Kelvins shall be particularly convenient in that absolute zero shall indeed be zero. At *zero Kelvins* shall a body have *no energy*.

## Chapter III: Space

Now man shall measure space. And to have the means to measure space, man shall have some units. A *fermi* shall be a femtometer, one millionth of a billionth of a meter, the size of nuclei. One-hundred-thousand fermis shall constitute an *Angstrom*, the size of a small atom. Ten Angstroms shall be a *nanometer*, a small molecule's diameter. One-thousand nanometers shall be a *micron*, which shall also be a *micrometer*, a typical cell's diameter. One-thousand micrometers shall be a *millimeter*, a toothpick's width. Ten millimeters shall be a *centimeter*, a thumbnail's width. A centipede shall be five centimeters long. Two-and-a-half centimeters shall be an *inch*. One-hundred centimeters shall constitute a *meter*, which shall be slightly longer than a yard. The length of a human foot shall be a *foot*, and three feet shall make a *yard*. A *kilometer*, which by definition is a thousand meters, shall be somewhat more than half a mile: 1.6 kilometers shall be a *mile*. An *astronomical unit* shall be one-hundred-and-fifty-million kilometers, the distance from the Sun to Earth. To man, an astronomical unit shall seem colossal; in the context of the Universe, it *shall* be minuscule – one-millionth of one-billionth of the width of the visible region of the Universe. A light year shall be an even longer unit. Now know that a light year is not an interval of time. Know that a light year is an interval of space. A *light year* shall be the distance that light travels in a year – almost ten-thousand-billion kilometers or ten-million-billion meters.

Square units shall be used to measure area. A square centimeter shall be the area of a square that is a centimeter by a centimeter. A square meter shall be the area of a square that is a meter by a meter. Thus ten-thousand square centimeters shall be the same as one square meter.

Cubic units shall be used to measure space or volume. A *cubic centimeter* shall be the volume of a cube that is one centimeter by one centimeter by one centimeter. A thousand cubic centimeters shall constitute a *liter*. A liter of liquid shall be about a *quart*. A *cubic meter* shall be the volume of a cube that is one meter by one meter by one meter. Thus a thousand liters shall be a cubic meter, while there shall be a million cubic centimeters in a cubic meter.

## Chapter IV: Time

Now man shall measure time. And to have the means to measure time, man shall have some units. A *Planck time* shall be ten-to-the-minus-forty-three seconds,[169] which is one-tenth of a millionth of a trillionth of a trillionth of a trillionth of a second. Thus ten-million-trillion-trillion-trillion Planck times shall pass each second. The Planck time shall be the smallest possible interval of time. And man shall be unable to deal with such tiny intervals of time; *quantum fluctuations* shall render times smaller than Planck units *meaningless.*

A *microsecond* shall be one-millionth of a second. Thus a million microseconds shall pass each second. A *millisecond* shall be a thousand microseconds or one-thousandth of a second. Thus a thousand milliseconds shall pass each second. A *second* shall be a second, the time between two typical heart beats. Sixty seconds shall constitute a *minute*, and sixty minutes shall constitute an *hour*. Thus an hour shall be three-thousand-and-six-hundred seconds. Thus there shall be more than three-and-one-half thousand heart beats in an hour. Twenty-four hours shall constitute a *day*. Each day, the Sun shall rise but once. Each day, the Sun shall set but once. Three-hundred-and-sixty-five days shall be a *year*. Each year, the Earth shall go but once around the Sun. There shall be roughly pi times ten-million seconds in a year. Thus, each year a heart shall beat more than thirty-million times.

And man shall live to seventy or so. Thus two-billion beats shall constitute a life or so. Yet how *short* a man's time *be*.

## Chapter V: Time Means Death

*Thus one should know that*
*one's heart beats are not forever.*
*Thus one should know that one will die.*
*One will sense this when one 's old.*
*So one should know it when one 's young,*
*for the heart shall beat whether one be young or old.*

And know in *Nature's world* that eternal life is a misguided lie. And one should not despair – there is the *Word*. And if you hear the Word, then cry. And if you cry, cry out. And if you cry out, then shout. And if you do shout perhaps you *will be heard*. Know that you will die, for nothing can survive. In the end will be *the Word*.

And death destroys – the self-organizing system is abolished and becomes chaotic. And if one is lucky, the molecules are scattered and become the sustenance of future generations.

Time and decay *guarantee* the death of all.

Thus the Earth is not forever. Thus the Sun is not forever. Thus the Milky Way is not forever.

---

[169] 1/(10,000,000,000,000,000,000,000,000,000,000,000,000,000,000)

If Earth were a human being, the age of Earth would be the age of man and four-and-a-half-billion years of real time would correspond to seventy years of geo-time. And a second of *geo-time* would be two years of real time. Thus the geological time scale is much longer than the temporal human scale. In terms of geo-time, a man lives for half-a-minute.

And perhaps even the Universe is not forever – as for the fate of the Universe, it is known *not*. But know that the human race and every form of life eventually will die. And for now, this very moment, ye have life and ye have Earth. Here on Earth can ye ignore *the destiny of galaxies*. Ye make the Earth thy little universe.

*A leaf floating in an ocean.*

## Chapter VI: Derived Units

Now the *fundamental* concepts shall be mass, length, time, temperature and charge. All other quantities shall be *derived* from these. And an example shall be *speed*: It shall be the distance travelled per unit time. Thus a man who runs fifty meters in five seconds shall have a speed of ten meters per second. A mile per hour shall be a little less than half-a-meter per second. Hence speed units shall be length units divided by time units. Hence speed shall be derivable from length and time.

And density shall be another example. *Density* shall be the mass per unit volume. The *density of water* shall be a gram per cubic centimeter, meaning that a cubic centimeter of water weighs a gram. A unit of density shall be a mass unit divided by a volume unit. And since volume is expressible in terms of lengths, density shall be derivable from mass and length.

## Chapter VII: Energy, Power, Force and Pressure

Now the unit of energy shall be the joule. A *joule* shall be the energy of motion of two kilograms travelling at a meter in a second. A joule unit shall be a kilogram times a meter-squared divided by a second-squared. When a book weighing a kilogram is lifted ten centimeters off a table and is dropped, it shall yield one joule of energy *when* it strikes the surface. An *erg* shall be one tenth of one millionth of a joule, so that ten-million ergs shall constitute a joule. A *calorie* shall be about four joules. A *food calorie* shall be a thousand calories, or about four-thousand joules. To burn a thousand calories of food, one shall need to do four-million joules of exercise.

Now power[170] units shall be watts. A *watt* shall be one joule of energy generated in a second. A *kilowatt* shall be a thousand watts. Now know that a *kilowatt-hour* is not a power unit, *nor* is it a time. It

---

[170] *Power* is the energy released or consumed per unit time.

shall be an energy, the energy outputted in an hour from a power source one-kilowatt in strength. Thus a kilowatt-hour shall be sixty seconds (to the minute) times sixty minutes (to the hour), or three-thousand-six-hundred kilowatts-seconds, which is three-million-six-hundred-thousand joules.

Now force shall be in newtons. A *newton* shall be the weight felt by a hand, here on Earth, holding up an object of a hundred-grams. Thus a one-kilogram book shall exert ten newtons. A newton unit shall be a kilogram times a meter divided by a second-squared. Thus a joule shall also be a newton times a meter.

Now *pressure* shall be the force per unit area. Pressure units shall be pascals, where a *pascal* shall be a newton divided by a meter-squared. One-hundred-thousand pascals shall be an *atmosphere*. The pressure of Earth's atmosphere shall be an *atmosphere* of pressure.

## Chapter VIII: Charge and Current

Now one elementary charge *shall* a proton have. That charge shall be the *fundamental unit charge*. An electron shall also have this fundamental unit, but negative shall be its charge. A *coulomb* then shall be six-billion-billion fundamental charges, an enormously large large quantity of charge.

*(And a voice spake, saying*
*"Where there be a coulomb charge,*
*do not touch that charge.")*

Now electric current, which is the flow of electric charge, shall be in amps or amperes – one *amp* shall be the movement of a coulomb's worth of charge per second past a point. Hence an amp unit shall be a coulomb divided by a second. Now electric charge shall flow because it shall be driven so. *Voltage* shall be the impetus, and volts shall be used to measure voltage. The unit of a *volt* shall be a watt divided by an amp. A coulomb's worth of charge driven by a volt of voltage shall gain a joule of energy. Now a current shall *not effortlessly* flow, for retarding forces shall try to slow it down. This resistance to the flow of charge shall be in *ohms*. The unit of an ohm shall be a volt divided by an amp. In a one-ohm-resistant wire, a one volt battery shall make one amp of current flow. And if the resistance in a wire is doubled, then the current shall be halved – this is Ohm's law. Thus with a one volt battery, half-an-amp will flow in a two-ohm-resistant wire. And if the voltage in the wire is doubled, then the current shall be doubled – this also is Ohm's law, for *Ohm's law* says that the current which shall flow shall be the voltage divided by resistance. So in a one-ohm-resistant wire, a two volt battery shall make two amps of current flow.

## Chapter IX: Energy Measured Electrically

Now an electron driven by a volt of voltage shall gain an energy much smaller than a joule – one-sixth of a billionth of a billionth of a joule, and this shall be an *eV*, or *electron volt*.[171] Thus an electron volt shall represent neither a voltage nor a particle – *it* shall be an energy. A few electron volts shall be the energy of a typical electron in an atom. A *keV*, or kiloelectron-volt, shall be a thousand eV units. An *MeV*, or megaelectron-volt, shall be a million eV units. A few MeV's and hundreds of keV's shall be typical nuclear binding energies.[172] A *GeV*, or gigaelectron-volt, shall be a billion eV units. A GeV shall be the energy in a proton if its mass were completely changed to energy. A *TeV*, or teraelectron-volt, shall be a trillion eV units. A TeV shall be the energy that scientists in the late twentieth century can give a proton in a tevatron. A *tevatron* shall be a machine that accelerates a proton to a TeV of energy.

---

[171] The word eV is pronounced "ee vee." The other units in this paragraph are pronounced "kay ee vee," "em ee vee," "gee ee vee" and "tee ee vee."

[172] Such energies are released when a nucleus fissions or when nuclei fuse. Excitation energies of nuclei are hundreds of keV's.

*The new testament book of*

# Tables

*And I will give thee tables of stone.*

*Table of the Fundamental Matter*

|  | Up-Type Quarks | Down-Type Quarks | Charged Leptons | Neutrinos |
|---|---|---|---|---|
| 1st Family: | u | d | e | nu-e |
| 2nd Family: | c | s | mu | nu-mu |
| 3rd Family: | t | b | tau | nu-tau |
| Electric Charge: | $+\frac{2}{3}$ | $-\frac{1}{3}$ | -1 | 0 |

*Table of Vector Gauge Bosons*

| Interaction | Vector Gauge Bosons | Gauge Group |
|---|---|---|
| electromagnetism | photon | U-one |
| weak nuclear force | W-plus, W-minus, Z | broken SU-two |
| strong nuclear force | gluons | SU-three |

**The Periodic Table of Elements**

Legend:
- symbol → C
- atomic mass of an isotope → 12
- atomic number → 6
- valence electrons → $2s^2 2p^2$

| 1 | 2 | 3 | 4 | 5 | 6 | 7 | 8 | 9 | 10 | 11 | 12 | 13 | 14 | 15 | 16 | 17 | 18 |
|---|---|---|---|---|---|---|---|---|----|----|----|----|----|----|----|----|----|
| H 1<br>1<br>$1s^1$ | | | | | | | | | | | | | | | | | He 2<br>4 |
| Li 3<br>7<br>$2s^1$ | Be 4<br>9<br>$2s^2$ | | | | | | | | | | | B 5<br>11<br>$2s^2 2p^1$ | C 6<br>12<br>$2s^2 2p^2$ | N 7<br>14<br>$2s^2 2p^3$ | O 8<br>16<br>$2s^2 2p^4$ | F 9<br>19<br>$2s^2 2p^5$ | Ne 10<br>20 |
| Na 11<br>23<br>$3s^1$ | Mg 12<br>24<br>$3s^2$ | | | | | | | | | | | Al 13<br>27<br>$3s^2 3p^1$ | Si 14<br>28<br>$3s^2 3p^2$ | P 15<br>31<br>$3s^2 3p^3$ | S 16<br>32<br>$3s^2 3p^4$ | Cl 17<br>35<br>$3s^2 3p^5$ | Ar 18<br>40 |
| K 19<br>39<br>$4s^1$ | Ca 20<br>40<br>$4s^2$ | Sc 21<br>45<br>$3d^1 4s^2$ | Ti 22<br>48<br>$3d^2 4s^2$ | V 23<br>51<br>$3d^3 4s^2$ | Cr 24<br>52<br>$3d^5 4s^1$ | Mn 25<br>55<br>$3d^5 4s^2$ | Fe 26<br>56<br>$3d^6 4s^2$ | Co 27<br>59<br>$3d^7 4s^2$ | Ni 28<br>58<br>$3d^8 4s^2$ | Cu 29<br>63<br>$3d^{10} 4s^1$ | Zn 30<br>64<br>$3d^{10} 4s^2$ | Ga 31<br>69<br>$4s^2 4p^1$ | Ge 32<br>74<br>$4s^2 4p^2$ | As 33<br>75<br>$4s^2 4p^3$ | Se 34<br>80<br>$4s^2 4p^4$ | Br 35<br>79<br>$4s^2 4p^5$ | Kr 36<br>84 |
| Rb 37<br>85<br>$5s^1$ | Sr 38<br>88<br>$5s^2$ | Y 39<br>89<br>$4d^1 5s^2$ | Zr 40<br>90<br>$4d^2 5s^2$ | Nb 41<br>93<br>$4d^4 5s^1$ | Mo 42<br>98<br>$4d^5 5s^1$ | Tc 43<br>98<br>$4d^5 5s^2$ | Ru 44<br>102<br>$4d^7 5s^1$ | Rh 45<br>103<br>$4d^8 5s^1$ | Pd 46<br>106<br>$4d^{10}$ | Ag 47<br>107<br>$4d^{10} 5s^1$ | Cd 48<br>114<br>$4d^{10} 5s^2$ | In 49<br>115<br>$5s^2 5p^1$ | Sn 50<br>120<br>$5s^2 5p^2$ | Sb 51<br>121<br>$5s^2 5p^3$ | Te 52<br>130<br>$5s^2 5p^4$ | I 53<br>127<br>$5s^2 5p^5$ | Xe 54<br>132 |
| Cs 55<br>133<br>$6s^1$ | Ba 56<br>138<br>$6s^2$ | La 57<br>139<br>$5d^1 6s^2$ (58-71) | Hf 72<br>180<br>$5d^2 6s^2$ | Ta 73<br>181<br>$5d^3 6s^2$ | W 74<br>184<br>$5d^4 6s^2$ | Re 75<br>187<br>$5d^5 6s^2$ | Os 76<br>192<br>$5d^6 6s^2$ | Ir 77<br>193<br>$5d^7 6s^2$ | Pt 78<br>195<br>$5d^9 6s^1$ | Au 79<br>197<br>$5d^{10} 6s^1$ | Hg 80<br>202<br>$5d^{10} 6s^2$ | Tl 81<br>205<br>$6s^2 6p^1$ | Pb 82<br>208<br>$6s^2 6p^2$ | Bi 83<br>209<br>$6s^2 6p^3$ | Po 84<br>210<br>$6s^2 6p^4$ | At 85<br>218<br>$6s^2 6p^5$ | Rn 86<br>222 |
| Fr 87<br>223<br>$7s^1$ | Ra 88<br>226<br>$7s^2$ | Ac 89<br>227<br>$6d^1 7s^2$ (90-103) | Rf 104<br>261<br>$6d^2 7s^2$ | Db 105<br>262<br>$6d^3 7s^2$ | Sg 106<br>266<br>$6d^4 7s^2$ | Bh 107<br>262<br>$6d^5 7s^2$ | Hs 108<br>265<br>$6d^6 7s^2$ | Mt 109<br>266<br>$6d^7 7s^2$ | | | | | | | | | |

Lanthanides (58-71):

| Ce 58<br>140<br>$4f^1 5d^1 6s^2$ | Pr 59<br>141<br>$4f^3 6s^2$ | Nd 60<br>142<br>$4f^4 6s^2$ | Pm 61<br>145<br>$4f^5 6s^2$ | Sm 62<br>152<br>$4f^6 6s^2$ | Eu 63<br>153<br>$4f^7 6s^2$ | Gd 64<br>158<br>$4f^7 5d^1 6s^2$ | Tb 65<br>159<br>$4f^9 6s^2$ | Dy 66<br>164<br>$4f^{10} 6s^2$ | Ho 67<br>165<br>$4f^{11} 6s^2$ | Er 68<br>166<br>$4f^{12} 6s^2$ | Tm 69<br>169<br>$4f^{13} 6s^2$ | Yb 70<br>174<br>$4f^{14} 6s^2$ | Lu 71<br>175<br>$4f^{14} 5d^1 6s^2$ |
|---|---|---|---|---|---|---|---|---|---|---|---|---|---|

Actinides (90-103):

| Th 90<br>232<br>$6d^2 7s^2$ | Pa 91<br>231<br>$5f^2 6d^1 7s^2$ | U 92<br>238<br>$5f^3 6d^1 7s^2$ | Np 93<br>239<br>$5f^4 6d^1 7s^2$ | Pu 94<br>239<br>$5f^6 7s^2$ | Am 95<br>243<br>$5f^7 7s^2$ | Cm 96<br>245<br>$5f^7 6d^1 7s^2$ | Bk 97<br>247<br>$5f^9 7s^2$ | Cf 98<br>249<br>$5f^{10} 7s^2$ | Es 99<br>254<br>$5f^{11} 7s^2$ | Fm 100<br>253<br>$5f^{12} 7s^2$ | Md 101<br>255<br>$5f^{13} 7s^2$ | No 102<br>255<br>$5f^{14} 7s^2$ | Lr 103<br>257<br>$6d^1 7s^2$ |
|---|---|---|---|---|---|---|---|---|---|---|---|---|---|

*The new testament book of*

# Fundamental Constants

*And they shall be immutable.*

## Chapter I: SI Units

N ow in October of the year 1960, in Paris, Système International, or *SI units*, were established: Length shall be in meters; mass shall be in kilograms; time shall be in seconds; and temperature shall be in Kelvins.

## Chapter II: The Constants

N ow the *speed of light* shall be approximately three-hundred-million meters per second. Thus in SI units this speed shall be three-hundred-million. Now *Newton's constant*, which controls the strength of gravity, shall be a tiny miniscule number – two-thirds of a tenth of a billionth in SI units. *Planck's constant*, which governs the effects of quantum fluctuations, shall be even smaller – in SI units two-thirds of a millionth of a billionth of a billionth of a billionth. And because Planck's constant is so very very very small, quantum effects shall be very very very small. *Boltzmann's constant*, which gives the energy of a molecule per degree in temperature, shall be in SI units fourteen trillionths of a trillionth. And this number is very very small because the energy of a molecule is very very small.[173]

Now the *fine structure constant* shall be one divided by one-hundred-thirty-seven.[174] And it shall control the quantum fluctuations in electromagnetism. And because the fine structure constant is relatively small, quantum effects in electromagnetism shall be relatively small. Thus the fine structure[175] in an atom shall entail only tiny shifts in energy. Now the *alpha strong coupling constant* shall control the strength of *the strong interactions*,[176] which are the forces binding quarks. Alpha strong shall *vary* according to the *energies of quarks*. This constant thus shall *not* be constant – it shall "run."[177] Now since it is one-ninth at the electroweak unification scale of a hundred GeV, the strong interactions shall be *moderate at such high energies* and temperatures:[178] At a hundred GeV, quarks in hadrons shall be loosely

---

[173] The four constants in this paragraph are $3.0 \times 10^{10}$, $6.7 \times 10^{-11}$, $6.6 \times 10^{-34}$ and $1.4 \times 10^{-23}$.

[174] The constants in this paragraph are discussed in the Book of *Subnuclear Physics*.

[175] The fine structure consists of minute shifts in atomic energy levels due to the effects of quantum mechanics.

[176] The strong interactions are discussed in Chapters V, IX and X of *Subnuclear Physics*.

[177] This is the language that physicists use: Alpha strong is known as a "running coupling constant."

[178] In the early Universe, temperature determined the energies of quarks. During the

tied together. Now *alpha strong* shall increase as energy is lowered. And so at a GeV, *it* shall be roughly one. And since it is roughly one, the strong interactions shall be *strong*, causing quarks to tightly bind through potent forces and wild quantum fluctuations. Now the *Fermi coupling constant* shall be a hundredth of a thousandth in units of the proton's mass. This constant shall control the strength of the nuclear weak interactions. And because the Fermi coupling constant is so small, weak interactions shall be weak.

## Chapter III: The 1983 Declaration of Dependence

And in the year of 1983, the speed of light was *declared* to be 299,792,458 in SI units. And the second was *defined* by means of an atomic cesium clock – a second became 9,192,631,770 radiation transition cycles of cesium-one-hundred-thirty-three. And this atomic quantum clock was accurate to one part in ten-trillion. And so the *meter* was the unit to be *measured* – it was defined to be the distance that a light beam travels in 1/299,792,458 of a second.

*The speed of light and time became the master of the meter.*

---

Big Bang when the Universe was hot, the quarks were so highly energetic that they were not tied together. As the Universe cooled, quarks lost energy and became bound, forming groups of a few quarks known as hadrons. See the Old Testament Book of *Exodus II*.

# The Books of Physics

*Religion is contemplation directed inward;*
*the objects of the contemplation are the soul and spirit.*
*Physics is observation directed outward;*
*the objects of the observation are the Universe and its contents.*
*Religion and science are complements.*

*These Books of Physics*
*are the scientific scriptures.*
*They contain the laws of Nature.*
*And with the knowledge of these laws*
*can a man or woman better understand.*

*The first book of Physics, called*

## Matter

*It shall matter what matter is.*

### Chapter I: Microscopic Matter

Now all microscopic matter shall be made from elementary particles. These *fundamental* constituents shall be the quarks and leptons. Leptons, meaning "light particles" in Greek, shall include neutrinos and electrons. Through the strong interactions, three quarks *shall bind* to form a proton or a neutron, and neutrons and protons *shall stick* together in a nucleus. Thus quarks shall also make up nuclei. Now an *atom* shall be a tiny nucleus surrounded by electrons. *Molecules* shall be two or many atoms bound together. And macroscopic matter shall be aggregates of molecules.

Now molecules of carbon, hydrogen and oxygen shall make *organic compounds*. And some such organic macromolecules shall constitute *the molecules of life*, such as proteins, lipids and nucleic acids. And the organic matter shall come together in a cell, and cells shall form the *building blocks of life*.

### Chapter II: Macroscopic Matter

Now ensembles of many molecules shall group together to form three generic kinds of macroscopic matter: solids, liquids, gases. Ice, water and water vapor are examples. The molecules in *solids* shall be frozen in fixed places, while the *molecules* in *liquids* shall be liberated: *They* shall flow around each other, mutually attracting and rubbing one another as they go. The molecules in *gases* shall move freely with *hardly* any interaction. Now a fourth state of matter shall exist, which is rarely found on Earth: A *plasma* shall be a hot gas in which constituents are charged.

*And special relativity shall stipulate*
*that energy be a form of matter.*
*Thus there shall be four types of matter:*
*fire, earth, air and water.*

Now a macroscopic state of a substance shall be called a *phase*. A *phase transition* shall occur when a substance changes state from one phase to another. An example is the melting of a piece of ice – water in the solid phase passes to water in the liquid phase.

## Chapter III: Solids

Now there shall be many *types of solids*. Electrons in a *metal* shall throughout the solid freely flow, so that metals shall conduct electricity if driven so. A *superconductor* shall be a material in which such charges (the electrons) move with no resistance. In an *insulator*, electrons shall be tightly bound to atoms. Now a *magnet* shall be a solid with a magnetic field microscopically created by electrons either through their circulating movements or their spin. A *semiconductor* shall be an insulator in which the addition of a little energy allows electron flow.

A *crystal* shall be a solid in which atoms are *like unto* soldiers ordered in formation. An emerald is an example. Now crystals shall be held together by different types of *binding*.[179] An *ionic* crystal shall consist of oppositely charged ions held in place by attractive *electrostatic force*. And table salt, whose chemical composition is NaCl, is an example – it is a three-dimensional array of alternating positively charged sodium atoms and negatively charged chlorine atoms. A *molecular* crystal shall bind by *van-der-Waals-type forces*. Solid krypton is such a crystal. A *covalent* crystal shall be held together by *covalent bonds*. Diamonds are examples. In a *metallic* crystal, the atoms shall be packed together as closely as is possible – *repulsive forces* shall prevent complete collapse. And in this dense arrangement shall electrons hop between the atoms and conduct. Magnesium crystals are examples.

## Chapter IV: Liquids

Now a liquid shall be a substance that can flow. Unlike solids, the molecules shall be free to move about. But atomic forces shall be strong enough to keep the molecules together. Water and mercury at room temperature are two examples. A *glass* shall be a liquid so thick it hardly flows, while a *superfluid* shall flow with no resistance.

A *liquid crystal* shall be a fluid of long rigid molecules, all approximately pointing in the same direction. Now the molecules *shall* be free to move about, but they shall hardly rotate. Thus in *some* direc-

---

[179] The chemical binding mechanisms of this paragraph are discussed in the New Testament Book of *Chemistry*.

tions, liquid crystals shall be like crystals. But in other directions, they shall flow like liquids. Often, calculators and laptop computers use liquid crystals in displays.

A *solution* shall be a liquid with another solid, liquid or gas dissolved in it. An example is the salt water of the ocean.

A *gel* shall be a quasi-solid rich in liquid – flexibility shall be a property. Gelatin and jellies are examples. A *sol* shall be dust-sized particles suspended in a liquid or a gas. A hydrosol shall be a sol in water, and an aerosol shall be a sol in air. An *emulsion* shall be a thickish liquid sol such as a cream or ointment. Mayonnaise and margarine are more examples. A *foam* shall be a gas dispersed throughout a liquid. Whipping cream and beer froth are typical examples. A *paste* shall be a thicker liquid sol such as a paint or putty. Gels constructed from long chains of molecules shall be called *polymers*. Proteins, rubber, nylon are examples.

## Chapter V: Gases

Now the molecules in a gas *shall not be bound together* – instead they shall collide and bump and tend to fly apart. They must be thus contained, or else they will diffuse away: Helium gas must be confined inside a tank or a balloon. The atmosphere is held down by the gravity of Earth, but molecules at high altitudes *still* shall manage to escape. In each cubic meter of air at the surface of the Earth shall there be more than twenty-trillion-trillion molecules.

A *plasma* shall be a gas of ions. It is produced by the heating of a gas – heat shall make the positive and negative charges separate. And know thee and all around thee that for the *first three-hundred-thousand years*, until Recombination, the entire Universe was such a plasma gas.

## Chapter VI: Astronomical Matter

Now solid compounds *shall clump* together in dust and grains and rocks. And rocks shall coalesce to form the planets. Dense plasmas shall make up the Sun and all the stars. A star with planets shall be a stellar-planetary system. And stars and planetary systems, dust, and gases shall be the composition of a galaxy. A *galactic cluster* shall be a group of galaxies and intergalactic dust and gas. And galactic clusters and empty voids shall constitute the Universe.

*The second book of Physics, called*

# Forces

*Forces shall compel the bodies in the Universe*
*to change their motions.*
*May the natural force in thee,*
*thy brethren and thy neighbors so be moved.*

## Chapter I: Fundamental Forces

*They shall act invisibly like wind.*

Now *four* fundamental forces shall control the motions of objects, mass and matter. And these are gravity, the strong force, the nuclear weak force and electromagnetism.

Gravity *shall act* on mass. The strong force *shall hold* the quarks together in a neutron and a proton. The weak force shall lead to certain rare decays of nuclei. Electromagnetism shall act on charges and on currents and *be the binding force* in atoms and in molecules.

## Chapter II: Macroscopic Forces

Now a macroscopic force shall be that which *pushes, pulls* and/or *compels.* Gravity, magnetism and the electric force shall *seem to act mysteriously* through empty space and at a distance.

There shall be many types of macroscopic forces. And one shall be gas pressure. Steam exiting a kettle shall create a force. An atmosphere of air shall constantly push down against the Earth, causing liquid in barometers to rise. And *wind blowing* against a window pane *shall make it rattle.* Now *friction* shall be another macroscopic force, arising when one thing comes in contact with another. Air friction shall retard the fall of a parachute or feather. Friction between two solid objects shall allow a car to move or a man to walk: Without such friction, the ground would be like ice – the wheels of a car would spin in place and the slightest movement of a foot would bring about a fall. Still another macroscopic force shall be created by the spring. Springs shall give beds their support, making them comfortable and soft. Now *in all these cases*, the forces shall be *created* by the interactions between *microscopic* molecules: Air pressure shall be caused by molecules rebounding off a surface; friction shall be created by the atomic interactions of molecules moving in opposite directions; and compressed springs shall push outward because *the bonds of molecules* are squeezed.

And let it be known to thee and all around thee that *all interactions among molecules* are created by *electromagnetism.* Thus electromagnetism shall create *all* macroscopic forces, save for gravity.

Now the four fundamental forces *shall govern all*, acting at distances which are close or far and controlling the motions of *both* the big and small. They shall be the forces that make galactic gas *collapse* to form a star. And they shall be the forces causing water in a waterfall to fall. And they shall be the forces that make the planets move around the Sun. And they shall be the forces that set *the continents adrift*. Or the forces allowing animals to walk and cars to run. And they shall be the forces that let helicopters lift. And they shall be the forces in a bomb that blast debris apart. And they shall be the forces *causing clouds to drift*. And they shall be the forces pumping blood cells through the veins and arteries and heart. Or pushing charges through a wire. And they shall be the forces that permit a bus to stop or start. And they shall be the forces that flicker flames in fire. And they shall be the forces that *move* the tides. Or make rubber bands rebound. And they shall be the forces controlling roller coaster rides. And they shall be the forces in a coil which is wound. And they shall be the forces ventilating air from a circulating fan. And they shall be the forces that *control* the winds and weather. Or the forces that allow a bridge to stand. And they shall be the forces binding molecules together. And they shall be the forces that cause a piece of gum to stick. Or propel a baseball which is struck. And they shall be the forces that turn the gears in watches and make them tick. And they shall be the forces that lead to a windshield wiper getting stuck. And they shall be the forces that make springs spring. Or the forces that keep the walls of cells intact. And they shall be the forces in the vibrations of a music string. And they shall be the forces that cause nuclei to interact. And they shall be the forces in an earthquake causing furniture to shake. Or the forces that *bind* the quarks in a pion or a proton. And they shall be the forces that trigger muons to *disintegrate*. And they shall be the forces generated by a graviton, gluon, massive vector boson or a photon. And they shall be the forces that induce a yo-yo to reverse. Or the forces that cause a pipe to burst. In short, they shall be the forces that *control the Universe*.

*The third book of Physics, called*

# Classical Physics

*Give thanks unto Nature.*
*Make known her laws among all men.*

*So it was written.*
*So it shall be.*

## Chapter I: The First Law

Now there shall be three fundamental laws of classical mechanics, known as *Newton's laws of motion.* And they shall govern the movement of macroscopic bodies.

Now the First Law shall say the following. Unless acted upon by an external force, an object at rest shall *remain* at rest. Or, if in motion, an object shall *continue* in that motion in a fixed direction and with a constant speed. And the First Law shall have a name. And the *law of inertia* shall be its name.

And the First Law shall reflect the *inherent and natural "laziness"* of things. Inanimate blocks and objects shall lack the will to act. Why change if one is not compelled to change? Thus any body, be it alive or dead, shall want to be infinitely lazy in its behavior under Nature.

*Why flap thy wings? Why walk the desert sand?*
*Why raise thy arms to heaven?*
*Why strive to strive to do such things?*

Now *acceleration* shall be the change in speed *or* the change in the direction of an object. Thus acceleration shall be *modification* of a motion. Thus acceleration shall represent a "lack of laziness." And it shall indicate motivation and desire for a change.

## Chapter II: The Second Law

Now the Second Law shall say the following. The acceleration of an object shall be proportional to the external force on it. And the acceleration of an object shall be inversely proportional to an object's mass. And this law shall be called $F=ma$, or the *law of force.*[180]

Thus forces shall *create* the motivation for change in motion, while mass shall measure "laziness." And heavy objects *shall* be very lazy, resisting change: They shall react to forces slowly. And light objects shall be less lazy: They shall react to forces quickly.

And if thou push a half-ton rock with all thy effort, *shall not* the rock but hardly move, if it move at all? But if thou push a book lying on a table with the same great effort, *shall not* the book fly off?

---

[180] In this equation, $F$ stands for force, $m$ stands for mass and $a$ stands for acceleration.

Thus the Second Law provides *a reason* for the seemingly random motion of a body. When a naturally lazy body speeds up or slows down, or swerves to the right or left or turns up or down, then it does so *not* on its own volition but because it was *compelled* to do so by a force. So when a coin is tossed up, turns over and falls to the ground, it does so *because* there is a force. And in this case, the force is gravity. Thus bodies that accelerate do so because of forces. And it is *as though* Nature mechanically compelled bodies to change behavior. Thus forces are the embodiments of *natural commandments*.

Now the First Law follows from the Second Law, for, if there *be* no force acting on an object, then no acceleration shall there be. And by definition, *without acceleration*, the speed and the direction of motion *do not change*.

*Motion without forces shall be free.*

## Chapter III: The Third Law

Now the Third Law shall say the following. When two bodies interact in isolation, the force that each exerts on one another shall be of the same strength, but opposite in direction. And this shall be the *law of action and reaction*.

And this law shall represent fair play among all heavenly and earthly bodies. And for example, if you hold a partner's hands and pull, you will move toward your partner, but your partner will also move to you. Hence you cannot exert a force on your partner without having a force exerted on you too. The push you give is the push he gives. The pull you tug is the pull he tugs. Thus the two forces shall be of equal strength. And this is fitting and is fair.

*Do unto others as you would have them do unto you.*

When push comes to shove, *neither* push nor shove shall win.

And for example, when you push on the surface of a wall, the wall pushes back. And this is why the wall does not move. And it shall seem *as if* the wall has hands.

## Chapter IV: Gravity

*Cupid shall forever fire arrows.*
*And this shall make loving bodies so attract.*

Now the law of gravity shall say the following. The *force of gravity* between two bodies shall be proportional to the product of their masses and weaken with the distance squared. And the force shall be attractive and directed along a straight line between the bodies. And this shall be *Newton's law of gravity*.

And what shall it mean for the force to weaken with the distance squared? It *shall* mean this: If the distance between the two objects is *doubled*, the force grows weaker by *four* times. And if the distance is *tripled*, the force grows weaker by *nine* times. And if the distance is *quadrupled*, the force grows weaker by *sixteen*. And so on. Thus only relatively *nearby* bodies *feel* the force of gravity. Thus the Moon is attracted to the Earth. And the Earth and Moon are attracted to the Sun. But the Earth and Moon feel a *miniscule* force from the nearest star, Alpha Centauri, because it is forty-trillion kilometers away.

And what shall it mean for the force to be proportional to mass? It *shall* mean this: If, for example, the mass of Earth were *doubled*, then Earth's gravity would *double*. In this hypothetical situation, thou would feel twice the pull beneath thy feet; thy weight, as measured by a weighing scale, would double. And if the mass of Earth were *tripled*, Earth's gravity would *triple*. And if it were quadrupled, the strength of gravity would likewise increase *four times. And* so on.

And a *fundamental* parameter shall control *the strength of gravity*. And it shall be the *gravitational constant*, also known as *Newton's constant*. And it shall be $6.67 \times 10^{-11}$ Newtons meters-squared per kilogram-squared. And because it is so small, gravity shall be significant *only* if a body has *huge* mass. Thus the Earth, Sun and Milky Way shall produce a sizeable gravity, but rocks, bricks and blocks shall not.

And gravity shall be the *universal* and obligatory "love" among all massive objects. All massive bodies shall feel a great attraction to each other. And it shall be mutual and unisexual – there shall be no female and no male mass, for there shall be *one and only one* type of mass.

> *The command from Heaven did in ancient times descend:*
> *Thou shalt love thy neighbor as thyself.*
> *Thou shalt love thy enemy as thy friend.*

Now the *weak equivalence principle* shall be inherent in Newton's law of gravity. It says that the mass in Newton's Second Law shall be the selfsame mass in Newton's law of gravity. Thus there really shall be one and only one *type* of mass.

Now the force of gravity can be understood *as though* there be a holy presence – a massive object shall create an *aura* all around. And this aura shall have a name – the *gravitational field* shall be its name. And a second object, in the presence of the first, shall feel the aura of the first. And the aura shall draw the second to the first.

## Chapter V: Planetary Motion

Now the movements of the planets around the Sun shall be explained by Newton's laws of gravity and motion. These four laws shall integrate to yield three *lesser* rules called *Kepler's laws*. Now the *first* rule says that a planet shall move in an *ellipse* around the Sun and that the Sun shall be at one of *its* two foci.[181] And the *second* rule says that a straight line drawn between the Sun and a planet shall

---

181 An ellipse, or "stretched circle," has two points called foci adjacent to its center.

sweep out equal areas in equal times. And the *third* rule says that the period squared shall be proportional to the mean distance cubed. Now the period shall be the time it takes for a planet to go once around the Sun, while the mean distance shall be the average of the perihelion and the aphelion.[182] And what shall it mean for the period squared to be proportional to distance cubed? If the distance is increased *four-fold*, then the period grows by *eight*. And if the distance is increased *nine-fold*, then the period increases *twenty-seven* times. And if the distance is increased *sixteen-fold*, then the period becomes *sixty-four* times bigger. *And* so on.

Thus the planets *farther* from the Sun take *longer* to go round the Sun. And Saturn is an example. Saturn, which is about nine times farther from the Sun than Earth is, shall take roughly twenty-seven times as long to go around the Sun. And since the Earth circles the Sun once a year, it shall take Saturn about twenty-seven years to go round the Sun.

Now Kepler's laws, which are derivable from Newton's laws, shall be *universal* rules. And so asteroids and comets shall *also* follow Kepler's laws. And these rules shall apply to *any* two-body system bound by gravity, such as the Moon and Earth.

## Chapter VI: Gravity on Earth

Now gravity shall govern *the fall* of objects at the surface of the Earth. And it shall make golf balls and basketballs come back to Earth. And what first goes *up* shall then come *down*. Now when air friction is insignificant, all bodies, independent of their mass, shall fall the *selfsame* way. And for example, a feather and an iron paper-weight fall in a vacuum chamber at *precisely* the same rate. And the distance that an object falls, when released from a tower or a cliff, increases with time squared. And in one second, five meters shall a body fall. So in two seconds, four times farther, or twenty meters, shall it fall. So in three seconds, nine times farther, or forty-five meters, shall it fall. *And* so on. Now *projectile motion* shall be the motion of any object, such as a spear, a ball or missile, through the air. The horizontal and vertical motions shall be independent. And for example, a projectile shall move horizontally with constant speed. But it shall move vertically with constant downward acceleration, falling five meters in the first second. And the acceleration shall be created by Earth's gravity, which shall *draw all objects* toward the center of the Earth.

## Chapter VII: Momentum

Now *momentum* shall be the amount of push a moving body can deliver on impact. More mass means more momentum. Given a

---

[182] The *perihelion* is the shortest distance between a planet and the Sun during the planet's orbit around the Sun. The *aphelion* is the opposite; it is the farthest distance.

truck and a leaf moving at the same speed, the truck has more momentum. Likewise, more speed means more momentum. A bullet from a gun has more momentum than a penny tossed into the air.

## Chapter VIII: Energy

There shall be two kinds of energy: kinetic and potential. Now *kinetic energy* shall be the energy of motion. When any object moves, it has kinetic energy, and the faster it moves, the more it has. Now *potential energy* shall be energy *stored* by a body in an interaction. A ball on a table has a certain gravitational potential energy; a ball on the floor has less. And when a ball falls, it picks up speed, as potential energy is converted into energy of motion. Objects shall *continually trade* kinetic and potential energy, but total energy *shall be conserved*, which means it shall *remain the same*.

Energy is *like unto* emotion. Kinetic energy is *like unto* outright agitation, the jumping up and down in a fit of rage. Potential energy is *like unto* pent-up emotions, where the outrage they will cause has yet to be released.

## Chapter IX: Angular Momentum

Now *angular momentum* shall be rotational momentum. Spinning tops and skaters have angular momentum, but a sprinter running in a line has none. Now *angular velocity* shall be the rate at which a spinning body turns. More angular velocity shall mean more angular momentum.

## Chapter X: Special Motions

A *vibration* shall be a movement back-and-forth. An example shall be the motion of a leaf *on* an autumn windy day. *Harmonic motion* shall be a repetitive and smooth vibration, like a guitar string that's been plucked. *Circular motion* shall be motion in a circle, such as the turning of a Ferris wheel or the motion of the Earth around the Sun.

## Chapter XI: The Electric Force

*And Cupid shall forever fire arrows.*
*And this shall make loving bodies so attract.*
*But evil daemons shall make enemies of men.*

Now the electric force shall be like gravity *except* that charges shall play the role of masses. But unlike mass, of which there is only one type, there shall be *two types* of electric charge: positive and negative. And unlike mass, which may have any value, electric charge shall come in *quantized bits*. Thus there shall be a minimal and fundamental charge. And the proton's charge shall be this *fundamental unit* — one-sixth of one-billionth of one-billionth of a Coulomb, a very small amount of charge. And on an electron shall also be the fundamental unit, but *negative* shall be it.

Now let the *law of electric force* be known: The force between two charged bodies shall be proportional to the product of their charges and weaken with the distance squared. And for example, if the distance between two charged objects is *doubled*, the electric force grows weaker by *four* times. *And* so on.[183] Now if the charges are of *opposite* sign, the force shall be *attractive*. And if the charges are of the *same* sign, the force shall be *repulsive*. And the force shall be directed along a straight line between the charges. And this electrostatic law shall have a name – *Coulomb's law* shall be its name.

Now a *fundamental* parameter, called *Coulomb's constant*, shall control the strength of the electric force. And it is nine-billion Newtons meters-squared per Coulomb-squared. And because it is *so big*, the electric force shall be quite *strong*. Thus it shall be difficult to separate charges that are positive from charges that are negative, so that matter shall usually contain equal amounts of positives and negatives – matter shall normally be neutral.

And the electric force shall be like a *universal* and obligatory "love" and "hate" among charged objects. All charged bodies shall feel a great attraction or repulsion to all other bodies that are charged. It shall be *as if* there is female charge and male charge. And *as* females are attracted to males, so shall charges that are positive be attracted to charges that are negative. And *as* males are attracted to females, so shall charges that are negative be attracted to charges that are positive. And as for like-signed charges, positives shall be repelled by positives, and negatives shall be repelled by negatives.

Now the electric force can be understood *as if* there *be* a holy presence – a charge shall create an *aura* all around. And this aura shall have a name – the *electric field* shall be its name. And a second charge, in the presence of a first, shall feel the aura of the first. And if the aura is *compatible* then the second charge shall be *attracted* to the first. And if the aura is *incompatible* then the second charge shall be *repelled*.

And the *electric force* shall be available to mankind for its benefit or loss. And man will use *it* to make electrons move through wires to create electric flows. And these electric flows will supply the world with power.

## Chapter XII: The Magnetic Force

Now some materials such as iron shall be magnetizable. And when such a material is magnetized, it shall become a *magnet*. Now magnetization shall be a consequence of *circulating charge*. And when

---

[183] For more examples on the strength of the force versus distance, see the case of gravity in Chapter IV, which is the same.

such currents flow in random ways, no magnetism shall be present. But when, like marching soldiers, the currents circulate in an ordered manner in the same direction, the material shall magnetize, and a magnet shall it be.

And a magnet shall have two poles: a north pole and a south pole. Now when soldiers march in rows there is a front row and a rear row. And the front row is *like unto* the north pole of a magnet, whereas the rear row is *like unto* the south pole. And if one separates these marching soldiers into two new groups, then the first group will have a front row and a rear row. But the second group will *also* have a front row and a rear row. And the strength of each group, as determined by the number of troops, will be divided into two. Now magnets *are like unto* marching soldiers. And so when a magnet is broken into two, each piece obtains *both* a north pole and a south pole. It is *impossible* to have a magnet with a north pole only. Likewise, it is *impossible* to have a magnet with a south pole only. Thus the breaking of a magnet into two shall not isolate the north pole from the south pole but shall create *two magnets*, each with north-south poles and with *half* of the original magnetic strength.

And like the electric force, the magnetic force may be attractive *or* repulsive. And if the north pole of one magnet is directed at the south pole of a second magnet, then the magnets *shall attract*. But if the north pole of one is pointed at the north pole of the other, or, if the south pole of one is pointed at the south pole of the other, then the magnets *shall repel*.

Now the magnetic force can be understood *as if* there *be* a holy presence. A magnet shall create an *aura* all around. And this aura shall have a name – the *magnetic field* shall be its name. And a second magnet, in the presence of a first, shall feel the aura of the first. And, if the aura is *compatible*, the second magnet shall be *attracted* to the first. And if the aura is *incompatible*, then the second magnet shall be *repelled*.

And the magnetic force shall be available to mankind for its ~nefit or loss. And, among things, magnets will make most motors ᴧork.

Now the magnetic and electric auras shall interact: A changing magnetic field *shall create* around it an electric field. And a changing electric field *shall create* around it a magnetic field.[184] And for example, a highly changing electric current will create a changing magnetic field, ⸝which, in turn, will create an electric force that can drive a second electric current. And this effect will make transformers work.

---

[184] The effect of changing magnetic fields creating changing electric fields and of changing electric fields creating changing magnetic fields is the basis of electromagnetic waves.

## Chapter XIII: Electromagnetism

And the relation between electric and magnetic forces shall be a fundamental fact of Nature. The two shall be manifestations of one principle and four equations. And the principle shall be called *electromagnetism*. And the equations shall be *Maxwell's equations*.

## Chapter XIV: Determinism

Now at the end of the nineteenth century, it was thought that if Nature's forces were all known, then Newton's laws could be exploited to determine all. So if thou knew the classical macroscopic forces, then thou, like a prophet, could foresee the future – thou *would* know all. And thou, like a prophet, could predict the motion of anything and everything.

Thus the goal of nineteenth century science was to determine the macroscopic forces, such as the *friction* between two objects in contact, the *tension* in strings and cables, the *support forces* of solids that prevent an object from penetrating them, the *elastic forces* in the compression or stretching of springs, the *forces in collisions* arising when objects bump, and the *cohesive forces* causing things to stick. And the goal was to understand the *gravitational, electric* and *magnetic* forces, which made Newton's apple fall, compelled lightning to flash and caused compass needles to deflect.

And it was thought that *if* ye knew and understood these forces, ye, like the gods, *could* foresee all things.

And in the late nineteenth century, it was known that, of the macroscopic forces, *only two* were fundamental: the electromagnetic force and gravity. And all other forces, such as cohesion, tension, friction, forces in springs, in supports, and in collisions, were *consequences* of the electromagnetic force at a *microscopic level*.

So it was thought that *if* ye knew and understood gravity and electromagnetism, ye, like the gods, would *be* clairvoyant – ye could see the future.

Now by the end the seventeenth century, Newton had determined and had *understood* the law of gravity. And in the eighteenth and nineteenth centuries, Coulomb, Ampère, Faraday, Biot, Savart, Lorentz and Maxwell had determined and had *understood* electromagnetism. And with the knowledge of these forces, the *mystery of macroscopic motion* seemed to disappear. And it was thought that all was known, that the golden age of omniscience had arrived. But *Nature's laws* had been indelibly engraved in sacred stone. And they were *more subtle* than what nineteenth-century man had thought. And no one, neither scientists, nor philosophers, nor holy priests could *alter* Nature's laws. And in the early twentieth century, *new* fundamental forces were uncovered which were microscopic *and not understood*. And special relativity was then discovered, rendering Newtonian gravity *incompatible*.

Next quantum mechanics was discovered and was understood. And for man's mind did *it* create new puzzles. And *uncertainty* and chaos so ensued. And hope for omniscience was consequently lost.

> *Predicting the future was no longer a question of information.*
> *Classical mechanics was inexact and sometimes inappropriate.*
> *But classical mechanics was often still a good approximation.*

> *And in the quantum-revolution aftermath,*
> *mankind discovered the randomness of paths.*

## Chapter XV: Classical Physics
## During the History of the Universe

And after the Planck time when *the wings* of quantum gravity ceased to flap, and after the Big Bang aftermath when subatomic particles self-annihilated or combined, and after nucleosynthesis when subnuclear forces began to play a *lesser* role, and after Recombination when atoms formed, and after other quantum fluctuations began to wane, and after hundreds of thousands of years when matter had spread thinly, *then* did Nature's classical laws and forces take control. And the Universe became *somewhat* predictable. And "$F=ma$" became the most important rule. And the three laws of Newton almost determined all. And macroscopic forces controlled the macroscopic motions. And gravitational collapse made giant structures in the Universe such as galactic clusters and great voids.

*The fourth book of Physics, called*

# Thermodynamics

*It was a land of heat and chaos.*

## Chapter I: Heat and Temperature

Now a *system* shall be a single object, like a block of wood, or a collection of objects, like a pile of sand, or everything there is, like the Universe itself. And the *constituents* of a system shall be the microscopic entities that make up the system, such as molecules, electrons, grains of sand or atoms. *Heat* shall be the *total* energy of motion of constituents. A warm glass of water *has* a certain heat. Two warm glasses of water have twice that heat, for there are twice as many water molecules. A hot pot of water has more heat than a cold pot of water, for hot water molecules move faster.

Now *temperature* in Kelvins shall represent the average energy of motion of constituents. An air molecule at the surface of the Earth, where the temperature is three-hundred Kelvins, certainly moves fast. But an air molecule in the lower ionosphere, where the temperature is six-hundred Kelvins or *twice* as hot, moves even faster and has *twice* the energy. Now the relation between the average energy of a constituent and temperature shall be governed by a fundamental constant. And this constant shall be *Boltzmann's constant*, $1.38 \times 10^{-23}$ joules per Kelvin. And this constant is *very tiny* because the constituents – the electrons, molecules and atoms – are microscopic and because such a microscopic entity can carry only *very small amounts of energy*. And for example, each molecule in a solid at room temperature vibrates with an energy of four-billionth of one-trillionth of a joule.

## Chapter II: Fluctuations

Now macroscopic systems will not be exactly uniform. Crystals, for example, usually contain a few tiny cracks and imperfections. Gases also exhibit *non-uniformities* – in a gas there will be *minute regions* containing molecules that are moving *relatively slower*: These regions will be *cooler spots*. And in a gas there will also be minute regions containing molecules that are moving *relatively faster*: These regions will be *warmer spots*. And such microscopic variations in temperature shall be *thermal fluctuations*. Likewise, there will be minute regions that contain *more molecules* than normal: These will be regions of relatively *higher density*. And there will also be minute regions that contain *fewer molecules* than normal. These regions will be regions of relatively *lower density*. And *density fluctuations* shall be the name for such microscopic variations in the concentrations of constituents. Now essentially, any feature of a macroscopic system will undergo microscopic variations. And these variations shall be *fluctuations*.

*May the wings of wasps,*
*bees and butterflies flap fast.*

Now statistical mechanics shall deal with *large numbers* and the consequences that follow from the laws of probability. If, for example, thou flip a coin a hundred times, roughly fifty times the coins will come up heads and fifty times the coins will come up tails. But rarely will it be exactly fifty-fifty. Sometimes it will be fifty-two heads and forty-eight tails. And sometimes it will be fifty-six and forty-four. And sometimes it will be forty-five and fifty-five. *And so on.* And the variations in such outcomes shall be called *statistical fluctuations.*

*Oscillations shall arise*
*between the Yin and Yang.*

In a play, two voices speak:

> G: *"Heads or tails?"*
> R: *"Heads."*
> G: *"Heads it is."*
> R: *"Good, I win"*

> G: *"Heads or tails?"*
> R: *"Heads."*
> G: *"Heads it is."*
> R: *"Good, I win."*

> .
> .
> .

> G: *"Heads or tails?"*
> R: *"Heads."*
> G: *"Heads it is."*
> R: *"Good, I win."*

And on a stage did Rosencrantz and Guildenstern flip in a row a hundred heads. Was it an enormous fluctuation, a statistical fluke, a *violation* of the laws of probability? No, it was *just a play.* In the *real world*, there are no Rosencrantz-and-Guildensterns – Rosencrantz and Guildenstern are dead.[185]

> G: *"Perhaps this is a play within a play."*
> R: *"Perhaps our Universe is a Universe among the Universes."*

And if a room is *divided into two*, then each air molecule may be on one side or the other. Thus there is a fifty-fifty chance that a particular molecule is on a given side. And it is *like unto* the flipping of a coin: Heads means on the right; tails means on the left. And so there is a *miniscule, almost infinitesimal, chance* that the *billion-billion-billion*

---

[185] This is the title of a Tom Stoppard play as well as a line from Act 5, Scene 2 of William Shakespeare's Hamlet.

molecules in a room will all *accidently* and simultaneously move to the right side of the room. And such a situation would be a super Rosencrantz-and-Guildenstern event – the flipping in a row of a *billion-billion-billion* heads. And if thou be sitting on the left side of the room when the super Rosencrantz-and-Guildenstern event occurs, thy lungs will suddenly collapse, and without air will thou be. But do not hold thy breath while waiting for the super Rosencrantz-and-Guildenstern event, for thou will have to wait a very very long long time – much longer than thy life; indeed, much longer than the lifetime of the Universe.

## Chapter III: Entropy

Now *entropy* shall be a measure of statistical possibility: A situation that is *highly probable* shall have *high entropy*, whereas a situation that is *highly unlikely* shall have *low entropy*. And for example, in flipping one-hundred coins, an outcome of fifty-two heads and forty-eight tails has high entropy. But as for one-hundred heads in a row, it has low entropy. And so, Rosencrantz and Guildenstern have negligible entropy: Their situation is preposterous, ridiculous, perhaps perilous, and, at the very least, improbable. *Chaos, disorder and even death* must be the *final outcome.*

And consider thou the room of gas again. Now a billion-billion-billion molecules distributed in a particular way but more or less *uniformly* has *high entropy*. But a billion-billion-billion molecules *all* in the right half of the room has *very very very low entropy*. And because highly probable situations are more likely to occur, the entropy of a system *shall evolve* from low to high. And *this* is natural. And this shall be the *second thermodynamic law*. And because macroscopic systems contain trillions of trillions of constituents, the odds in the "probability game" are *overwhelming* – like the flipping of a coin a trillion-trillion times.

But if, at first, thou not succeed, try, try and try again. And if thou flip a *coin* a billion-trillion-trillion times, there is a *chance* that, at some point, thou will flip *it* in a row a hundred times as heads. Rosencrantz and Guildenstern live on! But not for long.

## Chapter IV: The Four Laws of Thermodynamics

Now thermodynamics, which deals with macroscopic systems, heat and entropy, shall have *four* laws. And the zeroth thermodynamic law says that *two bodies in contact*, which interact efficiently, shall have *the same temperature*. And the first thermodynamic law says that total energy shall be *conserved*, and heat shall *be* a form of energy. And the second thermodynamic law says that the entropy of an isolated system shall *increase with time*. And the third thermodynamic law says that there shall be a temperature called *absolute zero* in which the motions of the microscopic constituents shall cease.

And how shall the zeroth thermodynamic law be *fulfilled*? When a cold hand grasps a warm cup of coffee, heat shall flow from the warm cup to the cold hand. Now the heat gained by the cold hand will increase its temperature, while the heat lost by the warm cup will decrease its temperature somewhat. And heat will flow between the two *until* they have the *same* temperature, at which point the flow of heat will cease. And the final unchanging situation shall be called *thermal equilibrium*. Thus thermal equilibrium is the consequence of the thermal interaction of two bodies.

And why shall heat flow from a hot body to a cold body and not the other way around? Because *interactions* shall distribute energy in a fair and democratic way: When the molecules in a hot body, which are moving quickly, come in contact with the molecules in a cold body, which are moving slowly, the quickly moving molecules will strike the slowly moving molecules and *make* the slowly moving molecules *move faster*. And the quickly moving molecules, when they bump the slowly moving molecules, will *lose* energy and thus move slower too. And eventually, collisions will make all molecules move at *roughly equal* speeds. And thermal equilibrium will so ensue. Thus thermal equilibrium shall be the consequence of *microscopic interactions*.

And the first thermodynamic law shall come from the Sixth Commandment and be embodied in the Uni-Law.

Now the second thermodynamic law shall *not follow* from a law of Nature – it shall be a consequence of *mathematical probability*, for, as explained above, systems shall evolve to *most probable* configurations. There shall be no Rosencrantz-and-Guildensterns. Rosencrantz and Guildenstern are dead. Now since the Universe itself is an isolated system,[186] the entropy of the Universe shall with time increase. And this shall have *profound* ramifications for the Universe's fate.

An egg is beautiful and round and *full of great potential*. And the molecules are arranged in cells in a *special* way: The DNA is ready to *produce a life*. How it reached this *highly* ordered state is what some might call an act of God. But when dropped on a floor, the egg, its yolk, and its shell are randomly scattered everywhere. Drop an egg a billion times and a *billion* different splattering patterns so appear – there are a *billion* different ways to break an egg. And although each one *be* highly *improbable*, a messy pattern is highly *probable*. How easy be it to *pass* from the *ordered* to the *random*. Just drop an egg.

> *And all the king's horses and all the king's men*
> *couldn't put Humpty Dumpty together again.*

Now it shall be *impossible* for an engine to do work solely by extracting heat and then returning to its original state. Such a process shall produce a *decrease in entropy*, which cannot be – it would *violate* the second thermodynamic law. Now such an *imaginary* machine that

---

[186] This is the current *belief* of scientists.

pumps away producing work from heat shall be performing *perpetual motion of the second kind*. The second thermodynamic law declares that such machines cannot be. Alas, cars shall not run from the heat in air. Alas, an idea of this kind shall not be able to solve mankind's demands for energy.

Now the third thermodynamic law shall describe the ultimate freezer, with a temperature so cold that *all* is motionless – such a body shall be *without* heat. *Absolute zero* shall be the name for such a temperature. And absolute zero in Kelvins shall be zero. So unlike other systems for measuring temperature, such as Celsius and Fahrenheit, Kelvin shall be absolute and fundamental.

## Chapter V: Speed Distributions

Now the motion of molecules and constituents shall be quite variable. *Most* molecules will move at some *average* speed. But *some* molecules will move more *slowly*, while others will move more *quickly*. And still others will move extremely fast, at least for brief intervals of time. But the number of extremely fast-moving molecules shall be quite small. And how small shall it be? It shall be *very small*, exponentially small. And the scarcity of high-energy molecules shall be called the *Boltzmann suppression factor*. And the number of molecules with a given speed shall be called the *Boltzmann distribution*.

Now quantum mechanical effects shall *modify* the Boltzmann distribution for systems of *high density* or of *low temperature*: For cold and/or dense substances, quantum statistics shall ensue. Fermions shall obey a *Fermi-Dirac distribution*, whereas bosons shall obey a *Bose-Einstein distribution*. And this means the speeds of these two constituents will be differently distributed. And what is the reason for this difference? It is that fermions and bosons do *not behave the same*: Bosons, being democratic, *maximally mix* among themselves. On the other hand, being highly individualistic, fermions, by the exclusion principle, do *not* get in one another's way.

## Chapter VI: Ideal Gases

*A false balance is an abomination,*
*but a just weight is a delight.*

Now gases shall obey *a special set of lesser laws*. And the first rule shall be that the pressure shall go *up* when the number of molecules in a closed container is *increased*. And why shall this be so? Because *gas pressure* shall be the push created when molecules *strike* the walls of a container. Hence an *increase* in the number of molecules creates an *increase* in the number of collisions at the walls. And for example, when one *doubles* the number of molecules, one makes the pressure *double*. And when one *halves* the number, the pressure drops *in half*. Now the second rule shall be that the pressure shall go *up* when the temperature is *increased*. And why shall this be so? Because an *increase* in temperature creates an *increase* in the speed of molecules and because faster-moving molecules strike the walls of the container *harder*. And for example, when one *doubles* the temperature of a gas, the pressure *doubles*. And if one *halves* the temperature, the pressure drops *in half*. Now the third rule shall be that *slowly increasing* the volume of the container shall make the pressure *drop*. And why shall this be so? Because it will take *longer* for molecules to strike the walls of the container. And for example, when one *doubles* the volume, molecules take twice as long to strike the walls and so the pressure drops *in half*. And if one *halves* the volume, one makes the pressure *double*. Now rules two and three imply a fourth. And the fourth rule shall say that the change in temperature must match the change in volume if the pressure is to *be* maintained the same. And for example, if one *halves* the volume, then the temperature must be also *halved* to keep the pressure constant. And if the volume of the gas is *doubled*, then the temperature must also double if the pressure is to be the same.

Now these four rules shall be summarized as one. And that one law shall be the *ideal gas law*. This law shall work *like unto* a weighing-balance scale: Pressure is placed in one tray, while density and temperature occupy the other tray. *Balance* must be maintained. Hence, when density or temperature or both are *increased*, pressure must also be *increased*. And when pressure is *decreased*, density or temperature or both must also be *decreased*. And if pressure goes unchanged, then a *decrease* in temperature must be matched by an *increase* in density or vice versa. And *density*, being by definition the number of constituents per unit volume, may be increased by increasing the number of constituents or by decreasing volume.

Now, in general, *collapsing* gases *shall heat up*. And why shall this be true? Because collapsing walls knock hard against the molecules and make them travel faster. And usually the pressure shall *go up*. And the density *shall increase*. Now an *expanding* gas, in general, *shall cool*, the pressure usually *shall drop*, while density *shall decrease*.

And the rules of the ideal gas law shall often apply qualitatively to *other* forms of matter. And for example, subjecting a solid to increased pressure shall warm it up.

## Chapter VII: Engines

Now thermodynamics will be available for human benefit or loss. And turbines, motors and combustion engines are examples. The engine in a car shall *make it move*. And it shall work as follows. A cylindrical chamber in the engine of a car is sealed by a movable-cover called the piston. An intake valve is opened with the position of the piston *in*. As the piston is moved *out*, gasoline and air *are so draw in*. After the intake valve is closed, the piston pushes in, thereby compressing air and gas. An electric spark is then *provided* and a chemical explosion follows. The hot exploding gas expands, pushing out the piston and providing power. Thus chemical energy in fossil fuels[187] is *converted* into heat and motion. As the moving piston turns an axle, the car *moves forth*. The gas, which has expanded in the chamber, cools. Next an output valve is *opened*. When the piston pushes *in*, the useless gases *are exhausted*. Next the output valve is *closed*. The piston is now at its original position, which is in. And the engine is now ready for the next influx of fuel. The procedure is repeated. And this process, which is called the *four-stroke cycle*, involves four operations: intake, fuel compression, power and exhaust.

## Chapter VIII: Thermodynamics in the Early Universe

And during the Big Bang and its aftermath, during the expansion of the Universe and *throughout cosmic history*, the Universe was a thermodynamic system with a declining temperature and an increasing entropy. In this hot dense gas system, the fermions in early times followed a Fermi-Dirac-type distribution, while bosons obeyed a Bose-Einstein distribution. And the Universe was, in *many* ways, like an ideal expanding gas with minute density and thermal fluctuations. The Universe obeyed the four thermodynamic laws, for there was *little choice* – extraordinarily improbable were all *other paths* of possibility.

## Chapter IX: The Second Law and Decay

And the second law of thermodynamics shall mean that *disorder shall prevail*. Order, by its very nature, is unique. *Rare* are diamonds. Dirt is everywhere.

And art, which is *supposedly eternal* and is often beautiful, is full of thermodynamic flaws. And for example, after several hundred years a painting will gather dust and fade, while ointments will crack and chip. In ten-thousand years, the painting will depict nothing but faint smudges and decay. Art, contrary to artists' aspirations, does *not* endure.

*And this is what is called the natural decay of all.*
*It can't be stopped.*

*And everywhere in the Universe,*
*in the past, in the present and forever,*
*eggs are being dropped.*

## Chapter X: Entropy and Life

Now life is a fluctuation in entropy – a *seemingly local violation* of the second thermodynamic law. Does this mean that life must be a *miracle*? Not so, for the second thermodynamic law is *still* obeyed:

---

[187] Fossil fuels involve hydrocarbons. See Chapter VII of the Book of *Chemistry*.

Life is *not* an isolated system. Food, light and water are *imported*. The local loss of entropy in a living organism is *compensated* by the gain in its environment. The total entropy within the solar system *is* indeed increasing. The gain occurring in the Sun is dominant. Life on Earth *can be* thanks to the Sun and its entropic gain. And let it be known to thee and all around thee that life is the ultimate entropic *exploitation*.

But how did life arise? The answer lies in flipping coins a billion-trillion-trillion times until a string of one-hundred heads occurred. The *hand of Nature* did the flipping in the seas. The ocean waters *were stirred* in a thousand-billion places; the mud and molecules *were mixed* a thousand times a second for a hundred-million years. And by trial and error and *chance* and lots of effort was the first cell made.

## Chapter XI: Entropy and the Universe

Now the Universe is thought to be a closed and isolated system. And so the Universe, unlike life, *must obey* the second thermodynamic law. So the Universe is *doomed*: It shall decay and die in an entropic death. And let it be known now and forever that there *be no physical eternal life – only decay and death*. Know ye this truth. The odds are verily against thee. The gods are verily against thee.

*The moment of highest symmetry was the Big Bang birth.*
*Since then, the seeds of chaos have spread across the Universe.*
*The extrinsic structural beauty of Nature is at best a temporary lie.*
*Disorder will* ultimately *everywhere prevail.*
*The effort to maintain organization is guaranteed to fail.*
*A living creature will fight a courageous battle to survive*
*but someday will die.*
*Great paintings will fade, chip, discolor and be destroyed,*
*even though preventative measures be employed.*
*Dust will collect in the corners of rooms and on window sills.*
*Oil will spread thinly over the oceans and the seas in oil spills.*
*Seemingly solid clay pots will get crushed or be broken.*
*The second law of thermodynamics will have spoken.*
*Pollution will be* unpreventable *like political corruption.*
*Floods, tornados, hurricanes will cause disruption.*
*Earthquakes will leave behind scenes of great destruction.*
*Probability and statistics will be the cause of Nature's sins.*
*Buildings will collapse, leaving rubble, like in Roman ruins.*
*That which will remain shall be stone bricks and columns.*
*Disorder and decay will* eventually *dominate all.*
*The ship will stray off course and stay forever in the doldrums.*
*A wall will stand for long but someday will fall.*
*From ceilings shall chip off paint and plaster.*
*Day shall end in night*
*and everything will meet a final natural disaster.*

*The Sun, like any other star, will die and cease to light.*
*The increase in the entropy of the Universe will be the reason why.*
*The world, as ye know it, is* destined *to disintegrate.*
*All, whether living or inanimate, will suffer the selfsame fate.*
*Arteries will harden, blood will clot, and cells will die.*
*Nature will toss die, shuffle cards, and continually randomize.*
*The Earth will someday be destroyed and pulverized.*
*Self-organizing systems such as life will be anesthetized.*
*All living creatures – whether big or small – will end up dead.*
*Interstellar gas and dust will forever spread.*
*The flipping of a coin will always produce some tails and some heads.*
*No matter how hard ye try it will be impossible to win.*
*The material in the Universe will continually thin.*
*Indeed, the end of all is guaranteed.*

*The fifth book of Physics, called*

# Special Relativity

*All is relative.*

## Chapter I: On False Laws

*Is this not the way that Nature works?*

Now let it be known to thee and all around thee that Newton's laws of motion have *slight* flaws. They are false laws, for they are not always true. Beware of flawed laws for they, like false prophets, [188] *may* lead one astray.

Now the true laws shall be Einstein's laws of special relativity. And they shall be *true laws* because they are *always* true. And thou and all others shall obey these laws, for it has been *commanded*.

And when an object moves *slowly*, the difference between Newton's laws and Einstein's laws shall *not* be noticeable. And because human beings are used to human motions, which are minuscule compared with the speed of light, many humans will *erroneously believe* that Newton's laws are always true. But the *extrapolation* of Newtonian law to extremely fast-moving objects shall be *not* correct. And since the human brain cannot resist extrapolation, humans will often be confused; small is the mind of man.

## Chapter II: The Six Principles of Special Relativity

And these shall be the six principles of special relativity, which govern all motion in the absence of the force of gravity: First, the laws of physics shall be the *same* for all constant-moving viewers. Second, the *constancy of the speed of light* shall be a law of physics. Third, *nothing* shall travel faster than the speed of light. Fourth, time and space shall be part of one four-dimensional manifold and this four-dimensional manifold shall be called *spacetime*.[189] Fifth, constant-moving observers shall *not agree* on the time interval and the space distance between two distinct events. But they shall agree on what is called the proper-spacetime interval. Sixth, mass and energy shall be *equivalent*, and the energy of motionless matter shall be the mass of the matter times the speed of light squared.

---

[188] There are many false prophets today, like those who try to predict the future by the position of the planets or with a pack of Tarot cards.

[189] A *manifold* is a smooth space with a particular dimension. For example, a curved wire is a one-dimensional manifold. The surface of a balloon is a two-dimensional manifold. A solid block is a three-dimensional manifold. And so on.

## Chapter III: The First Principle

Now the first principle of special relativity shall say that the laws of Nature are the same for all constant-moving viewers. And what shall be a constant-moving viewer? It shall be an observer with a *constant* speed moving in a *fixed* direction. And what shall the first law mean? It shall mean that an experiment performed at rest and an experiment performed while moving at a constant speed in a fixed direction shall yield precisely *same* results. And suppose thou live inside a rocket far in outer space. Then, billiard balls will deflect off one another in the same manner whether thy rocket *be at rest or moving*. Likewise, the decay of radioactive nuclei will proceed *in the same way*, whether thou *art at rest or moving*. And this is natural, for if thou live in the black of outer space, thou know not whether thou move or not. And so the behavior of objects under Nature shall be identical when viewed from constant-moving frames of reference.

## Chapter IV: The Second Principle

Now since the constancy of the speed of light is one of Nature's law, it shall be, by the first principle, the *same* for all constant-moving viewers. Thus *all* such constant-moving viewers shall measure the speed of light to be the same. In thy rocket, thou shall find light's speed to be the same, whether the light moves *at* thee, *away from* thee or *by* thee. And this speed shall be identical whether thy rocket *be at rest or not*. And since the speed of light is the same for every constant-moving viewer, it shall be a *fundamental* concept. And so the speed of light shall be a *universal constant* – a little less than three-hundred-thousand-kilometers per second. And *this* speed shall be labelled "c". Thus c shall be three-hundred-thousand-kilometers per second.

Now the first two laws shall be the most important laws – essentially all of special relativity shall follow from these two.

And the constancy of light's speed will be confusing to a man with a Newtonian mind-set, for *to him* an object's speed *will* depend on whether he *be* at rest or not.[190] But, in Nature's world, light shall not behave like such an object.

## Chapter V: The Third Principle

Now the third principle says that under no circumstances shall an object travel faster than the speed of light. *Instantaneous* communication shall be impossible. And this lack of instantaneous communication shall have great *implications* for causality, or cause-effect. And

---

[190] An example of this is as follows. A man *standing* by a highway sees eastward-moving cars travelling at the *same* speed as westward-moving cars. But a man *sitting in a speeding eastward-bound train* sees eastward-moving cars travelling *slower* than westward-moving cars. In fact, if the train moves somewhat faster than the traffic, the eastward-moving cars seem to him to travel slowly backward!

for example, actions in one part of the Universe cannot *suddenly* affect the actions in another part – only when such a distant action *propagates* and arrives at another part of the Universe can such a distant action have effect. And for example, when a supernova explodes ten-thousand-light years from thee, ye initially see nothing; ye must wait for the light to come to thee; ye must wait ten-thousand years to see the flash. Thus the supernova ye *see today* is a supernova that exploded *long ago*.

And this limiting speed will be puzzling to a man with a Newtonian mind-set, for he will *think* that it *be* always possible with effort to go faster and to faster go.

## Chapter VI: The Fourth Principle

Now the fourth principle says that time shall be *the fourth dimension*. And how can time, which is measured in seconds, be space, which is measured in meters? Time shall be *like unto* gold. Gold is a metal. But it is also money. And to convert gold into money one needs to know the exchange rate, the number of dollars that an ounce of gold is worth. So time, which is the ticking of a clock, can also be a meter stick. And what is the exchange rate for time? It shall be *the speed of light*. And so, to convert time into distance, one multiplies time *by* the speed of light. Thus one second of time shall be three-hundred-thousand kilometers, which is also called one light-second. Two seconds of time shall be six-hundred-thousand kilometers, or two light-seconds. And one minute of time shall be eighteen-million kilometers, which is sixty-light seconds, or one light-minute. And one hour of time shall be a little more than one-billion kilometers, which is three-thousand-and-six-hundred light-seconds, or sixty light-minutes, or one light-hour. And one day of time shall be twenty-six-billion kilometers, which is twenty-four light-hours, or one light-day. And one year of time shall be nine-and-a-half-trillion kilometers, which is three-hundred-and-sixty-five light-days, or one *light-year*. Thus a light-second, a light-minute, a light-hour and a light-year shall *not* be measures of time but distance. And for example, the distance to the nearest star, Alpha Centuri, shall be four-and-a-third light-years; the distance between Pluto and the Sun shall be almost six light-hours; and the distance between the Earth and the Sun shall be eight-and-a-third light-minutes. And time, when it is represented as a length, shall be called *c-time*.

And the fourth dimension will baffle a man with a "Newtonian brain," for his visual world is three-dimensional, and his brain-waves are three-dimensional, and his *imagination* is three-dimensional. But a man with an "Einsteinian brain" has a four-dimensional imagination and can picture a four-dimensional space.

*(And a voice spake, saying,*
*"Do not present a confused and contorted face*
*when physicists speak of manifolds of four-d space."[191])*

## Chapter VII: The Fifth Principle

Now the fifth principle says that time intervals and spatial distances shall *not* be universal concepts but *shall depend on the observer*. And for example, two observers, moving with respect to one another, will *not agree* on whether two events occur at the same time! *Nor* will they agree on an object's length! But they will agree on the proper-spacetime interval. And the situation shall be *like that unto* a triangle – the Pythagorean theorem says that, for a right-angle triangle, the length of the hypotenuse squared is the sum of the squares of the two smaller sides. And if two geometricians start with a common hypotenuse and draw two more sides to make two different right-angle triangles then the lengths of the shorter sides are *not equal*. But for both of them, the sum of the squares of the two smaller sides *is the same*. Now the hypotenuse of a right-triangle shall be like unto a *proper-spacetime interval – it* is something on which constant-moving viewers can agree. And the two shorter sides shall be *like unto* the time interval and the distance between two separate events. Now there shall be a relativistic hyperbolic Pythagorean theorem: The *proper-spacetime interval* squared shall be the spatial-separation squared *minus* the c-time-elapsed squared. And the relativistic hyperbolic Pythagorean theorem says that all constant-moving observers shall agree on the proper-spacetime interval between two separate events.[192]

Now because one *subtracts* c-time squared, time shall be distinguished from space. And this is something on which both Newtonian and Einsteinian thinkers can agree – although space and time form one unity, time shall indeed be different from space.

And still, even among intellectuals, the concept of length will be debated and the concept of age will be confused. But special relativity shall *precisely* specify the relation between the different spatial distances and the different temporal intervals that two constant-moving observers measure. And these relations shall be called *Lorentz transformation laws*. And so those who understand the transformation laws will *not* enter into debate and *will* not be confused.

And distances and time intervals will be perplexing for a man with a Newtonian mind-set, for he has always *thought* that times and distances were universal concepts. Indeed, when two observers have a *small* relative velocity, their "hyperbolic triangles" for two events shall be virtually the same. And the sides corresponding to space shall differ

---

[191] "Four-d space" is the phrase scientists often use for four-dimensional space.

[192] They will *not* agree, however, on the distance between the two events nor on the time elapsed between the two events.

*imperceptibly*. And the sides corresponding to time shall also differ *imperceptibly*. And Newtonian observers, whose perceptions are not sensitive enough, will not see that those times and distances are minutely different.

Now since one *subtracts* c-time squared in the computation of the proper-spacetime interval, spacetime *shall* not be Euclidean; *Minkowski space* is what it shall be called.[193] And so the four-dimensional manifold of spacetime shall *be* Minkowski space.

## Chapter VIII: The Sixth Principle

Now the sixth principle says that $E=mc^2$. And because c squared is ninety-million-billion meters-squared per second-squared, c squared shall be a *very large* number. Hence, conversion of a small amount of mass into energy shall produce a *lot of energy*. And this is why nuclear bombs, which are based on the conversion of mass into energy, shall produce enormous blasts.

> *And man will make "the bomb"*
> *although he might not need it.*

And the equivalence of energy and mass will be confusing to children with "Newtonian brains." But by the time such children are adults, they will have heard of Einstein and of $E=mc^2$ so many times they *will* believe it.

## Chapter IX: Albert, Isaac and a Sacred Creature

*He who hath an ear,*
*let him hear.*

Now is this the parable of Albert, Isaac and a sacred creature. Once not so long ago, Albert was camping with three physics friends, Peter, James and John. And Albert said to them, "Today I shall climb that mountain." And he pointed to the peak. "I want you three to stay here and wait for me. When I come back I shall *reveal* to you what I have *learned*. In the meantime, build tents so that we may camp here tonight."

And Albert, who was a young man, quickly climbed the mountain. And it came to pass that the weather changed suddenly from sunny to overcast. And clouds *engulfed* the mountain peak. And when Albert reached the summit, there was a *mysterious* dense fog around him.

And it came to pass that a particularly thick mist swirled about Albert's head. And after the mist dispersed, Albert had been changed: he had an Einsteinian brain.

---

[193] Euclidean spaces are the "worlds" in which Euclidean geometry and the ordinary Pythagorean theorem are valid. In non-Euclidean spaces, theorems such as "the sum of the interior angles of a triangle adds up to 180 degrees" no longer hold.

Now on the mountain Albert spied another man and a sacred creature. And the man was *quite old*. His name was Isaac. And he had a Newtonian brain. Now the sacred creature had *no age, no name* and no brain. But it *always told the truth*, always obeyed instructions and always *followed Nature's laws*.

Now both Isaac and Albert had been brilliant in their youth. Isaac, being a lot older than Albert, had considerably *more experience*. But Albert, being younger than Isaac, was a *quicker thinker*. Now Isaac believed in the *old law*, which was outdated. And Albert believed in the *newest law*. And Albert liked to play tricks on old believers.

So Albert, Isaac and the creature descended on the other side of the mountain, where a highway was. And Albert asked the creature to drive a truck at eighteen kilometers per hour. And in addition, he instructed the creature to throw a ball forward at thirty kilometers per hour when the truck passed them. And Albert turned to Isaac and asked him, "When we measure the speed of the ball, what will it be?" And Isaac, who had observed *many* such experiments, said, "Well, if the truck is moving forward and the creature throws the ball forward then the speed of the truck will *add* to the speed of the ball. Eighteen plus thirty is forty-eight. Thus the ball will travel forward at forty-eight kilometers per hour for us." "I don't believe you," said Albert. And Isaac replied, "You youth think you are so smart. Let's see. Let's have the creature drive the truck and see." And sure enough, when the creature passed by and threw the ball, Albert and Isaac measured the ball's speed and it was forty-eight kilometers per hour. "For an old guy, you're pretty smart," said Albert. And Isaac smiled.

"But what will happen if the ball is thrown back instead of forward?" questioned Albert with a puzzled look. And Isaac, who had observed *many* such experiments, said, "Well, if the truck is moving forward and the creature throws the ball back then the speed of the truck will *subtract* from the speed of the ball. Thirty minus eighteen is twelve. Thus the ball will travel backward at twelve kilometers per hour for us." "I don't believe you," said Albert. Again annoyed, Isaac snapped, "You youth are so inexperienced, yet you do not believe your elders. Let us have the creature drive the truck and see." And sure enough, when the creature passed by and threw the ball, Albert and Isaac measured the ball's speed, and it was twelve kilometers per hour. "You're right again," said Albert. And Isaac smiled.

"This is a little boring," said Albert. "Let's speed things up." And so Albert and Isaac put on space suits and helmets. And they got in a rocket and blasted into outer space. And there, Albert asked the creature to drive a space-jet at one-hundred-and-eighty-thousand kilometers per second. "By Jove," interjected Isaac, "That's three-fifths the speed of light. I've *never seen* an object go that fast." And Albert responded, "These are modern times, old fella. Technology has made great advances lately." And Albert instructed the creature to turn on a light and shine it forward when the space-jet goes by them. And Albert turned to Isaac and asked him, "When we measure the speed of the light, what will it be?" And Isaac said, "Well, the speed of the space-jet will add to the speed of the light. One-hundred-and-eighty-thousand plus three-hundred-thousand is four-hundred-and-eighty-thousand. Thus the light will travel at four-hundred-and-eighty-thousand kilometers per second for us." "I don't believe you," Albert said. Annoyed Isaac replied, "Again you *doubt* the thinking of an experienced one like me?" And Albert said, "Well, let's make a wager. I'll bet you a gold coin you're wrong." And the two men put on special space suits and got out of the space-jet. And each contributed a gold coin. And the two gold coins *floated* there in outer space. Then the creature fired the space-jet engine and did as he was told. And Albert and Isaac measured the speed of the light and it was three-hundred-thousand kilometers per second. And Isaac was *astounded* and upset, "The creature must not have followed your instructions correctly." But Albert replied, "Remember, this is a *sacred* creature and it *never* disobeys." And Albert snapped up the two gold coins and put them in his pocket.

"Well, let's have another bet," said Isaac, who wanted to win his gold coin back. "Only this time, I'll give the instructions to the creature." "OK," said Albert, "let's shine the light out of the back of the space-jet instead. What will the speed of the light be?" And Isaac said, "Well, the speed of the space-jet will subtract from the speed of the light. Three-hundred-thousand minus one-hundred-and-eighty-thousand is one-hundred-and-twenty-thousand. Thus the light will travel backward at one-hundred-and-twenty-thousand kilometers per second for us." "Well, I bet it will be three-hundred-thousand kilometers per second," Albert countered. And two gold coins floated in outer space, as the creature fired up the space-jet and carried out Isaac's orders. And Albert and Isaac measured the speed of the light and it was three-hundred-thousand kilometers per second. And Isaac was *astounded* and upset. But Albert simply snapped up the coins and put them in his pocket. And Isaac, now a bit shaken, asked Albert, "Why did you predict that the speed would be three-hundred-thousand kilometers per second?" And Albert replied, "Don't you know the new law? The speed of light shall be constant and always be three-hundred-thousand kilometers per second."

And Albert continued, "But did you notice *the color* of the light? When the space-jet was approaching us, it was *blue.* And when the space-jet was passing us, the light was *yellow.* Yet when the space-jet sped away, it was *red.* Creature, what color did you see?" And the creature answered, "The light was *always* yellow." "That's strange," commented Isaac, who, in his youth, had studied prisms and the spectrum. But Albert countered, "You know, there is *no law* which says the color of light is the same for everyone. Have you ever heard of the blue shift or the red shift?

"You look a bit upset, Isaac. I'll give you a chance to win your coins back. Light is *very special*. The pedantic teachers at my school even called it an electromagnetic wave. Waves behave *differently* from particles. Let's repeat the experiment with *particles*. Here I have an electron-gun which shoots electrons at three-quarters of the speed of light." "That's some gun," Isaac interjected. He seemed quite impressed. And Albert continued, "Let's instead have the creature shoot electrons out the front of the space-jet." And Albert turned and said, "Creature, run the space-jet at three-quarters of the speed of light, aim the electron gun forward, and when you pass us pull the trigger." And turning back to Isaac, Albert asked, "How fast will the electrons move?" "Well, the speed of the space-jet will add to the speed of the electrons. Three-quarters plus three-quarters is one-and-a-half. Thus for us, the electrons will travel at one-and-a-half times the speed of light or four-hundred-and-fifty-thousand kilometers per second." "Well Isaac, my answer is *different* from yours. I say they'll travel at four percent *less* than the speed of light, just a little less than three-hundred-thousand kilometers per second."

And to give Isaac the chance to win back his lost money, they each bet two coins. So four gold coins *floated* in outer space, as Isaac and Albert watched through their glass helmets the outcome of the experiment. And the space-jet sped by, and the creature pulled the trigger, and the speed of the electrons was measured by Isaac and by Albert. And it was four percent *less* than the speed of light. And two additional gold coins jingled in Albert's pocket.

"You know, Isaac, you could have *never* won that wager." There was a pause and then Isaac asked, "Why?" And Albert replied, "Because of the second principle of special relativity, which says that *nothing* can travel faster than the speed of light. You predicted that the electrons would travel faster than the speed of light." And Isaac inquired, "Is this a new law?" And Albert responded, "No. It's *always* been that way. I'm surprised that a wise experienced fellow like you didn't know about it." And Isaac answered, "Well, in my days we didn't have space-jets and electron guns."

Now inside, Isaac was *upset*. Never had he been so annoyed with himself. He hated to lose money. But he hated being wrong *even more*. He tried to smile to hide his *internal* irritation.

"Listen, Isaac, I think you had a little bad luck. These relativity principles are a bit peculiar when it comes to adding or subtracting speeds. I heard that you, in your old days, were an excellent measurer. Let's perform some measurements. Here are two sticks of the same length, *five* meters. The first is an ordinary stick and the second is a ruler. Let's put the first one on the space-jet and ask the creature to speed along at one-hundred-and-eighty-thousand kilometers per second. Then we'll use the ruler to measure the stick in the space-jet. What do you say?" Now Isaac was quite confused. He thought to himself, *Why do such a stupid experiment. A five meter stick is a five meter stick.* His thought was interrupted when he heard Albert say, "I bet the stick on the space-jet will measure only *four* meters." And Isaac responded, "You mean you think the stick in the space-jet will shrink a meter?" And Albert continued, "Not exactly. But I bet when we measure it, it will be four meters. In fact, to be sure, I want *you* to perform the measurement." Isaac agreed.

And floating there in outer space were eight gold coins. Now the first stick was placed in the window of the space-jet. And the creature fired the engines and sped by Albert and by Isaac. Isaac had to react quickly. Perhaps his hands shook a bit, but when he lined up the ruler with the stick in the window, the stick in the window was one meter less. And Isaac's mouth *opened* with astonishment. And four coins fewer *was* his purse.

"This is preposterous," sounded Isaac. "*Never have I seen* such magic." And Albert responded, "It is *not magic*, Isaac. It is a transformation law." Isaac rebutted, "Forget your laws. I want to know what is going on. I'll do *anything* to understand what's happening." And Albert, who had planned his actions in advance, answered, "I'll give you some insight if you agree to make two more bets." Isaac consented.

And Albert summoned the creature, "Creature, did you see Isaac measure the stick?" And the creature nodded his beastly head up and down. "Explain what you saw." And the creature answered, "Isaac put the two ends of the ruler next to the stick in the space-jet window. *First* he lined up the two front-most ends. *Then* he tried to line up the two rear-most ends. But he *didn't make* the alignment attempts *at the same time.* And during this time lapse, the rocket moved forward and the rear end of the stick in the rocket also moved forward. That's why he measured less than five meters."

Albert tried to comfort Isaac. "Perhaps you should have computed the proper-spacetime interval and corrected your measurement." And Isaac queried, "What are you talking about? Proper-spacetime interval?" And Albert continued, "Well, to help you understand, I'll *explain* why you measured four meters. Creature, how much c-time elapsed between the two alignment attempts?" And the creature, *who never lied,* responded, "Three meters." And Albert demanded, "Sacred creature of great creations, please compute the proper-spacetime interval between Isaac's two alignment-attempt events." And the creature began to calculate like a talking computer, "The proper-spacetime interval squared is the length of the stick squared minus the c-time elapsed squared. Hence, the proper-spacetime interval squared is five meters squared minus three meters squared. Hence, the proper-spacetime interval squared is twenty-five square meters minus nine square meters or sixteen square meters. Take the square root and you get four meters. The proper-spacetime interval is *four meters.*" And Albert explained, "Your problem Isaac, was that you didn't measure the length of the ruler.

You measured the proper-spacetime interval. That's why you got four meters. According to the creature, who never lies, you didn't line up the two ends of the ruler at the same time. Perhaps your hands shook a bit.

"Let's perform a *simpler* experiment. I have an accurate stopwatch here. The sacred creature has no brain but he does *have* a heart. His heart beats once *a second*. I bet that if the space-jet goes at one-half of one percent less than the speed of light, or 0.995c, then his heart will beat about once every *ten seconds*. So if I'm right, you'll have *lots* of time to make the measurement." And Isaac responded, "You talk nonsense. *If* there were two such creatures then the creature in the space-jet would live ten times longer than a creature sitting with us. But think of things from the point of view of the space-jet. If the creature in the space-jet looks at the creature with us, he thinks the creature in space sitting with us is moving at 0.995c in the opposite direction. Therefore, the creature with us should also live ten times longer. How can both creatures outlive each other by a factor of ten?" Isaac was getting quite worked up. His face was red as he *sensed* his world was falling all apart.

And Isaac continued, "If anything, the creature will get nervous and his heart will beat faster. I don't care about money. I just want to know *the truth*. Here are eight gold coins." And Albert contributed another eight coins. Hence there were sixteen gold coins floating there in space. Now the space-jet had never gone as fast as 0.995c. And the creature climbed into the space-jet and unbuttoned his shirt. And he strapped himself in and he tried to be calm. And he fired the engines and the space-jet roared loudly. And he re-fired the engines and the space-jet roared more. And the space-jet accelerated. And a *great* pressure was felt on the chest of the creature. But the creature survived. And eventually the spacecraft reached 0.995c. And since the space-jet now moved at a constant speed the pressure on the creature's body was entirely gone. And the creature calmed down and his heart pumped as normal. Now Isaac, with the stop watch in his hand, looked at the space-jet and not at the watch. He could see the heart throbbing and throbbing quite slow. And once roughly every ten seconds, the heart gave a pump. And Isaac in anger threw the watch down and the watch flew off into black outer space. And *Isaac*, not the creature, was near cardiac arrest. And Albert calmed Isaac. And Isaac was miserable both in his soul and in his head. He was an old man who just wished to be dead.

"Unfortunately you are an old three-dimensional man living in a modern four-dimensional world," commented Albert. And Isaac did *not understand* because his three-dimensional brain could not conceive of a four-dimensional world.

"And what is the last experiment?" asked Isaac sadly, "I have only sixteen gold coins left." And Albert took the coins and answered,

"Here are two piles of Uranium-235. You will hold one pile in your left hand and one pile in your right hand. Please hold your arms far apart. And you will walk off. And when you are thousands of kilometers away, you will bring your hands together. The divided substance will come *together as one*. And *if you come back*, I'll return to you all your gold coins." And Isaac, who was thoroughly distraught and mentally destroyed, *did* as he was told.

And as Isaac left, *thousands of others* with Newtonian brains joined him. And they seemed to emerge magically. And they came from *all directions* – they were *like ghosts* from the seventeenth, eighteenth and nineteenth centuries. And they lined up one after another in a long line with Isaac at the head – it was the procession of the old thinkers. And Isaac led them off into the *black wilderness* of outer space.

For Isaac, it was the beginning of *the end*. His confidence had been broken. His self-esteem had been shattered. No longer did he want to live. He couldn't care less about lost gold coins. And it was just as well because he *never* came back.

Somewhere it is written in a proverb of a sacred book, "A fool and his money are soon parted."

And Albert returned to the summit of the mountain. And the clouds *cleared*. He descended to the campsite of his friends. And Peter said, "We were worried. The mountain was engulfed in clouds and we saw some *flashes* like lightning." And Albert replied, "The flashes were not lightning. They were from a rocket."

And Albert brought the three inside a tent and said, "I have written a manuscript. It is entitled *The Special Theory of Relativity*. Please read it. Please try to understand it. And when you have understood it, explain it to others."

*And those who do not believe in Nature's Laws* will *be fooled.*
*And those who do believe will not.*

## Chapter X: The Parable of the Non-Believing Pharaoh

*Hearken unto these words.*

And the Pharaoh *was told* to release the slaves, and if he did not, then his rivers would turn to blood. And the Pharaoh did *not believe*. And the Pharaoh did not release the slaves. And the rivers turned to blood. And the Pharaoh *was told* to release the slaves, and if he did not, then frogs would invade his lands. And the Pharaoh did *not believe*. And the Pharaoh did not release the slaves. And frogs invaded his lands. And the Pharaoh *was told* to release the slaves, and if he did not, then lice would attack his people. And the Pharaoh did *not believe*. And he did not release the slaves. And lice attacked his people. And it continued as so. The invasion of flies was followed by the disease of the oxen, horses, asses, camels, sheep and cattle. Then came the outbreak of boils on the skin of the Pharaoh's people, the rain of hail, and the invasion of the locusts. And *still* the Pharaoh did *not believe*. And *still* the slaves were *not released*. And there were three days of darkness. And the Pharaoh *was told* to release the slaves, and if he did not, then the first born of each household in his kingdom would die. And the Pharaoh did *not believe*. And the Pharaoh did not release the slaves. And the first born of each household suddenly did die. And the Pharaoh's people cried up in anguish, for their leader *had led them astray*. And reluctantly, he released the *slaves*. Finally *they* were free. And they fled the land of the Pharaoh. But the Pharaoh and his warriors pursued the slaves. And a great sea *was divided and made dry* so that the slaves could pass. And the slaves *crossed* the dry divided sea. But when the Pharaoh's chariots and horsemen entered the divide, the sea *was restored*. And the horses, chariots and horsemen were engulfed in deep waters and all drowned. And this was the result of one *who did not believe*.

*The blind will lead the blind to death.*

And special relativity will be difficult to comprehend. But one should verily believe, for it *is* the truth.

Now all the forces of Nature shall conform to the principles of special relativity. And remarkably, Maxwell's electromagnetic theory is compatible with special relativity. But Newtonian gravity is not.

*The sixth book of Physics, called*

# General Relativity and Gravity

*And spacetime shall be curved.*

## Chapter I: The Equivalence Principle

And because Newtonian gravity and relativity are not compatible, Newtonian gravity is *slightly wrong* and it contains a lie. But the lie is *hard to see*. And when shall *not* the lie be visible? It shall *not* be visible when the gravitation force is weak. But when the gravitation force is strong, the lie will be exposed and the gravity of Newton will be wrong.

And in the past, it came to pass that Newton's gravity, a product of seventeenth century observation, *was superseded* by Einstein's gravity, a product of twentieth century thought. Thus a new and better theory of gravity was so created. And it was provided with a name. And *The Theory of General Relativity and Gravity* was its name.

And if thou be in outer space in a rocket *far from* the Earth, far from the Sun and far from other heavenly bodies, then thou art *weightless*. And thou floatest in thy cabin and objects also float about thee. And this is so because around thee there is *no gravity*.

And if thou be in an elevator on a high floor in a tall building and the cable suddenly should break, then thou, the others with thee, and the elevator cabin all fall. But since thou fallest *at the same rate* as the cabin, thy feet, with the slightest push, leave the floor, and thou floatest. And since the others with thee fall at the same rate as the cabin, they float too. Thus while thou art falling freely thou *seemest to feel no gravity*. And it is like being in a rocket in empty outer space. And it is *as if* some great being had suddenly *turned off gravity*.

Next *supposest* thou be floating in a windowless cabin in outer space. And suppose one end of a cable be attached to the cabin's roof and the other end be tied to a rocket. And suppose the rocket blasts its engines and begins to move. Then the cable will become taut and pull the cabin. And as the rocket accelerates, the cabin will accelerate with it. Then thou wilt *seem to stop floating*, and thy feet will touch the floor. And why shall this be so? It shall be so because of the First Law of motion: When the rocket moves and begins to pull the cable, thou remainest motionless because thou, who art a body at rest, shalt remain at rest. But the cabin, being pulled upward by the rocket, *will rise* until it hits thy feet. And from thy point of view, it will seem *as if* some great being had suddenly *turned on gravity* and made thou fallest to the floor. So now thou art standing and thy feet are on the floor. What dost thou feel? Thou feelest the floor *pushing against* thy feet with a force. And why is this so? It is so *because* of the Second Law of motion: As the rocket blasts its engines, it pulls the cabin so that the cabin does accelerate. And since thou standest on the floor, thou acceleratest with the cabin. Thus thou art compelled to change thy speed. Thus by Newton's Second Law a force acts on thee. And it is *the push of the floor* against thy feet that is this force. And thou, in thy *ignorance* and lack of perspective, dost not know of the rocket. And thou *thinkest* gravity be pulling thee down against the floor.

And in 1916, this new insight enlightened Einstein and mankind about the force of gravity – the insight into gravity was suddenly turned on, like *someone* turning on a light.

And the elevator cabin and rocket shall embody the *strong equivalence principle*, which says that it shall be impossible to distinguish gravity from an accelerating system.

## Chapter II: Curved Spacetime

Now how shall the strong equivalence principle be incorporated into general relativity? The answer shall be by making spacetime *curved*. Gravity shall be the result of *the curvature of space and time*. The First Law of Newton shall be generalized. A body, whether or not it be under the influence of gravity, shall follow a path of *minimum length in the geometry of spacetime*. And such a path shall be a *geodesic*. Now on a flat surface a geodesic shall be a line. Thus the shortest path between two points on a tabletop shall be a line. And when there is no gravitational field, spacetime shall be *flat*. And the straight lines in flat spacetime shall correspond to constant motions. Thus in the absence of a gravitational field, a body at rest shall remain at rest, or a body moving at a constant speed in a line shall continue to move at a constant speed in that same line. Thus *in the absence of gravity*, Newton's First Law of motion *shall follow* from general relativity. But when a gravitational field is present, spacetime shall be *curved*, and geodesics shall *not* be straight. Spacetime shall be distorted *as is like* a sphere – the shortest path between two points on the surface of a sphere is a great-circle arc.[194] And when a body moves along a geodesic in curved spacetime, it shall *accelerate* because it shall follow *a curved path*. And because it accelerates, a force shall be said to act upon it. And this force shall be Einsteinian gravity.

Thus in the absence of other forces but in the presence of gravity, bodies shall follow geodesics. And this motion shall be as *natural* as it could be.

And what shall cause spacetime to curve? It shall be mass. And *concentrated mass* shall make spacetime curve *a lot*. And lots of curvature shall make geodesics *highly* curved. And a *highly curved* geodesic shall correspond to *high acceleration* and hence strong force. And near a heavy object shall the curvature be great. But far from such an object

---

[194] Great-circle arcs are the arcs of the largest circles that can be draw on a sphere. For example, a segment of a line of longitude of Earth is a great-circle arc.

shall the curvature be weak. Thus the force of gravity shall diminish with the distance. And for weak gravitation, Einsteinian and Newtonian gravity *shall almost coincide.*

Now how shall Earth be attracted to the Sun? The Sun shall be *like unto* an iron cannon ball, the Earth shall be *like unto* a marble, and the surface of a bed shall be *like unto* spacetime. And if an iron cannon ball is placed upon a bed, shall not the surface of the bed depress? And if a marble is tossed, lands on the bed and rolls, shall it not roll toward the iron cannon ball? And why does the marble so behave? It does so due to the surface of the bed – the surface *is not flat.*

## Chapter III: Consequences of Einsteinian Gravity

And as for planetary motion, Einstein's theory of gravity shall produce *small differences* from Newton's theory of gravity. And for example, the orbit of Mercury, which is an ellipse, shall through Einsteinian effects rotate forty-three seconds of arc per century.

And let it be known to thee and all around thee that gravitational waves *exist.* A gravity wave shall be like an electromagnetic wave, but gravitational fields will oscillate instead of electric and magnetic fields. But alas, gravity waves will be *too weak* to be detected by feeble twentieth-century scientific instruments. But the binary pulsar 1913+16 will radiate such unseen waves. And the energy lost through gravitational radiations will cause minute changes in the pulsar's beats. And *with a radio telescope*, scientists will measure the minute effects and indirectly "sense" the waves. So scientists *will see* by listening.

And since, in the presence of a massive body, space is curved, light like matter shall be affected. Thus light *shall bend* around a heavy body such as the Sun, a galaxy, or a dark dwarf-star-sized body – light shall be deflected by the force of gravity. So starlight from a star behind the Sun shall be bent as the starlight *passeth* by the Sun. And distant light from a quasar when it *passeth* by a massive galaxy shall refract, thereby creating *a double image* of the quasar. And this shall be like the thick glasses on a person which produce a "double-eye" in the eye-glass lens. And when light *passeth* by a dwarf-star-sized dark body, it shall be *focused.* Thus such a body behaveth like a convex lens. And so when such a non-luminous body passeth in front of a star, the star shall *brighten.* And contrary to one's intuition, the starlight shall not be blocked by the body but shall be *focused* – the effect shall be *like unto* a magnifying glass which createth a bright spot of sunlight on a piece of paper.

And all these astrophysics objects shall be *gravitational lenses.* And *gravitational lensing* shall *this* effect be called.

Now gravity shall affect light *in other ways.* Light shall take *longer* to traverse a region of space where *there* is gravity. And it will seem *as if* the speed of light *be* less than in a vacuum. And for example, when light *neareth* the Sun, the light shall enter a region of curved space. And while passing by the Sun, the light shall travel a longer distance than if the Sun *were* not there. And it is *like unto* a marble which rolls down a bowl and out – such a path is longer than if the marble moved from brim to brim. Now a second Einsteinian gravity effect is this: Photons shall lose energy as they climb out a gravity. And so if one stands on Earth and "throws photons upward," then the photons, like rockets, balls or birds, shall lose kinetic energy. Now when photons lose energy, their wavelengths shall increase. And this shall render blue light a little yellow, and yellow light a little red, and red light even redder. Thus the spectrum shall shift a bit toward the red. This shall be called the *gravitational energy red-shift*. Thus light, originating on the surface of the Earth, shall be slightly red-shifted high above the Earth. And the same shall be true of light emitted from the surface of *any* massive body.

And let it be known to thee and all around thee that, as a consequence of general relativity, the Universe must either be expanding or contracting. And indeed, the Universe has been and is *expanding*. And the expansion of the Universe shall be because spacetime can bend and *be dynamic* – it shall stretch, twist and/or contract.

Now if a great quantity of mass *be* concentrated in a tiny space, spacetime shall curve *so much* as to *close* upon itself. And it shall be impossible for anything, including light, to then get out. Such an object *shall* be *a black hole*. And so in general relativity *shall* there be black holes. And indeed, black holes will be "seen by man," *not with his eyes but* by other means.

*The seventh book of Physics, called*

# Quantum Mechanics

*The hummingbird's wings flap fast and are invisible.*

## Chapter I: Quantum Versus Classical

Now all matter *shall obey* the principles of quantum mechanics. No object, particle, nucleus or atom shall violate its laws, for quantum mechanics shall be a fundamental consequence of the *unbroken part* of the broken Uni-Law.

Now classical mechanics and quantum mechanics are not compatible. One is half-truth. The other is the truth. And quantum mechanics *shall be the truth*.

Now classical mechanics leads to *no uncertainty*. Everything is *determined* by initial situations. In classical mechanics, the future is predictable given a complete knowledge of the present. But classical mechanics is *not valid*. And so the future cannot be foreseen, even with omniscience of the present.

Now classical mechanics shall be a good *approximation* for objects *larger* than the molecules. Thus macroscopic bodies, such as blocks, balls, living beings, planets, stars and galaxies shall move in conformity with classical mechanics. And because humans are *much bigger* than the atoms and because humans only see, feel and touch human-sized objects, humans will *think* that classical mechanics *be* absolutely true.

Now the quantum-mechanical behavior of a *microscopic* object such as an atom, a nucleus or a subatomic particle shall be *completely different* from the classical-mechanical behavior of a *macroscopic* object such as a solar system, a ball or a speck of dust. And this shall be true even though an atom is *like unto* a solar system, a nucleus is *like unto* a ball, and a subatomic particle is *like unto* a speck of dust. And the quantum-mechanical microscopic world shall be *unlike anything* a man has seen. To venture into the atomic and the subatomic shall be like entering the stately pleasure-dome of Xanadu – the scene shall be *unimaginable*.

And quantum mechanics shall be correct. So there shall *be* uncertainty. And classical mechanics shall be flawed. But it shall be just slightly flawed. And the flaws shall be so small that classical mechanics *shall* be almost true. And human beings shall believe it.

## Chapter II: Paths

*Ask among all paths, which is the good way?*
*And walk therein, for ye shall find there peace.*

Now quantum mechanics has two formulations. And the first is the path integral. Now the position of a moving particle as time evolves shall constitute the particle's *trajectory*. Thus a trajectory shall be a curve through space and time. And because it is a curve in space and time, it shall also be a *path*. And a point on the path at a particular time shall be the position of the particle.

And it is *as though* thou walkest along a wooded valley trail between two mountains. And thou beginst thy walk at the beginning of the trail. And thirty minutes later, thou hast traversed one mile of track. And one hour later, thou art two miles from the start. And two hours later, thou finishest thy walk. And since thou traverst the trail in a steady manner, *anyone* knows where thou art at any time. Thy motion is *predictable*. And thy positions at various times constitute a known trajectory. Thus in this example, the trajectory is the trail itself.

Now in classical mechanics, there shall be *but one* trajectory, or path. And this path shall be computable from Newton's laws. And it shall be called the *classical trajectory*. And knowledge of this path shall provide knowledge of the position of any object in the future, at the present, or in the past.

In classical mechanics, it is *as though* thou be infinitely lazy. And choosest thou the path of *least resistance*. And avoidest thou steep mountain slopes, so that thou walkest along the center of the valley. And though thou be *tempted* to take a short cut, it involves climbing and descending. And thou mightest want to pass along a longer, perhaps-more-scenic route, but lazy as thou art, takest thou the easy path, the lazy path.

*Only poets choose the path less travelled by.*

And for thee, the classical trajectory shall be the predictable, well-travelled trail. But in quantum mechanics, thou shalt be *free*. Thou shalt be allowed to walk along all paths.

Quantum mechanics – it *be the democratization*
*of dictatorial classical-mechanics laws.*

So in a quantum mechanical world, an object shall transverse *all paths*. But some paths shall be *more preferable* than others. And *the most preferred path* of all shall be the *classical trajectory*. And because *all* paths are included, it shall be *impossible* to predict *with certainty* where an object *be* at a given moment. Thus uncertainty shall be a property of quantum mechanics. And this effect shall have a name – the *uncertainty principle* shall be its name.

And *suppose* thou livest *in a quantum world* and thou beginst thy walk. Now in this quantum case, thou dost not plan thy walk. And thou art only somewhat lazy. So most of the time, movest thou along the local trail of least resistance. But *sometimes*, decidest thou to profit from a short cut. And *sometimes*, thou decidest to ascend a little hill. And *sometimes*, thou decidest to take a longer route. And these decisions are made randomly *but preferably*, because preferest thou the easy trails. And friends who are waiting for thee will be frustrated and annoyed because they do *not* know where thou *be* for sure. And although it is most probable that thou art on or near thy favorite well-travelled trail, thou perhaps hast gone *astray*.

And this formulation of quantum mechanics shall be called the *path integral* because "integral" means "to include all."

## Chapter III: Quantum Mechanics, Philosophers, Scientists and God

And philosophers will debate the *meaning* and implications of quantum mechanics and be particularly concerned about uncertainty. And many will be frustrated and annoyed. But, as for the uncertainty principle, scientists will understand it. And Nature simply shall obey it.

*To decide and then revise. To decide and then retreat.*
*Uncertainty will certainly confuse the wise.*

And theorists using the rules of quantum mechanics will carry out *countless* computations. And the computations will *all* agree with *countless* experiments performed by experimentalists. And scientists will develop a *great trust* in quantum-mechanical dynamics. And for some scientists, the faith will be as strong as a Christian's faith in God.

Now as a consequence of the uncertainty principle, it shall be impossible to know *simultaneously and exactly* the position and momentum of an object.[195] Thus position and momentum in quantum mechanics shall only *probabilistically* be known. And this shall be completely different from the notion of position and momentum in classical mechanics, where they are known with certainty.

## Chapter IV: The Planck Constant and Quantum Hills

Now quantum mechanical behavior and uncertainty shall be controlled by a *fundamental* number. And this fundamental parameter shall have a name – *Planck's constant* shall be called its name.

And theorists will *pretend* that they can control Planck's constant. And if they play the game of "god" and set the constant to zero, then the classical and quantum worlds will coincide. And making Planck's constant smaller shall be like making the slopes of hills and mountains steeper. And so a somewhat lazy walker will be *forced* to walk quite near the trail of least resistance. And if the theorists do play "god" and make the constant zero, then they make the slopes of hills and mountains infinitely steep – with giant hands they fold together mountains. And valleys turn into crevasses. Walkers become

---

[195] This effect becomes particularly important for microscopic objects, such as atoms and electrons.

completely trapped. And then even the most energetic motivated hiker
is compelled to traverse the crack *of least resistance*. And since this
crack is the classical trajectory, the motion shall be predictable and
classical.

But in the real world, Planck's constant is $6.6 \times 10^{-34}$ Joule-
seconds. Although miniscule, it is nonetheless not zero. And *nobody*,
neither scientists, nor philosophers, nor holy men, nor theorists can
make the constant zero. Such be written in firm stone. But since the
constant is *so small*, classical mechanics shall often be a *good approximation*. And because the constant is so small, quantum mechanical effects shall *only* in the *microscopic* world be manifest at all. Thus atoms,
nuclei, nucleons, electrons, quarks and other microscopic bodies *shall*
feel quantum effects, but living bodies, blocks and balls *shall not*. And
even in the microscopic world, the hills and valleys shall be very small.

And ants may struggle to pass around a tiny pebble, rock or
clump of dirt, but elephants do not.

*And quantum mechanics shall govern all –*
*All shall hearken to its song.*
*And quantum mechanics shall dominate the small.*

## Chapter V: Tunnelling

And quantum tunnelling and barrier penetration shall be a consequence of *the uncertainty of paths*. In the quantum world, a marble
in a coffee cup, in principle, may suddenly jump out. A path exists
which climbs the cup and spout. And from the spout, quickly *would* the
marble fall. But for this path, the probability is *very very small*. And
during the lifetime of the Universe, the marble will not jiggle its way
out.

But in *the subatomic world*, a body has a better chance to climb a
wall. And sometimes, like an army scout who leaves the troops and
climbs a little hill, a particle will jump and manage to get out. How
foreign from the world of man *be* the world of the quantum and the
small. And if a microscopic particle should suddenly surmount a wall,
one need not shout nor be alarmed – this is what barrier penetration is
about.

Now a process, which proceeds along a quantum path through a
classically forbidden region, shall by definition be *quantum tunnelling*
or *barrier penetration*. And the decay of a radioactive nucleus shall take
place by means of quantum penetration. Such a nucleus shall be *like
unto* a marble in a cup.

*Quantum mechanics shall be*
*full of fluctuations for objects of small size.*
*The quantum wings shall flap*
*like unto the wings of butterflies.*

## Chapter VI: The Wave Function

Now the second way to understand quantum mechanics is through the quantum wave equation. And although it is not obvious, this approach shall be entirely *equivalent* to the path-integral approach.

And let it be postulated that there *be* a wave function for an entity or object. And let it be further postulated that the wave function provides *the probability* of finding the entity at a particular position. Thus the *wave function* sums and incorporates all information of the quantum paths. Thus the wave function directly gives the position and momentum probabilities. And so the wave function, like the path integral, incorporates uncertainty. And to obtain the wave function, one must solve the *quantum wave equation.*

Now a wave function for an object shall be *like unto* a cloud of varying intensity. And the *brighter, whiter* regions shall indicate locations where the object is *most likely* to be seen. And places where the object is *less likely* to be found shall correspond to *fainter, less dense* regions of the cloud. And if the wave function *vanishes* somewhere, then cloudy mist shall not be there – *no chance* exists to find the object there. So this cloud shall not be an ordinary one, *but* a cloud of probability – intensity shall correspond to probability.

And although uncertainty shall prevail, quantum mechanics shall specify the uncertainty *exactly.* And *if* the wave function, which by definition is a solution to the quantum wave equation, is known, then the probability of finding an object at a particular place at a particular time shall be *exactly known.*

## Chapter VII: Quantum Waves

Now to understand the wave-function formulation one has to understand a wave. A *wave* is just an undulating motion such as the rise and fall of ocean water.

Now a wave shall have a highest point, which shall be called the *crest*. And a wave shall have a lowest point, which shall be called the *trough*. And let it be known to thee and all around thee that, unlike particles, waves *shall interfere*, and this shall be their *most important* property. And for example, when two water waves merge, their crests can coincide and the height of the wave can be increased – this shall be *constructive interference* because the displacement is enhanced. On the other hand, when two waves merge, the crest of one can coincide with the trough of the other and the waves can cancel – this shall be *destructive interference* because the wave motion is diminished.

Now wave functions shall function *like unto* water waves. And the *most likely position* of an object shall coincide with a point of *maximum displacement* such as at a crest or trough. And there shall be *no chance* of finding an object at a position where the wave is *not displaced* – such a point is sea level for ocean water waves.

And since wave functions *act as* water waves, wave functions *too* can interfere. Thus quantum waves shall undergo constructive and destructive interference. An object shall more likely be at constructive-interference points. And an object shall less likely be near destructive-interference points.

## Chapter VIII: Wave-Particle Complementarity

And the size of a wave unit shall be called its *wave length* – the distance between two crests. Now the length of a quantum wave shall have a special meaning – it shall determine *when* a wave function *functions* like a wave and is quantum mechanical and *when* a wave function *functions* like a particle and is classical. When the quantum wave length is *long*, the wave function shall be *like a wave*. And when the quantum wave length is *short*, the wave function shall be *like a particle* and not be like a wave.

Now when the quantum wave length is *short*, the spatial probability distribution shall be *localized* – the object must be near a tiny spot. And so the position of the object shall be known with greater certitude; there shall be *little uncertainty*, and classical mechanics shall be a good approximation. And the wave function shall behave like a classical object such as a macroscopic ball or block. And in this case when the wave length is very small, it shall be *hard to see* the crests and troughs. And it shall be *difficult* for such a wave to interfere constructively or destructively with another wave because its crests and troughs *are* so closely spaced. Such a wave function shall be like the wave around a fast-moving small torpedo – the entity shall behave more like a bullet than a wave. And if such a wave so strikes a wall, the destruction shall be localized in time and space. The impact shall be *like unto* the impact of a particle against a wall.

But when the quantum wave length is *long*, the position shall be *delocalized* – the object shall be located anywhere within a certain region. And so it shall be difficult to determine precisely *where* the object is. And constructive and destructive interference shall often naturally occur. And the wave function shall indeed act as a wave. Now when a long wave strikes a wall, it slaps against the wall *slowly* and the impact shall *not* be like a bullet or torpedo – this shall be the way a quantum wave collides. And using classical mechanics for such a long quantum wave would be *a bad approximation*.

And the contrasting behavior of short and long waves shall be called *particle-wave complementarity*.

And when shall an *object* have a long quantum wave? *It* shall have a *long* wave whenever it has low momentum. And when shall an *object* have a short quantum wave? *It* shall have a *short* wave whenever it has *high* momentum.

And since the momentum of an object is proportional to its mass, a *heavy body shall always* have a short quantum wave and thus behave *as if* it be a particle. Hence macroscopic bodies, such as blocks and balls and living bodies, never shall behave like waves. Only *lightweight* entities, such as atoms, nuclei, and subatomic particles, can have *long waves*. And when such lightweight entities have low momentum, they shall indeed have lengthy quantum waves and be wave-like. Thus, for example, shall the wave functions of low-energy electrons interfere. And when such electrons interfere, they shall create constructive and destructive interference regions – this shall be an *electron interference pattern*.[196] And since the electrons in the atoms usually have low momentum, such electrons *shall* behave like waves. And the collection of waves of atomic electrons shall be called the *electronic cloud*. Now when an electron has high momentum, it shall have a short wave *and* be like a particle. And high-energy electrons, when they strike a target, shall produce localized, bullet-like destruction.

*(And a voice spake, saying*
*"Beware of multi-MeV electrons and beta radiation.")*

## Chapter IX: Discreteness

Now often there shall be only *discrete* solutions to the quantum wave equation. And it is *like unto* the string of a guitar. And when the string is plucked, various vibrational motions are then possible. And if there be only one crest, then the crest appears in the middle of the string. And this is one solution. And if there be two crests, then a still point appears in the middle of the string and the crests appear on either side. And this is a second solution. And there can be vibrations with three crests. And in this case, one crest appears in the middle of the string and the other two emerge on either side of it. And between the middle crest and each side-crest is a still point. Thus there are two still points. And this is a third solution. And in general there can be solutions with *any number of crests*. And excluding the ends of the string, which are tied down and motionless, the number of still points on the string is one less than the number of the crests. Now for each type of vibration, there is a note. Thus there is a *discrete set* of sounds. And a guitarist with only these selected notes is unable to play tunes – to create other notes he uses his finger to shorten the string by pressing it against the neck of the guitar. But in the quantum world, there is *no such way* to shorten waves.

*(And a voice spake, saying*
*"Ye cannot put thy finger on a quantum wave.")*

Now a single vibrational motion of the guitar string shall in quantum mechanics correspond to what is called a state. A *state* shall by definition be a particular solution to the quantum wave equation.

---

[196] The situation shall be like the pattern of light one sees at the bottom of a pool when the water is agitated.

And a particle shall be in a particular state when it has a particular wave function. And the different notes of the guitar shall correspond to different energies. So each state shall have a unique energy – an *energy level* shall be the name for this. And since there are only *distinct* possibilities for states, there shall be only *distinct* possibilities for energies. And this is why the name quantum mechanics shall be used, for "quantized" means "discrete possibilities."

And for example, molecules shall have energy levels. And they shall be called *molecular energy levels*. And atoms shall have energy levels. And they shall be called *atomic energy levels*. And nuclei shall have energy levels. And they shall be called *nuclear energy levels*. And so on.

And among all states shall be one state *with lowest energy*. And it shall be the *ground state*.[197] The existence of such a state shall be essential for the stability of matter, for classically, electrons in an atom can lose energy by continually emitting electromagnetic radiation. In such a hypothetical classical world, electrons would spiral into nuclei and atoms would collapse. And once atoms did collapse, solids would fall in upon themselves. Then macroscopic objects such as planets, living bodies, balls and blocks, would so collapse. But *in Nature's quantum world*, electrons in atoms shall not spiral into nuclei – instead they shall radiate until they reach the quantum state of lowest energy. And once in this ground state, *there* shall they remain. And in this manner shall the stability of matter be maintained.

## Chapter X: Many-Body Quantum Mechanics

Now when many objects and/or particles are present, there shall be a quantum wave equation for *each* particle or object. But *only one* wave function shall there be. And it shall solve all the wave equations simultaneously. And it shall be called the *multiparticle wave function*. And a *multiparticle state* shall be a particular solution of the quantum wave equations.

Now in Nature's world, there shall *be* two kinds of particles according to their spin: fermions and bosons.[198] *Fermions* shall obey the Pauli exclusion principle: It says that two fermions of the same type cannot *be* in the same state. And for example, *all* the electrons in an atom cannot "sit" in the ground state. Now the Pauli exclusion principle can be understood as the *vanishing* of the multiparticle wave function when two identical fermions are "put" in the same place. And why is this so? It is so because a zero wave function means *zero probability*. Thus it shall be *impossible* for two identical fermions to occupy the same position or same state.

---

[197] Any state with an energy more than the ground state's energy is called an *excited state*. Excited states can lose energy and "tumble" to the ground state.

[198] See Chapter VII of the Book of *Subnuclear Physics*.

Now identical *bosons* shall behave the opposite of fermions. Not only shall they try to occupy the same position or same state, they shall do so maximally: The interchange of two selfsame bosons shall not change the state. And the situation shall be similar to that of identical red marbles: After putting all the marbles in a bag and shaking it, one shall no longer know *which is which*. Bosons are *like unto* red marbles; the multiparticle wave function for this system is *like unto* the bag. The *indistinguishability* of selfsame bosons shall make them behave in the most democratic way. And for example, if two neutral pions' positions are interchanged, the world shall not be changed.[199]

Now imagine ye a room of seats. Quantum states shall *be like unto* seats,[200] and fermions shall *be like unto* human beings: Once a person occupies a seat, another cannot sit in that same seat. And so a *second* person entering the room must search for a different spot, one where no one sits. And if there enters still a *third, that person* must find a space where the other two are not. And so by analogy, selfsame fermions may not be in the same place. But bosons shall be different; they shall be *like unto* ghosts: When the "cloudy image" of a ghost occupies a seat, another ghost can *sit* in that same seat. And if the two sit on top of one another, their cloudy images shall simply make a whiter cloud. And furthermore, it is possible for still a third ghost to sit down where the other two are sitting. Such ghosts do not get in each others' way in searching for a space. And so by analogy, bosons in the quantum world may *be in the* same place.

## Chapter XI: The Wave Equations

And quantum mechanics shall rule *all*. It shall manifest itself for objects that are small. Quantum mechanics shall govern atoms, nuclei, and subatomic particles like photons, electrons, neutrinos, quarks and gluons. Now subatomic particles shall obey special quantum wave equations called relativistic wave equations. And larger microscopic objects shall satisfy the ordinary quantum wave equation, the so-called *Schrödinger equation*.

## Chapter XII: Quantum Angular Momentum

And quantization shall apply not only to energy but to other quantum observables. And *quantum observables* shall be quantities that one can observe and measure, such as position, energy and momentum.

And the *amount of revolving* of an object shall be its *angular momentum*. And since angular momentum is an observable, it *shall be*

---

[199] Pions are elementary particles, which are bosons. See the Book of *Subnuclear Physics*.

[200] The periodic table can be understood as a particular arrangement of seats. See Chapters III-V of the Book of *Chemistry*.

*quantized.* And the possible amounts of angular momentum shall be limitless but yet discrete. And these amounts shall be multiples of a *fundamental unit*, which is Planck's constant. Thus there shall be states with angular momenta of zero, one, two, three, . . . multiples of this fundamental unit.

## Chapter XIII: Summary

*Quantum mechanics,*
*the poetry of physics,*
*sometimes classical and partially comprehensible,*
*often subtle and incomprehensible.*
*Some people think it mystical,*
*others call it philosophical*
*due to the quantum-mechanical violation*
*of foregone behavior and deterministic fate.*
*The rules are straightforward to formulate:*
*One solves the Schrödinger equation*
*and finds the appropriate energy state.*

*The eighth book of Physics, called*

# Electromagnetic Waves

*Understanding light –*
*what could be more worthy an endeavor?*

## Chapter I: Photons

Now electromagnetic waves shall obey a relativistic quantum wave equation. Thus light and other forms of *electromagnetic radiation* shall be quantum waves. And the quantum theory of electromagnetism shall be called *quantum electrodynamics*, or *QED*.

Now since electromagnetic radiation is quantum mechanical in nature, it can be *like* a particle or *like* a wave. And when the wavelength is *short*, the EM[201] wave shall then be *like unto* a particle. And such a particle shall be a photon. A *photon* shall be a concentrated pulse of EM energy, a "pellet" of electromagnetic radiation. Now when the quantum wave is *long*, the EM radiation then shall be indeed a *wave*. And classically it shall be the oscillations of electric and magnetic fields, *like unto* the undulation of an angel's hair in cosmic winds.

*For the human mind, the concept is somewhat radical:*
*Quantum complementarity means*
*that light is like a wave and light is like a particle.*

## Chapter II: Frequency

Now the *frequency* of a wave shall be the rate at which it "flaps." A high-frequency wave shall quickly undulate. A low-frequency wave shall slowly undulate. Now the frequency shall be measured in flaps per second, or *hertz*.[202]

Now the frequency of a wave shall *depend* on the motion of the source and the observer. And for example, when an observer and a wave source move *toward* each other, the observer shall see the waves go by *more quickly*, and so the frequency goes *up*. And when an observer and a wave source move *away* from one another, the waves shall go by *more slowly*, and thus the frequency goes *down*. And the *Doppler effect* shall be the name for this effect. And sound, which is a wave, like all waves shall undergo such Doppler shifts. And for example, the pitch of a whistle of a train will rise as it approaches thee. And the pitch will drop when the train passes and goes away from thee. And as for sound, higher pitch shall correspond to higher frequency. And if thou be standing by a highway, thou can hear the same effect: The pitch of engine noise of speeding cars will drop as they pass thee.

---

[201] EM, pronounced "ee-em," is short for electromagnetic.

[202] For example, a flag that flaps five times a second shall have a frequency of five hertz.

## Chapter III: Wave Speed

Now let it be known to thee and all around thee that the travelling *speed* of any wave shall be the *product of its frequency and length*. And if a train passes thee, how can thou find how fast it goes? Thou can count the number of train cars which pass per second. Next thou take this number and multiply it by a train-car's length. And think about it: This is the distance that the train traverses in one second. And *this* by definition is the speed. Now the number of cars, which pass per second, is *like unto* the frequency. And train-car length is *like unto* wavelength. Thus frequency times wavelength is the speed.

And because electromagnetic waves travel at a constant speed, which is the speed of light, or c, the frequency and wavelength shall *inversely* be related. Thus when the frequency goes *down*, the wavelength shall go *up*. And when the frequency goes *up*, the wavelength shall go *down*. And it is *like unto* a girl and boy upon a seesaw. When the girl goes up, the boy goes down. And when the girl goes down, the boy goes up. And they cannot both go up. Nor can they both go down.

## Chapter IV: Photon Energy and Momentum

Now let it be known to thee and all around thee that a *photon's energy* shall be *Planck's constant times the frequency*.[203] Thus an *increase* in the frequency shall mean an *increase* in the energy, while a *decrease* in the frequency shall mean a *decrease* in the energy. So energy and frequency shall walk together hand in hand. And for example, the waves of highest frequency, the gamma rays, are of the highest energy. And the waves of lowest frequency, the radio waves, are of the lowest energy.

And because, for electromagnetic waves, frequency times wavelength is a constant, which is c, the wavelength of a photon shall *inversely* be related to its energy. Thus an *increase* in its wavelength shall produce a *decrease* in its frequency and hence a *decrease* in its energy, while a *decrease* in its wavelength shall produce an *increase* in its frequency and hence an *increase* in its energy. Thus energy and wavelength shall be like children on a seesaw – when one goes up, the other shall go down. And for example, the waves of highest energy, the gamma rays, *have* the shortest wavelengths. And the waves of lowest energy, the radio waves, *have* the longest wavelengths.

And let it be known to thee and all around thee that the *momentum of a photon* shall be its energy divided by the speed of light. Thus a photon of low energy shall have a low momentum. And a photon of high energy shall have a high momentum and also have a stronger impact when it strikes another thing. And so a photon's energy and its momentum shall walk together hand in hand – when one goes up, the

---

[203] The presence of Planck's constant implies a photon is a quantum object – a photon is a quantum packet.

other shall go up; and when one goes down, the other shall go down. And for example, the waves of highest energy, the gamma rays, *have* the most momentum. And the waves of lowest energy, the radio waves, *have* the least momentum.

## Chapter V: The Electromagnetic Spectrum

*Light shall be the visible form of "light."*
*And other radiations,*
*such as microwaves and gamma rays,*
*shall be the invisible forms of "light."*

Now many kinds of *electromagnetic radiation* shall there be. And to each type shall be assigned a name. And from the most energetic to the least, from the shortest wavelength to the longest, they shall be gamma rays, X-rays, ultraviolet radiation, visible light, infrared radiation, microwaves and radio waves. And the *electromagnetic spectrum* shall be the name for this range of radiations.

*Electromagnetic waves*
*shall emerge invisibly from bodies,*
*like unto ghosts from graves.*

Now all gamma rays shall be particle-like and hence be photons. And X-rays shall *sometimes* be like particles and *sometimes* be like waves. And ultraviolet and the other low-energy electromagnetic radiations shall *always* propagate as waves.

Now *gamma rays* shall be like bullets. Such rays can knock an electron off its course like a truck colliding with a car. And *Compton scattering* shall be the name for this process in which an electron and a photon ricochet off one another. Now gamma rays shall be produced when nuclei decay, when matter and antimatter annihilate each other or when energetic elementary particles collide. As waves, gamma rays shall flap *extremely* fast, at more than thirty-billion-billion hertz. And their wavelengths shall be less than *one-billionth* of a centimeter, which is ten times smaller than an atom's size. As photons, their energy shall exceed one-hundred-thousand electron-volts, which is twenty-thousand times the energies of electrons bound in atoms. Per photon shall they be more powerful than lightning bolts.

Now *X-ray* photons shall have less energy than gamma rays but nonetheless *be* quite powerful – from one-hundred to one-hundred-thousand electron-volts. Typically, an X-ray shall be emitted when an excited nucleus decays or when an electron drops into a lower-most and empty level of an atom.

Likewise, ultraviolet and *visible light* shall be produced when an electron in an atom "tumbles" from an excited-energy level to a lower one. And the process will be *like unto* a ball that bounces down some steps; the electron being like a ball; an energy level being like a step;

and each ray of light emitted being like the sound that each bounce makes.

Now compared with visible light, *ultraviolet radiation* shall be several dozen times *more* energetic – the energy of visible photons shall be a few electron volts. And the wavelength of visible light shall be "invisibly small" – several hundred nanometers.[204] Now each *color* of light shall be a different wavelength. Blue light shall be around four-hundred-and-fifty nanometers long; green shall be around five-hundred nanometers long; yellow shall be around five-hundred-and-fifty nanometers long; orange shall be around six-hundred nanometers long; and red light shall be around six-hundred-and-fifty nanometers long. So colors shall be to light as notes are to a song.

Now the eye of man can see light waves with lengths between four-hundred and seven-hundred nanometers long. But man will be bat-blind to other EM waves. And since visible light constitutes a tiny band of the electromagnetic spectrum, man *will* be mostly blind. But man will think that what he sees is *all that can be seen* – man's perceptions will be small.

Now *infrared radiation* shall be emitted when warm gases and warm bodies cool – these radiations shall be associated with processes releasing heat. And microscopically, infrared waves shall be given off as fast-moving molecules slow down. And the wavelength of these waves shall range from seven-hundred nanometers to a millimeter. Now compared with visible light, millimeter-long infrared waves shall be a thousand times less energetic. And although it *be* invisible to thy eye, thy face will *feel* this heat of radiation if thou *be* by a fire.

Now microwaves and radio waves, which are the longest waves, shall be produced by currents. The length of a *microwave* shall be between a millimeter and two dozen centimeters. And *radio waves* shall be those EM radiations with wavelengths longer than the microwaves. And radio waves shall be the weakest waves – at least three-hundred-thousand times less energetic than visible light and at least *twenty-billion times less energetic* than the gamma rays.

## Chapter VI: Other EM Production Mechanisms and EM Applications

Now *accelerating charges* shall also make electromagnetic waves. And for example, the waving a rod of charge shall create changing electric fields that generate electromagnetic waves. And it is *as if* a witch waved a wand and cast out magic spells into the air. But Nature's radiations are not witchcraft; they are physical and real. Now *synchrotron radiation* shall be emitted by charges moving in a circle.

---

[204] A nanometer is a billionth of a meter, or about ten times an atom's size. The nanometer and other units of measurement in this chapter can be found in the Book of *Basic Units.*

And speeding charges, which suddenly are stopped, shall produce *bremsstrahlung*, or breaking radiation. Highly accelerating charges shall emit high-energy-type rays. And slowly accelerating charges shall emit low-energy-type waves.

Now electromagnetic radiation will be available to mankind for its profit or its loss. Radio waves will be the vehicle for TV and radio communication. Microwaves will be used for radar and in cooking. Infrared waves will be detected in special binoculars, permitting soldiers to see warm objects during night. Visible light will let humans see the world. Ultraviolet radiation will be used for fluorescence and in sterilization by killing germs. Invisible X-rays will make visible the skeletons and bones. And gamma rays[205] will be released in nuclear bombs and particle accelerators.

## Chapter VII: Electromagnetic Wave Properties

Now what are the features of the EM waves? They can constructively and destructively combine – *this* shall be called *interference*. They can bend around objects, like water waves around a dock – *this* shall be *diffraction*. They can bounce off objects – *this* shall be *reflection*. And for example, a mirror makes a good reflector. Electromagnetic waves can be deflected by tiny specks – *this* shall be called *scattering*. And for example, fog, haze, water droplets, clouds and smog can scatter light. The electric fields of EM waves can be made to oscillate in a common fixed direction – this shall be *polarization*. And for example, polarized sunglasses block out the light that does not oscillate in the polarizing plane. Electromagnetic waves can change direction when entering a medium – *this* shall be *refraction*. And a prism is a good example. And because different wavelengths are bent by varying amounts, a prism shall separate a beam of light into its colors. And as another example, lenses use refraction to focus or de-focus light. This leads to microscopes, eyeglasses, telescopes and magnifying glasses.

Now in a gas in which electrons are in excited atomic states, the passing of an EM wave can make electrons *drop* to lower states. And when an electron drops, it shall emit an EM wave. And this emitted wave can *spontaneously* stimulate emissions in another atom. And a chain reaction can ensue. And a powerful short burst of radiation *then* will be produced. And this will be how masers and how lasers work.[206]

## Chapter VIII: Black Body Radiation

Now all warm bodies, which are capable of radiating all frequencies equally and fully, shall emit the EM waves in a characteristic

---

[205] Gamma rays are sometimes used in the treatment of cancers. Directing such rays at a tumor or malignancy destroys the cancerous cells.

[206] MASER stands for Microwave Amplification by Stimulated Emission of Radiation. LASER stands for Light Amplification by Stimulated Emission of Radiation.

manner, called *black body radiation*. Now a hot body shall give off high-energy photons, but a hot body shall *also* give off some low-energy photons, although the number shall be fewer. In contrast, a cool body shall give off low-energy photons, but it shall *also* give off some high-energy photons, although the number shall be fewer. And quantum thermodynamics shall determine the distribution of these photons. And because photons are bosons, they shall obey a Bose-Einstein distribution. Now a deadly cold object at a few Kelvins shall mainly give off microwaves. An object up to four-thousand Kelvins shall mainly give off radiation in the infrared. *An object* at four-thousand-and-five-hundred Kelvins shall primarily be red. At four-thousand-and-eight-hundred Kelvins shall *it* be mainly orange. At five-thousand-and-three-hundred Kelvins shall *it* be mainly yellow. At five-thousand-and-eight-hundred Kelvins shall *it* be mainly green. At six-thousand-and-four-hundred Kelvins shall *it* be mainly blue. Now between seven-thousand and two-hundred-thousand Kelvins, a body shall primarily produce the ultraviolet radiations. And from two-hundred-thousand to two-hundred-million Kelvins, it shall mainly radiate X-rays. And finally, above two-hundred-million Kelvins shall gamma rays be mainly given off. Thus the *temperature of a black body* can be determined by which radiations it is giving off.

And let it be known to thee and all around thee that black body radiations are not some evil-spirit ghostly propagations. And let it be also known that most black bodies *are not black*.[207]

> *Red is hot.*
> *Green is hotter.*
> *Blue is hottest.*
> *Gamma-rays are death rays.*
> *X-rays are also waves.*
> *Ultraviolet is beyond the violet.*
> *Infrared is before the red.*
> *The eye is blind to microwaves.*
> *The ear is deaf to radio waves.*
> *Now with thy hand turn on the light.*
> *And now ye understand.*
>
> *Fluorescence, iridescence,*
> *incandescence, phosphorescence,*
> *they are a kind of light in essence.*

---

[207] One might ask: if most black bodies are not black, then why are they called black bodies? The answer is that black bodies at zero temperature *are* black. Not only are black bodies capable of radiating all frequencies, they are also capable of *absorbing* all frequencies. When they do not produce their own radiation, all impinging EM radiation is absorbed, rendering them invisible. Objects that are not black bodies are "visible" due to their ability to reflect EM waves.

*The ninth book of Physics, called*

# Subnuclear Physics

*Faith is the substance of things hoped for,*
*the evidence of things not seen.*

## Chapter I: Reductionism

It is the nature of the World that *small things* make up larger things, and that *even smaller things* make up the small. And this is true of many things. Letters make up words; words come together in sentences; sentences are organized in paragraphs; paragraphs are put together in a book; books make up the volumes in a library; libraries and private collections constitute all written work, the "universe" of printed text, which is a "universe" of knowledge.

*In the beginning were the Vowels and the Consonants.*
*Later came the Word.*

*So* be written text; so *be* the matter of the world. Nature's fundamental building blocks shall *be* the tiny quarks and leptons, the "letters" of the World. They shall be the basic fundamental units from which *all* is built. Now leptons, such as the electron and neutrino, shall sometimes live in "isolation" – *like unto* the letters "i" and "a", which also live as words, "I" and "a". In contrast, quarks must be combined – in hadrons,[208] together shall they *bind*. So hadrons are like words. And among the hadrons, two shall dominate thy lives – the neutron and the proton. But unlike the quarks and leptons, which are so small they seem "invisible," the hadrons shall have size – a *millionth of a billionth* of a meter in diameter. Now the neutrons and the protons shall *bind* to form the nuclei of Nature. And just as there are many ways to string a set of words together to formulate a sentence, so shall there be *many ways* for the neutrons and the protons to combine in nuclei. Now the next largest structure shall *be* the atom: A cloud of one or more electrons shall "swim" rapidly about the nucleus; the cloud *together with* the nucleus shall constitute an *atom*. And although the electron cloud shall be twenty-thousand times the nucleus's size, the nucleus shall be *almost* all an atom's weight.[209] Thus an atom's size, which is a few tenths of one-billionth of a meter, shall be determined by *its* electron cloud, while an atom's weight shall be determined by its nucleus. Now atoms, "the paragraphs of Nature," shall often bind to form an even larger structure: the molecule. And molecules shall make up microscopic structures, such as the constituents of gases, liquids, solids *and* the cells of Life. *Collections of molecules* shall comprise the things that

---

[208] Hadron means "heavy particle." Lepton means "light particle." In physics, words ending in "on" indicate an elementary particle. Such particles are microscopic point-like entities, such as electrons.

[209] 99.9% of an atom's weight is in the nucleus.

ye *so* well know: the air, the living creatures, the oceans and the rocks of Earth. Such *macroscopic structures* shall constitute entire worlds, with a myriad of variety – *they* are *like unto* the libraries of a thousand-thousand different books. And finally, worlds like thy solar system, shall fill the vacant spaces of the Universe.

Now *laws* shall govern how all things combine. Just as a random sequence of paragraphs *does not* a good book *make*; just as a random list of sentences *does not* a good paragraph *create*, so shall it be that atoms and molecules can combine in *only certain ways*. And the principles that govern how they bind are *the* domain of chemistry – atomic and molecular electromagnetic forces shall make the atoms bind; the chemical bond shall be the basic binding force.[210] Likewise, electrons and nuclei shall combine in *only certain ways*. And the principles that govern the formation and structure of the atom shall be the subject of atomic physics.[211] And atomic forces, created by electromagnetism, shall "hold" the electron cloud about the nucleus.

Now just as a random sequence of words *does not* a good sentence *make*, so shall it be that protons and neutrons bind in *only certain ways*. And it shall be the nuclear strong force which holds the nucleus together. Now the strong force shall be one of four fundamental forces. And these four interactions shall constitute the *basic laws of Nature*, the fundamental principles *that govern all*. Knowledge of these forces shall be of priceless scientific wealth, as valuable to scientists as the Ten Commandments are to priests.

And just as a random list of letters *does not* a good word *make*, so shall it be that quarks combine in *only certain ways*. And again, it shall be the strong force which holds the quarks together. So knowledge of the strong force shall tell ye *which* hadrons form and why. To know the strong force is to understand the nuclear and subnuclear. *So may* ye understand. Now the *dominion of the very small* shall be very different from thy macroscopic world on Earth of simple things like sticks and books and balls. The microscopic world shall be a foreign land where objects obey a very different set of laws.

*(And a voice spake, saying,*
*"May ye a new language learn.")*

## Chapter II: Subnuclear Forces

Now the forces that control the *subnuclear dominion* shall be the strong force, electromagnetism and the weak force. And the fourth force, gravity, can be *neglected* at these microscopic scales, because the masses of the elementary particles are miniscule.

Now the elementary particles and subnuclear interactions shall constitute the *Standard Model*, which is a consequence of the broken

---

[210] See the New Testament Book of *Chemistry*.

[211] See the New Testament Book of *Atomic Physics*.

Uni-Law. And the Standard Model shall possess a hidden symmetry called *SU-three-cross-SU-two-cross U-one*. But when the Universe was one-trillionth of a second old, part of the symmetry became destroyed,[212] as SU-two-cross-U-one was broken to U-one. And so, the explicit symmetry of the Standard Model shall be less – it shall be *SU-three-cross-U-one*.

Now the strong force shall operate at distances within a femtometer – *a millionth of a billionth* of a meter, which is the size of lighter nuclei. And the weak force shall only operate inside an even smaller *sphere of influence* – within one-hundredth of a femtometer.

Now the weak force shall be *so weak* that it hardly has effects. And this shall be true even in a nucleus. But the weak force shall induce some *rare decays*. And a neutron outside a nucleus shall be a typical example – such a neutron shall in fifteen minutes undergo a weak decay into an antineutrino, an electron and a proton.

## Chapter III: Subnuclear Particles

Now there shall be two types of elementary particles: the gauge bosons and the matter fermions. The fundamental *matter fermions* shall make up matter; the *gauge bosons* shall create the forces.

Now the gauge bosons shall be the eight gluons, the photon, the W-plus, the W-minus and the Z. And let it be known to thee and all around thee that *all particle interactions are produced through the exchange of bosons.*[213] And for example, an electron may emit a photon which is absorbed *subsequently* by a proton. And this shall create an electromagnetic force between the proton and electron. And in general, *electromagnetic interactions* shall be produced through the *exchange of photons.* Now one quark may emit a gluon which is absorbed subsequently by a second quark. And this exchange shall create a nuclear strong force. And in general, *strong interactions* shall be generated by *exchanging gluons.* Now a neutron may decay by emitting a W-minus and a proton. But this W-minus, being short-lived, does not last long and almost instantly decays into an antineutrino and an electron. And this W-minus, which is "born" from the proton and "dies" near the electron, shall create this weak decay. And in general, the *exchange of the weak vector bosons*, the W-plus, the W-minus and the Z, shall generate the nuclear *weak force.*

Now of the fundamental matter fermions, *some* shall interact by *the strong force* – and *they* shall be the *quarks.* And those matter fermions that do not feel the strong forces shall be *leptons.* Now the strong force shall be so strong that quarks shall bind in groups of two or three called *hadrons* – isolated quarks shall never be observed. But leptons

[212] See the Old Testament Book of *Exodus I: Electroweak Breaking.*

[213] Even the fourth force, gravity, is *believed* to be generated by the exchange of a boson called a graviton.

*shall* be free, "living" in isolation and sometimes being "seen." And for example, in a flash of lightning shall ye see countless leptons.[214] Now since no human being shall have seen a quark, many among thee shall doubt the quark's existence. But in thy body shall there be several million-trillion-trillion quarks.

> *Water, water everywhere,*
> *nor any drop to drink.*

Now particles shall have *"mirror" counterparts* – for every particle, there shall exist an *antiparticle*. And for example, the positron shall be the electron's antiparticle. And the antiproton shall be the proton's antiparticle. *And so on.* Now the antiparticle of an antiparticle shall be the particle. So the antiparticle of the positron shall be the electron, for example. Some particles shall be their own antiparticles. And the photon shall be but one example. The antiparticles of leptons shall be called the *antileptons*, while the antiparticles of quarks shall be the *antiquarks*. And these antiparticles of Nature shall make up fermionic *antimatter*. When antimatter and matter come together, they shall annihilate, producing energy often in the form of photons. Antimatter shall rarely manifest itself on Earth. Indeed, most of the Universe shall be made of ordinary matter. But when the Universe was less than a second old, matter and antimatter were present in almost equal numbers.

## Chapter IV: The Naming of Matter Fermions

And let the names of matter fermions be known. Let the "letters" of Nature's secret scriptures be revealed. Of the *leptons* shall there be two kinds: those that have a negative electric charge and those that are precisely neutral. And the charged leptons shall be called the *tau*, the *muon* and *electron*, the latter two also being known as "mu" and "e". Now a *neutrino* shall be a neutral lepton and also called the "nu".[215] Each charged lepton shall have its own neutrino. Thus there shall be three types of neutrinos: the *"nu-tau," "nu-mu,"* and *"nu-e"*.

Now the *antileptons* (the leptons' antiparticles) shall have their lepton's name *prefixed* with an "anti." They shall be called the "anti-tau," "anti-mu" and "anti-e," and the "anti-nu-tau," "anti-nu-mu," and "anti-nu-e."

Now there shall be altogether eighteen types of *quarks*. Eighteen shall be just three times six: Three "strong-colors" and six "flavors" shall distinguish quarks. The *flavors* shall be "top," "bottom," "charm," "strange," "up" and "down" and have *"no taste"* – they *simply* shall be names. So in Nature shall there be the *top quark*, the *bottom quark*, et cetera. Now each of these six "flavored" quarks shall come in three

---

[214] Lightning, a visible form of electricity, is composed of electrons. Electrons are leptons. Technically speaking, ye see the photons coming from the electrons.

[215] The thirteenth letter of the Greek alphabet is "nu."

*strong-colors* – "strong-yellow," "strong-red," "strong-blue."[216] And ye shall call them "yellow," "red" and "blue" for short. These strong-colors and the colors of light *are not the same,* for strong-colors shall be the SU-three charges of the nuclear strong force. Here are the eighteen quarks:

|                    |                 |                  |
| ------------------ | --------------- | ---------------- |
| the yellow-t quark | the red-t quark | the blue-t quark |
| the yellow-b quark | the red-b quark | the blue-b quark |
| the yellow-c quark | the red-c quark | the blue-c quark |
| the yellow-s quark | the red-s quark | the blue-s quark |
| the yellow-u quark | the red-u quark | the blue-u quark |
| the yellow-d quark | the red-d quark | the blue-d quark |

where the letters "t", "b", "c", "s", "u" and "d" stand for top, bottom, charm, strange, up and down.

Now since the *antiquarks* are the antiparticles of quarks, they shall also number eighteen. Their names shall be the names of quarks *prefixed* with an "anti": the "anti-t quark," the "anti-b quark," et cetera. And if ye need to specify the strong-color of an antiquark, ye shall speak of the "anti-yellow-t quark," the "anti-red-t quark," et cetera. And note ye that the strong-colors of the antiquarks are the *opposite* of quarks – these strong-colors are "anti-yellow," "anti-red," and "anti-blue."

Now antiquarks and antileptons shall *constitute* all fermionic antimatter. And anti-e, the antiparticle of the electron, shall be provided with a special name. And that name shall be the *positron.*

Now the quarks and leptons shall form *three* families, not of people but of particles. Each family shall have *four* members: two leptons and two quarks. And the first generation and lightest family shall consist of the electron, nu-e, u and d. And the second family shall contain the muon, nu-mu, s and c, while the third generation and the heaviest family shall have for members the tau, nu-tau, the b and t.

> *Mankind has its many generations.*
> *Quarks and leptons have just three.*

## Chapter V: Enumeration of Vector Gauge Bosons

And let the *vector gauge bosons* be enumerated – there shall be twelve particles of interaction. And of these, *one* shall be for U-one, *three* shall be for SU-two, and *eight* shall be for SU-three. Thus gauge bosons shall be associated with the Standard Model's hidden SU-three-cross-SU-two-cross-U-one symmetry. Now a vector boson of SU-three shall be a *gluon*. Gluons shall have one strong-color and one strong-anti-color charge, that is, a dipole-color-charge. And of the *eight* gluons,

---

[216] The strong-colors, also known as strong charges or SU-three charges, are conserved, meaning that they do not change with time: The total number of SU-three charges in the Universe is a constant. The strong-colors play an essential role in the strong force. See Chapter VII.

*six* shall have manifest strong-color, and they shall be the yellow-anti-red, the yellow-anti-blue, the red-anti-yellow, the red-anti-blue, the blue-anti-yellow and the blue-anti-red gluons. And the remaining *two* shall be made from yellow-anti-yellow, red-anti-red and blue-anti-blue.[217] And the SU-two vector bosons, of which there shall be three, shall possess *weak-isospin* or SU-two-type charge. And the U-one boson shall be alone and *neutral* in its charge.

And the above twelve vector bosons shall generate *all forces*, save for gravity. They shall be the instruments implementing Nature's laws and dictating how the quarks and leptons interact.

## Chapter VI: Mass Generation

Now in the early moments of the Universe, *one-hundredth of a billionth* of a second after the Big Bang, SU-three-cross-SU-two-cross-U-one spontaneously broke to U-one and to SU-three. And this electroweak breaking *gave masses* to three of the four SU-two-cross-U-one vector bosons – the *W-plus*, *W-minus* and *Z-naught*. And the fourth gauge boson, born as part SU-two boson and part U-one boson, remained massless – it was the *photon*.

At the same time, electroweak breaking produced masses for the quarks and leptons. But neutrinos were not given mass – they stayed massless. Now what are the masses of the quarks and leptons? The electron weighs half a million-electron-volts,[218] or a *billionth of a billionth of a billionth* of a gram. And the up quark weighs ten times this. And the down quark weighs twice the up-quark mass. And the muon weighs two-hundred times the weight of an electron – one-hundred-and-six million-electron-volts. And the mass of the strange quark is fifty per cent more than this. And the charm quark weighs twelve times the muon's mass. The tau lepton is fifty per cent heavier than the charm quark, or one-thousand-eight-hundred million-electron-volts, which is the mass of a deuterium. And the bottom quark is two-and-a-half times heavier than this. And the mass of the top quark is *enormous* – forty times the mass of the bottom quark, which is three-hundred-and-fifty-thousand times the mass of an electron, which is the weight of a tungsten nucleus!

Now the mass of a particle and its antiparticle shall be exactly *equal*. And for example, the positron's mass shall be *precisely* the electron's mass. And the anti-d-quark mass shall be the d-quark mass. *And so on.*

And let it be known to thee and all around thee that the exchange of a massive boson shall yield only *short-ranged* forces. Thus the

---

[217] The ninth combination, which is an equal admixture of these three dipole-color-charges, is not an SU-three gluon.

[218] Mass can be measured in energy units, such as electron-volts, by multiplying by $c^2$. This uses the formula $E=mc^2$.

exchange of the Z and W shall generate repulsions and attractions over distances *no bigger* than a hundredth of a femtometer. And because it is difficult to exchange very heavy bosons, these forces shall be weak. Thus these forces shall be *the weak interactions*.

So the vector bosons, which are *massless*, shall be the gluons and the photon. *Long-ranged* forces shall be created by these bosons. The photon shall be the source of all *electromagnetism*. Through its exchange shall the electric and magnetic forces be produced.

## Chapter VII: Non-Abelian Gauge Interactions

Let the laws of Nature's interactions – "the syntactic rules of sacred script" – *be known*. How shall it be that all interactions are generated through exchanging bosons? Suppose thou and thy friend stand on a lake of ice. And suppose thou throw a ball to him. Then thou shall *move away from him*. And why? Conservation of momentum shall be the reason why – in throwing him the ball, thou throw away momentum; so thou must recoil from the toss. And that gives thee momentum opposite to the direction of the ball. Now upon catching the thrown ball, what happens to thy friend? He *moves away from thee*. And why? Conservation of momentum shall be the reason why – in capturing the ball, he gains the momentum that thou have thrown away. Now he, in turn, may throw the ball to thee. And this will make him further move from thee. And when thou catch the ball, thou receive an impulse, *further* sending thee away from him. And so by throwing balls between thy friend and thee, the two of thee *create a force*. And Nature's forces shall *be* created in this way; balls shall be *like unto* bosons, while thou and thy friend shall be *like unto* fermionic matter.[219]

Now the *strong forces*, which are non-abelian gauge interactions, *shall* be generated by exchanging gluons, or SU-three-type bosons. Such exchanges shall transfer color charges, *while preserving total color charge*. And the following shall be examples of processes *permitted* by the strong-force interactions. (1) A quark can decay into a gluon and another quark: And for example, a *yellow* quark can decay into a *red* quark and a *yellow-anti-red* gluon. And indeed this process *shall* proceed. And note ye that strong-yellow-color charge is *perfectly conserved*: the *yellow* of the initial quark arises as the yellow in the final gluon. And note ye that likewise the strong-red-color charge is *perfectly preserved*: the lack of strong-*red* in the initial quark is reflected in the cancellation of strong-red between the final quark and gluon. And *the reverse* of this decay can also happen: (2) a quark and gluon can *fuse* into a quark: And for example, a *red* quark and a *yellow-anti-red* gluon can fuse into a *yellow* quark. And indeed this process *shall* proceed. And (3)

---

[219] From this analogy, it would seem as if only repulsive forces could be created. The analogy is not perfect – when Nature "tosses bosons" both repulsive and attractive forces can be generated.

an antiquark can decay into a gluon and another antiquark, or (4) the reverse of this can happen with a gluon and an antiquark fusing into an antiquark. Or (5) a gluon can decay into a quark and antiquark, or (6) the reverse of this can happen with a quark and antiquark fusing into a gluon. And indeed, *as long as strong-color is preserved*, all these processes proceed. So in total, six generic types of gluon-quark decays and fusions shall arise.

Now gluons shall also interact with gluons. A gluon can decay into two gluons. And for example, a *yellow-anti-red* gluon can decay into a *yellow-anti-blue* gluon and a *blue-anti-red* gluon. And note ye that all three strong-colors are perfectly preserved. And *the reverse* can also happen. Two gluons can fuse into a single gluon. And for example, a *yellow-anti-blue* gluon and a *blue-anti-red* gluon can fuse into a *yellow-anti-red gluon*. And so on. And indeed, *as long as strong-color is conserved*, these processes proceed.

And these interactions shall constitute *quantum chromodynamics*, or *QCD*. And since only quarks, antiquarks and gluons have strong-color, *only* quarks, antiquarks and gluons shall interact by *the* strong force.

Now gluon emission and absorption shall not change the flavor of a quark. So it is not necessary to specify the flavor of the quarks for SU-three-type processes. Since SU-three is "tasteless," the strong interactions shall be *flavor blind*. Hence when a yellow quark decays into a red quark and a yellow-anti-red gluon, it might be a yellow-d quark which decays into to a red-d quark and a yellow-anti-red gluon, *or* it might be a yellow-u quark which decays into to a red-u quark and a yellow-anti-red gluon, *and so on*. And as is evident, the gluons carry *no flavor* and hence are flavorless.

Now the SU-two interactions shall be *just like* the SU-three interactions *except* that different charges, called weak-isospins, shall be exchanged. All quarks, antiquarks, leptons, antileptons and SU-two gauge bosons shall possess weak-isospins, so that all particles *except* gluons and the U-one boson shall participate in SU-two-type interactions. SU-two forces shall be generated by *exchanging* weak-isospin through SU-two gauge bosons.

Now the *U-one interaction* shall be *different* from the SU-two and the SU-three interactions in that *it* shall be abelian. Furthermore, the U-one vector-gauge boson shall *not* carry its own charge and hence, with itself, it *shall* not interact – this shall be the meaning of *abelian*. And this lack of self-interaction shall be the *essential difference* between abelian and non-abelian gauge interactions: non-abelian gauge bosons shall *be* self-interacting, while abelian ones shall not. Now all fermionic matter particles shall carry U-one charge, while all gauge bosons shall be U-one neutral. Thus only quarks, leptons, antiquarks and antileptons shall participate in U-one interactions. And they shall do so by exchanging U-one vector bosons.

## Chapter VIII: The Spins of Particles

A nd know that particles *can spin*. And they shall spin *like unto* tiny
tops. Now quantum mechanics *dictates* that the spin must be in
quantized bits – multiples of half a fundamental unit, which is
Planck's constant. Thus particles may have zero, half, one, one-and-a-
half, two, et cetera, units of spin. Now a particle with an *integer* spin
shall be a *boson*, while a particle with a *half-integer* spin shall be a
*fermion*. Thus the essential difference between a boson and a fermion
shall be its spin.

And let the spins of particles be known. All the quarks and leptons shall have *half*-a-fundamental unit. Thus quarks and leptons
shall be fermions. And since fermions *must obey* the Pauli exclusion
principle, electrons, as well as quarks and other leptons, *shall obey* –
they may not occupy each other's space. Now the word *vector* shall indicate *spin one*. And so the vector gauge bosons, as the name implies,
shall *spin* with one fundamental unit.[220] Thus photons, as well as gluons, W's and Z's, shall indeed be bosons.

## Chapter IX: The Charges of Particles

A nd let the electric charges of the particles be known.[221] Now the
charge of the electron, the muon or the tau – the charged leptons –
shall be *minus one*. Neutrinos shall be neutral – they have *zero* charge.
And the u, c and t quarks shall have a charge of *plus two-thirds*. And
*minus one-third* shall be the d and s and b. Now an antiparticle and a
particle shall have charges that are *opposite*. And so the charges of the
charged anti-leptons, that is, the anti-tau, the anti-mu and the anti-e
(the positron), shall be *plus one*. And *minus two-thirds* shall be the
anti-u, the anti-c and anti-t. And *plus one-third* shall be the anti-d, the
anti-s and anti-b. And of the gauge bosons, all shall be neutral, save
for two: W-plus shall have a charge *plus one*, and the W-minus, which
is the W-plus's antiparticle, shall have a charge of *minus one*.

And note ye that the charges of all particles are *multiples of a
minimum amount*, which is one-third. This property of Nature shall be
called *charge quantization*. It shall not follow directly from the Standard Model, but be a consequence of Grand-Symmetry and hence the
Uni-Law.

Now photons shall be exchanged among electrically charged particles. Such exchanges shall produce electromagnetic interactions, causing *same-signed charges* to repel and *opposite-signed charges* to attract.
And since particles that are neutral, such as the photon, gluons and
neutrinos, do not partake in the exchange of photons, they shall have
no electric nor magnetic interactions.

---

[220] Unlike the gauge bosons, the graviton has spin two.

[221] Also see the Table of Fundamental Matter in the Book of *Tables*.

## Chapter X: The Strong Interactions

Now the SU-three interactions, which are based on the exchange of strong-color charge through gluons, shall grow *relatively weaker* when the quarks *approach* each other. And this behavior shall be named. And *asymptotic freedom* shall be the name.

Now what happens when two quarks are pulled part? The answer shall be that quarks exchange more rapidly the gluons. And this increase in exchange of gluons shall lead to *stronger* force. And so the strong interactions shall *get stronger* when two quarks are *move apart*.[222] And this shall be true of any two strong-colored objects that are pulled apart. And this behavior shall be named. *Infrared slavery* shall be the name. Now at a distance of one femtometer, the force shall become extremely strong. *Quite difficult* shall it be to separate strong-colored objects further than a femtometer. To move a quark even a picometer[223] from all other quarks shall be virtually impossible. And this property shall have a name. And *quark confinement* shall be the name. *In chains of glue* shall quarks be tied together.

And in the aftermath of the Big Bang, when the Universe was *small*, particles were *close* to one another. And due to asymptotic freedom, the strong interactions were *not* so strong and quarks were free to move about each other. But as the Universe expanded, the quarks were drawn apart and the strong interactions grew *much stronger*. And when the Universe was one ten-thousandth of a second old, the strong force became *so strong* that quark confinement came about. Bound states of quarks and antiquarks then formed. And isolated quarks could *be no longer* found.

Thus the quarks and antiquarks in Nature shall be *bound* in groups of two and three. And such a state shall be a *hadron*. And so quarks and antiquarks shall remain *unseen* in the macroscopic world. *Ye* shall see no quarks – *hidden* in the hadrons shall they be.

## Chapter XI: The Hadrons

Now a *quark and anti-quark* can form a strong-color-neutral state. And for example, a yellow quark can combine with an anti-yellow quark since yellow plus anti-yellow makes white, which is *strong-color neutral*. Or a red quark and an anti-red quark can combine. Or a blue quark and an anti-blue quark can combine. And indeed such pairs of quarks shall *bind*. And these "SU-three-white" states shall have a name. And the name shall be a *meson*.

And *three quarks* can form a strong-color-neutral state. Yellow, red and blue quarks can combine since yellow plus red plus blue makes white. And indeed three such quarks shall *bind*. And these

---

[222] This is the opposite of the other three fundamental forces – they weaken as the distance is increased.

[223] A picometer is one-trillionth of a meter, or one-thousand femtometers.

"SU-three-white" three-quark states shall have a name. And the name shall be a *baryon*.

And *three antiquarks* can form a strong-color-neutral state. An anti-blue quark, an anti-red quark and an anti-yellow quark can bind since anti-yellow plus anti-red plus anti-blue makes white. And these three-antiquark bound-states shall have a name. And the name shall be an *antibaryon*.

Now ordinary white light is an equal mixture of yellow, red and blue electromagnetic light. And a prism can split such white light into its separate bands of yellow, red and blue. But SU-three-chromatic light shall be *quite different* from electromagnetic light. At macroscopic distances, *only* shall there be white SU-three-chromatic light; this is known as gluon-quark confinement. Beyond atomic lengths, there is no yellow, red and blue for SU-three. So these SU-three-chromatic colors shall never fill the dark of night, for they shall simply *bind too tight*. And so the baryons, antibaryons and mesons shall *be* strong-colored white.

And let be known the names of mesons. The flavor content of the quarks shall indicate the type of meson:

*The meson made of b and anti-b shall be the Upsilon.*
*The meson made of c and anti-c shall be the psi.*
*That of s and anti-s shall be the phi.*
*The meson made of u or d and anti-u or anti-d shall be the pi or pion.*
*The one of u or d and anti-s shall be the "K" or kaon.*
*And the meson made of c and anti-b shall be the "B-sub-c."*
*That of s and anti-b shall be the "B-sub-s."*
*That of c and anti-s shall be the "D-sub-s."*
*The meson made of u or d and anti-b shall be the "B".*
*And the meson made of u or d and anti-c shall be the "D".*

And let the names of the baryons be known. Their names shall be capital Greek letters such as Sigma, Delta, Lambda and Omega. But the baryon made of u's and d's shall have a special name: the *nucleon*. *Two* u's and one d shall be the *proton*. *Two* d's and one u shall be the *neutron*. So a nucleon shall be a neutron or a proton.

Now inside hadrons, the quarks, antiquarks and gluons shall interact according to the SU-three strong force.[224] Thus the exchange of gluons *shall not stop* inside bound states. *Like unto* glue shall gluons act, as quarks and antiquarks emit the gluons at high rates. And the gluons, also emitting and absorbing gluons, shall *likewise* tie themselves "in chains of glue" and *not* be able to escape. And all these processes shall produce strong interactions and bound states. And so the strong interactions shall be *not* long-ranged but *be* contained within a femtometer. And this shall be a hadron's size.

---

[224] Chapter VII described these interactions.

And the quarks and antiquarks shall be *like unto* colored angels, wearing *gluonic halos. The cloud of gluons* shall move with quarks when quarks so move. So if a quark speeds to the left, the gluon cloud shall too speed to the left. And if the quark speeds to the right, the gluon cloud shall too speed to the right. And since the gluon halos are somewhat *heavy*, the quarks and antiquarks shall gain an extra mass. And *effectively* the up and down quarks shall *not* be light in weight.

Now the mass of a hadron shall be *the sum* of the masses of its quarks and the surrounding interactions. And so *the mass of a meson* shall be roughly the mass of its *two* component quarks. Similarly, the mass of a baryon shall be roughly the mass of its *three* component quarks.

And a hadron's *electric charge* shall be *the sum* of the charges of its component quarks. And for example, u–anti-d, which is a pion, shall be *pi-plus*. And its charge shall be *plus one*, for the charges of the u and anti-d are two-thirds and one-third, which sum to one. And the charge of the d-d-u baryon, which is the *neutron*, shall be *zero*, for the charges of the d, d and u are respectively minus one-third, minus one-third and two-thirds, which sum to *none*. Thus the neutron shall be neutral. And the charge of the u-u-d baryon, which is the *proton*, shall be *plus one*, for the charges of the u, u and d are two-thirds, two-thirds and minus one-third, which sum to one.

Now a bound state shall be a *boson* if the number of fermions in it is *even*. And for example, mesons such as pions, which are made from a quark and antiquark and thus two fermions, are bosons. Now a bound state shall be a *fermion* if the number of fermions in it is *odd*. And for example, baryons such as the neutrons and the protons, which contain three quarks and thus three fermions, are fermions. And since fermions *must obey* the Pauli exclusion principle, the baryons including the protons and the neutrons *shall obey*.

Now most hadrons shall *not be stable* but *decay*: All mesons shall disintegrate within a small fraction of a second into lighter particles. And pions, for example, shall decay: The pi-naught, the neutral pion, shall vanish into a pair of photons in *one-tenth of one-millionth of one-billionth* of a second. And this process shall proceed by quantum electrodynamics, or QED. And similarly, the negatively charged pion, pi-minus, shall disappear into a muon and an anti-mu neutrino in *one-hundredth of one-millionth* of a second. And the *muon* from this pi-decay, in the next one-millionth of a second, shall decay into an anti nu-e, an electron and a nu-mu. And the decays of both the pi-minus and the muon shall proceed by *the* weak interactions.

Thus *only a few* particles shall not decay. And they shall be the photon, electron, proton, neutrino and their antiparticles. As for the neutron, it shall be often stable in a nucleus.

Now save for the neutron and the proton, hadrons shall be rarely found on Earth. Indeed they shall not be too common in the Universe.

And even if they are produced, they die quite fast. But around one-millionth of a second after *the* Big Bang, countless particles like mesons filled the Universe.

Still exotic hadrons shall appear. Indeed, energetic protons in cosmic rays from outer space shall strike Earth's upper atmosphere, producing countless elementary particles. And among these particles shall be pions, muons and neutrinos. They shall rain down from heaven, passing through the clouds and striking Earth. Indeed, several rays shall pass through thy body every minute of thy life on Earth!

## Chapter XII: Antimatter[225] and C-Exchange

Now charge conjugation, or *C-exchange*, shall be the *hypothetical* process of interchanging particles and antiparticles – under C-exchange, a particle shall become its antiparticle and an antiparticle shall become the particle. And for example, under C-exchange, an electron shall become a positron, and an antiproton shall become a proton. And applying C-exchange *twice* shall do nothing because the antiparticle of an antiparticle is the particle itself. And it is like thou hast a single sibling – the sibling of thy sibling is thyself.

Note ye that C-exchange creates *a change of sign* of charge. And for example, under C-exchange, an electron, which is *negatively* charged, shall become a positron, which is *positively* charged.

Now gravity, electromagnetism and the strong force shall be C-exchange invariant, meaning that these forces shall *not be changed* when particle and antiparticle are interchanged. And for example, the gravity between a gram of matter and a kilogram of matter shall be the *same* as the gravity between a gram of antimatter and a kilogram of antimatter. Likewise, the electrical repulsion between two electrons shall be the *same* as the electrical repulsion between two positrons. And the strong force between a proton and an antineutron shall be the *same* as the strong force between an antiproton and a neutron.

A world of antimatter shall be *almost like* a world of matter. But a difference between these worlds shall be created by the weak force – it shall *not* be C-exchange invariant: The weak force *shall change* when particle and antiparticle are interchanged. And for example, the weak force between two electrons shall not be exactly the same as the weak force between two positrons.

Now if man, like a god, could *somehow* implement the C-exchange, the Universe would instantly become an anti-Universe. And all matter would turn into antimatter. But man is *not* a god.

Nor would this antiworld[226] be just like ours. Know ye and all around ye that an antiworld is slightly different from a world.

---

[225] One practical application of antimatter is the PET scan. It uses positrons to make images of brain activity.

[226] Current astronomical observations do not indicate the presence of anti-galaxies or

*(And a voice spake, saying,*
*"Do not shake the hand of thy antimatter counterpart.")*

## Chapter XIII: Time Reversal

Now *time-reversal exchange* shall be the *hypothetical* reversing of the flow of time. Under time reversal, an object moving *forward* shall become an object moving *backward*. Under time reversal, a movie film runs backward – the outcome of the saga is at the beginning, the initial scenes are at the end.

Now under time reversal, the four fundamental forces *shall* remain the same. Thus for every process that proceeds, there shall be a process that proceeds but *in reverse*. And for example, an electron and a positron can annihilate and generate a pair of photons. And since the four interaction laws are time-reversal independent, two photons can annihilate and yield an electron and a positron.

And in a world with time-reversal symmetry, the following would be possible *in principle*. If, by an act of god, time's arrow suddenly were flipped, then the velocities of all objects in the Universe would be instantly reversed. And the history of the Universe would be repeated, starting from the present and ending in the distant past. And water would flow from basins into taps. And babies would crawl back into their mothers' wombs. And the space-fabric of the Universe, instead of expanding, would contract. And the end of time would be *the* Big Bang beginning.

However, under time-reversal exchange the laws of Nature at a fundamental level shall not be the same. And why? The *interactions* leading to electroweak breaking[227] shall *in a small way* upset this symmetry. As a consequence, the masses and the interactions of quarks shall reflect a *tiny* lack of time-reversal symmetry. So *if*, by an act of god, the arrow of time suddenly were flipped, the history of the Universe would be *not* repeated in reverse.

*(And a voice spake, saying,*
*"Those who say that history* does *repeat* are wrong.")*

And *even* if the laws of Nature *were* time-reversal invariant, *Nature* would not be. And there are *two* reasons why. The *first* is that the Universe had a beginning, in which particles obtained particular initial motions. And these motions were not invariant under reversal of time's arrow. Thus a direction for time was *chosen* in *the* Big Bang beginning. Hence, the initial situation broke time-reversal symmetry: The Universe began thus by expanding.

---

(for that matter) much antimatter in the Universe. Perhaps, another Universe dominated by antimatter exits elsewhere. If so, that Universe will behave slightly differently from ours.

[227] See the Old Testament's seventh book of Creation.

And the *second* reason is connected to the second thermodynamic law. Processes related under time reversal are not equally probable, for *the availability of final states* is quite important. And suppose a jar is dropped and breaks into a dozen pieces. Then there are many possible positions for the pieces on the floor. Thus there are *many possibilities* for final states. And so the breaking of a jar, when dropped, is probable. But the time-reversed procedure is improbable. Ye cannot take the pieces, throw them back into the air, and have them come together in a solid jar. An unbroken jar is a unique configuration – there is only one possibility for such a state. Thus probability and availability of final configurations *do provide* time with direction. Time reversal cannot be a symmetry of Nature – only a symmetry of one of *Nature's laws*.

*Humpty Dumpty, do not fall.*

## Chapter XIV: Man, the Matter Maker

And man with his modern machines has accelerated protons and electrons to produce *several hundred* different types of particles.[228] By these means has man been able to decipher bits of Nature's basic scientific scriptures – man has discovered the "letters, words and language rules" of some of Nature's fundamental laws. And in the future, man will be driven to uncover more, as he seeks to find the rest of Nature's secret ways. And through his experiments, discoveries and theoretical investigations, *man* will better understand.

---

[228] Most of these particles are hadrons.

*The tenth book of Physics, called*

# Nuclear Physics

*Ye shall hear the small as well as the great.*

## Chapter I: Enumeration of Nuclear Elements

This is the book of nuclear elements. And there shall be ninety-two *naturally* occurring elements. And [1] *hydrogen*, consisting of a single proton and existing since the deconfining phase transition one-tenth of one second after the Big Bang, shall be number one. And it shall be the *lightest* element, the fuel for stellar radiation, and nuclear-matter's basic building block.

And it was seen that a Universe with only hydrogen would *be* a lifeless, listless world. And stars *were created* to fabricate the other elements. And the stars were allowed to *burst* in supernovas, to *spill* their contents, to *spread* the elements throughout the Universe and to *fill* the cosmic voids with dust and matter.

And for each nucleus, there shall be a name. And the name and type of nucleus shall be determined by the *proton number* in the nucleus.[229]

And the [2] *helium* nucleus shall be forged by fusing hydrogen with hydrogen. And to helium, a proton shall be added to yield the nucleus of [3] *lithium*. And hydrogen, helium and lithium shall be the *oldest* nuclei, manufactured in Big Bang nucleosynthesis when the Universe was just minutes old. And [4] *beryllium* shall contain four protons. And five shall be in [5] *boron*. And the [6] *carbon* nucleus shall have six protons. And seven shall be in [7] *nitrogen*. And [8] *oxygen* shall have one more or eight. And so on, until [92] *uranium* is so obtained. The number of protons in uranium shall number ninety-two.

And these ninety-two elements shall be *like unto* generations. And hydrogen shall be the eldest, the father of all fathers. And each subsequent element shall be made from the marriage of its father with a proton.

*Adam was like an atom. And so was Eve.*
*And Adam married Eve, and Sheth was so conceived –*
*this son was like a helium.*
*And others then begat.*
*And they were like the other elements.*

And in the twentieth century, man would *defy natural law* and go on making other nuclei. And so man made eleven heavy elements. And they were [93] *neptunium*, [94] *plutonium*, [95] *americium*, [96] *curium*,

---

[229] In this chapter, the proton number, which is also known as the atomic number, is indicated in square brackets before the nucleus.

[97] *berkelium,* [98] *californium,* [99] *einsteinium,* [100] *fermium,* [101]
*mendelevium,* [102] *nobelium* and [103] *lawrencium.*

And in modern times, man continued to make even heavier elements, [104] *rutherfordium,* [105] *dubnium,*[230] [106] *seaborgium,* [107]
*bohrium,* [108] *hassium,* [109] *meitnerium,* and so on. But these elements would only live a second, or for a fraction of a second, or for a
millisecond.

## Chapter II: The Binding in the Nucleus

A nd let it be known to thee and all around thee that the strong force
*shall hold* the nucleons together in a nucleus. But the strong force
shall not be strong enough to bind protons and *only* protons in a nucleus: A nucleus of only protons shall fall apart, for protons, which are
positively charged, *electrically repel.* And the strong force, although
strong, shall not be strong enough to overcome the electrical repulsion.

And it was seen that a world with only protons would be a listless and a lifeless world. And Nature was supplied with the neutron,
which is like the proton *but* is neutral. And the neutron *was permitted*
to interact strongly by the strong force. And so the strong force in a nucleus was enhanced by adding neutrons. And with the neutron, nuclei
were made. And this *happened* in the early Universe and in the stars.

And the nucleus of *helium* shall be two protons and two neutrons.
And *lithium* shall be three protons and four neutrons. And *beryllium*
shall be four protons and five neutrons. And *boron* shall be five protons
and six neutrons. And *carbon* shall be six protons and six neutrons.
And *nitrogen* shall be seven protons and seven neutrons. And *oxygen*
shall be eight protons and eight neutrons. And so on. Thus neutrons
shall *maintain* the attractive strong interaction while *weakening* the
repulsive electric force by spreading the proton particles apart.

And the constituents of the nucleus shall be called the *nucleons.*
And nucleons shall number two. And the names of the nucleons shall
be the proton and the neutron.

## Chapter III: Isotopes

N ow sometimes an *extra* neutron can be *added* to a nucleus. And
this shall be an *isotope.* And sometimes a neutron can be *removed.*
And this shall also be an isotope. And for example, *helium-three,* which
is two protons and one neutron, shall be ordinary helium with one less
neutron. And *deuterium,* which is hydrogen-two, or one proton and one
neutron, shall be hydrogen with a neutron added. And *tritium,* which is
hydrogen-three, shall be one proton and two neutrons. And *lithium-six*
shall be three protons and three neutrons. But beryllium shall have no
stable isotopes. And *boron-ten* shall be five protons and five neutrons.
And *carbon-thirteen* shall be six protons and seven neutrons. And *ni-*

---

[230] Dubnium is sometimes known as *hahnium* or *joliotium.*

*trogen-fifteen* shall be seven protons and eight neutrons. And *oxygen-seventeen* shall be eight protons and nine neutrons. And so on for the other isotopes.

Now the number of nucleons shall be the last word in a nucleus's name. And for example, *oxygen-eighteen*, which is eight protons and ten neutrons, shall have *eighteen* nucleons. And a nucleus with six protons and eight neutrons shall have *fourteen* nucleons – this shall be *carbon-fourteen*.

Now too many neutrons shall make the nucleus unstable, for there is the Pauli exclusion law, which governs *all*. And since neutrons are fermions, they cannot be in *the* same quantum state. Likewise, this law, which affects the physics of the nucleus and small, does not permit two neutrons to occupy the selfsame space. And in effect, this generates *repulsions*: With too many neutrons, one or more must be in higher-energy locations. But nucleons bind by achieving low-energy configurations.[231] Thus with neutrons, too many or too few make the nucleus unstable and it falls apart. And so the nucleus, which is an atom's heart, must have some balance of its parts.

> *(And a voice spake, saying,*
> *"Too many or too few*
> *simply will not do.")*

## Chapter IV: Fission

Now a nucleus with too many or too few neutrons shall be unstable and *decay* into two or more, lighter nuclei. And this process shall be *fission*. And since the sum of the masses of the final states will in general be *less* than the mass of the initial state, mass shall be *converted* into energy, according to the Eighth Commandment, that mass be a form of energy. And because a little mass represents a *great* amount of energy, a *great* amount of energy shall be released. And the energy released shall be approximately *one-million* times the energy released in chemical reactions. Nuclear energies shall be in keV's and MeV's.[232]

Now a nucleus that is unstable shall be *radioactive*. And the process of decay shall be called *radioactivity*.

And radioactivity shall sometimes proceed by quantum tunnelling.[233] And because it is *difficult* to tunnel quantum mechanically, nuclei shall decay relatively *slowly*. And since the quantum barriers to overcome do vary greatly, decay times for radioactive nuclei shall extend over a wide range. And the times shall range from seconds to several billions years. And for example, in one second shall half of krypton-

---

[231] In fact, *all* objects – quarks, atoms, molecules, sand, rocks, et cetera – bind by combining so as to lower energy.

[232] For an explanation of these units, see the New Testament Book of *Basic Units*.

[233] See Chapter V of the Book of *Quantum Mechanics*.

ninety-three decay away. But for example, uranium-two-thirty-eight shall take *four-and-a-half-billion* years for half of it to disappear.

Now some radioactive nuclei shall decay into another nucleus and an alpha particle.[234] And this fission shall be *alpha decay*, because an alpha particle is given off. And this process shall proceed by the SU-three strong interactions.

And let it be known to thee and all around thee that some nuclei shall decay by the intrinsic instability of neutrons. Now neutrons shall be *more stable* in a nucleus but not always infinitely so. And in such a case, the neutron shall decay as in a vacuum to an anti-electron-neutrino, an electron and a proton. And the electron, which weighs little, shall flee the nucleus with *enormous* speed. Now this electron shall be called a beta particle. And this process shall be *beta decay*, because a beta particle is given off. And it shall proceed by the SU-two weak interactions, which is a weak force of the subnuclear, which rarely manifests itself, and which is responsible for the slow disintegration of the neutron.

And let it be known to thee and all around thee that some nuclei *temporarily* live in excited states of higher energy. Such a nucleus shall emit a *highly energetic "particle of light,"* a gamma ray. And the excited nucleus shall emit a this ray, lose energy, and achieve a state of lowest energy. And in this lowest state shall the nucleus be tranquil – it shall shake no more. And this process shall be known as *gamma decay*, because a gamma ray is given off. Now this process shall proceed by the U-one electromagnetic force, which is responsible for interactions of electric charges and of magnets, and which governs the forces of atoms and of molecules, and which *also* is a force of the subnuclear.

And these three fission processes, named after the first three letters, "alpha," "beta," "gamma," of the Greek alphabet, shall be the most common way that nuclei decay.

## Chapter V: The Fission Chain Reaction

Now in some fission processes, neutrons shall be given off. And if *little* nuclear material *be* present, then the neutrons will escape *without* further interaction and the fission processes will cease. But if *much* nuclear material *be* present, then the neutrons will collide with other *nuclei*, causing *them* in turn to fission. And these nuclei, which have been struck by neutrons and have fissioned, will generate *more* neutrons through *their* nuclear decays. Then these new neutrons will strike *more* nuclei, inducing *more* divisions, which will create *more* neutrons and *more* fissions. Such a process shall be a *chain reaction* and will proceed until the nuclear material is finally exhausted.[235] A nuclear chain reaction, when uncontrolled, shall proceed rapidly and cata-

---

[234] An *alpha particle* is a helium-four nucleus: two protons and two neutrons.
[235] This is the basis for the atomic bomb.

strophically. And since the mass of the final material is *less* than the mass of the initial material, mass will be *converted* into energy, according to the Eighth Commandment, that mass be a form of energy. And because a little mass represents a *great* amount of energy, a *great* amount of energy will be released.

> *And this chain reaction*
> *shall be available to mankind*
> *for its benefit or its destruction.*

## Chapter VI: Fusion

And let it be known to thee and all around thee that two nuclei can *combine* to form a single larger nucleus. The merging of two nuclei shall be *fusion*. And fusion shall be possible because the mass of the final state of a single larger nucleus is *less* than the mass of the initial state, which consists of two smaller nuclei. Now fusion shall principally proceed through the *strong interactions*, although the electromagnetic and weak interactions shall sometimes play a role. And since, in fusion, the mass of the final nucleus is less than the sum of the masses of the initial nuclei, mass shall be converted into energy, according to the Eighth Commandment, that mass be a form of energy. And because a little mass represents a *great* amount of energy, a *great* amount of energy shall be released. Now fusion shall be the *fuel of stars* and of the Sun. In such stars, the elements from helium to iron shall be forged. And fusion shall proceed in the early Universe, one second after the Big Bang and thereafter for several hundred seconds. During the early Universe, the light elements and isotopes of deuterium, helium, helium-three and lithium were made. And fusion shall sometimes occur in man-made cyclotrons, atom smashers and tokamaks.[236] And in hydrogen bombs, it shall be the main explosive source of energy.[237]

And finally, by using fusion, man shall make new elements. And by experiments and by trial and error, man shall better *understand* the nature of the nucleus.

## Chapter VII: The Nucleus in the Atom

And let it be known to thee and all around thee that *nuclear matter* shall consist of nuclear elements and isotopes. And that a nucleus shall be the core-part of an atom and shall be responsible for *almost all* an atom's mass. And that the nucleus, because it is so heavy, shall sit at the center of the atom and *be* its heart.

---

[236] A tokamak is a man-made donut-shaped container of a high temperature plasma in which fusion reactions take place.

[237] Hydrogen bombs work as follows: Hydrogen-rich material is surrounded by ordinary atomic bombs. When the atomic bombs are detonated, they release energy through fission, forcing hydrogen nuclei to fuse. The resulting fusions release tremendous energy.

*The eleventh book of Physics, called*

# Atomic Physics

*Ye shall obey these laws*
*with all thy heart and all thy mind.*

## Chapter I: Structure

Now an *atom* shall be the smallest unit of matter that cannot be divided without dividing charge. And it shall consist of the tiny, heavy, positively charged *nucleus* and the *electron cloud*, which is the relatively large, light, negatively charged distribution of electrons.

Now the electrons in an atom shall orbit the nucleus as a *quantum cloud*, the densest parts of which are where electrons *shall* be most likely found. This cloud shall be a consequence of quantum physics, which rules the region of the atom and the small. Verily shall the electrons in an atom *not* be particles but pieces of a cloud.

Now the "heart" of an atom shall be the nucleus, which shall contain one or many nucleons. Thus a nucleus shall consist of neutrons and of protons. And the *atomic mass number* shall be the number of these nucleons. And since a proton carries one positive charge, the charge of the nucleus shall be the number of these protons. And the *atomic number* shall be this number.

## Chapter II: Charge

Now the *electron cloud*, which engulfs the nucleus, shall consist of one or more electrons. And since electrons are *negatively* charged, the electron cloud shall be *negatively* charged, the cloud's total charge being the number of electrons. Now an atom shall be neutral when the number of protons equals the number of electrons. And *normally* an atom shall be neutral, for Nature shall provide, by the attractive electric force, a great desire for opposite charges to come together. Thus electrons shall be attracted to the nucleus by the electric force. And the nucleus and electron cloud shall be bound together *like unto* a beetle in a spider web. But energetic agitation can sometimes separate the two. And so atoms in hot gases shall often lose electrons, for heat shall be like *a strong wind* which blows free some strands of spider web. And an atom that is not neutral shall be *charged* and called an *ion*.

## Chapter III: Size and Weight

Now since a nucleon weighs eighteen-hundred times the weight of an electron, the weight of an atom shall be dominated by the nucleus. Thus the *mass* of an atom shall be the atomic mass number times the mass of a nucleon. Now the size of most atoms shall be one-hundred-million times smaller than a centimeter. But the *size* of the atom, which is the size of its electron cloud, shall increase slightly with the number of electrons. And as the number of nucleons goes *up*, the size of the nucleus shall also *grow*. But the size of most nuclei shall be *twenty-thousand* times smaller than the atom's size.

And the existence of such tiny objects will sometimes be met with skepticism, for some among ye will *think* that what one cannot see cannot be. But scientists shall perform experiments that provide *overwhelming* evidence for nuclei and atoms. And such scientists shall believe in the atom and the nucleus. And others, who have not *witnessed* such experiments, shall have to rely *on faith*.

## Chapter IV: Energy Levels

Now because electrons weigh *so little*, they shall move *rapidly* about the nucleus. And since quantum mechanics shall rule the motions of electrons, each electron shall behave *both* like a particle and like a wave. And each electron in an atom shall satisfy the quantum wave equation and only be allowed to be in a specific quantum state. And given that there are only *discrete* possibilities for energies, only in certain *energy levels* may electrons be.

Now an electron shall travel over all paths around the nucleus consistent with its energy. Thus one shall *not* be able to say that an electron at a particular time *is* at a particular position. Rather one shall be able to say only that there is a certain probability that the electron *is* at a particular position. This lack of certainty shall be *represented* by the cloud. And *each* electron in an atom shall have a contribution to the cloud. Now the cloud shall be denser in some regions and less dense in others. And a *dense* region in the cloud shall indicate a *higher* chance of finding an electron there. And a *less dense* region in the cloud shall represent a *low* chance of finding an electron there.

## Chapter V: Angular Momentum States

Now the paths of an electron shall go around the nucleus. And the amount of *revolution* of an electron around the nucleus shall be its *orbital angular momentum*. Quantum mechanics shall permit only *discrete* possibilities for such revolutions.[238] Thus angular momentum shall be *quantized*: it shall be an integer times Planck's constant. Now an electron with *zero* angular momentum shall be an *s-wave*. And the electron cloud of such an s-wave electron shall be spherical in shape. Now the next-to-lowest angular momentum possibility of *one* unit of Planck's constant shall be a *p-wave*. And there shall be three different p-wave clouds, corresponding the three directions, x, y and z, of three space. The three possible p-wave electron clouds shall look like "dumbbells" oriented in x or y or z directions. And the next-to-next-to-lowest angular momentum state, corresponding to a value of *two* times Planck's constant, shall be a *d-wave*. And there shall be five ways to

---

[238] See Chapter XII of the Book of *Quantum Mechanics*.

orient d-wave clouds. And after d-waves there shall be f-waves, with seven different types of clouds. *And* so on. All this shall follow from *the quantum laws*, which reign over the region of the atom and the small, for quantum mechanics shall come from the Uni-Law, which, although broken, still rules all.

## Chapter VI: Spectrum

Now electrons shall change their energy by emitting or absorbing photons. And for example, when a photon strikes an atom, an electron can *absorb* the photon and *pass* from a low-energy level to a higher-energy configuration. Or the opposite may happen: An electron in an excited state can *emit* a photon and end up in a lower state. And when such an electron "tumbles," the photon's energy shall be the energy that the electron just has lost, for according to the Sixth Commandment, energy shall be conserved. Thus the photon's energy shall be the difference in the energies of two atomic states. But because there are only *particular possibilities* for atomic energies, the energies of photons emitted or absorbed shall be *discrete*. These discrete possibilities for photon energies shall be the *spectrum* of an atom.

Now when light or electromagnetic radiation *from* an atom is examined by separating it into its different energy components, the spectrum shall consist of *bright lines* against a dark background. And the bright lines shall be *at* the energies of photons *emitted* by the atom. And the *emission spectrum* shall be the name for this.

Now when light or electromagnetic radiation passes *through* a collection of atoms or molecules and is separated into different energy components, the spectrum shall consist of *dark lines* against a bright background. A dark line shall indicate an *absence* of a photon, for such photons shall have been *absorbed* by atoms. And the *absorption spectrum* shall be the name for this.

And the dark lines in the absorption spectrum shall be at the *same* locations as the bright lines in the emission spectrum. And why shall this be so? Because the energy needed to *raise* an electron from a low state to a high state is the *same* as the energy released when an electron *tumbles* from the high state to the low state. The absorption spectrum shall correspond to processes in which electrons *raise* their energy, whereas the emission spectrum shall correspond to processes in which electrons *tumble* and lose energy.

Now because the energy levels are *different for each type of atom*, the spectrum of a particular atom shall be *unique*. And for example, the spectrum of oxygen shall be different from hydrogen or carbon. Likewise, molecules shall have their characteristic and specific set of spectral lines. Thus the spectrum of an atom or a molecule shall uniquely specify the atom or the molecule, just as a fingerprint uniquely specifies a human being.

*The new testament book of*

# Chemistry

*Hearken unto these words.*

## Chapter I: Enumeration of Chemical Elements

This is the book of the chemical elements. Now the names of the chemical elements shall *coincide* with the names of the nuclear elements. But a chemical element shall be a nuclear element clothed in its electron cloud – an element shall be an atom.

Now enough electrons shall be added to the nucleus to make the atom neutral. Thus the number of electrons and the number of protons in a neutral element shall be the *same*. And so *hydrogen* shall have one electron. And *helium* shall have two. And *lithium* three. And *beryllium* four. And *boron* five. And *carbon* six. And *nitrogen* shall have seven. And *oxygen* eight. And *fluorine* nine. And *neon* shall have ten electrons. And *sodium* eleven. And *magnesium* twelve. And *aluminum* thirteen. And *silicon* fourteen. And *phosphorus* shall have fifteen. And *sulfur* sixteen. And *chlorine* seventeen. And *argon* eighteen. And *potassium* nineteen. And *calcium* shall have twenty electrons. And *scandium* twenty-one. And *titanium* twenty-two. And *vanadium* twenty-three. And *chromium* twenty-four. And *manganese* shall have twenty-five. And *iron* twenty-six. And *cobalt* twenty-seven. And *nickel* twenty-eight. And *copper* twenty-nine. And *zinc* shall have thirty electrons. And *gallium* thirty-one. And *germanium* thirty-two. And *arsenic* thirty-three. And *selenium* thirty-four. And *bromine* shall have thirty-five. And *krypton* thirty-six. And *rubidium* thirty-seven. And *strontium* thirty-eight. And *yttrium* thirty-nine. And *zirconium* shall have forty electrons. And *niobium* forty-one. And *molybdenum* forty-two. And *technetium* forty-three. And *ruthenium* forty-four. And *rhodium* shall have forty-five. And *palladium* forty-six. And *silver* forty-seven. And *cadmium* forty-eight. And *indium* forty-nine. And *tin* shall have fifty electrons. And *antimony* fifty-one. And *tellurium* fifty-two. And *iodine* fifty-three. And *xenon* fifty-four. And *cesium* shall have fifty-five. And *barium* fifty-six. And *lanthanum* fifty-seven. And *cerium* fifty-eight. And *praseodymium* fifty-nine. And *neodymium* shall have sixty electrons. And *promethium* sixty-one. And *samarium* sixty-two. And *europium* sixty-three. And *gadolinium* sixty-four. And *terbium* shall have sixty-five. And *dysprosium* sixty-six. And *holmium* sixty-seven. And *erbium* sixty-eight. And *thulium* sixty-nine. And *ytterbium* shall have seventy electrons. And *lutetium* seventy-one. And *hafnium* seventy-two. And *tantalum* seventy-three. And *tungsten* seventy-four. And *rhenium* shall have seventy-five. And *osmium* seventy-six. And *iridium* seventy-seven. And *platinum* seventy-eight. And *gold* seventy-nine. And *mercury* shall have eighty electrons. And *thallium* eighty-one. And *lead* eighty-two. And *bismuth* eighty-three. And *polonium* eighty-four. And *astatine* shall have eighty-five. And *radon* eighty-six. And *francium* eighty-seven. And *radium* eighty-eight. And *actinium* eighty-nine. And *thorium* shall have ninety electrons. And *protactinium* ninety-one. And *uranium* ninety-two. And *neptunium* ninety-three. And *plutonium* ninety-four. And *americium* shall have ninety-five. And *curium* ninety-six. And *berkelium* ninety-seven. And *californium* ninety-eight. And *einsteinium* ninety-nine. And *fermium* shall have one-hundred electrons. And *mendelevium* one-hundred-and-one. And *nobelium* one-hundred-and-two. And *lawrencium* shall have one-hundred-and-three electrons. And so on.

## Chapter II: Chemical Symbols

And each element shall have a one- or two-letter code, which indicates the element. And *chemical symbols* shall *be* these codes. Thus H shall stand for hydrogen; He shall stand for helium; Li shall stand for lithium; Be shall represent beryllium; and B shall stand for boron; and C for carbon; and N for nitrogen; and O for oxygen; and F for fluorine; Ne for neon; Na for sodium; Mg shall represent magnesium; Al shall represent aluminum; Si shall stand for silicon; and P for phosphorus; and S for sulfur; Cl for chlorine; Ar for argon; and K shall represent potassium; Ca shall stand for calcium; Sc scandium; Ti shall represent titanium; and V shall represent vanadium; Cr shall stand for chromium; Mn for manganese; Fe for iron; Co for cobalt; Ni for nickel; Cu for copper; Zn for zinc; Ga for gallium; Ge shall represent germanium; As shall stand for arsenic; Se shall represent selenium; Br shall stand for bromine; Kr for krypton; Rb shall represent rubidium; Sr shall stand for strontium; and Y for yttrium; Zr shall represent zirconium; Nb shall represent niobium; Mo shall represent molybdenum; Tc shall represent technetium; Ru shall represent ruthenium; Rh shall stand for rhodium; Pd shall represent palladium; Ag shall stand for silver; Cd for cadmium; In for indium; Sn for tin; Sb for antimony; Te shall represent tellurium; and I shall stand for iodine; Xe for xenon; Cs for cesium; Ba for barium; La for lanthanum; Ce for cerium; Pr for praseodymium; Nd for neodymium; Pm shall represent promethium; Sm shall represent samarium; Eu shall represent europium; Gd shall stand for gadolinium; Tb for terbium; Dy shall represent dysprosium; Ho shall stand for holmium; Er for erbium; Tm for thulium; Yb shall represent ytterbium; Lu shall represent lutetium; Hf shall stand for hafnium; Ta for tantalum; and W for tungsten; Re for rhenium; Os for osmium; Ir shall represent iridium; Pt shall stand for platinum; Au for gold; Hg for mercury; Tl for thallium; Pb for lead; Bi for bismuth; Po shall represent polonium; At shall stand for astatine; Rn for radon; Fr for francium; Ra for radium; Ac shall represent actinium; Th shall stand for thorium; Pa for protactinium; and U shall represent uranium; Np shall represent neptunium; Pu shall represent plutonium; Am shall stand for americium; Cm for curium; Bk shall represent berkelium; Cf shall stand for californium; Es shall represent einsteinium; Fm shall stand for fermium; Md for mendelevium; No shall represent nobelium; Lr shall represent lawrencium; Rf shall stand for rutherfordium; Db for dubnium; Sg shall represent seaborgium; Bh shall stand for bohrium; Hs for hassium; Mt shall represent meitnerium. *And so on.*

*The elements shall be like Nature's sons and daughters.*

And the string of elements "tritium-helium-barium-deuterium-oxygen-neon" shall describe a devil. And the string "tritium-helium-potassium-indium-deuterium-oxygen-neon" shall describe a god. And both shall simultaneously announce their earthly presence in the string "iodine-americium-nitrogen-oxygen-tungsten-helium-rhenium."

## Chapter III: The Periodic Table

*And in the first row shall be*
*a sardius, a topaz and a carbuncle.*

Now let it be known that the elements may be organized in a tableau. And the tableau shall be *like unto* an arrangement of chairs in rows and columns in a theater. And one element shall sit in one and *only one* designated chair. And there shall be *seven* rows. The number of chairs in the first row shall be two. And the number in the second shall be eight, which shall *also* be the number in the third. The number of chairs in both the fourth row and the fifth row shall be eighteen. And thirty-two shall be the number in the sixth and seventh rows. But *not* all the seats of the seventh shall have an occupant. And this arrangement shall be the *periodic table.*[239]

*The periodic table shall be Nature's temple.*

And let it be known to thee and all around thee that the periodic table shall be the consequence of *three* things: one force, one principle, one fact. And the one force shall be *electromagnetism*, which is responsible for the binding of electrons to the nucleus. Now the one principle shall be the Pauli exclusion principle of the Tenth Commandment, which *dictates* that identical fermions, such as electrons, may not occupy the selfsame state. Now the one fact shall be that electrons have internal spin *one-half*. And a particle of spin one-half shall have *two types* of spin: clockwise and counterclockwise spin, which is also known as *spin up* and *spin down*. Now electrons of spin up shall be *different* from electrons of spin down – they shall *not* be identical fermions. And so the Pauli principle shall apply *separately* to electrons of spin up and to electrons of spin down.

---

[239] See the New Testament Book of *Tables.*

## Chapter IV: Atomic Energy Levels

In an atom, the lowest-energy state shall be 1s. And the first row shall have two chairs *by reason of the fact* that the electron can occupy the 1s state with its spin up or its spin down.

And the next-to-lowest-energy atomic states shall be the 2s and 2p. Now since p-state rotations can be oriented in three possibilities,[240] there shall be three 2p states. And so four shall be the number of next-to-lowest states: one for 2s plus three for 2p. And because each electron can have its spin up *or* its spin down, there shall be *eight* next-to-lowest levels. And these shall be the chairs that form the second row.

And the next-to-next-to-lowest-energy states shall be the 3s and 3p. And again, there shall be four atomic states. And because the electron is of spin one-half, again *eight* levels shall there be. And these shall be the chairs in *the* third row.

And the next lowest-energy states shall be the 4s, 3d and 4p. And since the s, p and d states have respectively one, three and five rotation possibilities, there shall be one plus three plus five or *nine* atomic states. And because each electron can have spin up *or* spin down, there shall be *eighteen* levels. And these shall be the chairs in *the* fourth row.

And the next lowest-energy states shall be the 5s, 4d and 5p. And *again*, there shall be *nine* atomic states and *eighteen* levels. And these shall be the chairs in *the* fifth row.

And the next lowest-energy states shall be the 6s, 4f, 5d and 6p. And since the s, p, d and f states shall have respectively one, three, five and seven rotation possibilities, there shall be one plus three plus five plus seven or *sixteen* atomic states. And because each electron can have spin up *or* spin down, there shall be *thirty-two* such levels. And these shall be the chairs in *the* sixth row.

And the remaining energy states shall be 7s, 5f, 6d and 7p. And *again*, there shall be *sixteen* atomic states and *thirty-two* such levels. And these shall be the chairs that form the seventh row.

## Chapter V: The Arrangement of the Elements[241]

Now electrons shall occupy the states of *lowest energy* when atoms are in ground states. And so hydrogen, which has one electron, shall have its electron in the 1s state. And helium, which has two electrons, shall have two 1s electrons, one of which shall be *up-spin* and one of which shall be *down-spin*. And this shall be denoted $1s^2$ – the superscript following a state shall indicate the number of electrons in

---

[240] See Chapter V of The Book of *Atomic Physics* for the discussion of quantum angular momentum and s, p, d and f states. The numbers in front of s, p, d and f in this paragraph distinguish different states with the same angular momentum.

[241] See the New Testament Book of *Tables*.

that state. And hydrogen and helium shall be the elements *that sit* in the first row.

And when all the states in a row are filled, the electrons shall be said to *fill that shell*. Thus the electrons in helium shall fill one shell.

And lithium, which has three electrons, shall have two 1s electrons and one 2s electron, which is $1s^2 2s$. Now its third electron cannot be placed in the 1s state. Why *is* this so? It is because of the Pauli exclusion principle: The first two electrons, one of which is spin up and one of which is spin down, *already sit* in the 1s state, and the third electron *cannot occupy* its brethren's space. Now beryllium, which has four electrons, shall have two 1s electrons and two 2s electrons, which is $1s^2 2s^2$. And boron, which has five electrons, shall have two 1s electrons, two 2s electrons and one 2p electron, which is $1s^2 2s^2 2p$. And carbon, which has six electrons, shall be $1s^2 2s^2 2p^2$. And nitrogen shall be $1s^2 2s^2 2p^3$. And oxygen shall be $1s^2 2s^2 2p^4$. And fluorine shall be $1s^2 2s^2 2p^5$. And neon, which has ten electrons, shall have two 1s electrons, two 2s electrons and six 2p electrons, which is $1s^2 2s^2 2p^6$. And note ye that the electrons in the neon atom *fill* two shells. And these elements from lithium to neon shall be the elements *that occupy* the second row.

And so on.

Now the atoms in the *same column* of the periodic table often shall *combine in the same way* with other atoms – atoms in a column shall chemically be similar.[242]

Let the elements of columns so be known.

In the right-most column in the periodic table shall be the six *inert gases*: helium, neon, argon, krypton, xenon, radon. Thus neon, which is in the second row, shall *sit behind* helium, which is in the first row. And argon, which is in the third row, shall *sit behind* neon. And so on until one arrives at radon, which *is* in the sixth row. And the electrons of the inert gas of the nth row fill n *shells*.

And in the left-most column shall be the *alkali metals*. Behind hydrogen, which is in the first row, *shall sit* lithium, which is in the second row. And occupying rows three through seven shall respectively be sodium, potassium, rubidium, cesium and francium.

And next to the alkali metals shall be the column for the *alkaline-earth metals*. Behind beryllium, which is in the second row, shall be magnesium, calcium, strontium, barium and radium – radium shall sit in the seventh *and* last row.

And next to the column of the inert gases shall be *five* columns. *Nearest* the inert gases shall be the column of the *halogens*: fluorine, chlorine, bromine, iodine and astatine. And *next* shall be the five *chalcogens*: oxygen, sulfur, selenium, tellurium, polonium. *Then* shall come the family of nitrogen, phosphorus, arsenic, antimony, bismuth. In the

---

[242] This is explained in Chapter VII.

*next* column shall be the family of carbon, silicon, germanium, tin, lead. And *finally* shall be the family of boron, aluminum, gallium, indium and thallium.

Now in addition to the eight columns of the previous four paragraphs, *ten more* columns shall start in the fourth row. Next to the column of the alkaline earths shall be the column for the scandium family. And next to the column of the boron-aluminum family shall be the column for the zinc family. Next to the zinc column shall be the coinage metals: copper, silver, gold. Then shall come three columns for the metal triads, headed by nickel, by copper and by iron. And the four remaining columns shall be the ones for the four families headed by manganese, chromium, vanadium and titanium.

And starting in the sixth row shall be fourteen new columns, each of which shall have but *just two rows*. The *first* of these two rows shall be the *rare earth elements*, consisting of cerium, praseodymium, neodymium, promethium, samarium, europium, gadolinium, terbium, dysprosium, holmium, erbium, thulium, ytterbium and lutetium. And the *second* of these two rows shall be the *actinide series*, consisting of thorium, protactinium, uranium, neptunium, plutonium, americium, curium, berkelium, californium, einsteinium, fermium, mendelevium, nobelium and lawrencium. Some of these names of these elements shall be *derived* from people, gods and places.

Now the ten plus fourteen or twenty-four columns of the last two paragraphs shall constitute the *transition metals*. And in all, there shall be eight plus twenty-four or *thirty-two columns*, which is the number of seats in the sixth and seventh rows.

## Chapter VI: Ions and Small Molecules

*They are in bondage under the elements of the world.*

Now *sometimes* an extra electron can be added to render an atom negatively charged. Such an atom shall be a *negatively charged ion*, or an *anion*. And *sometimes* an extra electron can be removed to render an atom positively charged. Such an atom shall be a *positively charged ion*, or a *cation*. And atoms with deficit or excess electrons shall be chemically different from their neutral counterparts, even though the *nuclei* of such atoms are *unchanged*.

Now when atoms *come together*, they may *exchange and share electrons*. And in certain circumstances, the energy will be *lowered*, thereby *binding* atoms. When two or more atoms bind together, the object shall be called a *molecule*. And when precisely *two* atoms bind, it shall be a *diatomic molecule*; when *three* atoms join, it shall be a *triatomic molecule*. And in general can many atoms bind.

## Chapter VII: Valence Electrons,
## Chemical Families and Bonding

Now *bonds* shall be the "bridges" of the world of chemistry, the basic units that tie the atoms in a molecule together. To *understand* these bonds is to *know* the rules of one of Nature's sacred structures. The construction units shall of course be atoms. And with bonds and atoms shall the macroscopic world be built.

Now there shall be many types of bonds: ionic, covalent, coordinate, metallic and so on.[243] And atoms shall be sometimes tied to one another through other binding mechanisms: molecular orbitals, hydrogen bonds, van der Waals forces and so on.

And let it be known to thee and all around thee that the binding of an atom shall be determined by its *outermost electrons*, which shall be called the *valence electrons*. And the other electrons, the non-valence electrons, shall occupy filled shells.

Now helium shall have, for its outermost electrons, two 1s electrons, which are *tightly bound* in a filled shell and *thus* cannot be shared. Consequently, helium shall *not* form molecules. Likewise, no valence electrons shall have the other *inert gases*: neon, argon, krypton, xenon, radon. In these atoms, all electrons shall be *tightly bound*. And since these gases cannot share their electrons, they shall *not bind* in molecules – these gases shall remain inert.

Now the alkali metals – lithium, sodium, potassium, rubidium, cesium and francium – shall have, for their outermost electrons, a *single* s electron, which is loosely bound and *can be donated* to other atoms with little loss of energy.

Now the halogens – fluorine, chlorine, bromine, iodine and astatine – shall have, for their outermost electrons, two s electrons and five p electrons, which are *tightly bound* and cannot be donated to another atom. But a halogen *can accept* one electron from another atom and place it in its one available p state with little loss of energy. And for example, one alkali atom and one halogen atom *can combine* to form a diatomic molecule – such molecules shall make up *salts*. And table salt, being one chloride atom and one sodium atom, is an example. Now why *is* it these two bind? The answer is electromagnetism: The alkali atom shall be *positively* charged, having *given* its s electron to the halogen. And the halogen atom shall be *negatively* charged, having *accepted* the s electron from the alkali and placed it in its last available p state. And the electric attraction between charges of opposite sign shall bind these two to one another. And this shall *be* called an *ionic bond* because the constituents are charged and hence are ions.

Now hydrogen, which heads the column of alkali metals, shall have a single s electron, which is loosely bound and *can be donated* to other atoms with little loss of energy. But hydrogen, like a halogen, *can*

---

[243] Examples of these bonds are given below.

*accept one electron* and place it in its one available s state with little loss of energy. Because of atomic hydrogen's great flexibility in its donating and accepting of electrons, it shall be chemically *highly reactive* and shall bind readily to many other elements. And for example, two hydrogen atoms shall come together to form a molecule of hydrogen. And the two electrons shall form a quantum cloud of negative charge between the two separated positive protons, which constitute the nuclei of the two hydrogens. And *neither* atom can be considered charged. And *yet both* atoms can *sometimes* be considered charged. This bond shall be a *covalent bond* because the electrons are *shared* between the atoms. And the electromagnetic force, which is responsible for all chemical binding, shall hold the two hydrogens together. Now atomic hydrogen, having the ability to accept excess electrons, when excess electrons are present, and to donate electrons, when electrons are needed by other atoms, shall be *omnipresent* in organic substances. And furthermore, hydrogen, due to its unique ability to share electrons, can *itself* act as a bonding agent. And this bond, which is weak, shall have a name. The *hydrogen bond* shall be its name. Hydrogen bonds shall be common in biologically related substances, such as wood, silk and candle wax. And the two strands in each DNA molecule shall be held together by this bond – due to hydrogen bonding, ye and other living things shall *be*.

Now the chalcogens, which are oxygen, sulfur, selenium, tellurium and polonium, shall have for their valence electrons two s electrons and four p electrons, which are *tightly bound* and usually cannot be donated to another atom but *can be shared*. And furthermore, a chalcogen can accept two electrons and place them in its two available p states with little loss of energy. Thus two alkali atoms and one chalcogen can combine to create a triatomic molecule. And *water*, being one oxygen atom and two hydrogen atoms, is an example. And the two alkali atoms shall be positively charged, having given their s electrons to the chalcogen. And the chalcogen atom shall be doubly negatively charged, having accepted the two s electrons from the two alkali atoms and placed them in its two available p states. The *electromagnetic attraction* between charges of opposite sign *shall bind* the two alkali atoms to the chalcogen. And two chemical bonds shall be formed, both of which are ionic bonds because the atoms are electrically charged and hence are ions. Now two chalcogen atoms can combine to form a diatomic molecule. And oxygen gas, being two oxygen atoms, is an example. And *two* p electrons from one oxygen atom shall be shared with *two* p electrons from the other oxygen atom, so that a total of *four* electrons shall be shared. And the four shared p electrons shall fill the empty p states of the two oxygen atoms so that no empty p states shall remain. So oxygen gas shall be bound by *two* covalent bonds – a *double bond*, which may be denoted by two lines between the atoms as in O=O.[244]

Now the atoms in the column of nitrogen, phosphorus, arsenic, antimony and bismuth shall have, for their outermost electrons, two s electrons and three p electrons. And the *three* p electrons *can be donated* in a sharing process with other atoms with little loss of energy. However the nitrogen-family atoms *can also accept three electrons* in a sharing process and place them in its three available p states with little loss of energy. Thus this family shall bind by donating, accepting or sharing three electrons. And nitrogen gas, being two nitrogen atoms, is an example. And six p electrons shall be shared between the two nitrogens in three covalent bonds – a *triple bond*. And ammonia, being one nitrogen atom and three hydrogen atoms, is one more example. And the three p electrons of the nitrogen shall be shared with the three s electrons of the three hydrogens in *three distinct* covalent bonds.

Now the members of the carbon-silicon family of carbon, silicon, germanium, tin and lead, shall have, for their outermost electrons, two s electrons and two p electrons. And carbon, like hydrogen, shall exhibit *great flexibility* in its sharing, donating and accepting of electrons. Carbon shall bind to other atoms in *many* ways. And carbon monoxide gas, which is one carbon atom and one oxygen atom, is an example. The carbon shall share its two p electrons with oxygen, which wants two electrons to close its shell. And oxygen shall share two of its p electrons with the carbon atom. Thus a total of four electrons shall be shared in two covalent bonds. And all the p states of oxygen *shall* be filled, thus lowering its energy. But in this situation, two of the p states of carbon are unfilled. And to further lower the energy, oxygen shall share two more electrons with the carbon atom, so that the two unfilled p states of carbon *may* be filled. And these two electrons, coming from oxygen and occupying carbon's unfilled p levels, shall constitute two *coordinate bonds*, which is a subtle way of both sharing and donating two electrons.[245]

And carbon shall be *omnipresent* in organic substances, for it has the ability to form four covalent bonds. It shall often mix its two s electrons with its two p electrons in a hybrid manner so that its four valence electrons behave in a democratic way. And with its four bonds, carbon, linking with itself and with other molecules, *shall form chains and networks* of organic molecules. Thus carbon shall be the "backbone" of organic molecules.[246]

Carbons joined with each other in a tree-like chain with hydrogens attached "as leaves" shall *be* called *hydrocarbons*. Examples shall

---

[244] A single bond is denoted by a single line as in H-H, which is hydrogen gas, or $H_2$; a triple bond is denoted by three lines, and so on.

[245] The valence electrons in a coordinate bond are shared by the two atoms but are donated by *only one* of the atoms. Thus a coordinate bond is both covalent and ionic.

[246] For examples, see the Book of *Biology*.

be alkanes, consisting of a linear carbon chain: methane ($CH_4$), ethane ($C_2H_6$), propane ($C_3H_8$), butane ($C_4H_{10}$), pentane ($C_5H_{12}$), hexane ($C_6H_{14}$), heptane ($C_7H_{16}$), octane ($C_8H_{18}$), and so on.[247] Alkanes, being flammable, shall often serve as fuels. The natural gas and oil that heat thy home shall be predominantly made of hydrocarbons. Likewise, isooctane[248] shall be the anti-knock fuel-component of a gasoline that runs the engine[249] in thy car. Now the story of this gasoline begins about one-hundred-million years ago, at the *center of the Sun. There*, through nuclear processes, four protons fused to form a helium and *energy*.[250] For ten-million years, the energy was repeatedly absorbed and re-emitted in the Sun. Then having reach the surface of the Sun, it left *as photons* in the form of light. Eight-and-one-third minutes later, the photons struck the chloroplasts[251] inside a plant. The photons' *energy* was processed through photosynthesis and *stored in bonds* of some organic molecules. Then the plant died, rotted, was buried and was crushed with other plants.[252] During the next ninety-million years or so, geo-pressure squeezed the plants into petroleum. In modern times, man pumped the oil from the ground and processed it as gasoline. When the gasoline was "burned" by adding a spark and oxygen, the hydrocarbon bonds were broken, *releasing* carbon dioxide, oxygen and *energy*. So when thee put a foot upon a pedal to make a car go forth, remember thee the source of this form of energy.

Now the atoms of the boron-aluminum family shall have, for their outermost electrons, *two s electrons and one p electron*, which can be shared and donated with little loss of energy.

And the atoms in the column of alkali earths – beryllium, magnesium, calcium, strontium, barium and radium – shall have for their outermost electrons, *two s electrons*, which can be donated with a moderate loss of energy.

And the zinc-cadmium-mercury family shall have for valence electrons two s electrons and ten d electrons. And these twelve electrons *shall* participate in bonding. Now these atoms shall form *metals*: By giving up and losing some of their electrons, these atoms shall become cations. And their electrons shall "swim" throughout the metal attracted to the positively charged cations. *Metallic bonds* shall bind the

---

[247] The chemical symbols in the parentheses are explained in the next chapter.

[248] Isooctane, like octane, has eight carbon atoms and eighteen hydrogen atoms, but the atoms are arranged in a different structure. Two molecules with the same numbers of each type of atom but which are structurally different are called isomers. The other main ingredient in gasoline is heptane.

[249] See Chapter VII of the Book of *Thermodynamics*.

[250] See the Chapter VI of the Book of *Nuclear Physics* and Chapter IV of the Book of *The Sun*.

[251] See Chapter V of the New Testament Book of *Biology*.

[252] See Chapter VII of the Old Testament Book of *The Cretaceous*. Another important period of fossil-fuel production was four-hundred-million years ago during the Carboniferous. See Chapter III of the Old Testament Book of *The Carboniferous*.

metal. And in effect, the valence electrons of each atom in a metal shall be donated and be shared with all the other atoms.

And the atoms of the coinage metal family, copper, silver and gold, shall have for valence electrons one s electron and ten d electrons. And these electrons and especially the s electron *shall* participate in bonding. These atoms shall form metals.

And the atoms of nickel, palladium and platinum shall have for valence electrons a *total of ten* d and s electrons. And these valence electrons *shall* participate in bonding. These atoms shall form metals. *And so on.*[253]

Now since chemical behavior is determined by valence electrons and since atoms in the same column have *similar electronic valence structure*, atoms in the *same column* shall chemically behave the *same*.

Now sometimes electronic states shall appear due to the presence of a group of many atoms. In such a state, an electron through its quantum cloud shall *spread its presence* over two or many atoms. A *molecular orbital* shall be the name for this somewhat nonlocal state. And molecular orbitals shall help to bind the molecules.

## Chapter VIII: Chemical Formulas[254]

*When ye take in a breath of air,*
*it shall be 78% $N_2$, 21% $O_2$ and 1% Ar,*
*with small amounts of $H_2O$, $CO_2$, Ne, He and $CH_4$.*

Now the *chemical formula* of a molecule shall indicate its atoms. A chemical formula shall be *like unto* a word in which there are letters and are numbers. And the letters shall represent the elements,[255] while the number in a subscript after such a letter shall indicate the number of that atom present.

And for example, $H_2O$ is *water*, consisting of two hydrogen atoms and one oxygen. And when it is a gas, it shall be known as water vapor. Now *hydrogen gas*, also known as *molecular hydrogen*, shall be $H_2$. And it shall be made from two atoms both of which are hydrogen. And $O_2$, which is *oxygen gas* and also known as *molecular oxygen*, shall be made from two atoms both of which are oxygen. And $O_3$, consisting of three oxygens, is *ozone*. And *nitrogen gas*, also known as *molecular nitrogen*, shall be $N_2$ – two nitrogens. And $NH_3$ shall be *ammonia*. And it shall consist of one nitrogen atom and three hydrogens. And *carbon monoxide* shall be CO; and *carbon dioxide* shall be $CO_2$. And $CH_4$ is *methane*. And *sulfur dioxide* shall be $SO_2$, while $SO_4$ is *sulfur oxide*. Hy-

---

[253] The valence electrons for the rest of the elements are given in the periodic table in the New Testament Book of *Tables*.

[254] The chemical formulas for the molecules mentioned in *The Bible According to Einstein* can be found in this chapter.

[255] See Chapter II.

*drogen sulfide* shall be $H_2S$. And it shall have the smell of rotten eggs. And $N_2O$ is *nitrous oxide*. And it shall be known as *laughing gas*. And $NO_3$ is *nitrogen trioxide*. And $NH_4HS$ is *ammonium hydrosulfide*. And $NH_4OH$ is *ammonium hydroxide*. And it shall consist of one nitrogen atom, one oxygen atom and five hydrogens.

And $SiO_4$ is *silicate*. And $SiO_2$ is *silicon dioxide* – in rocks shall it be known as *silica*. And $Al_2O_3$ shall be *alumina*. And *iron oxide* may be FeO, $Fe_2O_3$ or $Fe_3O_4$. And FeO is *ferrous iron oxide*, while $Fe_2O_3$ is *ferric iron oxide*. And *calcium oxide* shall be CaO. And *magnesium oxide* shall be MgO. And $CO_3$ is *carbonate*. And $CaCO_3$ is *calcium carbonate*, or *calcite* when a crystal. Now *magnesium carbonate* is $MgCO_3$. And *hydrogen carbonate* shall be $HCO_3$. And *bicarbonate* shall be a metal plus $HCO_3$. And *sodium chloride* shall be NaCl. And *table salt* shall be another name for it.

And HCl is *hydrochloric acid*. And $H_2SO_4$ shall be *sulfuric acid*. And $H_2CO_3$ shall be *carbonic acid*. And *nitric acid* shall be $HNO_3$. And *hydroxy acid* shall be an acid containing a group of COOH *and* a group of OH. And $C_6H_{12}O_6$ is *glucose*. And $C_2H_6$ is *ethane*. And *hydrogen cyanide* is HCN. And HCOH shall be *formaldehyde*.

And so on.

## Chapter IX: Big Molecules

Now let it be known to thee and all around thee that small molecules can combine to form a giant molecule, which shall be called a *macromolecule*. And, like atoms, the smaller molecules shall bind by sharing, rearranging and exchanging electronic clouds. And nylon, DNA and RNA shall be examples of such macromolecules.

And let it be known to thee and all around thee that the ability to bind shall be *stronger* at *lower* temperatures and *weaker* at *higher* temperatures, for at higher temperatures shall atoms vibrate more. And such vibrating atoms shall find it *not so easy* to settle into states of lower energy. At *high* temperatures, chemical bonds *shall break* and molecules shall then unbind. And so, at sufficiently high temperatures, there shall be *only atoms*. This shall be the situation in the Sun – no molecules shall exist inside the Sun. Now temperature shall be *like unto* a wind which blows against a bubble: When the temperature is low, the wind is low, and the bubble, although distorted, shall remain intact. But when the temperature is high, the wind is high, and the strong breeze against the bubble shall *make* the bubble break. And this breaking shall be *like unto* the breaking of a bond.

And let it be known to thee and all around thee that, at lower temperatures, molecular *van der Waals forces* shall cause molecules to bind, for, although such forces are weak, they shall be *attractive and long-ranged*. And if the temperature is *low enough*, molecules shall join to form liquids, solids, jels and cells. And let it be known that *all bind-*

*ing* shall be *electromagnetic* in origin, for in the realm of the atom and the small, electromagnetism governs all.

## Chapter X: Chemistry and the Early Universe

Now before Recombination when the age of the Universe was less than three-hundred-thousand years, there were *no atoms*, for the Universe was *too hot*. And in this hot Universe, electrons and nuclei did swim in *separate* seas. And without atoms, there was no chemistry. But when the Universe sufficiently expanded and subsequently cooled, *then* the electrons and the nuclei did bind. And this moment was *Recombination* – from this point onward, the Universe had atoms. The forces that made *these first atoms* were atomic forces. And it was the electric attraction between negatively charged electrons and positively charged protons that *made* these particles combine. Now when the Universe cooled further, some atoms joined "hands" and molecules *were made* – these "hands" were just the bonds of chemistry. And so Nature began to build the microscopic structures that would *eventually* constitute the macroscopic matter of the Universe. And at first, these macroscopic structures *were* but gas and dust. But later, gravitational instability *caused* such matter to collapse. And stars and planets thus were *made*. In planets, chemical binding formed the rocks and dirt. And there, chemistry and carbon made organic molecules. And at least on one such planet, organic molecules organized themselves into mobile forms *called life*.

*The new testament book of*

# Biology[256]

*This is the book of original life.*

*A living being is but flesh,*
*like a wind that emergeth, passeth,*
*goeth away and cometh not again.*

## Chapter I: Living Systems

The science of life shall be *biology*. Biology shall be based on chemistry, whose foundation shall be physics. And physics shall be man's knowledge of the fundamental laws of Nature.

Now all living things shall respond to their environment, use energy, and reproduce. The *energy* shall come from chemistry through bonds of molecules, from the Sun by way of photosynthesis, from the heat of thermal vents in oceans in the Earth, and so on. Living things shall be highly opportunistic, *responding* to surroundings, sensing what is there, taking advantage of each special situation, seeking instant benefit, *and*, at a basic level, being as greedy as can be, for if the "profit" is not seized, it shall be lost and those that lose shall *die*. And finally, living things shall *reproduce* by splitting into two, by sex, by cell division, by "casting off" an offspring and so on.

Cells shall be the basic building blocks, the biochemical "factories" of life. Cells *shall* be made of molecules, which in turn are made of atoms. The atoms shall be nuclei surrounded by electrons. And the protons and the neutrons in the nuclei shall each be formed of three bound quarks. Ye, the living, shall be full of electrons and of quarks.

Although the *diversity* of life on Earth shall be quite great – several million different species shall exist and many millions more *shall* have gone extinct – all living things shall *share* the *same* genetic code, for all shall have descended from a *common* ancient primogenitor. Ye, the living, shall be related through a shared ancestry. Ye shall be complex *living systems* embedded in a larger ecosystem called the Earth.

---

[256] The *Book of Biology* is unfinished, for human knowledge about the living is limited. Each day a new page of biology is written. The pages are and will be assembled. And when the book is finished, man will have the understanding to answer the fundamental questions: What makes that which is dead, dead, and what makes that which is alive, alive? And when the book is finished, man will have the power to manufacture life. And man shall, at that point, have one of the great powers of a god.

## Chapter II: The Molecules of Life

*Fire, earth, air and water.*
*Brain waves, flesh, breath and blood.*

Now the body of an animal shall be made from the *organic compounds*, which are molecules of carbon, oxygen, hydrogen, nitrogen and other elements. Carbon shall be the backbone of organic substances: Through its ability to form *four atomic bonds*, it shall *chain* itself and other atoms together in organic compounds. Life shall be made of *macromolecules* that are made up of hundreds, thousands or sometimes tens of thousands of atoms. The main macromolecules of the body shall be *carbohydrates, lipids, proteins* and *nucleic acids*.

Now *carbohydrates* shall be macromolecules that store energy. And sugar, starch and cellulose shall be examples. The energy in carbohydrates shall be tapped by living organisms.

Now *lipids* shall be fats and fat-like substances with two main purposes: they shall store energy and they shall form building materials for cells.

Now *proteins* shall have a variety of purposes. Certain proteins shall be the building blocks for cells. And for example, *collagen* shall be used for bones, tendons, ligaments and skin, while *keratin* shall be in the outermost skin-layer, nails and hair. And proteins such as *myogen*, *actin* and *myosin* shall make up much of muscle tissue. And soluble proteins such as *albumins* and *globulins* shall appear in blood and milk. Now proteins shall be essential for building new tissue and for repairing injured tissue. And they shall also be a source of energy. Respiratory proteins such as *hemoglobin* shall carry oxygen in blood. Antibodies shall defend an organism against invading foreign agents.

Now certain proteins called *enzymes* shall stimulate and speed up *metabolic processes*, which are the processes creating biological changes from physical and chemical reactions in a living organism. Many enzymes shall be *like unto* business brokers who bring together two distinct bodies so that they more quickly interact. Some enzymes shall be *like unto* bankers who lend money so that business can be speeded up – the money shall be like the energy needed to activate a chemical reaction; such enzymes shall be catalysts, reducing barriers so that molecules can more easily react. In digestion shall enzymes *break down* nutrients, such as proteins, fats and carbohydrates, into smaller and more basic molecules. And some enzymes shall guide these more basic molecules until they reach the bloodstream, while others *shall assist* in the formation of larger complex molecules from smaller basic ones. And enzymes shall help in *storing energy* and help in *its* release. For life shall enzymes be essential. Thus for life shall proteins be essential.

Now *nucleic acids* shall instruct – they shall give *purpose* to a cell and tell cells what to do. And they shall encode information and then disseminate it to the other biological components. And during reproduction, nucleic acids shall *pass* genetic information from one generation to the next.

## Chapter III: Cells

*Ye shall be like living stones.*

Now *cells*, the basic building blocks of living things, shall be made of mainly proteins, water, lipids and nucleic acids. Cells shall be alive, for they shall take in food, get rid of waste and grow, and sometimes shall divide and reproduce. Lipids shall make up the *membranes* that encase a cell. And the lipid casing shall permit only certain substances to enter or to leave a cell. Now there shall be many types of cells with many features and with many functions. And for example, there shall be blood cells, nerve cells, muscle cells, et cetera.

And cells of the same type that are strung together shall be *tissues*. And there shall be four main types: (i) *muscle tissues*, (ii) *connective tissues*, such as those which support and join together body parts, (iii) *epithelial tissues*, which line the body such as skin, and (iv) *nerve tissues*, which make up the brain and nerves. A component of two or more tissues that performs an important biological function shall be an *organ*.

## Chapter IV: The Human Body

*The blood of thy body shall be like wine;*
*thy flesh shall be like bread.*

Now the *symbol of thought* shall be the brain. And the *symbol of love* shall be the heart. And the *symbol of vital force* shall be the lungs. And these symbols shall be *brought together* in a human body.

And the human body shall consist of *one-hundred-trillion* cells. And encoded in each cell shall be a text of a *hundred-million* pages of genetic information. The cells shall be organized in several sophisticated systems, which are as follows.

The *skeletal system* shall include all cartilage and bones. A *bone* shall be a dense, calcified, rather rigid tissue, while *cartilage* shall be more flexible yet still be capable of withstanding a substantial pressure. Now the skeletal system shall supply stability to the body, a framework to support the softer parts. One component shall be the *backbone*, which shall run down the middle of the back. And the skeletal system also shall provide protection, as illustrated by the *rib cage* – it shall protect the heart, the lungs and other vital organs. The bones of the movable joints, such as the elbows, knees and shoulders, shall be held together by the *ligaments* – they shall tie two bones together.

Now the *muscles* of the *muscular system* shall be made of fibers that are strung together like the strands inside a cable. Just as many strands give such a cable strength, many fibers shall *give* a muscle *strength*. But unlike a cable's strands, muscle fibers are elastic, enabling them to contract and then relax, so as to implement a motion. Thus the purpose of a muscle shall be to move a body part. Thus the purpose of the muscular system *shall* be movement. And the heart, being an example, shall *pump* to make blood circulate. Other internal muscles shall *move* food through the digestive tract. Still others shall be connected to the bones by *tendons*. Thus a tendon shall tie a *muscle* to a bone, enabling *it* to move a leg, an arm, a hand or jaw.

Now the *cutaneous system*, consisting of the skin, the hair and nails, shall have three main purposes: (i) *to protect* the body from external agents and from injury, (ii) *to provide* a region of receptors for the sense of touch, and (iii) *to regulate* the body temperature by retaining heat and by excreting sweat.

Now the *digestive system* shall process food by converting it into nutrients that cells shall use. The digestive system *shall* start at the mouth, where the teeth shall chew, tear and grind *food* into smaller parts. *Saliva* shall be added to lubricate the food, thereby making it somewhat easier to swallow. But the saliva shall also provide enzymes to commence the process of breaking down the food. Next the food shall enter in the stomach, where some acids and some gastric juices shall be added. The *stomach* shall serve as a storage tank until the food is *sent* to the intestines. In the *intestines*, digestive enzymes and bacteria such as *escherichia coli* shall completely break down molecules of food: The *pancreas* shall supply protein-digesting and sugar-splitting enzymes, while the *gall bladder*, by supplying *bile*, shall aid the digestion of the fats. Eventually, proteins shall be broken into amino acids, and fats and carbohydrates shall be decomposed into useful building blocks. Next cells along the walls of the intestines shall absorb the processed nutrients and supply them to the blood. And the blood shall carry nutrients throughout the body to the cells. Some digestive products shall be stored in the *liver* for further processing and later use. Waste food products shall first enter the *colon*, then the *rectum*, and finally exit by the *anus*.

Now the *respiratory system* shall process air. Air shall enter the nose and mouth, go down the trachea and pass into the *lungs*, where three-hundred-million microscopic *alveoli* shall permit oxygen to diffuse through membranes and to pass into the blood. And at the same time, the alveoli shall allow carbon dioxide in the blood to pass into the lungs, go up the trachea and exit out the nose and mouth. Thus old blood entering the lungs shall have its *carbon dioxide*, which is a waste of metabolic processes, *removed*, while *oxygen*, a fuel of these same metabolic processes, shall be *infused in it*. Man shall breathe in oxygen and exhale $CO_2$.

Now the *circulatory system* shall be the internal transportation system of the body. The heart shall pump *blood*, a cell-containing fluid, through the *arteries* and *veins* as follows. Blood enriched with oxygen shall exit the lungs and enter *the* left upper chamber of the heart, where it will be pumped to *the* left lower chamber. Then the blood shall branch out into the body, passing through arteries of ever smaller size. Eventually, it shall enter capillaries,[257] where the oxygen shall be distributed to cells and carbon dioxide shall be absorbed. The carbon-dioxide containing blood shall head back to the heart through veins of ever larger size. After entering the right upper chamber, it shall be pumped to *the* right lower chamber and then back to the lungs. Around and around the circulatory system shall blood flow. Now many cells in blood shall be either *white* or *red*, while the liquid in which they float shall be called *plasma*. And the blood shall carry nutrients, gases, hormones, wastes and other substances to and from the cells. The wastes shall be removed via the *urinary system*: *Kidneys* shall extract the waste by placing it in *urine* in a tank-like *bladder*. Now the *lymphatic system* shall be a subsystem of the circulatory system. *Lymph*, a clear watery fluid containing white cells, shall be transported through lymphatic vessels, thereby connecting certain tissues with the blood-stream. At various locations, *lymph nodes*[258] shall destroy bacteria and filter out foreign substances and bodies. Now the *spleen* shall regulate the red-blood-cell count, at times destroying red blood cells, at times storing them for later use. And the spleen shall also manufacture lymph and produce antibodies to attack the foreign substances and agents.

Now the *reproductive system* shall allow human beings to multiply their numbers. And females shall provide the *eggs*, which males shall fertilize with *sperm*. A fertilized egg shall develop in a woman's womb, first as an *embryo* then as a *fetus*. And the mature fetus shall exit from the *vagina* as a newborn human being.

Now the *endocrine system* shall consist of glands that regulate the body's functions using hormones. *Hormones* shall be messengers that trigger chemical reactions. Now the *hypothalamus* in the brain shall control the *pituitary gland* at the cranium's base. This shall control the other glands, such as the adrenal, parathyroid, thyroid and sex glands. The *thyroid gland* shall regulate the rates of metabolic chemical reactions; the *parathyroid* shall control the calcium metabolism; and the *adrenal glands* shall influence salt balance and control the metabolisms for carbohydrates and for water. And in emergencies, *adrenalin* shall be secreted to stimulate activity. The *pancreas* shall secrete *insulin* into the blood to assist in the metabolism of the carbohydrates.

Now the *nervous system* shall be the communication network of the body. The messengers shall be the *neurons*. The *brain* shall be the master center of control. And the signals shall be transmitted by the neurons as electrical and chemical *impulses*. Signals shall move through the nervous system *both toward* and *from* the brain. In the latter case,

---

[257] These are tiny thin-walled tubes.

[258] The human body shall contain about five-hundred lymph nodes.

impulses from the brain shall pass through the *spinal cord* in the backbone and be distributed to the body through a branch-like set of *nerves*. Among things, such impulses shall make muscles move. Now some signals shall *move toward* the brain. And for example, the sensory organs for touch, taste, smell, sight and sound shall send signals via *sensory neurons* to the brain. The sensory neurons shall have *receptors* that translate environmental information into *the* nerve pulses. The tongue shall taste. The nose shall smell. The ears shall hear. The eyes shall see. The skin and hands shall feel.

Now the human body shall be continually attacked by foreign organisms, such as bacteria and viruses, and non-living objects, such as dust. The *immune system* shall protect the body against such foreign substances. The first line of defense shall be the skin. Immune-defense cells such as T cells and B cells shall defend the body against invaders. And the *thymus*, in the chest, shall make T cells,[259] while *bone marrow* shall make B cells.[260] And when a foreign substance invades the body, *B cells* shall detect it and attack. And the B cells shall produce some *antibodies*. And antibodies shall latch onto a foreign body and attack it. And they shall label the foreign agent so that it becomes a target for other cells, such as the macrophages. *Macrophages* shall engulf a foreign agent and process it so that it may be targeted by *T cells*. Certain T cells shall divide and shall attack the foreign agent.[261] And other T cells shall aid and regulate the antibody production of the B cells. The antibodies shall then pass through the human body in search of similar foreign agents. And if a massive invasion *be* underway, the rapid deployment force shall then go into action. And B cells shall quickly divide and multiply. And they shall produce the antibodies in great numbers.

Each antibody shall be able to *attach* itself to only certain foreign agents. And for example, antibodies that defend the human body against polio shall be useless for defending it against typhoid. So it shall be necessary to have *many different types* of antibodies to attack the many different types of foreign agents. The immune-defense cells shall circulate through the human body in the bloodstream and in the lymphatic system.

Now there shall be three generic types of T cells: *Helper T cells* shall enhance the production of antibodies by B cells, *killer T cells* shall secrete chemicals that kill infected cells, and *suppressor T cells* shall suppress the generation of antibodies by B cells. The latter shall be instrumental in terminating B-cell and antibody production after the invading force has been destroyed.

---

[259] Actually, T cells are derived from bone marrow and only mature in the thymus.

[260] At any given moment, two-trillion B cells shall be in a human's bones.

[261] T cells are responsible for organ-transplant rejection.

And the immune system shall be *like unto* an army. The antibodies shall be *like unto* soldiers with *unique* fighting capabilities and carrying and deploying *different* armaments. And their armaments shall be effective against specific invading foreign forces. The lymphatic system shall function as supply lines. Now the B cells shall be *like unto* officers that recruit, equip and organize the antibodies. And these B cells shall be responsible for keeping the defense system well supplied with the appropriately trained forces. And *when* there is a war, B cells shall also participate in fighting. Now the T cells shall be *like unto* sergeants that direct the other cells but fight as well. And B cells shall communicate with T cells to assist them in their duties.

## Chapter V: Cellular Biology

*For the life of the flesh is in the blood.*

And since the cell is the basic building block of life, to understand the cell is to understand the "atoms" of biology. Now a living organism shall be composed of one or many cells. An *amoeba* shall be an animal consisting of a single cell. The smallest living organism on the Earth shall be the PPLO, or pleuropneumonia-like organism, with a diameter of one-tenth of a micrometer and a weight of a *millionth of a billionth* of a gram. And compared to the amoeba, the PPLO shall be lighter by a *million* times. On the other scale of things, a human being shall be composed of a *hundred-trillion* cells. Now the size of typical cells shall be small with diameters ranging from a fraction of a micrometer to several micrometers. Cells *shall interact* chemically with one another. And for example, certain cells shall adhere to certain other cells. Now cells shall be able to communicate by signals: One cell shall secrete signalling molecules such as the hormones, which shall then bind to the *receptors* of a second cell. And by these means, cells shall be able to send messages to one another, allowing growth to be initiated or causing metabolic processes to speed up or slow down.

Now each cell shall contain a watery substance, the *cytosol*, which shall be full of dissolved organic substances such as proteins, carbohydrates, lipids and so on. Thus the cytosol shall provide a medium in which organic substances and organelles can move about. Now *organelles* shall be components inside the cell that perform specific functions. And the most important organelles shall be the nucleus, the mitochondria, the lysosomes, the endoplasmic reticulum, the Golgi apparatus and the chloroplasts. Now the *nucleus* shall contain the genetic information – it *shall* be a cell's "brain." And the *mitochondria* shall provide energy – they *shall* be a cell's "battery." And the *lysosomes* shall digest organic materials – *they* shall be the "stomach" of a cell. And the *endoplasmic reticulum* and *Golgi apparatus* shall synthesize certain biological molecules, process them, sort them and direct them to proper locations in a cell. In plant cells, *chloroplasts* shall provide energy by photosynthesis. Now there shall be hundreds of lysosomes and thousands of mitochondria in a cell, but there shall be just one nucleus, because a cell with two nuclei would be *like unto* a creature with two brains. And like the cells themselves, organelles shall be encased by membranes that shall control, restrict and permit the flow of organic substances into and out of organelles.

And water shall be the major constituent of living organisms. And cells, for example, shall be three-fourths water. Thus the behavior and properties of molecules in water shall be important. An *acid* shall be a substance that produces in water excess hydrogen cations, that is, $H^+$'s.[262] And a *base* shall be a substance that reduces in water the number of $H^+$'s. In other words, an acid shall be a proton donor, while a base shall be a proton acceptor. Now *neutral* water shall neither be acidic nor be basic. Basic water shall try to react with substances to end up neutral. Likewise, acidic water shall try to react with substances to end up neutral. And biochemical molecules shall often be acids and be bases. And for example, an amino acid shall be an acid, and a nucleotide base shall be a base.

Now the nucleus shall house the molecules of DNA. A *gene* shall be a portion of the DNA chain that codes a protein. The total genetic information of an organism shall be its *genome*. In the genome of a bacterium, there shall be a couple thousand genes. In the genome of a mammal, there shall be a couple hundred-thousand genes.

Now every cell of a particular living organism shall contain the selfsame DNA. However, in a given cell, some genes shall be *inactive*, while others shall be *active*. Most importantly, different kinds of cells and their function shall be determined by which genes are *turned on* and which genes are *turned off*.

The DNA strands in a nucleus shall be millions of times longer than the cell's diameter. Thus DNA shall have to wind up into a compact form. And *histones* shall be small proteins around which the strands of DNA can wrap – a histone shall function for a strand of DNA as a bobbin functions for a thread. A DNA molecule wound up by histones shall be a *chromosome*.

Now plants, using the energy in sunlight and combining it with carbon dioxide and water, shall produce sugar molecules and *oxygen*, the *latter* as a waste. The sugar molecules shall store the energy of light for later use. And this process shall be *photosynthesis*.

Now when molecules meet within a cell, they shall chemically react. And "chemical pandemonium" *shall* ensue with atoms rushing to be rearranged. And molecules *shall* combine or split. The presence of enzymes shall assist and speed up these chemical reactions. But some reactions shall not proceed unless energy is *externally* provided. And the most important energy-providing molecule shall be *adenosine*

---

[262] $H^+$'s is pronounced "H pluses." An $H^+$ is a proton.

*triphosphate*, or *ATP*. ATP shall be manufactured in cells from sugars and other organic molecules such as fatty acids and amino acids. And energy shall be stored in the chemical bonds[263] of ATP. And when the bonds are broken, energy shall be released.

Now RNA shall perform two main purposes: to speed up reactions or *to* send messages. And the latter shall be *messenger RNA*, or *mRNA*. They shall allow the information in DNA to be disseminated.

One purpose of RNA shall be assisting *synthesis of proteins*. Now DNA shall act as a template where single-strand RNA *can* be manufactured. The process of producing a specific protein shall begin with enzymes that "unzip" a stretch of DNA by breaking bonds that hold the DNA's two strands together. With this part unwound, the DNA's genetic "protein blueprints" thus shall be exposed. Next, other enzymes shall use the exposed DNA region to build an mRNA that is encoded with the blueprints. When a *ribosome* in the cytosol comes in contact with this mRNA, it shall become a *programmed ribosome*. Then it shall begin to move along the mRNA, reading codons[264] as it goes. At the same time, a relatively short tRNA, or *transfer RNA* molecule, shall bring an amino acid to the programmed ribosome; the amino acid type being determined by a codon. The programmed ribosome shall assemble each amino acid to the next to form the protein. Remarkably the ribosome, the work-horse of protein manufacturing, shall itself be composed of proteins bound to molecules of *ribosome RNA*, or *rRNA*.

And the nucleus of a cell shall be *like unto* a library. And the DNA strands shall be *like unto* a stack of books, while a gene shall be *like unto* a single book. Messenger RNA molecules shall be *like unto* librarians. The ribosome shall be *like unto* a borrower of books.

A cook goes to the library to find a new recipe and requests a cookbook from the librarian. The librarian searches the stacks, finds the book and brings it to the cook. The cook upon returning to the kitchen of a restaurant, prepares a new entree. First, he calls on his assistants to fetch *certain* ingredients. They go and get them and bring them to him. Then the cook combines the ingredients to make the new entree.

After having read the recipe, the cook shall be *like unto* a programmed ribosome, while the assistants to the cook shall be *like unto* tRNA. And the ingredients shall be *like unto* amino acids, while the entree shall be *like unto* a protein.

Thus DNA, RNA and ribosomes shall manufacture proteins from amino acids. And *some* newly manufactured proteins shall directly enter a cell's cytosol. But *other* newly manufactured proteins shall pass to the endoplasmic reticulum where they *further* shall be processed, while certain proteins shall go to the mitochondria, the chloroplasts, the

---

[263] Such bonds are discussed in Chapter VII of the Book of *Chemistry*.

[264] Codons code animo acids. See Chapter VI.

Golgi apparatus and other organelles. And tens of thousands of different types of proteins shall be manufactured and distributed this way.

Now cells shall reproduce by growing and *dividing*. Growing shall be achieved by ingesting molecules from the surroundings and by processing them in biochemical reactions. After cell growth, DNA shall *reproduce itself*: Each of the *two* strands that make up the helix structure shall, with the help of enzymes, unwind, separate and reproduce a second strand. Then *these two* new strands shall combine with the old strands to produce two helix structures. In other words, each of the two new DNA's shall consist of an *old* strand and a *new*. Then when all DNA molecules are duplicated, the cell shall stretch and break in two. This process shall be *cell division*. And the cells resulting from division shall be the *daughter cells*. And when a cell divides, chromosomes[265] shall pass genetic information to the daughter cells.

## Chapter VI: Microbiology

*All flesh is not the same flesh:*
*but there is one kind of flesh of men,*
*another flesh of beasts,*
*another of fishes,*
*and another of birds.*

Now biological macromolecules shall be built from smaller organic molecules such as simple sugars, amino acids, nucleotides and fatty acids. *Simple sugars* shall be the constituents for carbohydrates, while *amino acids* shall be the basic building blocks for proteins. Thus a string of amino acids shall a protein be. A chain of *nucleotides* shall constitute a nucleic acid. And *fatty acids*, which involve hydrocarbon $CH_2$ chains, shall be the main components of lipids and fat molecules.

Now *carbohydrates* shall be molecules made from simple sugars. The word "carbohydrate" meaning "watered carbon" shall well describe their structure. Carbohydrates shall be the principle product of plant photosynthesis – in chemical bonds shall the energy of sunlight so be stored. Thus carbohydrates shall be an energy source for living organisms. And they shall be the most abundant organic compounds on the Earth. The smallest *shall* be simple sugars such as *glucose, fructose* and *galactose* – each of these contains six carbons, twelve hydrogens and six oxygens ($C_6H_{12}O_6$) but differs from each other in the way their atoms are arranged. Glucose, from the Greek word "glykys" meaning sweet, shall be found in honey, fruits and blood. And simple sugars such as *ribose* ($C_5H_{10}O_5$) shall appear as a component in molecules of RNA and DNA.

Now two simple sugars that are linked shall be a *double sugar*. And *sucrose*, which is common table sugar and is composed of one glu-

---

[265] In a human being, the number of pairs of chromosomes shall be twenty-three.

cose molecule and one fructose molecule, *shall* be an example. And *lactose*, which is a sugar found in milk, shall be another double sugar – it shall be made from a galactose and a glucose. *Maltose*, which is found in sprouting seeds and malt, shall be two glucose sugars bound together. It shall be a digestive product of polysaccharides. Simple and double sugars shall be sweet.

Now *polysaccharides* shall be macromolecules consisting of *many* simple sugars. And *cellulose*, the principal structural component of plants and wood, shall be a polysaccharide. It shall be a linear molecule composed of thousands of glucose units. *Starch*, which is found in seeds, roots and stems, shall be another polysaccharide, consisting of branch-like chains of glucose. And *glycogen*, which is found in the liver and the muscles of the mammals, shall be the analog of starch for animals. And *chitin* shall be an important polysaccharide for insects and for arthropods.

Now to tap the energy of a double sugar or a polysaccharide, an organism shall first have to break the molecule into the simple sugars. In the case of breaking starch to simple sugars, *dextrin*, which is a polysaccharide made *from* eleven simple sugars, shall often be produced at the beginning of digestion. And later, dextrin shall be further decomposed.

Now lipids, which are greasy to the touch, shall be organic compounds which store energy for long-term future use and which form certain structural components of an organism. Although they shall *not dissolve* in water, they *shall dissolve* in organic solvents such as alcohol and ether. *Triglycerides*, a major ingredient of animal and human fat, shall store twice as much energy as carbohydrates. And the lipid *lecithin* shall be a main component of the membrane of a cell.

Now a chain of methylene groups shall be the "backbone" of a fatty acid molecule. A *methylene group* shall be one carbon atom and two hydrogen atoms, or $-CH_2-$. Now the dash on each side of "$-CH_2-$" shall indicate a "dangling bond." The two dangling bonds in $-CH_2-$ shall join $CH_2$ to other atoms. An *unsaturated fatty acid* shall be a fatty acid for which at least one pair of methylenes, $-CH_2-CH_2-$, is replaced by a double-bonded $-CH=CH-$ group. A *saturated fatty acid* shall have no double-bonded groups. Now a fatty acid shall often begin with a *methyl group*, $H_3C-$, of three hydrogens *and* one carbon, and often end with a *carboxyl group* of $-COOH$. The carboxyl group shall be responsible for the acidity of *fatty acids*. Now some fatty acids shall have side groups attached to *the* main backbone chain. Triglycerides shall involve three fatty acids joined by a molecule of *glycerol*. To exploit the *energy* contained in lipids, living organism shall first store the energy in fatty acids in ATP, and later, they shall liberate this energy in metabolic processes.

Now *proteins* shall be fundamental molecules for life, the second largest ingredient in cells, and the dominant organic macromolecule in terms of its importance. A chain of typically, many hundreds of amino acids *shall* comprise a protein. Proteins shall be able to fold up into compact sphere-like structures: This *folding* shall be vital for their functions and their interactions. Now random chains of amino acids shall not fold into a useful form − such proteins are worthless for an organism's purposes. It was *evolution* that led to Life's selection of the useful proteins. And during hundreds of millions of years, Earth's life forms *learned* to manufacture beneficial proteins and to ignore the useless ones.

Although amino acids are made at random in minute quantities throughout the Universe, it shall be *plants* that produce amino acids on Earth in sufficient quantities to maintain life. Now an animal shall not be able to directly manufacture the amino acids − an animal shall obtain them directly from the plants or indirectly from the proteins of the other animals. Thus the original source of all amino acids shall be the plants. Now hundreds of amino acids shall exist in Nature, but only twenty shall be the building blocks for useful proteins. And they shall be *cysteine, proline, alanine, threonine, serine, glycine, aspartate, asparagine, glutamate, glutamine, lysine, arginine, tyrosine, histidine, tryptophan, phenylalanine, methionine, leucine, isoleucine* and *valine*.

Each of the twenty amino acids shall be assigned a letter code. And cysteine shall be C, proline P, alanine A, threonine T, serine S, glycine G, aspartate D, asparagine N, glutamate E, glutamine Q, lysine K, arginine R, tyrosine Y, histidine H, tryptophan W, phenylalanine F, methionine M, leucine L, isoleucine I, and valine shall be V.

And at one end of an amino acid shall be an *amino group* consisting of two hydrogens and a nitrogen, $H_2N$-. The dangling bond of nitrogen shall bind the $H_2N$ to the rest of the amino acid. At the other end shall be a carboxyl group -COOH. And the dangling bond of carbon shall bind the COOH to the rest of the amino acid. Between the two ends shall be a hydrogen atom, a carbon atom and a side chain. An amino acid shall be distinguished by its side chains, which provide for *different chemical capabilities*. The simplest side chain shall be one atom long − a hydrogen atom. And this amino acid shall be *glycine*, $H_2N$-$CH_2$-COOH.

And when a ribosome manufactures a protein from amino acids, it shall join the carboxyl and amino ends, and produce a waste water molecule of $H_2O$. Thus -COOH shall join with $H_2N$- to produce -COHN- and $H_2O$. And the linking group -COHN- shall be a *peptide bond*. Now when digestion breaks down a protein into amino acids, the process shall be reversed: Water shall be added to break the peptide bonds and form carboxyl and amino ends.

And amino acids shall be *like unto* a toy construction set of twenty types of basic building pieces. And it shall be possible to join the pieces using small universal linking tubes, the peptide bonds. And the structures so obtained by attaching pieces shall be proteins. And with many building pieces and unlimited linking tubes, the number of such structures shall *be* enormous. Thus the number of proteins *shall* be almost *limitless*.

And Nature shall utilize these structures to form the fundamental components of life and living organisms. The processes of eating and digesting food shall be like taking someone else's ready-made construction and tearing it apart to use the parts.

Now protein chains shall have names determined by the sequence of amino acids. And for example, the pancreas hormone protein glucagon shall be HSQGTFTSDYSKYLDSRRAQDFVQWLMNT. And although this "word" may not make sense in English, it shall biologically make sense. So "HSQGTFTSDYSKYLDSRRAQDFVQWLMNT" shall be in the biological dictionary of protein words. And it shall represent the protein chain histidine-serine-glutamine-glycine- . . . asparagine-threonine. Now although the protein glutamate-isoleucine-asparagine-serine-threonine - glutamate - isoleucine-asparagine-tryptophan-alanine-serine-alanine-glycine-arginine-glutamate-alanine-threonine-serine-cysteine-isoleucine-glutamate-asparagine-threonine-isoleucine-phenylalanine-isoleucine-cysteine-serine-alanine-isoleucine-asparagine-threonine shall *not* be in the biological protein dictionary, it *shall* make sense in English.

Now an antibody shall be composed of four small protein chains – two identical heavy chains and two identical light chains. These protein chains shall originate from four types of genes – *variety genes*, or *V genes*; *diversity genes*, or *D genes*; *joining genes*, or *J genes*; and *constant genes*, or *C genes*. Now there shall be more than a hundred types of V genes, a dozen types of D genes, four types of J genes and one C gene. And when V, D, J and C genes are assembled to make a heavy chain, they shall be thousands of different combinations. Thus there shall be thousands of different heavy chains. Likewise, when D, J and C genes are assembled to make a light chain, there shall be hundreds of different combinations. Thus there shall be hundreds of different kinds of light chains. And when the light and heavy genes are combined to make an antibody, the possibilities *shall number in the millions*, so that antibody types shall number in the millions.

Now a *nucleotide* shall be a sugar-phosphate[266] molecule attached to a nitrogen-containing base. And a chain of nucleotides shall be *a nucleic acid*; the phosphate of one nucleotide shall bind to the sugar of the next. And the most important nucleic acids shall be deoxyribonucleic acid and ribonucleic acid. In *ribonucleic acid*, or *RNA*, the *sugar* in the nucleotides shall be ribose ($C_5H_{10}O_5$), while in *deoxyribonucleic acid*, or *DNA*, *it* shall be deoxyribose ($C_5H_{10}O_4$).[267]

---

[266] The phosphate shall be negatively charged $PO_4$.

[267] This "sugar" is ribose with an oxygen removed. The "deoxy" in the name for DNA indicates that each "sugar" in the nucleotides of DNA is missing an oxygen.

Now DNA shall consist of *two long strands* interwoven in a helix. The bases in the nucleotides of DNA shall be four basic types: *adenine, cytosine, guanine* and *thymine*. And A shall stand for adenine, C for cytosine, G for guanine, and T shall stand for thymine. And a DNA molecule shall be specified by listing the nucleotides in *one* of its two strands – a *DNA sequence* shall be the name for this, a long list of letters that "codes" the DNA. And for example, the sequence for one DNA strand of herpes shall be CTATGATGACAC . . . CGACCCTGCAGC. Now the list of letters of the second strand shall be determined from the first, for the two strands shall fit together like two parts of a zipper – A and T shall fit together, and G and C shall fit together. And ye shall say that A is complementary to T and that T is complementary to A. Likewise shall ye say that G is complementary to C and that C is complementary to G. And for example, the other strand in the herpes DNA molecule shall be GATACTACTGTG . . . GCTGGGACGTCG. Now it shall be two hydrogen bonds[268] that bind the A and T. And three hydrogen bonds shall bind the C and G. But neither A and C, nor A and G, nor T and C, nor T and G shall bind. So hydrogen bonds shall tie the two strands in DNA together. And DNA shall be *like unto* a twisted ladder with double and triple bonds for rungs.

Now most importantly, DNA sequences shall encode biological instructions. The nucleotides shall *act as* letters of Life's alphabet. Three letters in a row shall be a *codon*. A codon shall be *like unto* a word. So DNA shall be *like unto* a text with a thousand or tenthousand words. And the sentences shall encode the information. A few codons shall be punctuation – they shall say when a sentence starts and when it stops.

Now RNA shall differ from DNA in three main ways: (1) the sugar in the nucleotides, (2) the replacement of thymine with uracil, and (3) the structure, which is single-stranded for an RNA. Hundreds or thousands of nucleotides shall be contained in a chain of RNA. The four nucleotides, *adenine, cytosine, guanine* and *uracil*, shall be the units in the chain. Now U shall stand for uracil. And U and A *shall* be complementary. Thus uracil in RNA shall play the role that thymine plays in DNA.

And when RNA is manufactured, DNA shall act as a template in which complementary nucleotides are made. Thus a DNA sequence such as . . . TACCCGAGGTAGCCGCGTCGT . . . shall produce an RNA molecule of AUG-GGC-UCC-AUC-GGC-GCA-GCA. And the codons AUG, GGC, UCC, AUC and GCA shall yield the amino acids methionine, glycine, serine, isoleucine and alanine. Thus the AUG-GGC-UCC-AUC-GGC-GCA-GCA series of RNA shall yield the protein chain methionine-glycine-serine-isoleucine-glycine-alanine-alanine. And so the

---

[268] See Chapter VII of the Book of *Chemistry*.

TACCCGAGGTAGCCGCGTCGT region of the DNA molecule shall provide the information for producing the protein chain MGSIGAA.

Thus the *codons* in a region of DNA shall *code* the letter words of proteins. And in this manner, the language of the DNA shall be translated into the language of Life, thereby allowing DNA to manufacture RNA, proteins and itself. And with proteins, RNA and DNA, *life* shall be. And let it be known to thee and all around thee that the "secret of Life" shall be hidden in the DNA: It *shall* contain the code of Life.

# The Books of the Solar System

*Lift up thy eyes to Heaven and behold.*

*The first book of Planetology, called*

# Mythology[269]

And long ago, an ancient civilization ascribed to objects in the solar system godly characteristics and assigned them mythological purposes. And the Sun, Helios, became the goddess of energy. And She was commanded to burn in Her *inside* and radiate from Her *outside*. And Her radiation swept across outer space *like unto* a chariot drawn by four horses. And the children of Helios, the nine Planets, *also* became gods and goddesses. Mercury became the god of cosmic transportation. And He watched over the motions of the other heavenly bodies. And He made sure that they *obeyed the laws of Nature* and conformed to the rules of fair exchange, such as the conservation of energy and momentum. And Venus became the goddess of *attractive forces*. And Venus made sure that two massive objects wanted to move toward each other. And Earth became the goddess of life and living things. And Mars became the god of violent activity, making stars *explode* in supernovas. And He caused galaxies to collide and undergo galactic war. And Jupiter became the god of electromagnetism. He caused lightning to flash in atmospheres. And Saturn became the goddess of cosmic dust and grain. And She created nebulae, planets and other non-stellar objects out of *the seeds of cosmic dust*. And Uranus became the goddess of the heavens. She calmed the Universe when it was in its quantum-gravity beginning and fueled Inflation when the Universe expanded exponentially. And She slowed Inflation to a graceful conclusion. Now Neptune became the god of cosmic seas. He watched over empty outer space, *created* giant voids among the galactic clusters and instilled in the fabric of space the desire to *stretch* and to *expand*. And Pluto became the god of far-away worlds. And wearing a helmet that rendered

---

[269] It is important to distinguish myth from reality. Likewise, one should know the difference between an *astronomer* and an *astrologer*. Now astrologers are *false prophets* (no different from those who play with Tarot cards). And he who knows the Universe knows why, for astrologers try to predict the future based on the positions of the planets. And this is nonsense, for the sphere of influence of the planets is *limited* – their weak gravities can be hardly felt on Earth. And so the positions of the planets can have little effect on events on Earth.

*(And a voice spake, saying*
*"Beware of false prophets.")*

Now on the other hand, astronomers are true prophets, for they predict the planets based on the laws of Nature. And they can do this because Nature's laws are *universal* and valid *everywhere*. Thus to predict the position of a planet is a worthy endeavor.

*(And a voice spake, saying*
*"Hearken ye unto these words:*
*omnipresent are the laws of Nature.")*

Him invisible to the unaided eye, He watched over the black holes in the Universe. Thus in ancient times, the assignment of attributes and duties led to the personification of the Planets.

*The second book of Planetology, called*

# The Sun

*She was the greater light.*
*And She was there to rule the sky.*

## Chapter I: Her Place in the Solar System

Now the Sun shall be the mother of the solar system. And she *shall shine* brilliantly and *supply sunlight and energy* unto her children, which are the planets. And she shall sit at the center of the solar system, while her children and companions shall revolve around her. Once every twenty-eight days shall *she* turn slowly *and* watch over them.

Now the Sun shall use her weight to *influence* her children and her friends. The Earth and others shall obey *her* pull of gravity. And they shall orbit the Sun in a common direction in circles or in ellipses in almost a common plane. In such elliptical orbits, the Sun shall sit at one of the two foci.

## Chapter II: Her Place in the Galaxy

And in the Milky Way galaxy, the Sun shall be *but one* of several hundred-billion stars. And the Sun and the rest of the stars shall march in great circles around the center of the Milky Way. She shall drag with her family and friends, moving at more than two-hundred kilometers per second. But because their journey *is so long*, it shall take them more than *two-hundred-million* years to circle once around the galaxy.

## Chapter III: Size, Shape and Weight

Now the Sun shall have an enormous spherical body with a radius more than one-hundred times the radius of Earth. And she shall weigh *two-million-trillion-trillion* kilograms, which is two-thousand-trillion-trillion tons. Ninety-nine percent of the solar system's mass shall reside within her body.

And *tremendous* amounts of energy shall flow outward from her surface – from each square meter shall radiate sixty-million watts, so that the total power output shall be *four-hundred-trillion-trillion* watts. But *less than* one-half of one-billionth of this energy shall be absorbed by Earth. Now the Sun shall shine light brilliantly – more than *three-billion-billion-billion* candles bright.

Now by weight, sixty percent of the Sun shall be of hydrogen, and forty percent shall be of helium. But trace amounts of almost all the elements shall reside within her body.

## Chapter IV: Structure and Energy Production

Now the Sun shall be divided into three layers: a core, a radiation zone and a convective shell. The two-hundred-thousand-kilometer spherical *core* shall be the Sun's most inner part. The three-hundred-thousand-kilometer-thick *radiation zone* shall surround the core. And the two-hundred-thousand-kilometer-thick *convective layer* shall constitute Sun's outer layer.

Now Sun's temperature shall be highest at the center and decrease toward the surface. The surface shall be just six-thousand Kelvins — a dozen times as hot as a hot oven. In contrast, the temperature shall be *fifteen-million* Kelvins *at the center*. *There*, Sun's density shall be one-hundred-and-fifty times the density of water, and the pressure shall be *four-hundred-billion* atmospheres.

Now in the core, which is Sun's heart, the Sun shall by burning nuclei make energy: Two protons shall *fuse* to generate a deuteron, a positron and a nu-e. And the positron shall *immediately* annihilate with an electron to make some energetic photons. And the deuterium nucleus shall *fuse* with a proton to *produce* a photon and a helium-three. The helium-three nucleus shall quickly fuse with another helium-three to *produce* two protons and a helium-four. And the net effect of these reactions shall be the conversion of four protons into helium-four-type nuclei. Now during these reactions, mass shall be *converted* into energy, according to the Eighth Commandment, that mass be a form of energy. And because the destruction of a little mass produces a lot of energy, a lot of energy shall be produced. Although *five-billion* kilograms of mass shall be converted into energy each second, the Sun shall be so huge that during its lifetime it will sacrifice less than one one-thousandth of its mass in energy.

Now the proton-proton fusions shall generate neutrinos in enormous quantities. Moving at the speed of light, they shall pass through the body of the Sun without *any* interaction. And they shall continue, passing undetected through the planets and the solar system. They shall be *lost* to the outer parts of outer space.

Now in the Sun, the outward pressure of the outward flow of heat and photons shall *balance* the inward pull of gravity. And neither shall the Sun expand nor shrink.

The energy generated in Sun's core shall be carried by photons through the radiation zone. And photons shall *scatter* often off ambient electrons and off nuclei. And photons shall be repeatedly *absorbed* and *re-emitted* by electrons and by nuclei. After many trillion-trillion scatterings, absorptions and emissions, the energy and photons shall be transported through the radiation zone. At the inner radius of the convective shell shall photons be absorbed. From there, the energy and heat shall *be lifted* to the surface of the Sun through the *motions* of electrons and of nuclei. In all, it shall take *ten-million years* for a bit of energy produced in Sun's core to reach the surface of the Sun, the *photosphere*. Now compared with Sun's gigantic body, the photosphere shall be skin deep – just five-hundred kilometers in thickness. At Sun's surface, *upon the wings of electromagnetic waves* shall the energy fly off. And the waves shall travel at the speed of light. Eight-and-one-third minutes later shall they arrive on Earth. Five-and-a-half-hours later shall they pass the planet Pluto and *escape the solar system*.

Thus the sunlight that one sees on Earth shall have been emitted from Sun's surface eight-and-one-third minutes earlier and shall have been generated in Sun's core *ten-million years ago*.

## Chapter V: Surface Activity

Now at *Sun's surface*, the entire photosphere shall be a single intense *gas-fire*. *There* shall it often come to pass that a small bright region of hot gas shall *balloon* into a cloud hundreds of kilometers in size. And it shall remain there *like unto* a parachute supported by an upward flowing wind. Then some minutes later, the gas cloud shall divide, spread and fade. And it shall collapse *like unto* the parachute of a person when such a parachutist lands. Now this hot cloud shall be a *granule*. And millions of granules shall cover the surface of the Sun *like unto* the kernels on a cob of corn. And they shall be irregularly shaped and often polygons. Thus the solar surface shall look *like unto* a bubbling overheated broth.

Now sometimes shall erupt *magnetic storms* with magnetic fields thousands of times the strength of the magnetic fields on Earth. These storms shall engulf *thousands of kilometers* of surface region. And since the temperature shall be *cooler* than in non-storm regions, *less* light shall be emitted from magnetic storms. And from afar and against the brighter background, such storms shall appear as spots of *black*. And these blemishes on Sun's surface shall be *sunspots*. They shall last for days or even months. Now the number of sunspots shall fluctuate from day to day, while the average number shall vary gradually with time. And every eleven years, the average shall significantly increase.

Now it shall sometimes come to pass that other regions of the photosphere *grow extra hot*. And since these *hotter* regions radiate more light, they *shall* be very bright. *Faculae* shall they be called. And they shall look like splotches of silver paint upon the solar face.

## Chapter VI: The Sun's Majestic Halo

Now the Sun shall be surrounded by an atmosphere, whose temperature shall increase with the altitude. A few million Kelvins shall be the thinner upper reaches. Now this upper atmosphere shall have a name. And that name shall be *corona*. It shall flare up and wildly flap *like long blond hair in a strong wind*. And the denser lower atmosphere shall also have a name. And it shall be the *chromosphere.*

Now it shall sometimes come to pass that an explosion shall erupt from the photosphere and produce a *gigantic upheaval* of glowing gas. *This* shall be a *prominence*. Prominences shall differ in nature, size and shape. From afar, the smallest shall look *like unto* a campfire. Others, created by the flow of plasma gas along the magnetic field lines of two nearby sunspots, shall *form* a loop. Larger ones shall look *like unto* flames along a brush fire. And the biggest shall be two-hundred kilometers in length, forty-thousand kilometers in height and six-thousand kilometers in thickness. Gas shall be tossed upward like the water splashing outward from a plunging whale.

Sometimes energy stored in magnetic fields shall be violently ejected into the solar atmosphere. Such an outburst shall be a *flare*. *Twenty-five-million Kelvins* shall the hottest regions be inside a flare. It shall appear as a bright filament extending outward *like unto* the silver tongue of a lizard reaching for an insect. Now some flares shall *flash* for seconds, while others shall *last* about an hour. Radiation throughout the entire electromagnetic spectrum, from radio waves to X-rays, shall be given off. Such flares shall cause an *outward burst* of cosmic rays full of particles of different charge. The very strongest flares shall be *heard* on Earth as radio static created by distortions of Earth's ionosphere by energetic X-rays. And sometimes they shall be *seen* as aurorae, when charged particles *enter* Earth's magnetic field.

Now two-hundred-thousand kilometers above the surface of the Sun, the corona shall thin into the *solar wind*. Each second from the edge of the corona, billions of trillions of trillions of protons and electrons shall stream outward at hundreds of kilometers per second. And the solar wind shall *flow* across the solar system and be *gone* into the wilderness of outer space. And when *comets* approach the Sun, this wind shall blow *their* tails long.

*The third book of Planetology, called*

# Mercury

*And the planet nearest the Sun was called Mercury.*

## Chapter I: Mercury's Position in the World

And Mercury, who was named after the messenger of Roman gods and who was himself a god of wealth, commerce, dexterity and eloquence, shall be the child closest to the Sun. And he shall *whiz* around the Sun at an average speed of forty-eight kilometers per second along an ellipse, while the ellipse *itself* shall rotate at a miniscule rate of one-sixth of a degree of arc per century.[270] Now Mercury shall speed up as he approaches the closest distance to the Sun of forty-six-million kilometers, and he shall slow down as he attains the farthest distance of seventy-million kilometers. Every eighty-eight Earth-days, Mercury shall orbit once around the Sun. Thus a Mercurian year shall be eighty-eight Earth-days.

## Chapter II: Structure

Now Mercury shall be a small body with a diameter two-fifths the diameter of Earth. And Mercury shall weigh eighteen times less than Earth.

Now from afar, Mercury shall *look like* the Moon except that Mercury shall have scarps, or steep inclines. And the scarps shall be tens and hundreds of kilometers long and have vertical drops as much as *three kilometers*. They shall have formed more than four billion years ago when faults occurred as the Mercurian body *cooled and shrank*. Now the craters of Mercury shall be similar to the craters of the Moon except they shall be on average smaller. But unlike the Moon, where craters often overlap, on Mercury shall be regions that are smooth.

And like the Moon, Mercury shall have no atmosphere. Now the bright side of Mercury, the side facing the Sun, shall be *hot* – seven-hundred Kelvins, almost twice as hot as a hot oven. In contrast, the dark side, the side facing away from the Sun, shall be *cold* – as low as one-hundred Kelvins, almost three times colder than cold ice-water, *almost as cold as liquid nitrogen*.

And Mercury shall spin in the plane of the solar system. And without atmosphere and no spin-tilt, Mercury shall have *no weather* and *no seasons*.

## Chapter III: Mysterious Motions

*So the Sun stood still in the midst of Heaven.*

And Mercury will make pre-Copernican thinkers scratch their heads and wonder. It shall spin so *slowly* that it shall take fifty-eight-and-two-thirds Earth-days to complete one turn. And this period shall be two-thirds of a Mercurian year. Thus Mercury shall spin one-and-a-half times faster than it revolves around the Sun. Thus it shall make one-and-a-half turns per Mercurian year.

And *if* Mercury *were* not spinning, then its different sides would face the Sun at different times, as it revolves around the Sun. And *if* Mercury *were* not spinning, then one particular side would face the Sun once a Mercurian year. And in such a case, a Mercurian day would last a Mercurian year. On the other hand, *if* Mercury *were* to spin *one turn*

---

[270] Most of this precession is due to the gravitational perturbations of nearby planets. However, one-fourteenth of it is unexplained by Newtonian gravity. The remaining unexplained precession is accounted for by Einstein's theory of gravity.

during one Mercurian year, then one particular side of it would face the Sun *all* the time. *But* since Mercury spins one-and-a-half turns during one Mercurian year, it shall undergo one-half turn relative to the Sun. Thus during one Mercurian year, the side of Mercury *facing away* from the Sun shall become the side of Mercury *facing* the Sun. Likewise, during one Mercurian year, the side *facing* the Sun shall become the side *facing away* from the Sun. Thus night on Mercury shall last one Mercurian year or eighty-eight Earth-days. And night time shall be followed by daylight. And daylight shall also last one Mercurian year or eighty-eight Earth-days. So one full Mercurian day, the time between two *successive* Mercurian sunrises, shall be one-hundred-and-seven-six Earth-days. *A Mercurian day shall last two Mercurian years!*

An intelligent post-Copernican observer on Mercury will realize that when the Sun is overhead at noon, and then sets, and night passes, and the Sun rises and appears overhead at noon again, his planet has gone *twice* around the Sun.

So a Mercurian day shall be *longer* than a Mercurian year. This *shall* not be a paradox – it shall *be* a fact of Nature.

On Mercury, the stars of the heavens shall appear to move through the sky at night *three times faster* than the Sun moves through the sky at day. And when the Sun sets in the west and night begins, *suppose* that the bright star Regulus in the constellation Leo is just rising in the east. Then Regulus shall continue to rise, arrive overhead, sink to the west and set twenty-nine-and-one-third Earth-days later. And twenty-nine-and-one-third Earth-days after that, it shall still be night, and Regulus shall rise *again* in the east. And Regulus shall continue to rise, arrive overhead, sink to the west, and set again twenty-nine-and-one-third Earth-days later. And just as Regulus is setting in the west, the Sun shall rise in the east and it shall be morning. And in another twenty-nine-and-one-third Earth-days, Regulus shall rise *for a third time* in the east. But it shall still be morning and the Sun shall have climbed two-thirds the way to the zenith. And due to the Sun's light, ye shall not be able to see it: But the invisible Regulus shall continue to rise, arrive overhead, pass by the Sun, sink to the west and set for a third time twenty-nine-and-one-third Earth-days later. And when Regulus is setting in the west, it shall be afternoon on Mercury, and the Sun shall be one-third the way down from the zenith and heading to the west. And twenty-nine-and-one-third Earth-days later, the Sun shall set, thereby completing one Mercurian day. And then just as the Sun is setting in the west, Regulus shall be rising in the east *again*.

And an intelligent post-Copernican observer on Mercury will realize that when the Sun is overhead at noon, and then sets, and night passes, and the Sun rises and appears overhead at noon again, his planet has spun *three full turns*.

Now because Mercury is closer than Earth to the Sun during its elliptic orbit, the *Sun's disk on Mercury* shall appear bigger than the Sun's disk on Earth: *On average, it* shall be *eight times bigger* than the Sun's disk on Earth.

And as Mercury *approaches* the Sun, the *Sun's* disk shall grow *larger*. At closest approach shall it be eleven times bigger than on Earth. And as Mercury *recedes* from the Sun, the *Sun's* disk shall grow *smaller*. At the farthest point shall it be five times bigger than on Earth. Mercury will make pre-Copernican thinkers scratch their heads and wonder.

Now because Mercury speeds up as it approaches the Sun and because it is spinning only a little faster than it is revolving around the Sun, an observer on Mercury shall occasionally see the Sun *zigzag*: The Sun, which had been moving forward, shall slow down *and* come to a *stop*. Then it shall move *backward* for a bit for eight Earth-days. And once more the Sun shall slow down *and* come to a stop. Then finally, the Sun shall move *forward once again*.

And the Sun's disk shall expand before a zigzag. During the zigzag, it shall be biggest. And afterwards shall it be shrinking.

Now the Sun shall do two zigzags per Mercurian day. But for most observers on Mercury, one zigzag shall occur at *night*, so that *it* shall *not* be seen. And one zigzag shall occur at *day* – that one *shall* be seen. Most observers shall see the Sun rise in the morning, grow in size, zigzag, shrink in size, and set eighty-eight Earth-days later.

However, for an observer at *a special spot* on Mercury, the zigzags shall occur *at sunrise and sunset*. Such an observer shall see in the east *a large Sun* rise above the horizon, then sink below it, and then rise above it once again. And forty-four Earth-days later, the Sun shall be overhead, at the zenith, and shall be *smallest*. Then forty-four Earth-days after that, or eighty-eight Earth-days after the Sun had first risen in the east, *a large Sun* shall sink in the west below the horizon, then rise above it, and then sink below it once again. On that day, such an observer shall have seen one, two or three sunsets, depending on how ye define a sunset.

Now if ye *be* an observer at the north pole or the south pole of Mercury, ye will see the Sun *all* one-hundred-and-seven-six Earth-days of a Mercurian day. And ye will see the Sun expanding and contracting before, during and after *both* zigzags. But *half* the Sun will be *above* the horizon and *half* the Sun will be *below*. And for thee, there will *never be* any sunsets or sunrises, for the Sun will, in some sense, *always be setting and always be rising*.

*The fourth book of Planetology, called*

# Venus

*And the second planet from the Sun was called Venus.*

## Chapter I: Venusian Motion

And Venus, named after the Roman goddess of love and beauty, shall be Sun's second child. And for an observer on the Earth, she shall be the *third brightest object* in the sky, after the Sun and Moon. And Venus, which is slightly smaller than the Earth, shall have a warm body engulfed in thick "perfume."

She shall zoom through the emptiness of space at thirty-five kilometers per second as she orbits the Sun at two-thirds the Earth-Sun distance. It shall take her two-hundred-and-forty-five days to complete one journey. Thus a Venusian year shall be a two-hundred-and-forty-five-day year.

Now Venus shall spin quite *slowly*: One revolution shall take two-hundred-and-forty-three days – almost the same as a Venusian year. Now if Venus *were* to spin in the same direction as she orbits the Sun then she would always hold the same face to the Sun. However, Venus shall spin in the *opposite* direction. And this shall be *opposite* to the spinning of almost all the other planets and *opposite* to the direction in which all the planets go around the Sun. Thus if ye be *on Venus* looking at the Sun's diffuse vague glow among the thick haze and clouds of Venus, then ye shall see the Sun *rising in the west and setting in the east.*

And so when Venus makes a one-quarter revolution around the Sun, she shall spin her body by one-quarter revolution, while at the same time she shall rotate her orientation to the Sun by another quarter revolution due to her movement round the Sun. Thus in one-fourth of a Venusian year, the side *facing away* from the Sun shall become the side *facing* to the Sun. So a Venusian night shall last one-forth of a Venusian year or sixty-one Earth-days. And after night time shall come daytime. And daytime shall last sixty-one Earth-days too. And so in all, a day on Venus shall last one-hundred-twenty-two Earth-days. A Venusian year shall be two Venusian days.

## Chapter II: The Surface

Now Venus shall have a rocky dry terrain. And the surface temperature shall be seven-hundred-and-fifty Kelvins – hot enough to melt a piece of zinc or lead. And Venus shall have a topography of lowlands and of highlands with canyons, rugged mountains, volcanos and some craters. If liquid water could exist on Venus, the lowlands *would* be oceans and the highlands *would* be continents.

## Chapter III: The Atmosphere

Now the Venusian atmosphere shall be ninety-six percent carbon-dioxide and three percent nitrogen with trace amounts of other gases. Venus shall have *one-hundred times* more atmosphere than Earth. The atmosphere shall be so thick that the pressure at the Venusian surface shall be *ninety-five Earth atmospheres* – the equivalent of what ye would feel one kilometer beneath an ocean on the Earth!

Now Venusian volcanos shall *occasionally* erupt, spilling molten sulfur compounds over the terrain. And *sulfurous gases* shall spew up. They shall react with the carbon dioxide in the atmosphere to produce *sulfur dioxide and sulfide gases*. And at higher altitudes, these gases shall combine with water vapor to yield sulfuric acid, which *shall condense* and help form clouds.

Venus shall be clothed in clouds which completely *hide* her body. These clouds shall retain quite well the heat within her body. And there shall be *three closely spaced cloud layers* between sixty and forty-five kilometers of altitude.[271] And above and below these layers there shall be haze, which consists of sulfuric acid vapor. Now the clouds shall be white with a *pale lemon hue*. And from Earth, ye shall see Venus as a brilliant bright and yellow star.

At fifty-five-thousand kilometers above the surface, *sulfuric acid rain* from clouds shall fall. But at forty-thousand kilometers, the rain shall dissociate into sulfur-dioxide gas and water vapor. Then these gases shall rise up, only to condense again in sulfuric acid droplets.

The temperature of the highest clouds shall be as *cold* as at the arctic circle on the Earth. But the temperature shall increase with decreasing altitude: The lower clouds shall be four-hundred Kelvins, the temperature of a warm oven. At lower altitudes shall the atmosphere grow even hotter.

Now strong *mysterious winds* shall blow from east to west. And at an altitude of sixty kilometers, they shall attain a maximum speed of *three-hundred-and-fifty kilometers per hour*. And these winds shall push the clouds so fast that, once every four days, they shall complete a circuit round the planet. Now the *circulating* atmosphere shall *circulate* Venusian heat. And so, the surface of Venus away from the Sun, which stays dark for sixty-one straight days, shall be almost *as warm* as the surface of Venus that faces to the Sun.

---

[271] These Venusian clouds are five times higher than the clouds on Earth.

*The fifth book of Planetology, called*

# Earth

*And the third planet from the Sun was called Earth.*

## Chapter I: Earth's Orbit

And Earth shall be the Sun's third child and second daughter. And Atlas shall shoulder Earth around the Sun and propel her forward at thirty kilometers each second. And it shall take Earth three-hundred-and-sixty-five-and-one-quarter days to make one revolution. And one complete revolution shall constitute a *year*. Thus three-hundred-and-sixty-five days shall *be* a year. And every four years shall one extra day be added to account for the four quarter-days left out. And such a three-hundred-and-sixty-six-day year *shall* be called a *leap year*.

The distance between the Earth and Sun shall be one-hundred-and-fifty-million kilometers, or ninety-three-million miles. One *astronomical unit* shall be this Earth-Sun distance.

## Chapter II: Size and Weight

Now thirteen-thousand kilometers shall be the diameter of Earth.[272] But the size of the Earth shall be *insignificant* compared to the Sun, for the volume of the Sun shall be more than a *million times* the volume of the Earth. Now the mass of Earth shall be six-trillion-trillion kilograms. But Earth's mass shall be *insignificant* compared with Sun's, for *three-hundred-and-thirty-thousand times* more mass shall have the Sun.

## Chapter III: Spin Effects

*And He called the light Day.*
*And the darkness He called Night.*

Now Earth shall spin from west to east. And in twenty-four hours shall Earth complete one turn. Such a turn shall constitute a *day*. Thus twenty-four hours shall be a day. Now to ye on the Earth, the turning of Earth shall *make it seem* like the stars in heavens turn. And like the viewpoint of a child on a merry-go-round, *the world shall spin and the surroundings shall revolve.* Thus the heavens shall turn from east to west. And this shall make Sun rise and set one time at day. Likewise shall the Moon and stars rotate at night. They shall *all* rise in the east and *all* set in the west.

Now the side of Earth facing to the Sun *shall* be lit by it. And the other side, in contrast, *shall* be dark. As Earth spins, the side that *was in darkness* shall become the side that *is in light*. And the side that *was*

---

[272] This yields a circumference of forty-thousand kilometers.

*in sunlight* shall become the side that *is in darkness*. And ye on the dark side shall call this darkness *night*. And since Earth spins, day shall follow night as night does follow day, *like unto* a cat chasing its own tail. Both nighttime and daytime shall last a half-a-day.

Now the spin-axis of Earth shall tilt twenty-three degrees with respect to the solar-system plane. Thus for a quarter of the year, the northern half of Earth shall *tilt toward* the Sun, causing Sun's rays to fall *perpendicular* onto the regions in the *northern hemisphere*. And warmer shall this be. And *summer* shall this be, for ye living in the northern hemisphere. Now summer shall be followed by a quarter-year interval of time in which *neither* the northern nor the southern hemispheres tilt toward the Sun. And the rays of Sun shall fall *perpendicular* in the *equatorial region* of the Earth. And *autumn* shall this be. Next autumn shall be followed by a quarter-year in which the southern hemisphere shall *tilt toward* the Sun, causing Sun's rays to fall *perpendicular* onto the regions in the *southern hemisphere*. And the northern hemisphere shall thus be cool. And *winter* shall this be. Then winter shall be followed by a quarter-year in which *neither* the northern nor the southern hemispheres tilt toward the Sun. And the rays of Sun shall again fall *perpendicular* in the *equatorial region* of the Earth. This *shall* be *spring*. And summer, autumn, winter, spring shall be the Earth's four *seasons*.

Now when the northern half of Earth tilts *toward* the Sun, the southern hemisphere shall tilt *away*. Thus it shall be winter in the southern hemisphere when it is summer in the north. And when the northern half of Earth tilts *away* from Sun, the southern hemisphere shall tilt *toward* the Sun. Thus it shall be summer in the southern hemisphere when it is winter in the north.

As Earth moves around the Sun in outer space, the dark side of Earth *shall face* the different parts of heaven. Thus the collection of stars in the black of night shall change: the constellations of the winter shall be *different* from the constellations of the summer; likewise for the constellations of the autumn and the spring. But the dark side of Earth shall point in the *same* direction at the *same* time of the year. Thus the constellations ye see this winter shall be the constellations ye saw last winter and shall be the constellations ye will see next winter too. And likewise for the other seasons. Earth's motion round the Sun shall produce the *seasonal rotation of the constellations*.

Since the planets of the solar system move *in a common plane*, they shall appear to thee on Earth to move in a narrow strip of nighttime sky – the *zodiac*. Sometimes over a period of months, the planets, against the backdrop of the stars, shall appear to thee on Earth to zigzag back and forth. And this shall be an *illusion* created by the motion of the Earth around the Sun, for the planets shall move in an obedient manner and in conformity with Kepler's laws.

## Chapter IV: Structure

*And I will show signs in Earth beneath:*
*blood, and fire, and vapor of smoke.*

Now the outer part of Earth shall be Earth's *crust*, a layer of dirt and rock several dozen kilometers in width. Below the crust shall be the *mantle*, three-thousand kilometers thick and containing two-thirds of the mass of Earth. And Earth's temperature shall initially rise rapidly with depth, so that at a few hundred kilometers below the surface, it shall be one-thousand-and-five-hundred Kelvins hot. Now below the mantle shall be the *core*, the inner sphere of Earth. And at the core-mantle interface, the pressure shall be great – *one-and-one-half-million* atmospheres. Now the core shall have two parts: an inner and an outer core. The latter, a liquid shell two-thousand kilometers in width with almost one-third of Earth's mass, shall consist of molten iron-nickel alloys. *Electric currents* in this liquid shall *manufacture* Earth's magnetic field. The inner core with a radius of one-and-a-half-thousand kilometers shall be subjected to *enormous* pressures, which shall render it a solid sphere of iron. And at Earth's center shall the pressure reach *three-million-seven-hundred-thousand* atmospheres. *There*, the temperature shall be six-thousand Kelvins – as hot as *the Sun's surface*.

Thus the interior of the Earth shall be *like unto Hell* – the heat shall be intense – if ye *were* there, thy bodily flesh would instantly be blackened to a crisp; at the same time, a great pressure would crush thy bones into a set of tiny stones.

## Chapter V: Earth's Atmosphere

Now seventy-eight and twenty-one shall be the percentages of nitrogen and oxygen in *the* Earth's atmosphere. Trace amounts of other molecules such as carbon dioxide gas and water-vapor shall play *vital* roles. Water-droplets and tiny ices shall often form white structures – *these* shall be called *clouds*. Now the pressure of the atmosphere at the surface of the Earth shall be one atmosphere by definition: One-hundred-thousand Pascals, or fifteen pounds per square inch, shall be *one atmosphere*.

Starting at one-hundred-kilometers above the surface of the Earth, the atmosphere shall thin into the *thermosphere*. Atoms of oxygen shall mostly make up the seven-hundred-kilometer-thick thermosphere. And when a high-energy ultraviolet ray or X-ray from the Sun does enter the Earth's thermosphere, the ray shall strike with an electron in an atom. And when the electron absorbs the ray, it shall be *ejected* from the atom. Subsequently, it shall be captured by an atom which is positively charged; in doing so, the electron shall *release* some energy as light. Thus the thermosphere shall *absorb all radiations of high-energy*, thereby heating it.[273] Now this absorption of high-energy electromagnetic radiation shall prevent such lethal radiation from striking *the* Earth's surface. But lethal lower-energy ultraviolet rays shall still pass through the thermosphere and reach the upper atmosphere. Such rays shall be absorbed by *small amounts of ozone* fifty-kilometers above the Earth. How shall this work? When an ozone molecule is struck by an ultraviolet ray, it shall *absorb* the ultraviolet energy and *separate* into one atom and one molecule of oxygen.[274] Then the atom of oxygen shall recombine with a molecule of oxygen to produce harmless electromagnetic waves *and* an ozone molecule. Thus ozone, like the thermosphere, *shall shield* the surface of the Earth from lethal solar radiation.

Now the atmosphere at eighty kilometers above the Earth shall contain mostly positively charged molecules and negatively charged electrons. The *ionosphere* shall be this region of the atmosphere.[275]

Now the Earth's magnetic field shall form a giant *magnetosphere* twenty-thousand kilometers in radius. And the magnetosphere shall deflect around the Earth most solar-wind charged particles. But some high-speed protons and electrons shall get trapped in the magnetic field and spiral in donut-shaped orbits called *Van Allen belts*.

## Chapter VI: Topography

Now the Earth shall not be *perfectly* spherical. Some regions shall *rise up* above surrounding regions, while others shall *sink down*. And depressed regions shall collect with water. And a large water region shall be called an *ocean*. Earth shall have four major oceans – the Pacific Ocean, the Atlantic Ocean, the Indian Ocean, and the partially frozen Arctic Ocean. And of Earth's surface, seventy-one percent shall be covered by more than a *billion cubic kilometers of water*. Now an elevated region shall, in general, be dry. And a small isolated land-mass surrounded by a sea shall be an *island*, while a large dry land shall be a *continent*. Earth shall have seven major continents – Europe, Asia, North America, South America, Australia, Antarctica and Africa. And in some spots, land shall have risen or been pushed to several thousand meters high. Such a high land-mass shall be a *mountain*. And a *volcano* shall be a funnel-shaped mountain created by molten rock, which has thrust up through the earth. And occasionally volcanos shall erupt, spewing smoke and spilling lava. Now other parts of continents *shall* be flat. A level land shall be a *plain*. All continents shall contain water-bearing narrow crevices. And these shall be Earth's *rivers*. They

---

[273] The temperature shall be about a thousand Kelvins.

[274] The process is $O_3$ plus ultraviolet-ray goes to $O_2$ and O. The ozone molecule consists of three oxygen atoms, whereas the oxygen molecule consists of two oxygen atoms.

[275] By bouncing short waves off the ionosphere, it is possible to send radio signals around the Earth.

shall carry water off and drain the continents. Rivers flowing from high to low elevations shall eventually find seas and oceans. A riverless rainless region shall be a *desert*. Thus Nature through natural processes *shall have given* the surface of the Earth a great variety of forms and structures.

And viewed from outer space, Earth *shall* be beautiful. Blue shall be the oceans. White shall be the polar caps. Brown, green and gray shall be the continents. White shall be the clouds – they shall paint the Earth a *saintly white*.[276]

## Chapter VII: Tectonics

Now the upper layer of the Earth shall be forever changing. The crust shall be broken into several large *tectonic plates* that tile the Earth. And the plates, fifty to one-hundred kilometers in thickness, shall constitute Earth's *lithosphere*. Now there shall be eleven major plates: the Eurasian plate, the Indian-Australian plate, the African plate, the Arabian plate, the North American plate, the South American plate, the Nazca plate, the Pacific plate, the Caribbean plate, the Cocos plate and the Antarctic plate. The Nazca plate shall be in the Pacific Ocean off the coast of South America, and north of it shall be the Cocos plate. In addition to the major plates, there shall be several smaller plates.

These plates *shall float* upon the solid mantle *like unto* giant icebergs on a sea. And they shall bump against each other at the boundaries. And over centuries, the plates shall move about in miniscule amounts. But over tens of millions of years, their motions shall be significant.

Two plates in contact shall either converge, diverge or slip. When two *converge*, they shall thrust up Earth's crust *and create great mountain ranges*. When they *diverge*, the lithosphere shall be *torn apart*, leaving hot molten mantle to rise up to fill the void. Such a magma upward thrust shall manufacture a volcanic ridge. And the submerged ridge in the Mid-Atlantic Ocean, which stretches for thousands of kilometers and is created by the divergence of the North American and Eurasian plates, *shall* be an example. Now when two plates at a boundary are *slipping*, there shall be a region of great seismic action. If a slip should suddenly occur, the earth shall shake. And this shall be an *earthquake*.[277]

---

[276] This picture of Earth as viewed from outer space shall compete with the finest works of abstract art for beauty and impression.

[277] The slipping that occurs along the San Andreas fault at the border of the Pacific and North American plates is an example.

## Chapter VIII: Air Currents

*The wind goeth toward the south*
*and turneth about unto the north;*
*it whirleth about continually,*
*and the wind returneth again*
*according to His circuits.*

And let it be known to thee and all around thee that *hot air expands*. And in expanding, *lighter* it becomes. And let it be known that lighter air *rises* for the same reason that a hot-air balloon does rise – it is buoyant. And let it be known that *cold air contracts* and becomes *heavier*. And being heavier, it *sinks*, for it is not as buoyant – *like* a bar of lead in water.

Now the Sun shall not uniformly heat the Earth. And the *variation in heating* of the Earth and Earth's spinning shall generate general *wind patterns* by causing air to rise, sink and rotate.

Now because the *equatorial region* is the hottest, air *there* shall rise. And cooler air shall take its place and sweep in from below. Now *half* the rising hot air at the equator *shall* move north. And as *it* moves north, *it* shall cool. And eventually it shall become cooler than the air below. And at a latitude of thirty degrees, *it* shall sink. And after sinking, it shall move south along the surface of the Earth. And it shall warm as it moves south. And when it reaches the equator, it shall become warmer than the air above. So it shall rise again. Thus this air shall circulate in a great oval.

And the other half of the equatorial hot rising air shall *southward* move. And it shall eventually cool and sink at a latitude of thirty degrees in the southern hemisphere. Then it shall move north along the surface of the Earth, warming as it reaches the equator, where it shall *complete the circuit*.

Thus there shall be winds which blow *toward* the equator at the surface of the Earth. And the winds above these winds shall blow *away* from the equator.

And because the north and south *poles* are cold, air *there* shall sink. Such sinking air shall *push the air beneath it*, forcing it toward the Earth's equator. In the northern hemisphere, the pushed air shall move south along the surface of the Earth. While moving south, it shall warm until it reaches a longitude of sixty degrees where it shall be warmer than the air above. Then *it shall rise*. And after rising, it shall move northward to the north pole to fill the space vacated by downward moving cooler air. So air shall circulate in *a great oval* in the arctic north.

And the same shall happen in the southern hemisphere: Cold air shall *sink at the southern pole*, move north to sixty degrees longitude, where *it shall warm and rise* and then move south to replace at the southern pole descending cooler air. So air shall circulate in *a great oval* in the antarctic south.

Thus there shall be surface winds which blow *toward* the equator in the arctic north and the antarctic south. And the winds above these winds shall blow *away* from the equator.

Now between thirty and sixty degrees longitude, air shall *also* circulate in *a great oval*: Some of the air, which rises at a longitude of sixty degrees in the northern hemisphere shall move south instead of north. At high altitude shall this air flow until it meets the descending air coming from the equator at thirty degrees longitude. And *this* air from the north then *also* shall descend. From there, it shall move northward to a longitude of sixty degrees *where it shall rise up*.

And the same thing shall happen in the southern hemisphere.

Thus between thirty and sixty degrees longitude, both in the northern and the southern hemispheres, there shall be surface winds which blow *away* from the equator. And the winds above these winds shall blow *toward* the Earth's equator.

And let it be known to thee and all around thee that the spin of the Earth shall cause the winds to swerve to the east and to the west.

And if thou be on a merry-go-round, turning counter-clockwise, and thou throw a ball, it shall appear to swerve toward your right. And this shall be an illusion because Newton's first law says that an object in motion shall move in a straight line unless compelled to change so by a force. But *no* horizontal force does act upon the ball. And so the ball *does* travel in a line. And it is *thou* who thus art turning. And it is *thy perspective* that is changing: The curving motion of the ball is *thy illusion*.

And the spinning of a merry-go-round shall be *like unto* the spinning of the Earth. Since *observers* on the Earth move with the Earth, *they*, like riders on a merry-go-round, *shall* go round and round. Thus the motion of the air along the surface of the Earth shall *swerve*. And air moving away from the poles and *toward* the Earth's equator *shall* swerve to the west. And air moving *away* from the Earth's equator and to the poles *shall* swerve to the east.

And since surface winds in the equatorial zone move toward the Earth's equator, they shall *also* move toward the west. And they shall constitute an east wind since *they* come from the east – they shall be the *easterly trade winds*.

And since surface winds between thirty and sixty degrees longitude move away from the equator, they *shall* swerve to the east. And they shall constitute a west wind since *they* come from the west – they shall be the *prevailing westerlies*.

And since the surface winds in the polar regions move toward the Earth's equator, they *shall* swerve to the west. And they shall constitute an east wind since *they* come from the east – they shall be the *polar easterlies*.

And where easterly and westerly zones do meet, winds shall swirl in *cyclones*.

Now when the winds encounter mountains, they *shall* be forced to rise. And when the winds encounter valleys, they shall *sink* into the valleys. Thus the topography of Earth shall affect the *movement* of the winds.

## Chapter IX: Weather

*And when ye see the south wind blow,*
*ye say, there will be heat;*
*and it cometh to pass.*

And air descending through the atmosphere shall constitute a *high-pressure region* because the air shall push down more. And upward moving air shall constitute a *low-pressure region* because the air shall push down less. Now upward moving air shall generally carry moisture into the cooler higher atmosphere. And such moisture shall condense in clouds. So low-pressure regions shall have clouds and rain and storms.

Earth's moderately thick atmosphere, clouds, oceans, continents, polar caps, air movements and surface topography shall yield a *variety* of weather. In some regions, usually associated with high pressure, it shall be cloudless and be sunny. And in other regions, it shall be overcast. In low-pressure regions shall the clouds be dense. And often shall these clouds let loose their moisture. And water droplets falling from the clouds shall be called *rain*. In colder regions shall crystals of water fall instead – as *snow*. Now the high- and low-pressure regions and the clouds shall move, diminish and intensify and lead to *ever-changing weather*. And sometimes, strong circulating winds and dark thick clouds shall form a *hurricane*, in which the winds shall blow more than one-hundred kilometers per hour.

Now a *front* shall be the interface between cold and warm air-masses. And warm moist air shall rise, lifting its water vapor up into the atmosphere. And it shall pass over and beyond the cold-air mass. Now the moist air, when it meets the colder air, shall condense to water droplets. And the droplets shall fall to Earth as rain. If the cold-air mass is advancing under the warm-air mass, then this shall be a *cold front*. And as the cold front passes, the temperature shall drop. If the cold-air mass is retreating so that the warm-air mass is advancing over the cold-air mass, then this shall be a *warm front*. And as the warm front passes, the temperature shall rise. At cold and warm fronts, rainy weather shall arise.

And sometimes the dynamics of Earth's atmosphere shall make a thunderstorm. The flash of electric current through the atmosphere shall be called *lightning*. And lightning shall produce a crack of strong deep sound, which ye call *thunder*. And the energy released during a thunderstorm and the energy released from a twenty-kiloton atomic warhead shall *on average* be the same. And fortunately the fallout shall be rain, not radioactive elements.

Now surface winds shall move the weather systems east or west, depending on the longitude. And for example, between thirty and sixty degrees longitude, weather systems shall move *from west to east*, as they follow the prevailing westerlies.

And warm rising air near *Earth's equator*, which carries the moisture in the oceans upward, shall make the rainfall heavy *there*. These equatorial land regions shall constitute the *tropical rain forests*.

And let it be known that *continents* reflect and radiate their heat relatively *quickly*, and that *oceans* absorb and radiate their heat relatively *slowly*. Hence the temperature above the continents shall vary more than the temperature above the oceans. And air over oceans shall be *more humid* than the air above the continents. As a consequence, lands with ocean winds flowing over them shall have *moist mild weather*. And for example, England and Vancouver, although far north, shall have such moist and mild climates. But northeastern North America and eastern China, although near oceans, shall have drier climates with large seasonal temperature variations since, *there*, the prevailing westerlies produce winds *originating over continents*.

And clouds shall block sunrays. Thus a cloudy day *shall* be cooler than a sunny day. But clouds shall also help retain the heat of Earth. Thus the mornings after cloudy nights shall be warmer than the mornings after cloudless nights.

Now the general features of weather, which follow from the principles of physics and fluid mechanics, shall be easy to understand and to predict. But *detailed* weather forecasting shall be *difficult*, for Earth's topography and atmosphere are *enormous and complex*.

## Chapter X: The Mother of Life

Now the land, oceans and atmosphere shall provide a *special* environment for living organisms. And of all Sun's children, Earth shall be unique in harboring a wealth of living organisms. Earth shall be the mother of solar-system life. Now a *living organism* shall be a self-organizing complex structure made from countless carbon-hydrogen-oxygen organic molecules.[278] And although there shall be an enormous variety of life forms, there *shall* be but two basic macroscopic types: plants and animals. *Plants* shall utilize the energy of sunlight, and in the process yield oxygen for *the* Earth's atmosphere. And *animals* shall exhibit many different characteristics and abilities, among which shall be the capacity to move. And remarkably, animals shall appear to be in control of their mobility.

*Pray ye a prayer for Earth.*

---

[278] See the New Testament Book of *Biology*.

*The sixth book of Planetology, called*

# The Moon

*And He was the lesser light.*
*And He was there to rule the night.*

## Chapter I: Moon Facts

Now a companion shall Earth have. And it shall *be* the Moon. To Earth, it shall be *like unto* a slightly younger brother. And it shall have a diameter *one-fifth* the diameter of Earth and a mass *one-eightieth* the mass of Earth. And the force of gravity at the surface of the Moon shall be *one-sixth* the force of gravity on Earth: If ye weigh sixty kilograms[279] on Earth, then ye would weigh ten kilograms[280] on Moon.

Now the Moon shall orbit Earth in an ellipse. And when the Moon is *closest* to the Earth, it shall be three-hundred-and-sixty-thousand kilometers from Earth. And when it is *farthest* from the Earth, it shall be four-hundred-and-ten-thousand kilometers away.

## Chapter II: Phases

And when the Moon is on the Sun-side of the Earth, the *dark* side of the Moon shall *face* the Earth. And *this* shall be a *new moon*. And when the Moon is on the other side of Earth, the *bright* side of the Moon shall *face* the Earth. And *this* shall be a *full moon*. And as the Moon does orbit Earth, different fractions of Moon's surface that are lit shall face the Earth. And *these* shall be the *phases* of the Moon.

Now it shall take twenty-seven days for Moon to orbit once around the Earth. But *during this period*, the Earth and Moon shall move *one-thirteenth* of the way around the Sun. And so the time between full moons shall be *longer* by one-thirteenth. Thus almost thirty days shall be the time between full moons. This interval shall be a *month*. And so the Moon shall pass through all its phases once a month.

## Chapter III: Eclipses

*And the Sun and Moon shall darken*
*and withdraw their light.*

Now sometimes the Moon shall pass between the Earth and Sun. And *dark* shall be the Sun as viewed from Earth. A *solar eclipse* shall be the name for this. It shall be *as if Rahu*, the Hindu Sun-devouring daemon, had consumed the Sun. Now sometimes a full Moon shall enter *the shadow of the Earth*. And the sunlight, which lights the

---

[279] One-hundred-thirty-two pounds.
[280] Twenty-two pounds.

Moon, shall then be blocked. Dark *shall* become the Moon. A *lunar eclipse* shall be the name for this.

## Chapter IV: Moon Affection

Now the Moon shall spin its body at the *same rate* at which it revolves around the Earth. This shall cause the Moon to keep the *same face* facing Earth. Thus the far side of the Moon shall remain *hidden* from thee on Earth.[281]

## Chapter V: Terrain

Now the surface of the Moon shall be full of dry dirt and loose rocks. From Earth, the Moon shall seem to have some dark and whitish regions. The whitish regions shall be uplands. And the dark regions shall be *maria* – they shall be smoother than the whitish regions as a result of *ancient lava flows*. Now the Moon shall be pitted with depressions, which are its *craters*. The craters, varying in size from dozens of meters to dozens of kilometers, shall be *the remains of impacts* of rocks from outer space. From some of them shall white rays emanate, due to material ejected by an impact. And the most prominent such crater shall be *Tycho*. One-thousand kilometers shall be the longest rays of Tycho.

## Chapter VI: Tides

Now Earth's oceans shall feel the pull of *the Moon's gravity*. And this shall lead to high tides and to low tides. The energy needed to generate such tides shall come from the energy of the Earth-Moon system. Now the Moon shall move away from Earth at a rate of a few centimeters per century. And it shall be *as if* the Earth is slowly losing *its* grip on the Moon. And furthermore, the Earth shall spin imperceptibly slower as time passes, as energy goes into motion of the tides. And so the *length of day* on Earth shall *gradually increase*. And it shall increase by two seconds every thousand centuries.

---

[281] The same shall be true of most large moons in the solar system – the force of gravity shall make *one side* of a moon face the parent planet. It would not be until the space program that man would gain a glimpse of the unseen side of Moon.

*The seventh book of Planetology, called*

# Mars[282]

*And the fourth planet from the Sun was called Mars.*

## Chapter I: Orbit

A nd Mars, named after the Roman god of war, shall be the fourth child of the Sun. And he shall circle the Sun at twenty-four kilometers per second, completing one revolution in a little less than seven-hundred days. And this journey round the Sun shall be *one-billion-and-four-hundred-million* kilometers in length. And Mars shall do this at fifty per cent farther from the Sun than Earth.

And Mars shall have a diameter of one-half of Earth's diameter and weigh one-tenth the weight of Earth. And since it spins a little *slower* than the Earth, a Martian day shall be slightly *longer* than a day on Earth.

## Chapter II: Appearance

N ow the color of Mars shall be ochre-red: The *red* shall be due to iron oxide, for *of thirteen percent iron* shall Martian soil be. And the soil shall also have a sulfur content ten times that of soil on Earth. And upon the martian surface shall in places be some boulders.

Mars shall have craters, chasms, gullies, plains and a few mountains. And the southern hemisphere shall be particularly crater-ridden – this region shall be like the Moon. In the northern hemisphere shall be large plains, a giant lava basin *and* extinct volcanos, of which the largest shall be *Olympus Mons*: The cone of Olympus Mons shall be two-thousand kilometers around the base and twenty kilometers in height. And Mars *shall* have several large canyons. And the largest, *Valles Marineris*, shall be five-thousand kilometers in length, two-hundred kilometers in width and six kilometers in depth. Mars shall have ancient dry river channels and beds *where water once had flowed*.

Now Mars shall *have* white polar caps of water-ice and dry ice.[283] Since Mars shall tilt twenty-five degrees, it, like Earth, shall have four seasons. And when winter comes, a polar cap *shall grow* as carbon dioxide from the atmosphere condenses and does freeze. And when summer comes, a polar cap *shall shrink* as dry ice does evaporate. And the southern cap entirely shall disappear in summer since it is almost completely of dry ice.

Now sometimes winds shall *strongly* blow on Mars. And dust shall swirl about. And for thee who are looking from the Earth, it shall

---

[282] Because Mars, like Earth, has water, scientists will *wonder* whether Mars once in the past had life. One day in the twenty-first century, man will explore Martian soil and hunt for microfossils. And that day will be a great day in exploration.

[283] Dry ice is frozen carbon dioxide.

*seem* like the shadings of the regions change. And dust shall sometimes be blown ten kilometers in height. And the dust filling the thin Martian carbon-dioxide-dominated atmosphere shall develop into yellow clouds. And some dust storms shall be so large that *all of Mars* shall be engulfed. During such events, all geological features on Mars, as seen from thee on Earth, shall be obscured.

## Chapter III: Martian Moons

Now two companions – *Deimos* and *Phobos* – shall Mars have. And they shall be the tiny moons of Mars. Deimos, an irregularly shaped ellipsoid thirteen kilometers in size, shall orbit Mars in thirty hours. And many of its craters shall be filled with dust and dirt, rendering Deimos *relatively smooth.* Now at a distance of only nine-thousand kilometers, Phobos shall orbit Mars in just eight hours. And Phobos shall be irregularly shaped[284] and covered with some craters, of which the largest shall be *Stickney* – it shall be one-forth the size of Phobos.

*The eighth book of Planetology, called*

# Jupiter

*And the fifth planet from the Sun was called Jupiter.*

## Chapter I: Orbit, Size and Weight

And Jupiter, named after the Roman god of the heavens, who was the god of all gods, shall be the fifth child of the Sun. And once every twelve years shall he complete his circuit round the Sun at a distance five times that of Earth. And every ten hours shall Jupiter complete a single spin. And so a day on Jupiter shall last ten hours. Now Jupiter shall be the largest and the heaviest of all the children of the Sun with a diameter of one-hundred-and-forty-thousand kilometers. So Jupiter shall be *thirteen-hundred* times more voluminous and three-hundred-and-twenty times more massive than the Earth. But Jupiter's weight shall still be only *one-thousandth* of Sun's weight.

## Chapter II: Jupiter's Body

Now *almost all of Jupiter shall be a liquid!* But at the planet's *center* shall be a relatively small-sized solid core. *There,* the temperature shall be *several times hotter* than the surface of the Sun, and the *pressure* shall be more than *fifty-million atmospheres.* A large layer of atomic hydrogen *shall* surround the core; the enormous pressure shall make the layer *liquid and metallic.* And this conducting fluid shall oc-

---

[284] It looks like a slightly deformed rugby ball.

cupy most of the planet, extending three-quarters of the way through Jupiter. At the three-quarters point shall the pressure drop to three-million atmospheres and allow a new fluid to appear, which shall make up the outer layer of mighty Jupiter. It shall be a mixture of liquid molecular hydrogen and liquid helium. Thus the surface of Jupiter shall be an ocean of helium and hydrogen!

Now in the conducting metallic middle layer shall *swirl* electric currents, which produce a magnetic field *nineteen-thousand* times stronger than the magnetic field of Earth.[285] And as the planet rotates, radio waves shall be produced by this magnetic field. And magnetic interactions shall create a *five-million*-Ampere electrical current between Jupiter and its companion Io. Thus an *invisible lightning* shall spark between the two.

Now heat from Jupiter shall rise into the atmosphere. More than one-third of the heat radiating from the planet into outer space shall come from Jupiter's hot liquid body – the rest shall come from re-radiated sunlight.

## Chapter III: Jupiter's Atmosphere

*And Jupiter shall wear*
*Joseph's multicolored coat.*

And Jupiter's treasure shall be its *atmospheric coat*. The atmosphere shall be one-tenth helium, nine-tenths hydrogen with trace amounts of water vapor, methane, ethane, ammonia and many other gases. And certain compounds shall *act* as *pigments* and provide the colors of the atmospheric coat.

Now the atmosphere shall have four layers of clouds. And the highest clouds shall be of frozen ammonia *white* crystals. There, the pressure shall be one atmosphere and the temperature shall be one-hundred-and-forty Kelvins, which is very cold. The next layer shall contain *tawny* clouds of ammonium hydrosulfide and other ammonia-sulfur compounds. And the next to lowest layer shall contain *brown* clouds, while the lowest layer shall be *blue* clouds of water-ice, water vapor and ammonium hydroxide. Now the temperature and pressure shall go up as one descends the atmosphere. And so at the *top of the lowest layer*, the pressure shall be ten atmospheres – ten times the air pressure at the surface of the Earth. There, the temperature shall be room temperature. And the blue clouds of the lowest-cloud layer shall extend downward toward the surface of the planet Jupiter, while the pressure and temperature shall both continue to increase.

Now the atmosphere of Jupiter shall be *chaotic, wild, violent and turbulent*. Gases shall rise up in certain places and sweep down in

---

[285] The magnetism shall weaken with distance from Jupiter's center so that magnetism at Jupiter's surface shall be only thirteen times stronger than magnetism at Earth's surface.

others. And a rising gas mass shall create a *great low-pressure region*. And in such a region shall white clouds appear. And a sinking gas mass shall create a *great high-pressure region*. And in such a region shall belts of brown and red appear. Thus the up-and-down motions of air mass shall produce an *atmospheric coat of many colors*.

## Chapter IV: Weather

Now the weather on Jupiter shall be *violent, unpredictable and quickly changing*. And lightning bolts shall often flash among the clouds. And Jupiter shall also have more orderly brisk winds, which at certain latitudes blow east and at other latitudes blow west. Now in a band centered at the equator, the *strongest* wind shall blow, flowing easterly at *three-hundred-and-fifty kilometers per hour*. And sometimes such winds shall tear a hole in the upper atmosphere and expose blue-gray and purple clouds. In other bands, winds shall blow less strongly: one-hundred kilometers per hour. And these winds shall produce other *colored bands* on Jupiter of yellow, brown and orange.

Now when a band of easterly winds meets a band of westerly winds, *giant eddies, braids and folds* shall form. The latter shall look *like unto* the folds and ripples in a curtain that is drawn aside. And in an eddy, the wind shall swirl in a *giant* hurricane. At any given moment, there shall be dozens of such hurricanes that swirl the clouds and gases of the atmosphere. And from Earth, ye shall see such a hurricane as an oval spot on Jupiter. And the spots shall be orange, yellow, white or brown. And some shall *shrink in size and disappear*, while others shall *suddenly* emerge. And the spots shall slowly move across the surface of the planet, sometimes dividing into two. And sometimes, two shall merge to one. And the larger spots shall be thousands of kilometers in size and live for decades and sometimes centuries.

And the largest spot shall be Jupiter's majestic red medallion. And it shall have a name. And the *name* shall be the *Great Red Spot*. It shall be *so large* that two entire Earths could fit inside it. And it shall extend high above surrounding clouds. Inside the Great Red Spot, winds shall blow at more than *three-hundred kilometers per hour*. And the Great Red Spot shall move slowly over the liquid surface of Jupiter at a few kilometers per hour.

## Chapter V: Many Moons

And Jupiter shall have *sixteen* companions. And the companions shall have names: Sinope, Pasiphae, Carme, Ananke, Elara, Lysithea, Himalia, Leda, Callisto, Ganymede, Europa, Io, Thebe, Amalthea, Adrastea and Metis. And they shall be the moons of Jupiter.

And the orbits of the outer eight, Sinope, Pasiphae, Carme, Ananke, Elara, Lysithea, Himalia, and Leda, shall trace out great ellipses. And they shall not orbit in the equatorial plane of Jupiter. Now Sinope shall be the *farthest* out, at *twenty-four-million kilometers*[286] away from Jupiter. And since it shall take two years to go around the planet Jupiter, a Sinope-month shall be two years. Now Leda shall be the closest of these eight, orbiting at eleven-million kilometers from Jupiter. And Leda's trip shall last two-hundred-forty days. So a Leda-month shall be two-hundred-forty days. Now Himalia shall be almost two-hundred kilometers in diameter. But the others shall be *small*.[287] And these eight shall be the companions which Jupiter acquired *in adulthood*.

Now the remaining eight companions shall move in circles in the equatorial plane of planet Jupiter. And they shall be the friends which Jupiter knew *from infancy*.

The inner four, Thebe, Amalthea, Adrastea and Metis, shall orbit at one-hundred-and-twenty-thousand kilometers to two-hundred-thousand kilometers from Jupiter. Thebe shall be one-hundred kilometers in size, while the *irregular and oblong Amalthea* shall be two-hundred kilometers in length and a hundred-and-fifty-kilometers in width. And Adrastea and Metis shall be smaller – twenty and forty kilometers respectively; these two shall be *shepherd boys*.[288]

And the moons between the inner four and the outer eight shall be Io, Europa, Ganymede and Callisto. They shall be the *prominent large moons* – a couple thousand kilometers in radius. And they shall be the *Galilean moons*.

Now it shall take *Callisto* seventeen days to orbit Jupiter. And Callisto shall have a *dark stone-ice surface* which is spotted with light patches and peppered with some craters.

And *Ganymede* shall be the largest moon in the entire solar system – fifty-three-hundred kilometers shall be Ganymede's diameter, rending it *bigger than* the planet Mercury! And its *ice-covered surface* shall be cratered and have dark patches, which are old, and light patches, which are young. And Ganymede shall circle Jupiter in seven days.

Now the interior of *Europa* shall be mostly rock. But just below its surface shall lie *giant water caverns*. At times, water shall be forced upward on the surface, where it shall freeze and leave Europa with a *smooth craterless ice-cover*. And the frozen water shall form crisscrossed patterns of dark stripes and curved ridges. Now gravity shall hold Io, Europa and Ganymede in resonance positions. And tidal gravity from Ganymede, Io and especially from Jupiter shall help draw water out onto Europa's surface.

---

[286] This is one-sixth the distance between the Earth and Sun.
[287] The sizes shall be tens of kilometers.
[288] See Chapter VI below.

*Io* shall be the *most active volcanic body* in the solar system. Now tidal forces from Ganymede, Europa and especially from Jupiter shall cause the body of Io to bulge and oscillate. These motions shall *squeeze the inner rock* of Io. And this shall press the rock against itself, creating friction and *great heat*. And the heat shall melt some rock. And this molten rock rich in sulfur shall be ejected out of holes in Io. And the largest holes, twenty kilometers across, shall be *mountainless volcanos*; and Io shall have *hundreds* of them. Now the smaller holes shall be like geysers except that, instead of water, compounds rich in sulfur shall be ejected out. In eruptions, material shall fly up at a kilometer per second, spurting hundreds of kilometers above the Io surface. Upon landing, debris shall paint *colored rings* on Io. So rings of red, orange, brown or yellow *shall be*. Now some soot, dust and gases *even shall escape* from Io, journey to Jupiter and rain down on Jupiter's atmosphere, three-hundred-fifty-thousand kilometers away. Eruptions on Io shall eject enormous quantities of gas, soot and magma-rock.[289] The land around volcanos shall *glow* from frequent lava flows. Thus Io's surface shall be continually resurfaced. And the craters, which Io once had had, shall be covered by lava, leaving Io smooth. And lava shall paint the surface red and black, while sulfur-dioxide frost shall paint other patches white.

## Chapter VI: A Miniature Solar System

And Jupiter shall have a *single bright ring-band* of reddish dust and grains. It shall be six-thousand kilometers in width and less than a kilometer in thickness. At sixty-thousand kilometers above the Jovian equator, the ring-band shall encircle Jupiter. And Jupiter's two closest companions, Adrastea and Metis, shall watch over this lone ring. And *like unto* two shepherd boys, they shall circulate on each side of it and help prevent material from leaking out.

So Jupiter shall be *like a miniature solar system*, with planets being moons, the asteroid belt being substituted by a ring, and the Sun being replaced by Jupiter itself.[290] But the *light* that Jupiter gives off shall not be starlight of its own; *it* shall be *reflected light*.

---

[289] In one second as much material is ejected onto Io as all the material ejected during the 1980 Mount Saint Helens eruption.

[290] This similarity is not an accident: The formation of Jupiter and its moons was similar to the formation of the Sun and its planets, the only difference being one of scale. See the Old Testament's *Exodus XI* and *XII* for solar system formation.

# Saturn

*And the sixth planet from the Sun was called Saturn.*

## Chapter I: Saturn's Body

And Saturn shall be Jupiter's twin sister. And at ten astronomical units shall she orbit in a circle round the Sun. Even moving at ten kilometers per second, it shall take her *thirty years* to complete one circuit. Now Saturn shall be the second largest planet of the solar system with a diameter of one-hundred-and-fifteen-thousand kilometers, nine times the Earth's diameter, which is *more* than one-forth the Earth-Moon distance. And Saturn shall be seven-hundred-and-fifty times more voluminous than Earth and weigh ninety-five times the weight of Earth. Now Saturn shall not be quite round but *bulge* by ten per cent about the middle. And she shall be the *least* dense planet; if she were placed in a giant pool of water, she would float with one third of her *above* the water. Now of Sun's children, she shall be the beauty queen. And she shall use makeup and jewelry to enhance her look. And every eleven hours, she shall spin her body once *as if* she were a dancer on a stage, *as if* she wanted thee to see all sides.

Now Saturn shall have a body and a structure similar to those of Jupiter except that *smaller* shall the metallic-liquid middle layer be. Thus Saturn shall have a small ice-rock core surrounded by metallic-liquid hydrogen, as well as a giant ocean of liquid molecular hydrogen and liquid helium. And the conducting metallic middle layer shall produce a *magnetism* a thousand times the magnetism of the Earth.

## Chapter II: Atmosphere

Now the warmth of Saturn's body shall warm the atmosphere, so much so that half the heat that radiates from Saturn into outer space *shall* come from Saturn's liquid body. The rest shall come from *re-radiated* sunlight.

Now the atmosphere of Saturn shall be similar to Jupiter's. Likewise the clouds of these two planets shall be much the same, but *thicker* shall be Saturn's layers of clouds. And the different colors of each layer shall paint the face of Saturn with hues of *yellow, orange, brown and blue.* And the atmosphere shall be chaotic, wild and turbulent, with gases sweeping up and down *in violent upheavals.* And lightning shall *flash* among the clouds.

Now Saturn shall have bands of winds *which* blow east or west. At the equator, the winds shall blow the strongest. And they shall blow there easterly at more than *fifteen-hundred kilometers per hour!* In the other bands, the winds shall reach three-hundred kilometers per hour. And these winds shall give rise to colored bands of yellow, orange, brown or blue.

Saturn, like Jupiter, shall have enormous cyclones. And from thy viewpoint far away on Earth, the cyclones shall be giant oval *spots*. And the largest spot shall be of color brown and half the size of Earth.

## Chapter III: Bands and Rings

And Saturn shall wear necklaces. And they shall be her *rings*. They shall come in *seven* bands and be labelled by letters of the alphabet. The main bands shall be A, B and C with a total width five times *the* diameter of Earth. But the bands shall be less than a hundred meters thick! And from thy far-away viewpoint, *razor thin* shall they appear. Now these three bands shall be fifteen-thousand to seventy-six thousand kilometers from Saturn's surface, with band C the closest. Band B shall be *the brightest and the widest*. A three-thousand kilometer gap of emptiness shall separate bands A and B. And these two bands shall be opaque and reddish, with each containing *several thousand rings* made up of bits of ice and rock. Most ice-rock shall be a dozen centimeters big. But bands A and B shall also contain truck-sized chunks. And bands B and C shall be *also* full of dust.

Now between band C and Saturn's upper atmosphere shall be a layer of *haze and particles*. And this shall be the D band, the band closest to the planet.

Now ring F, which is narrow, shall be three-thousand kilometers beyond band A. Beyond it shall be the fainter band called G. And beyond G shall be *sparse particles* that constitute the barely visible band E.

Now the narrowness of F shall have a reason: On opposite sides of F shall be the moons Pandora and Prometheus. And they shall "watch over" the material in F, making sure it does not go astray. Due to their motions, this ring shall sometimes *braid and twist*.

And Saturn's ring-bands shall be the crown jewels of the solar system. And from afar and lit by sunlight, they shall appear to thee *like unto* a phonographic record with both grooves and bands. Now Saturn and *her rings* shall lie in a plane, tilted twenty-seven degrees from the solar system plane. And during Saturn's thirty-year-long year, *they* shall rotate and appear at various perspectives, *as if* Saturn desires to display to thee her rings from every angle.

## Chapter IV: Saturn's Moons

And Saturn shall have a family of *nine children*. And their names shall be Phoebe, Iapetus, Hyperion, Titan, Rhea, Dione, Tethys, Enceladus and Mimas. And these nine shall be the *greater moons* of Saturn. In addition, Saturn shall possess *nine pet companions*. And they shall be the *lesser moons*: Helene shall be Dione's cat; Calypso and

Telesto shall be seen near Tethys; and Janus, Epimetheus, Pandora, Prometheus, Atlas and Pan shall be the rest. Janus and Epimetheus shall be twin cats; and Pan, which is twenty kilometers in size, shall be the smallest. And the remaining three, Pandora, Prometheus and Atlas, *shall* be shepherd dogs, for they are guardians of flocks of rocks. These *eighteen moons* of Saturn shall consist of approximately two-thirds water-ice and one-third rock.

Now *Phoebe* shall be the only one to be adopted. And all moons but Phoebe shall hold their faces to the planet Saturn. And all the moons shall move round Saturn in a circle except for Hyperion and Phoebe, who shall orbit in ellipses. *Pan* shall be the closest at one-hundred-and-thirty-thousand kilometers from Saturn's center.[291] And at *thirteen-million kilometers*, Phoebe shall orbit *farthest*. And all the moons shall travel in a common plane except Iapetus and Phoebe: Iapetus shall revolve at an angle of fifteen degrees from this common plane, while Phoebe shall not only orbit at an angle of thirty degrees but in the direction *opposite* to all the others. Now it shall take Phoebe five-hundred-and-fifty days to go *once* around the planet Saturn. And Iapetus, Hyperion and Titan shall go around respectively in eighty, twenty-one and sixteen days, while the other moons shall take even less: from half-a-day to several days. Now four-point-five billion years ago, it shall have happened that material collapsed and formed Saturn and her moons *except for Phoebe*: Phoebe shall have been made elsewhere in the solar system and been captured later. And *that* shall be the reason why Phoebe *is different* from the others. Now among the greater moons, Titan shall be biggest and Phoebe shall be smallest.[292] And the lesser moons shall be quite small.

Now *Iapetus* shall have eruptions in which ammonia, ice and dark organic substances ooze out. And these substances shall make the *back side black*, but leave the front side *gray and white*. And to thee who look at Iapetus from far away, Iapetus shall grow brighter and grow dimmer every eighty days.

*Save for Hyperion*, the greater moons shall all be spherical: the lesser moons and Hyperion shall be *irregularly shaped*.[293] Within the solar system, it shall be one of the most asymmetric objects of its size.

Now the giant *Titan* shall be the only moon within the solar system having a substantial *atmosphere*. Being thick and reddish, it shall obscure the Titan surface in an envelope of mostly nitrogen. On Titan's surface *shall* be oceans made of liquid methane. And the solid inner part of Titan shall *be* half-ice, half-rock.

And Rhea, Dione, Tethys, Enceladus and Mimas shall have icy, cratered surfaces. But *Enceladus* shall have smooth regions on one side,

---

[291] In other words, Pan orbits Saturn at only about twice Saturn's radius.

[292] Titan's diameter shall be five-thousand kilometers. Phoebe's diameter shall be two-hundred kilometers.

[293] Hyperion looks like a soccer ball that has been half deflated.

for tidal forces shall force water to erupt and wipe the craters clean. And the *ice-frost* on its surface shall reflect Sun's light, *as* a mirror does. And this shall make Enceladus more visible. Now it shall have come to pass that *Tethys* was struck by an object long ago: So Tethys shall have a crater *four-hundred kilometers in width*. And *Mimas* shall have a crater one-third of its diameter. The craters on these moons shall make them seem like *the* Earth's Moon.

Now *Helene* shall move along in *the same circle* as Dione but one-sixth the way around. And *why* shall this be so? And it shall so due to a "pocket" of stability created by the force of gravity. Likewise, *Calypso*, *Telesto* and Tethys shall orbit in a *common circle*, with *one* one-sixth the way *in front* and *one* one-sixth the way *in back*.[294] And both shall gravitationally be locked in a pocket of stability.

Now the lesser moons of *Janus* and *Epimetheus* shall play a game called *cat and cat*: At the beginning of the game, Epimetheus starts outside of and in front of *Janus*. Then *she* chases Epimetheus, gaining on him as the game progresses. Now *when* she gets near him, she crosses to outside, while he slips inside of her. Then she *shoots past him*. And as the distance between the two increases, she, compared with him, slows down. At that point, the distance between the two decreases. And it becomes his turn: he chases her until he *races by her*. And the game shall never stop: Every four years, in chasing one another shall the two exchange their places.

---

[294] In other words, the three are spaced around a circle separated by sixty degrees.

*The tenth book of Planetology, called*

# Uranus

*And the seventh planet from the Sun was called Uranus.*

## Chapter I: Orbit, Size and Weight

And Uranus shall be Sun's seventh child. And she shall orbit the Sun one time every eighty-four years at a distance *twenty times* the Earth-Sun distance. Thus Uranus shall have an eighty-four-year year. And it shall take Uranus seventeen hours to spin once. Thus a Uranus day shall be three-quarters of a day. And Uranus shall have a radius four times the radius of Earth and shall weigh *fifteen times* the weight of Earth.

Now unlike the other planets, which spin in the plane of their so-lar-system orbits, on her side shall spin Uranus. And she shall do this for a reason. And the reason shall be that at an early age she was struck by an Earth-sized object that *knocked her on her side*. And because she's on her side, the days and nights at the polar regions shall last long. And for example, during winter on the north pole, two-and-forty years of *darkness* shall there be. And this shall be followed by two-and-forty years of *light*.

## Chapter II: Atmosphere

And Uranus shall have a *solid-rocky heart*, which is surrounded by a liquid-molten body. Upon this body shall Uranus wear a dress. Superdense gases mixed with ices of water, methane and ammonia shall constitute this *dress*. And around *it* shall a *thick* perfume per-vade: an atmosphere of hydrogen, helium and methane gas. Now the methane shall absorb all yellow light and leave behind a *green-blue hue*. But the highest clouds shall shine the white of methane ice. And above these clouds to six-thousand kilometers in altitude shall be an envelope of hydrogen. And this hydrogen shall be twice as hot as a hot oven. In the ultraviolet shall Uranus *radiate*.

And Uranus shall *reflect* light rays from Sun. And these *reflected* rays shall so go out in all directions but *some* shall reach the Earth. Thus through a telescope shall ye see Uranus from the Earth. Now some reflected rays *shall not escape* the atmosphere but be *absorbed* as heat. And Uranus shall also heat its atmosphere from sources deep within its core. Such heat shall fuel *winds*, making them flow three-hundred to six-hundred kilometers per hour. Such speedy winds throughout the atmosphere shall blow.

Now Uranus shall have magnetic poles which point sixty degrees *from* the axis of rotation. And if ye were on the planet's surface, *this* would make a compass reading *vary* with the longitude.

## Chapter III: Many Moons

And Uranus shall have *fifteen* moons. And *five* shall be the *greater moons*. And *they* shall be Oberon, Titania, Umbriel, Ariel and Miranda. And *ten* shall be the *lesser moons*. And they shall be Puck, Belinda, Rosalind, Portia, Juliet, Desdemona, Cressida, Bianca, Ophelia and Cordelia.

Now the five greater moons shall orbit Uranus at distances in kilometers varying from one-hundred-thirty-thousand to five-hundred-eighty-thousand. Oberon shall orbit *farthest*. Miranda shall be *nearest*. At closer distances, the lesser moons shall circle round Uranus.

Now *Oberon, Titania, Umbriel* and *Ariel* shall have diameters somewhat greater than a thousand-thousand meters.[295] Their surfaces shall be rich in water-ice and rock. All shall look somewhat like the Earth's Moon but with blemishes from carbon-bearing compounds. All shall have craters from *ancient* meteoric impacts, while Titania and Ariel shall have volcanic pasts. Umbriel *shall* be dark and gray; Ariel shall have faults and valleys ten kilometers in depth; and *Miranda* shall have a rugged surface with mountains shaped like giant cubic chunks and with cliffs from ten to twenty-two kilometers in height. And like the others, *Puck* shall be of rock and ice. *It* shall be the *largest of the lesser moons*, yet still with only a one-hundred-and-sixty-kilometer diameter. The other lesser moons *shall* be even smaller.

## Chapter IV: Rings

And Uranus shall have *ten dark and narrow rings*, of which nine shall have the names of numbers and Greek letters: "epsilon," "delta," "gamma," "eta," "beta," "alpha," "four," "five" and "six." Now "epsilon" shall be the *farthest ring* from Uranus, while "six" shall be the *closest*. And the tenth ring shall be almost invisible, made of dust, and sit between the rings of "epsilon" and "delta." And *it* shall have *no name*. Uranus shall also have one-hundred almost transparent bands of dust.

Now the rings shall lie forty-two to fifty-two thousand kilometers from the surface of Uranus, while hundreds of kilometers of empty space shall be between the rings. Two kilometers to one-hundred kilometers shall range the *thickness* of the rings. And from a viewpoint far away, the rings shall seem extremely thin. To thee on Earth, *invisible* shall they appear.

And the nine rings with names shall contain *boulders, stones and rocks*, with sizes that vary from an apple to a truck. And they shall just contain a little dust.

---

[295] A thousand-thousand meters is a thousand kilometers.

*And some rings shall have widths that vary or that wiggle.*
*And some shall be ellipses and non-circular.*
*Others shall have sharp jagged edges.*
*A few shall be somewhat irregular.*
*And some shall be completely circular.*

*These rings shall constitute,*
*in some sense, a herd of rock.*
*And* Ophelia *and* Cordelia
*shall be the shepherd dogs for the "epsilon" flock,*
*for when boulders stray away,*
*these two shall bring them back.*
*The force of gravity and a resonance effect*
*shall be their method of attack.*

And the collection of satellites, rings and dust shall, like Uranus, *be* tipped on its side. And when viewed from far away, they shall seem to thee like *a flat disk*. And they, *like unto* a wheel, shall roll on edge perpendicularly in the solar system plane. And of the other planets, none shall orient themselves this way.

*These rings shall form a regal halo for Uranus.*
*And in recognition of Uranus's majestic nature,*
*the other planets shall address this planet as "Her Royal Highness."*

*The eleventh book of Planetology, called*

# Neptune

*And the eighth planet from the Sun was called Neptune.*

## Chapter I: Neptune's Motions

Now Neptune, who was named after the Roman god of seas, shall be the twin brother of Uranus.[296] And every *one-hundred-sixty-five years*, he shall orbit in a circle once around the Sun at *thirty* times the Earth-Sun distance. And every sixteen hours shall he spin exactly once. Thus a day on Neptune *shall* last sixteen hours.

## Chapter II: Atmosphere and Weather

Now Neptune shall have an atmosphere *like unto* its nearest siblings, Jupiter, Saturn and Uranus. And the atmosphere shall be of hydrogen, helium and methane gas. And the atmosphere shall be *quite turbulent*, with great storms which are intense and violent. Now one such storm shall be a giant hurricane as *wide* as Earth. And *it* shall have a name. And the name shall be the *Great Dark Spot*.[297] At one-thousand kilometers per hour shall it sweep across the surface of the planet Neptune. Now elsewhere, winds shall blow at up to *fourteen-hundred kilometers per hour*. And high above the thick and dynamic surface-clouds shall be *tranquil silver-colored cirrus clouds*.

And Neptune shall be *blue-green*, colored by the methane of its atmosphere, for the methane shall absorb red sunlight, leaving only blue and yellow light to be reflected. And this reflected blue and yellow shall combine to make a blue-green hue.

## Chapter III: Auroras and Rings

Now Neptune shall have a magnetic pole which points forty-seven degrees from its axis of rotation. So a compass needle on Neptune shall *not* point to the northern pole – the needle shall point half-way from the equator to the northern pole.

And Neptune, like Jupiter, Saturn and Uranus, shall have some rings. And the rings, which number only *four*, shall be of particles and dust. When viewed from far away, Neptune shall look *like unto* a king who wears a crown.

Now charged particles in the solar wind shall travel to this distant planet. And they shall swirl about Neptune's magnetic field and generate auroras of *iridescent flickering colored lights*.

---

[296] Neptune and Uranus are of comparable size, weight and structure.

[297] It is like the Great Red Spot of Jupiter but smaller.

## Chapter IV: Neptune's Moons

A nd Neptune shall have *eight* companions. And they shall be its moons. And *six* shall be quite *small* – less than two-hundred kilometers in size. Their names shall be Proteus, Larissa, Galatea, Despina, Thalassa and Naiad. Battering by meteors shall have transformed these six into *misshaped chunks of rock.*

Now the remaining two Neptunian moons shall be named Nereid and Triton. And *Nereid*, the most distant moon from Neptune, shall be three-hundred-and-forty kilometers in size. Like a comet shall it orbit Neptune in a very asymmetric-shaped ellipse: *Thirteen-hundred-thousand kilometers* shall be the *closest* distance that Nereid shall come to Neptune, while *ten-million kilometers* shall be the *farthest*. And since Nereid shall circle once a year, Nereid shall *visit* Neptune once a year.

Now *Triton* shall be the largest satellite of Neptune – somewhat bigger than Earth's Moon.[298] And Triton shall orbit Neptune at almost the Earth-Moon distance. But since *Neptune is heavier* than Earth, the gravity of Neptune shall be *stronger*. So Triton shall orbit in *six* instead of twenty-seven days: the Triton-Neptune month shall be a six-day month. Now Triton shall revolve in the direction *opposite* to the spin-direction of the planet Neptune, as well as opposite to the direction that the planets go around the Sun. No other large solar-system moon shall spin this way. And this *strange spin* shall have come to be because Triton was not made from the collapsing gas and matter that made Neptune. Rather, Triton was captured at a later stage.

Now Triton shall have a ragged surface with great canyons, craters, active volcanos, mountain peaks and lakes of liquid ethane. And from afar, the surface shall look *like unto* a rind of cantaloupe. This moon shall have polar caps of solid nitrogen and methane ice. They shall be extremely cold: *seven times colder than ice-water*. Thus the polar caps of Triton shall be the *coldest* spots on any moon or planet in the solar system.

---

[298] The diameter of Triton is two-thousand-and-three-hundred kilometers.

*The twelfth book of Planetology, called*

# Pluto

*And the ninth planet from the Sun was called Pluto.*

## Chapter I: The Twin Planet

Now Pluto, who was named after the Greek king of the underworld, shall be the child *farthest from the Sun*. And he shall have a twin sister, whose name is *Charon*. Every six-and-one-half days at a distance of twenty-thousand kilometers, Pluto and Charon shall revolve around each other. And since they shall spin at the same rate as they revolve, the sister's and brother's faces always face each other.

## Chapter II: Orbit

Now *usually, they* shall be the siblings farthest from the Sun. But since they move in an ellipse, they shall *sometimes* pass inside the orbit of the planet Neptune. Then Neptune shall *be* the farthest planet from the Sun, at least for several decades. And at an average distance of forty astronomical units from the Sun, they shall take *two-hundred-fifty years* to complete one circuit. And they shall move as one.

Pluto, like Uranus, *shall be tipped up on his side*, spinning in a direction perpendicular to his movement round the Sun.

## Chapter III: Their Bodies

And Pluto and Charon shall have common rocky cores. But the two, although similar, shall have some differences – Pluto shall have a *frozen* face of methane ice, whereas Charon shall wear a mask of water-ice. And these two icy surfaces shall be like a *tiny* pair of mirrors. And the two, *so far away*, shall reflect enough of the Sun's light to be just visible in telescopes on Earth.

Together, they shall weigh *one four-hundredth* of the weight of Earth. But Pluto shall be the bigger of the two – he shall be like Triton in density and size.[299] And Charon shall be half his size.

*And they shall hold their faces face-to-face.*

---

[299] See Chapter IV of the Book of *Neptune*.

*The thirteenth book of Planetology, called*

# Asteroids

*Salute the heavens.*

## Chapter I: Minor Planets

Now the Sun shall have *many* other companions. And these cold rocky bodies shall vary in size from a few hundred meters to hundreds of kilometers. And the larger bodies shall resemble smaller moons of planets. Now a few shall be shaped spherically. But most, and especially the smaller, shall be *irregularly shaped* – peanuts, potatoes, cigars, et cetera, shall be their shapes. Although there shall be more than a million such bodies bigger than a kilometer in size, most shall be too small, too dark, too far away to *have* been seen by thee. And these bodies or minor planets shall be the *asteroids*, for "asteroid" is Greek for starlike. Together all the asteroids shall weigh less than *one one-thousandth* of the weight of Earth.

## Chapter II: Names

Now the asteroids shall have their names often chosen from the Greek and Roman deities. And greet thee the asteroids:

*Salute Pallas, Hektor, Hermione, and Herculina.*
*Salute Patroclus, Amor, Euphrosyne, and Angelina.*
*Salute Icarus, Koronis, Iris, Hermes,*
*and Toutatis, Adonis, Themis, Ceres,*
*and Achilles, Arete, Ida, and Apollo.*
*Salute Pholus, Psyche, Hilda, Juno,*
*and Eugenia, Chiron, Gaspra, Geographos,*
*and Eunomia, Phaethon, Ursula, and Eros.*
*Salute Interamnia, Bamberga, Hygeia, and Hungaria.*
*Salute Betulia, Bettina, Astraea, Brucia,*
*and Siegena, Fortuna, Flora, and Camilla.*
*Salute Dembowska, Diotima, Daphne, and Davida,*
*and also Alauda, Nysa, Vesta, and Europa.*
*Et cetera, et cetera, et cetera.*

## Chapter III: Orbits

And the asteroids shall revolve around the Sun in circles *or* ellipses. Most shall wander in the wilderness of outer space between the orbits of Jupiter and Mars. But some shall orbit elsewhere, so that *in every region* of the solar system shall some asteroids be found.

Now some asteroids shall cross the orbits of the planets. And occasionally an asteroid shall strike a planet. And Earth, like any other planet, *shall* be struck by asteroids.[300]

## Chapter IV: Flocks

And a few asteroids shall be double-asteroids, in which two bodies wobble as they bump each other. And others shall move in groups like in *a flock of sheep*. And flocks[301] shall have the names

> *the Amors, the Eos,*
> *the Floras, the Apollos,*
> *the Koronis, the Trojans,*
> *the Themis, the Atens,*
> *et cetera, et cetera.*

And *each flock* shall have a *leader*. And the name of the flock shall be the same name as the leader. And for example, the Apollos shall be led by Apollo, the Amors shall be led by Amor, and so on. And many members *shall* be in a flock. The Atens shall number just about a hundred; the Apollos roughly seven-hundred; the Amors shall be around a thousand.

## Chapter V: Belts

Now there shall be *asteroid belts* between Jupiter and Mars, consisting of *tens of thousands* of these tiny bodies. Between the belts shall be *voids* with hardly any asteroids. Such voids shall exist because of the gravitation generated by the Sun and Jupiter. Now a belt shall be provided with a name. The names, which shall be selected from a member of the belt, shall be the Hungarias, the Cybeles, the Hildas, the Thules, and so on. *Ceres* shall lead the biggest belt with the assistance of *Pallas* and of *Juno*. These three spherical asteroids shall be the *three largest* with radii of hundreds of kilometers.

Now there shall be two flocks that move in the same circular orbit of the planet Jupiter. The Apollos shall be the name of both. At one-sixth of a circle behind Jupiter, one-third of the Apollo flock shall *follow* Jupiter. And at one-sixth of a circle in front of Jupiter, the rest shall *lead* the planet Jupiter. And these two flocks shall be held in place firmly by two unseen hands: One shall be force of gravity coming from the Sun, and one shall be the force of gravity of Jupiter. And in effect, Jupiter shall be the master *shepherd* of these flocks.

---

[300] On average, every four-hundred-thousand years, a one-kilometer-sized asteroid strikes Earth. The impact from such an asteroid resembles a nuclear explosion, in which, in a region of dozens of kilometers, land and life is completely destroyed.

[301] In scientific jargon, the flocks are called *families*.

*The fourteenth book of Planetology, called*

# Comets

*Verily in the heavens and the Earth*
*are signs for those who do believe.*

## Chapter I: Origin

*And the Sun shall have visitors*
*from the outer reaches of the solar system,*
*where, except for tiny spots of starlight,*
*darkness reigns.*

And *it shall come to pass* that, at thousands of astronomical units from the Sun, a ten-kilometer-sized body of ices, dust and grit shall be *knocked out of orbit* and toward the Sun. And several tens of thousands of years later, it shall pass by the planet Pluto. And as it nears the Sun, the Sun *shall warm* its body. And frozen gases shall evaporate releasing dust-particles and grains. And the gases shall reflect Sun's light and glow. And *this* shall be a *comet*.

## Chapter II: Structure

And luminous gas shall swell about its core. And this shall be the *coma* of the comet. And solar radiation shall blow the comet's dust. And the solar wind shall blow the comet's gas. And *like unto* the blue flame of a blowtorch, a long whitish streak of glowing dust and gas shall form. And *this* shall be the *tail* of the comet.

And when the comet arcs around the Sun and moves away from it, the tail shall not point toward the Sun – the tail shall *point away*. And to thee who hath not knowledge, this *shall* seem *strange*, for the coma shall be moving *at* its tail. But verily is this natural, for the tail shall be blown by *the Sun's wind* – the tail shall not be a trail of dust exhaust. And when the comet ventures far enough away, the Sun shall cease to heat the frozen gases. Then the comet shall grow *dark* again.

## Chapter III: Orbit, Size, Life and Death

Now some comets *perturbed by the gravity* of Jupiter and Saturn or bumping with asteroid shall be captured in the inner solar system. Moving in great ellipses, *they* shall visit Sun *every* few years, few decades, or few centuries. And *these* shall be the comets with short periods.

And those comets seen by thee from Earth shall typically have a ten-kilometer-sized body, a coma swelling to several thousand kilometers, and a tail often as long as *one-hundred-million* kilometers in length. Now ye who first sights the comet shall *claim the comet* and have the comet named for thee. So the names of comets shall be Tycho

Brahe, Halley, Encke, Tuttle, Pons-Winnecke, Wolf, Shoemaker-Levy, Whipple, Hale-Bopp and so on.

Now some comets, as they approach the Sun, shall heat sufficiently to *break up into pieces*. The destruction of such comets shall soon follow. Most comets shall make a thousand solar visits before their final breakup. And since every comet shall *eventually* breakup and disappear, comets shall have lifetimes. But clouds of debris in the outer reaches of the solar system shall from time to time supply new comets.

Now at any given moment, the number of comets shall be *more* than a trillion. But their mass, when all combined, shall total just a few times the Earth's mass. And they shall visit the Sun *so rarely* or be *so dim* that few of them *be* visible from Earth. And when they come, they shall remain for several months and then be *gone*. And in the night sky, ye on Earth shall see the biggest with tails stretching a dozen moons in length. But small ones shall be seen by thee only in a telescope. And the smallest *shall pass by unseen*.

*The fifteenth book of Planetology, called*

# Meteors

*And there fell a great star from Heaven,*
*burning as if it were a lamp.*

## Chapter I: Origin

*Now Earth shall have other visitors*
*from the solar system and beyond.*

And *it shall come to pass* that a pebble of debris in outer space shall pass the orbit of the Earth and pierce its atmosphere. And friction with Earth's air shall make it grow quite hot and glow. And it shall streak across the dark night sky *as* a streak of light. And *this* shall be a *meteor*. It shall be *like unto a shooting star*.

## Chapter II: Showers

*And rocks and bits of objects*
*shall from the heavens fall.*

Now during the year at certain times, Earth shall pass through a region filled with outer-space debris. And if ye *be* looking, ye shall see dozens of meteors each hour. A *meteor shower* shall be the name for this display of Nature's fireworks. Prominent showers shall have names. And for example, each year on January third shall the Quadrantid shower "rain." On April twenty-two shall come the Lyrid shower. And the Perseids shall transpire in a two-week interval peak-ing on the twelfth of August.[302] And the Orionid shower shall last a few days and peak on October twenty-one. On November seventeen shall the Leonid display its streaks of light. The Geminid shower shall last for a few days but on the fourteenth of December shall it show its real power. Now the debris of showers often shall have come from comets. And for example, the Orionids shall be associated with the comet Halley. An exception is the Geminid shower: its debris *shall* have originated from the asteroid called Phaethon.

## Chapter III: Meteorites

Less commonly, a meteor shall streak across the sky, burn and generate a glowing disk of red as large or larger than a quarter Moon. And *this* shall be a *fire ball*.

Now the energy released within the atmosphere by a one-gram meteor shall be equivalent to one-hundred grams of TNT. Such small meteors shall be *pulverized* and burn up in the atmosphere. And since most are small, almost all shall vanish in Earth's atmosphere. But those that do survive and *land on Earth* shall be called *meteorites*. And quite infrequently, Earth shall *encounter* one that is relatively large. Such a large meteorite *shall* create a crater. Now once or twice every hundred-million years, a meteor ten-kilometers or bigger *shall* strike Earth, creating a blast equivalent to *one-hundred-million megatons* of TNT or more. And great ecological damage shall ensue; and Earth shall have a *holocaust*.

---

[302] The first-three weeks of August are the best time to view meteors.

# The
# Old
# Testament

*The first book of Creation, called*

# Genesis I: The Planck Epoch[1]

*In the beginning,*
*the World was without form and void;*
*and darkness was upon the face of the deep.*

*– The Holy Bible*

In the "Beginning," there was *no beginning*. Before the Planck time, there was *no time* and there was *no space*. The Universe was in a quantum state[2] with wild fluctuations. (The hummingbird's wings flap fast and are invisible.) What one might have called spacetime was incomprehensible. The quantum Universe was a *trillion-trillion* worlds. Potential worlds were bubbling forth and were evaporating *like unto* the waters in a boiling pot. And tunnelling and fluctuations moved thy proto-World among these worlds. And quantum gravity wreaked havoc. The waves of gravity were everywhere. The Universe was like a thousand knots.

Near the "Beginning," there was almost nothing. The Universe was unimaginably hot and small. And somehow from this *senseless void* would emerge *thy World*. And somehow from this *emptiness* there would emerge a time and space. Thy Universe would soon conceive itself. And from the almost nothingness would soon come all.

*The second book of Creation, called*

# Genesis II: The Big Bang[3]

*Things were perfect then.*

## Chapter I: The Beginning of Time

The time was ten-to-the-minus-forty-five o'clock: The Universe had existed for one *Planck time* – one-tenth of one-millionth of one-trillionth of one-trillionth of one-trillionth of a second. Temporal history commenced.

Thy Universe, though very very very hot, began to cool so ever slightly. The quantum fluctuations began to *weaken*. Fate began to settle *on a path*. What might have been *could* no longer be. Thy Uni-

---

[1] The meanings of the metaphors in this chapter and the next ones as well as the definitions of the scientific words are explained in The Books of Physics of the New Testament. See in particular the books *General Relativity and Gravity* and *Quantum Mechanics*.

[2] For the definitions of technical words such as state, see the Index/Glossary.

[3] The *Big Bang* refers to the events immediately following the initial moment of Creation.

verse no longer moved among the quantum universes. The waves of gravity began to wane. Strings and knots began to form *a space-time fabric*. The wings of probability-uncertainty began to slow. The wings of time began to flap.

And know that space and time, which had been merged, *emerged*. And know that gravitons, the particles of gravity, were mostly gone. And know that those few gravitons, which still remained, became *too weak to interact*. And know that the tunnelling of worlds had ceased. And know the Universe had *picked* a path for gravity.

In the Beginning, there was almost nothing. The Universe was very very very hot and very very very small. From this *senseless void* emerged *thy World*. From *emptiness* emerged a time and space. The Universe conceived itself in embryonic fashion – the chicken and the egg at once. And from the nothingness *came all*.

> *Those who claim a paradox,*
> *speak not.*
> *Those who do not understand,*
> *speak not.*
> *Small is the mind of man.*

> *In the Beginning was the Big Bang.*
> *In the Beginning was the Big Bang.*
> *In the Beginning was the Big Bang.*
> *And somewhere voices sang*
> *the words of great Creation.*
> *The Universe was small and hot:*
> *infinitely smaller than a spot,*
> *infinitely hotter than an oven.*
> *And all the voices sang*
> *in Heaven*
> *the words of great Creation.*
> *In the Beginning was the Big Bang.*

## Chapter II: The Uni-Law

In the Beginning, the Universe was in a perfect state, *like unto* a flawless sphere. And the Great Hand held the crystal ball. And the Great Eye observed *roundness* and saw that the roundness *remained* when the ball was turned. And the Great Eye moved about and the roundness *still remained*. And the Great One knew that roundness indeed was *good*. And this roundness was provided with a name. And the name was Ultra-Super-Symmetry.[4] In the Beginning was Ultra-Super-Symmetry.

---

[4] Ultra-Super-Symmetry is not standard scientific terminology, but similar symmetries under various names are used by physicists.

At the Beginning, from the Beginning, after the Beginning and Forever there is only one law and one law only. It is the *Uni-Law*. It governs all. All shall respect it. When all obey the Uni-Law, the Universe is in a state of *perfect* Ultra-Super-Symmetry. In the Beginning, *all obeyed* the universal Uni-Law.

> *Let us rejoice this perfect state,*
> *a flawless ball of frozen mercury.*
> *All promise to obey the Law of Unity.*
> *All join the singing voices and all celebrate*
> *the beauty of Ultra-Super-Symmetry,*
> *Nature in its purest state.*

In the Beginning, there was energy, matter and spacetime. Energy made matter *move*. Matter and energy made spacetime *curve*. The curvature of spacetime made matter move in strange ways. In its inception, the Universe was *very very very hot*, a glowing broth of fire and light. In this great but tiny oven, processes proceeded rapidly at random: Matter forms *dissolved* to energy. Energy condensed to matter. Some matter and some energy disappeared in heightened space-time curvature. Changes in curvature *created* new matter and new energy. All these fundamental processes perpetuated. Matter, energy and spacetime were almost one. They all obeyed the Uni-Law. The World was in a state of *perfect* symmetry.

> *The holy fire.*
> *The quark-soup mire.*
> *The space-time cloth.*
> *The Big Bang broth.*
> *Voices in heaven.*
> *Bread in leaven.*

Let us pray.

> *We celebrate our birth*
> *in Heaven and on Earth.*

> *And translucent figures flapped their wings*
> *and fanned the cosmic fires.*

And let it be forever said that the Uni-Law *rules all*: matter, energy and spacetime. And let it be known that the Big Bang is *a consequence*. And that the character of space and time is just a corollary. And let it be known to ye and all around ye that in the Beginning and the aftermath, the manifold of space-and-time has ten dimensions. And time is one and space is nine.

And it came to pass that, in the Beginning and the aftermath, matter moved in *nine* directions. Ask ye not why. It follows from the Uni-Law. If thou dost not understand, remember that the mind of man be small. The Uni-Law *reigns over all*.

But, the Uni-Law does not determine all! The Uni-Law is quantum law.[5] And quantum laws encompass *randomness*. Probability and possibility play a role. The World evolves in part by dice and chance: In a road a fork is reached. And one must go *to the left* or *to the right*. The flow of time, also a consequence of Uni-Law, propels one forward. There is no turning back; *only forward* left and right. A die is thrown – a choice is made. And one goes to the left or right. So goes the World then to the left or right. No principle controls the choice, and *randomness prevails*. With many forks and many paths, the future is uncertain – a probabilistic evolution – a quantum evolution. The world of atoms and the small is foreign to the world of man. Alas, the Uni-Law does *not* determine all.

> *In the Beginning and the aftermath,*
> *there is the randomness of paths.*

And let it be known, for now and for forever, that the Uni-Law is a *single* law, though it encompasses *many* principles, which are its parts. And the principles are not fundamental but *consequences* of the Uni-Law. The Uni-Law is *like unto* white light. With a prism, white light becomes a rainbow. Each color is a type of light.

*The third book of Creation, called*

# Genesis III: Ultra-Super-Symmetry Destruction

*Then came the destruction of the temple.*

There was an apple, a perfect apple, an apple red and round. And someone held the apple. And someone bit the apple. And the apple was no longer perfect and no longer round.

And on a plate the Great Hand placed a pen on end. And the pen stood perfectly vertically. And the pen was in a state of *perfect* balance. And it *was thought* that the pen would not fall. How could the pen pick a particular direction to fall?! All directions were *possible and probable*, thereby making any one direction *improbable and impossible*. By symmetry the pen *could not fall*. But it fell.

> *An egg had broken.*
> *The Universe had been disturbed.*

In the Beginning, the Universe had been a *perfect* state, a *flawless* sphere. And roundness had been seen from *every* angle. In the Beginning had been Ultra-Super-Symmetry.

---

[5] Quantum mechanics governs the behavior of matter at short distances and leads to uncertainty and unpredictability.

And the Hyper-Sphere[6] began to change its shape by chance. And the Hyper-Sphere began to *flatten* and to *stretch*. And the Hyper-Sphere became a Hyper-Tube. And the Great Hand held the Tube. And the Great Eye observed *some* roundness and saw that this roundness remained when the Tube was turned. And the Great Eye moved about, and this roundness still remained at *certain* angles and at *certain* points of view. But the roundness was no longer the roundness of a Hyper-Sphere. The roundness was *reduced*. And the Great One knew that the remaining roundness was still good. And this remaining lesser roundness was provided with a name. And its name was Grand-Symmetry. In the aftermath was Grand-Symmetry.

> *Spontaneously,*
> *the Ultra-Super-Symmetry*
> *had broken into parts.*
> *The Universe had picked a path and fate.*
> *A lesser but still great*
> *Grand-Symmetry remained.*
> *The Uni-Law still governed all,*
> *but in a broken state.*
> *A pen lying flat upon a plate.*

And then *the character of space* began to change. And *six* of nine dimensions began *to shrink*. And the other *three* began *expanding*. The temperature began to drop. But thy Universe was still very very very hot.[7] The time was ten-to-the-minus-forty-four o'clock.[8]

And from this moment onward, three-space[9] would expand forever. And the World would in a way become *less round*. And six-space, which was of finite size and volume, would get forever *smaller*. And the temperature of the Universe *would* go down forever.

In the aftermath, there was energy, matter and spacetime. Energy made matter *move*. Matter and energy made three-space *expand*. The expansion of space made matter *move apart*. At this time, the Universe was still *very very very hot*, a glowing broth of fire and light. In this great but tiny oven, processes proceeded at a rapid rate. Matter forms *dissolved* to energy, and energy condensed to matter. All obeyed the Uni-Law, albeit in its *broken* state.

---

[6] A Hyper-Sphere is a nine-dimensional manifold of perfect symmetry. A Hyper-Tube is the nine-dimensional analog of a tube.

[7] $10^{30}$ degrees Kelvin = 1,000,000,000,000,000,000,000,000,000,000 degrees Kelvin. The temperature of the Universe at this time was a hundred-billion-trillion times hotter than the temperature at the center of the Sun. Of course, at this time, neither the Sun nor the Earth existed.

[8] In other words, the time was ten Planck units, or $10^{-42}$ seconds, that is, 1/(1,000,000,000,000,000,000,000,000,000,000,000,000,000,000) seconds or one-millionth of a trillionth of a trillionth of a trillionth of a second.

[9] This is three-dimensional space, the space with which *ye* are now familiar.

*The holy fire.*
*The quark-soup mire.*
*The space-time cloth.*
*The Big Bang broth.*
*Angels in heaven.*
*Bread in leaven.*

Let us pray again.

*We celebrate our birth*
*in Heaven and on Earth.*

Now, this is *the story of the ant.* On a ball, there lived an ant. At first, it walked in two dimensions. Its world had two directions, up-and-down and left-and-right, for the surface of a ball has two dimensions. And then it came to pass that the ball was squashed and stretched until the *ball* became a *tube.* And the tube was further squashed and stretched until the *tube* became a *wire.* Behold the ant. It was walking on the wire. It walked in one direction, for its world had only one dimension. The ant moved only left and right. A wire *seems* to have but one dimension.

And it happened that three-space grew again tenfold. And six-space, the internal and compact manifold, shrank further. And matter, like the ant, moved effectively *in only three directions.* And in effect, spacetime had four dimensions. And all the matter of thy World was concentrated in a little place. And as a consequence, thy Universe was very very very very very very very very very very dense.[10] And matter moved according to the rules of *broken Uni-Law* and interacted through the hot-gauge bosons of Grand-Symmetry. The Universe was a strongly interacting sea of glue and matter. The Universe *was* a hot gauge soup. The temperature did drop, yet still the Universe was *very very very hot.*[11] And the time was ten-to-the-minus-forty-two o'clock.[12]

---

[10] The presence of each instance of "very" represents a factor of approximately ten-billion, or $10^{10}$. Here and elsewhere, density is measured relative to water, that is, one gram per cubic centimeter. The density of the Universe at this time corresponds to taking the Earth with all its mass and shrinking it into a ball with a radius of one-hundredth of one-trillionth of one-trillionth of a meter, that is, a ball ten-trillion times smaller than an atom! Of course, at this time, atoms did not exist.

[11] $10^{29}$ degrees Kelvin = 100,000,000,000,000,000,000,000,000,000 degrees Kelvin.

[12] $10^{-40}$ seconds, or 1/(10,000,000,000,000,000,000,000,000,000,000,000,000,000) seconds.

*The fourth book of Creation, called*

# Genesis IV: Grand-Symmetry Destruction

*A strange wind blew the bubble*
*and the bubble changed its shape and burst.*
*And smaller bubbles floated in the air.*

And space continued *to expand and stretch*. And matter moved apart quite fast. And time continued *to push forward*. More than a thousand Planck times had already passed.

There was an apple, an almost perfect apple, an apple small and round. And someone held the apple. And someone bit the apple. And the apple was no longer almost perfect and no longer round.

And the Great Hand placed a pin on end on a plate. And the pin stood perfectly vertically. And the pin was in a state of *perfect* balance. And it *was thought* that the pin would not fall. How could the pin pick a particular direction to fall?! All directions were *possible and probable* thereby making any one direction *improbable and impossible*. By symmetry the pin *could not fall*. But it fell.

*Another egg had broken.*
*Once more, the Universe had been disturbed.*

In the aftermath, the Universe had been an *almost perfect* state, a flawless tube. And roundness had been seen from *many* angles. In the aftermath had been Grand-Symmetry.

And it came to pass that Grand-Symmetry spontaneously broke in parts. The Universe had *picked* another path and fate. A lesser symmetry remained – the *Standard-Model symmetry*. The Uni-Law still governed all but in a highly broken state.

*A pin lying flat upon a plate.*

And the Great Hand held the Universe and felt a little roundness and knew that this roundness, although little, gave rise to symmetry transformations. And the Great Hand felt about, and this little roundness still remained in some directions. But the roundness was not the roundness of Grand-Symmetry. The roundness was *reduced*. And the Great One knew that this roundness, although little and reduced, was good. And the Great One named this symmetry *SU-three-cross-SU-two-cross-U-one*.[13] After Grand-Symmetry was Standard-Model symmetry.[14]

And three-space grew again tenfold. And the six-dimensional compact space became an *even smaller* compact manifold. The tempera-

---

[13] This is pronounced "ess you three cross ess you two cross you one." *U-one* is the symmetry associated with a circle. *SU-two* is the symmetry associated with a sphere. *SU-three* is the symmetry associated with a certain high-dimension space. The word "cross" indicates the simultaneous presence of these symmetries.

[14] See the New Testament Book of *Subnuclear Physics*, which also explains the terminology in the subsequent paragraph.

ture kept going down. Then the broken vector bosons *acquired mass.* And many broken bosons died in self-destruction – vector-boson self-annihilation. And still all the matter of thy Universe was concentrated in a little place. And hence the Universe was very very very very very very very very very dense. And matter moved according to the *rules* of Standard-Model symmetry and interacted through twelve SU-three-cross-SU-two-cross-U-one vector bosons. The Universe was a strongly interacting sea of leptons, antileptons, quarks and antiquarks. The temperature was *very very very hot.*[15] The time was ten-to-the-minus-thirty-nine o'clock.[16]

*The fifth book of Creation, called*

# Genesis V: Inflation

*And He blew into the Universe.*

Now more than a million Planck times had passed. The Universe was still *highly curved and lumpy.* Space was full of matter: vector bosons, quarks, antiquarks, leptons, antileptons and massive cosmic relics such as monopoles and solitons.[17] The density of matter made *enormous* space-time curvature. And thermal fluctuations made chaotic bubbles and lumpy fire soup.

And it came to pass that the Universe was in a metastable[18] state.

A Marble on a Hill.

*So motionless and still
for epochs had it been.
And then there came a wind.
Although there was no storm,
the wind became quite strong.
The marble shook a bit.
No longer did it sit.
The marble turned some more.
The wind began to roar.
It rolled along a path
of dirt between the grass.
And soon it reached the edge.*

---

[15] $10^{28}$ degrees Kelvin = 10,000,000,000,000,000,000,000,000,000 degrees Kelvin.

[16] $10^{-37}$ seconds, or 1/(10,000,000,000,000,000,000,000,000,000,000,000,000) seconds.

[17] Monopoles and solitons are vast collections of elementary particles that move together as a unit. They themselves act as elementary particles except that, instead of being point-like, they are spread out in space.

[18] Metastable means temporarily stable.

*It passed a little ledge,*
*and down the slope it slid.*
*And like a wild kid,*
*and bouncing as it fell,*
*it tumbled down the hill.*
*Below it reached a pit.*
*Back-forth it rocked a bit.*
*There was a final roll.*
*It settled in a hole*
*down there below the hill.*
*Again, motionless and still.*

And the Universe, *like unto* a ball, began to roll. It was too late. The World began its fall. Thy Universe began to make a *transition* to another state.

*First there came a quantum fluctuation.*
*And then began the great Inflation.*
*The Universe was in transition.*
*And three-space underwent a huge expansion*
*as six-space made a great contraction.*
*Background vacuum energy was the explanation.*
*It fueled the great expansion.*
*It caused an exponentiation.*
*The Universe reached its final destination.*
*There was a final oscillation.*
*It settled in its new configuration.*

And during this brief moment, which was not so brief in some sense, being a *hundred times* the age of the Universe *at that time*, space expanded by a factor of ten-to-the-fifty.[19] And a microscopic patch of space stretched itself ten-to-the-fifty-fold and became the precursor of *thy visible Universe.*

*Internal space deflated.*
*External space inflated.*

And that tiny patch of space, which had been very curved, became *almost exactly flat.* A gnat crawling on a little ball knows its world is round and small. Make the ball as big as Earth, and the gnat thinks its world is flat.

---

[19] $10^{50} = 100,000,000,000,000,000,000,000,000,000,000,000,000,000,000,000,000.$

*And that tiny piece of space,*
*which had been very lumpy,*
*became almost completely smooth.*
*The bumpy parts were thus removed.*
*Three-space,*
*like unto a wrinkled sheet of silk,*
*was stretched and smoothed.*

*Inflation brought about a huge dilution*
*of soliton and monopole populations.*

And the Great One observed Inflation and knew that it was good, for a World without Inflation *would be* a listless, lifeless world. Inflation set the matter density at criticality. It eliminated any chance of luck, for if the mass were *more* than critical, the World would soon *collapse* and self-destruct – the World would die a few fractions of a second old. And if the mass were *less*, the World would someday expand too fast and then become *extremely cold* – for this fate, the World would never die but soon consist of emptiness; matter would spread too thinly; the Universe would be in essence matterless.

*These fleeting moments would never be repeated.*
*Inflation caused the Universe to overcool.*
*And when inflation stopped, the Universe reheated.*

And so it came to pass that thy visible Universe grew from *a small patch* of the full Universe. And, as for the rest of the Universe, know that it be vast and *be beyond* thy reach. And do not expect this to be sensible, but simply note that light from the outer Universe *shall never* reach thy World. Know that the outer Universe shall remain forever invisible and inaccessible.

*The sixth book[20] of Creation, called*

# Genesis VI: The Cosmic Sea of Particles

*They were as the grains of sand.*

## Chapter I: Matter-Antimatter Excess

Now the Universe had just recovered from Inflation and Grand-Symmetry destruction. And the Universe had been shaken and was *slightly* out of equilibrium.[21] The broken vector bosons,[22] though heavy and dilute, provided baryonic violation.[23] Some *extra* quarks and

---

[20] This book and the next four books involve many concepts explained in the New Testament Book of *Subnuclear Physics*.

[21] The phase "out of equilibrium" means that the situation was not the most natural and most probable one. See the New Testament Book of *Thermodynamics*.

[22] These gauge bosons were the ones associated with the broken symmetries of Grand-

leptons were induced. And a tiny *excess* of matter over antimatter was produced.

## Chapter II: The Grand Desert

A billion Planck times had already passed. The time was ten-to-the-minus-thirty-six o'clock.[24] The temperature was still *very very very hot*.[25] The Universe was a *thousand-million-million-million-million* times smaller than its present size. The University was very very very very very very very dense: twenty-five times ten-to-the-seventy grams per cubic centimeter, almost a *trillion-trillion-trillion-trillion-trillion-trillion* times the density of Earth.[26] And let the particles be counted: There were

*one times ten-to-the-eighty-three*[27] *leptons per cubic centimeter,*
*one times ten-to-the-eighty-three antileptons per cubic centimeter,*
*four times ten-to-the-eighty-three quarks per cubic centimeter,*
*four times ten-to-the-eighty-three antiquarks per cubic centimeter,*
*three times ten-to-the-eighty-three gauge bosons per cubic centimeter.*

Thus there were in all thirteen times ten-to-the-eighty-three particles per cubic centimeter.

And for the next *one-trillionth* of a second, which was *enormously long* for a new-born universe, the Universe cooled and grew in size. And *nothing* came to pass: no phase transition, no breaking of a symmetry. And SU-three-cross-SU-two-cross-U-one remained and ruled thy World. And matter moved considerably apart. And the matter in thy Universe became *considerably less dense*, for space expanded a hundred-billion fold.

And the Universe, in quantum terms, was very very very old: *Ten-million-billion-billion-billion* Planck-times old. It was ten-to-the-minus-fourteen o'clock.[28] The temperature had dropped but was still extremely hot.[29] And although the Universe had grown a *hundred-billion* fold, it was still a *thousand-trillion* times smaller than its current size. It was still very very very dense: *two-billion-billion-billion* times denser than the Earth. And let the particles be counted: There were

*one times ten-to-the-fifty-three*[30] *leptons per cubic centimeter,*
*one times ten-to-the-fifty-three antileptons per cubic centimeter,*

---

Symmetry.

[23] These are processes in which the total number of quarks minus antiquarks is changed.

[24] $10^{-34}$ seconds, or 1/(10,000,000,000,000,000,000,000,000,000,000,000) seconds.

[25] $10^{26}$ degrees Kelvin = 100,000,000,000,000,000,000,000,000,000 degrees Kelvin.

[26] Of course, Earth did not yet exist.

[27] This number is $10^{83}$, i. e., a one followed by 83 zeros.

[28] $10^{-12}$ seconds, or 1/(1,000,000,000,000) seconds, that is, one-trillionth of a second.

[29] $10^{15}$ degrees Kelvin = 1,000,000,000,000,000 degrees Kelvin.

[30] This number is $10^{53}$, i. e., a one followed by 53 zeros.

*four times ten-to-the-fifty-three quarks per cubic centimeter,*
*four times ten-to-the-fifty-three antiquarks per cubic centimeter,*
*three times ten-to-the-fifty-three gauge bosons per cubic centimeter.*

Thus there were in all thirteen times ten-to-the-fifty-three particles per cubic centimeter.

And now and forever, let the names of these particles be known to thee and all around thee. Of the leptons, there were those which were *electrically charged*. And they were the tau, the muon and the "e". "Electron" was another name for "e". And those leptons that were *neutral* were called *neutrinos*. Now there were many types of quarks. They came in *six* flavors: "down," "up," "strange," "charm," "bottom" and "top"; and they had *three* strong-color types: "strong-yellow," "strong-red" and "strong-blue." Thus there were *eighteen* types of quarks. And for *every particle*, there was an *antiparticle*. Thus there were three kinds of charged antileptons, the anti-tau, the anti-muon and the positron. And the antineutrinos were the neutral antiparticles of the neutrinos. And of the *twelve* vector gauge bosons, *eight* belonged to SU-three, and they were called the *gluons*. And of the remaining four, *three* belonged to SU-two, and *one* belonged to U-one.

So these were the particles that filled thy Universe.

And the quarks, antiquarks and gluons carried strong-color charges. And they continually and *rapidly* exchanged strong-color by emitting and absorbing gluons. And these exchanges created SU-three interactions, the strong interactions.[31] And the quarks, antiquarks, leptons, antileptons, and SU-two bosons carried SU-two weak-isospin. And they also continually and *rapidly* exchanged weak-isospin by emitting and absorbing SU-two bosons. And these exchanges created SU-two interactions. And the quarks, antiquarks, leptons and antileptons carried U-one-charge and continually exchanged U-one bosons. And these exchanges created U-one interactions. Thus all the SU-three-cross-SU-two-cross-U-one interactions were generated by *exchanging* vector bosons. And SU-two and SU-three vector gauge bosons were *self-interacting* because they carried *their own* charge.

Thus these were the interactions that prevailed. So thus it be. The Universe was a dense, *highly interacting* quark-antiquark-lepton-antilepton-vector-boson sea.

---

[31] The word "interactions" is synonymous with "forces."

*The seventh book of Creation, called*

# Exodus I: Electroweak Breaking

*And the vessel shall be broken to shivers.*

## Chapter I: The Acrobat

The time was one-trillionth of a second after the Big Bang. Known history commenced.[32]

*A tightrope walk. All viewers hold their breath.*
*He bounces on the wire, then balancing*
*maintains himself by leaning right and left.*
*A clown below is unaware of anything.*

*Almost a misplaced foot, he poles the air.*
*In the leotards bulge his calves and thighs*
*and other muscles, as he steps with care.*
*One hears among the crowd a unison of sighs.*

*And now for the climactic act. He calls*
*for silence, throws away the pole, salutes*
*the crowd. The wire flexes. He executes*
*a backward flip. He slips and almost falls,*

*then leaps to safety undismayed. How*
*the people cheer. He turns and takes a bow.*

The Universe was on a stage. The Universe was *still* in balance. But the balance was *about to* disappear.

Now this is the story of the bell. There was a bell that was held upside down on a plate. And the bell was released on end. And it stood perfectly vertically. The bell was in a state of *perfect* balance. And it *was thought* that the bell would not fall. How could the bell pick a particular direction to fall? All directions were *possible and probable* thereby making any one direction *improbable and impossible*. By symmetry the bell could not fall. But it fell.

## Chapter II: Electroweak Symmetry Destruction

And so it came to pass that Standard-Model symmetry spontaneously *broke in parts*. And because the weak and electromagnetic interactions had been united under Standard-Model symmetry, SU-two-cross-U-one became known as the *electroweak theory*. And the

---

[32] The writings of *Genesis I* through *Genesis VI* involve some scientific speculation. The history and development of the Universe and Nature in *Exodus I* and henceforth is established scientific knowledge.

spontaneous destruction of SU-two-cross-U-one was named *electroweak breaking*. And as for *SU-three, it* remained unbroken.

The World had picked a certain path and fate. SU-two-cross-U-one was *partially* destroyed. A *single* symmetry of it remained: electromagnetic-U-one symmetry. And the Uni-Law still ruled but *in a highly broken state.*

> *On its side a bell upon a plate.*

> *The audience was clapping – they wanted more.*
> *And what they wanted was what they got:*
> *There was an encore.*
> *He picked an act among the hardest.*
> *Some in the bleachers closed their eyes.*
> *And then the tightrope artist,*
> *who had hitherto performed his balancing act so well,*
> *fell.*
> *There were a thousand open mouths*
> *with a thousand "oh's", a unison of sighs.*

The Universe had lost its balance.

> *SU-two had died.*
> *Of SU-three-cross-SU-two-cross-U-one,*
> *only U-one and SU-three survived.*

## Chapter III: The Post-Electroweak-Breaking Period

And let it be known to thee and all around thee that henceforth SU-three-cross-U-one would *dominate* the dominion of the very small. SU-three-cross-U-one and gravity would now and forever *control* the behavior of all matter and all mass.

The history of the Universe's symmetry had been *like unto* successive waterfalls. The last waterfall had passed.

And spontaneous symmetry destruction gave masses to three of the four SU-two-cross-U-one vector bosons. And these three were given names. And the names were *"W-plus," "W-minus,"* and *"Z-naught."* And henceforth, the exchange of W's and Z's produced *short-ranged* repulsions and attractions. And *these* were the weak interactions.

And from two of the four SU-three-cross-U-one vector bosons, the *photon was thus born.* Out of electroweak breaking, "light" was formed. Thus the photon was the fourth SU-two-cross-U-one vector boson – the other three were the two W's and Z. And because the photon had *no mass*, it produced *long-ranged* repulsions and attractions. And *these* were the electromagnetic interactions.

And it came to pass that electroweak breaking gave birth to masses *for* the quarks and the charged leptons. Now the top did weigh *the most*. Then, in order weighing in, were bottom, tau, charm, strange and the muon. The down and up acquired smaller mass. The electron weighed *the least.*

*And thus it came to pass*
*through the breaking of SU-two-cross-U-one*
*that the quarks and leptons did acquire mass.*

And because the antiquarks and antileptons were the twin brethren of the quarks and leptons, the antiquarks and antileptons *also* did acquire mass. And their masses were the same as their twin brethren. The masses of the anti-t and t were thus *the same.*[33] The masses of the anti-b and b were thus *the same.* And so on.

## Chapter IV: Two Stone Tablets

A nd the Great One went to one corner of thy Universe where two stone tablets lay. And He etched in the tablets *the laws of Nature.* And He did so to halt the breaking of the Uni-Law, for *so much* destruction had occurred since the Big Bang beginning. Ultra-Symmetry had been thoroughly corrupted. In pieces was the Uni-Law. *Only four fragments* still remained intact – these were the fundamental forces, which *made* things interact.

And the Great One summoned from all parts of the Universe the holy and the wise. And He revealed to them the tablets. And He commanded them to bow down *and* obey the Word. And they bowed down and did obey. And they became disciples.

Now and forever after, the laws of Nature *would be fixed.* There would be *four* fundamental forces: gravity, electromagnetism, the strong force and the weak force. And these forces would constitute the *Standard Model.* The Great One had so spoken. And the Great One commanded His disciples to spread the Word. And spread the Word they did. And henceforth, all in the Universe, without exception, *obeyed* the Standard-Model Word.

*Nature's laws shall not be broken.*

## Chapter V: Annihilations

T he time was one ten-billionth of a second after the Big Bang. The Universe continued its expansion. The temperature continued its descent. It was a hundred-trillion Kelvins. The strong force was getting *stronger.*

And the top quark, which was the heaviest quark, could *no longer* swim in the primordial cosmic sea – its heavy mass became a *heavy* burden and it drowned. And the top *annihilated* with the anti-top, producing b's, gluons, photons, W's and Z's.

---

[33] The top, bottom, charm, strange, up and down are also called the t, b, c, s, u and d.

And soon the Z's and W's *also* self-destructed into photons, quarks and leptons. And the Universe continued to *expand*. And the temperature continued to *decrease* – it was ten-trillion Kelvins hot. The time was ten-to-the-minus-ten o'clock.[34] And the b annihilated with the anti-b. And the tau annihilated with the anti-tau. And the c annihilated with the anti-c. And these *self-destructing processes* produced strange, up and down quarks, and electrons, muons, as well as photons.

And as the temperature of the Universe went down, one by one the events of self-destruction came about. And each time, the entire Universe became a *matter-antimatter bomb*. And the explosion was stupendous, releasing *unimaginable amounts* of energy as mass was converted into energy according to the Eighth Commandment, that mass be a form of energy.[35] And during each event, one flavor of quarks annihilated with its anti-flavor counterpart, producing particles of lesser mass. So thus it be. The *lightest* particles *lived* on, while the *heaviest* particles *no longer* swam in the primordial cosmic sea.

*The eighth book of Creation, called*

# Exodus II: Quark Confinement

*And they were thrown into the house of bondage.*

## Chapter I: The Confining Phase Transition[36]

The time was one-millionth of a second after *the* Big Bang. The Universe *continued* its expansion. The temperature *continued* to descend – one-trillion Kelvins was it. And the Universe contained a million-billion grams of matter per cubic centimeter.

And earlier, when the temperature of the Universe was very very high, the strong interactions had not been so very strong – *asymptotic freedom* was the reason why. But as the Universe's temperature declined, the SU-three strong interactions *grew much stronger*.

And so it came to pass that the strong force grew in strength. And the strong force became *extremely strong*. And the quarks and antiquarks emitted gluons at *extraordinary rates*. And the gluons acted as microscopic glue. And quarks were *tied together* by different-colored glue. *In fetters* were quarks tied to antiquarks and other quarks. And gluons stuck to gluons too.

---

[34] One-hundredth of one-millionth of a second after the Big Bang.

[35] If a human-made nuclear bomb had been exploded during one of these cosmic annihilation events, it would have had the same effect as tossing a lighted match into the mouth of a volcano in eruption.

[36] The physics ideas and terminology of this chapter are discussed in Chapters IX and X of the New Testament Book of *Subnuclear Physics*.

And infrared slavery ensued. And *color confinement* came about. And it was declared that, henceforth and forever, there would be no colored-asymptotic states. Thus quarks and antiquarks and gluons formed strong-color-neutral entities. And these entities, these bound states, were provided with a name. And *hadron* was that name. And when these hadrons formed, *tremendous quantities of energy* were given off. And *every patch* of space within the Universe exploded as a hadron bomb. And know ye and all around ye that a hadron bomb *be* more powerful than a nuclear bomb – one-hundred times more powerful per gram of matter. Thus the Universe exploded in a *violent, unimaginable manner.* And energetic particles were generated. And gamma rays were given off. And the temperature of the Universe interrupted its descent.

And the quarks and antiquarks *paired themselves* in slavery. Yellow quarks *tied themselves* to anti-yellow quarks; red quarks *tied themselves* to anti-red quarks; and blue quarks *tied themselves* to anti-blue quarks. And these bound states were provided with a name. *And* that name was *meson.* And the lightest meson also was provided with a name: the *pion*, also known as *pi.* And so the Universe was full of pi's.

And three quarks *tied themselves in slavery*: Yellow, red and blue quarks formed entities containing three quarks. And these SU-three-strong bound states were provided with a name. And the name was *baryon*. And so the Universe contained some baryons.

And three antiquarks *tied themselves in slavery*: Yellow, red and blue antiquarks formed states containing three antiquarks. And these were *antibaryons*. And so the Universe contained some antibaryons.

And the quarks, antiquarks and gluons continued to interact inside baryons, antibaryons and mesons. And these hadrons interacted externally more weakly among themselves by exchanging pions. But because the pion *had a mass*, these residual strong forces were *short-ranged* – their effects extended over only *tiny distances.*[37]

And at one ten-thousandth of a second after the Big Bang, in self-destruction almost all remaining quarks and antiquarks *annihilated*: The s *annihilated* with the anti-s; the d *annihilated* with the anti-d; and the u *annihilated* with the anti-u. And during each of these events of self-destruction, every patch of space exploded in a violent, *unimaginable* matter-antimatter bomb. And tremendous amounts of energy and radiation were produced.

But because there was a tiny excess of quarks over antiquarks, complete annihilation was *not possible*. And these *remaining* quarks were in the nucleons.[38] And these nucleons were indestructible, for absent were the anti-nucleons with which they could annihilate.[39] Thus a few remaining nucleons *survived*. And the number of nucleons indeed

---

[37] These distances were a few fermis, that is, the diameters of typical nuclei.

[38] A *nucleon* is a proton or a neutron.

[39] A nucleon needs an anti-nucleon in order to undergo a matter-antimatter annihilation.

was relatively small – in the cosmic primordial sea was but one proton and one neutron for *every billion* photons.

And it came to pass that pions did *disintegrate*. And they decayed into muons, anti-muons, neutrinos, antineutrinos, electrons, positrons and photons. And then the muons and the anti-muons *also* underwent annihilation: The entire Universe became a muon-antimuon bomb. And *more* electrons, positrons and photons were produced.

> *They had once filled the cosmic sea.*
> *Gone are the W and the Z.*
> *Departed are the Deltas, Psi's and Phi's,*
> *As well as Upsilons and Pi's.*
> *Dead are the kaons and the B's.*
> *Lost are the Lambda's and the D's.*
> *Even nucleons number few,*
> *for there was hardly any excess d and u.*
> *And no more t and no more b.*
> *And no more s and no more c,*
> *for the antiquark had killed the quark;*
> *for the quark had killed the antiquark.*
> *Gone are the muons and the taus.*
> *All the result of cosmic laws.*
> *The World shall never be the same.*
> *Now hardly any quarks remain.*

*The ninth book of Creation, called*

# Deuteronomy[40]

*These be the words which Nature spake.*

## Chapter I: Big Bang Nucleosynthesis

And so the tiny excess of quarks over antiquarks had left *miniscule* amounts of quarks surviving in the cosmic sea. And these few quarks were now confined *inside* the proton and the neutron. So thus it be. The Universe was full of neutrinos, antineutrinos, electrons, positrons and photons. But only *one-billionth* of the cosmic sea was made of neutrons and of protons.

> *In the next three minutes*
> *would transpire a chain of nuclear events.*

Now this is the story of Big Bang nucleosynthesis. The story is full of accidents. It has seven episodes. It describes the creation of the lightest elements.

---

[40] The physics of this book is discussed in the New Testament Book of *Nuclear Physics*.

## Episode I: The Energetic Cosmic Sea

The time was one-hundredth of a second – thy Universe had existed for one-hundredth of a second. The cosmic sea was *agitating wildly*. Subatomic particles bounced off one another via strong, weak and electromagnetic interactions. In colliding, they exchanged their energy and their momentum. Thus the particles were "in contact" through their thermal motions and their interactions.

Particles underwent subatomic transformations. Photons combined and disappeared, and in their place electrons and positrons *suddenly* appeared. Positrons and electrons self-destructed into photons. Neutrons and neutrinos collided off of one another, ending up as protons and electrons. Protons and electrons smashed and *reemerged* as neutrons and neutrinos. Neutrons and positrons met and *metamorphosed in particle alchemy* as antineutrinos and as protons. Antineutrinos and protons underwent transcendental transformations into positrons and neutrons. But among all these particle conversions, those *involving neutrinos* proceeded relatively *slowly*; the others proceeded rapidly.[41]

Now the Universe's temperature in Kelvins was a hundred-billion.[42] In these hot conditions, there was a thermal equilibrium among the nucleonic states. And as a consequence, the numbers of protons and of neutrons were essentially *the same* – the thermal cosmic sea had *so much* energy to give that the protons and the neutrons were created and destroyed at *equal rates*.

## Episode II: Protons Come to Outnumber Neutrons

Now time advanced and temperature decreased. Soon the protons numbered more than neutrons, for the thermal cosmic sea had *less energy* to give and gave it to the lighter particles: So *protons*, being a little lighter than the neutrons, were *produced* more easily. So *neutrons*, being heavier than protons, were *destroyed* more easily. The neutrons disappeared through sacrifice by giving up their mass in making lighter particles and energy. And thus it came to pass that, when the Universe was one second old and the temperature was ten-billion, there were *six times* as many proton particles as neutrons.

## Episode III: Nucleons Cease Their Subatomic Transformations

Since Episode I, the width of the Universe had grown tenfold. The volume of the Universe had increased a thousandfold. The temperature had dropped tenfold. And the density of particles had declined a thousandfold.

As the Universe got cooler, the weak interaction grew *much weaker*. Since space had pulled the particles apart, particles encoun-

---

[41] Neutrinos only interact through the weak force.

[42] This is about a thousand times hotter than at the center of the Sun.

tered one another less: Collisions among the nucleons decreased. So rare were these collisions and so feeble was the weak force that the proton-neutron particle conversions *ceased*. At this moment, there were six protons for each neutron.

### Episode IV: Neutrinos Decouple and Escape

Now the neutrinos, which only interact through the weak interactions, *no longer* interacted, for the weak force was too weak. Henceforth and forever, these neutrinos *would move freely* through the Universe. The story of these particles would be incredible. They would become *a cosmic non-interacting relic*, a ghost in space and of the past. For eternity would they fill three-space. Though omnipresent, they would be for the rest of time *invisible*.

### Episode V: Positron Annihilations

The age of the Universe increased tenfold. The time was ten seconds. The temperature of the Universe dropped threefold.

And the cosmic sea could *no longer hold* the light charged leptons. Thus electrons and positrons annihilated into photons, as the primordial sea purged itself of positrons. There was a *tremendous flash* of gamma rays. The Universe exploded inside itself as a matter-antimatter bomb *once more*. This would be the last such matter-antimatter bomb.

Now the tiny excess of matter over antimatter, which had existed since Grand-Symmetry destruction, remained as a tiny *excess* of electrons over positrons. And since not every electron found a positron with which it could annihilate, minute amounts of electrons consequently stayed. But the Universe was basically charge-neutral: The number of electrons which survived *equalled* the number of protons in the primordial heat bath, though this number was relatively small – in the cosmic sea, there was but one electron for every billion photons. Thus, in the dense hot-gas bath of photons, there was a *dilute* plasma of positive and negative electric charges in the form of minute protons and electrons. And all this took place in the arena of the Big Bang aftermath.

### Episode VI: The First Deuterons and First Nuclei

Now from time to time, a proton and a neutron merged and formed a *deuteron*. So in the cosmic sea were traces of deuterium.

Now the primordial sea had a strong natural tendency to make helium-four, for helium-four was the *most stable* of the lighter nuclei. But *rarely* did two protons and two neutrons come together to make such helium directly. *Instead*, miniscule amounts of helium-three were manufactured when a proton struck a deuteron or when a neutron and two protons met by chance.

## Episode VII: The Light Nuclei Are Made

Three minutes slipped away. During this long interval, in which thy Universe aged a *dozen-fold*, a fraction of the neutrons did decay – when such a neutron disappeared, an antineutrino, an electron and a proton in its place appeared. And so it came to pass that there were *seven* protons for each neutron.

The temperature dropped further – it was a billion. At this lower temperature, particles swam the cosmic sea with lower energy. And since nucleons *more slowly* moved, strong forces made them *stick together* when nucleons encountered one another. Thus in "nuclear matrimony" did a neutron and a proton merge to make a deuteron. But the deuterons, which were being readily produced, disappeared at almost equally rapid rates, for *instantly* did they combine to forge the heavier light-nuclei: And for example, in the heat bath gas, a deuteron and a deuteron merged to make a proton and a tritium. And nearby, another deuteron and a neutron stuck to form another tritium. One such tritium and a deuteron *instantly* were drawn together by the strong force, and after the two nuclei had merged, a neutron and a helium-four were forged. Elsewhere in the heat-bath gas, one deuteron banged into another deuteron, producing a neutron and a helium-three. In still another place, a deuteron and a proton merged and directly made a helium-three. Then a helium-three and a deuteron collided and emerged as a proton and a helium-four. Elsewhere in the cosmic sea, two deuterons directly forged a photon and a helium-four. And all of these processes proceeded *everywhere* in space.

And the Universe blew up inside itself as an *enormous* fusion bomb. And almost all the neutrons ended up in nuclei of helium-four. And so the neutrons became *enslaved in nuclei*. And miniscule amounts of lithium-seven were fabricated, for a helium-four and a tritium, on rare occasions, made a photon and a lithium-seven.

*And with a few embellishments,*
*in seven stages and three minutes,*
*at a temperature of a billion Kelvins,*
*Nature made the lighter elements.*

## Chapter II: Taking Count

And what was the nuclear score? For weight, one can *ignore* the leptons and the photons, for they are relatively *light*. By weight, seventy-six percent of matter was in protons and twenty-four percent was in the form of helium-four. All neutrons were in helium cores. And as for the other elements, by number, deuterium was one part in ten-thousand, helium-three was ten parts per million, and lithium-seven was one in ten-billion.

Now during the three-minute epoch of nucleosynthesis, the width of the Universe increased a *hundredfold*. And the particle density dropped a *millionfold*. And the energy density of the Universe fell a *billionfold*.

The primordial cosmic egg, which had been so *round and perfect*, had been *broken*. And its contents had been spilled and scattered throughout the vastness of thy Universe – the beginning of the process toward chaos had commenced.

*Humpty Dumpty had a great fall.*

*The tenth book of Creation, called*

# Exodus III: The Radiation-Dominated Universe

*A mysterious wind blew through the Universe,
casting its dust in all directions.*

## Chapter I: The Expanding Universe

*And Nature spread Her wings like a giant albatross,
and space, like air, was pushed apart.*

And during the next twenty-thousand years, *very little* would unfold: there would be no self-destructing annihilations of a particular form of matter with its antimatter, no spontaneous symmetry breakings, no phase transitions, nothing. But the diameter of the Universe would *increase a hundred-thousand fold*. To thirty-thousand degrees the temperature would drop; particles would be pushed apart; and the density of matter would thin to a mere ten-to-the-minus-twenty[43] grams per cubic centimeter.

And as the Universe expanded and cooled, the energies of photons did diminish. And through quantum physics, the character of photons changed[44] – they *passed* from particles to waves: Photons faded into gamma rays, the most energetic form of electromagnetic waves.

And space stretched. And as it stretched, its contents stretched. Thus the *wavelengths* of electromagnetic waves grew *longer*. And the *energies* of such waves *diminished*.[45] And those waves that were gamma rays turned into X-rays. And those waves that were X-rays turned into ultraviolet radiation. And ultraviolet radiation became blue light. And blue light turned into yellow light. And yellow light became red light. And red light faded to the infrared.

And later, when the Universe expanded more, infrared radiation *would* turn into microwaves. And some microwaves would degrade in energy, and radio waves would they become.

---

[43] $10^{-20}$, or one-hundredth of a billionth of a billionth.

[44] See the New Testament Book of *Quantum Mechanics*.

[45] See the New Testament Book of *Electromagnetic Waves*.

Thus the entire electromagnetic spectrum faded, for wavelengths grew as the Universe expanded waves of light. And this effect was provided with a name. And the *red shift* was the name because visible blue light shifted to the red.[46]

And the relic neutrinos of the Universe underwent a red shift of their own – the quantum waves of neutrinos *elongated*, as the Universe expanded and space stretched. And as the wavelengths of neutrinos grew, their energies diminished. And the invisible neutrino-antineutrino gas thus cooled.

And so the energy of the *massless matter* – the photons and neutrinos – *lessened*. As space expanded more, their energies continued to diminish. Thus the energy in massless matter composed an ever dwindling fraction of the Universe's total energy.

In the energy battle between the massless and the massive particles, the massive lagged behind the massless but were quickly catching up. Eventually, the massive would surpass the massless. The massive would ultimately win the race.

*It was like the story of the tortoise and the hare.*

## Chapter II: The Radiation-Matter Demarcation

*Even angels seemed to languish.*

It was twenty-thousand years after the Big Bang. Thy Universe was thirty-thousand Kelvins hot. And the energy in photons and neutrinos *dropped* below the mass-energy of nucleons. And the mass-energy of nucleons became the driving impetus in the expansion of the Universe. The expansion of the Universe *increased somewhat*. Henceforth, the Universe would grow at a relatively slightly faster pace. Henceforth, the protons and the neutrons in nuclei would determine thy Universe's fate. And mass would dominate and drive the *stretching* of expanding space.

And twenty-thousand years was declared to be a demarcation point. And the old Universe, the Universe up to this point in time, was provided with a name. And the name was the *radiation-dominated Universe* because hitherto radiation, travelling at the speed of light, drove the expansion of the Universe. And the new Universe, the Universe henceforth, was also provided with a name. And the name was the *matter-dominated Universe* because matter, in the form of protons and of neutrons, henceforth would drive the expansion of the Universe.

*Translucent wings no longer fanned the cosmic fire.*
*Twenty-thousand years of flapping had diminished their desire.*
*The Universe had simply grown too large.*
*Now husky blacksmiths with bellows were in charge.*

---

[46] There are several different types of red shifts. This one is the *cosmological red shift.*

*The eleventh book of Creation, called*

# Exodus IV: Recombination

*Let there be light.*
*And there was light.*

## Chapter I: The Blindingly Bright Universe

Now the Universe was a *brilliant* glowing bath of *light*. Any light that was created was *instantly destroyed*, for it was absorbed by protons or electrons. And light re-emitted by these particles had hardly any time to move. If ye had been there it would have been impossible to even see an atom's length away, for the fog of light did fog the "sight" – it was a bath of light too bright to see; the World was *blinded* by its own brilliant light.

Now thy Universe consisted of a plasma – space was *filled* with charge. And negatively charged electrons and positively charged hydrogen and helium nuclei were everywhere. And although these changes swam in *separate* seas, together did they form a neutral gas. So protons moved about electrons, and electrons moved about the protons. And now and then did an electron and a proton bind. Thus *for a moment* did an atom form.[47] But such an atom did *not last*, for instantly a ray of light knocked the two constituents apart. The Universe was "blinded" in its light, for electromagnetic waves were constantly *absorbed, reflected* and *emitted* by the charges in the plasma gas.

The Universe was three-hundred-thousand years in age. And the temperature was eight-thousand Kelvins – slightly hotter than the surface of the Sun.[48] And since the matter-radiation demarcation point, space had grown sixfold.

## Chapter II: Atom Formation

And electromagnetic radiation continued to red shift. And when it shifted to the red, it cooled. And as it cooled, it *lost* its energy and struck electrons with *less force*. And electrons in the gas lost energy and moved about less vigorously.

And it came to pass that rays of light had *insufficient energy* to kick electrons out of nuclei, when electrons bound to nuclei. And so, when electrons tied themselves to nuclei, they *stayed* – it was the electric force of Nature that made them stay. And thus it came to pass that electrons orbited the nuclei *and atoms formed*. And when an electron and a proton bound, an atom of hydrogen appeared. And with one plus charge in the nucleus and one minus charge in the electron, such a hydrogen atom had *no net charge*. And when an electron and a helium

---

[47] By definition, an atom consists of one or more electrons surrounding a nucleus.
[48] The Sun, of course, did not yet exist.

nucleus did bind, a helium-plus atom formed. And with two plus charges and one minus charge, such a helium-plus was positively charged. And when an electron and helium-plus atom bound, an atom of helium appeared. And with two plus charges and two minus charges, such heliums had *no net charge*. And so it came to pass that electrons and nuclei tied themselves together, until all atoms had *no net charge. Thus* it came to pass that the plasma changed into a *neutral gas*.

*And it was declared that positive charges*
*and negative charges*
*would no longer swim in separate seas.*
*Now electrons still repelled electrons.*
*And protons repelled protons.*
*But pluses moved about in search of minuses.*
*And minuses moved about in search of pluses.*
*And all this happened because the Universe had cooled,*
*and as a result, a kind of cosmic mating-dance of charge ensued.*
*And electrons swirled about prospective proton spouses.*
*Their motions and their movements unrehearsed*
*took place in the theater of the Universe.*
*Electrons danced about the protons,*
*ignoring neutrinos, neutrons and the photons.*
*In the beginning, electrons were rather energetic.*
*And the protons tried to trapped them in an orbit.*
*But the electrons seemed not very sympathetic,*
*for there was too much commotion in their motion.*
*But then the temperature did drop a bit.*
*And the electrons tired and they became less frantic.*
*They felt the pull of the electric-charge attraction.*
*The electrons could no longer live in isolation.*
*There came about the largest ever wedding ceremony.*
*And particles paired in holy cosmic matrimony.*
*It was a splendid moment in atomic history.*
*Each marriage of a pair produced a little scintillation.*
*And all this was due to the electromagnetic interaction.*

And when electrons were captured by the nuclei in atoms, light *was* emitted. And since there were so many electrons and so many nuclei, light *was* produced profusely. There was a *tremendous flash* throughout the Universe. And the radiation was ultraviolet, blue, yellow, red, and infrared. All this lasted for several thousand years as ten-to-the-eighty[49] electrons paired with ten-to-the-eighty protons to form ten-to-the-eighty atoms of hydrogen and helium. And this event in

---

[49] $10^{80}$, or one-hundred-million-trillion-trillion-trillion-trillion-trillion-trillion.

cosmic history was provided with a name. And *Recombination* was the name.[50]

*And a few protons and electrons found no lover.*
*And a few separated charges would remain left over.*

## Chapter III: The Last Light

*Thy Universe turned dark.*

And during Recombination, the Universe *scintillated* in radiant brilliant light. Now at the end of Recombination, when almost all electrons were bound to nuclei, the production of light gradually stopped. And eventually, the Universe turned *dark and black*. Henceforth, the Universe would continue to be *dark and black*. And *the first day for the Universe*, which had lasted three-hundred-thousand years, was over. And *the first night for the Universe* began. And this night would last for the next fifteen-billion years or so, for the first day of the Universe was *its last day*. Forever forth would it be night.

And the black of sky, which ye see after the Sun sets, is the black of the Universe, *as it was* three-hundred-thousand years after the Big Bang, *as it has been* for the last fifteen-billion years, *as it is* unto this day.

*On the last day of Recombination,*
*the last light was made, and there was darkness.*
*Let there be light and darkness.*

## Chapter IV: The Cosmic Background Electromagnetic Radiation

*And the gate of it shall not be shut at end of day,*
*for there shall be no day.*

And *so it had come to pass* that the Universe had undergone a phase transition, from a plasma to a gas. And the formation of atoms had rendered matter neutral. And so electromagnetic radiation interacted weakly with the atoms.[51] And these interactions were *so weak* that electromagnetic waves were *liberated*. Thus photons travelled *undisturbed* – their fate became the same fate of the Deuteronomy neutrinos.[52] And cosmic photons, like cosmic neutrinos, became invisible and formed a *cosmic relic*, travelling through the Universe without disturbance *for the rest of time*.

---

[50] Recombination signifies the coming together of electrons and nuclei to form neutral atoms. Although the two had never been bound before so that "combination" would have been a better name, the word "recombination" was selected just the same.

[51] Neutral matter interacts more weakly than charged matter, for it is charge that creates electromagnetic interaction.

[52] These neutrinos were discussed in the ninth book of Creation.

Thy Universe was one one-thousandth of the size it is today.

*And husky blacksmiths pounded at the anvil*
*and fanned the hearth*
*and kept the Universe expanding at a steady pace.*

And whereas the first few minutes of the Universe had been a series of events in which symmetries were broken, the next fifteen-billion years would be characterized by *the collapse of matter* under gravity at different distance scales in space.

*The twelfth book of Creation, called*

# Exodus V: Large-Scale Structure

*The seeds were cast out into a vast field.*

### Chapter I: Density Inhomogeneities

Now after Recombination, the Universe was highly homogeneous – matter was *evenly* dispersed throughout the Universe. And after Recombination, the Universe was also isotropic – it appeared the same from *every point of view*. Thus the Universe was in a democratic state – no particular point of space could claim to be its center.

*The Universe was not self-centered.*
*The Universe was center-less.*

Thus matter, energy and radiation were very *evenly distributed*. And over great distances were they uniform to less than one part in ten-thousand. But there existed smaller than one-part-in-ten-thousand fluctuations – such regions of tiny variation were *density inhomogeneities*. And so the Universe possessed pockets of space that were *less dense* by one part in one-hundred-thousand. And so the Universe possessed pockets of space that were *denser* by one part in one-hundred-thousand.

Now these density inhomogeneities would play a crucial role – they would shape *the structure* of the Universe; they would govern the formation of its contents, for they would become the *seeds of galactic superclusters* and *of giant voids*.

### Chapter II: Proto-Galactic-Superclusters

Now it happened that in one particular region of the Universe, there was a *denser* spot. And the matter in that region, being more, *attracted* by its gravity more matter. And the region *gained* a little mass. And when it gained more mass, its gravity grew *stronger*. And the stronger pull attracted *even more* material. Thus the dense spot grew more dense.

Now the matter in this region would eventually come together and form a giant structure – a *galactic supercluster*. Within it, dozens of galaxy clusters would there be. And in each *galaxy cluster*, hundreds and even thousands of galaxies would be. Thus tens of thousands of galaxies would arise from each dense density-inhomogeneity.

And there were *hundreds of thousands* of dense density-inhomogeneities within the Universe. Thus there would eventually be *hundreds of thousands* of galactic superclusters in the Universe.

## Chapter III: Proto-Giant-Voids

Now it happened that there was a particular pocket in the Universe where matter was *less dense*. And the matter in that region, being less, did *not* attract more matter. Instead, the matter in it was attracted to surrounding denser regions by Nature's force of gravity. And the pocket *lost* a little mass. And when it lost a little mass, its gravity grew *weaker* so that it attracted surrounding matter *even less*. Now the mass which the pocket lost was accumulated by surrounding regions. Thus surrounding regions *gained* more mass. And the stronger pull of gravity from nearby regions *pulled* more mass away. Thus the less-dense pocket grew less dense. Eventually would it become a *giant void*, containing few if any galaxies.

And there were *hundreds of thousands* of less-dense density-inhomogeneities within the Universe. Thus there would eventually be *hundreds of thousands* of giant voids within the Universe.

*Thus Nature's force of gravity*
*began to shape the Universe.*

## Chapter IV: Structure Formation

Now the Universe would expand *a hundredfold* during the next fifteen-billion years. And density inhomogeneities expanding with expanding space would be stretched *a hundredfold*. And so a region of an inhomogeneity, which measured a few million light years across, *would grow* to be a few hundred-million light years. And in several billion years, the *large-scale structure of the Universe*, which would consist of galactic superclusters and of giant voids, would indeed be large.

And the *dense parts* of the Universe would grow *more dense*. And the *less-dense parts* of the Universe would grow *less dense*. Thus it would come to pass that the smoothness of the Universe *would* not last.

*It was written in a sacred text:*
*"The rich get richer and the poor get poorer."*
*And in the Universe,*
*the rich got richer and the poor got poorer too.*

*The thirteenth book of Creation, called*

# Exodus VI: Quasars

*Let there be lights in Heaven – candles for the night.*
*And this happened on the fourth day*
*of the first month of a long lost year.*

## Chapter I: A Cloud of Gas Collapses

Now the Universe, which had had so much light, was black as night. And it was *as if* the Christian, Roman, Greek, Tibetan, Hindu, Moslem and Egyptian gods joined in prayer and prayed for light. And it was *as if* in darkness they nodded heads before the sacred walls of stone that housed the Universe. And Nature *seemed* to hear their prayers. And Nature so responded.

Now it was five-hundred-million years after the Big Bang. And it came to pass that, in one black region of the Universe, there was a *cold cloud* of atomic hydrogen and helium gas. And the gas of the outer parts of the cloud *felt* the pull of gravity from the gas of the inner parts of the cloud. And the gas of the outer parts moved in. And the cloud became *smaller* and more dense.

And in the gas, a hydrogen atom bumped another hydrogen atom. And the two *stuck together*, making a molecule of hydrogen. And there was a "pop," as the binding process released energy. And the molecule spun and shook. And elsewhere in the cloud, other atoms of hydrogen combined as $H_2$ molecules were made.

And the cloud continued getting smaller and more dense. And *many* atoms came together and made molecules. The chemical energy *released* was converted into thermal energy and heat. And the temperature of the cloud increased.

## Chapter II: The Cloud Gets Dense and Hot

And tens of millions of years went by. And it had come to pass that the cloud was much smaller than before – the cloud had undergone *collapse*. The cloud's center, which was its *core*, had the highest density of gas. *There*, molecules moved, bumped and pushed against each other. And so the pressure there was high.

Now gas in the outer parts of the cloud was *drawn inward* by the force of gravity. And gas surrounding the central region accelerated and *struck* gas in the core. And the helium atoms and molecules of hydrogen so shook. And the temperature in the center rose – the temperature was much higher than before. Thus it came to pass that, in the center of the cloud, there was a *dense hydrogen and helium hot core*.

And gas continued to *pour* into the core. And the pressure and the density increased more. And the temperature increased as well. And it happened that the two atoms in a hydrogen molecule shook *so violently* that they did separate. And the same was true for other molecules. Thus in the core, molecules of hydrogen *broke up* into atomic hydrogen.

And gas continued *flowing uncontrollably* into the center of the cloud. And as the core's mass grew, the force of gravity increased. And as the force of gravity increased, the acceleration of surrounding gas grew stronger. And surrounding gas struck core gas *with great force* – it was *like unto* a blacksmith striking iron; the iron warmed. *Thus* the core grew warm. And more collisions of gas molecules did make it heat. And eventually, it grew so hot *it glowed*. And light, infrared and ultraviolet radiation were produced. And the radiation was *absorbed* by surrounding gas. And as light and ultraviolet radiation struck electrons, the electrons *were ejected* out of atoms: Atoms in the core dissociated into electrons, helium nuclei and protons. It was the reverse of what had happened in Recombination. And the outward flow of radiation created a pressure, which tried to slow the inward flow of gas. But the core was *so dense and so massive* that its force of gravity overwhelmed the outward pressure. And gas continued to pour relentlessly into the core.

And the central density grew great – the contents of the gas were *squeezed together*. And the central pressure increased more, as the contents of the gas rammed against each other forcibly. And the central temperature in Kelvins reached a million. The heat *ignited* thermonuclear reactions: In the core, through fusion processes, the nuclei of deuterium and hydrogen combined, making helium-four and *destroying mass*. Thus mass turned into energy as heat and radiation. But the surrounding gas was so dense and vast, that the heat and radiation *did not escape* the cloud but were absorbed by it. And although thermonuclear fusions created great amounts of heat, energy and radiation, the *acceleration of gas* into the center generated *even more*. And although heat, radiation and pressure tried to slow the inward flow of gas, the core was so massive and so dense that *gravitation overpowered all*. And gas continued to pour relentlessly into the core.

## Chapter III: The Core Neutronizes

And tens of millions of years did pass. And the pressure in the core became *immense*. And the pressure pushed the protons, neutrons and electrons into one another. Particles were *crushed together*. And for example, in one spot in the core, an electron was *squeezed* into a proton – a neutrino and a neutron were produced. And the neutrino at the speed of light streamed out the core. But the neutron stayed behind. As other protons and electrons fused into neutrons and neutrinos, a *kernel* of neutrons formed at the center of the core.

And the collapse of matter under gravity continued. *Overwhelming* was the pressure. In the core, the protons, neutrons and electrons everywhere were squeezed together. And the neutron kernel grew, becoming *a giant nucleus of neutrons.*

> *The circus strongman*
> *in a theatrical act of magic*
> *squeezed a rock.*
> *It was mystical:*
> *Out of the rock seeped water –*
> *the rock* seemed *to be a sponge.*
> *In his hand, the rock transformed into a crystal.*

And in great numbers streamed neutrinos out the core. Some scattered off of neutrons, protons and electrons just outside the core. These neutrino interactions caused a pressure that *tried* to slow the inward flow of matter. But the neutron kernel and the core were so massive and so dense that *gravitation overpowered all.* And matter continued to pour relentlessly into the kernel and the core.

Gas half way out in the middle of the cloud flowed into the central region at a steady pace – in the core *so much* matter was swallowed *in such a tiny space.*

## Chapter IV: A Giant Black Hole Forms

And tens of millions of years went by. And it came to pass that the kernel did contain incredible amounts of mass. It was *so dense* – unimaginably dense. And in a region the size of the solar system – five-billion kilometers[53] across – a mass of *two-hundred-million* suns had been accumulated. The force of gravity in the core was strong – incredibly, unimaginably strong.

And a light ray was emitted from a neutron in the kernel core. And the ray rose, slowed and then fell back into the kernel, *like unto* a ball thrown up on Earth. And elsewhere, light rose, slowed and fell back down – it was like a fountain not of water but of light. And *nothing*, not even light, escaped the core – the accumulation of concentrated mass had made a *black hole* in the core. The cloth of space was torn – it had been ripped apart. And a piece of the visible Universe was gone.

And so it came to pass that the kernel was one immense black hole. Around it was the cloud of gas, which stretched out in space two-hundred-thousand light years.

The *collapse* of gas and matter, the *increase* in temperature, the *bending* of three-space – all these things made it seem as if this tiny section of the Universe had undergone a Big Bang in miniature and *in reverse.*

---

[53] A kilometer is about 0.6 miles so that five-billion kilometers is about three-billion miles.

## Chapter V: A Quasar Is Made

*And there was a great light*
*in this piece of the Universe.*

And the gas around the central region tumbled *inward*. And atoms of hydrogen and helium moved faster and faster, as they fell in. And within the inward flowing gas, the atoms bumped each other, and in doing so they shook. And when they shook, electrons bounced about and were *ejected*. So the atoms separated into helium nuclei, protons and electrons. And these particles sped faster and faster as *they* streamed in, almost reaching the speed of light when deep inside the cloud. And it was *like unto* a shell of lightning collapsing and converging on the kernel core. And *enormous* quantities of energy and radiation were produced. As gamma-rays, X-rays and other electric-and-magnetic rays struck surrounding gas, they were deflected and reflected, *and* they were absorbed and re-emitted. And the flow of proton and electron charges created *strong* magnetic fields. And these fields were *squeezed* and focused by the black hole's gravitation. And the squeezing of magnetic fields created further rays and radiation.

As the *surrounding gas* absorbed the rays and radiation, *it* grew *hot*. And the gas got *so hot* that it *too* emitted rays and radiation. And these rays and radiation were absorbed again by gas surrounding the surrounding gas. And so, this gas grew hot and it *too* emitted rays and radiation. These *rays and radiation* were absorbed and re-emitted in the *next* gas layer. And so on did they propagate until they reached the outer limit of the cloud. Then they were *free* to speed across the emptiness of space.

And the giant cloud glowed with a brightness of a *hundred-billion* stars – the luminous output of a galaxy. And the cloud, the kernel and the core were provided with a name. And they were named a *quasar*. A quasar had been born.

And the *blackness* in this part of the Universe *partially* was gone. In one dark corner of the Universe, a *bulb* had been turned on.

*And in the Heavens did sound a trumpet*
*to celebrate a cosmic triumph.*
*A translucent figure flapped its wings and blew a horn.*
*And still another figure sang a song,*
*"In a corner of the Universe, a quasar has been born."*

## Chapter VI: The Quasar Evolves

And twenty-five million years went by. The quasar still shone with the brightness of a *hundred-billion* stars. Now the *outer region* of the quasar cloud was *lumpy*: There were *dense regions* of hydrogen and helium, which constituted countless minute[54] clouds of gas. But elsewhere, there were *voids*. And it was during the past few million years that these voids and lumpy structures had developed. And what had happened was *like unto* an overcast day on Earth in which a cloud cover broke and thinned and left behind a bunch of little clouds.

Now the *middle region* of the quasar, which engulfed the core, had no voids. However *there*, the gas was also lumpy – some parts were dense, while other parts were thin. The *dense parts* were *high concentrations* of gas and mass; the *thin parts* were *low concentrations*. And the dense parts looked like bright minute clouds against the thinner less bright background.

And the entire quasar system slowly turned about its center, *like unto* the waters in a whirlpool but the rotation speed was slower. Now regions of gas revolved at different rates. And the regions that revolved the *slowest* moved *almost directly at* the center. And when the protons, neutrons and electrons in such gas reached the central region, they were accelerated. And they produced *enormous* quantities of rays and radiation. And the rays and radiation struck surrounding gas, thereby producing an outward force, which slowed the inward flow of gas.

And each year, the black-hole kernel swallowed mass equivalent to several dozen suns. And the matter that the kernel swallowed fueled the quasar, for such accelerating matter did release enormous quantities of radiation. And the quasar shone with the brightness of a *hundred-billion* suns.

## Chapter VII: The Quasar Ages

And twenty-five million years went by. And it came to pass that the huge black hole had swallowed all the slowly circulating matter. And gas continued to trickle in but at a *slower rate*. And rays and radiation were generated but at a *lesser pace*. And the central region still shone but it no longer was so blinding bright. Thus the power of the quasar had subsided – less light flowed from it to outer space. And from afar, it seemed *like unto* a five-watt light-bulb in the black of night. A weakening of the active core had taken place.

> *The bonfire burned its wood*
> *until the wood was gone.*
> *But some hot coals still glowed.*

And it came to pass that the quasar cloud was ellipsoid-shaped with several fin-like structures. And it came to pass that the thinner regions thinned and had less gas.

---

[54] Minute here means in relation to the size of the giant quasar system. On a human scale, these clouds were huge.

## Chapter VIII: A Galaxy Would Be

And in another two-hundred-million years, the quasar would die out. And another system would evolve from it and take its place. Denser regions would condense. There, *stars* would form. And so a galaxy would be. And its shape would be a spiral pie. A gigantic black hole *would* be hidden in its center. And galactic gas and stars would circulate around. And the black hole and the core would anchor all – they would be the *galactic active nucleus* of the new-born galaxy.

## Chapter IX: Quasars and Proto-Galaxies Are Made

And *elsewhere* in the Universe, other *giant clouds* of gas collapsed. And *those*, in which the mass of the central core was more than a hundred-million solar masses,[55] turned into quasars. And those that had less mass became proto-galaxies without a quasar infancy.[56]

And during the first few billion years or so, a quasar every several years was made by Nature.

And during the first ten-billions of years or so, a few proto-galaxies each year were fabricated by the hands of Nature.

## Chapter X: Nature Lights Up the Universe

And thy Universe was *like unto* an enormous black room with billions of unlit light bulbs. And the bulbs varied in wattage from one watt to five-hundred watts. And *randomly* a mysterious being turned on the bulbs. And one by one and sometimes two at a time, bulbs lit up. And the bulbs that burned the *brightest* burned the *quickest* and became dim bulbs. And the bulbs that burned dimly burned steadily and lasted *for a longer time*. And eventually, almost all bulbs in the room were lit. But the room was *very large* and, even with all bulbs on, the room was *nearly black*.

*The blackness of the Universe was in part gone.*
*All over the Universe, bulbs were turning on.*

And know thee and all around thee for now and for forever that, at the heart of almost every galaxy, there is an anchor. And that the anchor *be* a dense black hole.

---

[55] One solar mass is equivalent to the mass of the Sun.

[56] In most proto-galaxies, the collapse of matter still formed a black hole at the central core. Often the black hole had a mass of many million solar masses. Thus the key difference between a non-quasar proto-galaxy and a quasar was the quantity of central mass. In the case of a non-quasar proto-galaxy, less mass in the core produced a weaker gravitation force. Although the gravitational force was still fairly strong, the pressure of outward flowing radiation was able to better match the inward pull of gravity. Thus at a primordial stage, a balance was obtained and the uncontrollable flow of gas into the core was slowed. In place of a blindingly brilliant quasar core, an active proto-galactic nucleus arose. Thus in the blackness of the Universe, the proto-galaxies still glowed but significantly less brightly than their quasar counterparts.

*The fourteenth book of Creation, called*

# Exodus VII: Stellar Birth

*Let there be one candle to light the night.*

## Chapter I: A Gas Cloud

It was a billion years after the Big Bang. Now it so happened that *a cold dark cloud* of hydrogen and helium gas several hundred-billion kilometers in size floated in a region of the wilderness of space. And primordial hydrogen and helium were densely concentrated at the *center* of the cloud. Thus much mass was in the middle of the cloud. And there, Nature's force of gravity *pulled* in surrounding gas. And the amount of hydrogen and helium in the middle grew. But gas in the outer reaches of the cloud did hardly move – it floated *as if unaware* of what was happening inside.

## Chapter II: The Core Heats Up

And several hundred-thousands years went by. And it came to pass that the central region of the cloud was *very dense* – large amounts of hydrogen and helium had been accumulated there. And the pull of gravity *being strong* drew nearby gas into the center. Thus the central region gained more mass.

Now hydrogen and helium halfway from the center slowly drifted inward. But the gas in the outer parts did *hardly* move. And the flow *was as* that of water in a bathtub when the plug is first removed – the water near the drain goes quickly down, but the water far from the drain does hardly move.

Deep inside the cloud, molecules rushed to the center. And *molecules* gained speed and bumped. And as they sped and bumped, *they* gained thermal energy. And the center of the cloud, which had hitherto been cold, did warm. And as the central region warmed and grew *more dense*, the pressure rose. And the increased pressure slowed the flow of gas into the center. But the cloud of gas *continued* to collapse. And as more gas fell toward the center, the cloud began to rotate slightly – the effect was *like unto* a skater who draws in her arms and spins a little faster, but this cloud spun much more slowly than a skater.

And somewhat later, it came to pass that the central core *grew hot* enough that it began to *glow* – infrared and red light were produced. And as this radiation was absorbed by surrounding gas, surrounding gas began to warm.

And several hundred-thousand years did pass. And the temperature in Kelvins at the center was three-thousand: The core glowed *like unto* a kiln. But the light and radiation were absorbed by gas in the colder outer parts. And since the core was covered in cold dense gas, the light did not leak out. And from far away, the black cloud *was in-*

*visible* against the black backdrop of outer space – it was *as if* the door of a hot kiln were closed.

## Chapter III: The Cloud Collapses and the Core Heats More

Now *hydrogen molecules* just outside the core were struck by light and radiation. And energy was absorbed. And when it was absorbed, the two hydrogen atoms in a molecule did *fly apart*. Thus hydrogen molecules broke up, as *molecular* hydrogen became *atomic* hydrogen – the molecules were split.

Now since this breakup of molecules absorbed much energy and heat, the growth in temperature did slow. And this also eased the rise in pressure. But as the core acquired mass, the force of gravity continued to increase. And soon gravity did *overpower* pressure. And *suddenly* the core *collapsed*; the temperature and pressure *surged*. And when the pressure was enough, *the* collapse subsided. And it came to pass that the central temperature was ten-thousand Kelvins hot. And electrons in absorbing both light and radiation were *knocked out* of atoms. Thus atoms dissociated – each became an electron and a nucleus. And the central gas became a plasma of alpha particles,[57] protons and electrons.

Now the separation of atoms into nuclei and electrons absorbed a lot of energy, which slowed the rise in temperature and pressure. But the core *continued to accumulate* material. And the force of gravity continued to increase. And gravity once more did *overpower* pressure. Again the core did suddenly *collapse*. And as it fell in upon itself, the temperature, the pressure and the density shot up; the latter reached the density of water. And when the pressure increased enough, *the* collapse subsided. The central temperature was *one-hundred-thousand* Kelvins – the core was very hot.

Yet farther from the core, the temperature was low. And the outer parts of *the* gas cloud were even colder. And it came to pass that the collapse had shrunk the *cloud's* diameter – fifty-billion kilometers was now *its* size.

Now it was ellipsoid-shaped. And slowly did the cloud rotate. Most gas circulated round the center like planets moving round the Sun. But as the core gained mass, the force of gravity increased. And so the gas *also* drifted in. Thus most gas slowly *spiralled in* toward the center of the cloud. But gas *above* the main bulge of the cloud and *above* the core did hardly turn. And this gas was drawn directly down and *quickly* to the core. Likewise, gas *below* the main bulge of the cloud and *below* the core was drawn directly up and *quickly* to the core. Thus it came to pass that the gas cloud did get flatter. The cloud's shape was pancake-like.

---

[57] An *alpha particle* is a helium-four nucleus.

*The hand of gravity did mold the cloud.*

And through the force of gravitation, the mass within the core continued *pulling in* more gas. And as the gas approached the core, it sped up, moving faster and still faster till it struck the core. And when it struck the core, a *shock wave* of pressure was produced. The shock wave's energy was great, causing a rise in temperature of a *million* Kelvins in some places. In the region where the shock wave sped, hot gas radiated *brilliantly*, then cooled to the surrounding temperatures, which were ten-thousand Kelvins. Although the surface of the core glowed *ten times brighter* than the Sun, its light and radiation were repeatedly absorbed and re-emitted by surrounding cooler gas. And almost all the energy in radiation ended up in the enveloping gas cloud. And from afar, the cloud was *visibly dark* but glowed in infrared.

## Chapter IV: A Star Is Born

And several million years went by. And it came to pass that the core shrank considerably. The temperature in Kelvins at the center reached a *million*. And deuterium nuclei, which were dilutely present in the gas, *fused* with protons to produce nuclei of helium-three.[58] Then helium-three nuclei combined, forming nuclei of helium-four. And the conversion of deuterium into helium-four *destroyed some mass*. Thus mass was converted into energy. And because the destruction of a little mass produced a lot of energy, a lot of energy *was* produced. So in the center of the core, *thermonuclear fusion* generated energy. The core was now a *star*. A star had thus been born. And although there was little deuterium – two nuclei for every hundred-thousand protons – deuterium did fuel the star.

Now the thermonuclear ignition of deuterium did cause a *fusion bomb*: The reactions *raised* the temperature. As the temperature did rise, reactions took place *even quicker*. And boom! The fusion bomb went off. A pressure wave swelled from the center. The star's outer layer blew off. Electromagnetic radiation blasted hard against surrounding gas. Gas was propelled outward and dispersed throughout the wilderness of outer space. All that remained were the inner core of the star and heavy cloud debris.

And the star swelled to *thirty* times the volume of the Sun. And then the star regained stability. It radiated *brilliantly*. And from trillions of kilometers away and farther, the star was *highly visible*.

*A tiny light in a dark, tiny part of outer space*
*had been turned on.*
*The blackness in this small region of the Universe*
*partially was gone.*

---

[58] For more information about the physics processes and terminology in this chapter and the next, see the New Testament Book of *Nuclear Physics*.

And deuterium continuously burned at the *center* of the star. And this thermonuclear energy was absorbed by plasma gas. And in growing hot, this gas expanded. And in expanding did its pressure drop. And in expanding did *it* get relatively *light* as well. And *like unto* a hot-air balloon, the bubble of hot gas *did rise*, surging to the surface of the star. There, it radiated and it *cooled*. And when it cooled, it did contract. And when it contracted, it grew relatively *heavy*. And the cooler, relatively heavy gas *sank* toward the center of the star and filled the places vacated by hot, expanding rising gas. Then thermonuclear reactions in the core heated this relatively cooler gas. And it grew hot, expanded, rose and radiated. Thus the star convected – the star boiled *like unto* boiling water.

And as the star radiated, it lost energy. And when it lost energy, it shrank somewhat. And when it shrank, the pressure rose a bit. And when the pressure rose, the temperature grew slightly. Thus the star slowly *decreased* in size and slowly *increased* in temperature. And the slow gravitational collapse heated the interior of the star and became its principal source of energy.

## Chapter V: The Star Heats Up

And thirty-million years went by. The star was somewhat smaller than the Sun. The central temperature attained *ten-million*, initiating new thermonuclear reactions: the helium-four production from four protons. The process was as follows. Two protons *fused* and made a deuteron, a positron and a neutrino. The neutrino streamed out the star and into outer space. The positron immediately *annihilated* an electron, producing *energetic* photons. The deuteron quickly did absorb a proton and become a helium-three, while another energetic photon was emitted. Helium-three *fused* with itself, producing a helium-four nucleus and a pair of protons.

And this process was named the *proton-proton chain*. And in effect, six protons in the core were processed into two photons, two positrons, two protons, two neutrinos and a helium-four.

And in the proton-proton chain, mass was verily *destroyed*. And the destruction of mass generated great outputs of all types of energy. And the energy was transmitted to the photons and the protons, heating up the star. And as the temperature increased, the protons fused *more rapidly*. And this caused the energy output to increase and made *more radiations* in the core. Such radiations created a stronger outward pressure, which *pushed* the star apart. And as the star expanded, the rise in temperature did slow. And an equilibrium was then achieved. And to fifteen-million Kelvins did the central temperature so settle. And the star became of solar size.

And henceforth for billions of years, the star would burn its protons in its core and radiate light brilliantly.

*The fifteenth book of Creation, called*

# Exodus VIII: Galactic Birth

*These stars would be the candles –*
*they would light the way.*

## Chapter I: A Galaxy Is Born

And within two-hundred-thousand light years of the new-born star, *other* dense clouds collapsed and glowed. And each year, a hundred new such stars appeared. And after millions of years, there were several hundred million stars. And if ye had been there, it would have looked *like unto* a city in the evening, seen from far away: Initially, a few lights turned on. Then more. Then still more. And gradually spots of lights filled what once had been black void. And this collection of stars was provided with a name – the name was *galaxy*. A galaxy was born.

And gas in the galaxy was consumed to form new stars. And after a billion years, the galaxy held a *hundred-billion* stars. As gas was consumed, the *gas available* for making stars *decreased*, and so the production of new stars did slow. And so it came to pass that only a few new stars per year were made. And some of the older and more massive stars *quickly* burned their nuclear fuels and thus *died out*. And the number of stars in the galaxy did hardly increase.

*And in the Heavens did sound a trumpet*
*to celebrate a cosmic triumph.*
*A translucent figure flapped its wings and blew a horn.*
*And still another figure sang a song,*
*"In a corner of the Universe, a galaxy 's been born."*

## Chapter II: The Starlit Universe Appears

And *elsewhere* in the Universe floated another giant cloud hundreds of thousands of light years across. And under its gravity, the giant cloud *collapsed*. And as it collapsed, denser regions formed. And it came to pass that there were hundreds of millions of such denser regions. And each one turned into one or many stars. Thus *hundreds of millions* of stars were born. Thus from a giant cloud of primordial hydrogen and helium, *another* galaxy was formed.

And the Universe contained *billions* of such giant primordial gas clouds. And throughout the Universe, which was just a few billion years old and a few billion light years big, *billions* of galaxies were born.

And it was *like unto a vast forest* wherein each hundredth tree was decorated with *countless* unlit candles. And in the center of each tree was a *powerful bulb*. Now in the beginning, the forest was completely black. And randomly a mysterious being *seemed* to turn on lights. And the first object on a tree to glow was the central bulb. And one by one and sometimes two at a time, bulbs throughout the vast black forest did start to glow. Now the brightest bulbs burned quickly, subsequently dimmed and less brightly shone. And shortly after the central bulb of a tree turned on, nearby candles began to burn with flames. And randomly a mysterious being *seemed* to light the candles – a few at a time did light, sometimes a dozen lit at once. And gradually all the candles in a tree had flames. Thus throughout the vast forest randomly did trees become completely lit. And eventually, almost every one was lit. But the forest was *vast* and its blackness *great*. And even with such lighted trees *was* the forest fairly dark.

*The darkness of the Universe partially was gone.*
*All over the Universe lights were turning on.*

*The sixteenth book of Creation, called*

# Exodus IX: A Special Spiral Galaxy

*Out of the dust emerged a mighty structure.*

## Chapter I: Two Gas Clouds Merge

It was three-billion years after the Big Bang. And it so happened that a one-million-light-year-wide *cold gas cloud* sped across an empty region of the Universe. Now three-million light years away, a *second huge cold cloud* floated motionless.

And five-hundred-million years went by. And during this time, both clouds shrank in size, so that each was half as big. And each had a central region, which was *dense* with gas. Now the distance between the two clouds had verily decreased – in light years it was one-and-one-half million.

And another five-hundred-million years went by. And it came to pass that the first cloud *collided* with the second. Their central regions *merged*. And two clouds turned into one – it was the *union of two great gas clouds*. And their hydrogen molecules and helium atoms mixed. The merging of the clouds made gas and matter *twice as dense*.

And more matter meant more gravity. And the force of gravity increased significantly. And gas throughout the giant cloud felt a *stronger pull*. And gas sped toward the center of the cloud, causing it to decrease in size and grow *more dense* – the cloud was undergoing a *collapse*.

## Chapter II: A Proto-Galaxy Appears[59]

And one-hundred-million years went by. And it had come to pass that *great amounts* of matter had fallen into the center of the giant cloud, which was its *core*. The core was dense and hot and glowed. And for millions of years, hydrogen and helium gas did pour into the central core.

Another hundred-million years went by. And it had come to pass that a *huge black hole* had been created at the center of the core. And around this core, hot dense gas did *glow* and *radiate*.

Now when viewed from far away, the core was just a *small* part of the giant cloud: Elsewhere were comparatively small but dense gas regions, which looked like white flakes against the less dense regions of the gas. And these denser regions joined to form a shape and structure *like unto* an octopus. And the white octopus-like structure was engulfed in an even larger *sphere-shaped halo* of thin gas four-hundred-thousand light years in diameter.

*It was* like unto *a giant embryo.*

A proto-galaxy had formed. And the active central core was its proto-galactic nucleus.

And several hundred-million years went by. And it came to pass that the giant gas cloud grew smaller, with a diameter of one-hundred-thousand light years. When viewed from far away, its shape was somewhat irregular but basically ellipsoidal – like a *sphere* that has been *squashed*. And the middle section of the cloud consisted of a single gaseous structure of *concentrated* matter, while the outer regions were thinner and were unevenly distributed. And the flake-like parts had grown narrow, white and dense. And the entire system *slowly turned*. And if ye had seen it from afar, ye would have said that it looked *like unto* a hurricane.

And *in the outer reaches* of the proto-galaxy, the dense-cloud flakes revolved at *different* rates. And those cloud flakes that revolved the *quickest* orbited in giant *circles*. And those cloud flakes that revolved *less fast* moved inward and around – they travelled in great *spirals*. And those flakes that revolved the *slowest* sped almost *directly at* the proto-galactic nucleus.

And the gas that revolved the *slowest* was drawn steadily and quickly *inward* by the strong force of gravity generated by the massive proto-galactic nucleus – such gas flowed inward *like unto* water down a drain. And as the gas got *closer* to the center, *faster* did it flow. And in the central region, it accelerated to high speeds. And inside it, molecules did bump, heat and radiate. And the heat and radiation were *absorbed* within the central region. And there, the temperature and pressure rose. And the high pressure and high density did retard the

---

[59] The collapse of this proto-galaxy was similar to the one described in *Exodus VI*.

inward flow of gas. And outward-flowing electromagnetic radiation created an *outward-pushing* force, which inhibited surrounding gas from drifting in. Thus moderately or quickly revolving gas did *not* flow in.

And the black hole sitting at the center of the proto-galactic nucleus *pulled* at all surrounding mass, causing gas to trickle in. And atoms in such gas were *torn apart*, becoming neutrons, protons and electrons. And X-rays and gamma rays were copiously emitted. And the high-energy *outward-flowing* rays created a strong *outward-oriented* pressure, which *prevented* most gas from falling in. Thus the black hole drew in only relatively small amounts of matter and of mass.

And viewed from far away, the proto-galaxy appeared hazy white against the blackness of the Universe. And it was *like unto* an egg of great potential. And as gas well above and well below the main bulge was *drawn* toward the central region, the ellipsoid flattened.

And several hundred-million years went by. And it came to pass that the shape of the proto-galaxy was like a thick pancake. But around the proto-galactic nucleus was a dense and smaller sphere. This was the *central bulge*. Inside it, a million stars had formed – within the bulge were a million points of light. But the light from these points was refracted, absorbed and re-emitted by surrounding gas. Thus outside the bulge, there was a *diffuse* bright glow. And the effect *was as* a soft-white light bulb in which the filament is blurred by coated glass.

Now the pancake-like structure was surrounded by a giant *halo sphere* two-hundred-thousand light years in diameter. Although it consisted mostly of dilute helium and hydrogen, in some regions were countless small dense clouds of gas. And they travelled in *all directions* and at *different* speeds. And sometimes two such clouds moved *near* each other; in such a case, the force of gravity *drew* them even closer, and they merged.

And several hundred-million years did pass. And the proto-galaxy did flatten more. And the central bulge was like a bright squashed sphere. And in the outermost region of the thin pancake-like structure, some stars did *twinkle*. And the middle and the central sections glowed with the light of several hundred-million stars.

And hundreds of millions of years went by. And the proto-galaxy became a galaxy. And apart from the central bulge, the pancake had flattened to a *disk*. And dense gas in flake-like regions had collapsed and given birth to groups of *countless* point-like shining stars. And in the disk, they had formed long luminous curved arms. A *spiral galaxy* had so been made. And a name was given to it. And the name was *Milky Way*. It was thy galaxy, the place where one day thee would live.

*Nature had made a great construction*
*of a hundred-billion brilliant stars.*
*And the Milky Way was beautiful*
*to behold from distances afar.*

At the center of the Milky Way was a black hole no bigger than the Sun but weighing *two-million* solar masses. And the black hole was provided with a name. And the name was *Sagittarius A-star*.

And it happened that some matter passed near Sagittarius A-star. And the black hole, through its strong gravity, *pulled* at the matter, rapidly accelerating it until it almost reached the speed of light. As in a particle beam of a man-made cyclotron, it collided with itself and created exotic forms of matter, including anti-matter positrons. *Almost instantly*, these positrons annihilated with electrons, thereby producing *highly energetic* gamma rays – they had two-hundred-fifty-thousand times more energy than ordinary light. And an *outburst* of radiation and of energy consequently *flashed*.

And this would happen from time to time: Into the black hole, material would trickle. And typically ten-trillion kilograms of positrons would annihilate with ten-trillion kilograms of electrons. And there would be *an outburst and a flash of radiation*. Thus Sagittarius A-star functioned as *atom smasher*, generating all types of electromagnetic radiation from microwaves to gamma rays.

And nearby the black hole in a relatively tiny one-billion-kilometer region[60] of the galactic center, *intense radio waves* were given off. And some such radio waves passed through surrounding material and gas and into outer space.

And in the same vicinity, gamma rays scattered off surrounding matter and triggered *X-ray radiations*. Now some nuclei *absorbed* the gamma rays. And this made the nuclei unstable. And subsequently they decayed, while giving off *more* X-rays.

And within three-hundred light years of Sagittarius A-star, ultraviolet radiation ionized atoms as electrons were *torn out* of atoms and charged nuclei were left behind. In subsequent collisions, the electrons and the nuclei made *microwaves* and other radiations. And in ambient and weak magnetic fields, electrons *spiralled* in helicoidal orbits. Such circulating electrons produced *more* microwaves. And some microwaves, after passing through surrounding gas and matter, entered empty space. Now the more-energetic charged particles, which circled in magnetic fields, produced *X-rays*, some of which *escaped* and passed into the black of outer space.

Now occasionally, *violent explosions* ejected ionized material and gas. The explosions produced great structures that resembled streamers, filaments, rings and lobes, some of which were several hundred light years long. And they were Nature's *galactic fireworks*.

And surrounding ions, atoms, molecules and dust *absorbed* the energy from the galactic center. And they absorbed ultraviolet radiation from the nearby stars. In the atoms and the molecules of gases, electrons in excited energy levels emitted *visible light* and *infrared radiation*

---

[60] This is the size of the orbit of Jupiter around the Sun.

when they *decayed* to lower levels. And warm dust and hot molecules gave off more radiations in the infrared. And some of these infrared waves *passed through* surrounding cool thick clouds of hydrogen and *exited into* the black of outer space.

And this three-thousand-light-year-sized region of activity was the *galactic nucleus* – the Milky Way's essential heart. It contained a *dense* amount of ions, gas and dust. And in addition, millions and millions of stars were packed inside the heart. And the light outputted from these stars was *so intense* that, between the stars, normally black space was as bright as twilight on the Earth. One-twentieth of the total luminosity of the Milky Way was there. Now the galactic nucleus weighed *ten-billion* solar masses. And at its center was Sagittarius A-star. Thus Sagittarius A-star was the galactic nucleus's heart – it was the Milky Way's heart's heart.

Now the galactic nucleus was surrounded by the central bulge. And it sat at the center of the galactic disk whose diameter was *one-hundred-thousand light years*. Yet the disk was only two-thousand light years thick. And the disk contained *one-hundred-billion* stars. Now this entire structure slowly revolved, taking *two-hundred-and-fifty-million* years for it to make one turn. Compared with the galactic nucleus, the disk was relatively calm.

And an ellipsoidal halo with a diameter of *one-hundred-and-fifty-thousand light years* surrounded the galactic disk. And in the halo, stars and star clusters were scattered randomly about. And the stars were point-like shining *specks*, while the clusters, which contained several thousand stars, *sparkled* like crown jewels.

> *The Milky Way was* like unto *a giant angel,*
> *beautifully dressed in lace.*

And a large spherical dark corona of *mysterious, nonluminous* material surrounded the halo and the Milky Way. And because this material was invisible and its nature was unknown, *it* was named *dark matter*. And the diameter of the corona measured *four-hundred-thousand light years*. And it weighed *one-trillion* solar masses – five times the weight of the mighty Milky Way.

And the Milky Way would become a *special galaxy*, for several billion years later at a distance twenty-five-thousand light years from the galactic center and in the plane of the galactic disk, a *star* would form. And that star would *be* the Sun. And the Sun would heat a planet called the Earth. And Earth would be *provided* with a suitable environment for complex and gargantuan self-organizing molecules – they *would* be living organisms. And among the living would be one called man. Thus billions of years later, the Milky Way would become the home for the Sun and Earth. Thus billions of years later, the Milky Way would become the home for life and man.

*The seventeenth book of Creation, called*

# Exodus X: Nucleogenesis

*Ah Nature, the Almighty Alchemist.*

## Chapter I: On Stars and Living Creatures

Now let it be known to thee and all around thee that a star is *like unto* a living creature. It has a birth, a childhood, an adolescence. It matures, grows old and dies. And like any living creature, it needs food to support its activities and functions. Now a star's principal function is *to radiate.* And to radiate, a star processes nourishment and turns it into motion, energy and heat. But unlike a living creature, which takes its sustenance from its surroundings, a star feeds itself by burning in its core *its nuclei.* Thus the core at the center of a star is *both* its stomach and its food. In some sense, a star *consumes itself* to shine.

And just like there are *many kinds* of living beings, there are *many kinds* of stars: red supergiants, red giants, yellow Sun-like stars, blue giants, cepheids, white dwarfs, subdwarfs, and many more. And stellar luminosities, temperatures and masses vary greatly. The white dwarfs *are* the ants of stars. The red giants *are* the elephants.

## Chapter II: A Giant Energetic Star

It was nine-billion years ago. And in a remote region of a galaxy, a cloud of gas collapsed and made a star.[61] And the star was *very heavy*, weighing eighteen times a solar mass. Now for a living creature, the larger it is the more it eats. And let it be known to thee and all around thee that the same is true for stars. And this star had an *insatiable* appetite for its sustenance, its own nuclei.

And let it be known that a star *supports* its weight with pressure from outward-flowing heat and radiation. Thus without heat and radiation to *counteract* the force of gravity, a star would uncontrollably collapse.

And it came to pass that the giant star *devoured* its nuclear fuel in supporting its enormous mass. Hydrogen nuclei[62] constituted its main source of nourishment: In the core, protons *were consumed* and converted into helium-four. And the fusion of four protons produced both heat and radiation. And to speed the processes, a "digestive enzyme-analog" substance was employed, consisting of the nuclei of carbon-twelve. Thus small quantities of carbon in the core expedited fusions of the protons into helium-four.

---

[61] The collapse was similar to the one described in *Exodus VII*.

[62] A hydrogen nucleus is also a proton. For the terminology and processes in this chapter and the remaining ones in *Exodus X*, see the New Testament Book of *Nuclear Physics*.

Now carbon catalyzed the processes as follows. A carbon-twelve nucleus absorbed a proton and metamorphosed into a nitrogen-thirteen nucleus. The nitrogen-thirteen decayed to carbon-thirteen, which in turn fused with a proton to produce nitrogen-fourteen. Then the nitrogen-fourteen absorbed another proton and became oxygen-fifteen. The oxygen-fifteen decayed into nitrogen-fifteen. And finally, the nitrogen-fifteen merged with a proton and produced helium-four and carbon-twelve.

And these processes constituted the *carbon cycle.* During the cycle, a carbon-twelve nucleus was destroyed at the beginning and recreated at the end. And in effect, a carbon-twelve in the core absorbed four protons and produced a helium-four.

And in these processes, neutrinos, electrons and *energetic photons* were produced. And the neutrinos, being massless and weakly interacting, streamed *out* of the giant star at the speed of light, and they were lost. Nor did the positrons last long – they *instantly* combined with electrons in matter-antimatter annihilations which generated gamma rays. Thus the carbon cycle destroyed mass, created photons, and generated energy. And the photons and the energy, which were *absorbed* inside the star, produced great quantities of *heat and radiation.* And the outward flow of radiation was *so intense* that it counterbalanced the enormous central pull of gravity. And so the mass and matter of the star did *not* collapse upon itself.

Now the heavy weight of the giant star pushed down strongly on matter in the core, creating a *great pressure* there. And as the pressure pushed the protons and the nuclei *together,* they *merged* quite readily. Thus high pressure and high density made fusion processes *proceed quite rapidly,* and vast quantities of energy were generated. The star was hot both radioactively and thermally, the central temperature being *forty-million* Kelvins. And the star's surface radiated light brilliantly and blindingly at *thirty-thousand* times the brightness of the Sun.

Thus protons were *vigorously consumed* and converted into helium by the hungry star. Compared with other stars, this giant was a reckless *squanderer* of nuclear fuel and food. And like a greedy individual, it would someday pay the penalty.

## Chapter III: No More Protons in the Core

Two-million years passed by. And it had happened that all hydrogen was *depleted* at the center of the giant star – a tiny core of nuclei of helium-four was there. And the star began to digest protons at the *surface* of the sphere of helium. And as the star digested more, so grew the helium core. The star *was* a hungry one and was shining *seventy-thousand* times brighter than the Sun.

*And he who devoureth during the first seven years of plenty*
*shall starve in the second seven years of famine.*

Then *ten-million* years went by; the giant star had consumed
what an average star consumes in *ten-billion* years. And the innermost
one-quarter of the star had been converted into helium.

The hydrogen in its stomach was exhausted – the proton food
*was gone.* Suddenly did the energy output drop. The radiation pressure
plunged. And with *little* to support the star, it shrank. And as it
shrank, the central temperature surged to *two-hundred-million* Kelvins[63] and the density climbed to a thousand times the density of water.

## Chapter IV: The Helium Flash

And suddenly, *helium fusion* activated. And in the core, three helium-four nuclei *merged* into a carbon-twelve, while ejecting energetic photons. And everywhere within the central core, helium nuclei
did *fuse.*

And the entire core ignited. And the energy from the new nuclear
reactions *fired*, creating a burst of outward-flowing radiation. And as
the core *expanded quickly*, a *wave* of heat and radiation surged outward through the star. And the star's outer shell did swell. And a layer
of hydrogen was *blasted* into surrounding empty space.

Deep inside the star, as the core expanded, reaction rates did
drop. And eventually the expansion slowed and stopped.

## Chapter V: A Red Supergiant Arises

And the star's new size was great – a *red supergiant star* had it become. And with a radius of *three-hundred-million kilometers*, it was
large enough to hold within its body the orbits of the Earth and Mars if
they had been in that vicinity.[64]

Now the swift expansion cooled the stellar surface to five-
thousand Kelvins. And less light was emitted per unit region of the
surface than before. But the star was *so voluminous* that it still shone
*one-hundred-thousand* times the brightness of the Sun. Now hydrogen
composed the outermost three-quarters region of the supergiant star.
And at the inner parts of this three-quarters region, hydrogen continued *fusing* into helium. And this was the main source of energy for producing the star's heat and light. But in the core, helium fused to carbon-twelve. And further fusions by absorptions of helium-fours slowly
produced oxygen-sixteen, neon-twenty and magnesium-twenty-four.
And in these processes *energetic* photons were ejected. And as the photons heated the surrounding gas, the star got *hot* inside.

---

[63] This is fifteen times hotter than the temperature at the center of the Sun. Collapsing
systems tend to heat up as constituents bump against each other. See the Book of *Thermodynamics.* In this case, gravitation potential energy is converted into heat.

[64] Of course at this time, the solar system did not yet exist.

The star had had no choice but *to consume its stomach*. The burning of helium and heavier nuclei was *like unto* an ulcer. The star was sick inside.

And for hundreds of thousands of years did helium so burn while making carbon in the core. And the amount of carbon at the center of the star increased. And a small sphere of carbon in the core appeared.

## Chapter VI: No More Helium in the Core

One million years went by. Having been converted into carbon, the *last nuclei of helium* in the central core were finally exhausted. And a sudden drop in energy resulted in a drop in outward-flowing radiation pressure. And so the star did *shrink*. And as it shrank, the central density soared to *two-hundred-fifty-thousand* times the density of water and the central temperature climbed to *seven-hundred-million* Kelvins.

## Chapter VII: The Carbon Flash, the Neon Flash

And suddenly did *carbon fusion* activate – in the core, two carbon-twelves combined, producing nuclei of neon, magnesium, oxygen and sodium. And these reactions also generated energetic photons, neutrons, helium-four nuclei and protons. And for a second time, there was a *flash*, as the entire carbon core ignited. And the inner region of the star exploded in an enormous blast. And the core shook back and forth. But eventually did the star obtain an equilibrium.

In a shell, helium closest to the carbon core did fuse and make more nuclei of carbon-twelve. And so the carbon core grew *bigger*. Likewise, protons just outside the shell of helium did fuse. As they made more nuclei of helium, the helium-shell's outer radius *grew out*. And the fusion into helium did fuel the outer regions of the star.

Now the carbon, which burned *deep* inside the star, was *like unto* a stomach cancer. The star was like a human with a *hidden tumor*. Outside the core, the star seemed unaware of anything – it *even* radiated *stronger* than before.

Now the central region was *so hot* that highly energetic photons made matter-antimatter positron-electron pairs. And the positrons annihilated quickly with electrons, most often generating gamma rays but sometimes producing neutrino-antineutrino pairs. And such antineutrinos and neutrinos *were so weakly* interacting that they streamed out the star without a single interaction – they left the star and entered outer space. Thus neutrinos *robbed* the core of energy; they were *like unto* parasites.

*The cancer had begun to* drain *the star of strength.*

And carbon burned for *just* two-thousand years. And when the carbon in the core was gone, the star contracted, the central temperature doubled to *one-and-one-half billion* Kelvins, and the central density surged to *seven-million* times the density of water.[65] And neon fusion in the core commenced.

## Chapter VIII: The Energy Drain

And the *sizzling* core produced such *highly energetic* photons that *photonuclear dissociation* did begin – a highly energetic photon struck a nucleus and *tore* the nucleus *in two*. Now in this fission process, energy from photons was *absorbed*. Thus photonuclear dissociation *sapped* the core of energy.

And the sizzling core created positron-electron pairs at *a prolific rate*. In matter-antimatter annihilations, sometimes antineutrinos and neutrinos were produced. And out of the star did go these massless weakly interacting particles. Henceforth the star would lose more energy in neutrinos than in light and radiation.

Now the *structure* of the star was this: The core contained the nuclei of medium-light elements. Around the core were four concentric shells: an inner shell of oxygen, magnesium and neon; a second shell of oxygen and carbon; a third shell of helium; and an outer shell of hydrogen. Negatively charged electrons were distributed everywhere and neutralized the nuclei throughout the star.

And through neutrino radiations and photonuclear dissociations, the core's energy *was being drained*. Fusion had to sustain these energy-consuming processes *and* to support the star's enormous weight. The "energy engine" in the core was being strained.

## Chapter IX: Heavier Elements Feed the Star

And in *just* twelve years, the neon in the core was *gone*! The energy output in the core declined. And since the outward flow of radiation no longer could support the heavy star, the core *contracted*. The central temperature did increase to *two-billion* Kelvins; the central density did double. And oxygen nuclei began to "burn." Two oxygens merged and made magnesium, sulfur, silicon and phosphorus. Thus *oxygen fusion* fueled the core, providing energy for heat, for radiation, and for the parasitic processes of neutrino emission and photonuclear dissociation.

And in only four short years, the core's oxygen completely was depleted. And so again the core *contracted*. At *sizzling* temperatures and *tremendous* densities, the neutrino drain accelerated while *silicon* became the core-producing fuel: Silicons fused into nuclei of nickel-fifty-six, which subsequently did decay to nuclei of iron-fifty-six, neutrinos, positrons and energetic photons. *Iron* thus began to grow within the core. And in small quantities, heavier elements such as titanium, vanadium, chromium, manganese and cobalt were created.

And the neutrino drain on energy took off.

---

[65] Compared with the conditions at the center of the Sun, the star at this point was one-hundred times hotter and more than forty-thousand times denser!

In its core, the star was *starving*. The core burned anything to satisfy *its need* for energy. But iron would not burn. Now let it be known to thee and all around thee that iron is the *most stable* of all nuclei. When iron fuses, energy is absorbed and *not* released. Thus for a star, iron is like dead material.

## Chapter X: The Nuclear Rainbow

Now the star had lived for only thirteen million years – yet it was *old*, for its body had *severely* aged, and its structure had *severely* changed: There were an iron core and five concentric shells. And the inner shell was made of silicon and sulfur; the second shell contained oxygen, magnesium and neon; the third was made of oxygen and carbon; the fourth was formed of helium; and the outer shell was hydrogen. Thus the star was *like unto* an onion – the onion layers were layers of elements.

## Chapter XI: The Core Goes Critical

Now with little radiation to support the core, the core *contracted*. And iron nuclei were *squeezed* together. Likewise, electrons were pushed against each other. And this squeezing of electrons led to pressure. And the dead core shrank until the pressure from electrons matched the force of gravity. Thus *electron-pressure* counterbalanced weight and did prevent complete collapse.

*The ants were holding up the elephant.*

And time ticked *like unto* a sparking fuse of dynamite. As silicon which burned around the core turned into iron, the dense dead core accrued more mass. And the *core's weight* upon itself *increased*. And this caused the electrons and the iron nuclei to squeeze together *more*.

Now silicon burned for two straight days,[66] during which the iron core grew to one-thousand kilometers in radius. The iron therein weighed as much as the Sun and one-third more. And then it came to pass that the core's enormous weight *matched* the maximum-achievable electron pressure; the core was *critical*. And the gravitational analog of an atomic bomb was *ready* to take place.

## Chapter XII: The Inner Core Collapses

And in the next split second, weight overwhelmed the pressure. Thus the *mighty* force of gravity had won the war against the miniscule electrons.

*The elephant, of course, had triumphed.*

---

[66] Here and below, a day refers to a unit of time – twenty-four hours – that is, the time it takes the Earth to rotate once in the third millennium AD. Since the Earth did not yet exist, one might wonder whether concepts such as year or day make sense.

Now in the onion-structured shells outside the core, the star *kept fusing nuclei.* And these fusions generated heat and radiation and supported the weight of the outer regions of the star. And at the stellar surface, light *continued* to be emitted brilliantly, but the star *was* as good as gone.

*The ill-tempered star would die*
*not with a whimper but a bang.*

The core collapse commenced. As electrons and iron nuclei were *squeezed together* at the center of the star, electrons merged with protons, producing neutrons and neutrinos. Electron disappearance in the core *reduced* the pressure more. In contrast to most situations, the collapse of matter made the pressure *drop* instead of rise. The internal resistance was *completely gone.* The fist of gravity was free to pound the floor. The hand of gravity accelerated matter to the center of the core. The central temperature did soar.

*The foundation of a tall building is dynamited.*
*The lower floors free fall and crash to earth.*
*Momentarily, the higher floors remain in place.*
*And then they too free fall.*

And the core collapsed in an implosion. And it was like a movie running backward of an explosion.

And a few milliseconds passed. And three-fold did the core reduce in size. The nuclei became *so closely packed* that even weakly interacting neutrinos interacted. Thus in the core, neutrinos bounced off nuclei and scattered. And some neutrinos were absorbed and re-emitted. Eventually they did escape the core, but they did so much more slowly than before.

And a few more milliseconds passed. The innermost fifteen-kilometer region, which contained one-fifth a solar mass, *contracted further* until the iron nuclei were crushed together. The density skyrocketed *six-hundred-fold,* attaining that of pure nuclear material – *two-hundred-and-fifty-trillion* times the density of water. The iron nuclei melted into a single ten-kilometer nucleus of electrons, neutrons, protons and neutrinos.

And the inner core was *spinning:* The collapse had set it spinning – it was *like unto* a skater bringing in his arms. The bringing in of mass had made the core-ball spin.

And a few more milliseconds passed. The protons and the neutrons in the ten-kilometer nucleus were together crushed *beyond* the density of normal nuclear material. And let it be known to thee and all around thee that nuclear matter is highly incompressible. And so the inner core could squeeze *no more.*

## Chapter XIII: The Inner Core Rebounds

And *like unto* a ball *bouncing* off a wall – deforming, squashing then expanding – the inner core *rebounded*. And nuclear matter halted in its tracks and then drove out. And there was a thunder-deafening ring. And from the center did emanate a *wave of pressure* at the speed of sound. But the iron in the outer core continued to fall in at *one-fourth the speed of light*. And the outward-moving pressure wave pushed against the flow of inward-falling nuclei. And it *was as* walking through a wind of raining iron.

And the pressure wave plowed out, moving *against* a moving medium. And at thirty kilometers from the center, iron fell so fast the wave could *hardly* move at all.

*It was* like unto *a rower rowing in a stream against a current,*
*in which the current* almost *flowed as fast as rower rowed.*
*To an observer on the river bank, the rower* barely *moved.*

At the center of the star, nuclear material *continued* to compress. The compression produced more pressure waves. These secondary pressure waves pushed out and joined the original principal pressure wave, *adding energy and pressure* to that wave. And a bulge of *tremendous pressure* and great energy developed there. And energy furnished to the wave *propelled* it through the heavy rain of iron. And the pressure-build-up-point sped out at *one-twentieth the speed of light*.

*The rower was given help and strength*
*to row against a strongly flowing current.*

A millisecond passed. Deep inside, the protons and the neutrons in the iron rained in and joined the other nucleons. The giant nugget of a nucleus *grew* to twenty-two kilometers in size. Inside the nucleonic nugget, intense pressure and high density did push electrons *into* protons. And as the electrons and the protons merged and disappeared, neutrons and neutrinos took their place. Thus a metamorphosis of *charged* particles to *neutral* ones took place. And the sizzling *forty-billion-degree-hot* nucleonic nugget profusely spit out positron-electron pairs; energy was *converted* into matter in the form of e-minus–e-plus[67] pairs as "E turned into mc-squared." As positrons and neutrons merged and disappeared, antineutrinos and protons took their place.

Thus antineutrinos and neutrinos were made in subatomic metamorphosis. And as antineutrinos and neutrinos *scattered* randomly off matter, they moved in *jagged paths*. Now some made it to the surface of the nucleonic nugget and escaped. But most, like drunken individuals, simply staggered aimlessly about and did not reach the surface – they were *trapped* inside the nucleonic nugget.

---

[67] An electron is also called an e-minus. Likewise, a positron is also called an e-plus.

Now *outside* the core, all was calm, with light radiating from the surface of the star as it had done for a hundred-thousand centuries before. The giant star still shone eighty-thousand times the brightness of the Sun. And the onion layers of elements moved *imperceptibly, unperturbed* by any agitation in the core.

## Chapter XIV: The Wave Becomes Destructive

And another millisecond passed. At seventy kilometers from the stellar center, the pressure wave had amassed extraordinary energy and pressure. And now the pressure was *so strong* that iron nuclei, passing through, disintegrated; they completely fell apart, crumbling into protons, helium-four nuclei and neutrons. And it was *like unto* rock being blasted into pieces by a drill – the rock was like the iron; the drill was like the pressure wave. And *tremendous* was the noise – so whopping was the sound that nuclei did pop. The pressure wave had changed its character; it was a *shock wave*, a destructive wave of *enormous force* and energy.

And deep inside, the helium-proton-neutron fragments *struck* the surface of the nucleonic nugget core, suddenly being *halted* in their tracks. And pressure waves *rebounded* and sped out until they reached the *wave of shock*. And there, they joined and energized the wave. And some of the *antineutrinos and neutrinos*, emerging from the center of the core, struck the wave of shock, and they too *helped to push it out*.

And another millisecond passed. Now half the iron nuclei had fallen in and had been crushed to nucleons. And the innermost seventy-kilometer region of the star contained three-quarters of a solar mass.

And it came to pass that, in one-tenth of a second, the wave of shock, propelled by its enormous energy, *drove out*. And it battled the inward-falling iron nuclei, which were *ripped apart* while passing through the shock. Like a tornado, the shock wave left behind a trail of nuclear destruction. At two-hundred kilometers from the stellar center, it plowed *forth* and tore the core apart.

Thus the shock wave *undid* what the star had done before, for iron nuclei were being *fissioned* into smaller parts.[68] But to fission iron, energy was needed. Thus the destruction of the iron nuclei *sapped* the wave of energy.[69]

And the nucleonic fragments and debris[70] created by the shock wave streamed in until they *struck* the giant nucleonic nugget. And they were flattened, squeezed and crushed, and *added* to it. And the giant nucleonic ball grew bigger.

---

[68] Previously the star had assembled protons, neutrons and small nuclei into the larger nuclei.

[69] The shock wave was also so hot that some neutrinos were produced. The production of neutrinos also sapped the wave of energy.

[70] These were protons, neutrons and helium-four nuclei.

## Chapter XV: The Shock Wave Stalls

One tenth of a second suddenly went by. At three-hundred kilometers from the stellar center, the shock wave did inch forward. The destruction of nuclei had *robbed* the wave of energy. And with the loss of energy, the *driving force* behind its motion *dropped*. And so the wave slowed down; hardly was it moving.

And in another tenth of a second, the debilitated shock wave *weakened more* and *stopped*. Only fifteen kilometers of iron lay between it and the shell of sulfur-silicon. But the wave had lost the battle against the inward flowing iron nuclei. It was *like unto* a battered boxer, punch-drunk and too weak to move. It *even* started drifting slightly in. And nuclei continued to flow through it, rob it of its energy and push it in.

*At sunrise, the plow began to till the soil.*
*In the morning were the oxen fresh –*
*the tilling of the earth went well.*
*But at sunset did the oxen tire,*
*for the same animals had pulled the plow all day.*
*And the plow dug deep, too deep into the earth.*
*It hit a rock and it got caught.*

And *deep inside* the dying star, the nucleonic nugget ball accumulated mass. And with a radius of seventy kilometers, the ball was of enormous weight. As its mass *weighed down and crushed* its nucleons, the ball contracted. And this created heat. And the rate of neutrino-antineutrino-pair production soared. But the ball was *so dense and hot* that only a fraction of the antineutrinos or neutrinos could escape.

## Chapter XVI: A "Neutrino Star" is Born

One tenth of a second passed. And the ball contracted – fifty-kilometers was now its radius. Countless neutrinos and antineutrinos were *packed within the ball*. And some, like drunkards, staggered to the surface and escaped. And there, they streamed outward at the speed of light – a *"neutrino star"* had formed. The *outward* neutrino-antineutrino flow created pressure[71] which matched the force of gravity and slowed the compression of the ball. At its surface, antineutrinos and neutrinos, instead of light, were shining out.

## Chapter XVII: The Wave Is Revitalized by Neutrinos

*The elements shall melt with fervent heat.*

And *like unto* water spraying from a geyser, enormous quantities of antineutrinos and neutrinos so poured forth. And after travelling

---

[71] This pressure arose when some neutrinos and antineutrinos were converted into electrons and positrons after striking nucleons.

almost three-hundred kilometers, some *struck* the floundering shock wave, which was much hotter and much denser than surrounding matter. And the wave absorbed neutrinos, gaining their energy and their momentum. And so the wave edged out – the neutrino-antineutrino flow was pushing on the shock wave like unto a *wind which blows against a sail.*

> *In the field, the rock was overcome.*
> *It no longer blocked the plow.*

And in less than one-tenth second, the shock wave reached the outer surface of the iron core.

> *The army of destruction had been liberated.*
> *It was free to march.*
> *And forward did it march,*
> *transfiguring everything*
> *that lay in its way.*

Now the shock wave, which was *five-billion* Kelvins hot, ascended through the layer of silicon and sulfur. And in the region of the wave, silicon-twenty-eight fused with itself, thereby creating nickel-fifty-six and energetic photons. Thus the shock wave *stimulated fusion* and left behind a trail of radioactive nickel in its wake. And the fusion furnished energy which *fed* the wave.

> *The army robbed and plundered victims,*
> *and it grew stronger.*

And the wave travelling at one-fiftieth the speed of light took several seconds to pass the shell of silicon and sulfur. And a tenth of a solar mass of nickel-fifty-six was left behind. Electrons as well as nuclei of nickel, silicon and sulfur were *exploding out*. The wave reached the base of the magnesium-oxygen-neon layer. And in the region of the wave, oxygen fused with oxygen, thereby producing magnesium, sulfur, silicon and phosphorus. Heat and energy were released which further fueled the wave. And the wave grew *even stronger*.

And the nuclei of neon, oxygen, magnesium and other elements ,oined the material behind the wave *which* was being *blasted out*.

And throughout the inner layers, nuclear processes in the region of the shock wave made minute amounts of potassium, fluorine, chlorine, argon, calcium, aluminum and scandium. And all these nuclei were ejected and sent flying out.

## Chapter XVIII: The "Neutrino Star" Contracts

And it came to pass that, deep inside the star, the nucleonic nugget ball grew smaller, hotter, denser – forty-kilometers was now its radius, while its temperature was *one-hundred-billion* Kelvins.[72] And enormous quantities of antineutrinos and neutrinos continued to be produced by a thermal bath of liquid nucleons. It was *like unto* a pot of boiling water – the water molecules were like the nucleons; the antineutrinos and neutrinos were like the bubbles and the steam. In *colossal* numbers, antineutrinos and neutrinos at the surface of the ball poured out. And through the star and at the speed of light did they stream out.

And since neutrinos carried energy, they robbed the ball of energy. And gradually the temperature *declined a bit*. And so production of neutrinos *eased somewhat*.

The neutrino-antineutrino blast lasted for ten seconds. Thus the lifetime of the "neutrino star" was *just ten seconds*. During its existence, *ten-billion-trillion-trillion-trillion-trillion*[73] antineutrinos and neutrinos were emitted.

And the temperature of the nucleonic ball dropped further. And the neutrino-antineutrino output sharply fell. The "neutrino star" *shut down*. Now almost all the protons had been *transformed* to neutrons, so that the ball was *a giant nucleus of neutrons*. At several times a second did it spin.

And the antineutrinos and neutrinos in the burst flowed out the star and into outer space. And they passed *undisturbed* through intergalactic dust and gas. They formed a giant shell, like the surface region of a giant sphere. Three-million kilometers in thickness was the shell.

## Chapter XIX: The Star Explodes

*And forces shall cause the stars to burst.*

Now deep inside the star, the shock wave did rage on. And as it sped *through* the giant star, it spread a bit in width. Thus a thin spherical shell was the region that it occupied. *And* as it moved out, the shell expanded, and its volume did increase. And as its volume did increase, the energy diluted, causing the wave of shock to *cool* and to *lose speed*.

*As the wild army conquered many distant lands,*
*the battalions spread out near and far.*
*The troops were getting tired.*

And the shock wave *struck* the layer of oxygen and carbon. And the shock wave's temperature declined below the limit needed for inducing fusion. And nuclear alchemy then *ceased*. But the wave continued plowing through the oxygen and carbon nuclei.

---

[72] This is more than six-thousand times the Sun's core temperature. At this stage, the nugget ball was a billion-billion times denser than the Sun.
[73] $10^{58}$.

Three dozen minutes passed. As the shock wave swept throughout the star, electrons and nuclei were *blown about*. And interior to the
wave, all matter, save the central nucleonic ball, *exploded out*.

And in the inner layers, some nuclei and neutrons merged. And
minute amounts of all the elements heavier than iron formed.

And the wave of shock swept through the layer of helium and
blasted electrons and alpha particles about. And they too went *streaming out*. Yet still the surface of the star was undisturbed – just as before, it radiated light at eighty-thousand times the brightness of the
Sun.

> *When the heart of a man stops,*
> *the eyes may close but the body functions still continue.*
> *If the heart can be restarted within seven minutes,*
> *the man can even then be resurrected.*
> *The cells in such a dead man absorb*
> *the little oxygen that still remains in non-circulating blood,*
> *and only later do they die.*
> *The organs are non-operational*
> *but remain functional for several hours.*
> *The corpse stays warm and only slowly cools.*

Three dozen minutes passed. The shock wave reached the inner
edge of the layer-shell of hydrogen. It started *plowing* through the protons and electrons.

.    .    .    .    .    .    .

It was three hours after the iron-core collapse. And the shock
wave rushed out through the very outer edge of hydrogen, the surface of
the star. Boom! The star exploded. It was a *supernova*.

And the supernova was classified. And its classification was *type-
two* because it exploded alone under its own weight.

The star's pent-up energy was finally *thrown out*. The pent-up
insides of the dead star were tossed with vigor into space. The star,
which had previously so greedily consumed, was *dead*.

> *He who hath taken away shall give back.*

And the nuclei and hydrogen exploded outward at one-tenth the
speed of light. The gas leading the advance was one-hundred-thousand
Kelvins hot. And the ballooning supernova sphere emitted heavy *ultraviolet radiation*. And the ultraviolet burst shot out at the speed of light,
while the exploding gas was left behind.

And in outer space around the supernova were two *expanding*
spheres: the outer neutrino-antineutrino shell and the inner ultraviolet-
radiation shell. And three-billion kilometers of distance *were* between
the two. And both of them ballooned *outward* at the speed of light.

*A pebble fell into a pond of perfectly quiet water.*
*A ring went out.*
*A second pebble fell into the pond.*
*A second ring went out.*

## Chapter XX: The Aftermath

And near the defunct star, a giant shell of gas swelled out. And as the gas *expanded*, it did *cool*. And after several hours, the temperature at the surface of the supernova sphere declined a dozen-fold – six-thousand Kelvins hot was it. And at this lower temperature, ultraviolet radiations *dropped*, and visible emissions took their place. Thus the expanding gas profusely radiated *light*. And to an eye, the supernova *brightened*.

Now *inside* the exploding gas, gamma rays repeatedly scattered with electrons and *lost energy* and degraded into X-rays. And through repeatedly scattering off electrons, these X-rays *too* lost energy. And the lower-in-energy X-rays were absorbed by electrons, nuclei and protons in the gas, causing these particles to move faster and get hot. And such particles gave off visible light and ultraviolet radiation. But deep inside the gas, material was *so dense* that electromagnetic radiation was repeatedly absorbed and re-emitted – it was trapped by the material that had created it. Unable to reach the outer surface, *it* did not escape.

And *the surface* of the outward-moving front did cool a bit – five-thousand Kelvins was it. And protons and electrons *came together* and formed *atomic* hydrogen. And the story of Recombination, which had taken place when the Universe was three-hundred-thousand years old, was told again. As electrons tumbled to atomic orbits, photons were ejected – *light* was thus emitted. And to an eye, the supernova *brightened*.

Five days went by. At ten-thousand kilometers per second, the hydrogen gas front *zoomed* through space. But the exploding gas inside sped *more slowly*, at several thousand kilometers per second. And when the *outer regions* of the gas expanded more and cooled, recombination also started *there*. Thus near the surface of the gas, protons and electrons recombined, ejecting photons and *releasing light*. Atomic hydrogen was made. And the outer layer of the exploding gas became *transparent*. And the radiation that had been trapped inside was *liberated*. The supernova *strongly* brightened.

And far inside the explosion, nickel-fifty-six, which had previously been generated in the shell of silicon and sulfur, decayed to cobalt-fifty-six, a neutrino and a positron. And the decay released *great energy*, which propelled the cobalt nuclei to several thousand kilometers per second. Now the positrons annihilated with electrons into *energetic* photons, which scattered off exploding gas and heated it.

Two weeks went by. And it had come to pass that each electron in the exploding gas had found a partner. And recombination was *complete*. And so electrons and the nuclei formed neutral atoms. And the advancing gas became *entirely* transparent. The supernova shone the brightest it would shine – *five-hundred-million* times the brightness of the Sun.

And one month went by. Now it had come to pass that most of the energy of the shock wave had been *dissipated* in escaping radiation or high-speed ejected matter. And the exploding supernova sphere, which was four times the solar system size, had *dimmed a bit*.

And two months went by. And in the wilderness of outer space, the advancing gas front *further cooled*, and *light output* diminished. Radiation in the infrared did dominate, as the gas front copiously radiated heat.

Now *deep inside* the supernova, a cobalt-fifty-six *decayed* into a positron, neutrino and excited iron-fifty-six. And the excited iron nucleus tumbled to its lowest-energy configuration by hurling out a *gamma ray*. And the positron annihilated an electron and produced *another* gamma ray. And these subatomic processes were happening everywhere within the defunct star. Now as gamma rays did *scatter*, they lost energy in heating up the gas. And they *soon* degraded into X-rays of energies a thousand times the energies of light. And the supernova *copiously* emitted energetic X-rays.

And another month went by. Cobalt-fifty-six, zooming at three-thousand kilometers per second, *passed* the innermost envelope of gaseous hydrogen. And decaying cobalt nuclei produced gamma rays with energies a *million* times the energies of light. Now *some* gamma rays passed through the surface of the exploding gas and *into outer space*. But *other* gamma rays *scattered* off of matter, lost energy and degraded into X-rays, some of which escaped the envelope of hydrogen and entered into outer space. Thus the supernova *profusely* radiated gamma-rays and X-rays. But visible emissions continued to descend – the brightness of the supernova visibly *declined*.

And what was the final energy score? In electromagnetic radiation, the supernova produced *thirty-trillion-trillion-trillion-trillion* ergs, the equivalent of *one-trillion-trillion-trillion tons* of TNT. The energy in motion of ejected matter was ten times this. But the energy in the neutrino-antineutrino burst was even greater – a thousand times the output of ejecta, or *ten-thousand-trillion-trillion-trillion tons* of TNT! The total energy unleashed *matched* the production of one-hundred Sun-like stars for their entire lifetimes of *ten-thousand-million* years.[74]

---

[74] The supernova explosion was Nature's nuclear-bomb blast, except Nature had been more powerful than modern man, for it had produced the output of *one-billion-trillion-trillion* H-bombs. The four large numbers in this paragraph and the one in this footnote are $3.0 \times 10^{49}$, $10^{36}$, $10^{40}$, $10^{10}$ and $10^{33}$.

## Chapter XXI: A Neutron Star Is Born

And what was left? At the center of the mushrooming radioactive and radiating gas-sphere spun a relatively tiny ball twenty kilometers wide containing a *billion-trillion-trillion-trillion-trillion* neutrons. It was a giant neutron nucleus, a *neutron star*. Thus all that remained of the defunct star was *its* charred stomach. And Nature had rolled the star into a black and tiny ball.

And the neutron star was forty percent *more massive* than the Sun – yet seventy-thousand times *smaller* was its radius. So it *was* the size of a metropolis – yet the force of gravity on its surface was *two-hundred-billion* times the force of gravity on Earth.

And the body of the neutron star was mostly liquid with a solid outer layer; the liquid was a *superfluid,* in which neutrons swam about with *little friction.* Now the neutron star contained some protons and electrons, but neutrons did outnumber protons and electrons twenty-one to one.

As the neutron star spun at thirty times a second, currents of electrons and of protons generated a magnetic field a *trillion* times the strength of Earth's magnetic field. Now the spinning-axis and magnetic field were aimed at *different* angles. Thus the spinning of the neutron star made the direction of its magnetic field trace out a circle.

*The beacon of a light house is turned toward the sky at night.*
*On the dark night clouds, it makes a disk of white.*
*Along a circle in the cloud-covered sky revolves the disk of light.*

Outside the neutron star, in outer space, were particles. And of the particles, *some* were charged. And these charged particles were *caught* in the neutron-star's magnetic field. And as the field revolved, so *did* revolve the charges. And those charges that were trapped at a thousand kilometers away from the neutron star moved *almost at the speed of light.* And they generated long-wavelength radiations[75] in collimated waves. And these waves of radio noise *beamed outward in a cone,* which circled with the circulating field of magnetism, *like unto* an upward-pointing light-house beam. Now this neutron star was special – it was a *pulsar*; it was *Nature's* broadcast station. Nature was *sending sounds* throughout thy Universe to announce the neutron star's existence.

## Chapter XXII: A Collision With a Gaseous Cloud

It was one year after the explosion. Debris ejected from the supernova polluted a six-hundred-billion-kilometer interstellar region. And the exploding giant sphere of gas and matter was *still* ballooning outward at ten-thousand kilometers per second.

---

[75] These radiations were radio-frequency synchrotron emissions.

And the remaining minute amounts of cobalt-fifty-six decayed and generated gamma rays and X-rays. But the production was significantly *lower* than before. The supernova star had *dimmed* considerably. Yet still it shone ten-million times the brightness of the Sun. But all emissions of electromagnetic radiation were *dropping quickly* in an exponential fashion.

And many years went by. And trillions of kilometers away from the explosion site did sit a cool gas cloud. And the leading front of the exploding supernova gas struck the almost idle cloud. And it was *like unto* the clapping of two hands. And two shock waves materialized and moved apart. Between the two did gas grow hot. At a *million Kelvins*, atomic chaos followed: In the hot shock region, an electron of a heavy atom was *ejected* from an inner shell. With the *emission* of an X-ray, another electron *fell* into the vacant shell. And these processes did happen everywhere between the waves of shock. Thus there were energetic X-rays and electrons *everywhere*. And free electrons[76] *spiralling* around the lines of magnetic interstellar fields acted as tiny broadcast stations and *emitted* synchrotron-type radiations, which were mostly noisy radio-type waves.[77] In unison, the "noise" was *great*. Now in the hottest regions, the gas emitted ultraviolet radiations. And less-hot gas emitted visible and infrared. And all these electromagnetic waves, *like flocks of birds*, took flight, speeding outward at the speed of light.

*And the supernova* signalled
*throughout the Universe to those who watched and listened*
*the destruction of its sins.*

And the collision of the supernova gas with the cool idle cloud did dent the leading supernova front. And the multi-trillion-kilometer-sized sphere developed a dimple in its shape.[78]

And for thousands of years, the exploding supernova gas would expand, thin, cool and fill a certain void of outer space. And when collisions with interstellar clouds occurred, the clouds and gas would *heat*. And there would be renewed emissions of radio waves, X-rays, infrared and ultraviolet radiations, microwaves and light. And the exploding gas, *like unto* a broom, would sweep up interstellar gas and leave behind a trail of disruption and electromagnetic radiation. And the clouds and supernova remnant would be visible, *like unto* gigantic fingerprints, for several times ten-thousand years.[79]

Now eventually, collisions would *retard and cool* exploding supernova gas. And electrons, nuclei and atoms from the supernova would

---

[76] These were electrons outside atoms that moved freely through the medium.

[77] There were also some synchrotron radiations in the visible, infrared and microwave regions of the electromagnetic spectrum.

[78] Later, more collisions with interstellar gas would produce more dimples in the sphere of supernova gas and it would eventually look like a giant gaseous walnut.

[79] The emissions would be readable by those who *chose* to read. And the supernova remnant would recite a tale to those who *chose* to listen.

*mix* with interstellar clouds of molecules and dust. And a dim but luminous nebula would then *remain*. And a distorted supernova remnant several times ten-light years wide would then prevail.

## Chapter XXIII: The Supernova: The Almighty Alchemist

A nd the nebula would *contain* a legacy of elements from hydrogen and helium, from carbon through uranium. Thus this and other supernovas would *provide* the interstellar regions of the Universe with almost all the non-light elements.[80]

For millions of years would the pulsar beam its signal. And the loss of energy in emissions would *slow* its spin.[81] And eventually, only once every several seconds would it spin. And its broadcast signal then would *cease*. And the pulsar *would* become a quiescent neutron star.

Now the stellar death, which had been *disruptive and destructive*, produced a benefit. And *like unto* dead vegetation, which rots and forms the soil for other plants, the supernova would become a source for *new creations*. Now Big Bang nucleosynthesis made the first three elements, hydrogen, helium and lithium. And the giant star made medium-weight elements like carbon, oxygen, nitrogen and iron. And the explosion scattered them through outer space, where they settled and joined intragalactic gas and dust. And eventually, the mixture would *collapse* and form a planetary-stellar system. And a *new star*, rich in medium-weight elements, would thus be *born*.

*Daffodils shall bloom*
*around the tombstones of the dead.*

## Chapter XXIV: Other Supernovas

A nd let it be known to thee and all around thee that supernovas exploded often in the early Universe. And that supernovas have exploded throughout cosmic history and *will* continue to explode. And that they will erupt wherever stars are found – in galactic active nuclei, in the spiral arms of galaxies, in globular and open clusters, in starrich nebulae, in stars within galactic halos, and so on. And let it be known that supernovas supply material and elements to build *new stars*.

*Dead plants shall leave behind*
*the seeds for future generations.*

And the supernova in this Book of Exodus was *relatively* mild. Now *if* the mass of the original star had been less, smaller would have

---

[80] Exceptions would be for beryllium and boron. Most beryllium and boron would be made by cosmic ray collisions of protons with nitrogen-fourteen and carbon-twelve.

[81] In the supernova explosion of this Book of *Exodus X*, the initial spinning rate was thirty times a second. In other cases, the initial rate varied from one time to one-hundred times a second.

been its iron core. The initial shock wave would *not* have stalled inside the iron core. And it would *not* have rested and lost energy. Instead, it would have passed directly through the iron core and out. And the pressure of the shock wave *would* have had more power, the force on nuclei and gas *would* have been much stronger, and material would have been ejected outward harder. Thus the explosion would have been *severer* – the supernova would have been significantly brighter.

And *if* the mass of the original star had been larger, twenty-five solar masses or more, the iron core *would* have been a little bigger. And the neutron star would have weighed *twice* the Sun or more. In cooling and contracting, it would have shrunk *significantly smaller*. And its pull of gravity would have been *so powerful* that *nothing*, including light, would have been able to escape. A black hole a few kilometers in size *would* have been produced. It would have been an *invisible* stellar cinder.

And let it be known to thee and all around thee that a star with less than eight solar masses shall collapse but *not* explode. And it shall burn its hydrogen, and perhaps some helium and carbon, but when its nuclear fuel is spent, the pressure of electrons shall *prevent* complete collapse. Such a star shall shrink until quite small. A *white dwarf* shall be its name. And it shall burn its nuclei until it is *too cool* to burn them any more. And then its light shall be *extinguished*. And the glow shall fade and disappear like the embers in a fire. And without light, a star is by definition *dead*. The corpse of such a star shall be a *brown dwarf*.

Now among white dwarfs, which do not explode when they collapse, some *barely* shall support their heavy mass. And of these stars, *some* shall have a binary companion. And if the white dwarf's force of gravity draws matter from its companion into the white dwarf's oxygen-and-carbon core, and if the accretion of this matter pushes the white dwarf's mass beyond its critical mass limit so that the pressure of electrons can no longer maintain weight, then the white dwarf shall contract and heat up quickly. And the nuclear chemistry of the star shall be upset. And higher temperatures shall provoke a *flurry* of nuclear-fusion chain-reactions. And *tremendous* energy production shall *blast* the star apart. And this shall be a *type-one supernova*. And although the total energy released shall be one-hundred times smaller than in a type-two supernova, more *visible light* shall be emitted. Thus optically, a type-one supernova shall typically outshine a type-two supernova by five times.

## Chapter XXV: Supernovas and Life

And in the *first three minutes*, *Nature* made the hydrogen and helium, which *would* make stars. And in the billions of years thereafter, stars made the moderately heavy elements from carbon all the way to cobalt. Next Nature *made* some stars collapse and then explode in supernovas. And the elements were spilled in outer space. And Nature *took* the elements from all the corners of the Universe and *made* dust, atoms, molecules and protostars.

And someday the hydrogen, nitrogen, iron, carbon, oxygen and other elements, which supernovas tossed into the open spaces of the Universe, *would come together* in the form of planets like the Earth. And later, carbon, oxygen and hydrogen would form organic molecules. And such organic molecules would mix and make a macroscopic structure *which* would be a form of life.

*The eighteenth book of Creation, called*

# Exodus XI: A Dust Cloud Formation

*They pitched their tents where the cloud abode.*

## Chapter I: A Special Cloud of Molecules Is Made

*And Moses led his people out of the land of slavery.*
*And they wandered in the desert wilderness for years.*
*And one day they reached the Promised Land.*
*And there they battled with the local tribes.*
*And finally they settled there.*
*And a new covenant was conceived in the land of Canaan.*

It was five-billion years ago. And a star exploded thirty-thousand light years from the center of the Milky Way – it *was* a supernova. And gas and debris were ejected out, as the supernova spilled its contents into space. And the ejecta travelled for thousands of millenniums through voids. And it moved through the Milky Way in a particular direction, *as though* it had purpose.

And forty-thousand years went by. And it came to pass that the debris of the supernova met a dense cloud of hydrogen and helium. Atoms and molecules of light- and medium-weight elements *merged* with the dense interstellar hydrogen and helium. And they swirled and intermingled. And it was *as if* a mysterious finger stirred the soup of elements and mixed the contents.

And two-hundred-thousand years went by. And the hydrogen and helium gas *circulated* in a giant swirl. And there were *small amounts* of molecules containing oxygen, magnesium, carbon, sulfur, silicon and iron. And atoms of neon and argon floated without interacting. And also present were molecules containing nitrogen, nickel, sodium, aluminum and calcium. A cloud of molecules had formed in interstellar space. Ten-thousand astronomical units[82] *was* its size.

---

[82] One astronomical unit is the Earth-Sun distance of one-hundred-and-fifty-million kilometers.

## Chapter II: Dust Develops

A nd *the cloud* was thin and slowly turned. Against the backdrop of
the Universe, *it* was black, floating lifelessly in the *emptiness* of
space.

And two water molecules within the cloud bumped against each
other and they *stuck* – molecular forces held the two together. And they
stayed together because the temperature was low: In such a cold environment, molecules had little thermal motion and hardly any agitation.[83] And a molecule of methane and a molecule of hydrogen collided.
And they too *stuck together*. And a helium atom and a silicon-dioxide
molecule bumped and separated; the helium atom continued floating in
the cloud in isolation. And when a molecule of hydrogen hit a molecule
of ammonia, they joined and made a larger molecule. Elsewhere, $H_2O$
and $FeO$ combined.

And other molecules within the cloud did bump and make *new
molecules*. And in joining, they created molecules of larger size. And
molecules kept sticking to each other until microscopic particles were
formed.

Thus it came to be that the cloud was filled with helium and hydrogen gases, with molecules and with particles of micron size. And the
cloud of gas and dust did slowly turn. It was *like unto* a pot of soup.
And it seemed *as if* someone with a ladle stirred the soup.

And gas and dust not only did revolve around but also *drifted in*
somewhat. The contents slowly spiralled to the center of the cloud. The
cloud had started to collapse.

And from a viewpoint far away, the cloud was verily invisible.
But one could *sense its presence*, for the central region blocked out background stars. Against the backdrop of the Universe, the cloud was
black. And it floated there mysteriously *as if* it had a purpose.

---

[83] If the temperature had been higher, the motions of the molecules would not have allowed them to combine.

*The nineteenth book of Creation, called*

# Exodus XII: Geogenesis I

*They were given a place called home.*

## Chapter I: The Cloud Gets Lumpy

It was a little more than four-billion-seven-hundred-million years ago. And in the vast wilderness of outer space, *the giant disk-shaped cloud*[84] of gas and dust did slowly turn. And the center of the cloud contained a *small* dense, warming core. Toward the core, material slowly drifted *inward*.

In the outer regions of the cloud, one dust particle bumped against another. And when they bumped, they *stuck together*. And they did so in the same way that two snow flakes do. And in adhering, the particles made a *larger* piece of dust.

And elsewhere, other particles through random motions came in contact. And through touching, sticking and combining, *larger* particles did form. As several million years went by, millimeter-sized grains *were grown*. And so the contents of the cloud got lumpy. Slowly did the giant spiral cloud of helium and hydrogen, of molecules, of dust and grains revolve around the central core. The seeds for cosmic creations were contained within the cloud.

And a piece of dust came in contact with a grain. And it *adhered to it*. And the grain continued moving through the cloud. As it met other particles of dust, they *adhered to it*. And this grain thus *grew* in size.

And as they swept through space, so did other grains increase in size.

## Chapter II: Macroscopic Objects Form

And millions of years went by. And it had come to pass that the cloud in the black of outer space contained helium and hydrogen gases, pellets, ices, molecules, dust particles and grains. The pellets, grains and ices ranged in size from millimeters to centimeters.

And it happened that two ice-pellets struck each other, ricocheted and moved *apart*. And it happened that an ice-grain touched an ice-pellet. And they remained in contact for a second and they *fused*.

And elsewhere, pellets, grains and ices moved through space, collecting dust and molecules and sometimes fusing. And *they* increased in size. They were *like unto* small snowballs moving through a snowstorm; when a snowflake comes in contact with a snowball, it sticks to it, adding to the snowball's mass.

Now innermost material in the cloud *was drawn into* the central core[85] by gravity. Material far from the center slowly drifted both in-

---

[84] This is the same cloud as in *Exodus XI*.

ward and around. And during many million years, the cloud *collapsed* and grew denser and more lumpy.[86]

As the matter in the cloud converged, the contents of the cloud were merged. And it came to pass that *macroscopic* objects formed, so that the cloud contained helium and hydrogen, grains, pellets, ices, molecules, dust particles and ice-rock boulders; the largest of latter were a meter long.

## Chapter III: Asteroids Appear

And ice-rock boulders revolved around the core in the outer regions of the cloud. The pellets, ices, dust and grains that touched the boulders stuck to them through cohesive forces. These boulders swept through space, *aggregating* mass.

And it *happened*[87] that a smaller boulder struck a larger one and stuck to it. And the larger boulder continued to accumulate more mass. And eventually, it grew into a *massive chunk*. And elsewhere in the cloud, other massive chunks *were forming*.

And the cloud of helium and hydrogen, molecules, dust, pellets, ices, boulders, grains and massive chunks revolved *as a gigantic slowly turning disk* in outer space. And the massive chunks *were* of different shapes and sizes, ranging ten to several hundred meters long.

And during the next few million years, the processes of aggregation generated even larger objects. And truly *sizeable* ice-rock structures formed. And such an object was provided with a name: the *asteroid*. And in the giant disk-like system, there were asteroids from one to ten kilometers in size. Some asteroids were made of mostly ices, grains and dust – they were comet-like.

## Chapter IV: Asteroids Grow Larger

And it *happened* that a boulder struck a ten-kilometer-sized asteroid and broke in several fragments. And the fragments rebounded, rose, slowed down, and fell, striking the asteroid again. And they bounced *several* times before they settled on the surface. And as this asteroid sped through space, other boulders rained down on it, breaking and *settling* on its surface.

Now it *happened* that a one-hundred-meter ice-rock chunk struck the asteroid. And the asteroid shook but *stayed intact*. However, the chunk broke into many *pieces*; it *was like* the dropping a clay pot on a concrete floor, except the pieces bounced up higher. Now some small pieces rose so high that they escaped to outer space. But most slowed and fell and struck again. And these pieces broke in even smaller

---

[85] At this stage, the core was hot. The processes leading to the heating of the core were similar to those described in Chapters I-III of *Exodus VII*.

[86] The diameter of the cloud was still large – five-hundred astronomical units.

[87] More often, two boulders simply rebounded when they collided.

pieces, which bounced several times but eventually *settled* on the surface of the asteroid.

And as this asteroid *advanced through space*, boulders rained down on it, struck and broke in fragments. And less frequently, the asteroid was hit by chunks tens of meters wide. And the fragments from collisions ultimately settled on the asteroid.

And it *happened* that a two-kilometer-sized asteroid struck this ten-kilometer-sized asteroid. And thousands of pieces *broke off* the two. But the bulk of these two asteroids *remained intact*. And they bounced off each other. The smaller moved away, then stopped and began to slowly moved toward the larger one. And it struck again; the two asteroids "bumped heads" the way rams do, except more slowly. And although the impact speed was low, *hundreds* of smaller pieces still broke off. The pieces rose, slowed and rained down upon the two. And the asteroids bumped heads a few more times then stopped. The *impact area* was glowing slightly red. And in outer space, the two asteroids hung together loosely, not cohesively, but by a feeble *force of gravity*.

And elsewhere in the giant cloud, other multi-kilometer-sized asteroids collided. And in colliding, sometimes they deflected, continuing to move as independent asteroids. But sometimes, they combined. And gradually, by accumulating massive chunks and boulders, and sometimes by combining, the asteroids did grow in size.

## Chapter V: The Cloud Is Cleansed and Seen

And hundreds of thousands of years did pass. And suddenly at the center of the giant cloud, a *glow* appeared. As it grew bright, a *great wind* emerged from the region of the glow, speeding *outward* through the cloud. And much of the helium, hydrogen gas, molecules and fine dust were blown out, swept away *like unto* dust beneath a broom. And they travelled for hundreds of millions of kilometers, moving to the outer regions of the cloud. And some material was even blown beyond the system, disappearing in the wilderness of outer space. It was *as if* a powerful explosion had occurred. And there in the central region was a luminous bright disk three times bigger than the modern Sun – a star was born.

Now in the cloud, the debris of grains, rocks and asteroids remained; all revolving in a swirl, each one *reflecting* starlight from the star. And for the first time, all the asteroids were seen. And from afar, it *looked like* confetti reflecting sunlight in a ticker-tape parade.

Now the cloud was full of asteroids. Most were a few to several hundred kilometers in size. And in the cloud were also loosely connected pairs of asteroids that floated *as a unit*. These pairs *were bound together* through the force of gravity. And from a viewpoint far away, they *looked like* two irregularly shaped large marbles held in the fist of an invisible huge hand.

## Chapter VI: A Planetesimal Appears and Heats Up

A nd one-hundred-and-sixty-million kilometers from the center of the
system was a body with a three-thousand-kilometer diameter.[88]
And since it was much larger than an asteroid, it was called a *planetesimal*. And it orbited around the star with the other asteroids and rock
debris. Now it *happened* that a fifty-kilometer-sized asteroid did pass
nearby. And propelled by Nature's force of gravity, it accelerated and it
struck the planetesimal. A powerful collision and explosion shook that
area of outer space. It was *like unto* the denotation of countless warheads loaded with atomic bombs. But the energy unleashed was not
nuclear in nature, but mechanical. And the asteroid *vibrated violently*,
then *broke in pieces*. Huge rocks were tossed onto the surface of the
planetesimal. Pieces of the asteroid *glowed red and melted*. Shock
waves speeding through the planetesimal *shook* its core. Rock-ice inside
*absorbed* the waves. And inner regions of the planetesimal were
*warmed*. And dust and debris rose above the planetesimal, then fell
and struck its surface. And after half a minute, all debris had settled
on its surface. Lava *bubbled* at the impact site. Steam and gas *spewed
out*. As surrounding rock absorbed the heat of molten rock, the lava
cooled and froze in place. On the surface of the planetesimal was *an
enormous crater*.

Now the planetesimal revolved around the star, while boulders,
debris and massive chunks, drawn by Nature's force of gravity, *rained
down* upon it. And when they struck the surface, dust flew up, the surface shook and craters were created. Sometimes comet-like objects
smashed into the planetesimal; they deposited ices, gas and dust.
Less frequently, an asteroid approached and crashed. In this case,
there was a violent mechanical explosion. And *great quantities* of energy *passed* into the planetesimal. And it *was warmed*.

And through these impacts, the planetesimal did *grow in size*.
And as it grew, inner rock was crushed by weight of outer rock. And the
weight created monumental pressure which *squeezed and heated* inner
rock. And so the core *was warmed*.

Now uranium *inside* the planetesimal decayed to energetic products. And the products *struck* surrounding rock, *depositing* their energy.
And surrounding rock got hot. Hidden in the planetesimal was *faintly
glowing rock*.

And elsewhere in the planetesimal, radioactive materials and
elements decayed and heated rock. And so the planetesimal *was
warmed*.

---

[88] Even farther from the center were several larger bodies, tens of thousands of kilometers in diameter.

## Chapter VII: An Atmosphere Forms

And when the planetesimal was struck by boulders, massive chunks and asteroids, gases at the impact sites *spewed out*. And gas with high velocity *escaped* the planetesimal. But less energetic gas rose up and *stayed* – the planetesimal's force of gravity retained it. And so it came to pass that the planetesimal *obtained* an atmosphere of nitrogen gas, carbon dioxide, water vapor, methane and ammonia.

And in time, the *atmosphere* grew thicker. And light rays from the central star did warm it from *above*. And heat from the surface of the planetesimal did warm it from *below*.

And it happened that a bit of rock from outer space was *drawn* toward the planetesimal. And when it *hit* the atmosphere, *it* burned up and glowed – a *meteor* was it.

And from time to time, other meteors did *strike the atmosphere* and glow. Now hitherto, outer space debris had struck the surface of the planetesimal and often had created craters. But now *small* comet-like objects and rock bits burned up before they struck the surface. And so the atmosphere served *as a blanket of protection*.

And the planetesimal continued spewing gas. As the atmosphere obtained more mass, *it grew very thick*. And so it came to pass that the atmosphere grew superdense. It acted *like unto* a giant sleeping bag, for it retained the warmth of its enormous occupant: Heat originating from the planetesimal was trapped by atmospheric gas. And the lower atmosphere got particularly hot.[89]

## Chapter VIII: The Atmosphere Survives Bombardment

And *it so happened* that a two-hundred-kilometer-sized asteroid, having *ventured near* the planetesimal, was drawn to it by Nature's force of gravity. And the asteroid pierced the atmosphere. As it descended, it created *a great wind*, which swept off some atmospheric gas, dispersing it in outer space. Then, with mighty force, the asteroid *struck* the planetesimal. The *thermal violent explosion* generated enormous quantities of heat. And during the next several hundred-thousand years, many such medium-sized asteroids did strike the planetesimal.

And *it came to happen* that an asteroid with a nine-hundred-kilometer diameter *passed near* the planetesimal. And it was drawn to the larger body by the force of gravity. And it smashed into the planetesimal, blowing much of its atmosphere away, as pressure waves and winds sent gases flying into outer space. And when the asteroid struck the surface of the planetesimal, there was a *thermal vio-*

---

[89] It was one-and-a-half thousand Kelvins, which is three times hotter than a hot oven.

*lent intense explosion.* Rock turned into red hot magma[90] at the impact site.

Now although some atmospheric gas remained, the *atmosphere* was *thin.* And it no longer held the heat so well. And the surface of the planetesimal and its atmosphere both *cooled.* Four-hundred Kelvins was the lower atmosphere.[91]

> *It was* as if *someone stole a sleeping bag*
> *and left behind a sheet.*

And it happened that a rock from outer space was *drawn* toward the planetesimal. And the rock passed through the atmosphere. And it glowed somewhat but did not vaporize. And the rock hit the surface of the planetesimal.[92]

And with so *thin an atmosphere,* the planetesimal was verily exposed: Rocks tumbled down from outer space and struck its surface. And at the impact sites of meteorites, *gas spewed out and up.*

And since the atmosphere was *thinner* than before, impacts occurred *more frequently.* As more gas from impacts rose into the *atmosphere, it* regained its mass. And so it came to pass that the atmosphere grew superdense again.

> *It was* as if *someone took the sheet*
> *and left behind a sleeping bag.*

And the planetesimal was warm in its thick gaseous blanket. And the atmosphere grew hot again.

And during the next several hundred-thousand years, a few large asteroids struck the planetesimal, each time, *blowing off* the *atmosphere.* And when *it* blew off, it thinned and cooled. And *each time,* after it had thinned, emissions at the surface released new gas into the atmosphere. And consequently the atmosphere grew dense again and was renewed.

## Chapter IX: A Planet Called Earth Appears

Now the planetesimal had absorbed much of the matter in the region of its orbit. And during hundreds of thousands of years, it had grown to a sphere with a ten-thousand-kilometer diameter. It had become a *planet.* And the planet was provided with a name. And the name was *Earth.* It was four-and-a-half billion years ago.

And the *bright disk* in the daytime sky, which was three times bigger than the modern Sun – *that star* was the Sun.[93]

---

[90] *Magma* is liquid rock.

[91] This is the temperature of a warm oven, about 170° Celsius, or 250° Fahrenheit.

[92] When outer-space debris *hits* a planetismal or planet, it becomes a *meteorite.*

[93] Although the disk of the Sun was bigger, visible light emissions at this time were about thirty per cent lower than in modern times; ultraviolet radiation was about twenty per cent higher.

Now the numerous impacts from asteroids and meteorites as well as gravitational squeezing of its body had significantly heated Earth. Ices long ago had melted and had vaporized. And most rock had also melted. Earth was *very hot*. Indeed, it was a giant globe almost entirely *of magma rock*.

And molten drops of heavy metals such as iron *sank*, drifting to the center of the Earth. But compounds containing lighter elements such as silicon, sodium, aluminum, magnesium, potassium and calcium *rose up*, drifting to the surface of the planet. And so the force of gravity did *separate* the elements.

Thus it came to pass that Earth contained *all elements*, among which were *rare ones* such as silver, platinum and gold. And eventually, small bits of these three precious metals would surface to the surface of the Earth. And they would *sparkle* on a sunny day from Sun's reflected light.

## Chapter X: The Earth Gives Birth: the Moon Is Made

And *it came to happen* that a planetesimal with a three-thousand-kilometer diameter *passed* near thy planet Earth. And the planetesimal, feeling the force of gravity, charged toward the Earth, *like unto* a bull toward a matador. And the planetesimal *smashed* into the molten Earth. And if ye had been watching it from far away, the collision would have looked like a slow motion movie of a droplet dropping into water: The sphere of Earth did stretch in one direction – it became egg-shaped. A giant molten sphere with a three-thousand-kilometer diameter *broke off* and was ejected into outer space. Then the elongated part of Earth collapsed toward the center while the shorter part expanded. And Earth was squashed the other way. And several oscillations followed. And *then* the Earth was spherical again.

Now during the impact, enormous magma spheres were tossed about. And they moved away from Earth, slowed, fell back and struck the Earth. And Earth's molten body *shook*.

But the three-thousand-kilometer-sized molten sphere *swung out* from Earth. And there it slowed as the Earth's gravity took hold. At twenty-thousand kilometers away, it began *to move about the Earth* in a distorted circle. And since it had no atmosphere, heat readily *radiated* from its surface. And the magma sphere then *cooled*. And eventually did it *solidify*. And the giant sphere was named. And it was named the *Moon*.

And viewed from Earth, the Moon was *twenty times* its modern size, for the Moon was closer than in modern times. And during the next few billion years, it would spiral *outward* from the Earth.

Now the Moon was spinning fast. But *eventually* its spin would slow and synchronize with Earth. And then the Moon would hold a *single face* to Earth.

And it came to pass that another giant asteroid struck the Earth, but this time with a *glancing blow*. And Earth was turned a bit. And Earth, which had been spinning in the plane of its orbit round the Sun, spun at an angle *of twenty-three degrees*.

Now daylight on Earth lasted just three hours. And nighttime also lasted but three hours. Thus *six hours long* was day. And this was so for Earth was *spinning faster* than in modern times – the World was very different in four-billion-and-five-hundred-million years BC.

## Chapter XI: The Birth of Other Planets

And elsewhere, the largest planetesimals aggregated the matter in their regions of the solar system *and evolved to* planets. And there were nine such planets, named as so: The one nearest to the Sun was *Mercury*; the next was *Venus*; the third was *Earth*; the fourth was *Mars*; the fifth was *Jupiter*; the sixth was *Saturn*; the seventh one was named *Uranus*; the eighth was *Neptune*; and the ninth one and farthest from the Sun was *Pluto*.

Now these planets had formed in a manner *similar* to Earth. However, Mercury and Venus encountered no truly cataclysmic impacts. Thus Mercury and Venus had no moons. And since Mercury was small, it had less gravity. And since Mercury was near the Sun, it was hot and felt a strong solar wind. Thus Mercury retained no atmosphere. And Uranus, Saturn, Jupiter and Neptune aggregated much more material than Earth and grew to be quite large – the formation of *these larger four* was similar to the formation of the solar system. Thus each developed miniature solar-system-like configurations in which the planet acted as the Sun. And so, *they* had satellites, debris and dust. But unlike the Moon, satellites were not produced in cataclysmic impacts – rather, at the same time that the planets formed, the satellites *accreted mass* while orbiting their planets. And this was true of most moons.[94] And Jupiter and Saturn, which were respectively three-hundred and one-hundred times *heavier* than Earth, retained through their strong gravities more hydrogen and helium.

Now not all multi-kilometer-sized objects were incorporated into planets. And *those* that were not captured and remained were named. And *asteroids* were they so named.

Thus a little more than four-billion-five-hundred-million years ago, *Nature*, during millions of years, made the molecular cloud that condensed to make the Sun, the planets, the Earth and Moon. And these bodies collectively were called the *solar system*. And so through natural processes and forces was the solar system made.

---

[94] A few moons were captured later. An example is Phoebe. See the Book of *Saturn*.

*The twentieth book of Creation, called*

# Geogenesis II: The Infant Earth

*And the dry land was called Earth.*
*And the gathering together of the waters was called Seas.*
*And this happened on the third day*
*of the first month of a long lost year.*

## Chapter I: The Earth Cools

*The hills melted like wax at His presence.*

This is the beginning of geo-history. It is the path among the *possible* paths which thy planet Earth has picked. It was four-billion-four-hundred-million years ago. And the last impact of a *super giant* meteorite on Earth had passed.[95] And the original superdense atmosphere had to a large extent been blown away – the original primordial gases had long been lost. But the thinner atmosphere which remained was *still many times thicker* than the atmosphere in modern times.

Now the formation of the Earth from smaller parts had left it in a *hot and violent* state – almost all of Earth was molten rock. And so Earth began the processes of cooling off.

And it came to pass that, deep inside the Earth, a *hot molten region* swelled and rose. And it *drifted up* toward the surface of the Earth where it released its heat and cooled. And a *cooler* but still quite hot region near the surface slowly *sank*. And near the center of the Earth, it absorbed heat, and it grew hot. And when it grew hot enough, it swelled and rose.

And such circulating, up-and-downward-moving currents were happening everywhere within the Earth. Molten Earth was in a turmoil. And *currents* slowly moved Earth's heat from its center to its outer layers. Thus convection[96] over distances of thousands of kilometers was occurring in the Earth.

And the heat that reached the outer layers moved to Earth's surface and escaped. And after passing through the atmosphere, the heat *entered into outer space* as radiation.

Now the surface of the Earth was solid. But it was very hot and glowing red. And it was dry – the surface was *so hot* that no *drop* of water could exist on it without *it* being vaporized.

*Water, water, nowhere.*

Now the *crust*, the very outer layer of Earth, was fragile and in fragments. And it was *like unto* an oven-heated pie. In many places just beneath the surface of the Earth, molten rock meandered in a ran-

---

[95] During the next several hundred-million years, many impacts would still occur but by objects smaller than multi-hundred-kilometer-sized asteroids.

[96] The flow of heat by motion of the medium is called *convection*.

dom way. And crustal pieces floated on a liquid Earth *like unto* ice-bergs on a sea.

And it came to pass that a *giant lobe of magma* surged toward Earth's surface and broke the crust in two. And lava *flowed* profusely, spilling onto nearby solid earth. And gases such as carbon dioxide, hydrogen sulfide, nitrogen, sulfur dioxide, water vapor, hydrogen, ammonia and methane spewed into the atmosphere.

And thrusts of magma *through* the crust were happening everywhere on Earth. And from a viewpoint far away, it would have seemed *as if* the skin of Earth were scratched and bleeding red. Now some magma movements pushed the earth into a funnel – these were thy planet's first *volcanos*. And from a viewpoint far away, they would have looked like pimples on the surface of the Earth. And *hot and liquid rock* poured out the central tunnels, while gases rich in carbon-sulfur compounds spurted up into the air.

And it happened that one particular spot on Earth's surface was *not solid* – it was a pool of red hot magma. And steamy gases made a cloud above the pool. Elsewhere did it come to pass that one patch of crust suddenly *gave way and sank*. And another pond of lava formed and cooled. And Earth had yet another scar. Thus the surface of the Earth had many pools of liquid rock.

And two adjacent crustal pieces *moved apart*, causing a giant rift between the two to form. And the region cracked and bled. And magma flowed up through the rift and onto nearby thin dry crust, while hot gases *spewed* into the atmosphere. And the lava cooled and finally solidified. And the rift froze over *like unto* a winter stream.

And elsewhere did it come to pass that a lobe of magma surged. And a volcanic blast spit bits of liquid rock *into the air*. And lava from the volcano flowed and spread to nearby land. But this land *could not support* the lava weight. And so, through Nature's force of gravity the lava *sank* into a molten pool. And then the volcano followed suit and sank below the surface too.

The surface of the Earth was full of scars. And *everywhere*, gases poured through holes in hot thin crust.

And it so happened that a boulder, speeding through the black of outer space, struck Earth's upper atmosphere. And the boulder's surface melted, burned and vaporized. And a brilliant glow ensued. Then the object *struck* the Earth itself. And at the impact site, lava oozed, hot gases spurted up, and another magma hole was *upon the face of Earth*.

And so it came to pass that the surface of the Earth was pitted, not with craters, but with volcanos and with red-hot lava holes.

And in many places in the Earth were concentrations of short-lived radioactive elements. And those just below Earth's surface decayed, created heat and led to small hot spots. And above such spots, liquid rock and gases oozed out *like unto* sweat from pores.

And by an *act of Nature*, two crustal pieces *pushed against* each other, leading to a mountain ridge. But the mountains *did not long endure*, for within a million years did they dissolve away *like unto* butter in an oven.

And Earth's hot surface heated nearby air. And as such hot air rose up above the Earth, it expanded and it *cooled*. Then this cooler air *descended* until it reached the surface of the Earth. There, it warmed. And when it had warmed enough, it rose *again*.

And everywhere in massive movements, air was heaving up and down – it was convection of the atmosphere.

Now the heat in the upper atmosphere was released to outer space as radiation in the infrared; the waves sped out *in all directions* at the speed of light.

## Chapter II: The Early Atmosphere

And behold, one-hundred-and-fifty-million kilometers away there sat the Sun, thy planet's nearby star. And it was *less brilliant* than in modern times. In this ancient past was Sun a lesser sun.

And gases rising from Earth's surface formed *dense clouds*. And the highest clouds were struck by ultraviolet light. And such light often broke the molecules apart. Now the destruction of a molecule by light was called *photodissociation*. And for example, carbon dioxide was converted into carbon monoxide and $O_2$; and ammonia was broken into gases of nitrogen and hydrogen; and water, when destroyed by ultraviolet rays, became gases of oxygen and hydrogen. Now the pieces of the broken molecules often quickly *recombined*. And the oxygen gas, which was produced by photodissociation, did not last, for it was rapidly *incorporated* into other molecules. And free oxygen near Earth's surface was *absorbed* by metals in the earth – the glitter of such metals disappeared as rust was made. Thus Earth's atmosphere contained *very little diatomic oxygen*. Now hydrogen gas, being light, rose to the upper limits of the atmosphere and fled the Earth. And so it came to pass that the atmosphere evolved, becoming mainly carbon dioxide, water vapor, nitrogen, ammonia and methane, with small amounts of carbon monoxide, sulfur dioxide, hydrogen sulfide and other toxic gases.

Now the Sun was not visible from the surface of thy planet Earth, for the atmosphere was *thick*. Sunrays were diffused and were absorbed by clouds and atmospheric gas. And during day, the sky was bright but always overcast. And in the air was always haze. And during night the Earth was *dark* – even the Moon could not be seen.

Now most solar radiation directed at the Earth struck the outer atmosphere, thereby heating it. As hot air molecules moved rapidly, they sometimes reached high altitudes and fled the Earth *to outer space*. In effect, the Sun was burning off some outer atmosphere.

And although little light reached the lower atmosphere, the air there *was* still very warm – heat from the surface of the Earth *was trapped* by the carbon-dioxide-dominated atmosphere and water-vapor clouds. And bound to Earth by gravity, these clouds and gases acted *like unto* the canopy of a hot-air balloon tethered to the ground – hot air rose but was contained within the canopy.[97]

Now these were times in which the atmosphere functioned as a factory for chemistry. When carbon dioxide, hydrogen sulfide, water, methane, nitrogen, ammonia and hydrogen were mixed, *new* molecules were made. And these new molecules combined with old molecules and even *more* new molecules were made.

And let it be known to thee and all around thee that oxygen reacts quickly with substances containing carbon; so oxygen inhibits many carbon-based reactions. But with hardly any atmospheric diatomic oxygen, the production of certain organic molecules *did* indeed proceed. And among these molecules were formaldehyde, hydrogen cyanide, hydroxy acids, glucose, fructose and amino acids. Thus the lack of atmospheric oxygen was a *blessing* for organic molecules.

And tens of millions of years went by. And it happened that a *giant* meteor passed through the upper atmosphere. And it *fortunately* missed the Earth. But it swept away a little atmosphere, leaving a region rarified of air. And quickly *through this hole*, heat and radiation in the infrared escaped, until air currents brought in air to fill the void. Now the atmosphere lost many molecules, but *still* did it remain quite dense.

And what had happened *was like* a tiny pellet that pierced the plastic of a hot-air balloon. And the balloon lost gas *through* a tiny hole. But the balloon almost instantly repaired itself. And so not a lot of gas was lost.

## Chapter III: The Earth Solidifies Somewhat

*Mountains shall be thrown down*
*and every wall shall fall unto the ground.*

And tens of millions of years went by. And the molten body of the Earth continued radiating heat. Such heat rose *upward* through the atmosphere and was released. And bit by bit, the Earth did cool.

And it came to pass that, during millions of years, sections of the Earth's crust rose up, turned over, sank and disappeared. Crust was thus repeatedly folded *like unto* the dough between the palms of a great baker who kneaded it to make a bread. These were times in which thy planet Earth was in a state of instability.

Now there happened to be radioactive matter near the surface of the Earth. And one nucleus in this matter decayed into an alpha particle and other products. And the particle's double charge produced a *local strong electric force*. And two nearby electrons, feeling the force, were

---

[97] This is the *greenhouse effect.*

drawn toward the alpha particle and captured by it – atomic helium was thus created. And elsewhere, other alpha particles appeared and grabbed electron pairs. And so it came to pass that helium gas inside the Earth *was being made*. But the gas *did not* often last too long, for much of it slipped through the cracks in crust and entered air. From there, it *ascended* to the upper limit of the atmosphere, where it escaped to outer space. Thus helium created at the surface of the Earth did disappear.

And tens of millions of years did pass. And Earth continued *cooling*. And it had happened that the outer part of Earth had become a thicker solid sheet. And this outer layer was provided with a name: the *lithosphere*. Compared with modern times, the lithosphere was thin. Now inside Earth, solidification under a high pressure made some crystal structures. And certain heavy elements, such as uranium and thorium, *were squeezed* and forced to migrate. And *some* such migrating heavy elements *rose up* and lodged themselves in open cracks of crystalline oxides and silicates of crustal rock.

And somewhere in the lithosphere was a speck of uranium-two-thirty-eight. During the next two-billion years, about one quarter of the uranium *would turn* to lead. And in four-billion years, almost another quarter would turn to lead. Thus the speck of uranium-two-thirty-eight was *like unto* an hour glass. And the sand in the upper chamber was uranium. And when the sand passed to the lower chamber, it *turned* to lead. And by examining how much uranium and lead were present, one could tell the time.

And elsewhere in the lithosphere were other specks of uranium-two-thirty-eight. Thus *many* radioactive time-pieces were buried in Earth's crust. And when thy planet's crust was made, the radioactive chronometers began to tick. And they would tick *throughout* the history of Earth and *to this day*. And geologists in modern times would collect selected samples of Earth's earth. And they would examine them and read the times. And samples from Mount Narryer in western Australia would read *four-billion-and-three-hundred-million* years. Thus scientists would conclude that the first bits of solid Earth appeared over four-billion years ago.

And scientists would inspect the Moon, meteorites and other objects in the solar system. And these objects would contain some radioactive elements. And scientists would examine them and tell the times. And four-and-a-half-billion years would be the times. Thus scientists would conclude that the *ages* of the Sun, Earth, planets, comets, Moon and asteroids, which make up the solar system, were *four-billion-and-five-hundred-million years*.

Now the lithosphere, which first appeared four-billion-and-three-hundred-million years ago, was made of solidified magmatic rock. Dark igneous rock,[98] which cooled quickly, was called *basalt*.[99] In some places, basalt did crystallize. Such crystal magma rock was *gabbro*. And sometimes other igneous rocks richer in alumina and silica, such as *andesite*,[100] were forged. And still others, high in silica and low in magnesium and iron oxides, formed such as *granite*, in which seventy-five percent was silica, and such as *granodiorite*, in which sixty-five percent was silica. And these igneous rocks were *the first rocks* on Earth.

And during the next four-billion-and-three-hundred-million years through unto this day, magma *in* the Earth and lava *on* the Earth would flow, eventually solidify and make magmatic rock.

Now *crustal movements* led instantly[101] to valleys, plains and mountains. And impacts from meteorites created craters. But the surface of the Earth was *in a constant flux* and, in a million years, the craters, valleys, plains and mountains were regurgitated and destroyed. And new structures were continually arising to replace those that had been lost.

And Earth continued *cooling*. And eventually it came to pass that a *new solid layer* appeared below the lithosphere. And it was provided with a name: the *asthenosphere*. Now the rock making up the asthenosphere was predominantly *peridotite*, which was a magnesium-rich olivine.[102] And the border between the lithosphere and asthenosphere a few dozen kilometers below the ground was provided with a name. And the *Mohorovicic discontinuity* was its name.

And it came to pass that a meteorite struck Earth. And a *great sound wave* propagated through the Earth. And when it went below the "Moho," its speed suddenly *increased*.

And these were times when the land of Earth was *constantly* in motion, when major earthquakes often made land shake, when volcanos came and *disappeared*, when Earth's land was badly bruised and blistered, and when hills and valleys sometimes suddenly[103] *appeared*.

---

[98] *Igneous rock* is magma that solidifies.

[99] It consisted of approximately fifty percent silica ($SO_2$), fifteen percent alumina or ($Al_2O_3$), ten percent iron oxides, ten percent calcium oxide (CaO), and ten percent of other metal oxides. The iron oxide was mostly FeO, but there was also some $Fe_2O_3$ and $Fe_3O_4$.

[100] Andesite consisted of approximately fifty-five percent silica, seventeen percent alumina, nine percent iron oxide, eight percent calcium oxide, four percent magnesium oxide (MgO), four percent of $Na_2O$ soda, and a few percent of other metal oxides.

[101] "Instantly" in this geo-historical context means thousands of years.

[102] *Olivine* is a green-colored rock-forming silicate of $Mg_2SiO_4$, $Fe_2SiO_4$ and $Ca_2SiO_4$ with lesser quantities of other minerals.

[103] "Suddenly" here means during hundreds of years.

## Chapter IV: The Earth Acquires Water

*Let the waters under Heaven be gathered in one place,*
*and let the dry land appear.*
*And it was so.*
*And this happened on the third day*
*of the first month of a long lost year.*

And it came to pass that a heavy cloud in the lower atmosphere *let loose* its water drops. And the water droplets fell naturally to Earth – it was a rain. Indeed, it was *the first rain*. And carbon dioxide, sulfur dioxide and other chemicals were *absorbed* into the falling droplets thereby forming acids. And for example, carbon dioxide combined with water to form carbonic acid. And as the acidic droplets fell *toward* the Earth, an *upward-moving* hot-air current met the rain. And the water droplets vaporized. And these vapors were carried *back* up to the lower atmosphere.

And henceforth during this period of geo-history, everywhere within the atmosphere it was raining but never did the droplets reach the ground.

And tens of millions of years passed by. And the outer part of Earth continued cooling: Five-hundred Kelvins was the surface temperature of Earth. The land was *dry* and hot. And the atmosphere was thick and toxic.[104]

Now solar cosmic rays and radiation hastened the release of atmospheric gases *into outer space*. And they rubbed away the outer atmosphere the way sandpaper rubs away a surface. Thus atmospheric gas was lost. But outgassing *at the surface of the Earth* replenished lost carbon dioxide, water vapor, nitrogen, ammonia and methane.

And the lower atmosphere did manufacture *certain* complicated molecules, with lightning and ultraviolet solar radiation *aiding* the production. And *minute* amounts of biological building blocks, such as nucleotide bases and porphyrins,[105] were made. And energy-rich organic molecules more primitive than but similar to adenosine triphosphate were produced.

And thy planet Earth was cooling *like unto* a giant radiating furnace. And with the loss of heat, the lithosphere grew thicker. But most of inner Earth was molten liquid metals.

And one-hundred-million years went by and disappeared. And then *it came to pass* that a dark cloud let loose its acid rain. And from the heavens did the pristine, clear round drops *descend to Earth*. And the first drops *landed* on hot rock. And they sizzled and evaporated instantly. And more drops did land – it was the baptism of the Earth. And steam rose up above the rocks.

---

[104] The Earth at this time was like the planet Venus of today.

[105] Porphyrins are organic light-absorbing nitrogen-containing compounds.

*And there went up a mist out of the earth,*
*and watered it the face of Earth.*

And the rain continued falling. Some rocks *cooled off* somewhat. And puddles formed. And little pools of water stayed. But within a day, the rocks were reheated from within the Earth. And so the pools evaporated, relinquishing their liquid bodies as *vapors* rising *up into the sky*. And the vapor carried heat into the lower atmosphere. And there, the moist air cooled and droplets formed. And another heavy cloud developed.

And roughly every other day, it *rained* almost everywhere on Earth. And the vapors *carried heat* into the atmosphere; it was a steamy scene. And the heat released by condensation *warmed* the atmosphere. And the rate of radiation in the infrared from Earth to outer space *increased*. And so the Earth began to cool *more* rapidly.

And tens of millions of years passed by. And where it rained, it did rain hard. Rain *fell upon* the mountains and the hills. Waters rushed down slopes, *tumbled over ledges* and flowed in crustal cracks. And the water dug gullies in the ground and made pools in indentations on the rocks. And it collected in the valleys. And so the surface of the Earth *was full* of puddles and of ponds.

And acids in the pools ate minerals in rocks, making such minerals *dissolve*. And for example, carbonic acid became aqueous bicarbonate and carbonate. And the carbonate combined with calcium ions thereby forming calcite, which *then precipitated* out – particles of calcite settled on the bottom of Earth's ponds as sediments.

Now the waters in the pools and ponds absorbed the heat from Earth's interior. In many places, *steam and gases rose*. And so the evaporation pace was rapid – it was a time when Earth's surface was a steamy place. The temperature of Earth continued its decline.

And tens of millions of years came and went. And it *happened* that, inside the Earth, more molten rock *solidified*. Beneath the asthenosphere, a *new* solid layer had formed. And the asthenosphere plus this new layer were provided with a name. And *that* name was the *mantle*. And the *region below this mantle* would be called Earth's *core*.

Now on the surface, warm acidic water *cut through* the lower parts of land, and *rivers* formed. They flowed into the countless ponds that filled the lowest parts of Earth. And the World had its first *real* rivers. And these rivers would be the veins and arteries of Earth.[106]

And warm water collected in the valley regions *and* made lakes. Thus Earth acquired *its first lakes*. And as Earth cooled, the rate of evaporation slowed and lakes enlarged. And tens of millions of years

---

[106] Later, such rivers would be barriers to the creatures that crept on Earth. But much later, one among these creatures – man – by the dexterity of his mind and hand would build bridges so that rivers could be crossed.

went by. And it came to pass that lakes joined, and there were seas. And Earth had *its first seas.*

And the Earth continued cooling. And as tens of millions of years went by, it came to pass that seas *increased in size.* And seas joined, and there were oceans. And as tens of millions of years went by, it came to pass that all the oceans joined and formed a *single giant ocean.* And this mighty ocean was provided with a name. And it was called the *Panthalassa Ocean.* Water had inundated the *entire* globe except in certain high-land regions. And these remaining lands were *microcontinents.* And in addition to the microcontinents, volcano tops above the ocean surface constituted islands.

*Earth possessed a* single *mighty sea.*

And when it rained, water droplets *absorbed* particles and toxic gases in the air. And such drops became *acidic.* And acid rain landed in the ocean. Then acids involving carbon, sulfur and other elements reacted in the ocean with bases built from calcium, magnesium and sodium as well as silicates. And *salts* were made. Now some salts were particles suspended in the sea. Such particles were *precipitates.* And gravity took hold of them and sent them drifting down. And in settling on the ocean floor, precipitates turned into *sediments.*

*It was snowing in the ocean,*
*snowing particles and sediments.*

Now rain, streaming through the air, *washed away* complicated molecules, which had been manufactured in the "atmospheric factory." Among these were organic compounds. And they *fell into* the Panthalassa Ocean. The *seeds* for life were sitting in the sea.

*The Garden of Eden lay dormant*
*at the bottom of the Panthalassa Ocean.*

And each time it rained, a little carbon was removed. It ended up *in* and *on the bottom of* the ocean. Thus the amount of carbon dioxide in the atmosphere was slowly *going down.* And the same was true for methane and ammonia and many other gases. But nitrogen remained. Thus the rain-evaporation cycle, the *hydrologic cycle,* acted as an atmospheric purifier. And during the next three-hundred-million years, carbon dioxide in the atmosphere decreased five-fold.[107]

*(And a voice spake, saying,*
*"All the rivers run into the sea;*
*yet the sea is not full;*
*unto the place from whence rivers come,*
*thither they return again.")*

---

[107] However, the carbon dioxide in the air was at this time still extremely high – it was hundreds of times the modern atmospheric level.

*The first book of Geo-Evolution, called*

# The Archean Eon I

*And as for Earth, every precious stone was in its covering:*
*the sapphire, emerald, and carbuncle,*
*the beryl, onyx, and the jasper,*
*the sardius, topaz, and the diamond.*

## Chapter I: The Skin of Earth Matures

It was four-billion-and-three-hundred-million years ago – the *Precambrian* time commenced. It would last almost four-billion years. And the first part of Precambrian time, the *Archean Eon*, began. And the Archean would last until two-and-one-half-billion years BC.

Now Earth had matured somewhat – it had reached a semi-stable state. Mighty Earth was *in its youth*.

And it *happened* that a ten-kilometer meteor penetrated the Earth's outer coat, its atmosphere. And a *tremendous* glow arose – if ye had been there, ye would have seen a second moon that night. But this "moon" was red and streaked *across the sky*. And it descended to the Earth and struck a shallow part of Panthalassa. And a gush of water spurted in the air. And the meteor's outer layer broke off, as it *plunged* into the sea and *struck* the ocean floor. The surrounding region *shook*. Then gases bubbling out of the ocean floor ascended to the surface of the sea. There, in turmoil, waves and bubbles churned *like unto* boiling water. Now Earth was wounded *only slightly*, for Panthalassa functioned as a shield.

Now the meteor impact had made a *giant* wave, which was speeding off, followed by large but smaller waves. And *thousands of kilometers* the giant wave did travel. As it swept over small volcanic islands, *momentarily* they disappeared. Large tongues of water lapped the coasts of microcontinents, as the wave sped half-way round the globe. *Eventually* did it diminish.

And during the next three-hundred-million years, *many* meteors struck Earth, with a particularly large one striking roughly every million years.

And thy planet Earth *cooled further*. And it had come to pass that lower temperatures inside the Earth had caused a three-hundred-kilometer-thick layer of magma to solidify. Under great pressures due to rock above it, the mantle of the Earth had *grown*. It consisted predominantly of crystalline peridotite rocks of fifty percent olivine, thirty percent pyroxenes, fifteen percent garnets and five percent of other igneous-type rocks. Now the microscopic binding of the rock was provided by tetrahedral *silicates* of $SiO_4$.[108]

---

[108] In these silicates, four oxygen atoms are at the corners of a tetrahedron while the

Now the *lithosphere* and *mantle* conducted heat more poorly than the molten, metal-rich interior of Earth. Thus these two outer layers functioned *as unto* an insulator. And with a thicker mantle, heat inside the Earth *no longer fled so fast*, and the cooling of the hot and liquid core slowed down.

## Chapter II: Underwater Vulcanism

*When the melting fire burneth,*
*the fire causeth waters to so boil.*

And one day it came to pass that a *crack* five meters long opened on the ocean floor, from which balloons of gas emerged. And the *giant bubbles* rose until they reached the surface of the sea. And there, the surface water foamed *as if* a creature were below. But such was not the case, for the gas was $H_2O$ vapor, carbon dioxide, hydrogen sulfide, and other toxic fumes.

And the crack grew longer. And soon *particles* poured out. And a cloud of black engulfed the crack. And the crack got wider and started ejecting fist-sized rocks. And slowly, the rocks rose several meters up, before tumbling to the ocean floor.

*It seemed* as if *the Earth was sick.*
*At this spot, the Earth was coughing rocks.*

Then the ocean floor pushed upward, bulged and formed a mound. And gases, particles and rocks spewed out. And the mound grew slowly bigger.

Now the next day in a hundred-meter region of the crack, the sea was black. And candles seemed to light the crescent fissure of the underwater mound, giving it *an orange glow*. And then the glow began to flow. And down the slope edged liquid rock; it was an *underwater lava flow*. And water adjacent to the lava *vaporized* to bubbles, which joined the other gases exiting the fissure. And the bubbles rose and reached the ocean surface, where they generated one-half-meter waves. And the spreading ringlets formed a pattern that looked *like unto* a halo on the surface of the sea.

Now *deep below the ocean floor*, at a temperature of fifteen-hundred Kelvins, a slice of the asthenosphere partly melted, making a basaltic magma. And some magma had a *reddish glow* while other parts were *orange*. Now the heating of the magma caused it to *expand*; and the expansion naturally forced it through a conduit in the crust.[109] And so the magma rose *like unto* oil in a well. And *hot magma* reached

---

silicon sits at the center. In crystals of *pyroxenes*, oxygens are shared by several tetrahedrons, thereby reducing the ratio of oxygen to silicon from four-to-one to three-to-one. In other words, the chemical composition of pyroxene consists of a metal plus $SiO_3$. The metal is magnesium, iron, calcium or aluminum. As for *garnets*, they are five metals plus three silicates.

[109] A *conduit* is a pipe-like tunnel.

the opening upon the mound. Now some of *it* cooled quickly, solidifying into spheroid shapes called *pillow-lavas*. And pillow-lavas tumbled down the mound's sides while liquid lava followed suit. And repeated lava flows built up the cone-shaped mound. Thus the magma rupture had made an undersea volcano.

Elsewhere in the ocean floor, magma solidified in cracks of crustal rocks. And in one spot, a vertical sheet-like structure formed, called a *dike* due to its shape. And several dikes were forged there in the ocean crust. And some magma forced its way horizontally through loosened rock and solidified into a one-hundred-meter-thick formation – it was a *sill*. And many sills were made. And some magma was captured in a five-hundred-meter-sized dome-shaped cavity. It solidified into a *lac-colith*.[110] And still a deeper, larger subterranean magma intrusion slowly crystallized into coarse-grained igneous rock. And it was twenty-kilometers wide and irregularly shaped – it was a *batholith*.

And during the next several hundred years, lava periodically pushed its way through earth, oozed out of the undersea volcano, flowed down its slopes and solidified as rock.

And eventually it came to pass that the pressure from the magma melt subsided and the lava ceased to flow. But the volcano had already grown in size, becoming one-thousand meters high. And this underwater mountain was provided with a name – *it* was called a *seamount*.

And elsewhere on the Earth, *undersea volcanos* spontaneously emerged. And *some* rose up above sea level, and volcanic islands formed. And occasionally, a volcano blew its top, creating kilometer-sized craters where peaks had been – *caldera* was the name for such a crater.

And the particles and lava from eruptions filled the waters of the sea *with minerals*. And among the minerals were metal cations such as doubly positively charged ferrous iron, magnesium and calcium, as well as some singly charged potassium and sodium.[111] And some cations *joined with* anions such as singly negatively charged sulfur oxide, chlorine, hydrogen carbonate and nitrogen trioxide to form *precipitates and salts*.[112] But most metal cations remained dissolved in ocean water. Thus the seas were thoroughly polluted with iron, magnesium and calcium.

---

[110] Laccoliths and the other intrusive igneous bodies mentioned here most frequently appear in continental crust. However, at this time when Earth was almost entirely engulfed in water, such formations occurred at the bottom of the ocean.

[111] These cations were $Fe^{++}$, $Mg^{++}$, $Ca^{++}$, $Na^+$ and $K^+$.

[112] These anions were $SO_4^-$, $Cl^-$, $HCO_3^-$ and $NO_3^-$.

## Chapter III: The Making of More Microcontinents

*And the sea was opened up,
and a new land appeared.*

And it came to pass that, two-thousand kilometers beneath the surface of the Earth, there lay a two-hundred-kilometer-sized liquid
blob which happened to be *lighter and hotter* than surrounding molten
matter – it was a *hot spot*.[113] And like a bubble in a jar of honey, it
very slowly rose. And as it rose, the pressure on it dropped. And the
drop in pressure caused it to expand, rendering it more buoyant. And
as it rose, it came in contact with surrounding cooler molten rock and
metals. And they were *heated* by the giant bubble and grew hotter.
And they were *added* to the bubble. Thus the giant liquid blob grew
*bigger*.

Now in giving heat to surrounding molten matter, the blob lost
energy and cooled. And in addition, expansion kept the bubble light
and cooled it. Thus as the bubble did ascend, its temperature declined,
but still at every depth it was *lighter and hotter* than surrounding molten rock.

And the hot spot rose, expanded and grew bigger. And it moved
*toward the surface* of the Earth.

And after two-million years had passed, the hot blob *was* five-
hundred kilometers in size. And it came to pass that it *collided* with
the solid mantle. And the hot liquid bubble mushroomed outward,
spreading a thousand kilometers horizontally beneath the mantle. And
it acted as a buoy underneath a bather, as it put upward pressure on
the mantle.

And in one place, which *was* in contact with the hot spot, the
mantle heated and formed a blob of semi-molten rock.[114] And as tens
of thousands of years went by, this new blob rose *slowly* through the
mantle, heating nearby rock. And eventually it reached the Earth's asthenosphere, *where* it spread out horizontally, curling over *like unto* a
mushroom. Thus a tube-shape region through the mantle had been
heated – it was a *mantle plume*.

And *elsewhere* at the liquid solid-mantle interface, the hot spot of
molten matter generated plumes, which made their way through channels in the mantle. And *throughout* a one-thousand-kilometer-sized region, plumes sprouted up *like unto* flowers.

And it came to pass that, in one extra hot place in the upper region of a plume, rock melted into magma which pushed up and pene-

---

[113] This hot spot is different from modern ones. In modern Earth, hot spots occur in the
mantle and are solid not molten. They are nonetheless able to rise slowly through the
solid mantle because on geological time scales the mantle behaves as pitch in that it con-
vects like a fluid. Only when hot spots and plumes reach a depth of one- or two-hundred
kilometers do they melt to magma.

[114] It was solid but could move through the mantle given enough time.

trated the Earth's lower lithosphere. And it collected in a pocket in Earth's crust – this pocket was a *magma chamber*.

And elsewhere above the one-thousand-kilometer-sized region, magma filled the pockets in the lower lithosphere. And magma chambers *everywhere* appeared.

> *The empty spaces of a sponge*
> *were injected with a fluid.*

And magma *flowed through* conduits in the lithosphere. And after the magma reached the ocean floor, *dozens* of undersea volcanos broke through the crust and suddenly appeared.

> *The sponge was saturated.*
> *Fluid* now *was flowing out.*

And this region of the mantle was full of plumes. Their heat made upper mantle rise, expand and flex. And lighter matter in the region buoyed up the upper mantle. And *it* arched up, *pushing earth* above it.

And one-million years went by. And it came to pass that the crust above the region rose above the sea. And its surface *dried* and land appeared. A microcontinent[115] a thousand kilometers in size emerged – it was a piece of southern proto-Africa.

And during the next several hundred-million years, *other giant hot spots* developed in the liquid core of Earth. And they rose up, collided with the mantle and created plume-filled regions, which eventually made microcontinents. And the less dense microcontinents would last *unto this day*.

## Chapter IV: Ancient Rock

And during geological processes, *liquid magma* in cooling did *solidify*. Thus *igneous rock* was made. And the lightest magma rose to upper levels of the crust, so that near the surface of the Earth, the rocks were predominantly of granite and of andesite – they were rich in silicon and also did contain aluminum. And *heavier* magma solidified to form the rock in *lower* levels of the crust. Now being subjected to strong forces and high pressures this rock often crystallized into gabbro and basalt. *These deeper rocks* had silicates but much less compared with surface rocks. They contained more iron, magnesium and calcium, but they had less potassium.

And Earth's magnetic field made bits of iron in the magma turn and all line up – each was *like unto* a compass needle. And when the magma cooled and finally solidified, the iron filings *froze in place*, still pointing to the Earth's magnetic poles. Now when a microcontinent moved, the frozen filings *also* moved. And when a microcontinent

---

[115] A *microcontinent* was a solid piece of lithosphere which floated on the asthenosphere *like unto* foam on water. It was a smaller version of a continent.

turned, the frozen filings *also* turned. Thus the tiny bits of iron tracked the motion of the microcontinents. And later, when microcontinents had merged to form the *continents*, the iron bits would also track *their* motion.

Now the surface rocks on Earth were *broken into particles and pieces* by erosion. And rocks also were destroyed when the crust in which they were embedded was destroyed by geological processes such as deep burial. And such destruction would occur throughout Earth's history. But a small fraction of the rocks survived. And for example, $ZrSiO_4$ zircon crystal grains in granite rocks were *particularly robust* and were *resistant* to erosion. And some such ancient zircon grains did survive *unto this day*. And in modern times, a geologist would discover them near Great Slave Lake in northwestern Canada. And he would take them to his laboratory. And under a microscope would he examine them and see Earth's rock *as it had been four-billion years before*, when Earth's age was only five-hundred-million years.

And geologists would find zircon crystals in other places, such as Montana, Labrador, western Australia, southeastern Africa and western Greenland. And these samples would provide a picture of Earth's rock *almost four-billion years ago*.

And high pressure in Earth's rocks created crystal gems. And among them, there were some which would be *highly sought*, such as sapphires, rubies, emeralds and diamonds. And in the modern times would man exploit the Earth for gems.

And in Earth's rocks were other precious stones, among which there were twelve that would be held *in great esteem*: emerald, sardius, sardonyx, *chrysoprase*, chalcedony, sapphire, jasper, beryl, topaz, jacinth, amethyst and *chrysolite*.

## Chapter V: Islands Come and Go

*And islands fled away,*
*and mountains were not found.*

And *suddenly it came to pass* that a volcano *lifted up* and created a small island in the ocean. And ten-million years later, the magmatic activity below it did subside. And the island started *sinking*, for the magma pressure from below had ceased, and the cone could not support its weight.

And when it rained, acid in the droplets ate the island's rock. And the *surfaces of rocks dissolved*. And dirt and grains ended up in streams. And as such streams flowed toward the ocean, they *carried off* the dirt and grains. So eventually the grains were deposited offshore. Thus it came to pass that the island was surrounded by a beach of sand.

And every several seconds, waves beat relentlessly against the coastal rocks. And after millions of such poundings, tiny bits of rock *wore off*. And the bits were washed onto beaches and into nearby seas.

And after ten million years went by, the island slipped *below* the surface of the sea – the island was *no longer* – it was a mountain under water. A seamount it would be.

And elsewhere in the Panthalassa Ocean, islands were created, only to *later sink and disappear* below the sea.

## Chapter VI: Sedimentary Rock

And eruptions of volcanos on microcontinents produced lightweight, porous matter known as *pumice*, as well as igneous gravel, soot and ash. And rain washed them into streams and lakes. Now at this time, there were *neither trees nor grass* to anchor dirt in place. Indeed there were no plants on land at all – Earth was *barren* and was bare. The dry parts of Earth looked like the land on Moon. Boulders, pebbles, dust and grains *slid unimpeded down* the sides of hills and mountains. And winds blew dust in desert plains. And rain flowed over rocks and *wore away* small bits of silt and clay. And such debris was washed into the valleys or collected in the beds of rivers, ponds and lakes. Thus sediments *did settle* in the waters of the lowlands of the Earth.

And to the ocean did the *rivers* carry pebbles, mud and sand. And as *waves* beat coastal rocks, they broke off bits of grains and sand and sometimes rocky fragments. And *winds* did blow the sand in beaches. And *waves* washed the sand and pebbles off into the sea. Thus sediments settled *on the shores and off-shore shelves* of microcontinents.

And *precipitates and soot* from eruptions underwater collected on the ocean floor. And rain washed *particles* in air into the sea. And currents eroded basins thereby creating *mud and sand*. And strong tides transported off-shore sand and mud. Thus sediments accumulated *on the ocean floor*.

Now some sediments *lithified into sedimentary rocks* by physical and chemical effects. There was solidification through evaporation, crystallization through precipitation, compactification through pressurization and aggregation through cementation. Thus through *lithification* sediments turned into rocks. Granules, particles and pebbles, which cemented together like bricks, became breccia stones and conglomerates. And calcium-carbonate precipitates changed into *limestone*, while siliceous sediments formed *chert*. And laminated sludge solidified to *shale*. And mud turned into *mudrock*; silt turned into *siltstone*; clay turned into *claystone*; and sand turned into *sandstone*. Thus the sedimentary rocks of Earth were made.

And for the next four-billion years, erosion and weathering would continue making sediments. And the sediments would settle and lithify to produce Earth's sedimentary-type rock.

## Chapter VII: More Hot Spots, More Islands

And it came to pass that just *beneath the mantle* was a two-hundred-kilometer-sized hot spot full of molten rock. And it was lighter than surrounding liquid rock. And magma seeped into the mantle, forming semi-molten plumes. And this section of the mantle edged slightly up and *pushed against* the ocean crust above, causing it to uplift.[116] And on the floor of Panthalassa was an *underwater elevated plain*, an underwater mesa.

And some magma seeped into the lithosphere, *filling* cracks in upper ocean crust. And magma was thrust[117] *through* a conduit of the lithosphere; the molten rock flowing through it like a liquid through a straw. And lava oozed out of a hole, spilling onto the ocean floor and creating pillow-lavas, which collected in a pile. And so beneath the sea, *a volcano had appeared*; the underwater mesa had a mound upon it. And pillow-lavas flowed onto the mesa and down its sides, adding a little height and width to it.

And a hundred years went by. And it came to pass that magma flowed through *another* conduit of the lithosphere and spilled onto the ocean floor. And a *second* undersea volcano formed. And another hundred years went by. And still a *third* volcano formed. And from time to time, magma pushed its way through earth and then flowed from these three volcanic holes. And down the slopes the magma slid, where it solidified and added mass to the volcanos. And *wider* did they grow. And as the magma provided pressure from below, the volcanos grew a little *taller*.

And several hundred years went by. And it came to pass that one volcano rose *above the sea* – an island formed. And in the next few hundred years, as the volcanic cone ascended, the island grew a little larger. And it came to pass that the other two volcanos poked their summits *up above the sea*. And two more islands formed. And so this part of Panthalassa contained a volcanic island chain.

And below, in Earth, light magma accumulated in a chamber. And rising heat and magma *pushed against* the ocean crust. And the ocean floor ascended slightly.

And several thousand years went by. And this section of the ocean floor *emerged above the sea*. And the island chain became connected, as a *single* island formed. And land continued to emerge above the sea. And it came to pass that an island half the size of modern Iceland was created.

And *elsewhere* at the bottom of the Panthalassa Ocean, mesas, mountains and volcanos were conceived. Some stayed below sea as

---

[116] This type of uplifting does not occur today because the mantle is much thicker.

[117] Usually magma flows less abruptly through such conduits. This is especially true in modern times. But geological forces were stronger in the Early Archean.

seamounts. Others rose above the ocean, as they turned into islands of many *different sizes*.

## Chapter VIII: Proto-Tectonic-Plates Collide

And it came to pass that underneath the ocean were *two plates* of lithosphere. Each was a thousand kilometers in size. And one was two-hundred kilometers east of the other. Now these plate moved as a unit – they were proto-*tectonic-plates*.[118] Now each plate was supported by the asthenosphere, which, for these plates, was slippery.[119] And so the lithospheric plates floated *like unto* icebergs in an arctic sea. And every dozen years, the east plate slid half-a-meter to the west, while the west plate slid half-a-meter to the east.

And in twenty-million years, it came to be that *the plates touched*. And they continued to *push against* each other. And the crust between them buckled, producing folds in Earth.

Now the crustal movements led to *friction*. And friction led to *heat*. And heat *melted* an upper region of asthenosphere. And there the magma swelled. And one great ball of magma, found a crack, and through it did it thrust. And the pressure was so strong that the crack grew wider. And the magma lifted crust, drove *through* the earth and broke the surface *like unto* a ground hog burrowing upward through a sod. And a volcano instantly appeared, erupting with *tremendous* force. And lava spilled onto the ocean floor, and it sizzled, flowed and froze.

And elsewhere *along the common boundary* of the two colliding plates was crust uplifting, magma flowing and volcanoes forming. And lava spread profusely. And layered basaltic rocks were built.

Now the momentum of each lithospheric plate was *huge*. As the plates pushed against each other, internal forces *tried* to slow the motion. But the plates maintained some forward motion and momentum and *continued* to collide. And it came to pass that after one-hundred-thousand years, the crust from one plate slid *over and above* the other. And there appeared a *long large island* – fifty kilometers in width, five-hundred kilometers in length – with *dozens of volcanos*.

And during the next one-million years, the plates continued to collide and slide. Now a name was given to the process in which one plate did *slide beneath* another. And that name was *subduction*, which in Latin means "to lead under." And the thickness of the crust doubled *where* the two plates overlapped. And in this region was a microcontinent – it was proto-West-Australia.

Now the collision of the plates had caused Earth's crust to fold in places. A crest of such a fold was called an *anticline*, while a trough

---

[118] Tectonic means "builder." The surface of the Earth would eventually be built from tectonic plates, and tectonic processes would someday build the largest lithospheric structures.

[119] On time scales of several hundred-thousand years, the asthenosphere, although solid, is more like butter than like rock.

was called a *syncline*. And among the anticlines was one that was folded on its side – it was an *overfold*. And in places had crust cracked and fractured. And eventually crust would slip along such cracks, which *also* were called *faults*.

And during the hundreds of millions of years that followed, *other* proto-lithospheric-plates collided, and *other* microcontinents were made.

And so it came to pass that heat and pressure from beneath the surface of the Earth produced *mighty* crustal movements. And they created anticlines, synclines, faults and mountains. And sometimes such movements led to microcontinents.

## Chapter IX: Metamorphic Rock

And throughout the life of Earth and in its youth, geo-physics *changed* the face of rock within the crust. And for example, *hot* magma raised the temperature of nearby rock; *percolating* water mixed different minerals and sediments; the *movement* of crust created enormous pressure zones; the *folding* of crust caused rock to fold; and the *slipping* at a fault produced friction, heat and pressure. And *downward* crustal movements transported rocks to lower depths where higher pressures and higher temperatures prevailed – this was *burial*. And *upward* movements carried rock to the surface of the Earth – this was *uplift*. And *compression* squeezed Earth's rock. And *tension* pulled the rock apart – *it* was like the pull produced when rope was tugged at both its ends – the rope was rock. And *shear* stretched the rock at angles, while *torsion* twisted rock. Thus compression, tension, shear and torsion were among the forces shaping rocks.

And when geo-processes like these occurred, *old rock* turned into *new rock*. It *was* like magic. Rock *metamorphosed*; it *changed* from one form to another. And this new rock, obtained from old rock by chemical reactions and physical processes, was provided with a name. That *name* was *metamorphic rock*.

The tools of metamorphism were pressure, heat and mixing. Now *mixing* created chemical reactions and led to *different compositions*. And *heat* catalyzed chemical reactions and generated phase transitions. And *pressure*, the consequence of force, squeezed rocks of different types together and caused *structural transformations*.

And when a rock of one type was heated with another type, new rock appeared *at that place*. And when a rock of one type was placed next to another type, new rock was made *at that interface*.

And chemical reactions produced new types of rock. So Earth became a chemist. And pressure, heat and mixing transformed rock. So Earth became an alchemist. Thus basalt became *amphibolite*. And under higher pressure, basalt turned into *eclogite*. And Earth would engage in other alchemies: granodiorite to *gneiss*, granite to *granulite*, limestone to *marble*, shale to *schist*, and so on.

Thus *through metamorphism*, new minerals, such as garnet and mica, were manufactured. Thus *through metamorphism*, new rocks were made like marble, slate and gneiss.

*Crustal subduction generated dramatic transformations.*
*Plate collisions produced widespread pressure variations.*

*Stress spawned structural deformations.*
*Burial and uplift led to phase transitions.*
*Heat generated dehydrations.*
*Pressurization and evaporation created crystallizations.*
*And these were the processes of metamorphic mineral creation.*

*Juxtaposition set off chemical reactions.*
*Chemical reactions created new mineral concentrations,*
*which underwent migrations.*
*Mineral migrations made new distributions,*
*which created new rock combinations.*
*These new rock combinations appeared in juxtaposition.*
*And so on.*

*Fragmentation of conglomerates led to new rock formations.*
*Diffusion of rock formations created new rock concoctions,*
*which occurred in varying proportions.*
*Varying proportions brought forth density fluctuations,*
*which created new rock compositions.*
*These new rock compositions underwent fragmentation.*
*And so on.*

*And these were the situations*
*that made new metamorphic rock formations.*

*Thus metamorphic rock resulted from varying conditions.*

And even metamorphic rock *was subjected* to metamorphism. Thus metamorphic metamorphic-rocks were made.

And for the next four-billion years through *unto this day*, heat, pressure and mixing would continue to transform rocks. And the result of these transformations would be metamorphic rock.

## Chapter X: Rock Dynamics

Thus there were *three* types of rock – igneous, sedimentary and metamorphic. Igneous rock came from magma generated by heat in Earth's interior. Magma was the *origin of all rock*, while sedimentary and metamorphic rock were both *derived*. Erosions, weathering and solidification generated sedimentary rock. Metamorphism made metamorphic rock.

And for the next four-billion years through *unto this day*, all types of rocks and minerals were manufactured. And Earth did *this* through rock dynamics. And it was *like unto* a game. And the game was simple. It had a board with *six squares, which* were labelled. The labels were (1) magma, (2) igneous rock, (3) surface rock, (4) sediments, (5) sedimentary rock, and (6) metamorphic rock. And certain moves between the squares were so permitted. All play began with square (1), magma. Now one could move between squares (1) and (2) by solidification. Uplift took one from (2) to (3). One went from (3) to (4) by weathering and by erosion. The path between (4) and (5) was lithification. Burial led one from (5) to (6). High heating sent one back to (1) from (6). Now these six paths formed a circle. But there were other moves that were permitted. Remelting reversed the movement between (1) and (2), thus allowing one to also go from (2) to (1). Folding, pressure, stress and other geological forces provided a way to pass from (2) to (6). Uplift could then take one from (6) to (3). One went from (5) to (4) through fragmentation. And then there was a special move called volcanic eruption – one went from (1) to (2) and immediately passed to (3). And from the start, Earth has played this game. It played it in three-billion years BC, and it is playing it today.[120]

## Chapter XI: Land-Mass Subduction

And it came to pass that a hundred-kilometer-sized island in Panthalassa was sitting on a proto-lithospheric-plate, *like unto* a napkin on a tablecloth. Now five-hundred kilometers north of the island, there was a subduction fissure. And on each side of it, crust was drawn *into the Earth*. At the subduction zone, proto-lithospheric-plates turned over and went down like cloth at a table's edge. And geo-forces pulled each plate like a child tugging on a tablecloth. And just as a napkin would travel with a moving tablecloth, so did the island *travel with* the proto-lithospheric-plate.

And the plate drifted slowly over *the* asthenosphere. And with it went the island. And ten-million years went by. And it came to pass that the island reached the fissure of subduction. And it *sank into the Earth* like a body sinking in a quicksand. And in a hundred-thousand-years, the island *disappeared.*

And *elsewhere*, land masses were drawn into subduction zones and vanished from the Earth.

## Chapter XII: Spreading from Mid-Ocean Ridges

*And fire was cast into the sea.*
*And part of the sea became blood.*

Now it had happened that much heat had accumulated in a region of the upper mantle. And the heat drove through an ocean proto-

---

[120] And in modern times, humanity participates. Prospectors play; their goal is gold. And oil companies also play; their goal is oil and coal.

lithospheric-plate and cracked it in the middle, forming what is called a *rift*. And all along the three-thousand-kilometer-long rift, earthquakes *shook* the ocean floor. And as millions of years went by, the ocean plate *broke into two*. And the two pieces edged *apart*, and a large fissure opened up along the two. And magma in the lithosphere pushed up into the ocean crust creating dikes. And pressure from below *lifted up* the ocean floor, forming a three-thousand-kilometer-long ridge in the middle of the rift. Particles and lava flowed out of the fissure, hot gases were absorbed in water, and pillow lavas tumbled down the ridge's sides. Particles and precipitates settled on the pillows. And this long underwater mountain range and fissure were provided with a name – a *mid-ocean ridge* was it.

And one year later, the two ocean proto-plates suddenly did shift *apart* by several centimeters. The flows of lava escalated. And more pillow lavas tumbled down the ridge's sides. Magma forced its way into the crust, creating many dikes.

Now *sudden movements* of the two proto-plates continued for several hundred-million years. As the two edged away from one another, dikes and pillow lavas were transported. And so it came to pass that a *four-layered* crustal structure formed. It extended for several hundred kilometers on both sides of the ridge. Now the *first layer*, the sedimentary layer, contained eroded rocks, precipitates and sediments, all lying on the ocean floor. It thickened with distance from the ridge; at the ridge, it was several meters thick, while at a hundred-kilometers, it was two-hundred meters thick. Now the *second layer* was full of pillow lavas, lying beneath the ocean floor *like unto* marbles in a jar. Lava which had solidified in horizontal sheets was interspersed among them. Next came a layer of sheeted dikes, stacked against each other as in a deck of cards. This *third layer* was a *dike swarm*. Together the sheeted dikes and pillow lavas were one-thousand meters thick. And finally below the dikes was the *last layer* of several kilometers of gabbro rock.

Now each year, several centimeters of ocean crust inched out of *the* mid-ocean ridge, spreading horizontally. Thus near the ridge the crust was young, while farther from it, it was old. And for example, the age of crust one-hundred kilometers away was half-a-dozen million years.

*From the ridge the ocean floor flowed forth*
*like unto a ticker tape of time.*

And *in several places* in Panthalassa had mid-ocean ridges formed. Now some heat from the Earth's hot core passed through the mantle and the oceans. But mid-ocean ridges were *like vents* which let much heat escape.

## Chapter XIII: The Lower Mantle Forms

And it came to pass that the temperature of the outer liquid core of Earth went down. *Under enormous pressure*, magma and molten metals solidified, adding to the mantle from below. And gradually the mantle thickened. And eventually, it extended two-thousand kilometers into the Earth. Now *high pressure* below four-hundred kilometers caused the crystal structure of peridotite to change into a denser form. The oxygens of the silicon-oxygen tetrahedrons of $SiO_4$ *were squeezed* into a position of cubic closest packing.[121]

Now below eight-hundred kilometers, the pressure was *so great* that silicon-oxygen octahedrons[122] became the basic binding blocks – the octahedrons allowed an even denser packing. And the mantle below eight-hundred kilometers was given a specific name – the *lower mantle*.

## Chapter XIV: Creation and Destruction of Earth's Surface Structure

Now in a few hundred-million-year period, much ocean crust, numerous islands and some microcontinents *were made*. And one-hundred-million years later, the self-same crust and islands were subducted into the mantle and *disappeared from Earth*. And over several hundred-million years, geo-processes destroyed most microcontinents. And so, during the Early Archean Eon, that which was created *at one time* was to a large extent demolished *at a later time*. In its youth, thy planet Earth was ever changing and dynamic.

And let it be known to thee and all around thee that although they would slow down, the *processes of creation and destruction* of Earth's crust would continue beyond the Archean and through *unto this day*.

## Chapter XV: Variations in Earth's Motion

Now Earth's gravitational interaction with the Sun, the Moon and planets caused *tiny variations* in its motions. And for example, Earth's *orbit* varied from almost a perfect circle to an oval.[123] And the orbit fluctuated between these two shapes. And when the orbit was an oval, Earth moved around the Sun in an *ellipse*. And as a consequence, once[124] a year the Earth drifted *slightly farther* from the Sun – this was

---

[121] This is a special way of densely packing spheres. Within a plane, each sphere is surrounded by six others in a honeycomb-like arrangement. The next plane of spheres fits into the depressions of the first, and so.

[122] The six oxygens in the silicon-oxygen octahedrons of $SiO_6$ are located at the faces of a cube while the silicon sits in the center.

[123] The oval however was almost circular.

[124] If the Sun were in the middle of the ellipse, this would happen twice a year. However, since the Sun sits off-center at one of the two foci of the ellipse, it happens only

the *aphelion*. And once a year the Earth drew *slightly closer* to the Sun – this was the *perihelion*.

Now the *tilt* of Earth's spinning axis also *varied very slightly*. *Sometimes* Earth spun a bit more vertically. And *sometimes* it spun a bit more horizontally. And this variation would continue *unto this day*. Thus in modern times, the tilt angle would range between twenty-four-and-a-half and twenty-two degrees.[125] Earth's spinning axis would oscillate between these two angles with a period of forty-thousand years.

Now the *direction* of the spin axis also varied with respect to distant stars. Over a period of thousands of years, it changed *significantly*. And this effect was called *precession*.[126] Earth was *like unto a top* in outer space, so that its spinning axis did precess. And so the star ye would have called the "north star" was forever changing. And in modern times, one precession cycle would last twenty-thousand years.

And throughout Earth's history, these three variations of Earth's motions would have climatic implications. And throughout Earth's history, Earth's weather would exhibit frequent global fluctuations.

---

once.

[125] The angle is measured with respect to the common orbital plane of the planets.

[126] Precession occurs for all spinning objects such as tops. When a tilted toy top spins on the surface of a table, two things turn: the top and the spinning axis, for the top spins, and the spinning axis revolves about the vertical. Thus the direction of the spinning axis traces out a small circle.

# Biogenesis

*Let there be life.*
*And there was life.*

## Chapter I: The Long Experiment

*His lightnings enlightened Earth.*

The air was warm and moist. The ground was wet and warm. And everywhere was fog. *Steam* lurked over the dark waters of the Earth; valleys held cradles of *white fog*; and the mountains were clothed in clouds. Black and hardly visible was the land. Steam floated above the ocean. The Earth was in a foggy cloud. *And darkness was upon the face of the deep.* For millions of years, it was thus so.

And the *winds* began to lightly blow and swirl the fog. And the clouds moved about in mysterious ways, as white patches *swirled around* the peaks of mountains. The mist collected in the valleys and floated among the hills.

And a *wind with purpose* began to swirl a fog. And this fog took shape and formed a tube, which then changed shape becoming arm-like. And the arm seemed to grow protrusions, which looked *like unto* fingers. And the wind blew and moved the elements, *stirring the waters* there below. And at the bottom of the shallow waters, mud, sand and earth were *mixed*. As a finger of the fog moved in circles, it *seemed* to stir the waters and mud too. And different molecules in mud were merged. And the molecules combined in many ways. And new molecules emerged.

And for millions of years, the muddy waters turned and molecules were mixed and made.

And one day near a hydrothermal vent rich in minerals, organic matter containing hydrogen, oxygen and carbon atoms combined to form a complex molecule. And the complex molecule captured the chemical energy of its parent molecules. And it pulsated *like unto* a tiny heart. And it breathed the energy of life, vibrating several seconds under its own power. But soon the power was exhausted and the molecule stopped beating.

*And the Great Eye observed the tiny vibration,*
*and it was seen as good.*

*The mist and fog*
*no longer reign.*
*The muddy waters*
*have been stirred.*
*The seas will never be*
*the same again.*

*The Earth has been disturbed.*
*A molecule was kindled in the sea*
*and seemed to be alive*
*for several moments.*
*It lingered in dark waters*
*but did not survive.*

*In Heaven*
*wingèd figures sing.*
*"Below there is a miracle of fate.*
*So rare and fragile be.*
*So strange its movement be.*
*So precious be its state:*
*Just a speck, a heart, a source of energy."*

And for tens of millions of years the muddy waters *turned*, and energy-producing molecules were made and shook for only moments.

And more millions of years went by. And the Sun grew slightly brighter. And as the *light of Sun* did slightly warm the Earth, the fog began *to rise above the ground*. And it rose beyond the highest mountains, collecting in the clouds. And the air in valleys and above the lakes and oceans *became* clear and dry. But clouds covered Earth and kept it dark and gray.

And the clouds grew heavy, and sky was black. *Dark* was the ground; *black* were the waters of the Earth. And the clouds could no longer hold their moisture; heavily it rained. And *thunder resounded* and *lightning flashed*. And in the air, lightning made new molecules.

And *the rain* filled existing lakes and oceans. And as water collected in the valleys, new lakes formed. And it rained until the clouds grew thin and *light seeped* through the clouds. And when the light rays reached the *waters* of the Earth, *they* were warmed. And the warm water evaporated, forming new mists which rose and made new clouds. And the clouds again grew heavy, and then again was thunder and was rain.

For tens of millions of years, it was thus so.

And the winds of Earth continued *blowing gently*. And the waters of the Earth were *continually stirred*, while the mud of shallow lakes and pools was *continually mixed*. And nucleotides, amino acids and minerals were intermingled. And new molecules were made. And among them were *certain organic complex molecules*. And these complex molecules were proto-proto-cells. And they were continually being formed. But the proto-proto-cells often existed only for brief moments.

For tens of millions of years, it was thus so.

Then one day, when clouds had cleared and *rays of light* had fallen on a valley with a lake below, and when a wind had blown *a little stronger* and had stirred the waters so, two molecules combined to form a special proto-cell. And the proto-cell *received* the rays of light.

And the proto-cell absorbed *the energy of light*. And it shook. And then it moved itself. And throughout the day, it shook and moved about. Then came night, and *motionless* was it.

And in the morning when there *fell some light* upon the face of Earth, the proto-cell began *to shake again*. And when some clouds blocked out the rays, it ceased its motion. And when the heavens cleared, the proto-cell rekindled. And it "lived" and "died" a thousand times, until one day it met destruction.

> *And the Great Eye observed the motion,*
> *and it was seen* as good.

> *The mist and fog*
> *no longer reign.*
> *The muddy waters*
> *have been stirred.*
> *Rays of light*
> *stream through the clouds.*
> *The seas will never be*
> *again the same.*
> *The World has been disturbed.*
> *On Earth there is a proto-cell which "lives,"*
> *and it is His.*

> *In Heaven*
> *wingèd figures sing and*
> *celebrate the new creation.*
> *"So joyous is a proto-cell.*
> *So rare and fragile be.*
> *So strange its motion be.*
> *So precious be its state:*
> *The proto-cell, a spark,*
> *a heart, a source of energy.*
> *The Garden of Eden, be it*
> *at the bottom of the sea."*

> *The gift of life is what He gives.*
> *Below there is a proto-cell which "lives."*

Henceforth, the sea produced a *billion-billion* proto-cells which "lived" a billion-billion "lives." But proto-cells could *not beget* themselves.

And tens of millions of years did pass and disappear. Then one day by chance a *mutant proto-cell* was formed. And it *floated* in the sea absorbing light. Then, as a certain molecule passed by, the mutant proto-cell *absorbed* it. And the proto-cell became a little larger. And other nearby molecules were soon absorbed. And the proto-cell became a giant proto-cell. And it grew in size until, too large, it fell apart.

*And the Great Eye observed this growth,*
*and it was seen as good.*

Henceforth, the sea produced a billion-billion proto-cells which did grow big but did not procreate.

## Chapter II: Self-Sustaining Cells

And millions of years passed by. And the sea teamed with proto-cells which grew and did absorb the energy of light. Then one night, a certain group of molecules *combined*. A miracle was in the making. First, like its predecessors, the cell absorbed other molecules and grew in size. But then, spontaneously did it *divide in two*. And from one large cell, *two* were born – the cell had *made its image*; it had reproduced. And these two cells also grew and then divided. And soon the seas *were filled* with many many living and dividing cells.[127]

*And the Great Eye observed division,*
*and it was seen as good.*

*A new cell came,*
*which could divide.*
*The ocean waters*
*teamed with microscopic life.*
*The Earth will never be*
*again the same.*
*The Universe has been disturbed.*
*On Earth there is a cell that can survive.*
*This is His gift.*

*In Heaven*
*wingèd figures sing and*
*celebrate the great creation.*
*"A living cell is born.*
*So strange is its conception.*
*So wonderful is life.*
*So rare and fragile be.*
*So precious is its state:*
*The cell, a life, a heart,*
*the first to replicate.*
*The gift of life is what He gives.*
*Below there is a cell which lives,*
*a cell which can divide,*
*a cell which can survive."*

Let us pray.

---

[127] The cells at this time in geo-history were much simpler than modern cells.

*We celebrate our birth*
*in Heaven and on Earth.*
*Give us each day*
*our daily breath.*

Thus Nature, through years of trial and error, produced an ocean full of life. And on thy planet Earth, *verily were* living things: cells that tapped the energy of light, cells that could divide and grow.

*In the muddy waters*
*move the molecules of life.*

*And the Great Voice gave life His blessing, saying*
*"Be fruitful, multiply and fill the waters of the seas."*

And it was so, for the new cells grew and multiplied. The seas were filled with life – a million-million, then a billion-billion, and then a trillion-trillion living cells. And then the growth began to slow.

And millions of years passed by. And the *currents in the seas* were moving fast. And there were *many many* living and dividing cells at last.

## Chapter III: Natural Selection

And so the seas teamed with microscopic living organisms. And one organism floated just below the surface. And when a wave rose, *it rose*. And when a wave sank, *it sank*. And when a current flowed, it flowed *with the current*. And sunlight did the cell absorb. And sunlight was converted into energy, which was used for growth and reproduction. And this organism was a *proto-plant*.

And the seas were filled with *many different kinds* of one-celled proto-plants. And they had *no means* to move about. And most absorbed sunrays as their source of energy, but a few used the chemicals and heat in muddy ocean floors. And proto-plants were plentiful.

And another organism lived below the surface of the sea. And it consisted of a single cell. And by means of successive contractions of its cell, *it moved* albeit slowly. And it propelled itself *to just below surface of the sea*. And *there* did it engulf a proto-plant. And the proto-plant was processed. And chemical reactions did occur, which generated energy. And this energy would be used for motion, growth and reproduction. And this creature was a *proto-animal*.[128]

And the seas were filled with *many different kinds* of proto-animals. And they moved about by any means they could. They all consisted of a single cell, and most *ate of* proto-plants. But some *ate of* other proto-animals. And a few fed off the mud and dirt at the bottom

---

[128] In this Book of *Biogenesis*, the division of life into plants and animals is based on function. Other more sophisticated classification schemes exist, some of which are used in the subsequent books of the Old Testament.

of the ocean floor. And what they ate was chemically digested and *converted into energy.*

And the proto-animals were plentiful, although not as plentiful as proto-plants. And the sizes of these living organisms varied greatly. But all were microscopic. And most were just a micron big.

And the proto-plants *that survived* were the ones that reproduced *quickly* or had effective *protective means.* And the proto-animals *that survived* were the ones that had the *best means* of avoiding being eaten by other proto-organisms.

> And the Great Eye observed the *resourceful mechanisms*
> *which living creatures had acquired.*
> *And it was seen* as good.

For millions of years, it was thus so.

And the ocean's waves undulated endlessly. And *ocean foam* sprayed into air. And the seas were full of biological material. And one such bio-molecule *floated listlessly* about. And a cell did bump into that molecule. And to the cell the bio-molecule attached itself. And chemical reactions occurred *within the bio-molecule,* and energy was generated. Then the molecule and cell did separate. And the bio-molecule floated listlessly *again.*

Now the bio-molecule was *not* a living cell – it had no means of moving and had no energy-producing capacity *within itself:* It was a *proto-virus.* And it "survived" by latching onto cells and by extracting chemicals and energy.

And millions of years passed by. And there were *countless types* of proto-viruses. And they *attached* themselves to cells, extracting energy and sometimes even growing.

And more millions of years went by. And a cell and proto-virus joined. And the proto-virus extracted energy, and it began to grow. And after it had grown a bit, *it* divided into *two.* And the two parts were *copies* of the original proto-virus. Then these two copies attached themselves to other cells. And they in turn did grow and did divide. And so the *first disease* developed in the seas.

And soon the seas were full of proto-viruses that could divide. But they were not alive, for outside a host, they neither moved, nor grew, nor divided, nor generated energy – they were the *lifeless parasites* of the micro-biotic world.

Now there were *many varieties* of proto-viruses. And to a proto-plant, it happened that one strain attached itself. And *violent* chemical reactions did ensue, which *destroyed* the cell *before* the proto-virus could grow and duplicate. And this proto-virus attached itself to a proto-animal. And *violent* chemical reactions did ensue, which *destroyed* the cell *before* the proto-virus could grow and replicate. And so this proto-virus could not multiply its numbers.

Thus after thousands of years, those types of proto-viruses that were *non-lethal* dominated the proto-virus population. And usually when a proto-virus attached itself to a host cell, the cell performed its biological functions at *reduced capacity*. But sometimes the cell did function very badly; and in this case, the host *was sick*. And sometimes when the cell and proto-virus interacted, the cell was *changed*. And if the cell was changed too radically, then the host, be it a proto-plant or proto-animal, did die.

Now it *happened* that in the center of a proto-plant, there was a section of a cell converting sunlight into energy. And a proto-virus attached itself to this energy-producing part. And chemical reactions did ensue; and molecules within the cell were rearranged somewhat. And the cell was *changed*. And surprisingly, it converted sunlight into energy *more efficiently* than previously.

And on rare occasions did other proto-viruses induce a "positive" transformation in a cell. Henceforth, proto-animals and proto-plants evolved at a *more rapid pace*.

And thousands of years passed by. And *ocean waves* undulated endlessly. And it happened that a proto-virus attached itself to one section of a proto-plant. And in the cell, chemical reactions fired. And the cell performed its biological function badly. The proto-plant was sick. But then nearby molecules expanded and swarmed the proto-virus and *ejected* it.

And soon the seas were teaming with living organisms which *could expel* many strains of proto-viruses. And those proto-virus strains that were *easy to expel* did number *few*. And those strains that were *harder to expel* did number *more*.

And millions of years went by. And it came to pass that a large one-celled proto-animal propelled itself toward the surface of the sea to eat, but it *collided* with a microscopic particle. And the particle struck *with force* the proto-animal, causing damage to a small section of the cell. And the damaged part performed its biological function *badly*. But then a nearby macromolecule passed over the small damaged spot. And it was like magic, for when the macromolecule did move away, the damaged spot was *changed*. And it began *again* producing chemical reactions. And that section of the cell performed its previous biological function, although at *a reduced capacity*.

And the ocean teamed with proto-animals and proto-plants of varying sizes and *abilities*.

And the seas were a *mighty battle field*. It was a time when proto-animals ate proto-plants, when proto-animals ate proto-animals, and when proto-viruses attacked both proto-plants and proto-animals. Some species died; others survived; some disappeared; new ones appeared; others did dissolve; and species *did evolve*.

*And the Great Eye observed*
*the development of living organisms,*
*and it was seen* as good.

## Chapter IV: Three Fables

O n a flat land lived wolves and sheep. And on this flat land did grow grass. Now in the beginning the wolves and sheep were *few*. But the grass was *green and abundant*, for during day the Sun was bright, and during early morning the Earth was moist with dew. And the sheep *ate of* the green grass which grew long. And the sheep prospered and *did grow in number*. And each day, they moved to new pastures where the grass was green and long. And the grass they left behind replenished itself using bright sunlight and the morning dew. And so the sheep grew *numerous*, while still the wolves were *few*. And the wolves *ate of* the sheep, for the sheep were good and succulent. And the sheep continued to procreate. And the wolves did *also* reproduce. And the wolves continued to eat the fat of sheep. And the wolves did not go hungry, for the sheep were *fat and plentiful*. And the wolves mated more, and their numbers did increase. And from these predators, the sheep did *try to hide*. But the land was flat, without caves and without rocky slopes. And since the sheep could not find protection from their predators, their numbers did begin to *wane*. And the wolves became aggressive. And their numbers rose. And the wolves continued to copulate. And the number of sheep *grew less*. And the wolves grew large in number. And the wolves continued to eat the sheep, who numbered now quite few. And so it came to pass that the wolves were very aggressive and were hungry. And then it happened that the *last sheep* was devoured. And the wolves had *no more food* to eat. And they, in desperation, began to eat each other. The strongest ate the weakest. The biggest ate the smallest. And the wolves grew *few in number*. And then the last male wolf ate *the last female wolf*, who held within her womb an unborn pup. And the last male had no more to eat and died.

. . . . . . .

In a rocky countryside, there were only cows and weeds. And since the land was dry, the weeds grew only slowly. Now in the beginning, the cows were *few*. And they fed on the weeds and *prospered*. And as the cows begat more cows, their numbers *grew*. And the cows continued to feed from the vegetation of the land. And the weeds grew sparse and numbered few. And the cows were hungry and their flesh hung thin. And some cows died. And just a few survived. Then only a single cow remained. But that cow begat no calf and the last cow died.

. . . . . . .

In a mountain-valley region, there were goats, sheep, coyotes, lions, grass and trees. In the beginning, the coyotes and lions numbered few, the mountains and valleys were green, and so the goats and sheep *prospered* and their numbers grew. Now the goats and sheep ate grass off the land and leaves from lower branches of the trees. And when the goats and sheep became numerous, the vegetation vanished, and they had less to eat. But the coyotes and lions who fed off the goats and sheep had *plenty* of meat to eat. And the coyotes and lions ate and they began to thrive. And they grew in number, while the goats and sheep diminished. And the predators prospered, while the herbivores suffered. And the goats and sheep grew still fewer, as the predators proliferated. Now some sheep and goats climbed the mountain to find *new pastures*. And since the sheep and goats were just a few, the coyotes and lions had but little meat, and their numbers so declined. And it came to pass that the grass grew long again and the lower branches of the trees grew back. And some sheep and goats *came down from the mountain*. And while the coyotes and lions suffered, the sheep and goats did prosper.

And the fable at this point repeats, "In a mountain-valley region, there were . . . ." Thus the species of aggression lived in oscillating balance with the species of non-aggression in the varied terrain of the mountain-valley of trees and grass. And *neither* prey nor predator prevailed.

## Chapter V: Four Sayings

*Blessed is he who keepeth
the sayings of this book.*

And he, who is betrayed by his brethren and is thrown into a pit and is sold as a servant, but who survives and has the will, shall return as the ruler of his brethren.

And he, whose back is bent but not broken, shall eventually be strong.

And he, who is a slave and is oppressed, but who escapes, shall be the master of his master.

And he, who is without money or wealth of *any kind*, but who has the desire, will and know-how, shall be rich.

## Chapter VI: Life Develops

And it came to pass that cells became more complicated and performed sophisticated functions. Now it happened that some *oxygen gas* approached the cell of a proto-animal.[129] And when one $O_2$ molecule touched the cell, a proto-receptor received it. Then a signal, consisting of a wave of chemical reactions, passed along a chain of molecules within the cell. And the signal caused some filaments to flap, and the cell propelled itself *away*.

---

[129] Oxygen was toxic to life at this point in geo-history.

And a *food particle* of biomatter was near a proto-animal. And an organic molecule from the food broke off and touched the cell. And a region of the cell, a proto-receptor, reacted with a site of the organic molecule. And a chain of chemical reactions followed. And a signal passed from molecule to molecule within the cell. And the signal caused some filaments to flap, and the cell *approached* the particle of food.

Now the proto-receptors of the cell constituted its sensory system. Thus the cell could *sense* some chemicals and could *respond*. And this response was *reflex* – a given molecule produced a deterministic chain of chemical reactions and a fixed responsive motion. And this sense, based on chemical detection, was, in some sense, microscopic proto-smell and taste.

And sensing systems would evolve. And there would be two basic types, *chemical* and *physical*. Thus there would be *chemical* and *mechanical* receptors.

And *someday* living organisms would develop *many* physical and chemical senses. And certain life forms would "smell" and "taste" chemicals that other living organisms, including man, could not.

And for some living creatures, the contact with an object would be "felt." And this would be the *sense of touch*. And for some creatures, electromagnetic radiation would be "detectable." And if the radiation were light, this would be *vision*. Now some early species would be sensitive to ultraviolet waves, for in the early days of Earth ultraviolet radiation was strong and dangerous and worthy of detection; those without such ultraviolet sensors often died. And several billion years later, some predatory animals would "see" the infrared, for infrared radiation would mean heat, possibly the indication of a warm live prey. And if the rapid motion of molecules in a medium could be "felt," *this* would be the *sense of hearing*, for the propagation of knocking molecules is sound. Eventually some animals, including man, would be sensitive to sound. And many marine creatures would be able to "feel" pressure, allowing them to judge how deep below the sea they were. And this would be a sense that humans would not have. And other such senses would exist – such as sensing magnetic fields, in particular, Earth's magnetic field.

And *much later on*, as life forms grew bigger, communication of sensory signals would need to be more complicated. And a *nervous system* would develop. And neurons would pass biological messages between a creature's cells. Within a neuron, charged waves, like electricity, would be the means to signal a transmission. Now a stimulus would provoke a signal detected from the sensors. And the signal would pass to a central system for evaluation, processing and a response decision. Then after the response signal passed out along the nervous system, a reaction would ensue. And for *coordinated responses*, hormones would be released, and chemical reactions would produce a biological response.

And so creatures not only lived in their environment, they learned to react and to respond to it. And this added thus a new dynamics to the bio-world.

.     .     .     .     .     .     .

Now it *happened* that a particle of food passed through the outer membrane of a cell. And the particle was manipulated by the mucus in the protoplasm until it reached a certain region of the cell – the food was thus *ingested*. Next, *one part* of the particle was processed into energy-storing molecules – the food particle was thus *digested*. And the *other part*, being waste, was manipulated by the protoplasm until it reached the membrane of the cell, through which it passed. And the protoplasm moved the energy-storing molecules to another location in the cell. There, bonds were broken, releasing energy, *which* was put to use. Thus the protoplasm of the cell *moved and manipulated molecules*.

And *later*, more sophisticated means would be achieved to ingest food, nutrients and molecules. And for example, the lung and gill *would eventually appear*, allowing life forms to take in air and water. And mouths and tubes would take in fluids, food and air. And other organs, such as lungs and stomachs, would process them. And vascular systems would move the processed intakes, such as oxygen and proteins, to other places. Finally waste materials would be excreted. And for example, respiratory animals would breathe out $CO_2$.

And for large animals, *efficient means* for locomotion would be needed. Eventually, muscles would appear, allowing limbs and body parts to move.

And more sophisticated reproduction methods would arise. One day, simple cell division would *be replaced* by a variety of duplicating processes. And there would be mitosis. And there would be meiosis.[130] And reproduction through sex would be a great success.

*So it would come to pass* that all living things, from the simple uni-celled microorganism to the sophisticated human being, would have their methods for internal communication, digestion, energy production, transportation, reproduction and external motion.[131]

---

[130] Mitosis and meiosis are two methods of cell reproduction. Both begin when chromosomes are duplicated in a mother cell. Mitosis is simple cell division: the mother cell splits in the middle, dividing into two daughter cells, each of which has the same number of chromosomes as the original mother cell. Meiosis prepares for sexual reproduction. In meiosis, two divisions take place, leading to four daughter cells with half the number of chromosomes. These daughter cells are then ready to combine sexually with meiotic cells of a partner.

[131] For more on this, see the Book of *Biology*.

## Chapter VII: Bacteria

*And one man built a house, dug deep,*
*and laid the foundation on a rock;*
*and when the flood arose,*
*the stream beat vehemently upon that house,*
*it could not shake,*
*for it was founded upon a rock.*
*And another man built a house*
*without foundation and upon the earth;*
*against which the stream did beat vehemently,*
*and immediately it fell;*
*and the ruin of that house was great.*

Now *microbes* were among Nature's most basic and most early forms of life. In the beginning more than three-and-a-half-billion years ago, there were primitive *hyperthermophiles*, microorganisms that thrived in extremely heated waters. And with time, microbes evolved. And what was their phylogenic tree? Embryonic microbes branched out to two main types: *archaea* and *bacteria*. And archaea would survive more than three-billion years of biological battles to become a modern phylogenic kingdom. They would dwell in the harshest of environments – hot springs, extremely salty waters, sulfurous pools, in mineral-laden sea-deep vents, and in ecosystems almost devoid of diatomic oxygen. They would be the great survivors, living where no others could. Now after several hundred-million years, the primordial hyperthermophilic archaea would branch into *methanogens*, which produce methane as a waste, and hydrogen-sulfide feeding microorganisms, which use sulfur instead of oxygen for metabolic processing. Eventually after hundreds of millions of years, some archaea would evolve to salt-loving halophiles, among which would be *halobacteria*, capable of performing photosynthesis based on *carotenoids*, yellow pigments that function as a weaker form of chlorophyll.[132] And some species of methanogens, halophiles, archaeal hyperthermophiles and mineral-processing archaea would survive several billion years and *unto this day*. Now bacteria would have an even more "successful" history. Not only would they survive in harsh environments, but they would spread throughout the World. After several hundred-million years, green bacteria would emerge, some using sulfur in their metabolic processes, others using chlorophyll to photosynthesize. Now eventually, *cyanobacteria* would arise, which not only photosynthesized but produced $O_2$ as waste.[133] And later, purple

---

[132] *Chlorophyll* is the green pigments in a plant that photosynthesize.

[133] Most bacteria do not produce oxygen gas as waste. For this reason, cyanobacteria are sometimes called *blue-green algae*. Certain cyanobacteria would eventually become incorporated into cells of plants as chloroplasts.

photosynthetic bacteria emerged.[134] And species of cyanobacteria as well as thermophilic, green and purple bacteria would survive for billions of years to become a modern phylogenic kingdom.

Now it would take almost two-billion years for a third group of microbes to emerge. They would be the eukaryotic microorganisms with sophisticated cells. And they too would survive *unto this day*. Hence, in modern times there would be three main types of microbes: archaea, bacteria, and eukarya.

And throughout geo-history, each microbial type would *branch out* into more specific forms – *simple and complex types* would be achieved. Their numbers would increase steadily with time. They would become the common denominator of all life, the biological base – the pyramids of life would be constructed on their backs. Bacteria would be basic. Microbes would *be* the masters of the World.

And throughout geo-history, sometimes mass extinctions would strike Earth's life. And many forms of life would disappear forever. And among the fauna and the flora, there would be many losers and few winners. But *among the winners* would be microbes – they would always win the battles, for they would be most robust. Thus microbes would survive the mass extinctions.

And trilobites would one day dominate the sea but later die. And dinosaurs would one day dominate the land but later die. But *microbes* would *verily survive*. And feeding on the dead remains of others, *they* would even thrive.

And in modern times, man would think he was the master of the World. Microbes would verily "know better." They would *really rule* the World.

*Microbes have built the strongest house.*

---

[134] Later, purple bacteria descendants would be incorporated into cells as mitochondria.

*The second book of Geo-Evolution, called*

# The Archean Eon II

*And the clouds did cast long shadows*
*upon the face of Earth.*

## Chapter I: Rock Belts and Cratons

*And mountains were raised*
*so that lands may be divided.*

Now *throughout geo-history*, the continental crust of Earth was continually regurgitated. And with each passing of a billion years, one-third of it was destroyed and returned to the mantle, for that which wind did not wear off, the rain wore off, and that which rain did not wear off, the sea tore off, and that which the sea did not tear off, earthquakes broke apart, and that which earthquakes did not break, subduction ate, and when subduction ate the earth, *that earth* was lost. Thus the earliest history of Earth, some four-billion years ago, which was written in the crust and in the rock, was largely lost.

Now between four-billion and two-and-a-half-billion years BC, significant events shaped Earth. And during the Archean Eon, magma flows were creating *giant belts of rock*. Those belts in the upper crust were predominantly greenstone-granite, while those below were granulite-gneiss. Now *greenstone-granite* was granite and granodiorite rock with a greenish tinge, while *granulite-gneiss* was the lower-in-silicate metamorphic equivalent of greenstone-granite created by high heat and pressure.

*These were the ancient belts of Earth,*
*beautiful to behold.*
*They were ribbons of rocks woven in a robe.*
*And they were made by Nature,*
*the almighty master of all architects.*

And then it came to pass that in three-billion-and-eight-hundred-million years BC, a *giant slice of crust* thrust through a slab of gneiss. And the metamorphic rock combining with flows of lightweight magma made the Selukwe belt. And a billion years later by similar means, the Belingwean belts were born nearby. And two-hundred-million years thereafter, the Bulawayan-Shamvaian belts were built. And these belts were then united into a solid almost indestructible core of crust. And it was called the *craton of Zimbabwe*.

Thus belts of rock were bound in *cratons*, the robust cores of future continents.

*The Archean was an eon*
*of craton-type creation.*

*Thus it came to pass* that the one-thousand-kilometer by two-thousand-kilometer Superior Province craton of central proto-Canada was built. And this craton would later fragment, thereby producing crustal parts of Greenland, northeast Canada and Scotland. *Thus created* were the cratons of Kaapvaal in proto-South-Africa, Dharwar in proto-India, and Hopeh-Liaoning in proto-China, as well as many other smaller crustal cores. *Thus created* were the Ukrainian shield, the Wyoming Province, the Pilbara and Yilgarn blocks in western proto-Australia, the Aldan and Ananbar shields of proto-Siberia, the Slave Province in northern proto-Canada, and the Baltic shield of proto-Sweden, proto-Finland and the proto-Kola-Peninsula. Now *shields*, *blocks* and *provinces* were massive robust regions of crust and rock. And they were shaped like what their names suggest.

*The Archean was an eon*
*of shield, block and province building.*

And cratons, rock belts, giant batholiths, blocks, provinces, mountain ranges, shields and surface sedimentary rock *combined* to form the microcontinents. And Earth possessed two dozen microcontinents. Most were half the size of modern Greenland.

## Chapter II: Micro-Life

Now the world of micro-life was flourishing. But most microorganisms were only microns big. And they floated *in the ocean*, or they lived on floors of *shallow* seas, under a layer of water that protected them from lethal ultraviolet light. Now those that lived near the surface used sunlight for their energy – they were *photoautotrophs*. And the cell of each such microorganism was encased in a robust membrane which protected it from its surroundings and helped to shield it from Sun's ultraviolet rays. Now other micro-life dwelling deep below the sea lived in hot hydrothermal vents – they were *thermophiles*. Others processed minerals such as sulfur – they were *chemoautotrophs*. Now an organism that acquired energy from a non-organic source was called an *autotroph*, for "autotroph" means self-nourishing. And if the source was sunlight, it was a photoautotroph. And if the source was chemical, it was a chemoautotroph. Now some microorganisms used two sources – and for example, there existed photochemoautotrophs. And some microorganisms ate organic matter – they were *not autotrophs* but *heterotrophs*.

Now at this time, all life forms were prokaryotes, meaning "before the nucleus" in Greek. *Prokaryotes* were simply structured one-celled living creatures, such as archaea and bacteria. By definition their cells possessed no special regions with specific functions. And for example, a prokaryote contained *no nucleus* where genetic code was stored. The *protoplasm*, which was the essential bio-matter of the cell, performed all biological activities. Now reproduction for a prokaryote was simple – it pinched in the middle and divided, thereby splitting its protoplasm *into two*.

*A prokaryote was like unto a business*
*that operated from a single all-purpose room.*

And then as unto today, proto-plants produced *oxygen as waste*. But for the microorganisms of these ancient times, *oxygen was toxic*, for it reacted with organic molecules and disrupted metabolic processes. Some microorganisms would have perished in their own oxygen excrement had the ocean water *not been full* of metal cations; the cations captured oxygen and then precipitated out. And for example, aqueous iron $Fe^{++}$ combined with $O_2$ to make iron oxide rust of $Fe_2O_3$ and $Fe_3O_4$. But the rust did not dissolve in water. Instead, it sank and settled on the ocean floor as reddish dust. And in locations full of microorganisms, biologically generated iron-band formations were created.

And so the waste disposal system for early life was simple: Metal cations collected garbage and placed it in the garbage dump, *the ocean floor*.

## Chapter III: A Meteorite-Induced Extinction Event
*Then it rained brimstone and fire out of heaven.*

*A giant meteor struck Earth.*
*What was to follow*
*was like unto a bullet piercing flesh.*
*And Earth shook and trembled.*
*And the heavens seemed to move and shake.*
*Magma blood gushed from the gash.*
*Smoke went out its nostril.*
*Fire came out its mouth.*
*Coals were kindled by it.*
*Ash rode the wings of all four winds.*
*And burnt dust filled the skies.*
*It assembled in thick clouds above.*
*And darkness was under its feet.*
*The voice of thunder uttered.*
*Like warrior's arrows, lightning bolts descended.*
*Seas rose and islands disappeared.*
*And waves of death surrounded all.*
*The oceans bowed and dry-land strips appeared.*
*The blast in its nostrils so continued.*
*Destruction was delivered.*[135]

And a volcano erupted at the impact site. And a *mighty piece of pumice* was ejected into Panthalassa. And behold, it was three-

---

[135] Throughout Earth's history, cataclysmic meteors would strike Earth many times.

hundred half-meters long, fifty half-meters wide and thirty half-meters deep. And *like unto* a ship, the porous pumice floated on the sea.

And ash and dust, which filled the skies, travelled *all around the globe*. And these particles became the seeds for rain. And during the second month of a long lost year did it begin *to rain*. And waters fell upon the Earth for forty days and forty nights. And it seemed *as if* the heavens were a liquid ball that had been broken open.

And water *flooded* microcontinents. And islands *drowned*. And as sea level rose, all land masses *disappeared*.

And the giant piece of pumice *floated* in the Panthalassa Ocean. Now it was rich in minerals and ash. And primitive ocean microorganisms *clung unto* its underside, feeding on its nutrients.

And after forty days and forty nights, the rain *subsided*. And sea level stopped ascending. And the Sun broke through the clouds. And hot weather followed suit. *Steam* was upon the face of Earth. And the sea began *descending*. And after one-hundred-fifty days went by, the microcontinents did drain and islands *reappeared*.

And during the seventh month of a long lost year, the giant piece of pumice *settled on* a shallow ocean shelf. And mud filled the pores and holes. And the microorganisms, which had been clinging to the pumice, quickly *reproduced*.

And the *Sun* rose as before at dawn – Earth had survived the cataclysmic meteor attack. And life on Earth went on.

*(And a voice spake, saying*
*"Go forth and multiply.")*

## Chapter IV: The Biosphere is Born

And a couple of hundred-million years went by and disappeared. And life progressed. Proto-algae generated bio-matter by primitive photosynthesis. Now in *photosynthesis*, energy from light was used to combine carbon dioxide with water to produce organic compounds. And oxygen as waste was also made. And the oxygen combined with metal cations in the oceans. However, small amounts of oxygen *seeped into air*. And much of this oxygen was absorbed by minerals and metals in Earth's surface rocks. And so, *little oxygen* did the atmosphere possess.[136]

Now proto-algae were prolific and productive. They breathed in $CO_2$ and breathed out oxygen. And over time, the atmospheric $CO_2$ declined somewhat. And over time, the amount of *metal cations* in the sea *declined*. And methanogens in swamps made methane gas in small amounts, which then escaped and entered air. Thus *life* began to change the chemistry of Earth.

---

[136] At this time in geo-history, some oxygen was produced by photodissociation of carbon dioxide, water vapor and sulfur dioxide in the upper atmosphere.

Now some underwater vents spewed out $H_2S$. Near such vents *sulfur-loving* microbes thrived, for they used $H_2S$ for photosynthesis instead of $H_2O$.[137] And instead of oxygen, sulfur was produced as waste. And this made these microbes mildly tolerant of diatomic oxygen, for sulfur could combine with oxygen to cleanse their system of this toxic molecule. Now the *sulfur wastes* were used by other microorganisms. And for example, certain microbes used sulfur for energy-producing fermentation, in which the sulfur was converted into $SO_4^{..}$ sulfate ions. And these sulfates then combined with metal cations in the ocean and precipitated out. And for example, $Ca^{++}$ calcium and $SO_4^{..}$ made calcium sulfate, or $CaSO_4$.

## Chapter V: Ancient Bio-Relics

### *What mean ye by these stones?*

N ow it came to pass that some microbes *colonized* warm shallow waters. And they organized themselves in layers and matted dome-like structures called *stromatolites*.

And eventually some stromatolites would be compressed and be incorporated into rock. And the layered structures *would* so be preserved. And nearby, microscopic twisted stalks of dead bacteria would likewise *be* pressed into rock. And such tiny imprints would be *microfossils*.

Thus microscopic creatures created a work of art, *a biological relic* that would survive for several billion years through *unto this day*. And three-and-a-half-billion years later in Western Australia and elsewhere, paleobiologists[138] would discover the stromatolites. And they would see life *as it was* three-and-a-half-billion years ago.

Now it came to pass that most of the atmosphere was nitrogen. And carbon dioxide in the atmosphere *continued to decline*, but still the $CO_2$ was dozens of times the modern atmospheric level – the greenhouse effect was operating still. And in its atmospheric blanket, thy planet Earth *was warm*. And there were *no polar caps*.

And as several hundred-million years went by and disappeared, microscopic heterotrophs *turned into* prokaryotic proto-animals. Thus Earth possessed new forms of proto-animals and proto-plants, two of Life's six major kingdoms.[139] And that which was animal was called *fauna*. And that which was plant was called *flora*.

---

[137] Some $H_2S$ combined with cations in the oceans. However, the concentrations of $H_2S$ were so high near the vents that plenty of it was available for sulfur microbes. $H_2S$, or hydrogen sulfide, has the smell of rotten eggs.

[138] The prefix "paleo" means "historical."

[139] The other four are archaea, bacteria, protists and fungi. Protists include eukaryotic microorganisms such as protozoans and most algae. Since the division of life into groups is highly dependent on the criteria used, other classification schemes are possible.

And it came to pass that the remains of some *dead prokaryotes* settled in siliceous sediments, which solidified to chert. And the microbodies made imprints in these rocks.[140]

## Chapter VI: Ancient Rifts

*And the mountains shall be molten,*
*and the valleys shall be cleft,*
*as was before the fire,*
*and as the waters that are poured*
*down a steep slope.*

It was three-billion years ago. And it came to pass that a dense, *overthick* crustal region in southern proto-Africa began to sink. Now the region's rock had been made from *heavy* magma. And during the next ten-million years, as the hand of gravity pulled on the land and rock, the region *sank*. And a rift one-hundred kilometers long and thirty kilometers wide between proto-South-Africa and proto-Swaziland developed. And the newly created lowland was provided with the name *Pongola Rift*.

*The Earth did open up.*
*But Earth's time had not yet come,*
*for all of Earth was not ripped up.*

And during the next few billion years, the Pongola Rift would *survive* all geological encounters. Thus it would be *not* destroyed in subsequent collisions of the continents. Thus it would be *not* significantly reshaped by regional subduction of nearby ocean crust. And magma upheavals would occur *close by*, but none would wipe it out. And three-billion years later, it would become the *oldest continental trough* on Earth.

And elsewhere on Earth were other overthick and heavy crustal regions. And at certain times in geo-history, they sank. Thus Nature and the hand of gravity made other giant rifts on Earth.

## Chapter VII: Solar System Mysticism

Now during the Archean, the Sun was growing *brighter*. But even by the end of the Archean, it would still be radiating light fifteen percent less brightly than in modern times. And at night the patterns of the stars, as viewed from Earth, were different.[141] And the moonlit sky

---

[140] *Three-billion-and-one-hundred-million years* later in the *Fig Tree chert* in Swaziland, in Africa, paleobiologists would discover some of these small fossilized remains. And they would know that sophisticated prokaryotes, such as cyanobacteria and bacteria, existed *then*.

[141] Most of the stars in the night sky are from the Milky Way. Since the Sun orbits our galaxy once every quarter-of-a-billion years, star patterns continually change with time. The modern constellations would not have been familiar to an observer on Earth until the Late Cenozoic Era!

was brighter, for the Moon's disk was *four times bigger* than in modern times – the Moon was two-hundred-thousand kilometers from Earth, half of what it is today. And the *closer distance* provoked *stronger ocean tides*.

And Earth was *spinning faster* than in modern times. And in six hours did rise and set the Sun. Likewise, six hours *did* night last. Thus the hours in a day were twelve. And a month, as defined as the time for the Moon to pass once through all its phases, was *just ten days*. Thus the day and month in three-billion years BC were different from the day and month in two-thousand years AD.

And during the next three-billion years, the Moon would slowly *spiral out* a few centimeters every year. And Earth gradually would spin a little slower. A few milliseconds per century would the length of day *increase*. Now an angular momentum transfer was the reason for these changes: The spin lost by Earth *was given* to the Moon, the transfer being caused by tidal torque of Earth-Moon gravity.

> *The invisible hand of Nature passed rotation between bodies.*
> *And know that this not be created by some axiom of Zen.*
> *Time was constant, but a month was less, a day was less.*
> *This was not meaningless – the World was very different then.*

## Chapter VIII: Ancient Sedimentary Basins

And two-hundred-million years went by. And it came to pass that there was a wet lowland[142] adjacent to some highlands. And in the highlands did wind, rain and weathering produce dirt, grain and pebbles, some containing minerals, including uranium and gold. And streams carried the mud, grains, uranium and gold into the *wet lowland*. The sediments did settle *there*. And it came to pass that lava flowed and covered all the sediments. And during the next million years, erosion produced *another* layer of sediments. And it came to pass that *lava flowed again*. And once more the sediments and minerals were covered by basalt. And the layers continued to accumulate for millions of years until an eleven-kilometer-thick structure was established.

Now during this period, microorganisms feeding on minerals and organic molecules *thrived* in the muddy waters of the wet lowland. *Most* were only microns big, but some thread-like species grew to several millimeters long. And they were proto-algae, proto-fungi and proto-lichen. And when they died, the microscopic carbon remnants *settled in the sediments*. And when the sediments solidified, *imprints* were so made. And these were microfossils – fingerprints in time.

And the two-hundred-kilometer-by-three-hundred-kilometer region was given the name *Witwatersrand Basin*. And like the Pongola

---

[142] This lowland region was *north of* and *not far from* the Pongola Rift.

Rift, it would survive the next few billion years to become the *oldest sedimentary basin of its size* on Earth. And in modern times, it would be mined for minerals. But uranium and gold would not be the richest find: Paleobiologists would collect some samples of the sedimentary rocks. And with a microscope, the scientists would scrutinize the rocks for microfossils. And scientists would see life *as it was* two-billion-and-eight-hundred-million years ago.

And elsewhere on Earth during the Archean Eon, Nature built sedimentary basins and provided habitats for primitive and microscopic life.

## Chapter IX: Microcontinental Drift

Now previously, in three-billion-and-five-hundred-million years BC had proto-Africa consisted of *several separate* microcontinents, all located far *into the northern hemisphere*. Now iron filings frozen in basaltic rock would allow future scientists to *track* the motion of these microcontinents. During the next three-hundred-million years, these land masses *drifted* slowly south and eventually arrived *at the equator*. Now at this time, proto-Africa was *"on its side"* – southern proto-Africa *was west* of central proto-Africa, and western proto-Africa *was north* of eastern proto-Africa. Now it came to pass that the motion *was reversed*, so that during the next three-hundred-million years, proto-Africa did wander *north* – three-thousand kilometers it journeyed. Then it began to rotate and head south again. And as it drifted south, the Pongola rift and Witwatersrand Basin in southern proto-Africa, also drifted with it, being transported *like unto* cargo in a barge. And it came to pass that by the year two-billion-and-seven-hundred-million years BC, proto-Africa arrived *once more* at the equator. And it was *on its side again*. But one-hundred-eighty degrees had *it rotated*, for southern proto-Africa *was east* of central proto-Africa, and western proto-Africa *was south* of eastern proto-Africa.

And during the next few billion years, proto-Africa would continue to so *drift about*. And where it travelled, the Pongola rift and Witwatersrand Basin would travel *with it*.

And during the Archean Eon, other microcontinents *drifted* from place to place. And a part of Earth where *there* had once been sea there now was land. And a part of Earth where *there* had once been land there now was sea.

Now some microcontinents gained mass as pieces of Earth's crust were added. And a few microcontinents did merge. And intense mountain building around two-billion-and-six-hundred-million years BC added height to many microcontinents. Thus during the Archean Eon, many microcontinents *increased in size*.

## Chapter X: Igneous Layer Complexes

And it came to pass that around two-billion-seven-hundred-million years BC, there was a *giant magma movement* beneath the Beartooth Mountains of proto-Montana in proto-North-America. And magma flowed through crust, spreading horizontally for fifty-five kilometers. And the magma made an underground lava mare like a mare on the Moon. And when the six-kilometer-thick flow solidified, it *crystallized* into a fractured structure with large layers. And in one layer was a three-meter-thick deposit of minerals enriched in platinum.

And elsewhere on Earth during the Archean Eon, igneous layer complexes like the one below Beartooth were made.

## Chapter XI: Stromatolites Proliferate

And stromatolitic microorganisms such as cyanobacteria did *flourish* in Earth's waters. They strung themselves together in green living strands. And it came to be that stromatolites *three meters high and wide* were built!

And for the next two-billion-seven-hundred-million years through to modern times, stromatolites would continue to be built by microscopic life.

*Stromatolites were like beams of light,*
*illuminating insights into ancient life.*

## Chapter XII: The Great Dyke

And then it came to pass that by two-and-a-half-billion years BC had the Zimbabwe craton *rifted*, as a crack five-hundred-kilometers in length appeared. And magma flowed, filled the crack, *solidified* and formed an eight-kilometer-wide dam-like structure in the crust of Earth.

And this structure would survive the next few billion years of geological activity. And when the microcontinent in which it was embedded ⌐oved, it *would move with* the microcontinent. And it would travel over ⌐ceans *like unto* a tiny sail upon a giant boat, eventually, settling in the lower hemisphere as part of modern Africa. And in the Late Cenozoic Era, weathering would wear away some earth around the *dam-like structure*, exposing some of it. And geologists upon discovering it near a lake in southern Africa would name it. And the *Great Dyke* would be the name they gave it.

## Chapter XIII: Great Mineral Riches Are Made

Now the crust, which Nature did create in the Archean, was *rich in minerals*. During this eon, most of thy world's heavy precious metals such as silver, gold and platinum *were planted* in the earth. And the same was true of other less-precious-but-more-important minerals such as nickel, copper, iron, zinc and chromium. Most heavy metals that had *not been captured in the crust* had sunk to the center of the Earth and had been lost.

And for example, during the Archean Eon, the gold in South Africa and at Kalgoorlie, Australia and at Val d'Or, Canada and in veins at other places was *embedded in Earth's crust*. And likewise other metal mines were made – chromium at Selukwe in Zimbabwe, nickel at Kambalda in Australia, copper and zinc at Timmins and Noranda,[143] iron in the Hopeh[144] and Liaoning provinces of China, nickel and copper in Botswana, tantalum in Monitoba, Canada, and so on.

---

[143] Timmins and Noranda are both in Canada.
[144] Also spelled Hebei.

*The third book of Geo-Evolution, called*

# The Proterozoic Eon

*And the crust of Earth squeezed the rock*
*until the rock gave up its waters.*

## Chapter I: Earth's First Supercontinent

Now it was *two-and-a-half-billion years ago*. And the Archean Eon ended and Earth became an adolescent. And the second half of the Precambrian time, the Proterozoic Eon, started. And this eon would last till five-hundred-and-seventy-million years BC.

And it came to pass that the microcontinents amalgamated and made a *large land mass*. Now the collision of theses microcontinents caused crust to *buckle and uplift*; when two land masses merged, *rugged* mountain ranges did rise up. And bands of rock, called *orogenic*[145] *belts*, were forged beneath. This was orogenesis – mountain-making.

And so the coming together of the microcontinents produced Earth's *first supercontinent*. And this supercontinent covered fifteen percent of Earth, while oceans occupied the remaining eighty-five percent.[146]

## Chapter II: The Structure of Earth's Body

Now during the previous eon, the Earth had cooled considerably, achieving a form similar to modern Earth. During two-billion years, a layered structure like an onion had been made.

Now the external part of Earth was *crust*, which was of two main types: continental and oceanic. Earth's new supercontinent was made of *continental crust*. It was light, floating on the Earth *like unto* cream on milk. Its average depth was thirty-five kilometers. But under mountain ranges did its thickness often almost double. Now *ocean crust* made up the ocean floor. And compared with continental crust, it was denser, more uniform and thinner – approximately six kilometers in thickness. And the ocean crust, *like unto* outstretched hands, *cradled* the waters of the Earth.

Now the *mantle* lay beneath the crust.[147] And the mantle's outer region and Earth's crust made up the *lithosphere*, the outer lip of Earth. And the *asthenosphere* lay below the lithosphere. It was hot and pliable, and it terminated two-hundred kilometers below the surface of the Earth. The rest of the mantle was below.

Under tremendous pressure, the most inner part of Earth, the *inner core*, was compressed into a solid ball a thousand kilometers in

---

[145] Orogenic comes from "oros," meaning mountain.

[146] Nowadays, water covers about seventy-four percent of Earth.

[147] The mantle was two-thousand-and-five-hundred kilometers thick.

radius. And between this ball and mantle sat the *liquid outer core*. There, electric currents swirled and generated Earth's magnetic field.

## Chapter III: On Earth's Crust

And let it be known to thee and all around thee that henceforth continental crust would be permanent and *indestructible*. And its low density would provide stability. And being somewhat buoyant, *like unto* cork in water, it *would* be unsubductible.[148] And at times, tectonic forces would push down some continental crust, but it eventually would *pop back up*. And sometimes, continental crust would get eroded at the edges, but the bulk of it would virtually remain intact. And if it broke in two, the pieces *would* survive. And its margins might get flooded periodically, but when the floods subsided, always would the margins *reappear*. And continental crust would have an intricate structure and a varied composition created by geological dynamics over *extended times*.

Now during the last four-hundred-million years of the Archean Eon, fifty percent of *modern continental crust* was made − *most of the rest* would be forged in three distinct two-hundred-million-year-long periods at around one-billion-and-eight-hundred-million, one-billion and six-hundred-million years BC.

Now in contrast to continental crust, ocean crust was rather uniform and did not last: Its lifetime of several hundred-million years was *relatively short*. Now the ocean crust was fragmented into *pieces* − each piece acted as a mosaic unit, a tectonic plate. Ocean crust was conceived in the upper asthenosphere as magma melt, *born at mid-ocean ridges* where it came out. And during millions of years, it travelled underneath the oceans, shuttling forth islands and seamounts, *like unto* objects on conveyor belts. Eventually the ocean crust *subducted* into trenches at the edges of Earth's continents. There, it *sank*, disappeared and was recycled to its originator, the asthenosphere. Thus unlike continental crust, ocean crust was born to be and bound to die.

## Chapter IV: Continental Water Flow

*He cutteth out rivers among the rocks.*

Now when it rained *upon* the supercontinent, water *flowed down* the sides of high plateaus and mountains. And water *collected* in small streams. And the smaller streams *flowed into* larger streams, which *meandered* through the countryside along the *paths* of lowest elevation. And the large streams entered rivers. And the rivers *flowed unto* the Panthalassa Ocean. Now the branch-like complex of streams and rivers looked *like unto* a network of arteries or nerves. It was the drainage system of the supercontinent. Thus water that landed on the supercontinent was collected and dispersed to Panthalassa.

---

[148] Impossible to be drawn into the Earth.

Thus it came to pass that pebbles, mud and particles were transported from inner lands by rivers and deposited in deltas and in the margins of the supercontinent. Now *margins* were the surrounding regions of a continent, for a continent was *like unto* a page's text, and the continental margins were *like unto* the margins of the page. And so it came to pass that the depositing of sediments added matter to the margins.

## Chapter V: Subduction at Continental Margins

And during millions of years, ocean crust *flowed slowly* from the ocean ridges of Panthalassa to the margins of the supercontinent. This crust was transported by the ocean plates. And when the ocean plates drew near the supercontinent, they were subducted. And subducted with them *was* the ocean crust.

At subduction zones, the plates deeply cut into the lithosphere. And they carried sea water *downward* to the "wound" and rubbed it in. And the asthenosphere bled magma badly. And this magma – rich in calcium and alkalis – pushed through crust, creating *igneous intrusions* in it. And some magma bubbled up and filled large cavities. And it was *as though* Pluto, the *Greek god* of the underworld, breathed fire through the rock. And when the magma solidified deep below the surface, *plutonic rock* was made.

And above subduction zones, *volcanos* rose up along the coasts and inland from the sea. And volcanos ascended also in the margins, creating *island-arcs*, which are off-shore island chains. And lava *oozed* out of the volcanic cones and flowed down slopes and *into lower lands*. There, the lava cooled, solidified and darkened. And scabs of igneous rock were *upon the face of Earth*.

And the rise of magma underground did *raise the margins*, while the solidifying lava *added mass*. And gradually, as the margins grew and rose, *they* turned into *continental shelves*. And rivers from the supercontinent deposited quartz salt,[149] carbonate and shale on the continental shelves.

## Chapter VI: Mutation

Now it *happened* that a cosmic ray struck a proto-plant. And a proton was transformed into a neutron – it was nuclear alchemy. And a molecule of genetic code did *break* in two. And when the proto-plant divided and reproduced, a mutant offspring did appear. And the offspring proto-plant in several minutes died.

And a proto-virus attacked a proto-animal. But when the proto-virus entered the protoplasm of the proto-animal, the proto-virus died. And its molecules *merged* with molecules of protoplasm of the proto-animal. And *a new protoplasm* was obtained.

---

[149] Quartz is an abundant mineral whose main chemical compound is silicon dioxide.

And an ultraviolet ray descended from the sky and struck a molecule in a bacterium. And the molecule was *split in two*. Thus one organic molecule was converted into two. And the bacterium did die.

And it happened that a dead organic molecule bumped into a proto-plant, *stuck* to the outer membrane wall and was incorporated in it. Thus the cell wall grew a little thicker. And later it so *happened* that a poisonous molecule did *touch* the cell. But the molecule could not penetrate the thicker wall. And so this proto-plant survived. And soon there were *other* proto-plants with *thicker* outer membrane walls.

And it came to pass that a proto-animal was in the act of reproduction when toxic *oxygen* did enter in its protoplasm. And some molecules of the proto-animal reacted with the oxygen. And the cell divided as intended into two. But the two mutant off-spring proto-animals that were produced simply *floated* lifelessly upon the sea.

And so during the Early Proterozoic Eon, constantly being produced were *mutant* microorganisms, which almost always quickly *died*. They were the monsters of Nature's trial-and-error experiments. But Nature had hundreds of millions of years to tinker with *trillions of trillions* of cells. And on *rare*, remarkable occasions, a "mutation" made a *better cell*.

And what made a "better"[150] cell? Nature naturally knew *what was better*. And cells knew too, without consciously knowing. It was simple: If a cell was better, it functioned well, and the cell and its brethren-cells *survived*.

And so it came to pass that, randomly and rarely, a mutation did occur which made a better microorganism. And if the change was great, a *new strain* of life emerged. But new strains were also made more slowly, often over countless generations, as small "positive" changes accumulated and created a new species.

Thus Proterozoic micro-life evolved. And evolutionary "progress" did proceed. And, compared with later times, the pace was *very slow but steady*.

Now these were the good old days, when life was relatively calm and natural nutrients were *plentiful*. These were days when the variety of species *was low*, predatory cells were rare, and competition among the living was largely lacking. These were the days when life's enemies were few and far. These were the good old days, when the generations of a species could endure for *half-a-billion years*.

## Chapter VII: Photosynthesis

And it came to pass that proto-plants made better use of energy from sunlight. And they began to manufacture energy-rich sugar molecules, such as *glucose*. Now making glucose was relatively complicated: Hundreds of millions of years of trial, error, accidents and luck

---

[150] Of course, "better" is a human judgement.

had helped perfect the process. Now to produce a sugar, a proto-plant arranged more basic organic molecules in certain combinations and supplied the energy from sunlight. And chemical reactions so ensued, in which *bonds were made* that tied the atoms of the sugar molecule together. Now these bonds *stored energy* for later use. And the energy could be released by breaking bonds.

> *Nature, through trial-and-error experiments,*
> was *refining biochemistry.*
> *Nature, the Almighty, became a* biochemist.

Now the construction of a molecule by bonding smaller parts was called *metabolic synthesis.* And when photons from the Sun supplied the energy, the process was called *photosynthesis.*

And many microorganisms ate proto-plants for food. And they *took the sugars* from the food, added water and used chemical processes to *break* the bonds. And each time a *bond was broken*, the bond *released some energy.* And this process was *metabolic fermentation.* Thus metabolic fermentation supplied the energy for microscopic Proterozoic life.

## Chapter VIII: Heat Breaks Up the Supercontinent

*Fire mingled with blood was cast upon the Earth.*

Now the radioactive *decay of elements* such as potassium-forty, uranium and thorium *produced heat* inside thy Earth. Thus the interior of Earth was in part a nuclear reactor.

And the Moon tugged on Earth through gravity. And the tugging caused the Earth to *strain and stretch.* And the stretching led to friction. And friction led to *heat.*

And heavy matter *sank toward* the center of the Earth. And in sinking did the matter rub against surrounding molten metals. And this generated heat. And when such falling matter struck the solid inner core, heat also was produced. Thus gravitational potential energy was converted into kinetic energy, and kinetic energy was converted into *heat.*

And molten liquids at the surface of the inner core *solidified.* And in solidifying, *heat was given off.*[151]

Thus the inner part of Earth was *like unto* a furnace. Verily was the inner Earth a hell. And like all furnaces, heat went out in all directions and escaped. But the heat escaped by different means at different depths in Earth. And it passed through Earth's liquid inner core to the mantle in convective circulating flows. And then some of it passed through the mantle to the crust steadily, smoothly, and microscopically – one oscillating molecule bumping with the next. Thus the thermal

---

[151] It takes heat to melt a solid and so, conversely, the solidification of a liquid gives off heat.

motion of one molecule was given to the next. And *this* was heat *con-duction*.[152] But some heat in the mantle convected through *hotter long thin tubes* – they were giant *mantle plumes*; the matter in such plumes, although solid, was so hot it slowly rose. Now to escape the very outer layer of Earth, much heat seeped through mid-ocean ridges – these cracks in crust provided *paths of least resistance*. But some heat also conducted through the ocean crust. And *still less heat* passed through continental crust, since the thicker, lighter continental crust *conducted poorest*. Thus the heat of inner Earth passed to the surface via different means and paths.

And it came to pass that *heat* amassed beneath Earth's super-continent. Now the supercontinent acted as an insulating cap. And so the temperature below it *grew steadily*, albeit slowly. And matter melted in the asthenosphere beneath the supercontinent. Such melts made magma rich in iron and magnesium. And the heavy magma *rose and surged* through certain spots. There, mountains and volcanos formed.

> *The supercontinent was* like unto *the crust of pie.*
> *The pie was in the oven being baked.*
> *The hot, expanding filling lifted up the crust.*

And twenty-million years went by. And it came to pass that heat forcing its way through the supercontinent had *cracked* it a half-a-dozen places.[153] And fault lines formed, through which magma *surged*. And lava did flow out of cracks and onto land, and chains of mountains and volcanos formed.

Thus the supercontinent had fractured: It was *like unto* a jigsaw puzzle with seven pieces, for the supercontinent had *seven* sections. And each was bordered by volcanic-mountain chains, which discharged lava, gas and steam. And as the lava froze and formed heavy basaltic rock, dense mass was added to the supercontinent along its fracture zones.

And during the next twenty-million years, heat rising through the faults did *push the land apart*. And the seven sections *separated* slightly. Then it came to pass that the heavy rock in earth adjacent to volcanic-mountain chains *collapsed*. Thus on both sides of mountain chains were rifts and valley plains.

Now there was one rift-valley that emerged between a high pla-teau and mountain range. And when it rained, water flowed *down* both slopes into the lowland region of the rift and flooded it. And wind and weather generated dirt and grains on mountains. And rain *washed* the

---

[152] Heat conduction is like electricity with heat instead of charges flowing.

[153] It has been suggested that because the supercontinent had a higher elevation, the spinning of the Earth would subject it to extra stress, like the centrifugal force on the clay of a spinning potter's wheel. However, it seems likely that this played a minor role, if at all, in cracking open the supercontinent.

dirt and grains into the lowland region, making it *a basin*. And sediments collected there. And microorganisms *flourished* in the dark and murky waters. And cyanobacteria did multiply in marshes, bacteria did *thrive* in swamps, and tiny spore-like life forms *floated* in the pools and ponds. The air above the basin was both moist and musty. And this sedimentary basin, which *was* in southern proto-Ontario, was provided with a name. And the name was the *Huronian Basin*.

And it came to pass that rain collected in all the rifts of the fractured supercontinent. Thus narrow seas *surrounded* all seven continental sections. And microscopic life did *flourish* in these seas. The supercontinent had rifted into *seven* giant sections.

*The pie had over baked.*
*The crust had cracked in several places.*
*Steam seeped out.*
*Filling spurted through the cracks.*

And during the next forty-million years, the *seven sections* moved apart. And the seas between them *joined*. And these seven pieces were thy *Earth's first continents*. Each was made of thick and light and elevated crust.

Thus the *heat* that had amassed beneath the supercontinent some one-hundred-million years before had detonated an "explosion." And it was of *enormous energy and force*, for it had cracked the supercontinent into the smaller continents. And it had propelled the continents *to drift apart*. And yet it had happened *so extremely slowly* – during many million years. And if ye, at any given year, had been there, ye would have noticed nothing. Indeed the continents were moving at several *centimeters* every year! And although the speed of each was slow, the momentum was enormous, for a continent's tiny speed was compensated by *its giant mass*. And it would take many million years and great geo-forces to reduce a continent's momentum. Indeed, the motion *would* be hard to stop. And for tens of millions of years, each continent would drift in its particular direction. And so it came to pass that *full-fledged* plate tectonics was established.

And the *intercontinental volcanic-mountain chains* remained in the middle of the newly opened seas. And some were underwater, while others stood as island chains. But *all* were sinking – the severing of the old supercontinent had left them no support.

## Chapter IX: Plate Tectonics

And millions of years went by. And it came to pass that the continents drifted *against and over* the ocean plates of Panthalassa. Now the boundary between two such *colliding* plates was called *convergent*. At convergent boundaries, the subduction of the ocean plates produced a rise in continental shelves, *as though* the shelves were shovelled onto land. And as the shelves became incorporated into continents, the amount of continental crust on Earth increased.

And subducting ocean plates slid *into* Earth's asthenosphere, pulled by Nature's force of gravity. They were like *knives* cutting flesh. They carried ocean water to the "wound" and rubbed it in. And the asthenosphere bled magma badly. And again it seemed *as if* Pluto, the *Roman god* that ruled the underworld, breathed fire through the rock. And when magma rich in calcium and alkalis bubbled up in chambers and solidified, plutonic rock was made.

And faults formed along the Panthalassa coast. And earthquakes shook these coastal regions, while eruptions added much basaltic rock and ash.[154]

And as millions of years went by, the continents *closed in on Panthalassa*. And it *shrank* somewhat in size, and some deep waters disappeared. Now the spreading of the continents did *open up the intercontinental seas*. And these seas turned into shallow oceans. And water flowed through channels from Panthalassa to the newly fashioned shallow oceans. And *sea-level* subsequently *rose*.

And the intercontinental volcanic-mountain chains, the remnants of the rifts of the old supercontinent, slipped below the sea and became *mid-ocean ridges* for the new-born oceans. And *hot dense magma* emerged through underwater cracks and fissures and manufactured new and heavy ocean crust. And it was *heat* beneath the Earth that fed the ridges.

And the newly constituted ocean plates slid along the asthenosphere and ferried continents apart. Thus mid-ocean ridges marked the boundary between *separating* ocean plates. Now this boundary was *divergent*, for from this boundary did the sea-floor spread and ocean crust diverge.

Now what were the forces causing ocean plates to move apart? The basic source was *heat*; *its* energy supplied the plates with motion. Now the weakest force was *push*: As heated magma flowed through *the* mid-ocean ridges, it pushed the plates apart *a little*. Another force was *gravity*: Heat had uplifted regions near mid-ocean ridges, causing plates to simply *slide away*. But the strongest force arose from heat convection: Some of the heat that rose beneath mid-ocean ridges curled over and flowed horizontally away. And the moving medium of heat did *drag* the plates along.

And as millions of years went by, the continents were *pushed*[155] by intercontinental ocean plates, so that they *drifted into* Panthalassa. And the subduction of the ocean crust along the coast of Panthalassa

---

[154] The earthquakes were similar to those in modern-day California, but they were more frequent and robust. The eruptions were similar to the one of Mount Saint Helens in 1980 AD.

[155] Later, continents would also be *pulled* by ocean plates.

produced a rise of land inland. And *new mountains*, similar to the Rocky Mountain Range of modern times, *were made.*

And it came to pass that an island-arc in Panthalassa stood *in the way* of an approaching continent. And after several million years, the continent did strike the island-arc. And as more years went by, the island-arc was *thrust* into the land. And metamorphic rock and a mountain range *were made.*

And it also came about that a continent *drifted into* a Panthalassan *island*. And after many million years, metamorphic rock and local coastal mountain peaks *were made.*

And *elsewhere* along convergent boundaries, continents at random and from time to time collided into ocean island-arcs and islands. And *many island-arcs and islands*, made by Earth two hundred-million years before, were thus destroyed. *They* were buried in the crust of continental coastal regions. And mountains, *like unto* tombstones, *towered* over them.

And at one interface, two plates slid by each other *without* converging or diverging. And this was a *transform strike-slip boundary*. And each time there was a sudden slip, a strong earthquake shook this region of the Earth.

And throughout the rest of geo-history, plate tectonics would *shape the surface* of thy Earth. And the face of Earth would be determined by the motion of the plates. And *divergent boundaries* would cause *lava flows*. At mid-ocean ridges would they most frequently occur. But when a divergent boundary emerged upon a continent,[156] the continent would rift apart and open up, and then a sea would form. Now motions of the plates at *transform boundaries* would cause *earthquakes*. And at *convergent boundaries* would be both *earthquakes and volcanos*. Often would convergent boundaries occur at edges of a continent where ocean crust subducted. And *sometimes* a convergent boundary would draw two continents together, eventually causing them to *bump* into each other. And such a slow powerful collision would produce the *highest and most rugged* mountain ranges on the Earth.[157]

> *Tectonic plates did cover Earth*
> *like a mosaic of a dozen tiles.*

It was two-billion-and-three-hundred-million years BC. And it came to pass that the seven continents were *well dispersed*.

And millions of years did pass and disappear. And the *aging* intercontinental oceans assumed a certain profile shape[158] determined by the dynamics of tectonics. Now a mid-ocean ridge was *uplifted and buoyed* by strong magma flows. And each year, out of the "womb" of a mid-ocean ridge, *dense ocean crust* was born. And as it moved outward

---

[156] Most divergent boundaries originated within a continent.

[157] The Himalayan Range is a modern example.

[158] This is the height profile of the ocean floor, as viewed from the side.

from the ridge, it aged and cooled. And in cooling did it grow a *little denser*. And being dense and heavy caused it *gradually* to sink. Thus an intercontinental ocean was most shallow near its mid-ocean ridge,[159] and depth *increased with distance*. And for example, the ocean four-thousand kilometers from the ridge was *twice as deep* as the ocean one-thousand kilometers from it. And so ocean crust was oldest, densest and *deepest* just off the continental shelves. But at the continental margins, the ocean floor *curved up and joined* the continents. And from the ocean profile, it looked *as if* the continents were weighing down the ocean plates. But the opposite was true – the lighter continents *were holding up* the heavy ocean crust. And so geologic forces provided the ocean floors with profiles that were similar.

And sea-floor spreading from mid-ocean ridges continued to ferry forth the continents. And Earth's continents so very slowly *moved apart*.

And several tens of million years went by. And larger did the intercontinental oceans grow. Likewise, the intercontinental ocean crust increased.

And it so happened that a few hundred-million years had passed since the breakup of the supercontinent and the opening of the intercontinental seas. And at one continental shelf, old *heavy* ocean crust, which had been joined to continental crust deep below the sea, had *broken off*. Thus the oceanic lithosphere was severed from the continental lithosphere, as one tectonic plate broke into two. And as millions of years went by, the ocean crust drawn by the force of gravity slid *beneath* the continent, eventually piercing Earth's asthenosphere. And a *new* subduction zone arose. And a *new* convergent boundary appeared. And the coastal region of the continent, which had been previously so quiet, began to "rumble." And volcanos rose and *sputtered lava*; and offshore island-arcs appeared; and earthquakes *shook the coast*.

And a new force began to act upon the fractured ocean plate. It was *pull*: At the subduction zone, Nature's hand of *gravity* tugged at the *heavy* ocean plate. And the convection cycle was "completed," as the colder medium beneath the plate was recycled to Earth's mantle, where it would sink, then turn, move horizontally through Earth, and after being heated finally rise up.

Now the ocean plate *no longer pushed* the continent. But the continent continued drifting in the same direction.[160] And although the force behind the continent was gone, the momentum *still* was there.

And as millions of years went by, the continent continued drifting, but it did so *at a slower rate*. And a trail of off-shore island-arcs was left behind it in its wake.

---

[159] In places, the ridge even pushed above the sea and made islands.

[160] The situation was analogous to a speed boat that suddenly runs out of gas. Even without motor power, such a boat continues sliding forward over water.

And it came to pass that, in *other places* in the World, old heavy ocean crust broke off of continents and starting sinking down.

## Chapter X: The First Proterozoic Ice Age

*And from the heavens shall snow fall*
*in flakes of pristine white.*

And the Sun brightened somewhat, but its radiation was still *ten percent less* than that of modern times. And rain continued to wash carbon dioxide from the atmosphere. And microorganisms continued to breathe in $CO_2$. And while some carbon dioxide was being recycled to the atmosphere, levels of $CO_2$ were *dropping*. And Earth was *cooling*. Now at this time, the North Pole was covered by one continent, while the South Pole was partly covered by another. And ocean currents no longer circulated warm water from the tropics to the polar regions. And gradually the poles turned *cold*. And eventually at the North Pole and the South Pole, water turned to ice.

*Earth was wearing polar caps*
*on both its crown and chin.*

And sea level went down slightly. And many microorganisms that could not stand the cold or wound up stranded on dry land did quickly die. Now the substantial *difference in temperature* between the equator and the poles created robust ocean currents. And a few life forms adapted to the changing world and thrived, while others that could not cope with swirling currents *died*.

And in the *summer* months, the northern polar cap dissolved and *disappeared*, while ice at the southern pole increased. And in the *winter* months, arctic ice and snow *returned*. And while the northern polar cap grew larger, the southern polar cap dissolved and disappeared.

*And the old man,*
*with the white beard and gray hair,*
*cut his hair and let his beard grow long each summer*
*and cut his beard and let his hair grow long each winter.*

And millions of years went by. And it came to pass that Earth's climate *further* cooled, and most markedly in the northern hemisphere. And ice formed in northern proto-North-America. And snow *fell* to Earth from heaven and *accumulated* on the ice. Embedded on the underside were pebbles, rocks and dirt. And on the mountains, *glaciers grew*. Then gravity took hold and made the glaciers *slowly* slide down mountain slopes. And as the glaciers slid, ice eroded rock, and stones were polished by the ice and snow. But grains and pebbles in the glaciers also *scratched* such surface rocks, while surface rocks ground glacial pebbles into grains and small grains into dirt.

And in summer, *ice retreated* some. And left behind were pebbles, dirt and boulders. And in winter, *ice advanced*. And the ice was *like unto* a paw that clawed the Earth. And boulders broke, and stones got scraped, and pebbles cracked. And a layer of clay and silt was placed on top of last year's scratched and broken rocks.

And during hundreds of years, the ice went back and forth, building laminated *layers* of clay and grains. And when ice in summer melted, lakes appeared. And clay and pebbles from the ice did settle in the beds of lakes. Such annually deposited sediments were *varves*.

And it happened that a boulder lay upon a glacier. And as the glacier inched like a snail forward, the boulder too *inched forward*. And when ice melted in the summer, the boulder fell *onto* a varve, depressing all the layers of sediments below. And such a boulder was a *dropstone*. And in many places in the glacial varves were dropstones so deposited.

And ice sheets travelled *three-thousand kilometers* from proto-Quebec, through proto-Ontario, through proto-Michigan, and into proto-Wyoming. And in some cases, large boulders were transported lengthy distances *like unto* cargo in a barge. And elsewhere in the World did glaciers form. Ice and snow ventured into proto-Siberia and eastern proto-Finland; and ice sheets covered southern proto-Africa, for continental drift had once again positioned proto-Africa well to the north.

And this was Earth's *first extensive glaciation*. And it lasted a *few hundred-million years*, and then the polar caps did disappear.

And when the ice age ended, some earth-pebble-rock layers lithified to *tillite*. And it would happen that certain tillite would survive to modern times. And for example, two-hundred-meter-thick tillite in a twenty-thousand-kilometer region of Ontario would one day tell the tale of Earth's *ancient* Proterozoic glaciation, a glaciation that took place *more than two-billion years ago*.

And this would not be the only Proterozoic ice age – the next would come six-hundred-million years thereafter, at around one-billion-seven-million years BC.

## Chapter XI: Oxygen in Earth's Atmosphere Increases

*He poured out the contents of his vial upon the beasts.*
*And they gnawed their tongues for pain.*
*And the kingdom was full of darkness.*

And a hundred-million years went by and disappeared. And it came to pass that metals in surface rocks *completely oxidized* – no more gaseous oxygen could be absorbed. And the face of Earth possessed no spotless shiny metals, *only rust*. And for example, earth contained red beds of rocks, due to the iron which was dirty red. And the oxygen released by micro-life at the surfaces of seas was finally set *free*. And $O_2$ rose into air *like unto* spirits from a grave. And *for the first time*, there was more than a little oxygen in air.

*The poison which had been released*
*would someday be a blessing.*
*That which was bad* at *one moment*
*could be better later and* even *good.*

And during tens of millions of years, *minute* amounts of oxygen collected in the atmosphere. And life on Earth was visibly disturbed. Those prokaryotes that floated on the surface of the seas *succumbed*, for oxygen disrupted their biochemical reactions, and metabolizing failed. And a *mass extinction* of surface micro-life took place. On the seas, scum was everywhere. Earth's oceans had a putrid smell.[161]

But some surface-sea prokaryotes with thick cell walls endured. And life in the *ocean deep* survived, essentially unscathed. *There*, the processes of oxidation still persisted, for deep-sea metallic cations captured oxygen and made precipitates of it.

## Chapter XII: Proterozoic Igneous Complexes

And a hundred-million years went by. And Earth bled as it had done in the Beartooth Mountains six-hundred-million years before. But this time Earth bled *more*: In proto-South-Africa, magma flowed uncontrollably over a region of *sixty-thousand square kilometers*.[162] Now the magma carried in it minerals such as vanadium, titanium, nickel, iron, platinum and chromium. And when the hemorrhaging ceased, the liquid rock solidified into a *nine-kilometer-in-depth* deposit – the largest layered igneous intrusion in Earth's crust. And someday it would become among the richest mineral deposits in the World. And it would be called *Bushveld Complex*.

And during the Proterozoic, as in the Archean, igneous complexes were forged, albeit at a slowing pace.

## Chapter XIII: Heterocysts

And it *happened* that a new type of thick-walled proto-green-algae came about – during the previous one-hundred-million years, it had been engineered by Nature and by evolution. And it was a *heterocyst*, a cell with a robust outer membrane which protected the organic molecules inside.[163] And for life, the heterocyst was a revolution, for metabolic processes *were shielded* from lethal non-organic molecules like oxygen. And new proto-green-algae dwelt on the surface of the sea where other non-heterocysts could not.

Now the heterocyst was a crucial step for future life, *preparing* organisms for the impending $O_2$-*filled* environment. Starting around one-

---

[161] This *would* not be the only mass extinction – many would follow. The most recent would be in the Recent.

[162] So much lava poured out that it would have covered the entire United States in a layer one-hundred meters thick!

[163] The heterocyst actually arose as a reaction to nitrogen starvation.

and-a-half-billion years BC, levels of oxygen would *everywhere become significant*. And at that time, many creatures without heterocysts would perish in the oxygen. Thus without the new cell-wall protection, *few* living species could survive beyond one-billion-and-five-hundred-million years BC. Thus without this natural invention, *little life would be*.

Now it so happened that *life rebounded* from the mass extinction that had struck the Earth a hundred-million years before. And micro-flora *flourished*; and proto-micro-fauna *multiplied*; and stromatolitic microorganisms continued to proliferate. And the variety of biota indeed was great. And some cells were shaped like *spheres*, some like *rods*, some like *disks*, some like *tubes*, and so on. And certain cells were *long thin filaments*. And there were microscopic creatures with curved *cocoon-shaped* cells and even large[164] spore-like prokaryotes up to twenty micrometers in diameter. And many of the Proterozoic bacteria assumed a form that looked like modern-day bacteria.

And when *some* organisms died, they *drifted to the surface* of the seas and decomposed. And when *others* died, they *sank* and settled on the bottom of the ocean floors or in the sediments of wet lowlands. And when rain washed sediments into a wet lowland, the bodies of the microorganisms were interred in mud. And for example, basins such as the Huronian became giant natural burial grounds for Proterozoic life.

And during millions of years, the deeper sediments solidified to chert, forming *small casts* around remains of certain heterocysts. And some such casts survived the destructive geologic forces of the next two-billion years, being preserved *unto this day*. Thus the casts turned into ancient microfossils – the microscopic versions of Egyptian mummies – time capsules of paleontologic information. And the ancient burial ground in the Huronian Basin was assigned a name. And the *Gunflint iron formation* was the name.

## Chapter XIV: Ophiolites

And one-hundred-million years went by. And ocean crust *crept* toward the eastern coast of proto-North-America, where it subducted. And it so happened that a *small piece of upper ocean crust* severed from the other ocean crust below. And when this small piece reached the northeast coast of proto-North-America, it slid up and *settled on the continental margin*. Thus instead of sinking with the other ocean crust and disappearing in the lithosphere, it found a home *on land*. And this relatively rare process was provided with a name. And *obduction* was the name.[165]

And this particular piece of ocean crust, which was incorporated in the continent, would survive destruction. And geologists would dis-

---

[164] Large for this time in geo-history.
[165] Obduction is the opposite of subduction.

cover it in modern times in Cape Smith on the Hudson Bay in Canada. And they would call it an *ophiolite* from the Greek "ophios" meaning serpent. And the Cape Smith ophiolite would be the *oldest* known to man. And by inspecting it, geologists would deduce the composition of the ocean crust *as it was two-billion years ago.*

And throughout geo-history, ophiolites were occasionally deposited on continents. And some survived geological destruction, becoming records of the ancient Earth.

## Chapter XV: The Kangamiut Dike Swarm

And it happened that one-thousand kilometers away from the continent containing proto-Greenland stood a mid-ocean ridge, where magma *surging into the lithosphere* solidified in dikes. And every year, when *ocean crust* was created at the ridge, *it inched out* in opposite directions, transporting the dikes with *it*. And new dikes were made and filled the spaces where old dikes had been. Thus the ocean crust contained a *swarm of dikes*. And as millions of years passed by, the leading front of the dike swarm *inched toward* the continent containing proto-Greenland. And eventually dikes were subducted with the ocean crust just off the proto-Greenland coast.

Now it so happened that the swarm passed *above a hot spot* in the upper mantle, causing a three-hundred-kilometer-long section of the swarm to rise. And when this elevated section reached the coast of proto-Greenland, it was obducted and incorporated in the continent. And miraculously would it survive *unto this day*. And two-billion years thereafter in western Greenland, *it* would be discovered by geologists and called the *Kangamiut swarm*, the World's densest continental swarm of dikes.

## Chapter XVI: The Atmosphere Obtains Some Ozone[166]

And while the continents were moving about and the face of thy planet Earth was changing, microorganisms *continued to produce* diatomic molecules of oxygen. And the oxygen passed into the atmosphere. And the amount of oxygen in air became about one percent of the modern atmospheric level.

Now some oxygen in the *upper* atmosphere was *struck* by radiation from the Sun, causing molecular oxygen, or $O_2$, to split into atomic oxygen, or $O$.[167] This was *molecular photodissociation* – the division of a molecule by the absorption of electromagnetic radiation. And when photodissociation produced $O$ atoms, some of them combined with $O_2$ to make $O_3$, which is *ozone*. And this was *molecular recombination*.

---

[166] The time at which the Earth acquired a significant ozone layer is not exactly known – it could have happened earlier.

[167] Of course, two atoms of $O$ were produced each time an $O_2$ was split.

And so the atmosphere of Earth obtained an ozone layer, which was thin but nonetheless absorbed Sun's ultraviolet light: When an ultraviolet ray struck an $O_3$ molecule, the $O_3$ broke into $O_2$, O and heat. Now the heat was passed to the surrounding gas. And the O soon recombined with $O_2$ and remade an ozone molecule. Thus in effect, *ultraviolet radiation was converted into heat* through ozone photodissociation and recombination. And throughout the upper atmosphere of Earth, ozone, being continually destroyed and made, *filtered out* the solar ultraviolet rays. And the amount of ultraviolet radiation striking the surface of the Earth *went down*.

## Chapter XVII: Earth's Thermostat

And a hundred-million years went by. And it came to pass that an asteroid *traversed* Earth's path. And the asteroid *struck* land in proto-North-America at Sudbury, Canada. And rock fragments scattered hundreds of kilometers in what was *like* a nuclear explosion without radiation – dirt, debris and dust *mushroomed up* into the atmosphere. And pressure from the impact made metamorphic rock. And heat did *cook* Earth's crust. And magma melted. And the surface of the Earth was bruised: Out of it was carved a crater one-hundred-ten kilometers across. And in certain places, lava flowed profusely. Now below the surface, magma carrying copper, nickel, cobalt, gold and platinum filled a sixty-five-kilometer-sized dome-shaped chamber and solidified. And a rich deposit of these minerals *was made*.

And at the impact site, carbonic and sulfuric gases spewed into the air. And as in a broken hydrant, steam sprayed *out and up*. And the gases *rose* into the atmosphere and joined the dust. And a large dark cloud was so created. And it did cast long *shadows* on the face of Earth. And thousands of kilometers of ocean and of land *were dark*.

And weeks went by. And as gas and dust did spread around the globe, sunlight *was blocked out*. And rain did come and wash the dust away. But lots of $CO_2$ and other gases stayed.

And with more $CO_2$, the temperature of Earth *increased* a few degrees. And ponds, lakes and oceans *warmed*. And water thus evaporated *faster* than before. Such vapors rose and carried heat. And in the upper atmosphere the $H_2O$ released its heat. And infrared emissions from the Earth to outer space *increased somewhat*. And rain clouds *appeared more often* than before. Likewise it rained more often than before. And atmospheric $CO_2$ dissolved in drops of rain. And carbonic acid raindrops landed in the seas.

*The hydrologic cycle was Earth's air conditioner:*
*When the temperature went up,*
*it seemed as if someone turned up the cooling rate.*

And as many years went by, the atmospheric $CO_2$ *decreased*, reaching the levels of before. And Earth's temperature returned to *normal*.

Thus Earth's thermostat was in its $H_2O$. And so the rain and water vapor *regulated* temperatures on Earth. And throughout the rest of geo-history, they would continue *to do so*.

## Chapter XVIII: Aerobic Life

And it came to be that a *new microorganism* from the heterocystic population did appear.[168] And it lingered on the surface of the sea *absorbing* minute amounts of oxygen. And *like* many other microorganisms, it *ate of* proto-plants for food and processed energy-rich glucose by metabolic fermentation. But *unlike* other microorganisms, it *used oxygen* to further break some bonds. And to break these extra bonds, a primitive *enzyme*[169] was employed. And this new oxidizing metabolic method was called *respiratory metabolism*; it produced *twice* as much energy from glucose than fermentative metabolism. And so this *new microorganism* had better energy production. And soon it and others like it became the rulers of the seas.

*And Earth possessed its first oxygen-employing life.*
*And Nature took in a breath of air.*

Now old floral life and new faunal life combined to create a *metabolic cycle*, which worked as follows. Micro-proto-plants took in carbon dioxide, processed it and expired oxygen, while respiratory micro-proto-animals inhaled oxygen and exhaled $CO_2$. Thus the waste of proto-plants was "air" for proto-animals. And what proto-animals breathed out was food for proto-plants. And plants and animals thus formed a *partnership*. And eventually respiratory proto-animals would multiply, becoming numerous enough that an oxygen–carbon-dioxide balance between animals and plants could be established.

*This partnership would last a lifetime,*
*the lifetime of the Earth.*

Plants *were as* an arc of a circle – they were half a circle, a semicircle. And animals *were as* an arc of a circle also – they too were half a circle, the other semicircle. Thus plants with animals and animals with plants did make a circle whole.

---

[168] Here and elsewhere, words such as "appear" and "emerge" in regard to life forms do not indicate a sudden process. New organisms and species usually take millions of years to evolve and are often continually changing. As one turns the pages of *The Bible According to Einstein*, millions or tens of millions of years go by. On these time scales, new life forms seem to "instantly" arise. The same applies to geological processes such as mountain building, sea formation, continent movements, et cetera.

[169] An enzyme assists a biological process. It itself remains unchanged.

## Chapter XIX: Micro-Merging

And it so *happened* that a micro-proto-animal ate a micro-proto-plant. But because the micro-proto-plant was big, the micro-proto-animal could *not ingest* the bio-matter of the micro-proto-plant. And the microorganisms existed for a while as part proto-animal, part proto-plant. And soon they died.

And two microorganisms bumped each other, and they fused. And they struggled to get free but stuck as one. And they too, after a short time, did not survive.

And it came to pass that two microorganisms joined and fused, but did not die – *they lived as one*.

And *elsewhere* on the Earth and randomly in time, microorganisms so combined. And this was *micro-merging* of divergent species. And it almost always caused disaster – the microorganisms almost always died. But on rare occasions, the microorganisms did survive. Thus micro-merging *began* occurring on a microscopic scale.

And even more *common* were symbiotic partnerships, in which for their mutual benefit two creatures *lived together*. And for example, certain microscopic proto-animals and proto-plants dwelt in colonies, exchanging oxygen and $CO_2$.

## Chapter XX: The Sun and Earth Cool Slightly

And it came to pass that the temperature inside the Sun *decreased a little*. And as the energy production in the core *slowed down a bit*, the Sun did shine less brightly. Likewise, a *little less light* reached Earth. And the temperature of Earth descended slightly then. And near the South Pole and the North Pole did *snow and ice* emerge again.

And *fluctuations* in the brightness of the Sun would cause the polar caps to wax and wane. And glaciers would advance, retreat, advance and so on. But for several hundred-million years, some ice and snow on polar caps would nonetheless remain. And then, after three-hundred-million years, the snow and ice would disappear.

## Chapter XXI: The Second Mass Extinction from $O_2$

It was one-billion-and-seven-hundred-million years BC. And it came to pass that most aqueous positively charged metal cations of ferrous iron, magnesium and calcium[170] had combined with oxygen and other elements and had *precipitated out* – over the past billion years or so, ocean life had cleaned the seas of metal cations. Thus all ferrous iron now was ferric iron. And rust lay on the bottom of the seas.

*The ocean floors were* red *with rust*.

---

[170] These cations are $Fe^{++}$, $Mg^{++}$ and $Ca^{++}$.

Now proto-plants produced oxygen, as they had done before. But since cations in the water were *relatively* rare, *oxygen dissolved* in water. And this *was* occurring everywhere. And even more $O_2$ did enter air.

And oxygen reacted with organic molecules in cells and *disturbed* their biochemistry, causing cells to die in *countless numbers*. And at all depths did sea life perish, with cells disintegrating into plain organic matter – everywhere did dead biota fill the seas. And many microorganismal species disappeared. And on the floors of seas, dead microcells thus lay.

*A second oxygen-induced mass extinction*
*now was underway.*

But not all life died out. Some microorganisms huddled *around the vents* of mid-ocean ridges where minerals and metal cations continued pouring out. But such *safe havens* were a tiny fraction of Earth's former fertile habitats. And *certain* thick-walled microorganisms that had oxygen-protective heterocysts *survived*. And among the species that continued to live on were surface proto-green-algae which had faced and overcome the threat of poisoning by oxygen a half-a-billion years before. And another group of life forms that survived were respiratory microorganisms that used oxygen for metabolic processes – *they even thrived*.

And so dead biota and organic matter *filled* the ocean water. How rich the oceans were in such organic food! And those microorganisms that survived soon multiplied. And the seas were full of proto-plankton, bacteria and other microorganisms. And although the number of species was now *few*, those species that remained did number *quite a few*. And these survivors were *more robust*, having become resistant to oxygen and many other poisonous biological and chemical materials. And some life forms, like respiratory microorganisms, put $O_2$ to productive use.

*He, whose back is bent but is not broken,*
*shall rebound and shall be strong.*

## Chapter XXII: Subduction Begins Off the Coasts of Proto-North-America

And *proto-North-America* moved *westward* into Panthalassa. It was being driven by tectonic forces coming from the *other* side of it. There, on the eastern coast, it joined an ocean plate. And as the intercontinental ocean crust spread forth from a mid-ocean ridge, the ocean plate *slid westward*, driving proto-North-America with it.

And for *several hundred-million years*, the ocean plate was pushing proto-North-America. And along the eastern coast, the crust was old and *heavy* when compared with other ocean crust. And it was sinking slowly.

And it came to pass that ocean plate *broke off* the eastern coast of proto-North-America. And subduction of the ocean plate along the eastern coast commenced. And proto-North-America continued drifting to the west but *at a slower pace*, no longer being driven by the intercontinental ocean plate.

## Chapter XXIII: Primitive Eukaryotes

And a hundred-million years did pass. And as proto-plants produced $O_2$ at rapid rates, the amount of oxygen in air *increased* to a few percent of modern atmospheric levels. And a significant atmospheric ozone layer arose, which blocked out solar ultraviolet rays. And it was *as if* a filter had been placed around thy Earth, for hardly any ultraviolet radiation reached the surface of the Earth.

And micro-merging was *taking place* on microscopic scales. And life evolved, as cells combined. And *larger* prokaryotes developed under the atmospheric ozone, which helped *protect* the life on Earth.

And tens of millions of years went by. And it came to pass that some microorganisms continued growing bigger. And among the larger ones was *one that had a nucleus* – the nucleus was *like unto* a holy temple for genetic codes. And this new cell was furnished with a name. And the name was *eukaryote*, which means "good nucleus."

And soon Earth was full of eukaryotic cells. They contained *centers* with specific functions, called *organelles*.[171] And organic molecules protected and enclosed each organelle. The organelles floated in a mucous substance which permitted them to move about.

Thus a cell with organelles *was* a eukaryote. Thus organelles were *smaller crucial parts* of eukaryotic cells.

*A eukaryote was like*
*a business office with several rooms:*
*The office was the cell.*
*The organelles were rooms.*

And in the sea, a eukaryote *received the stimulus to replicate*. And organic molecules raced to reproductive sites. And into place did move genetic codes – they unfolded, stretched, aligned and broke. And like magic did a *second* set of codes appear.[172] And the nucleus inside the cell stretched and split *in two*. And each nucleus contained a copy of the codes. And other organelles did also split *in two*. And as the cell elongated, the protoplasm severed and the mother cell was gone. Two off-spring cells remained.

Thus reproduction for eukaryotic cells was not so simple – unlike prokaryotes, the cell did not simply separate in two. But the *new* re-

---

[171] Organelles had originated as independent living cells.
[172] The replication of genetic codes was simpler than in modern times.

productive process had "advantages" in the way it *passed genetic information* to succeeding generations.

Now a cell with special bio-centers, each performing a specific bio-task, was more biologically efficient. Thus eukaryotes proliferated. And since they *consumed* more energy than prokaryotes, they ate more food. And they processed food in both respiratory and fermentative metabolisms. And the prokaryotes, which used *only* fermentation, *were less energy efficient*.

And many eukaryotes did eat prokaryotes. And prokaryotes declined. And it came to pass that prokaryotic species *numbered less*, falling victim to "evolutionary progress."

But prokaryotes did not die out – their small size and their great numbers guaranteed survival. Thus prokaryotes lost the war among the "karyotes" but *still* endured.

## Chapter XXIV: The Making of Laurentia

*Nature's mountains stood there high*
*like giant altars unto the heavens.*

Now on *both* the eastern and the western coasts of proto-North-America was ocean crust subducting. And proto-North-America was drifting westward *very slowly* – each year it only budged a fraction of an inch.

And millions of years passed by. And *static friction* suddenly[173] took hold. And the continent of proto-North-America *stopped drifting* to the west. And eventually it happened that a piece of Panthalassan lithosphere *bonded* with the plate of proto-North-America along the western coast.

Thus instead of sinking into Earth, the Panthalassan ocean crust pushed proto-North-America *like unto a tugboat* nudging forth a giant barge. And the motion *was reversed*, for proto-North-America started drifting *to the east*. It was heading now *toward* the continent containing proto-Greenland. And it so happened that proto-Greenland was heading in proto-North-America's direction.

And a hundred-million years went by – it was around one-billion-and-five-hundred-million years BC. And the continents of proto-North-America and proto-Greenland *touched* – a *collision* of two continents commenced.

And the margin of proto-Greenland *merged* with the margin of proto-North-America, as offshore sediments began to *pile up*. And as millions of years went by, the margin of one continent was shovelled onto the margin of the other.

And several million years went by.

*The bulls began to butt their heads.*

---

[173] "Suddenly" in geological terms means during several thousand years.

And the rock of proto-North-America and the rock of proto-Greenland drove into each other.[174] And the landscape was *distorted* – it was orogenic torture. And during countless years, rock was *twisted and contorted* and was "squeezed to death." And rock was crushed so hard that "liquids trickled out." And rocks near the surface rubbed against each other, crumbled and were even pulverized. The erosion was enormous.

And below the surface, granite became granulite, and granodiorite transformed to gneiss. And rock belts buckled and they folded over. Synclines, anticlines and overfolds were everywhere. And the belts that folded down were *forced into the Earth*. And the belts that buckled up *made mountains*.

And during the next four-hundred-million years, the collision of the continents continued.

Now some crust of proto-Greenland was thrust *onto* proto-North-America, thereby making continental crust *there* thicker. And a long mountain range arose. Starting in proto-Labrador, it ran along the proto-Adirondack Mountains, continued through the coastal plain of proto-eastern-USA and ended finally in proto-Texas. This was the origin of the *Grenville Orogen*.

Now lots of surface rock were shattered into *fragments*. And rain washed away loose rocks. And what remained were *rugged* mountains *like unto* the modern Himalayas. But such rugged peaks would not endure, for a half-a-billion years of weathering would wear away the edges, and another half-a-billion years of geological activity would wipe out many mountain belts. And so the original Grenville Orogen *would* be largely lost. And that which would remain would be *buried* under eastern North America.

Now the collision of the continents caused proto-North-America to split apart inland. And so the *Midcontinental Rift* was made. It was a thousand-kilometer-long lowland region, which extended south from proto-Lake-Superior. And later the Midcontinental Rift would fill with water.

And proto-North-America and the continent containing proto-Greenland were compressed into a single land formation. And a new continent called *Laurentia* was created.

## Chapter XXV: Primitive Organelles

And it came to pass that eukaryotes became *increasingly complex*. Many were now fifty micrometers big. Evolution had "progressed."

---

[174] Of course, this collision happened very slowly – during thousands and thousands of years.

And through environmental pressure and through natural selection, proto-green-algae *evolved* to modern-like green algae with eukaryotic cells. And other proto-micro-plants evolved to micro-plants.[175]

Now the cells of eukaryotes contained sophisticated organelles of which the most important was the *nucleus* – it housed genetic codes. And in the nucleus, instructions for cell functions were copied and sent out. Now one round green organelle converted sunlight into energy – it was a primitive-type *chloroplast*. And another elongated oval organelle generated energy by biochemical reactions – it was a primitive *mitochondrion*. Now these two organelles were essential, for a cell could not function without energy. And there were other organelles. The *lysosome* broke down proteins and primitive carbohydrates. And the primitive *Golgi apparatus* and the primitive *endoplasmic reticulum*, a network of microtubes, assembled, modified and exported proteins. And the rod-shaped *centrioles* assisted in the division and reproduction of a cell.

And it happened that the protoplasm of a one-celled eukaryote contained an empty hole – it was a *vacuole*. And this eukaryotic micro-organism filled its vacuole *with gas*. And the vacuole inflated. And the eukaryote *ascended* through the waters of a deep blue sea. Then the eukaryote *expelled* some gas, and the vacuole deflated. And the motion was reversed; the eukaryote *descended*.

And vacuoles of other cells were used for other purposes such as engulfing nutrients, discharging waste and storing bio-matter.

*And the eukaryote was like unto a factory*
*with many floors and sections for specific tasks.*
*Each section of the factory involved a different-type activity.*
*Such specialization led to better productivity.*

## Chapter XXVI: The Mackenzie Swarm

And several hundred-million years went by – it was around one-billion-and-two-hundred-million years BC. And it came to pass that a *dike swarm formed* from suboceanic magma flows. And *heat* inside the Earth *uplifted* a *relatively light* five-hundred-by-three-thousand-kilometer-sized piece of ocean crust containing many dikes. And it joined the continental crust of northern proto-North-America. And it survived *unto this day*. And so in modern times from the Great Lakes to the Arctic, there would *be* a land of dikes. And it would be the *Mackenzie Swarm*, the World's largest continental swarm of dikes.

---

[175] The process by which proto-life-forms change into life forms is gradual, taking thousands to tens of millions of years. Since the process is slow, one cannot say exactly when the transformation takes place.

## Chapter XXVII: Evolution Begins to Accelerate

*And the microscopic creatures of the World*
*were given great desire unto intercourse*
*so that they may make their numbers multiply.*

And it came to pass that an algal eukaryote began to replicate. The organelles did duplicate, and the cell did *stretch* into an oval. But a section of the membrane wall was *extra thick*. And the left half of the eukaryote tugged on the right half, while the right tugged on the left. But the tug of war *did not break* the cell apart, and the protoplasm *did not* split in two. A peanut-shaped eukaryote emerged – it was a Siamese-twin of the micro-world. And the poorly functioning, defective eukaryote did die.

And during millions and millions of years, short-lived two-celled microorganisms did arise. And all of them did die.

. . . . . .

And then it came to pass that a two-celled algal eukaryote, a proto-seaweed, *did survive*. It was a functional bio-freak of micro-life, a microorganism no better or no worse than a single-celled eukaryote.[176]

And a hundred-million years went by. And it came to pass that one-celled *micro-animals* appeared. And they were *the first protozoa*. And there were other evolutionary changes too: Proto-viruses *evolved to* viruses, and proto-plankton *became* plankton. Now *plankton*, from the Greek word "planktos," meaning "wandering," were free-floating forms of ocean life. And some of the eukaryotic cells did fossilize. And among the fossils were some spherical ones called *acritarchs*, meaning "of uncertain origin."

And a hundred-million years went by. And it came to pass that in the waters of a sea two eukaryotes *intermingled* and then coalesced. And a hole between the two emerged and formed a passageway, through which protoplasm flowed. And a larger organism with twice as many organelles appeared. And the two nuclei moved randomly about until they met. Then they merged into a single nucleus. And molecules of genetic codes from each eukaryote lined up. And by folding, turning, merging, bending, joining and then breaking, the molecules produced a *new third set* of codes. And after the nucleus had split in three, the cell stretched into a three-pod structure. Then the protoplasm also *split in three*.

Through this encounter, three were made from two. And so it came to pass that eukaryotes did interact before they replicated. And this was a new mode of reproduction was uni-sexual cellular duplication.

Now the new mode resulted in a revolution in life's evolution. Why was this so? In *two-body reproduction, not* every organism of a

---

[176] At this stage in evolution, having more cells was not an advantage.

species was the same, so that this form of reproduction brought about a large variety of members of a species. And furthermore, it was *impossible* to replicate exactly, especially in the more complicated two-body process: Cells were not robots coming off an automated factory assembly line; cells were intricate. And so there *always* were some microscopic *differences*. And the differences in parent cells *were combined and passed* to offspring cells. Now most of the time the differences were not significant. And *occasionally*, the differences resulted in a "poorer cell." And *occasionally*, they made a "better cell." Significant changes sometimes arose in the metabolic mechanisms, in the ability to move about, in the make-up of the protoplasm, in the nature of the outer membrane wall, and so on. And those cells that functioned *poorer* lived for *shorter* times. And those cells that functioned *better* lived for *longer* times. And those cells *that* lived longer *mated more*, producing offspring *that*, on average, functioned better. Thus two-body reproduction led to a more progressive evolution. Now changes in a species might be imperceptible and even random from generation to generation, but during millions of years the changes *could be* dramatic and "for the better."

And so it came to be that *steady* evolutionary progress was obtained for life on Earth. And the more rapid rate of evolution led to more biotic *competition*. And those organisms that obtained a "biological advantage" *conquered* those creatures that did not. And the seas became a giant bio-battle ground.

And it was a ruthless world for life. It was a time when *the weak were killed.* It was a time when the strong were "nicely compensated" for their conquests. And species that were rulers at one evolutionary moment became slaves at a later stage, as *new ruling species* suddenly[177] arose. And old-life forms became the food for new-life forms. From now on, the average life-span of a species shrank. And for a plankton species for example, it shortened to a hundred-million years.

The law of the survival of the fittest fell on all on Earth. The law of evolution cast a *shadow* on the Earth. Henceforth, the world of life and evolution would proceed in a wild, *almost random way*. Thy Earth would never be the same again.

And competition among the living was cruel but had a benefit: it sped up the evolutionary process. And new forms of life appeared *every several million years*. And so it came to pass that there was a quantum *jump* in evolutionary progress.

## Chapter XXVIII: The Longest Ice Age

It was one-billion years BC. And it came to pass that the South Pole was *covered* by a continent. And equatorial warmer ocean currents could not flow freely in the lower southern-hemisphere. And waters there turned *cold*.

---

[177] "Suddenly" here means during hundreds of thousands of years.

Now at this time, Earth was geologically quite quiet. Eruptions of volcanos were *uncommon*. And the coming together of some continents had closed a few mid-ocean ridges, so that *gas emissions* from them had *declined*. Thus carbon-dioxide sources were *reduced*, while photosynthesis and rain *continued to remove* Earth's atmospheric $CO_2$. And $CO_2$ descended to its lowest level yet. And heat and radiation from the surface of thy Earth were *no longer* trapped by it. It was *as if* thy Earth had lost its insulating blanket. And heat was lost to outer space more easily and readily. A *new cooler climate* was established. And the *most widespread, longest ice age* in geo-history began – it would go on and off for the next *four-hundred-million years*.

And *ice and snow* covered all the continents. And glaciers everywhere left tillite sediments and scratches on the rocks. And the temperature of oceans *also* dropped, causing a decrease in the metabolic rate of cells and life. And some species could not stand the cold and went extinct. It was another *mass extinction* in the making.

## Chapter XXIX: The Sexual Revolution

*And the twain shall be one flesh.*

And a hundred-million years went by. And Earth warmed up a bit – a pause in the ice age did take place. And glaciers *retreated* toward the poles. And as with *warming* ocean waters, microorganisms multiplied and multicellular algae did appear. And proto-seaweeds turned into Proterozoic seaweeds.

And it came to pass that a *mutant* strain of a spore-like microflora formed. Now the original strain was microflora X. And the new form was microflora Y. And microflora X and microflora Y were *not too different*: Although their cells contained the same kinds of organelles, microflora X was *slightly* smaller than microflora Y. And a few sections of genetic code were also different.

Now the microflora reproduced as follows. When microflora X mated with microflora X, a microflora X emerged, as was the case before. And when an X mated with a Y, a Y emerged. But when a Y mated with a Y, *no* offspring microflora were produced. Thus the reproduction and survival of the microflora Y depended on the microflora X.

And microflora X was designated *female*, while microflora Y was designated *male*. And a new revolution in evolution did commence – it was the *beginning* of the sexual revolution.

Thus sexual liberation in the Late Proterozoic Eon started. And it would lead to the longest, greatest orgy-like encounter of life forms ever, lasting more than *half-a-billion years*.

Now *some* species developed *several sexes*. And for example, one microorganism had W, X, Y and Z strains. Thus there were six mating possibilities among the *different* strains, so that mating for this microorganism was quite complicated. More sexes were not necessarily "better," just more complex.

And some multi-sexual organisms would survive to modern times. And for example, modern paramecia *would* have half-a-dozen sexes.

*Now the sexual revolution had lit a fuse.*
*A flame was burning on a thread*
*whose end was fastened to a bomb,*
*a bomb that would create a burst in evolution.*

And after fifty-million years went by, Earth's temperature *declined again*. And glaciers filled the continents. And ice sheets several kilometers in thickness formed. And the temperature of ocean waters *also* went way down.

And once more, microorganisms *suffered from the cold*. And metabolic fermentation slowed. And bacteria did not multiply so fast. And since fewer microorganisms meant less food for heterotropic life, some species *went extinct*. And the *potential* evolutionary blast was put on hold. And for the next fifty-million years, the Earth continued to be cold.

*It seemed* as if *the flame had dwindled to a cinder.*

## Chapter XXX: The Ever-Changing Face of Earth

And during the Proterozoic Eon, greenstone-granite and granulite-gneiss belts continued to be built. And *some new cratons* were created. And ancient mountain chains and orogenic rock *were made*. And for example, subduction in the Arctic in northwest proto-Canada had *earlier* produced the Wopmay Orogen, at around one-billion-and-nine-hundred-million years BC. And at the same time in proto-Scandinavia, the Svecofennian Orogen was created in a collision of two continents.

Now the plains of continents were vast deserts of *dust and sand*. And when the wind blew, particles filled the air. And when strong winds blew, *dust storms* did engulf entire plains. And visibility dropped to a few meters – it was like a fog, not of mist but *dust*.

And *plate tectonics* dominated the geo-physics of thy Earth. Continents did *move about*, being shuttled by adjacent ocean plates. Continental coasts, when fused to ocean plates, were geologically quite quiet. Now sometimes *two continents* closed in upon an ocean and made it disappear. And if *they* continued to collide, they merged to make a larger continent. Such collisions generated *rugged mountain ranges*. But sometimes the opposite occurred: A large continent rifted, separating into smaller continents, which then diverged and opened up; and when the rift regions filled with water, *new seas and oceans* came about. And at the same time, mid-ocean ridges formed which then supply new ocean crust. Now from time to time, a continent slid away from an adjacent ocean plate at a subduction zone. And such a movement created volcanos, island-arcs and faults. And sometimes a continent passed over an adjacent ocean plate. And such a movement swept up continental shelves and built up *coastal mountain ranges*. And the continent occasionally overran old island-arcs and islands. And earthquakes often shook the coastal regions.

And such tectonic processes would continue through the rest of time. And the shape of continents and oceans would be forever changing. And continents would from time to time combine. And sometimes oceans would close up. And now and then new seas and straits would form. And every several hundred-million years, the face of Earth *would change*.

## Chapter XXXI: Some Parts of Proto-Africa Join

Now *earlier*, in about one-billion years BC, subduction off the coast of northern proto-Africa had produced a two-thousand-kilometer-sized stretch of *island-arcs*. And during the subsequent half-a-billion years, these island-arcs and northern proto-Africa *collided*. And as ocean crust was thrust up between the island-arcs, the richest stretch of Proterozoic ophiolites resulted. And a *new shield*, the Arabian-Nubian shield, was made. And later this core of continental crust would become Saudi Arabia, Egypt and Sudan.

And at the same time, the continents of proto-east-Africa and proto-central-Africa *collided and produced* the Pan-African orogenic belts in what would become Tanzania, Kenya, Mozambique and Ethiopia.

Gradually the pieces of proto-Africa were being put in place.

## Chapter XXXII: Great Proterozoic Sedimentary Deposits

And sediments were *deposited in basins* in many places during the Proterozoic Eon. And for example, for eight-hundred-million years starting around one-billion-seven-hundred-million years BC, layer after layer of shale, sandstone, siltstone and conglomerates was laid down in the *Riphean* in proto-northern-Asia. And likewise, around seven-hundred-million years BC, a ten-kilometer-thick sedimentary basin, the *Sinian*, in proto-China, was created.

And in the sediments were *several types* of stromatolites. And some were shaped like domes, while others were like columns and like cones. And all were built in mat-like layers each a millimeter thick by colonies of algae, interspersed among fine sediments. Now some large stromatolites *tilted to the Sun*. And the tallest of these temples reached *eleven meters high*. And in terms of diversity and numbers, the stromatolitic "empire" peaked around nine-hundred-million years BC.

## Chapter XXXIII: Bio-Feedback

And it came to pass that *two continents* approached each other. And as many million years went by, the sea between them narrowed. And the mid-ocean ridge was squeezed.

*It was* like unto *a doctor pressing skin together
and sewing up a laceration.*

And there was a sudden movement of a crustal plate. And a powerful, unfathomable earthquake shook the region near the ocean ridge.

*The stitching slipped apart.
The laceration opened up again.*

And magma just below the crust burst *upward* through one fault. And surrounding crust surged up above the sea. Molten rock was tossed into the air; smoke and gases mushroomed to the clouds; and dirt, dust and broken rocks rained down upon the land for hundreds of kilometers.

And within hours, a volcano was created where *no* volcano was before. And this was not the only one, for another six had surged above the fault and were spitting out their magma.

And all around the globe, air was full of dust and dirt and carbon-sulfur gases. And the face of Earth was *dark*: No sunrise could be seen for days. And each week for weeks, the rain which fell on Earth was brown. And eventually, the dust and dirt in air were rinsed away, but lots of $CO_2$ remained.

And because Earth possessed a *heat-retaining* coat of $CO_2$, the temperature on Earth increased. And with warmer waters and more $CO_2$, certain microorganisms *multiplied*. And in the oceans, seas and lakes, such warmer waters did evaporate more quickly. And rising vapors made Earth's clouds appear repeatedly. *Frequently and heavily* did such clouds let loose their rain. And this helped to wash away the atmospheric $CO_2$.

Now photosynthesizing microorganisms, such as *phytoplankton*, *breathed in* the excess $CO_2$. And their metabolisms *did speed up*. And lots of $CO_2$ went into making biomass and $O_2$ gas.

Now much of the extra atmospheric $CO_2$ was removed in the hydrologic cycle of rain, run off and evaporation. But a little extra $CO_2$ *remained*. And as hundreds of thousands of years went by, bacteria and microorganisms *breathed in* the $CO_2$. Profusely did these organisms multiply.

And plankton consumed the carbon dioxide and processed it into organic molecules containing carbon, which were then *deposited on ocean floors* as calcium-carbonate sediments. And during hundreds of thousands of years, the micro-organisms *reduced* the atmospheric $CO_2$ to normal levels. And this process was called *bio-feedback*.

Thus bio-feedback and the rain-cycle did *regulate* the temperature on Earth.

And micro-animals feasting on the lush plankton populations prospered. And micro-faunal numbers multiplied. And this increase in biotic populations led to an *increase in mutations*, which, in turn, led to *new varieties* of species.

And millions of years went by. The *two continents* were pushing *once again* against each other.

## Chapter XXXIV: Micro-Multizoa

And it came to pass that two protozoa stuck together, forming a *two-celled* micro-animal, *a bizoon*.[178] And the bizoon functioned poorly, for *it* had difficulty moving. But the bizoon did not die. And although, after millions of years, the seas contained great populations of bizoa, protozoa numbered more.

And thousands of millenniums went by. And it came to pass that a new bizoon symbiotically emerged. Now its *left cell* was good for locomotion, while its *right cell* was efficient in metabolism. And the two together made a *more mobile energetic* organism. And the new bizoa prospered, multiplied, and soon[179] they *ruled* the seas.

And fifty-million years went by. And the seas were full of micro-multizoa – *micro-multizoa* were micro-animals with *many* cells.

And it came to pass that stromatolites, being *rich* in minerals and bio-matter, became the feeding grounds for several types of micro-multizoon. And the ancient colonies of the stromatolitic algae dwindled: It was the *downfall of an ocean empire* – a hundred-and-fifty-million years earlier, stromatolitic life had been the ruler of the seas. Now the micro-multizoa nibbled at the temples. And the great biological palatial wonders of the World turned into ruins – it was *like unto* the Europeans conquering the Incas. And stromatolitic algae almost disappeared from Earth.

And plants continued outputting oxygen to oceans and the atmosphere. And $O_2$ in air reached seven percent of the modern atmospheric level. And respiratory organisms *breathed* more easily. Correspondingly, there was an increase in their metabolic rates.

And species struggled in the war of the survival of the fittest: The "race" was on to obtain the most efficient metabolic systems. Now better metabolic systems permitted bigger species to exist. But bigger species required a more rapid metabolic rate. And so a vicious circle was created. A battle to be biggest followed.

---

[178] Pronounced bye-ZO-en.
[179] "Soon" here means during thousands of years.

And improvements in oxidation-based metabolism allow respiration to produce *ten times* the energy of fermentation. And the mitochondrionic organelles became a potent power source for cells.

## Chapter XXXV: Metazoa

And millions of years went by. It was seven-hundred-million years BC. And it so happened that the ice age paused, and the climate of thy planet Earth warmed up a bit. Seas teamed with floating protozoa and green algae. The *golden age for plankton* came about, as their populations peaked.

And the sexual revolution, the struggle to survive, and the battle to be bigger led to rapid evolution. And the micro-multizoa grew into the *metazoa*, animals with many many cells, each performing different functions. And marine life flourished in *shallow off-shore margins* where nutrients were readily available. And thousands of millenniums went by. And many different metazoa – all with *soft* bodies – occupied the oceans: tiny proto-worms, proto-sea-pens, proto-sponges, proto-jellyfish and so on. Now many metazoa floated on the sea *basking in the sunlight*. But proto-sea-pens grew in the muddy ocean floors in colonies. And there existed pipette-like metazoa which siphoned water through theirs straws extracting food and oxygen.

And the plankton, algae, metazoa and aquatic-life assumed a *variety of forms* – triangles, rectangles, stars, cups, folded leaf-like structures, octahedrons, vases, hollow cylinders, et cetera. And one micro-metazoon was structured like the branches of a tree. Another species had a *micro-pod*, which was an elongated blob that propelled a micro-animal about by waving up and down *like unto* the tail of a porpoise. Now many metazoa were several hundred micrometers long. But the largest were a millimeter. And one plankton species had a cone-like collar – this heterotrophic plankton was a tiny ocean carnivore. And it moved about collecting algae in its cone, which it *then* ingested and consumed.

And tens of millions of years went by. And some Proterozoic metazoan animals *ballooned in size*. The "elephants" of the micro-world had so arrived. The largest stretched to several centimeters. And some, like pteridinium, were shaped like worms, while others, like tribrachidium and parvancorina, were flat and multipodal.

And many forms of micro-life had groups of cells that *functioned as a unit*, such as tiny tissues.[180] And each tissue had a particular purpose, such as a protective outer cover, a pod, a filament and so on. And many forms of micro-life had microscopic organs.[181]

---

[180] A *tissue* is a structure made from similar cells that are strung together with an intercellular material.

[181] An *organ* is a group of cells that performs a specific and important function.

And *as if* to sunbathe, a jellyfish-like metazoon floated on the surface of the sea. Below it, a metazoon crawled along the ocean floor, leaving tiny tracks behind.

And although the air had oxygen, $O_2$ was *rare* – still less than one-tenth the modern atmospheric level. But enough oxygen was there to be dissolved in water. And animals and plants fought for food, organic-matter, $O_2$, minerals and nutrients. And this caused many organisms to develop flatter bodies, for the larger *surface area* permitted higher food intake and better aqueous oxygen absorption.

And one flat metazoon living at the surface of the sea surprisingly was *green* – it had *teamed up* symbiotically with multitudes of micro-algae. In fact, its surface membrane was infested with the algae, which were photosynthesizing and releasing oxygen as waste. Now the $O_2$ was *inhaled and used* in respiratory metabolism by the metazoan host. And this partnership provided protection for the algae – to eat the algae, a plankton-feeding organism would have had to eat the bigger metazoan host.

And similar symbiotic partnerships existed for certain deep-sea metazoa living near mid-ocean hydrothermal vents.

And it came to pass that some fauna died and *fossilized* in the Ediacara Hills in proto-South-Australia. And more than sixty species were preserved. And the fossils of these soft-bodied metazoa of the Late Proterozoic Eon, the *Ediacaran fauna*, would survive *unto this day*.

## Chapter XXXVI: Two Supercontinents Are Made

And it came to pass that the motion of the continents moved the continents *toward each other*. And during many million years, the continents of proto-Siberia, proto-Kazakhstan[182] and proto-Baltica collided with each other to form proto-north-and-central-Asia. And the seas between them closed, and the Riphean water basin narrowed. And as coastal waters disappeared, mobile marine biota migrated, searching for new habitats. And some plankton found themselves on land and died.

. . . . . . .

And as the continents continued *to close in*, the Riphean waters disappeared, and all large forms of life within it perished. And the Riphean filled in further, lifted up and joined the continent of proto-Asia.

And elsewhere intercontinental ocean floors rose up, taking hold of all the life within them *like unto* giant fishing nets. And as the "nets" were slowly raised, sea life was caught and cast onto the sandy lands.

And the Sinian basin also *drained*: A land emerged where waters once had been. And it became a part of proto-Asia.

---

[182] This land mass was also known as Kazakhstania.

And *everywhere* the intercontinental seas did drain and disappear. And in their place *dry land appeared*. And life sought out "new pastures," but they were disappearing almost everywhere: Shallow ocean habitats *were* becoming rare. And organisms found themselves *on land*. And dead biota and organic matter made the coastal regions smell.[183]

And elsewhere on thy Earth were *other continents colliding*. And in the southern hemisphere, proto-Australia already had struck proto-Antarctica. And proto-India was bumping into eastern proto-Africa. And the intercontinental seas were being *sealed up*. And when continents did join, mid-ocean ridges were destroyed and continental shelves dried up. And during all this time, fertile ocean habitats were disappearing from the face of Earth.

And twenty-million years went by. And the continent containing proto-north-and-central-Asia had crashed into Laurentia and formed a *giant continent*. And proto-South-America had reached the western coast of proto-Africa.

And many million years went by. And the continent containing proto-South-America and proto-Africa was *colliding with* the continent containing proto-Australia and proto-Antarctica. And then proto-southern-China bumped with them to forge an even larger continent, a supercontinent. And the supercontinent was furnished with a name. And *Gondwana* was its name. Thus a second *coming together* of continents produced a second supercontinent.

Thus in the southern hemisphere, Earth possessed *two giant continents* which had been built in one-hundred-million years starting in seven-hundred-and-fifty-million years BC. And the ocean of *Iapetus* filled the two-thousand-kilometer-wide void between the two. And Panthalassa occupied the northern hemisphere and *some parts* of the southern hemisphere.

Now the closing of the intercontinental seas produced a *mass extinction* – mighty tectonic forces overwhelmed Earth's life. And those species that *died* during the formation of the supercontinents were *those* that could not make the changes in a changing world. And those which *did survive* were mobile and *more versatile*.

And a thousand-thousand years went by. And Life's survivors battled over habitats and nutrients. And those that lost the battles *died*. And those that won the battles *lived*.

## Chapter XXXVII: Late Proterozoic Life

And it came to pass that many metazoa ate the ocean's plankton. And since numerous shallow ocean basins had vanished when the

---

[183] Just previous to the disappearance of the intercontinental seas, the coasts smelled only of fresh sea air, a situation very different from the one ye know today, in which coastal sea life creates a strong odor.

continents had made two supercontinents, many fertile plankton habitats had disappeared. And so plankton populations, which had peaked just thirty-million years before, *decreased* dramatically, and half the species *went extinct*.

Now some metazoa fed on other metazoa. With *soft* bodies, these creatures verily were *easy prey*. The battle to survive again was driving evolution.

And it so happened that the Laurentia-proto-Asian supercontinent moved south, cutting off the ocean currents from the middle region of the Earth that *used to warm* the waters of the southern pole. And as the South Pole region cooled, ice began to grow.

Now the coming together of the continents had closed up many ocean ridges, thereby sealing shut the carbon-dioxide emissions from these sources. And the amount of atmospheric $CO_2$ *went down*.

And it was *as though* thy planet Earth had *taken off* a winter coat. And Earth, which was radiating heat more easily, turned *cold*. It was the Late Proterozoic, and the coldest period in geo-history arrived – the *Varanger Ice Age*. And during its eighty-million-year-long reign, Gondwana was buried under multi-kilometer-thick glacier ice, snow landed even in the equatorial regions of the Earth, and icebergs floated in Panthalassa in the northern hemisphere. Half the globe was under ice and snow!

And many plankton, protozoa, metazoa, algae and microorganisms could not stand the cold. And the number of organisms went way down. And the development of new forms of life was put on hold.

And with a cooler climate, the waters in the seas evaporated *slower*, so that it took *longer* for Earth's clouds to form. And although it rained and snowed on Earth, it did so less frequently, so that atmospheric $CO_2$ washed out *more slowly*. And this helped to moderate the drop in $CO_2$. And since there were fewer photosynthesizing organisms, *less* carbon dioxide was *absorbed* by micro-plants. And this also eased the drop in $CO_2$, albeit in a meager way.

And while the surface of the Earth was cold, heat was accumulating *underneath both supercontinents*.

Now some metazoa survived the frigid climate. And among them were *cloudina* and *sinotubulite*, with tube-shaped bodies of a millimeter wide and several centimeters long. And through the tubes, which *had* hard outer casings, these metazoa filtered nutrient-rich water. Thus the outer section of a tube was for protection, while the inner part was used for taking in $O_2$ and food.

And many metazoa *increased in size* while remaining *flat or thin*. And for example, some proto-jellyfish were a meter wide but only several centimeters thick. And likewise, the stems of some proto-sea-pens were a meter long but just a centimeter in diameter. And from their stems, flat "leaves" stuck out like in a fern. And the pancake-shaped *dickinsonia* was half-a-centimeter thick and half-a-meter wide with special tissues all along its body to assist in oxygen collection. And long proto-worms, which were everywhere, dug into the seabed mud or floated in the ocean water. And the flat and "furry" *spriggina*, which looked like a silver-fish, wiggled on the ocean floor. And eventually the descendants of spriggina would grow hard casings and evolve to some of the mightiest and most dominating creatures of the ancient seas, the trilobites.

Now *weaker species went extinct* from lack of fertile habitats, from the cold climate, from wars among life forms, from biological competition, and so on. But the stronger species did continue on. And among them were the *metazoa*, who through their *respiratory* metabolism were benefiting from a world with an increasing prevalence of oxygen. *They* began to prosper.

## Chapter XXXVIII: A Supercontinent Breaks Up

And fifty-million years went by — it was six-hundred-million years ago. And heat and magma *pushed up* through the Laurentia-proto-Asian supercontinent. And rifts appeared. And volcanos surged up suddenly. And during the next thirty-million years, the supercontinent *broke into* the continents of proto-Siberia, Laurentia, Baltica and Kazakhstania.

And mid-ocean ridges in Iapetus emerged, out from which magma made new ocean crust. And as ocean plates diverged, they *pushed* the four new continents apart. And after many millions of years, proto-Siberia, Laurentia, Baltica and Kazakhstania *drifted north*, left the Antarctic Circle and were isolated in Iapetus. And while these four moved north, the other supercontinent, Gondwana, *headed south*.

Now the *shallow off-shore margins* of proto-Siberia, Laurentia, Baltica and Kazakhstania provided fertile habitats, which *teemed* with ocean life. There, *new species* soon[184] developed. Now the flora and the fauna *within* a continental margin fought and battled one another. But those *from different* continents did not, for the vast seas between the continents were barriers. And so it came to be that life in the coastal waters of different continents developed into different forms. For many millenniums henceforth, life would evolve in *isolated* ways.

And carbon dioxide from the newly formed ocean ridges rose into the atmosphere. And the slow rain-cycle *helped* the atmosphere maintain this $CO_2$, while the $CO_2$ helped Earth *retain its heat*. Thus Earth had its carbon-dioxide blanket back. And as the temperature of Earth increased, the *warmer* climate caused sea waters to evaporate more quickly. And the rain-cycle rate returned to what it had been four-hundred-million years before. And with a new milder climatic equilibrium established, algae and micro-plants began to flourish once again — they breathed in $CO_2$ and breathed out oxygen.

---

[184] "Soon" here means during hundreds of thousands of years.

*The first tome of the trilogy of geo-history, called*

# The Paleozoic Era

*Speak to the Earth and it shall speak to thee.*

## Introduction

*Ye can see words in these stones.*

The Proterozoic Eon ended. It was five-hundred-and-seventy-million-years ago. Earth became adult. And the *Phanerozoic Eon* started. And the Phanerozoic Eon would last *unto this day*.

Now the name Phanerozoic means "to reveal life" in Greek, for from this point onward, prolific *fossils* would etch in Earth its history. And henceforth, biological dating would be possible. And it would be the invention of the shell that would initially make this feasible, for shells would *be* pressed into mud, *which* would harden into molds that preserved the images of ancient life. And each period of geo-history would have its tell-tale flora and its tell-tale fauna. And younger sedimentary fossils would be laid *on top of* older sedimentary fossils. And sedimentary rock *would* read like a book: Each layer of sediments was *like unto* a chapter; each fossil was a paragraph containing words somewhat like hieroglyphics, strange patterns to be deciphered. And like priests, paleontologists in modern times would read the pages and interpret them. And like detectives, paleobiologists would deduce how life had been. Ancient fossils would *be* like fingerprints in modern crimes; petrified remains would be like hair and body fibers; and stony bones would be like bloodstains. Even DNA analysis would be undertaken. Thus the sedimentary layers of earth would *reveal* the history of Earth.

Now the Phanerozoic Eon would have *three eras*. And the first would be the Paleozoic, meaning "ancient life," the second would be the Mesozoic, meaning "middle life," and the third would be the Cenozoic, meaning "recent life."

Thus in five-hundred-and-seventy-million years BC, *a new era*, the Paleozoic, started. And it would last three-hundred-and-twenty-five-million years. And it would be divided into *six* periods: the Cambrian, the Ordovician, the Silurian, the Devonian, the Carboniferous and the Permian. Thus in five-hundred-and-seventy-million years BC, a *new period*, the Cambrian, also started. And it would last for the next sixty-five-million years.

Now the Cambrian sedimentary rocks had the *oldest* tale to tell – these rocks were the "Dead Sea Scrolls" of paleontology.

*The first book of the Paleozoic, called*

# The Cambrian

*And let the waters bring forth abundantly
the moving creatures that have life.
And this happened on the fifth day
of the first month of a long lost year.*

## Chapter I: The Cambrian Face of Earth

And the continents of proto-Siberia, Laurentia, Baltica and Kazakhstania continued drifting *north*. And it came to pass that Laurentia and proto-Siberia were positioned at the equator. And Kazakhstania was southeast of proto-Siberia, while Baltica was in the middle of the Iapetus Ocean south of the Tropic of Capricorn. And Laurentia was *on its side*, for western proto-North-America was north of eastern proto-North-America. And proto-Greenland was east of proto-North-America.

And Gondwana stretched from the Tropic of Cancer to the Antarctic Circle. And the pieces of proto-modern-continents in Gondwana were in *different* places. And for example, proto-Australia and proto-Antarctica were in the southern northern-hemisphere, while proto-Arabia was near the southern pole. And proto-China was west of proto-India which was southwest of proto-Antarctica. And proto-South-America and proto-Africa were positioned in the middle of the super-continent in the southern hemisphere. But both were *upside down*, for northern proto-Africa was south of southern proto-Africa, and southern proto-South-America was north of northern proto-South-America. And proto-Africa and proto-South-America fit snugly into one another, *like unto* two lovers in each other's arms.

Thus the map of the world in five-hundred-and-seventy-million years BC was not the same as the map of the world in modern times. The World was very *different* then.

And it came to pass that the seas were on the rise. And coastal regions *flooded*. And all the continents possessed extensive margins with *shallow* seas, which provided *fertile* habitats for life, for there were nutrients in muddy ocean floors and much more oxygen in surface water than in deeper water.

And skies were often clear; and days were often *warm*. And a pleasant climate over Earth prevailed.

## Chapter II: Cambrian Life and Evolution

*Now a strange wind blew the dust of Earth in swirling clouds,
as if someone were blowing it.
And in one place, where dust did settle,
was a peculiar pattern made –*

*It looked like unto a candelabra with eleven arms.*
*And each arm seemed to hold a candle.*

Now evolution was proceeding at a rapid pace. The fire on the fuse was burning. The fuse itself was almost gone. And everything was *perfect* for a biological explosion, an *evolutionary radiation*:[185] The geology was right; the chemistry was right; the climate was right; the atmosphere was right; the biology was right; and the recent evolutionary past was right, for sea level had risen and the continents had separated, providing new shallow-water habitats; for circulating ocean currents were full of nutrients; for the seas and air had warmed; for the atmosphere had oxygen; for eukaryotic cells had previously appeared and the sexual revolution in evolution had occurred.

*And it was* like unto *mixing*
*gunpowder, gasoline and fire.*

And in five-hundred-and-seventy-million BC – the evolutionary "big bang" went off!

*There was a sudden burst in evolution,*
*the beginning of a bio-revolution.*

And the *diversity* of animals on Earth *exploded*. There were annelids, arthropods, brachiopods, onychophores, ctenophores, cnidarians, echinoderms, chordates, mollusks, graptolites and sponges.[186]

Now some Cambrian creatures created shells, while other creatures had hard bodies – the battle was on to build effective *protective shields*. And the metazoa made their shells and casings by secreting minerals such as calcium carbonate, calcium phosphate and/or silica. Now hard external casings were called *exoskeletons*. And shells made from the minerals of calcium were *calcareous* shells, while those from the minerals of phosphorus were *phosphatic* shells. And hard parts made from minerals of silicon were *siliceous* parts. And when the creatures died, their shells and exoskeletons collected on the *bottom of the sea*. And they were crushed and eroded into sediments of limestone, chert and phosphate rock, often becoming underwater carbonate platform-belts. And sometimes the ocean floor rose up above the sea, and off-shore reefs were made.

Now some metazoa were mobile – they moved or floated. And some metazoa were *sessile* – they were *fastened to* the ocean floor.

Now *annelids* were segmented worms whose bodies came in pieces that were tied together. The annelids had developed from their Ediacaran counterparts, the primitive sea worms. And some Cambrian annelids would evolve and *eventually* end up *on land*. And they would

---

[185] This use of the word "radiation" indicates the outset of a great diversity of new life forms.

[186] These are eleven major animal phyla. They are described below.

become the modern earth worm and the leech. But others would remain at sea as ocean-dwelling worms.

Now *arthropods*[187] were animals with hard and jointed exoskeletons whose bodies were in segments and who had matching pairs of jointed arms, appendages, antennae, legs or wings. And *one day*, they would be the first creatures on Earth to walk on land. Now at this time, on short stubby legs, or *pods*, they crawled on seabed floors, often leaving trails behind them. And so it came to pass that the tracks of arthropods were everywhere upon the ocean floor. Now eventually these ancient creatures would evolve to *crustaceans* such as barnacles, lobsters, crayfish, crabs and shrimp and to insects such as grasshoppers, crickets, aphids, ants, lice, earwigs, butterflies, bugs, beetles, dragonflies, wasps, fleas, flies, termites, moths and bees, and to other creatures such as scorpions, ticks, spiders, mites and centipedes.

Now *onychophores* were half annelid and half arthropod – worms with pods. And they looked *like unto* many-legged salamanders.

Now *brachiopods*, also called the *lamp shells*, were small marine metazoa who were filter feeders living in a two-pieced shell. And the *top shell* protected the metazoa *from above*. And the *bottom shell*, which in general was bigger, protected the metazoa *from below*. And the shells were *bilaterally symmetric* – the left and right halves were mirror-image look-alikes. But still the shells had many shapes – some looked like tongues, moths, stop-watches, butterflies or bats. Many shells were oval shaped. And their colors varied – brown, green, red, gray, pink or white. And some had spots and some had stripes. Now inside, the shell contained a tiny fleshy body with *cilia*, or hair-like filaments. And brachiopods fed through a crack between their shells by combing minute-organism-bearing currents with their cilia. Now at the beginning of the Cambrian, the shells were phosphatic and *inarticulate*, meaning that the two shells were *locked in place*. But as millions of years went by, many shells became calcareous. And at the end of the Cambrian, a few types of brachiopods became *articulate* – they had a muscle that could make the shells *swing open or shut close*.

Now a *ctenophore*, also called a comb jelly, was *like unto* a vase-shaped jellyfish. The closed end contained a sense organ from which many comb-like strands emerged, which *flapped* to make the creature move. And as it moved, living organisms *were* swept in the open end, its orifice.[188] Thus the comb jelly functioned *like unto* a living floating vacuum cleaner.

Now not all the *cnidarians* were newcomers to the Cambrian – some had existed in the Late Proterozoic Eon. They were jellyfish, proto-sea-anemones, primitive coral, hydra, sea pens, sea fans, and so on. And they had two-layered epidermis, or "skin," and were carni-

---

[187] Arthropod means "jointed feet."

[188] Some ctenophores had two tentacles to clasp food to place it in their orifices.

vores, feeding mostly on sea plankton. Now the bell-shaped jellyfish and hydra floated with their tentacles dangling down. And the proto-sea-anemones were cylindrically shaped and sessile, rooted in the muddy ocean floor. And their mouths and brightly colored tentacles *were* directed upward. Each looked more like a flower than a fauna. And cnidarians were often *radially symmetric*, like a disk.[189] And sea pens seemed *like unto* feathers, growing in the ocean floor. And the sea fan was more irregular – instead of a single stalk, it had several stems that formed a branch-like structure, giving it the *appearance of* a spider web.

Now the *echinoderms*, whose name means "spiny skins," were scavengers with hard prickly casings.[190] And while crawling on the seabed or floating in sea water, they ate decaying bio-matter. And in doing so, they *cleaned* the ocean floors and waters. Now many looked like delicate glass ornaments, with stems, cups, spines and leaf-like pods. And many looked like underwater flowers. And *later*, the ancestors of the echinoderms would evolve into sand dollars, sea cucumbers, sea urchins, starfish, and into exquisite, almost brittle creatures such as feather stars, sea daisies and sea lilies.

Now Cambrian proto-chordates were quite *rare*. But some soft-bodied metazoa from the Ediacaran fauna developed hard protective outer plates and swam, albeit crudely. And these were jawless proto-fish. But other swimming soft-bodied creatures obtained phosphatic cone-like "teeth."[191] And when such proto-chordates died, their teeth turned into fossils, known as *conodonts*. But in the Cambrian, such conodontal creatures were not common.

*Deep swimming proto-chordates*
*churned the muddy sea floor sediments.*

Now during the rest of geo-history, proto-chordates would undergo *extensive* evolution, eventually becoming *chordates*. The first chordates would be proto-fish. Now some fish would grow limbs, evolving into tetrapods, who would, in turn, branch out into amphibians and amniotes, the vertebrates that lay land eggs. And amniotes would develop into warm-blooded animals, the mammals, and into reptiles. And some reptiles would grow wings and fly as birds, while others would remain on land or *go* back to the sea. Thus chordates would include amphibians, fishes, reptiles, birds and mammals. Thus *man* would be a chordate.

Now the *mollusks* were of three main types: proto-cephalopods, gastropods and bivalves. The primitive scallops and oysters would

---

[189]In other words, when turned about their centers they looked the same. This phylum of animals is called radiata.

[190] Some echinoderms grouped together in small colonies.

[191] It is not clear that the teeth were used for chewing; they more likely were a support structure.

later "join" the *bivalves*, the invertebrates with two-hinged shells, such as clams and mussels. And at this time, the *gastropods*[192] were underwater proto-slugs and proto-snails, while proto-*cephalopods* were proto-octopuses, proto-squids and proto-nautiloids.

Now a *graptolite* was a string-like metazoon that looked *like unto* a twig. And graptolites lived colonies in harmony, joined in branch-like structures, some of which looked *like unto* a net. And they filtered water for particles of food and plankton.[193]

And by the hand of evolution, the Ediacaran proto-sponge became the *sponge*,[194] organisms that filtered food through pores with thin skeletons made of fine siliceous or calcareous protective *spicules*.[195]

## Chapter III: Cambrian Sea Creatures, Part A

Now soft-bodied Proterozoic fauna, being *easily* consumed, often *were* the food for Cambrian hard-shelled metazoa. And so it came to pass that most Proterozoic fauna *went extinct*. But a few tube-shaped metazoa managed to survive by developing solid outer-layer casings. And they became the Cambrian tube-like metazoa. And for example, anabarite was a tiny animal with a shell resembling a garden hose with three lengthwise indentations. The tube was *open* at one end; *closed* at the other. And like its predecessors, cloudina and sino-tubulite, anabarite filtered *ocean water*, removing from *it* organic matter, nutrients, and particles of food.

And a spiny creature several centimeters long *inched* its way across the ocean floor. And it was covered entirely with countless *tiny leaf-shape plates*, which made it look pineapple-like. And on its back stood two rows of *spines*, like two arrays of swords to threaten those above. And in the front and on its underside, two arc-shaped bars containing teeth were clawing at the seabed for algae and for bits of food. And the creature was wiwaxia, the "porcupine" of ancient annelids,[196] the "tiny stegosaurus" of the Cambrian seas. And a slow current flowed between its spines *like unto* a weak but steady wind. Now nearby, sluggishly crawling forward *like unto* a snail another wiwaxia had a tiny brachiopod clamped onto its last and eighteenth spine. And still

---

[192] Gastropod means "belly-footed."

[193] Cambrian graptolites were sessile and relatively rare.

[194] A sponge is a creature half-way between a multicellular organism and a colony. Possessing no tissues or organs, it has relatively few types of cells, which, although they can live independently of each other, organize themselves in specific macroscopic structures. Some sponges when dissociated into individual cells will, after a few days, reorganize themselves into a macroscopic creature again. Some jellyfish can perform the same feat.

[195] Some sets of spicules formed exoskeletons that could open up and close. Other spicules were needles randomly arranged.

[196] Wiwaxia is so different from any modern metazoa that, rather than being an annelid, it might represent a unique ancient phylum. Recent studies suggest that it is linked to the modern scale worm, the sea mouse.

another smaller wiwaxia had *spines one-third* the size of its two bigger brethren. And still a smaller one had none.

And a *daisy-like* dinomischus undulated with the movement of the ocean waves above, its thin stem tethered to the ocean floor. And upon the stem, some twenty upright *grass-like blades* protruded from a bulb. And hidden by the blades and *on* the bulb were two small openings, one through which dinomischus took in bio-matter and one through which it discharged wastes.[197]

And isorophus, a spherically shaped echinoderm with a diameter of two centimeters, was covered in countless tiny crusty plates. And on one side, *like unto* a starfish, *five arms* with grooves in them radiated from a mouth. And food particles were moving through the grooves toward the mouth.

And protohertzinas were tiny but ferocious predators. Like the modern earwigs, they had *pincers* that could squeeze their prey to death as in a vise. Now when protohertzinas died, they left behind their tiny tusks. And some such tusks became phosphatic fossils, *imprints* that protohertzinas left behind in hardened mud.

Now many types of inarticulate brachiopods dwelt in Nature's seas: lingulids with oval-shaped phosphatic shells and acrotretids with calcareous round shells. And although the *lingulids and acrotretids* would be dominated by other species and decline in number, they *would* endure. And unlike other inarticulate brachiopods such as obolellids and paterinids, they would survive *unto this day* to become the *oldest lamp shell species* on the Earth.

Now a pear-shaped *helicoplacus*, half-a-dozen centimeters in diameter, sat upright, slightly embedded in the mud. And *like unto* a modern armadillo, it was completely covered by a multitude of tiny *plates* – it wore a helicoidal hard mosaic coat. And as it sat there, food particles were moving between the plates through grooves which, *in a spiral*, wound entirely around its body.

Now a few predators drilled holes in shells of brachiopods and mollusks and sucked out the meat inside. But some brachiopods adopted skunk-like tactics by *discharging chemicals and irritants* that repelled such predators. And some prey, like phycoides pedum, escaped by *burrowing* into the muddy ocean floor. And sea worms such as ancalagon, ottoia, selkirkia, louisella, peronochaeta and burgessochaeta did the same.

And it so happened that a swift sea current came. And an eocrinoid,[198] with a stem emerging from the mud and ending in a cup which held about one-hundred feeding fiber-threads, waved back and forth but *was not* swept away – *strong roots* did hold it in the seabed floor.

---

[197] Although dinomischus seemed like a plant, it was not. It was a stalked animal.

[198] An *eocrinoid* was a stalked echinoderm, having roots and stems much like a flower.

And an aysheaia, an onychophore which looked *like unto* an underwater caterpillar, was crawling on the ocean floor on twenty tiny *cone-shaped pods*, on which many even smaller spikes stuck out. And two antennae on its head were moving left and right, feeling things to help it find its way. And elsewhere, aysheaias were crawling and were feeding on a sponge.

*They were* as unto *bridges*
*that spanned* two *different lands.*
*And* one land *was the kingdom of the arthropods.*
*And* one land *was the kingdom of the annelids.*

And hyolithes lived in cone-shaped shells. And as these tiny mollusks grew, they grew their shells by adding to the open end.

And a phyllocystis, an asymmetrical echinoderm encased in plates and without five-fold symmetry,[199] sat feeding through its stem. It was Nature's version of an underwater apple, but somewhat smaller, flatter and with a thicker, longer stem.

And sticking out of muddy seabed were seven pairs of "toothpick" *spikes* – each pair forming an upward pointing "V". Now these fourteen spikes emerged from fleshy sockets of a half-buried worm-like onychophore.[200] And this creature was hallucigenia, for the body of this highly structured animal was so bizarre it *seemed to be* an apparition. On its underside were *seven tiny tubes* that probed the muddy earth for nutrients – it was *as if* the creature had seven necks and seven mouths. And at the rear were half-a-dozen tiny tentacles all grouped together. And the body of this spiny scavenger ended in a long thin open tube, *which was used* for getting rid of wastes. And at the creature's other end was an ellipsoidal blob, an eyeless head.

And it came to pass that pikaia did emerge – it had a notochord, a stiffened rod, along its back. And this tiny eel-like proto-chordate, with forked tail and soft but scaly skin, was *swimming through Earth's waters*. Thus pikaia was a kind of tiny jawless proto-fish. Now since its descendants would *one day* grow a bone along their backs, *pikaia and its brethren* were the Adam-Eves of all the vertebrates.

And off the coast of proto-Siberia did dwell the multi-centimeter-sized *archaeocyathan*. Shaped like a wine glass, archaeocyathan possessed a porous double-walled calcareous shell *like unto* corrugated cardboard. And although it *looked* like coral and although it *was* like sponge, it belonged to *neither* phyla – it was unique, *a candle unto itself.* Now it and others like it lived in the warm and shallow waters of the tropics, where they sometimes joined together "*hand in hand,*" us-

---

[199] Most echinoderms, such as the starfish, have five-fold symmetry, meaning that they look the same when rotated by seventy-two degrees.

[200] Scientists believe that this creature was not an arthropod but a primitive version of the modern velvet worm. Some think the creature could have walked on its seven pairs of "stilts."

ing calcareous needles as a glue. And archaeocyathids and communities of algae built porous rock-like structures. And so it came to pass that Panthalassa possessed its *first organic reefs*.

## Chapter IV: Cambrian Sea Creatures, Part B: Trilobites[201]

*And they scuttled across the floors of not-so-silent seas.*

And a creature crawled along the ocean floor on several dozen legs. And then it paused; when motionless, its encrusted legs looked *like unto* a cage of ribs. Now the creature had *three lobes* like unto a butterfly – a worm-like central core[202] along with two flat, shield-like sides. And it was moving *now* its head[203] from side to side. And it began to crawl again. And on grainy underwater sand, it felt about to find its way. And it was called a *trilobite*, named as such because it had *three* lobes. Now it happened that the seas were *full of* trilobites. And there were a *myriad* of different types – countless shapes for lobes and legs and shield-like sides.

Now an exoskeleton encased the lobes. And as they grew, the trilobites did *shed* their exoskeletons and grow new ones. And so it came to pass that the ocean floors were full of empty exoskeletons of many different shapes.

Now it happened that a discarded exoskeleton was *pressed* into some sludge. And eventually the sludge solidified to shale, leaving an imprint of the exoskeleton. And the imprint looked *like unto* a moth with wings replaced by ferns. And elsewhere at the bottom of the sea, exoskeletons were pressed in mud and *fossil imprints* made.

And it came to be that one light and tiny trilobite[204] developed thin crude fins instead of legs. And instead of crawling like a crab, it floated and it swam.

## Chapter V: The Eye

And the hand of Nature touched an ostracod, an ancient version of the modern mussel shrimp. And the *ostracod* evolved in the middle of its head *a single eye* – the creature *was as* cyclops. And many trilobites and other metazoa did acquire eyes. Thus life saw *light* and objects that were lit; the sense of sight had come about.[205]

Now the shrimp-shaped opabinia was encased in overlapping armored plates that fanned out on both sides. And a *long tube* that extended from its head was slowly moving. And at the tube's end, a pair

---

[201] The trilobite was the most famous and common Cambrian arthropod, becoming the symbol of Cambrian life.

[202] This body part had three segments – a head, a thorax and a pygidium, or tail region.

[203] Its head had sense and feeding organs so that it could seek and eat its food.

[204] This was the millimeter-sized *agnostoid*.

[205] The development of the eye occurred during dozens of millions of years, beginning with light-sensitive tissues and eventually evolving into a sophisticated organ.

of tiny claws did open up and clamp down on a bit of floating biomass. Then the tube twisted back, bent down and curled around.[206] And the biomass was place inside a hole beneath its head. And the biomass passed through a U-shaped channel which led to opabinia's cylindrically shaped gut, a gut that started at its neck and ran down the length of its entire body to the tail, where two side fins stuck out. Now opabinia had *five raised and knob-like eyes.*

*And why did it have five?*
*Why not?*
*This was a time, like many other times,*
*when evolution was exploring all sorts of possibilities.*
*And Nature was venturing down many evolutionary paths,*
*some less travelled by.*

## Chapter VI: The Waste Land

And though the seas were *full of* living creatures, *barren* were the lands. And on the plains were only desert, wind and dust. On land was no discernible movement of a living form at all. Nor was there any plant or tree. And without trees and vegetation, Earth fell victim to erosive forces, when wind and rain *eroded* continental lands. And as dirt, pebbles and particles were transported in Earth's streams and rivers to the continental shelves, the shelves did grow in size. And so there was a general movement of material from inland highlands to the off-shore margins. And as the continents declined in height, *wider* did they grow. And this continental widening would continue during the rest of the Cambrian, then *through* the Ordovician and Silurian.

## Chapter VII: Cambrian Sea Creatures, Part C

And as it swam just above the ocean floor, an *anomalocaris* flapped two side fins of pleated cloth-like folds. Now for Cambrian times, its body was enormous – *half a meter long.* And the body was shaped *like unto* a submarine except it narrowed in the rear. And beady, disk-shaped eyes on each side of its head searched the ocean for any sign of movement. And the anomalocaris spied a tiny crawling trilobite, maneuvered to it and then hovered over it. And underneath anomalocaris's head, *two claws*, consisting of segmented tubes with jagged spikes, curled opened and unfolded down and did embrace the smaller trilobite. Spines then impaled the prey. The two claws contracted, curled and lifted up the squirming trilobite. And on anomalocaris's underside, a *mouth*, shaped like a slice of pineapple and lined with teeth, *did open up.* And the ring of jaws collapsed upon the trilobite. The prey was so consumed.

---

[206] The motion was similar to the that of the trunk of a modern elephant when it feeds itself with grass.

And elsewhere *trilobites* fell victim to large predators. And it came to pass that some grew *pointed spines*. And a few trilobites, when bitten, were able to survive and partially repair the wounds.

Now anomalocaris was a strange and almost dream-like creature, *unlike* any modern metazoon – it was an ancient, long-lost phylum, *a candle unto itself*. It was one of Nature's experiments in bigger body size. But if longevity be the judging factor, then anomalocaris was not "successful," for in five-hundred-and-ten-million years BC, this "shark of Cambrian seas" did go *extinct*.

Now the creatures of the Cambrian possessed *almost all* the body shapes that future forms of life would have. The variety was *enormous*. Often there were ornamental structures. Some creatures were adorned like Gothic churches and cathedrals.

And a molaria was momentarily motionless, looking *like unto* an underwater fly. And growing in the seabed, chancellorias, piranias and vauxias had acquired shapes like cacti. And all these vauxias had *hollow* limbs. And a swimming amiskwia *seemed like* a miniature seal with two antennae, a tail fluke and two side fins. And several pea-shaped micromitra sticking on the needles of piranias *used* it as a host. Nearby, a mackenzia seemed driven into soft mud *like* a post. And upon the seabed were choias, "little balls of needles." And crawling nearby them were the bug-like naraoia and the shrimp-like canadaspis – they looked *like unto* beetles. Now "blooming" in the seabed was the flower-like echmatocrinus, a "frozen torch-flame wrapped in lace." And dwelling next to it was an eiffelia, a "hollow oval vase." And with the motion of the water, suspended sarotrocercuses undulated *like unto* tiny kites. And olenellus and callavia were just two of many types of trilobites. And *these* were just a few of the *countless* creatures which did occupy Earth's seas.[207]

## Chapter VIII: Cambrian Flora

And sea flora also flourished, although not as spectacularly as fauna. Now many Cambrian photosynthetic organisms, including bacteria and many algae, were *still* a single cell. But the diversity of algal species doubled at this time. And one strain of cyanobacteria, or blue-green algae, *thrived* in sediments of off-shore limestone platforms, building large laminated mounds of many shapes. And one green algal species, margaretia dorus, was a goliath – although a centimeter wide, it grew to be a *meter long*. And phytoplankton such as those producing acritarchs diversified and thrived.

And the pace of algal evolution *sped up* as the battle field for life became complex and fierce. And the expected lifetime of an algal spe-

---

[207] Many Cambrian creatures in remarkable detail would be preserved *unto this day* in the Burgess Shale of British Columbia.

cies shrank to *just ten-million years*.[208] And the number of types of plankton skyrocketed as well, for they flourished in the *warm waters* of the tropics. And the variety of plants in Panthalassa and in Iapetus *grew exponentially*.[209] And since these marine plants converted carbon dioxide into oxygen, the growth of atmospheric oxygen was *also* exponential, with $O_2$ soon achieving one-fourth the modern atmospheric level. And through absorption in the air, the oxygen in water near the surface grew quite *high*. But deeper in the ocean, oxygen was rare.

## Chapter IX: The Food Chain

A nd it came to pass that the *predatory food chain* was established: The micro-metazoa fed on micro-plants and plankton. Small creatures fed on micro-metazoa. Big creatures fed on smaller ones. The biggest ate the big.

## Chapter X: A Fluctuating Sea

*The tree, which bendeth in the wind, breaketh not.*

N ow in five-hundred-and-forty-million years BC, it so happened that sea level *dropped* abruptly. And shallow continental shelves dried up. With disappearing habitats, many metazoa died. And the archaeocyathids that *dwelt in the shallow waters of the tropics* went extinct. And near Laurentia the olenellid trilobites *succumbed*, the holmiid ones near Baltica were killed, and the redlichiids perished near Gondwana. But the swimming agnostoid trilobites survived and even thrived.

And when sea level dropped, some bacteria, fungi and ocean plants were stranded on dry land. And unlike their predecessors, *they did not immediately die*, for *low* was their metabolism.[210] And sea mist spraying over them revived a few of them. And without water, barely could the *living* live, but nonetheless some life on land eventually survived. Thus life invaded land.

And ten-million years went by. And sea level *rose again*. And having more shallow-water habitats, the metazoa were revived. And for example, it happened that some trilobites did grow quite large: Paradoxides harlani off the northeast coast of proto-North-America was *half-a-meter long* and weighed five kilograms!

And ten-millions years went by. And sea level *dropped again*, causing the *extinction* of another group of metazoans. And hardly any archaeocyathids survived, inarticulate brachiopods declined, and many echinoderms did die. And for example, helicoplacus disappeared.

And ten-million years went by. And then sea level *rose again*.

---

[208] Recall that in the Early Proterozoic Eon the lifetime had been five-hundred-million years!

[209] Increasingly fast.

[210] The ozone layer also protected them from ultraviolet rays.

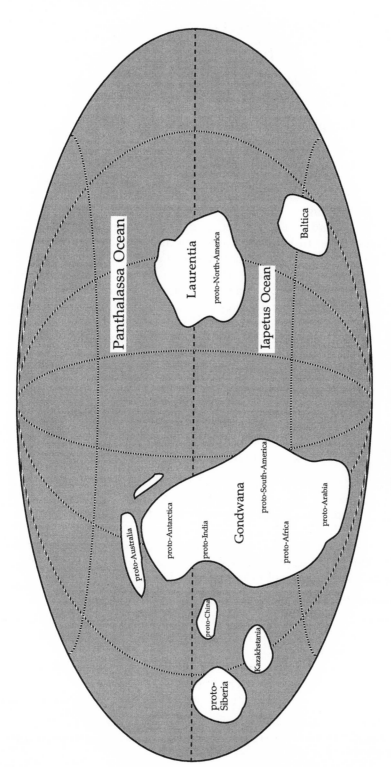

The World in 525 million BC

*The second book of the Paleozoic, called*

# The Ordovician

*And so another branch was added
to the tree of Life.*

## Chapter I: The Ordovician Face of Earth

It was five-hundred-and-five-million years ago. The Ordovician Period
began. And sixty-seven-million years would it endure. Now it came to
pass that Baltica, Kazakhstania and proto-Siberia were *drifting* north,
while the giant continent Gondwana was drifting to the south. And so
Baltica was heading *at* the Tropic of Capricorn in the northern southern-hemisphere and *at* the east coast of the continent Laurentia. And
so the Iapetus Ocean between Laurentia and Baltica was *narrowing.*
And at the equator did Kazakhstania so arrive. And a *new sea* was
opening up between Gondwana, Baltica and Kazakhstania – the *Paleo
Tethys Sea.*[211] And proto-Siberia was passing over the equator. And the
northern part of Gondwana, proto-Australia, had slipped just south of
the equator. And the southern part of Gondwana, proto-Arabia, had
reached the southern pole. And proto-Arabia had obtained a covering in
ice.

And as ocean plants continued to produce $O_2$, the oxygen in air
became one-third the modern atmospheric level.

## Chapter II: The Early Ordovician

*To be risen from the dead,
ye first must die.*

Now since the water in the *polar ice* came from the *water in the
ocean*, the growing southern polar cap *made* sea level *drop* one-
hundred meters. And *cooler seas* flowed in the Antarctic Zone. And
many species died, including countless trilobites – the golden age of trilobites *was over*. And with fewer prowling predators, certain other species flourished. And in particularly, articulate brachiopods, graptolites,
nautiloids and bivalve mollusks multiplied.

*The nature of Nature – be it to raze and to renew.*

And so *new ocean species* did develop which were more adaptable
to changes in the level of the sea. And life forms began to spread to different ocean depths.

And flapping back and forth, fleshy pods propelled a shell
through clear blue shallow water. And *this* "true shellfish" was a *nautiloid*. Inside the shell there lived an elongated cephalopod which

---

[211] The Paleo Tethys Sea is named after Tethys, the Greek sea-goddess, daughter of Uranus and wife of Oceanus.

looked somewhat like a squid. And *elsewhere* in Earth's shallow seas did nautiloids swim slowly with their pods protruding out a small hole in their shell.

And the graptolites, which had survived the newer, colder climate, were planktonic, *floating* in the ocean water. And this made them less susceptible to the vagaries of the sometimes rising, sometimes sinking seas. Now there were two generic types of graptolitic colonies – those which had their branches *pointing up* and those which had their branches *pointing down.*

And it *happened* that an onychophore crawled from the ocean onto sand. And it baked in sunlight on the beach for several seconds. Then *instinct* drove it back into the sea.

And throughout the rest of geo-history, sea level would *fall and rise* and *fall and rise.* And in the Ordovician, as in the Cambrian, as in other periods, life would have to adapt to changing situations and environments or die.

And it came to pass that algae-like organisms stranded on moist land *evolved* to tiny plants. And non-vascular and leafless, they reproduced asexually with *spores* – they were rudimentary forms of moss. And they grew on wet rocks and on the earth of coastal regions. Thus Earth had *its first plants* on land.

And echinoderms progressed: Proto-sea-lilies and proto-feather-stars *evolved to* sea lilies and to feather stars; proto-starfish *became* brittle stars and starfish; and proto-sea-cucumbers, proto-sand-dollars and proto-sea-urchins *became* sea cucumbers, sand dollars and sea urchins. Now sticking out of one spot on the ocean floor in shallow waters was a *feather star*, a star-like "wreath" of plankton-feeding feathers. And nearby it, a similarly "feathered wreath" was supported by a *stalk* – a *sea lily* was this creature. Now both looked much liked flowers. But both were metazoa. And a *sea cucumber* floated just above them. And its main body was a cylinder, open at both ends. But the larger end was *lined* with sticky tentacles that were flapping through the water and collecting floating plankton. And the tentacles were curling in and out, placing plankton food inside its mouth. Now another sea cucumber moved across the ocean floor, using its tentacles to stir up organic matter, mud and sand. And this *material* was swept into its mouth and travelled through its gut and *out* the other end. And some particles of mud landed on a half-hidden, flat and star-shaped creature – it was a *starfish*. And it was wrapped in *bristles*. And nearby it, there was a *brittle star.* It was like the starfish, but *its five arms* were longer and more slender, and its body was a disk. And two other metazoa were dwelling in these shallow waters. One was a spherical in shape, the other ellipsoidal. And both *these sea urchins* were encased in spines. And a similar but flat disk-like echinoderm lay motionless – a *sand dollar* was this creature.

And Earth had new scavengers: Among the gastropods, underwater slugs and snails evolved.

And it so happened that a *monoplacophoran* did appear – a mollusk with a simple, single cap-shaped shell. And soon the seas were full of monoplacophorans. And for eighty-million years or more, they dwelt on Earth. Then their numbers *notably declined*, and the fossils from their shells did disappear.[212]

And it came to pass that, in the waters over proto-China, a new plankton-feeding metazoon, the *moss animal*, or *bryozoon*, did appear. And so another branch was added to *the tree of Life*.[213] And bryozoans were colonies that looked *like unto* a piece of branch without the leaves, with thousands of tiny holes each housing a small *filter-feeding* bryozoon. And they covered submerged surfaces such as rocks, shells, stones and seaweeds. And so Earth possessed another faunal phylum.

*And a* twelfth *arm to the candelabra was set in place.*

And proto-coral evolved to *coral*, a tiny hollow living cylinder. And corals attached themselves together to form *complicated structures*.[214] And with bryozoas and sponges, corals constructed reefs, the largest of which were several meters high and many dozen meters wide. Now there was a great variety of coral. Some were soft and some were hard. And they were honeycombed, feathery, horny, and/or stony.[215] And they were yellow, brown, black or blue. And they were ribboned, weblike, rust-like and/or thorny.

And these metazoans were just some of the *countless* Ordovician creatures that swam the seas and stirred the muddy waters of the Earth.

## Chapter III: The Middle Ordovician

*The fish passeth through the paths of seas.*

And thirty-million years went by. Sea level rose. And waters did invade the continents, and many lands were *flooded*. And it came to

---

[212] It would be *presumed* by scientists in modern times that all monoplacophorans died when they disappeared from the fossil record, for that which cannot be seen cannot be – at least that is sometimes what one *thinks*. But in 1952 AD, a fishing trawler would be dredging off the coast of Costa Rica in deep waters. From four-thousand meters deep, a monoplacophoran would be pulled on board. And it would *not* be dead. Thus monoplacophorans did not die in the Devonian but *descended to the deep*. Thus off the coast of Central and South America, monoplacophorans would continue to exist *unto this day* six-thousand meters undersea on dark seabed. Monoplacophoran would be the quintessential Lazarus – a creature taken to be dead in the Devonian and then, from the human point of view, brought back to life *four-hundred-million years thereafter*.

[213] The bryozoon would survive to modern times. People would think it was a plant rather than an animal until the middle of the eighteenth century!

[214] They acted somewhat like the construction pieces in certain children's toy sets.

[215] The "horn corals" were called rugosids; the "honeycombed corals" were tabulates.

pass that the articulate brachiopods, those whose shell could open, thrived in these shallow waters, *covering* in some places ever inch of ocean floor. For brachiopods, it was *their golden age*.

And trilobites on shallow shelves of Gondwana south of the Tropic of Capricorn began to multiply – in the battle for survival, trilobites were trying to fight back.

And it seemed *as if* a scorpion were crawling sluggishly upon the ocean floor – it was a *eurypterid*. And elsewhere in the seas did these predators with pincer claws crawl and seek out prey. And they would grow in numbers, flourishing in the Silurian as the dominating predators. And their descendants would exist for a *quarter-of-a-billion years* and then would disappear.

And jawless proto-fish evolved to jawless fish, or agnathans. And so another branch was added to *the tree of Life*. And *these first fish* were *ostracoderms* – primitive jawless fish with outer armored plates.

And flapping its tail, which was free of plates, an ostracoderm moved irregularly through waters over what eventually would be Australia. And its head, covered in a thin and bony shield, had openings for its nostrils, eyes and gills. And this fish was *tadpole-like* in shape and in the way it swam. Now as water entered and passed through its gill,[216] oxygen was extracted and used for metabolic processes, while waste gases were dissolved in water and ejected out. Its eyes, set on the sides and far apart, were moving, *looking* for some particles of food. Now nearby, some dead organic matter floated aimlessly about. And when its nostrils smelled the food, it *awkwardly*[217] maneuvered to the food, and had it pass into its circular, small mouth. And it so happened at this moment that below this fish was another ostracoderm half-a-dozen centimeters long. And it was swimming *with its jaw ajar*, rummaging the mud for food.

Now Nature had provided ostracoderms with well-developed brains and nervous systems, and *primitive* hearts, glands, kidneys, livers and digestive tracts. And for living organisms and evolution, these sophisticated organs were a remarkable advance.

Now the ostracoderm was *the first vertebrate* on Earth – it had a *notochord*, a flexible stiff rod to brace the body.[218] And this was just the beginning, for someday *vertebrates*, the animals with *backbones*, would dominate sophisticated life on Earth.

Now from old fish, *new* fish would evolve. And what would be the pattern of their evolution? Newer, "better" species would emerge and swim with older, well-established fish. And what would "better" mean? It would be *more efficient* ways of breathing, swimming, feeding and other aspects of existing. And when the newer fish did come, the older

---

216 It was the invention of this gill that made fish life feasible. For this ostracoderm, there were just two gill slits, one on each side.

217 The early ostracoderms had no fins.

218 The internal skeleton of the ostracoderms was made of cartilage not bone.

fish would gradually decline. They would be eaten, be forced to leave their habitats or become victims of environmental factors. And *they* would go *extinct*. And after tens of millions of years, the new fish species would "grow old," and even newer fish would come. And the process would continue through the rest of time.

And the same was happening with all of Nature's life. And so *new faunal species* were evolving from the older species. And for example, the cyclocystoid, a new echinoderm, looked *like unto* a "flying saucer" with several dozen dangling pods hanging from its rim. And on its underside and in the middle was a hole, which was its mouth. And its pods moved *back and forth*, as it "danced" across the ocean floor; a trail of particles and dirty water did it leave behind, as it moved and sucked up food and mud into its mouth.

And small non-vascular plants and microscopic animals occupied the coastal regions of the tropics. And so the invasion of the continents by life *continued*.

## Chapter IV: The Late Ordovician

And thirty-million years went by. And as Gondwana drifted south, proto-northern-China *broke off from* proto-southern-China and remained behind at zero latitude. And proto-Arabia, northern proto-Africa and northern proto-South-America covered the southern cap of Earth. And there, as *great glaciers* formed, sea level dropped two-hundred meters. And water currents flowing from the tropics to the Antarctic Circle were disrupted by Gondwana. And the climate in the lower southern-hemisphere turned *cold*. And plankton numbers dropped. And the micro-metazoa that fed on plankton starved, and so *many* micro-metazoa died. And quite a few small ocean animals that fed on micro-metazoa perished. And since larger creatures, which ate small ocean animals, could find no food, many larger creatures went extinct. And the *largest*, which ate the larger, *also died*. And with the habitats in the southern hemisphere cold and hostile, one-eighth of all species *went extinct*. All graptolites, except those in the tropics, disappeared, and one-third of coral, trilobites and bryozoans died. And although brachiopods did suffer, their numbers were so great that they survived.

And among the brachiopods, *lingula* was perhaps the *most* robust of all. Its inarticulate shell, long and *like unto* a tongue, was brown with dark-green splotches – all for camouflage. And a worm-like "stalk," called a *pedicle*, that stuck out of lingula's shell was used to dig into the mud and sand of shallow seas, where lingula made its home. Now the pedicle also *tied* lingula to its burrow. And when *swift sea currents* came, some sessile ocean life *would* be swept away, but lingula would remain.[219]

---

[219] For the next four-hundred-and-fifty-million years, lingula would maintain its form

*The third book of the Paleozoic, called*

# The Silurian

*A wreath was set upon the tomb.*

## Chapter I: The Silurian Face of Earth

It was four-hundred-and-thirty-eight-million years ago. The Silurian Period began. And it would last for thirty-million years. And Laurentia began to rotate counterclockwise. And northern proto-North-America was northeast of southern proto-North-America. And proto-northern-China *drifted north* of the equator. And the Paleo Tethys Sea, which was surrounded by Laurentia, Baltica, Kazakhstania, proto-northern-China and Gondwana, was now *widening*. And proto-Siberia had arrived at the Tropic of Cancer, north of Laurentia. And compared with modern Siberia, proto-Siberia was *upside down*. And the giant ocean of Panthalassa still occupied the northern hemisphere and most of Earth.

And Baltica was drifting north and *heading at* the east coast of Laurentia, with which it would eventually collide. And so the Iapetus Ocean *narrowed*. And during millions of years, volcanic island arcs were thrust against and onto East Laurentia, producing mountains, earthquakes and other geological activity. And for example, mighty rocks and sentiments were squeezed and raised, thereby forming the Taconic Mountains, which extended from the proto-Hudson-Valley to northeastern proto-Canada.

And it so happened that thy planet Earth did *warm* somewhat. And glaciers in proto-Brazil and proto-West-Africa in Gondwana, which were on the southern pole, did shrink a bit. And ice turned into *water* and sea level rose. And warm waters at the equator evaporated into *steamy mists*. And trade winds in the tropics carried water vapor up. And thunderclouds formed regularly, dumping rains onto Laurentia, proto-northern-China, Baltica and Kazakhstania. And as for Laurentia, two-thirds of it was *flooded* – these shallow waters *provided fertile habitats* for life.

And in the southern hemisphere, monsoons prevailed in certain places in Gondwana. Now *monsoons* were long, *strong*, steady winds: In summer, hot air over continents rose up, while cooler off-shore ocean air *rushed in*. And in winter did the flow reverse. Higher cooler air over continents sank down, *pushing* low-lying continental air out *to the sea*.

And the equatorial continents were *eroded* by strong rains and floods. And sediments collected everywhere. And in many places, sand and sediments lithified to sandstone and to shale. And *calcareous shells*

---

and shape. Paleobiologists would discover the Ordovician fossil shells of lingula and compare them to the shells of modern times, and they would be the same. Lingula during four-hundred-and-fifty-million years of evolution has hardly changed. Thus paleobiologists are able to see an ancient fossil that is still alive today. For this reason, lingula is called "a living fossil."

*and exoskeletons* from ocean life collected in the shallow waters. And some such shells were *crushed* and then *compressed*; and limestone usually was made, but where magnesium was present, dolomite did form instead.[220]

And coral in conjunction with other metazoa made rock-like mounds called *bioherms*. And soon it came to be that Earth had many such organic mounds. And ocean floors were "littered" with the bioherms and reefs. And near proto-Chicago, the Thornton Reef Complex, a *huge* region a kilometer in diameter, was an example of extensive coral growth. But the largest organic complex at the time was a *three-hundred-and-fifty-kilometer* reef barrier off northern proto-Greenland. Now *some* round mound reefs would survive *unto this day*. And ten-meter-tall limestone "hay stacks" would stand in modern times along the shores of Gotland, Sweden.

And so, life joined geology in shaping the continental shelves and Earth.

And sometimes, water with sediments in flooded lands evaporated. And dry sediments, called *evaporites*, were left behind, often as salt deposits on the continents. And for example during the Silurian, *several-hundred-meter-thick* salt beds from proto-New-York through proto-Ohio to proto-Michigan became embedded in the Earth.

## Chapter II: Biological War

And as Baltica drove farther into Laurentia, the continental shelf of Baltica *merged with* the continental shelf of Laurentia. And it came about that a trilobite *indigenous to Baltica* bit an annelid *indigenous to Laurentia*. And the dark body fluids of the annelid drifted through the clear blue water. And the trilobite did bite again. And it grabbed the annelid and shook it. Then another trilobite approached. And the two ate the pieces of the annelid. And it happened that bacteria *indigenous to Laurentia* multiplied on a coral *indigenous to Baltica*. And as the bacteria consumed the coral microorganisms, the coral structure fell apart. Now these were not the only battles between marine life forms – on the ocean shelf between Laurentia and Baltica, a million metazoa fought. And it looked *like unto* the bloody clash of two great armies.

Thus the biota of the eastern coast of Laurentia battled with the biota of the western coast of Baltica. And Laurentian predators ate prey of Baltica, and Baltica predators ate Laurentian prey. And the predators of both continents *attacked each other*. And it was biological warfare at its worst. And many species *specific to Baltica* went extinct; the same happened to many species *specific to Laurentia*. And those that did survive were verily the strongest.

And throughout the history of Earth, other continents would come together and biological battles would ensue. And "weak" species would

---

[220] *Dolomite* is part calcium carbonate and part magnesium carbonate.

be defeated *and* disappear from Earth. And only those species that were "superior" would so endure. And these encounters would not be governed by a law of physics but by the *laws of evolution and survival*. And setting aside suffering, cruelty and moral judgement, biological war was *natural*, being driven instinctively by Nature's laws.

And it would be *no different* in modern times, when people of *two* different lands first met. And for example, when Europeans would *come* to the Americas, they would bring European-type diseases. And the immune system of the Indians would not be able to cope with new diseases. And millions of Indians would get sick and die. Then the Europeans and the Indians would battle over land. And the Europeans with their *superior* guns and with their horses would defeat the Indians. And almost all Indians would die. Now the times and the participants would be different in the Silurian and other periods, but the principles would *be the same*.

Now ye may ponder whether wars are right or wrong, but the *instincts* of the insects, mammals, reptiles, birds, amphibians, and fish, and in fact all life is to fight – to battle to survive – to fight and not to die.

And it was only after a long period of time, in which the life forms in the Baltica-Laurentian region were forced to live together, that stability was achieved, and communities of metazoa adjusted and "learned" to live more or less in harmony.

Now other bio-struggles would occur *throughout* the history of Earth. And typically would some external destabilizing event take place, or perhaps a species would evolve a novel "weapon." And battles would resume. And "suffering and cruelty" would once again ensue. And particular life forms would die. And certain species would consequently *go extinct*. And sometime thereafter, a readjustment would take place. And a new stability and "harmony" would be achieved again, and war would be *replaced by peace*.

## Chapter III: Silurian Waters

And it came to happen that a hot *low-pressure* weather system developed in the northern Paleo Tethys Sea. And warm circulating winds carried upward humid air. And heat was converted into motion and to wind. And when vapor in the rising air condensed to water droplets, more energy became released in wind. And the winds swirled in a five-hundred-kilometer circle at *three-hundred-kilometers* per hour – a typhoon thus was born. And as the typhoon struck the coast of Baltica, giant waves did slap the coast. And currents caused an off-shore *shale-and-sandstone platform* to collapse. And in an underwater avalanche, a kilometer of sediments slid down a seamount into a nearby underwater valley. And all marine life in the valley and the slope was buried. And *like unto* tombstones, boulders sat on top of sediments. And eventually the sediments solidified into a structure called Aberystwyth Grit Formation. And it was located in western central proto-Wales.

Now the atmosphere of Earth was heading to its modern composition. And oxygen in air was now one-half the modern atmospheric level. And the oxygen *dissolved* in water, making it plentiful at the surface of the seas. But $O_2$ also penetrated *deeper* ocean waters. And respiratory sea life extended farther off the coast to lower underwater habitats.

## Chapter IV: Fossils as Time Pieces
*What mean these stones?*

*And new life forms
evolved from old life forms.*

And graptolites underwent a *rapid evolution*. And some twig-like graptolites grew into narrow leaf-like forms of many shapes. And for example, there were the genera monograptus, neocucullograptus, bohemograptus, cucullograptus, lobograptus, pristiograptus, cyrtograptus, monoclimacis, coronograptus, et cetera. And each genus had *many species*. And behold, graptolites in one colony had formed *a central cup*, and other leaf-like graptolites had attached themselves to *it* to form a wreath. And such graptolitic wreaths with central cups were common in Earth's seas. And as time went by, even multiple-cup graptolites appeared. Now some graptolitic colonies floated *in the middle or on the surface* of the sea, while others, which lived in particular geographical locations, colonized *sea floors*. Now it happened that a graptolite died, fell to the bottom of the sea and lay there as a *single leaf*. And it was not alone, for indeed the ocean floor was covered with such graptolitic leaves. And some such leaves were pressed into the mud. And in certain places mud solidified to rock. And *imprints* of the leaves were made.[221]

And it came to pass that a nautiloid developed a shell with *separate chambers* which could be filled with gas. And the nautiloid removed some gas, and it descended. And then it added gas, and it ascended. Thus the nautiloid, *like unto* a submarine, moved up and down by adding or removing gas.

And soon the seas were filled with *other* nautiloids with chambered gas-filled shells. And many nautiloids had simple, elongated shells. And for example, the bactrite's shell was straight.

And during the Silurian, the brachiopods became the dominating metazoan creatures. Now the *pentamerids*, whose shells were teardrop-shaped, were particularly prominent for their size – almost ten centi-

---

[221] Graptolitic fossils became a biological dating clock for paleontologists because different graptolitic species came and died every million years. The parakidograptus acuminatus marked the start of the Silurian. The monograptus uniformis marked its end.

meters.[222] And the *spiriferids*, whose filter-feeding fibers were arranged as in a spiral, had shells that looked like butterflies. And the strophomenids, with shells like praline chocolates, and the rhynchonellids, with shells like tiny fans, both became *exceptionally abundant*. And some brachiopods fought the swift counter-clockwise-circulating currents of the Paleo Tethys Sea by anchoring themselves with a fleshy pedicle to pebbles, stones and rocks.

Now it happened that, in the tropics, some fish *developed jaws* – during millions of years, the first pair of gill arch supports had moved forward and had folded over, joining in the middle. And such jaws would revolutionize Earth's life, for henceforth fish could feed on larger prey.[223] A battle to be bigger and be stronger would be waged. Now the first jawed fish were *acanthodians*, also known as "spiny sharks."[224] And the large heavy shield plates, which ostracoderms had had, were gone – instead the acanthodians were covered with *smaller bony scales*, allowing them to swim more rapidly. Now later during the Devonian, they would colonize Earth's streams and rivers – *each continent* would contain *its own* group of acanthodians. And the seven-centimeter climatius was an example of a "spiny shark." On its back two dorsal fins were supported by some bony spikes. And on its underside, a row of spines protected it from predators like larger squid-like creatures. And only in its lower jaw did it have *teeth*, and they were *tiny*.[225] Now its *large* eyes spied an annelid below. And it swiftly darted down, and bit and chewed the worm. And moments later, the annelid was gone.

And it came about that conodontal creatures became quite common. And when they died, their fleshy bodies did decay away, but their *teeth*, the conodonts, *remained*. And the conodonts were of different shapes – cones, bars, blades and cubes. And being hard, *many* did "survive" as fossils. And in modern times, for paleontologists, these fossils told a tale. And among the tales they told was *time*. And it was *as if* the teeth stuck up *like unto* markers on a sundial, except that time was not read in hours but in units of a million years. And for example, the conodont, disfomodus kentuckyensis, pointed to the beginning of the Silurian. And icrioddus woschmidti pointed to its end.

## Chapter V: Silurian Ocean Colonies

And from old species, *new species* did emerge. And for example, several intricate cnidarians arose. Now halysites were coral that constructed ten-to-twenty-centimeter structures of a wide variety of shapes. And in one Silurian community forty meters underneath the

---

[222] Other brachiopods were typically several centimeters long

[223] Previous to this, fish were filter feeders, eating only small particles of food.

[224] Despite the name, the acanthodians were not members of the shark family. The acanthodians, which ranged from five to fifty centimeters long, had an internal skeleton of cartilage.

[225] Some acanthodians had no teeth.

sea, the halysites had folded back and forth *like unto* corrugated cardboard sheets bent back. And in another community, the halysites were
cylinders which emerged from ocean mud in tightly bundled groups of
several dozen.[226] And nearby them and stuck in mud was a streptelasmatid. *Like unto* a carrot, it possessed a fat stalk on which many
worm-like short appendages[227] were waving with the ocean current.
And also in this community were a heliolite and favosite. They were
coral spheroids which were rough and honeycombed. And *orophocrinus*,
a flower-like echinoderm a quarter-meter tall, had a dozen plates making up its holding cup, from which emerged a *hundred* thread-like arms.
And one sea-lily looked *like unto* a tiny palm: Upon its fifteen-
centimeter stem, five feathers "sprouted" out. And a dalmanite, a trilobite that had survived the tribulations of its species' troubled times,
was *crawling* on the ocean floor. Above it swam a horizontal cone-
shaped shell – an orthocone, a kind of nautiloid – propelled by a dozen
worm-like pods. And a *pterygotus buffaloneis*, a giant eurypterid *three
meters long*, scuttled across the seabed floor. And at the time, this
ocean scorpion and others like it were the *largest* arthropods on Earth.
And during the Silurian, there were innumerable other *novel species*
born.

Now fifty-meters beneath the sea, where stormy weather did not
disrupt the ocean floor, calcareous green algae, stromatolitic microorganisms, echinoderms, corals, brachiopods and bryozoans *lived together*
in the fertile muddy habitats and bioherms. And these diverse and different forms of life lived as a community *in harmony*.

## Chapter VI: High Waters, Low Waters

Now during the Silurian, over a period of several million years, *sea
level* sometimes rose or fell by up to fifty meters. And for example,
high seas appeared in four-hundred-and-forty, four-hundred-and-thirty-
six, four-hundred-and-thirty-three, four-hundred-and-thirty, four-
hundred-and-twenty-eight and four-hundred-and-twenty-four *million
BC*. And particularly prominent *low seas* occurred in four-hundred-and-
eighteen-million BC and in four-hundred-and-eight-million BC. And
when seas were high, deep-sea algae suffered and died out, only to
have new species take their place when seas returned to normal
height. And for example, in four-hundred-and-thirty-four-million BC,
*new acritarchs* appeared. And when sea level fell, mobile metazoa
moved from very shallow off-shore margins to the deeper waters. And
when sea level rose, the mobile metazoa once again moved in.

And it came about that a centipede-like onychophore crawled out
of the sea and *onto land*. And it stayed on land and did not die, for it
possessed a primitive aerobic-intake system. And this was a tiny step

---

[226] They looked like packs of cigarettes.

[227] These made the streptelasmatid look somewhat like a mop.

for this onychophore but a giant step for animals. And soon other onychophores were living on and in the earth. Now eventually other creatures would invade the continents; each would try to claim a plot of land. And it would be *like unto* the colonization of the Americas in modern times, in which England claimed northeast North America, France claimed parts of Canada and the Louisiana territory, Spain claimed South America, and so on. Eventually these countries battled over land. *Likewise*, creatures would occupy a spot of earth and battle for it. But for the "moment,"[228] territory was *plentiful* and land was for the taking.

## Chapter VII: The Late Silurian

*Let the Earth bring forth
creeping creatures and beasts of the earth.
And it was so.
And this happened on the sixth day
of the first month of a long lost year.*

And ostracoderms, the jawless "shell-skinned" fish, in adapting to a changing world, diversified, *evolving* to smaller and to larger forms. Now most had heavy *outer bony plates*, but some such as pharyngolepis were covered in thin scales. And in waters nearby proto-Norway, a pharyngolepis plowed its head through mud, scooping it into its rounded mouth, as mud was tossed about. Then it rose above the dirty waters. Along its back stuck out a row of tiny plates, while on its underside it had a long but narrow fin, which helped to stabilize it when it swam. And it flapped its downward-curving tail as it floundered awkwardly around.[229] Now in waters over proto-England, a hemicyclaspis[230] *propelled* itself *quickly* through the water as it waved its upward-curving tail. And behind its head plate on each side, two scale-covered flaps served as *pectoral fins*, while *on its back* a single fin, or *dorsal* fin, helped stabilize it vertically. And its *single nostril*, which was between its eyes, *smelled* for particles of food. Now off the coast of proto-Germany, a drepanaspis moved slowly while scavenging the seafloor mud for food. And it was flat *like unto* a flounder and well encased with plates of different shapes. Its eyes, which were set on either side of a wide and upturned mouth, seemed to rotate randomly about. And these three fish, pharyngolepis, hemicyclaspis and drepanaspis, were just a few of the *many* ostracoderms that swam the seas.

---

[228] "Moment" here means a geological moment, or roughly ten-million years.

[229] The descendants of pharyngolepis would survive four-hundred-million years to become the modern jawless fish, such as the worm-like scavenging hagfish and the parasitic eel-look-alike lamprey.

[230] Hemicyclaspis was larger than most ostracoderms at this time. It was twelve centimeters long.

Now ostracoderms occupied all ocean waters in the equatorial middle third of Earth. But eventually it came to pass that they moved into streams and rivers, and later into lakes. Thus they populated the waters of the continents. And Earth possessed its *first freshwater fish*.

Now during the Silurian both jawed and jawless fish evolved some bone *inside their body* – it existed as a coating on the cartilage of skeletons.

And the evolutionary pace of terrestrial floral life increased. And proto-mosses *multiplied and spread*. And *vascular plants* – only centimeters big – emerged on land along seacoasts. They had *vascular systems*, networks of tissues for transporting fluids, so that they were able to absorb nutrients and water *from the soil*. Now at this time, photosynthesis was executed *in the stem*. Nature had not yet *provided* plants with leaves – the World was very *different* then.

Now the plants on Laurentia, Baltica and proto-Siberia *differed from* the plants on Kazakhstania, which in turn *differed from* the plants on proto-southern-China and proto-Australia of North Gondwana, which in turn *differed from* the plants on proto-northern-China. The *southern part* of Gondwana was without flora, for *there* it was too cold. Now the *cooksonias*, which were half-a-dozen centimeters tall, were indigenous to Laurentia, Baltica and proto-Siberia. And they were among the first to colonized the earth *inland*. They had smooth branched stems, on which there were spore-bearing sacs – they reproduced by spreading spores. Thus spores caught *winds and drifted so*. And spores found barren lands in fertile and unpopulated earth. And cooksonias by these means *spread wide and far*. And so they escaped the battle of the wild by staking out *new lands*.

*The fourth book of the Paleozoic, called*

# The Devonian

*Be fruitful and multiply,*
*and fill the waters in the seas.*
*And it was so.*
*And this happened on the fifth day*
*of the first month of a long lost year.*

## Chapter I: The Collision of
## Two Continents Is Completed

It was four-hundred-and-eight-million years ago. The Devonian Period began. And Earth, which had spun so fast during its early history, had *gradually slowed down*. Thus the number of hours in a day was twenty-two. And because a day was shorter than in modern times, there were more days per year. Each time thy Earth went once around the Sun, thy Earth spun *four-hundred times*. Thus during the Devonian, each year there were *four-hundred days*.

Now the last stretch of the Iapetus Ocean disappeared, as Baltica completed its collision with Laurentia. And a new continent, *Laurussia*, formed from the two. And the collision continued producing earthquakes, mountains and volcanos. Thus lava *flowed over* the protolands of Newfoundland, New England, Nova Scotia, Scotland, Scandinavia and eastern Greenland. Thus rose up the Caledonian Mountains, which were *rich in iron oxide*. And peaks appeared from proto-Greenland and western proto-Scandinavia through the northern proto-British-Isles to eastern proto-North-America along the proto-Hudson-River. And in this region, igneous intrusions beneath the Earth *built a base* that would support the growth of mountains.

And on the west coast of Laurussia, subducting ocean crust *pushed up the continental crust*. And the foundation of the Cordilleran Mountain Chain was formed in western proto-North-America.

And proto-Siberia – now just north of Laurussia – was drifting eastward. And *west-to-east* directed currents flowed between the two through the Pleionic Ocean Strait. And Kazakhstania, inching northward, was east of the Laurussian continent and somewhat north of the equator. And proto-southern-China had broken off Gondwana and was joining proto-northern-China. At this time, proto-China was a *long and narrow* continent.

And as proto-South-America and proto-Africa swung north, the sea between Laurussia and Gondwana narrowed to a strait.

Now the Paleo Tethys Sea *was surrounded* by four continents: Gondwana, Kazakhstania, proto-China and Laurussia. And these continents were separated by four narrow seas.

Now *carbon dioxide and sulfurous gases* spewing out of the volcanos of the Caledonians replenished greenhouse gases. And as Earth's temperature increased, Gondwanian glaciers almost disappeared, and sea level, which had been relatively low, began to rise. And Gondwana gained extensive continental shelves. Most of proto-South-America was *underwater*, northern-proto-Africa and all-but-eastern proto-Australia were flooded, and seas covered southern proto-Siberia and the proto-Mississippi-Valley. And parts of proto-Russia, proto-China and proto-India were also underwater.

And volcanic activity would go *off and on* during the Devonian as land masses merged. And severe atmospheric pollution *would* suddenly ensue. And Earth's white limestone *would turn black*. And this would happen many times. And when it happened, the oxygen–nitrogen–carbon-dioxide–sulfur content of the atmosphere would change. And the oxygen in oceans *would go down*. And faunal life would be disturbed.

And for the next eighty-million years would the climate be on average warm and wet. Land plants would flourish in a $CO_2$-rich[231] atmosphere and in a wet warm climate. A *green and golden age* for plants began.

## Chapter II: The Old Redstone Continent

Now Laurussia was in the tropics. And during the rainy season, evening thunderstorms struck daily. And the Caledonian Mountains were eroded frequently by *heavy rains*. And earth, pebbles, particles and sediments rich in iron oxide poured down their slopes and onto plains, causing flatlands to turn into wetlands. And during the other seasons, the plains were *often dry*. Now sediments, which were carried by rivers to the seas, accumulated near the coast. Then coastal currents carried particles to off-shore margins. Thus *iron oxide* from the Caledonian orogeny was mixed with beach and desert sand to make *red sediments* that covered the proto-lands of Scandinavia, North America, the British Isles and Greenland. And the sediments eventually solidified and made sedimentary bedrock. And among the sedimentary rocks, sandstone did stand out. And *iron* in it made it *red*. Thus much of Laurussia contained a layer of red sandstone. And Laurussia obtained the nickname of *Old Redstone Continent.*

And in proto-Devonshire, England, three-thousand-meter thick *deposits* were built up of shale, limestone, sandstone and conglomerates. And the rocks were full of fossils. And in the middle of the nineteenth century, paleontologists would discover the lithified deposits between Silurian and Carboniferous rock layers. Thus the Devonian Period *derived* its name from Devonshire.

And elsewhere on the Earth, *loose sediments were lithified* to limestone, sandstone, shale and slate. And some of these sedimentary rocks metamorphosed into schist and *marble*. And for example, marble belts were formed in proto France and Belgium.[232]

## Chapter III: The Graptolites Are Gone

And as fish and other predators ate graptolites, the graptolites declined in number. And by four-hundred-million years BC, the *last one* died. And graptolites *were* forever gone.

---

[231] The atmosphere was rich in $CO_2$ compared with today. However, carbon-dioxide levels would be steadily dropping as land plants absorbed the gas. When they were buried, some carbon would be buried with them.

[232] In modern times, man mined the marble. Thus Devonian stones were used as building stones. In medieval times, German kings had their castles clad in slate of these four-hundred-million-year-old stones.

## Chapter IV: Life Evolves

And it came to pass that a plant grew to thirty-centimeters tall. And its stem had tiny modules which *collected light and photosynthesized*. The part of the plant *above the ground* was supported by a horizontal rooty network *just below the ground*. And the roots, full of hairlike filaments, absorbed the moisture in the earth.

And on Earth were other leafless plants that photosynthesized. And for example, *zosterophyllum* was a twenty-centimeter creeping plant with thin branched stems. And it and its descendants would eventually evolve into the family of club mosses. Now *ryhnia*, which was smaller than zosterophyllum, was slender and reed-like. Plants like it would become the Carboniferous horsetail trees and ferns. And some species of club mosses, ferns and horsetails would survive four-hundred-million years and *to until today*.[233]

And it came to be that oxygen in air *attained its modern atmospheric level*. Henceforth, the amount of oxygen in air would more or less remain the same.

And giant eurypterids, such as pterygotus buffaloneis, which had appeared in the Silurian, began to feed on fish. And fish were verily both predators and prey.

And life forms that had arisen in the Cambrian, Ordovician and Silurian continued to multiply, evolve, prosper and "progress." And in sandy underwater coastal habitats, burrowing creatures, coral, brachiopods and bivalve mollusks were *abundant*. And in offshore reefs, the communities of coral, sea lilies, sea feathers, brachiopods, bivalve mollusks, trilobites and gastropods *abounded*. And bioherms were also being built. And stone-like forms and netlike forms of bryozoans overran the shallow seas of continental shelves. And above them, hydra and jellyfish floated aimlessly about.

Now one type of microorganism, the *foraminiferan protozoa*, grew hard casings. And there were thousands of different species types. And when these protozoa died, the *crusty calcareous casings* of their microscopic bodies collected on the ocean floors. And the foraminiferan particles often *calcified to limestone and to chalk*.

And radiolarian protozoa, which were spherical and microscopic and which had already populated Earth for more than one-hundred-million years, also multiplied and lived and died. And their *tiny siliceous exoskeletons* also settled on the ocean floor. And the radiolarian ooze often *solidified to flint and chert*.[234]

---

[233] The modern horsetail has a jointed stem from which spore-bearing stalks and leaves stick out. It is called the "scouring rush," a name that arose when settlers came to America. Silica crystals in the plant allowed them to use it for scouring cooking pots.

[234] *Flint* is dark-colored chert.

And as *conodontal metazoa multiplied*, the number of new species types diversified. And seabeds were covered with teeth from conodontal creatures that had died.

And among the echinoderms, some starfish, sea cucumbers and brittle stars did dwell in Nature's oceans. But most abundant were the sea lilies and the feather stars. Some floated *just above the ocean floor*, using an organic claw-shaped anchor to combat the ocean current. Others grew in mud and sand. Now wheat-like stalked echinoderms, similar to the eocrinoids and the orophocrinus, which had appeared in the Cambrian and Silurian, developed into *different forms*, distinguished by their feeding fibers and their fiber-holding cups. And some of these echinoderms developed *complicated stalks and roots*.

And it happened that some giant *sixty-centimeter* trilobites appeared. And it was *as if* Nature knew that primitive elongated simple shells of nautiloids were awkward. And some nautiloids adapted by adopting *coiled shells*.

## Chapter V: The First Leaves

And it came to pass that, in the battle to obtain Sun's energy, tiny photosynthetic modules of plants grew larger and grew flatter. And these were *the first leaves*. Now the appearance of the leaf was *natural* – plants with leaves were better photosynthesizers, for they collected *more sunlight* than the plants that had no leaves. And as time passed, the plants with leaves prospered and grew taller. And "soon" some stems developed forks, and branch-like structures came about.

Now there existed some plants that were solely tubular tissue networks. And the tubes *above the ground* were stems, while the tubes *below the ground* were roots. And still other plants had dense and leafy stems. And asteroxylon, a "relative" of zosterophyllum, had simple, spiny leaves. And at this time, the "descendants" of rhynia grew taller and more branched.

Thus it had come to pass that plants were quite *diversified*. And there were reed-like, moss-like, fern-like, grass-like, vine-like *and* small shrub-like forms. And species were distinguished by their *different types* of leafs, stems, roots and spores.[235]

## Chapter VI: Fish Flourish

*And they had breastplates,*
*as it were the breastplates of iron.*

And the ostracoderms during the Devonian diversified. Indeed *all* fish were flourishing. And so began *a golden age for fish*. And particularly prolific was *pteraspis*. It was a member of the jawless fish, whose armored head-shield had two plates, one above and one below,

---

[235] Later, paleobiologists would use the spores as micro-chronometers.

that came apart for feeding. And though it had no fins, it darted through the water with amazing speed. All its features were "hydrodynamically designed" for rapid swimming: a *curved knife-like* bone above its head *served as* a dorsal fin; a *long cone-like beak* protruding from its mouth deflected water; two side bone flaps acted as pectoral fins; and a flexible, long tail provided thrusting power.

And a fish two-meters long cruised the sea *in search of prey*. And it had a triangular-shaped tail fin, a powerful jaw and well-developed *sharp enamel teeth*. And five gill slits furnished it with oxygen. And it bore two dorsal fins above its notochord and four pectoral fins – a large pair behind the gills and a small pair halfway to its tail. And this creature was a *proto-shark*.[236] And at this time in geo-history, many proto-sharks swam rapidly through the waters of Earth's seas. Now it would take *two-hundred-million years* of evolution for proto-sharks to change to sharks. And later, during the Jurassic Period, bottom-dwelling sharks *would* develop into skates and rays. And species of sharks, skates and rays would survive *unto this day*, retaining ancient features such as skeletons of *cartilage*.

And whipping a long and eel-like tail, a heavily armored fish was cruising just above the ocean floor. And its mouth opened to engulf a shell. Instead of teeth, it had two jagged dental plates. And the upper and the lower plates came together, crushing instantly the shell. Particularly sophisticated jaws and hinges provided all the crunching power. Now this fish was a *placoderm*, which means "plate skin." And the seas at this time were filled with placoderms of many types; some were long and thin, while other were wide and flat, but all had interlocking bony plates that encased the front half of their bodies. And some such as the antiarchs were dwelling in freshwater streams and lakes. Now the thirty-centimeter-sized gemuendina was flat and roundish *like a flounder*. Except for its body plates, it looked like the modern ray or skate.[237] And its features – eyes and nostrils on its upper side, a protruding lower jaw – were designed for diving vertically for food. And it flapped its tail and wing-like sides to search the seabed for such food. Now almost two-thirds of the placoderms were *arthrodires*, which means "jointed necks," for ball-and-socket joints permitted certain plates to move. These creatures cruised the ocean floors in search of trilobites and shellfish.

And *ray-finned fish* arose, named as such because their fins were supported by a *comb-like set* of bones. They were members of the class

---

[236] Some paleontologists consider such creatures already to be sharks. However, there were differences in shape and in other features. Since cartilage rarely fossilizes, it is possible that proto-sharks swam the seas as early as the Silurian.

[237] That two completely unrelated fish could obtain the shape body shape is an example of *convergent evolution*: An attractive feature can be obtained by different species even though they are unrelated. The wing, used by such different creatures as the bat, the bird and butterfly, illustrates this idea.

called osteichthyans.[238] It had taken one-hundred-million years for fish to developed bones *within their body*. First had been the skin bones, notochords and cartilage. Then bone had formed around the *cartilage* inside a fish's body, eventually replacing *it*, so that fish obtained a *bony skeleton*. Thus the hand of Nature worked the body of the fish. And life achieved one more *new building block* – the internal bone was born.

Now the palaeoniscids, the earliest *ray-finned fish*, were swiftly swimming predators with *tiny pointed spikes* for teeth, big eyes, and mouths so large that some species could swallow fish one-third their size. And they dwelt in all the waters of the Earth, using a pair of air sacs to control their buoyancy.[239] And their streamlined bodies were designed for swimming speed – *stiffened tails* provided power; dorsal, pelvic, anal and pectoral fins ensured stability; enamelled scales could supply protection with low friction. Now during the next four-hundred-million years of evolution, ray-finned fish would radiate into *twenty-thousand different* types of fish, their descendants being essentially all modern bony fish.

And during millions of years of evolution, there came to be the *lobe-finned fishes*, named for their long and fleshy fins. And though their pelvic and pectoral fins were supported by a core of bones, *muscles* in these lobes allow these fish to move them independently.[240] And among the lobe-finned fish were the *crossopterygians*. Their jointed skull increased the biting power of their jaws. Now they would have a *long and stable history* – in the Devonian would they flourish in fresh-waters. In the Permian, they would increase in size and move into the oceans. And they would evolve during the Triassic and the Jurassic. Then at the end of the Cretaceous they would, with other creatures such as dinosaurs, decline. And after sixty-five-million years BC, they would be *absent* in the fossil record.[241]

And after several million years, among the lobe-finned fish were some whose air sacs had *developed into lungs*. And these freshwater fish were *lungfish*. Now it happened that a lungfish was dwelling in a pond, breathing through its *gills* extracting oxygen. And with the coming of a dry spell, the waters of the pond went down. And the lungfish poked its snout and nostrils *out of water and* it gulped the air. And by these means it breathed in oxygen.[242] Now the *lung* would appear in

---

[238] Osteichthyan means "bony fish."

[239] Later, fish would have *one sac*: In most, its purpose would remain for buoyancy, but, in the dipnoans, it would develop into lungs.

[240] In contrast, the ray-finned fish do not have muscles in their fins.

[241] In 1938 AD, *latimeria chalumnae*, a strange one-and-a-half-meter fish was caught off the coast of southeast Africa. Surprisingly, it was a crossopterygian, and it was *alive*. Thus latimeria chalumnae was "a living fossil." In the next twenty years, fifty such "living fossils" were caught. It is one of the few bony fish to give birth to live young.

[242] Eventually some lungfish "could hibernate" during a period in which the water in a pool dried up; when rain returned, they were "revived."

other animals as well. And so it came be that Nature provided life with still another fundamental organ. The lung would *someday* be important, enabling vertebrates to occupy Earth's land.

## Chapter VII: Devonian Life Diversifies

And during millions of years, environmental pressures caused crustaceans to develop into more sophisticated forms. And the *number of types* of arms, legs, limbs, antennae and other appendages *increased enormously*. Now the body of the shrimp-like *ten-legged* palaeopalaemon had *half-a-dozen* thoraxes and abdomens. And *each* had a pair of arms or limbs or legs. And it burrowed into mud, leaving its two beady eyes above to look about. Now nearby was lepodicaris with its *dozen* crusty arm-like limbs of different shapes and sizes. And though it only was three-millimeters long, it had *twenty* segments to its body! And its branch-like antennae were so large in relation to its body that they were able to assist it when it swam. But most of the swimming thrust came from *ten* rear limbs. And this lepodicaris settled on some algae-covered stones. Then its three pairs of jagged arms started scraping them for particles of food. And after its frontal paws[243] had grabbed some particles of food, the particles were passed forward to the mouth with *many little bristles*.

And it happened that *new forms* of coral came about. And for example, amphipora produced spaghetti-like organic structures. And steadily with time did coral forms evolve. As old species died, new species came about. Thus coral, like conodonts, turned into dating clocks.[244]

And through natural selection did brachiopods diversify. And for example, new shell-types for the spiriferids appeared. And productids and terebratulids became prolific. Now the spiny productids hid in mud to avoid such predators as placoderms. And the *terebratulids* had a calcareous loop, which in the Early Devonian was *small*. But by the Carboniferous, some loops would grow quite large. And even some giant terebratulids would eventually emerge. And terebratulids would persist *unto this day*, surviving *four-hundred-million years* of geo-history to become the dominant lamp shell of modern times.

And it came to pass that clams occupied the *coasts of continents*. And during the Devonian, their numbers did increase enormously. And by three-hundred-and-seventy-million years BC, clams had *moved into the continents* and settled in the waters of Earth's streams and rivers.

And *several thousand kilometers* below the surface of the sea, the scaphopods did dwell. They were gastropods with tusk-like shells open on both ends.

---

[243] These paws were large in males and small in females.

[244] In modern times, corals would be used by paleontologists for dating and for correlation.

And it came to pass that *ostracods* diversified into *several thousand* species. These shrimp-like creatures who dwelt in casings were also called the *mussel shrimps*. Like other crustaceans, most *crawled* upon the ocean floors and *scavenged* for their food. But some millimeter-sized ones with a *single* beady eye floated in the open sea. And some fed on microorganisms, while others ate organic matter. And some were predators, and some were parasites.

And it came to pass that *the first ammonoids* appeared. Now ammonoids were like nautiloids but with thinner and more highly ornamental shells. And so the seas were full of swimming shells of countless different shapes.[245] Now ammonoids developed *rapidly*, with a new species emerging every million years. And when one died, its shell settled on the ocean floor and *sometimes fossilized*. And these fossils dated time. It was *as if* the shells were round wall-clocks, and when a clock randomly fell off the wall and broke, the hands no longer turned but simply pointed to the time of death. And for example, rocks with shells of probelaceras lutheri indicated three-hundred-seventy-two-million years BC.[246]

And rhyniella, the *first insect*, a collembolan, or springtail, "exited the sea." And another branch was added to the *tree of Life*. Just a millimeter long, it *was as* a wasp without its wings. And it crawled awkwardly over dirt as it *invaded land*. Now eventually it would evolve a forked limb at the rear, which like a spring could be compressed. And when the forked limb was released, the collembolan would then jump forward. Now the springtails would survive *unto this day*. And so the first insect species *would* be found among the last.

And it came to pass that plants *spread over continents*. And mosses, lichen, tiny plants and low-growth vegetation covered hills and plains. And shrubs appeared. And thy Earth had *its first flowerless green gardens*. And millipedes multiplied and soon became abundant.

Now the stems of some plants *thickened*. And some thickened stems did harden to a form of wood. And these small plants were *proto-trees*. And forests formed of proto-trees.

And some sexually reproducing plants emerged with male and female spores. These *heterosporous* plants lived *near wetlands*, where water could transport the spores of different sexes. And cross fertilization soon occurred, as spores of different types of plants combined. And this *caused* a revolution in plant evolution. The *diversity* of plants exploded.

And in millions of years, some plants would drop spores on moist land surfaces. Then spores would grow into match-stick forms containing both female eggs and male sperm. And the male sperm would

---

[245] *Goniatites*, for example, had coiled shells with zigzag shaped sutures.

[246] In modern times, paleontologists would use the fossil shells of ammonoids to tell the date.

swim through moisture in the earth and seek out female eggs. And fertilized female eggs would grow into new plants.

## Chapter VIII: A Continental Collision
## Causes an Extinction

And Baltica continued to *press into* Laurentia. And as folding rock belts made more mountains and magma flowed through earth, the bedrock of the Catskill Mountains formed. And new volcanos spit out gas and ash. And soot did cover Earth and block the Sun. And for forty days, the Earth was *dark*, and photosynthesizing stopped. And animals and plants breathed in the *bad* air and the soot. And algae *died*, and plankton *died*, and the bottom of the food chain shrank in size. The base of the pyramid became a pinnacle; and the pyramid tipped over. And other animals joined the list of dead.

Suddenly *the climate of the Earth had changed.*

And a minor extinction of many metazoa followed. And certain coral, brachiopods and trilobites died off. And during the Devonian, there would be several such "eruptions of black death."

## Chapter IX: More New Fish Appear

And swimming in Earth's seas were fish that looked *like unto* rats with *long and flag-like tails.* And they were proto-ratfish. Now during the Mesozoic Era, they would evolve into elephant fish, chimaeras, ratfish and ghost sharks.

And a certain lob-finned fish began to change: The muscles in its four lower fins were stronger than before, and it had developed lungs. And it swam in water, breathing with its gills. But rising to the surface, it sometimes *gulped in air.* Now it happened that the pool in which it dwelt dried up. And the fish waddled in the mud and flapped its fins and *waited.* And it was waiting for a rain to fill the pool again.

And soon it came to be that Earth had many kinds of fish which swam in ponds with limb-like fins and breathed in air.

And it happened that some arthrodires grew large. And dunkleosteus was an example – verily a giant serpent of the sea, on average *four meters* long was it.[247] And of its scaleless body, just the head and neck were clothed in plates. And its forceful jaws and ferocious jagged dental plates could *crush the strongest bones and shells.* It was a mighty predator, the dreaded swimming "jaws" of the Devonian that would have even terrified the proto-sharks.

And it so happened that the phacopids, a type of trilobite, began to lose their eyes. And *helpless without sight*, the phacopids began to die.[248]

---

[247] Some dunkleosteuses eventually appeared which grew to be eight meters long.

[248] It is possible that it was a disease that led to their blindness.

## Chapter X: Late Devonian Life

*Let the herb yield seed. And it was so.*
*And this happened on the third day*
*of the first month of a long lost year.*

It was three-hundred-and-seventy-million years BC. And in proto-Greenland, there appeared a fifteen-centimeter-long creature with four stubby limbs with toes. And it was a *tetrapod*, which means "four feet." And it was like a fish in many ways: its tail fin, vertebrae, outer bony scales, web-like limbs and cranium were all like those of lobe-finned fish. Now the pool in which it swam *dried up*. And it waddled, dragging its belly to a nearby lake. And on the way, it paused and raised its head, and out of its mouth went air. Then it dropped its head, and air went in its mouth. And by these means it breathed, for its rib-cage was of solid bone *unable to expand*. Now when it crawled into the waters of the lake, an enormous fish with sharp teeth happened to be swimming there. And when the fish approached the *tetrapod*, quickly did it exit from the water and escape. Now this creature was provided with a name. And *ichthyostega* was its name. And it was *the first chordate* that did walk on land. And since it could live *both* in water and on land, it was the *first amphibian*. And when ichthyostega stepped on land, it was a small step for it, but it was a giant step for vertebrates, for soon amphibians would populate Earth's ponds and pools. And they would feed on smaller arthropods. And although they could survive on land, *they* would spend *most of their time* in water.

*And so another branch*
*was added to the* tree of Life.

And amphibians would inherit features of ichthyostega such as scales, relatively large skulls, enamel teeth and tails.

And it came to pass that protective casings enclosed the spores of certain plants. And these were *the first seeds*. Thus Earth possessed its first seed-bearing plants.[249]

And seeds were cast into the air and *fell in diverse places*. And some seeds fell by the way side. And insects came and did *devour them*. And some seeds fell upon the stony ground. And they withered *for lack of earth* in which to root. And still other seeds fell among thick thorns. And the thorns grew up and *choked the seeds*. But some seeds fell in a moist dark soil. And it was *these seeds* that sprang up and bore good growth.

And in one plot of land, proto-trees grew taller. And among these trees, *one* must have been the *first*. And soon *elsewhere on the Earth* did

---

[249] These plants are called gymnosperms, or "naked seeds." Modern day gymnosperms include conifers, cycads and ginkgoes. The egg-bearing seeds are fertilized by male pollen grains carried by the *wind*.

proto-trees turn into trees. And they grew tall and wide, with some trunks two meters in diameter. And they colonized the land of Earth, giving it its *first true forests*. And for example, in proto-New-York-State, which was in the warm wet tropics at the time, a forest full of ten-meter-tall tree ferns did form.

## Chapter XI: A Mass Extinction

*The smoke of the country went up
as the smoke of a furnace.*

And it came to pass that proto-Siberia and Kazakhstania began colliding. And they were heading at Laurussia from the north and east. And the merger of these three continents created folds in continental crust. And the *Ural Mountains* rose along the junction.

And in this region, magma flowed in earth below, while lava flowed on earth above. And off and on for seven-million years, the atmosphere became polluted with *volcanic fumes and ash*. And the chemical composition of Earth's air was always changing. Likewise, the temperature of Earth went up and down, depending on eruptions. Sometimes thy planet grew quite cold, and on average there was a cooling trend. And there were short periods of violent rains, interspersed between intense long droughts. Vast regions of certain continents turned to deserts, as rivers ceased to flow. And when shallow lagoons warmed up, the oxygen levels in the waters dropped. And the biochemistry of plants and animals was verily disturbed. And many species *disappeared*: All Devonian trilobites succumbed except one group. And lopodicaris, an ancient insect, died – but its "brethren" would endure and become the modern water flea. And placoderms *died out*. All jawless fish did meet a similar demise, save for a few bottom-dwelling types. And certain ammonoid species such as clymenid and anarcestid vanished from the Earth – but others, such as prolescantites and goniatites, managed to persist. And all wheat-like stalked echinoderms, save for orophocrinus and its family, were too frail to survive. Likewise certain coral, primitive fish, brachiopods, sponges and floating algae *went extinct*. And the biggest of the brachiopods, the pentamerids, *disappeared from Earth forever*.

And there seemed to be *no logic* as to which species died – it was *as if* Nature tossed dice to decide who would live and who would die. And the concept of "the survival of the fittest" seemed to play a minor role, as every living creature was forced to participate in evolution's Russian roulette game. And "the unfortunate," be they strong or weak, still did succumb. And "the lucky ones" lived on. But life would *never* be again the same.

*The fifth book of the Paleozoic, called*

# The Carboniferous

*It was a land which flowed with milk and honey.*

## Chapter I: The Early Carboniferous

*It is Nature which doeth great things and unsearchable;*
*marvellous things without numbers:*
*who giveth rain upon the earth, and sendeth waters upon the fields.*

It was three-hundred-and-sixty-million years ago. And the conodont siphonodella sulcata appeared – the Carboniferous Period commenced. And the period would last for seventy-five-million years.

And although thy planet Earth was *warm*, some ice persisted on southern proto-Africa in Gondwana at the southern pole. And the level of the sea was *high*. And Laurussia was often flooded.

And it came to pass that in the seas appeared the *fusulinids*, a new class of foraminiferan protozoa. And they produced tiny, tightly coiled, calcareous, chambered structures. And when the fusulinids died, their remains settled *on the ocean floor*, and layers of limestone formed.

And there were *thousands* of fusulinid species. And they "rapidly" evolved in time: *New species* came about and died, often lasting a few million years. And since each produced a *characteristic* calcareous structure, it was possible to know the age of Earth through fusulinids. Now some of the calcareous structures fossilized and were preserved *unto this day*.[250] And calcium-carbonate-producing algae and other foraminiferans *added to the limestone* on the bottom of the seas.

And it came to pass that feather stars *and* sea lilies flourished. In certain places, these flower-like echinoderms overran the ocean floor. It was *as if* the seas had underwater meadows. And as the current flowed, the feather stars and the sea lilies waved back and forth *as if in wind*. And in shallow waters, the calcite[251] of their "petals" sparkled in the sunlight. Now when these fragile creatures died, their crystal petals settled on the ocean floor. And calcite collected there and lithified to limestone. And so *vast quantities of calcium carbonate* were created by these creatures of the seas: In certain places, one-hundred-meter layers of limestone lined the ocean floor.[252]

And in other underwater places, bud-like stalked echinoderms and fanlike bryozoans joined the "meadow." And lamp shells attached themselves to seabeds with their tethered pedicles. And when all these creatures died, their bodies *piled up*, and bioherms were built.

---

[250] In modern times, paleontologists would use fusulinids as clocks to date the rocks.

[251] *Calcite* is a crystal formed from calcium carbonate.

[252] For example, at this time was Indiana limestone made. In modern times, the Indiana limestone would be mined in quarries and be used for buildings in, for example, Washington, DC, and New York City.

And nautiloids and ammonoids swam the seas, searching for organic wastes or catching prey. And as they propelled themselves with mop-like *wiggling limbs*, streams of bubbles and swirling water followed them: They zoomed through the ocean blue and leaving short white trails of gas. As millions of year did pass, these creatures did evolve: It happened that giant *three-meter* nautiloids emerged, and the number of different ammonoids increased enormously. And particularly prolific were goniatites with coiled and ornamental shells.

And new types of fish appeared. And old species did increase their numbers – the seas were *full of fish*. But some marine organisms, such as sponges, corals and trilobites, declined. And at this time, Earth began to lose its reefs.

And meanwhile on land, when plants did die, their remains decayed and made loose, dark organic matter. And the organic matter mixed with grains and dust. And light dirt became dark dirt. And dark dirt turned into soil. And *Earth had real earth*, soil that provided *rich organic matter* for further growth of vegetation – from the dead did sprout new life.

Now at this time the number of amphibians that dwelt on Earth was relatively low. But many *new species* nonetheless arose. And some had lost their legs so that they looked *like unto* eels and snakes; they slid to move on land. But others evolved short sprawling limbs: They were thirty centimeters to two meters long and *salamander-shaped*. Some spent almost all their time on land, but when the sun grew strong and caused their skin to start to dry, they plopped *back into water*. Thus they lingered near Earth's oceans, streams and lakes. And it was in such places that they fed, preying on aquatic creatures. And it was *in such places that laid their eggs*. Thus amphibians were *unable to venture* into arid lands.

And spore-producing plants dominated Earth's swamps and water regions, while seed-producing plants dominated drier spots. But mosses, lichen, ferns, vines, shrubs and trees covered plains, valleys, hills, the sides of mountains and *almost every* hospitable square foot of land. And vegetation was particularly rich and thick in the warm and humid tropics of proto-North-America and proto-Europe in Laurussia. Now plants in the *shade* of other plants grew relatively poorly. And the forms of vegetation that grew the tallest were rewarded in *receiving light*. And so it came to be that trees strove to be the highest trees. And some grew to thirty meters tall. Earth had *its first jungles*.

And seed ferns, which reproduced with seeds instead of spores, spread across Earth's land. And proto-conifers appeared – they were tall plants with *cones* and *needles*. Now the *variety* of Nature's vegetation was enormous. And save for ferns, clubmosses and horsetails, few plants and trees resembled modern plants and trees. And since ferns were particularly numerous, the Carboniferous is called the "Age of Ferns."

Now it happened that some gastropods developed small membranes that could breathe in air. And with a shell upon their back, they crawled out of water onto land. These were *the first gastropods to live on land.*

And as insects multiplied, *new insect species* came about. And most were a few millimeters long. All had a head, a thorax and an abdomen. Many had antennae for feeling and six legs for crawling. Hence they were *hexapods*, for hexapod means "six-footed." And they fed on leaves and bio-matter in the soil. And mites, wingless cockroaches,[253] proto-crickets, scorpions and proto-bugs infested forests, vegetation, grass-like lands and swamps. And a *new food chain* began on land involving amphibians, gastropods, insects, bacteria and plants.

## Chapter II: The Middle Carboniferous

And by three-hundred-and-twenty-five-million years BC, the temperature of Earth had dropped significantly. And a *new ice age* was upon the face of Earth. Glaciers spread through the Antarctic region of Gondwana. And proto Australia, Antarctica, southern-South-America, southern-Africa and India were *under ice*. And in such snow-laden lands did flora and did fauna die. But some land life persisted in the cold climate just north of where the glaciers stopped.

At times, the ice advanced, and sea level dropped a bit. At times, the ice retreated, and sea level rose a bit.

Now the tropics had shallow wetlands *full of vegetation*. And these were *swamps*. They were particularly dense with life – full of insects, amphibians, small fish and plants. And when plants died, their organic matter sank. And *black ooze* accumulated in the swamps.

And some swamps dried up, and the black organic ooze solidified. And new rains came, and *some* swamps were *renewed*.

And in the jungles of the tropics, when ferns, trees, and small plants died, their biotic matter rotted in the rain and humid air. And *dark organic matter* accumulated everywhere.

And it came to pass that primitive crickets evolved from proto-crickets. Likewise primitive forms of grasshoppers did appear. And in the jungles of the tropics, the *sounds* of chirping insects would have heard at night, had ye been there. And during day, in open fields, the trajectories of leaping insects *would* have so been seen.

And with few large predators on continents, *amphibians did multiply*: They populated pools, ponds, swamps and land. Now many were about two meters long and salamander-shaped. But the fish-eating *pteroplax* was huge – five meters long.

Now it happened in proto-Novia-Scotia that a twenty-centimeter-long tetrapod laid some eggs *in earth*. And unlike the eggs of the am-

---

[253] Cockroaches would become so prevalent that the Late Carboniferous is called the "Age of Cockroaches."

phibians, these eggs did not dry out, for they were *covered* in a *special shell*: The shell allowed Earth's air and *oxygen to enter* but permitted *hardly any water to escape*. Thus an embryo could live within its "little bio-world" inside the shell. And this natural creation was the *amniotic egg*. And it began a revolution in the evolutionary *tree of Life*, for henceforth *amniotes*[254] – the animals that laid such eggs – could dwell away from water habitats. Now having laid its eggs, this tetrapod ran off to search for insects and invertebrates. Its *thick skin* glistened in the sun, for it was lined with *keratin*, a substance that, like oil, repelled water and prevented dehydration. And this lizard-looking creature was called hylonomus, *the first reptile*. It was a *cotylosaur*, the earliest of *reptiles*. And although such vertebrates could live on land without a water habitat, cotylosaurs often at this time still lingered near Earth's oceans, streams and lakes, for many fed on fish.

And soon – within a dozen million years – in proto-Novia-Scotia, hylonomus was joined by *archaeothyris*. It was twice the size of hylonomus and similarly shaped, but it had snapping jaws with canine teeth, which were used to prey on smaller creatures. Now archaeothyris was a member of the *pelycosaurs*, amniotes that on the *outside* looked like lizards, but on the *inside* had synapsid skulls,[255] similar to the type of skulls that the first mammals would possess. Indeed, the descendants of pelycosaurs would develop hair and chambered hearts and be warm-blooded. And so on Earth, there had appeared a *new amniote*, which *was* both like a reptile and a mammal.[256] And these pelycosaurs ventured into high plains and arid regions searching for their prey.

## Chapter III: The Late Carboniferous

*Let there be wind, and there will be wings.*

Now it happened that a great amount of biomatter from dead plants in jungles and in swamps was buried and *compressed*. And during millions of years, powerful geological forces *crushed* the biomatter further. And black carbon rock was fabricated – this was *coal*. And such rock was made in many places in the tropics. And for example, in proto-eastern-Pennsylvania, thirty-meter biomatter was crushed to ten-

---

[254] The amniotes include reptiles, birds and mammals.

[255] There are three main types of animal skulls: anapsid, synapsid and diapsid. The *synapsids* have a *single* opening in the skull behind *each* socket of the eye; the *anapsids* of which the cotylosaurs were an example have *none*; and the *diapsids* have *two* such pairs of openings. Crocodiles and dinosaurs are examples of the simple diapsid skull. Over time, these skulls have evolved. In birds, the two openings join to a make a single large opening; in lizards the lower opening is enlarged; and in snakes not only are the openings enlarged but they are joined. These openings allow muscles to attach to tendons, leading to stronger jaws with greater movement. Lacking such openings, anapsids have relatively weak jaws. The large diapsid opening in snakes provides them with the flexibility to swallow large creatures.

[256] The pelycosaurs and their descendants are sometimes called the "mammal-like reptiles," although strictly speaking they are not reptiles.

meter seams of coal to become the Mammouth Coal Bed, which were preserved *unto this day*. And in proto-western-Pennsylvania, a four-meter-thick sixteen-thousand-square-kilometer layer of coal was made. And *coal beds* also formed in the proto-British-Isles, in proto-Belgium, in proto-France, in proto-Germany, in proto-Poland and in proto-Russia. And smaller veins appeared in proto-Korea, proto-North-Africa and proto-northern-China. Now more coal formed between three-hundred-and-thirty-million years BC and two-hundred-and-eighty-million years BC than in any other time of geo-history. Thus came the name Carboniferous, meaning "carbon forming."

And in the oceans, limestone continued to be made. And in certain places, Earth had alternating layers of white and black — perhaps this rock was the most beautiful of all.

Now at this time, Gondwana was drifting slightly north. And as Gondwana and Laurussia merged, the strait between the two did disappear. A *new giant continent* was forming; it was proto-Pangaea — Pangaea in its embryonic stage. And the collision of the continents led to orogenies in proto-Europe, proto-North-America and proto-Africa. During tens of millions of years this is what transpired: First, northern proto-South-America struck southern proto-North-America, forging the Ouachita Mountains. Then proto-Africa struck Laurussia, and three mighty mountain ranges rose: the Appalachians in eastern proto-North-America, the Variscan Mountains in western proto-Europe, and the Mauritanides in northwestern proto-Africa. And all these mountain ranges were rugged *like unto* the modern Rocky Mountains of today.

And Kazakhstania and proto-Siberia collided, making a new continent, *Angara*. And as a consequence, more mountains formed in proto-Asia.

And the *first diapsid* did emerge. It was petrolacosaurus, a lizard-like reptile forty centimeters long that chased small vertebrates and insects on the dry and elevated plains of proto-Kansas. And in proto-North-America, it was "soon" joined by others like it.

Now it came to pass that a certain insect developed a web-like structure between a pair of legs. And when the web did catch the wind, the insect fluttered in the air a bit. And "soon" the web evolved. And the web became a *wing*. And Earth had its *first life that flew*: It was a mayfly, an insect like the dragonfly but with a single pair of wings.

Thus Nature through evolution *had given life* a new device, the *wing*. With it, movement through the air was *possible*. And it came to pass that other insects such as grasshoppers, crickets and cockroaches did develop wings.

And time went by. And one type of mayfly evolved a second wing above the first, so that it grew *two pairs* of wings. And it became the dragonfly. And soon it came to pass that Earth had many flying insects. *And* the air of Earth was *full of life*.

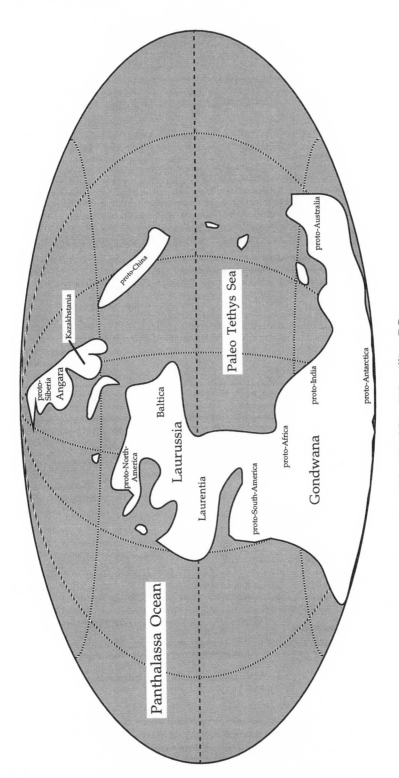

The World in 300 million BC

*The sixth book of the Paleozoic, called*

# The Permian

*The parts all came together.*
*And it was whole.*

## Chapter I: The Early Permian

*The wild beasts of the desert*
*shall meet with the wild beasts of the island.*

It was two-hundred-and-eighty-five-million years ago. The Permian Period began. And it would last for forty-million years. And as Angara, the continent containing northeast proto-Asia, drifted south, its margin started *merging* with the margin of northern proto-Pangaea near the Ural Mountains. Only a narrow shallow strait between the two remained. And as the long thin continent of proto-China drifted west, its margin *joined* proto-Pangaea's eastern margin in the north. And the Paleo Tethys Sea opened up and joined the Panthalassa ocean.

And with the merging of the margins of the continents, *battles* between the species indigenous to each broke out. Now this was not the first time such battles had occurred – it had happened in the Silurian when Baltica collided into Laurentia. And in fact, it had happened every time two continents collided. But what was different now was that *all the continents* were approaching one another. And this battle was just the beginning of a war. And no ordinary war was this – it was verily *world war*.

Now the *glaciers*, which had started in the Middle Carboniferous, *persisted* in the Permian: Within the Antarctic Circle, they covered continental land. But the North Pole had also grown a polar cap: northeastern proto-Siberia was *under ice*. And during the Permian, the temperature of Earth would slowly rise, and the glaciers would retreat somewhat.

And those life forms that had survived the drop in water temperature *moved into* the burial grounds of ancient extinct habitats, for these life forms were more robust and more tolerant of cold. And they multiplied in the cool but warming waters. And *new species* of foraminiferan protozoa, bivalve mollusks, bryozoans, brachiopods and ammonoids arose.

And the types of vegetation of the Carboniferous *persisted* in the Permian. Thus ferns, seed ferns and spore-bearing vascular trees and plants continued growing in moist earth. And for example, *glossopteris*, a seed fern with tongue-shaped leaves, dwelt in Gondwana *everywhere*. But with a drying trend, the pattern of Earth's vegetation would experience a change: wind-blown seeds would prevail over spores. And for example, lycopsids – trees with diamond-shaped scaly bark of the club moss family, which had grown densely in the swamps of the Carboniferous, sometimes reaching heights of thirty meters – would begin to be *replaced by seed-bearing* trees. And by the middle of the Carboniferous, the gymnosperms would dominate Earth's land. And *conifers*, the trees that reproduced with *cones*, would spread wide and far.

And in the forests of the tropics, insects multiplied, with plants provided food and/or protection. And giant dragonflies with *half-a-meter* wing spans fluttered among the trees and over grass-like lands. And joining them were *primitive* moths, butterflies, and two-winged crane flies with spider-like thin legs. And they and others like them would eventually evolve into mosquitoes, midges, fleas and many types of flies. And some insects ate the wood of trees – these primitive types of termites digested cellulose. And other insects – primitive plant lice and aphids – sucked on plants. And *dwelling in the plants and trees* were leafhoppers, planthoppers and sound-producing primitive cicadas. And *crawling* through the low-growth vegetation were many types of bugs and beetles. And webs were spun by spiders between the stems and leaves of plants and trees – the water droplets on such webs reflected sunlight in the early morning dew. And from time to time when proto-flies and proto-fleas got *trapped* in spider webs, they struggled in the filaments until they died. Then a spider ate the proto-flea or proto-fly.

And although insects originated in the Carboniferous, it was in the Permian Period that insects *greatly multiplied*. And from this point onward, enormous insect numbers would make them pests for animals and plants.

And it came to pass that in Gondwana, a salamander-shaped reptile developed *webbed* feet and hands. It was half-a-meter to a meter long and dwelt *in water, not on land*. As it bent its body back and forth and paddled with its feet and waved its tail from side to side, it swam. And before taking a deep dive, it rose to the surface to breathe through nostrils high upon its snout. As it descended, it spied a school of tiny fish. And its cage-like jaw of teeth did open up, come down and trap some of the fish. Now this swimming reptile was a *mesosaur*. And the waters near Gondwana were full of these swimming crocodile-like reptiles, with interlocking teeth and long broad flapping tails.

Now it was early morning and still dark. And *the* night air was cool. And amongst some ferns, a three-meter-long pelycosaur was sleeping. Upon its back a "sail" sat, supported by a row of vertical long spines, making it look more like a marlin than a reptile. As the Sun did slowly rise above the lip of Earth, the first beams of light *streamed* through trees, and this pelycosaur woke up. It moved *into the open* so that light could strike its sail. And it basked in the sun for half an hour. And blood circulating through its sail was *warmed*. And when the pelycosaur was warm enough, it trotted off and started chomping on some plants. And because it fed on vegetation, it was a *herbivore*. Now other pelycosaurs with "marlin sails" and *large* sharp teeth did prey on smaller animals. And since they ate the meat of other creatures, they were *carnivores*.

And the limestone and coal production, which commenced in the Carboniferous, *continued* in the Permian Period. And some iron-rich red shale was also made.

## Chapter II: Pangaea

A nd twenty-million years went by. And as Angara pushed into proto-Pangaea, a *new belt* of mountain ranges was added to the Urals. And as the strait between these continents did *disappear*, marine life there was pushed to other waters. Now at the same time, the shallow margin between proto-Pangaea and proto-China was becoming narrower. And bio-battles for the fertile off-shore habitats *ensued*. And ocean life declined, as war among the living so continued.

And the *last trilobite* died off, ending what had been a mighty reign. For a while, trilobites had been the *most* sophisticated dominating form of life on Earth – once the tiny ocean versions of the dinosaur. But attrition, competition and environmental changes killed them off.

And several million years went by. The long continent of proto-China finally collided with the eastern part of proto-Pangaea. And so the continents were *all* united. Thy planet Earth possessed a *single supercontinent*. And it was provided with a name, which was *Pangaea*, or "all lands."[257]

Now Pangaea had an indentation south of proto-China and north of proto-Africa. And this was the *Tethys Sea*. And besides this sea and Pangaea, the rest of Earth was ocean, the Panthalassa Ocean. And except for islands in Panthalassa, all land was in Pangaea.

Now the creatures from Angara *battled* with the creatures of Laurussia. And the stronger creatures won. And similar battles were happening in many places, as Pangaea was assembled. And while fierce competition and a changing land environment decimated animals, *some new species* did emerge, particularly larger ones.

And in proto-Africa, some parseiasaurs gulped leaves and stems of plants, then chewed the vegetation with serrated leaf-shaped teeth. These reptiles had *hippopotamus-like bodies*, massive legs and bony armor. And their heads had bumps and spikes.

And in proto-Germany, a *protorosaurus* sprinted after insects – it was two-meters long and lizard-like. Elsewhere, some crocodile-like thecodontians were floating in a swamp; unlike modern reptiles, they had bone plates upon their backs. Now these creatures were the Earth's first *archosaurs*, or "ruling reptiles," for soon[258] would their descendants rule the World.

---

[257] The formation of Pangaea was perhaps the greatest geological event on the face of Earth during the Phanerozoic Eon.

[258] I.e., twenty million years.

And more advanced synapsids did appear. And these half reptile, half mammal creatures were *therapsids*. Most therapsid species would die off within the coming twenty-million years, but among the few that would survive would be some dog-like ones that would evolve to mammals.

And in proto-southern-Africa, it looked *as if* a pack of wolves were running through woods. Each, a *lycaenops*, was a meter long and had the body of a panther; two fangs pointed downward from their upper jaws. Perhaps these predators would attack the moschops, which was feeding on some vegetation in a nearby field. Now it so happened that a second moschops joined the first. Both were bulky, massive, three meters long and looked like a hippopotamus. And the two faced off and starting butting heads; a thickened upper bony forehead cushioned blows. Now two other therapsids were dwelling not so far away: One had fang-like teeth similar to those of lycaenops, but was twice as big as it and crocodile-like; the other, a small pig-like creature with a beak-like mouth,[259] was chewing on some cones.

## Chapter III: The Great Extinction Event

*A fire goeth before Him
and burneth up His enemies.*

A nd it came to pass that hot and dry conditions prevailed near the tropics. And some regions were *too hot and dry*. And green plants, ferns and forests bent over, turned yellow, died and disappeared. And in their place did deserts form.

And the merging of all land into a single supercontinent brought diverse habitats *together*. And this led to battles between Earth's life, as species from divergent regions merged and fought for limited resources. And those life forms that were adaptable and robust managed to survive. But those that were inflexible or weak *succumbed*. And many species *went extinct*.

Now the coming together of the continents produced mighty mountain ranges and volcanos. And in a region of proto-Siberia, where the underlying upper mantle was particularly hot, the lithosphere *broke open*. And magma pushed through cracks and flowed profusely over land. And *smoke, carbon dioxide and sulfur gases* filled the atmosphere. A black cloud surrounded Earth, and darkness was upon the face of Earth. The Sun did disappear for weeks. Plants did *cease to photosynthesize*, and algae *died*. And those marine creatures that fed on algae perished. The bottom of the food chain broke. And many large invertebrates went hungry and subsequently died. Only a few survived.

Then the Sun appeared again. And the environment of Earth recovered. And a thousand years went by. Then proto-Siberia erupted for

---

[259] Its beak-like mouth made its head seem like the head of a turtle.

a second time, spilling lava on the land and filling skies with ash. And the shadow of death was cast upon the face of Earth again.

And during the next million years, eruptions came and went. Repeatedly the Earth deteriorated and recovered. Only in between eruptions could the Sun be seen. And life on continents and in the oceans *suffered*.

And layers of lava flowed on top of layers of lava, forming giant *flood basalts*. In all, two-million cubic kilometers of lava was produced, which covered three-hundred-thousand square kilometers of land. And this giant igneous geo-structure was provided with a name: the *Siberian Traps*.

Now the activity of the Siberian Traps made the temperature of Earth go up and down. And this *caused* the polar caps to wax and wane and sea level to go *up and down*. And when sea level dropped, shallow off-shore habitats did disappear. And some marine life found itself on land and died. Organisms battled with *environmental and climatic change*. And those life forms that could adapt survived. And those that could not cope succumbed. And many species *went extinct*.

And so there came to be the *greatest mass extinction* of Earth's ocean life of any time in geo-history, caused by a changing hostile world. This change had been brought about by the coming together of the continents, for this event had led to vulcanism and to reduced off-shore habitats. The lack of fertile habitats had led to struggles among Earth's species. And so a *widespread death* fell upon the face of Earth. And all the stalked echinoderms, horn corals, eurypterids, goniatite ammonoids and fusulinid protozoa disappeared *forever from the face of Earth*. And almost all sea feathers, netlike and fanlike forms of bryozoans, mollusks, gastropods, sea lilies, nautiloids and brachiopods died out. And coral reefs decayed and disappeared. And *ninety-five percent* of non-fish species in the oceans *went extinct*.

And with the food chain snapped, the number of fish declined. Predators, like proto-sharks, were starved. And many died. And the acanthodians, the first jawed fish which had appeared in the Silurian, *forever disappeared*.

Thus fish, the food for many vertebrates, diminished. And for example, mesosaurs went hungry and they *all* died off. Other reptiles suffered from a lack of food and from a hostile quickly changing world. Many reptiles and *three-fourths* of the amphibian orders *vanished* from the lands of Earth. And the number of synapsids nose-dived; hardly any did live on.[260]

> *And the life that did survive*
> *became the seeds for Mesozoic life.*

---

[260] The synapsids came *very close* to being wiped out. Had this lineage been lost, mammals, including man, never would have appeared on Earth!

*The second tome of the trilogy of geo-history, called*

# The Mesozoic Era

*And giant serpents came to dominate the Earth.*

## Introduction

The Paleozoic Era ended. It was two-hundred-and-forty-five-million years ago. And the *Mesozoic Era* started. And it would last one-hundred-eighty-million years. Now Mesozoic, which means "middle life," was the second era of the Phanerozoic Eon.

And the Mesozoic was divided into three periods: the Triassic, the Jurassic and the Cretaceous. Thus in two-hundred-and-forty-five-million BC, the Triassic Period *also* began. And it would last thirty-five-million years.

*The first book of the Mesozoic, called*

## The Triassic

*The World was very different then.*

### Chapter I: The Triassic Face of Earth

Now the giant continent Pangaea covered *one-fourth* of the surface of thy planet Earth, while oceans covered the remaining part. And Pangaea stretched from pole to pole. And the snow caps that covered Pangaea's crown and chin were in retreat and soon would disappear. And in the tropics was the climate *relatively* warm and dry. Meanwhile, *heat* inside the Earth was accumulating *underneath* Pangaea.

### Chapter II: Triassic Ocean Life

And Earth's environment and climate *stabilized*. And sea level rose a bit. And the ocean life that had survived the Late Permian extinction soon rebounded. And bryozoans, gastropods, echinoderms and foraminiferan protozoa reproduced and *multiplied*.[261] And although brachiopods rebounded too, the golden age for them had passed.

And *coccolithophores*, which were spheroidal single-celled algae encased in calcium carbonate, drifted in the seas. And when they died, they settled on the ocean floor and then combined with shells of foraminiferan-type protozoa. And *chalk*[262] did form.

---

[261] Bryozoans and other ocean life forms would diversify greatly in numbers and in species types during the Mesozoic Era. In several ways, bryozoans would be as successful as the ruling reptiles, except that, from the point of view of man, the latter would "overshadow" the former due to the latter's larger size.

[262] Chalk is a powdered form of limestone.

And new species of corals colored the ocean floors with reefs.

And ray-finned fish, which had developed in the Devonian, diversified enormously. And proto mudfish, gars and dogfish swam the seas. And it came to be that fish species had acquired many *diverse* body shapes, bone structures, fins, tails, eyes, gills and scales. And the slender pike-like saurichthys, the vertical disk-shaped dapedium, the herring-like pholidophorus and leptolepis, and the freshwater sharp-toothed perleidus were just *some* of the thousands of species of ray-finned fish that swam Triassic seas.

And new bivalve mollusks propelled themselves up and down and sideways *through Earth's water*. And some bivalve mollusks by attaching to a piece of floating seaweed spread throughout the World. And sometimes they dug into the mud to hide. Now among the survivors of the Late Permian extinction, the ammonoids, Earth's swimming shells, rebounded well, emerging in enormous numbers and *new forms*. They had distinctive ornamental shells with chambers containing fluids and/or gas. The ammonoids were verily *crown jewels* of the oceans. And so it came to be that *agile-swimming* ammonoids and bivalve mollusks thrived and dominated seas.

## Chapter III: Triassic Reptiles

And it so happened that the ocean-dwelling reptiles did diversify. And a *three-pronged* fork in a path of Nature's evolutionary tree produced ichthyosaurs, placodonts and nothosaurs.

And in the ocean, the flapping a powerful tail fin propelled a large sleek creature rapidly through water, *like unto* a tuna or a marlin. It was *ichthyosaur*, and it had the profile of a dolphin. Its *large wide eyes* were searching for a squid-like belemnite. And soon it had one in its mouth: the belemnite and its shell were crushed and chewed to pieces in its long-toothed jaws. Next the ichthyosaur dove above the surface of the sea to breathe in air through a pair of nostrils just in front of its two eyes.[263]

Now just offshore, in the shallow waters of the Tethys Sea, there *seemed* to be a giant turtle swimming. And it dove, paddled to the seabed and dislodged a mollusk. And after *strong jaws* broke the shell apart, it chewed the prey inside with broad blunt teeth. And this swimming armored-body reptile was a *placodont*.

And a little farther from the shore, a *nothosaur* was "crawling" through the water, swimming rapidly with long paddle-limbs instead of arms and legs. And this long-tailed long-necked reptile opened up a jaw of interlocking teeth and trapped a baby ray-finned fish inside.

Now at this time in geo-history, *therapsids* were the *dominating* creature of Earth's lands, although no vertebrate could really claim to

---

[263] Ichthyosaurs were *so acclimated to the sea* that they did not venture onto land to lay their eggs. Instead, these reptiles gave birth to young directly in the water.

rule Pangaea. And for example, the "half reptile, half hog" lystrosaurus browsed on all lands of the southern hemisphere.[264] And it was joined by other herbivorous therapsids, with body shapes like oxen, pigs and hippopotami. Meanwhile the carnivorous therapsids terrorized the lands, sometimes hunting in a pack.[265]

Now *new species* of four-legged lizards crawled through the low growth vegetation of Earth, while other lizards occupied the deserts, swamps and streams. Insects were the food of many lizards, and many lizards were the food of larger vertebrates.

The Sun had set, and it was dark. And there was the rustling sound of a creature moving through the leaves. It was a primitive-type *tuatara*. It looked like a lizard but with a row of spines from head to tail. And it was chasing bugs, snapping at them with its beak-like mouth.

Now the legs of most reptiles were directed outward – such reptiles moved over land *with a sideways twisting gait*. But certain thecodontians had developed legs that were directed down. And such reptiles ran instead of sprawling like a lizard.[266] And it even came to pass that certain reptiles leaned back and walked on *just* two feet. And these reptiles learned to quickly run. And by running quickly did they catch more prey. And their numbers consequently multiplied.

And in another dozen million years or so would reptiles dominate the land on Earth – the *golden age for reptiles* was about to start.

## Chapter IV: Triassic Plants

And tree ferns and large conifers covered the *fertile lands* of Earth. And in their shadow were seed-bearing ferns and plants. And growing near to horsetails were palm-like plants with short, thick and unbranched trunks. And these were *cycads*; at their tops were large, leathery and pointed leaves and giant seeds. And some such cycads species would survive *unto this day*. And lands were also populated with multi-branched tall trees with foul-smelling seeds the size of cherries. And these were *ginkgoes*. They had fan-shaped leaves, which grew large in summer and fell off in winter. And while many ginkgo species would appear in the Mesozoic Era, only one, ginkgo biloba, would survive *unto this day*.

---

[264] Lystrosaurus played a crucial role in convincing scientists in the 1960's that the supercontinent Pangaea existed and that continental drift did indeed occur. Fossils of lystrosaurus were found in Africa, India and Antarctica. If these lands had not been together, it would have been difficult to understand how such a heavy creature could have swum the seas between these continents. The wide distribution of the seed fern glossopteris also provided convincing evidence.

[265] These reptile-like creatures had body forms of weasels, dogs and bears. It is probable that some of them had a little hair and could control in part their body temperature.

[266] This type of reptile would eventually evolve into the dinosaurs. Reptiles with legs positioned more under their bodies than to the sides would have two advantages: They would be able to run faster and they would be able to support more weight.

## Chapter V: The Manicouagan Crater

And thirty-million years went by. And in northeastern proto-Quebec, a large meteor struck Earth. And a *tremendous* explosion shook thy planet. And it was similar to what had happened in the Archean and Proterozoic eons, when such impacts had been frequent. And debris was scattered everywhere. And bedrock *melted down*, exposing Proterozoic rock. And a sixty-kilometer crater was created. And for forty days and forty nights, Earth's weather was disrupted. And the depression in the ground, the crater, collected water when it rained. And so a lake was *made*. And the lake was provided with a name. And the name was Lake Manicouagan.

## Chapter VI: Triassic Life Evolves

*In the habitation of the dragons, where each lay,*
*shall be herb with reeds and rushes.*

And new forms of life emerged. And two-legged fast-running reptiles *grew larger* and did dwell in proto-South-America. And soon they spread to other places in Pangaea. They were proto-dinosaurs. And those that ate of animals were carnivores; and those that ate of plants were herbivores. And for example, *prosauropods*, which were two to seven meters long and weighed a ton, looked like small "brontosaurs" – "giraffes with reptile skin." Now their hind legs were large and thick, while their forearms were moderately weaker. Five clawed toes on limbs provided balance and support.

And there on Pangaea, one prosauropod feasted on some conifers. And it sat tripod-like on its two rear feet and its long strong tail, while its forearms dangled in the air. And its *long neck* stretched up and disappeared among the branches of a conifer. Seconds later did its head emerge, with its flat, leaf-like teeth munching leafy matter. The sound of crunching cones would have been heard, had ye been there. Bits of leaves and cones slipped from its mouth and fell to Earth. And a minute later, the prosauropod leaned forward *on all fours* and trotted off. Now in proto-Brazil, a two-meter-long *staurikosaurus*[267] spied a small therapsid. And lunging forward, it caught the smaller creature. The creature writhed within the larger reptile's mouth. And *ferocious teeth* pierced through flesh and brought about *quick death*. Then the staurikosaurus on just its two rear legs ran off to seek another prey.

And it happened that a small light lizard grew some skin between its body and its limbs. And wind caught the skin and made the lizard *lift into the air* and glide somewhat. And soon other lizards awkwardly did glide short distances, but to move about, they mostly

---

[267] Some other proto-dinosaurs of the Triassic were eoraptor, *coelophysis* and herrerasaurus. Many paleontologists consider these reptiles to already be dinosaurs.

walked on feet. And one such reptile was *icarosaurus*, named after Icarus who used wax and wings to fly.

And other reptiles developed bat-like rigid webs for wings. And they were called the *pterosaurs, the first vertebrates to occupy the air of Earth*. Now at this time, they had long and bony tails, short necks, and beaks with many teeth. At first, they struggled with their wings and flight: mostly gliding when they flew – some launched themselves from cliffs. Now they used *sight* to spot insects such as crickets, roaches, bugs and beetles; their method of attack was from the air. And as time went by, the *sharp-eyed* ones did thrive, while those with weaker eyes died out. And so eventually, the pterosaurs developed keen eyesight. Likewise with time, their webs began to bend a little better. And "soon" pterosaurs did flap their wings and fly.

And by a pond, a shell with four protruding legs was crawling over land. And nearby it, there was a second "walking shell." And these were *Earth's first tortoises*. They differed from their modern counterparts in that they still had a few teeth in the upper jaw and they could not retract their legs and head into their shells. Now eventually some turtles would live in water, using feet as paddles when in oceans and in ponds. And they would float upon the surface or swim at shallow depths, with their shells providing *good protection* from the crocodiles and predators.

Now Triassic proto-crocodiles were small, lightly built and lizard-like. And they lived on land in dry landscapes. Upon four long legs and *like unto* a greyhound dog, they sprinted after large insects and small lizards, sometimes running for short spells on just their two hind legs.

Now as reptile numbers grew, the therapsids did decline. But among those that did survive were some which were *more mammal-like*: obtaining hair and multi-chambered hearts; evolving a lower jaw that hinged directly to the skull; acquiring *three* types of teeth: molars, canines and incisors. Now it came to be that one small shrew-like animal *nursed* its young at birth, after they – weak and immature – had hatched from leathery shelled eggs. And this *triconodont*, as it was called, was *the first mammal* to reside on Earth. It was an *insectivore*, for it fed on crickets, roaches, termites, ants and beetles. And so in the Late Triassic period, another branch was added to the *tree of Life*.

## Chapter VII: Environmental Changes
## Lead to Mass Extinctions

*And Earth's creatures shook their heads in agony,
for their grief was very great.*

And it came to pass that heat below Pangaea melted rock along the fracture lines of *least resistance*; the same had happened to Proterozoic supercontinents – history was repeating. And volcanos rose between Gondwana and proto-North-America. And as they separated, a *rift* between the two developed. And magma pushed up through the rift. And lava flowed, forming great basalt plateaus in southern proto-North-America. And *gases* from volcanos filled the skies. And as the waters of the oceans rose, seas inundated proto-Europe.

And water inundated forests full of confers. Then strong winds *blew them over*. And trunks were mixed with dirt and buried. And later, in some places, when pressure petrified the wood, it *turned to stone*. And some stone conifers would survive the geo-forces of the next two-hundred-twenty-million years: These tree-statues would exist *unto this day*.[268]

And environmental and climatic changes led to loss of life. And the thecodontians, nothosaurs, placodonts and certain amphibians gradually did go extinct. And many bivalved mollusks disappeared, *all* conodontal creatures vanished, and *only one group* of nautiloids survived. And snails also suffered, *almost disappearing from the Earth*.

---

[268] An example would be Petrified National Park Forest, in northeastern Arizona. It would contain six separate lots of ancient conifers.

*The second book of the Mesozoic, called*

# The Jurassic

*There were giants on the Earth in those days.*

## Chapter I: The Early Jurassic Environment

It was two-hundred-and-ten-million years ago. The Jurassic Period began. It would last fifty-five-million years. And it came to pass that the rift between proto-North-America and Gondwana widened. And water entered there. And a *new strait* connected Panthalassa to the Tethys Sea. Pangaea had become two pieces – Gondwana in the south and Laurasia in the north. And *Laurasia* was the union of three large lands: proto-Europe, proto-Asia and the ancient continent of Laurentia, which included proto-North-America.

.      .      .      .      .      .      .

And as millions of years went by, Laurasia and Gondwana *further* moved apart. And westward-moving currents flowed between the two from the Tethys Sea to Panthalassa. All along the shore, new continental margins formed, making new water habitats *available* for life.

And volcanic emissions steadily supplied the atmosphere of Earth with greenhouse gas. The temperature of air was warm, and there were no polar caps. As Earth's tectonic plates did move about, *deep waters* were displaced. And as sea level rose, water *flooded* proto-Europe, southwest proto-Asia, southern and eastern proto-North-America and parts of proto-Africa. And there were sands and sediments laid down. Later, they solidified to sandstone, salt and clay. And in pools, *organic matter* rotted. Later, it was crushed and pressurized. And eventually did it turn into *coal and oil* in proto-Siberia, proto-England, proto-China, proto-Gulf-of-Mexico and northern proto-Germany.

And it came to pass that Laurasia, in the northern hemisphere, was drifting north and west.

## Chapter II: Early Jurassic Life

And marine life flourished once again. Shellfish, foraminiferan protozoa and coccolithophores made more limestone and more chalk. And for a second time, ammonoids underwent a *remarkable recovery* from almost sure extinction:

> *The walls shook.*
> *And the clocks fell down and broke.*
> *And mysteriously new clocks appeared*
> *where old clocks once had been.*

And bivalve mollusks diversified. And oysters grew *white pearls*. And *new* gastropods with complicated shells crawled on the floors of shallow seas, oceans, lakes and ponds. Above the gastropods swam *modern forms* of bony fish. And crabs and lobsters crawled on underwater sand.

And mid-depth swimming proto-sharks evolved to sharks. And flat bottom-dwelling proto-sharks evolved to rays.

And on the land and in the air did life develop. And many beetles, flies, wasps, ants and bees assumed their modern form. And some land creatures took to water – they were *the new amphibians*: the frog, the toad and salamander.

And in proto-Europe did dwell the sphenodontal tuataras. These lizard-like reptiles did grow to a half-a-meter long. And they dug *into the ground* to make their homes in earth; during day, they *hid in holes*, thereby avoiding predators. And they came out at night to feed on crawling bugs. But even then, they dared not venture more than a few meters from their burrows. And they were robust creatures that could endure month-long droughts or bad climatic times. Now the Mesozoic Era, tuataras would spread from proto-Europe to proto-North-America and proto-Asia. And paleontologists in modern times would find their fossils *there*. And during the Cenozoic Era when rodents became rampant, *tuataras* would fall prey to these assertive predators; decimated, *they* would *almost* go extinct. But some tuataras would survive on isolated islands in New Zealand in the Recent.[269] And during two-hundred-million years of evolution, in which the world and life would undergo dramatic transformations, they would *hardly change*.[270]

## Chapter III: The First Dinosaurs

But unlike tuataras, other reptiles underwent enormous changes. Thus came the reptile evolutionary revolution. And the golden age of reptiles gathered force as archosaurs, the ruling reptiles, which included crocodiles, pterosaurs and dinosaurs, *reigned over Earth*.

And there emerged the modern forms of crocodiles with longer snouts. And they were the *masters* of Earth's marshes and its swamps.

And some pterosaurs grew larger, achieving wing spans of a meter. And they had hollow bones, large eyes and long thin tails. These agile flying creatures spread to all four corners of the World. And they *patrolled* the skies of Earth.

Now the nothosaurs of the Triassic were replaced by long-necked reptiles that had paddle flippers for their arms and legs. They were the *plesiosaurs*.[271] And plesiosaurs and ichthyosaurs *controlled* the oceans and the seas.

---

[269] The Recent, also known as the Holocene, is the most modern epoch on Earth.

[270] To see a breathing modern tuatara today is to see a reptile representative as old as the oldest dinosaurs. The same is true for crocodiles.

[271] During the Mesozoic some plesiosaurs would develop extremely long necks: Elasmosaurus of the Late Cretaceous was *fourteen* meters in length; *eight* of which was in its

And dinosaurs emerged, *dominating* lands on Earth. And with well-developed tendons and strong, sophisticated ligaments and muscles, they thundered as they walked or ran; the earth beneath their feet did *shake*. And their powerful, multi-chambered hearts pumped blood to all the limbs and body parts. Now there were two main types of dinosaurs – *saurischians* with lizard-hips and *ornithischians* with bird-like hips.[272]

And it had happened that Triassic reptiles such as staurikosaurus and coelophysis had evolved into the *theropods*, the carnivorous saurischians. Although the smallest weighed a kilogram and were no larger than a chicken, most Early Jurassic theropods were several meters long. And compared with the rest of their body, their heads were large but light. And their mouth, when closed, displayed an "evil smile." And their mouth, when opened, revealed two long rows of narrow, pointed and *serrated teeth*. Now all theropods ran on two legs containing hollow bones. And although their arms in front were small and short, their hands were clawed *like unto* those of hawks. With tails raised for balance and on light legs, theropods swiftly darted after smaller lizards, infant dinosaurs and shrew-like mammals at up to *forty-five kilometers per hour*. And once a prey was caught, powerful large jaws and strong sharp teeth tore and ripped the prey apart. Now *all* the bones of *coelurosaurs* were hollow, and their hands had three-pronged curving claws. These theropods – half-a-meter to two-meters long – walked on relatively long, thin legs, which left their small arms dangling free. Now *megalosaurs*[273] were the largest of the early theropods – six to nine meters long; two to three meters tall. And they stood on strong and sturdy legs.

Now also dwelling on the lands of Earth were *sauropods*, with their massive elephant-like bodies. Powerful huge tails acted as counterweights to compensate the long thick necks.[274] Now the early sauropods were about six meters long and weighed ten tons; few predators

---

neck! It looked roughly like a snake attached to a seal.

[272] Dinosaur hip structure is an important classifying feature. Saurischians include theropods and sauropods. Typical ornithischians are armored, horned and duckbilled dinosaurs.

[273] Megalosaurs were a member of the carnosaur infraorder of dinosaurs. The *carnosaurs* were the large carnivorous dinosaurs of the theropod suborder. The word carnosaur means "flesh lizard." The first dinosaur bone on record to be discovered by man belonged to a megalosaur. The bone was found in 1676 in England. At that time, no one knew the significance of this bone. Only two-and-a-half centuries later would scientists come to realize the existence of dinosaurs. At an 1841 meeting of the British Association for the Advancement of Science, the great paleontologist and anatomist Richard Owen announced the existence of a class of fossil reptiles, the "terrible lizards." In 1842, the word "dinosaur" appeared for the first time in print, in the proceedings of that meeting.

[274] It would be too simplistic to have called sauropods Nature's version of the seesaw, for the balancing mechanism was more dynamic. They had sophisticated body structure, a flexible backbone of intricate vertebrae, and *complex muscles and ligaments* surrounding the entire skeleton. More engineering went into them than in any modern man-made suspension bridge of girders, cables, grids and struts.

did dare attacked *such* huge and mighty creatures. Their barely bending legs were *like unto* the columns of a temple – looming strong and solid. And broad feet with five blunt toes supplied them with support. Some had a claw in one toe, which provided extra traction when they walked.[275] And when a sauropod did walk, it walked on all four legs, and the *ground around it shook*; and the tail was lifted up for balance and to avoid it being stepped upon by other members of the herd. Now sauropods could move no faster than an elephant. And *few* large sauropods could raise their legs in front to feed.[276] But their necks were *long and flexible*, allowing their small heads to sway and reach into the trees. To satisfy huge appetites, they spent endless hours ripping leaves and trigs off forest trees, and with little chewing, they simply swallowed them.

Now *pisanosaurus*, the first ornithischian, appeared around two-hundred-and-ten-million years BC in proto-Argentina. And "soon," it was joined by fabrosaurs and related dinosaurs. Although lizard-like in shape, *fabrosaurs* walked on two hind legs, while their shorter arms were used for grabbing leaves, seeds and other vegetation. The fabrosaurs were *light and hollow-boned and fairly small* – about a meter long. Later, Jurassic ornithischians would grow to several times this size. Now all ornithischians were *herbivores*, often having beak-like mouths. And although they had the large supporting tails and strong hind legs to stand upright, many walked or ran on all four limbs. And through natural selection due to evolutionary pressures, some such as the heterodontosaurs,[277] would eventually develop different types of teeth for cutting, crunching and for chewing vegetation. Now certain ornithischians had bony plates to protect them from flesh-eating dinosaurs. And for example, *scelidosaurus* had several rows of triangular studded plates running from its neck to tail tip, while much of the rest of its body was covered with bony pointed plates, or scutes. It tore off vegetation with a toothless beak and then chewed it with its weak[278] and leaf-shaped teeth set back in its jaws.

## Chapter IV: The Russet West

And thirty-million years went by. And it came to pass that *water invaded* western proto-North-America from the Arctic Circle to the proto-Gulf-of-Mexico. This *was* the Sundance Sea. And sediments collected and made sandstone, shale and limestone. And iron-oxide-rich sediments painted proto-Colorado, proto-Arizona and other places red. And rivers flowed into the swampy regions of the *Morrison Formation*,

---

[275] The claw was also sometimes used for defense.

[276] Some sauropods could balance tripodally to reach into high trees.

[277] Fabrosaurs and heterodontosaurs are members of the *ornithopod* suborder of plant-eating bird-hipped dinosaurs capable of walking on their hind legs. The word ornithopod means "bird footed."

[278] Weak relative to other dinosaurs.

depositing mud, silt and sand. And in time, the mud, silt and sand turned into mudstone, siltstone, shale and sandstone.

## Chapter V: Reptiles Evolve

And as millions of years went by, *new* saurischian dinosaurs emerged from older ones. And in general, they grew larger: some were even *thirty meters long*, a dozen meters tall, and weighed several dozen tons. And brachiosaurus was such a heavy giant sauropod,[279] weighing more than *fifty tons*! And as time advanced, it happened that a carnosaur grew to be five meters tall, ten meters long. And its skull got larger and its jaw got stronger. And its *teeth* curved back, *each one* finely serrated *like unto* a steak knife. And its three-pronged claws grew longer. And it became an *allosaur*, a ferocious theropod and predator.

And one day in proto-Connecticut, a herd of dinosaurs ran through some mud. And within a week, the mud had solidified and become as *strong as stone*. And the footprints were preserved *unto this day*. And elsewhere on Earth, dinosaurs ran through muddy earth. And some of those turned into holes in stones.[280]

And pterosaurs soared through the air *above the reach of predators*. And they developed larger hawk-like claws to grab their prey and sometimes grasp a branch. And as millions of years went by, some species of these flying reptiles grew longer beaks and lost some teeth, their eyes moved inward and above the beak, their tails got shorter, and their necks got longer. And these new pterosaurs were *pterodactyls*. Some flew over waterways, catching fish in beaks of teeth.

## Chapter VI: Pangaea Breaks Apart

And twenty-million years went by, during which heat below the pieces of Pangaea made the pieces *crack in places*. And as magma rose between Laurentia and proto-Europe, earthquakes shook the earth and volcanos suddenly[281] appeared. And in southern Gondwana, magma was ascending through the earth. And giant rugged mountain ranges and volcanos did rise up. And it had happened that a mantle hot spot, the *Walvis Hot Spot*, had rifted the southern halves of proto-Africa and proto-South-America apart. Elsewhere, a piece of *land mass* of Gondwana, which was south of the Tethys Sea and in the middle of

---

[279] Another example was the twenty-meter-long ten-ton cetiosaurus. Its bones were discovered in 1809 before the concept of a dinosaur had been conceived of by man. Since people at the time thought that the bones were of a giant marine animal, they named it cetiosaurus, which means "whale lizard."

[280] Nowadays in Dinosaur State Park, in Connecticut, there are hundreds of such prints. In Peace River Canyon, in British Columbia, there are thousands of dinosaur footprints that have survived! By inspecting tracks, paleontologists have come to know how dinosaurs ran and walked.

[281] Within years.

the southern hemisphere, had *broken off*. And it was India. And to the north did India begin to drift. And water filled the void where it had been and made a sea – the proto-Indian-Ocean was this sea.

## Chapter VII: The Making of the Rocky Mountains

And as proto-North-America drifted north and west, it happened that the west coast struck an island arc. And folds in Earth arose, *and rock rose up*. They were the Sierra Nevada peaks, pointing to the sky *like unto* towers of cathedrals. And from proto-British-Columbia to northern proto-California, other collisions with island arcs made faults and rugged mountains. And these upliftings were the beginnings of the Rocky Mountains.

And during the next one-hundred-and-fifty-million years, proto-North-America would drift over a tectonic plate of Panthalassa. And this Panthalassan plate would be subducted. And *most of it* would sink below the continent of proto-North-America. But sometimes, light and elevated parts of ocean crust, seamounts and islands would scrape *up* on land. And it was *like unto* a shovel passing over dirt – the dirt accumulated in the shovel. Thus crust was added bit by bit to western proto-North-America. And during the next one-hundred-and-fifty-million years, western British Columbia, Oregon, Alaska, California, Washington and Baja California would be assembled *out of scraps of ocean crust*.

And during the Mesozoic, as proto-North-America drifted over Panthalassa, the Panthalassan tectonic plate would push against it to the east and from below. And the western third of continental crust of proto-North-America would be compressed and would be *lifted up*. And *this* would make the Rocky Mountains higher and add more mountains, rocks and mass. And *this* would *elevate the land* and make plateaus elsewhere in the western part of proto-North-America.

## Chapter VIII: The Evolution of Earth's Life Continues

*Let there be fowl that may fly above the Earth*
*in the open firmament of Heaven.*
*And this happened on the fifth day*
*of the first month of a long lost year.*

And life evolved. And the *hand of Nature shaped* sharks and rays into their modern forms.

And during several million years, certain ornithopods evolved: Mouths *turned into* beaks, and teeth of many types arose. The upper and the lower teeth did meet instead of interlock. And well-developed cheeks appeared which hindered vegetation, plants and leaves from falling out when such ornithischians did eat. And hips pushed forward; *thick muscles* joined the hips and thighs; and bones in legs got *lighter*. Thus lightweight, speedy dinosaurs "*were made*." And they were *hyp-*

*silophodonts*. At this time, they were just one meter to two meters long.[282] Now these hypsilophodonts lived in herds together. And when threatened, they would stampede, running swiftly on hind legs. In calmer times, they fed on ferns and other vegetation. And when a female did give birth, she produced a dozen eggs or more, arranged them *in a circle* and took care of them. Now during the Jurassic, other ornithopods evolved, growing into giant beasts half-a-dozen meters long with *thick bones* in the legs to support their bulky bodies – these *slowly moving* ornithischians often walked on all four limbs. They had developed pointed beaks for mouths, inside which were grinding teeth *like unto* modern-day iguanas. And these heavy herbivores were provided with a name. And *they* were named *iguanodonts*.

And in proto-North-America, a three meter tall, eight meter long, bulky creature slowly walked on all four legs; it must have weighed three tons. Along its spine was a row of movable *diamond-shaped bone-plates*, while on its tail were several pairs of *long sharp spikes*. And it had a relatively tiny head and hardly any jaws. It was a *stegosaur*.[283] And it happened that an allosaur approached and opened up a jaw of mighty teeth. The stegosaur turned away and *swayed* its tail from side to side. And the allosaur drew closer, moving in a circle. But the stegosaur turned and kept its sharp-spiked tail between itself and the approaching allosaur. And the allosaur remained two body's lengths away, waiting and maneuvering. Then after half a minute, the allosaur did turn away, and it marched off.

And some coelurosaurs, the Early Jurassic carnivorous theropods, shrank in size, while their arms grew relatively longer. And during the Jurassic, a few became almost warm blooded: They could in part control their body temperature.

Now since the tallest herbivorous dinosaurs had more available trees and leaves to eat, there were evolutionary pressures to be bigger; the smaller members of a species ate less food, grew weak and sometime even starved. And so it came to be that sauropods grew *longer necks*,[284] as they diversified to many *different* species. And for example, the thirty-ton *apatosaurus*, also known as *brontosaurus*,[285] emerged in proto-North-America. It could reach to feed off leaves on top of trees

---

[282] In the Cretaceous, larger ones would form, averaging three meters in length. Tenontosaurus would be among the biggest – seven meters long.

[283] Although the bone-plates on its back provided some defensive protection, they were mainly used for regulating heat. Blood circulated through them. To warm itself, a stegosaur would move into light, letting the plates receive sunrays, as in "solar panels." To cool itself, it would move into shade.

[284] One-hundred-million years later, the same evolutionary effects would cause giraffes to evolve longer necks.

[285] Brontosaurus means "thunder lizard," reflecting the sound that brontosaurus must have made as it walked through proto-North-America. "Brontosaurus" is the popular *misnomer* for apatosaurus. For many people, the term "brontosaurs" has become synonymous with the long-necked browsing "sauropods."

ten-meters tall! Now Nature had provided apatosaurus with only peg-like teeth, so that, although it easily could tear off leaves, it had diffi-culty *crushing* them. Thus much tearing action often wore teeth down. And when they did wear down, the teeth fell out and new ones *did grow in*. Now it happened that an apatosaurus died. And its bones were buried and preserved *unto this day*. And elsewhere in the earth were apatosaurus bones preserved or petrified.[286]

And other new four-footed long-necked sauropods, such as the camarasaurus and diplodocus, *emerged on Earth*. And they were simi-lar in shape to "brontosaurus," but camarasaurus was smaller, while diplodocus was longer and was lighter.[287] In proto-New-Mexico, one "relative" of diplodocus grew to forty meters long![288] Now *camarasaurus* had a wide rectangular head with two bumps on top with *large nasal openings* – the holes helped cool a small but active brain. And in herds of just a few, camarasaurs stood side by side *patiently* chewing plants and leaves with spoon-shaped teeth – in a sluggish manner did they eat. Now it came to pass that a camarasaurus swallowed several rough stones. And they descended to the gizzard, where they *rubbed against half-digested vegetation*, crushing and pulverizing it. And such stones were *gastroliths*. And it would come to pass that other herbivo-rous dinosaurs would use gastroliths to aid digestion of plant matter.

And "brontosaurs," camarasaurs, iguanodonts, diplodocuses, stegosaurs and allosaurs were just a few of *many kinds* of dinosaurs that rumbled as they walked on Earth.

And it came to be that more therapsids did evolve to mammals. And Earth had *several* different types. But during the Jurassic, Na-ture's mammals numbered few, and all were small and mouse-like. And plant-eating species had appeared, some of which climbed trees. And all mammals at this time laid eggs to reproduce.

And it also happened that lizards looked more like modern liz-ards, both in form and shape.

And it came to pass that a coelurosaur-like reptile developed into *archaeopteryx, the first bird*. And in proto-Bavaria, in southern proto-Germany, an archaeopteryx sat waiting in a tree. Now a tiny lizard was crawling on some pebbles just below. And archaeopteryx leaped from the tree and landed on the ground. But the lizard disappeared into a hole. Then archaeopteryx spied a worm, pounced on it and ate it. And it walked back to the tree, and using all its claws, it climbed the trunk. And several minutes later, it was on a branch again.

---

[286] Later, one-hundred-million years and more, paleontologists would collect "bronto-saurus" bones and reconstruct the giant creature. In modern times, such whole skeletons would become the prized and omnipresent pieces in museums of natural history.

[287] Many of the long-necked browsing sauropods, such as diplodocus, had depressions, known as pleurocoels, carved out of their vertebrae as a weight-saving device.

[288] This length is measured from crown to tail tip. Diplodocus and similar dinosaurs were most likely the longest creatures to ever live on Earth.

And it would not be long before archaeopteryx became an agile airborne creature. And instead of gliding, it would flutter feathers and would really fly.

Now archaeopteryx had *features like a reptile*: teeth, scales, and bones along its tail. Half-way to each wing tip were three claws. But archaeopteryx *was* indeed a bird, for it was *warm blooded* and its wings had *feathers*.

> *And soon the skies of Earth*
> *were filled with many flying birds.*
> *And so another branch*
> *was added to the tree of Life.*

## Chapter IX: The Last Jurassic Day

> *And the sound of their wings was as*
> *the sound of chariots of many horses running to do battle.*

The *first rays* of sunlight beamed upward just above the Earth's horizon. The air was cool and moist. A *mist* covered the face of Earth. An allosaur woke up and roared. Pterodactyls fled the trees. The sound of flapping wings was heard. Then there came the screams of a baby brontosaurus[289] being clawed by the hungry allosaur.

The mist rose up above the palm-like cycads. At the edge of a conifer forest, a camarasaurus *calmly* chomped away at leaves. Sunlight sparkled off the drops of dew in ferns. A bug crawled on the moist, musty-smelling earth. A fly struggled in a spider's web. And just a foot away, a lizard had a smaller lizard in its mouth.

The air began to warm. The earth began to dry. The mist began to lift. And that *was* the way it was at the beginning of that day, *the last Jurassic day*.

And then the last Jurassic day did pass away.

---

[289] More precisely, a baby apatosaurus.

*The third book of the Mesozoic, called*

# The Cretaceous

*And one day, the mighty shall be powerless.*

## Chapter I: The New Continents Move Apart

*He clave the rock
and waters did gush out.*

It was one-hundred-and-forty-five-million years ago. The Cretaceous Period began. It would last eighty-million years. And cretaceous in Latin means "making chalk," for during the Cretaceous Period *more than half* the chalk on Earth was made.

Now the breakup of Pangaea *into pieces* was proceeding.

And it came to pass that a *mid-ocean ridge* emerged between Gondwana and proto-North-America. *There*, magma thrust its way up through the Earth, creating ocean crust. And the crust spread outward from the ridge, as Gondwana and proto-North-America were drawn *apart*. And the North Atlantic Sea, the Gulf of Mexico and the Caribbean Sea came into being. And these seas would remain *unto this day*.

And during millions of years, it came to pass that geo-forces tore apart Gondwana *like unto* a person ripping cloth. Southern proto-South-America pulled *away* from southern proto-Africa. And a sea, similar to the Red Sea of the Holocene, arose between the two. And magma ascended in the Earth and cracked apart the southern region of Gondwana: Proto-Antarctica and proto-Australia *broke from* proto-South-America and proto-Africa. And water filled the void between the two – the Drake Passage was this waterway. And Cape Horn was also born.[290]

As ocean crust spread from the proto-Mid-Indian-Ocean-Ridge, India drifted north at a relatively rapid rate, transported by a lithospheric plate.

Thus Earth had many *new* mid-ocean ridges. And at these underwater rifts, where the skin of Earth was pulled apart, magma flowed continuously, thereby creating twenty cubic kilometers of new ocean crust a year. And minerals poured from the ridges, filling seas with *nutrients* for life. And underwater magma warmed the ocean waters near the ridges. And carbon dioxide and sulfur gases bubbled out of cracks and ascended through seawater. And greenhouse gases entered air. And Earth grew very *warm*.

And as Pangaea broke in pieces and the pieces moved apart, the level of the sea began to rise.

---

[290] Actually, during the rest of geo-history, a peninsula would sometimes connect proto-South-America to proto-Antarctica.

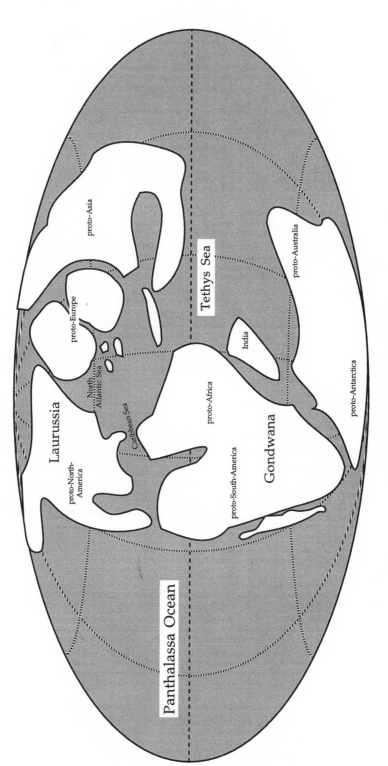

The World in 130 million BC

## Chapter II: Early-Cretaceous Life

Now the waters of the Earth contained *many types* of modern bony fish. In the oceans, lakes and seas swam proto anchovies, carps and eels. And they were joined by *primitive forms* of perch, butterfly-fish, pike, piranhas, catfish, whitefish, salmon, herrings, minnows, tarpons, smelt and trout. And countless other fish *unique to the Cretaceous* were dwelling in Earth's waters: a long round fish of blue with yellow spots; a half-meter version of a pollywog of checkered green and brown; a red fish with purple stripes that was flat, vertical and small; and so on. And so it had come to pass that Earth's seas contained fish of *many colors, shapes and sizes.* And *xiphactinus,* which grew four meters long, was at this time the largest bony fish of all.

And at the bottom of the Tethys Sea, large bivalve *rudists* built reef-like structures. Now rudists were strangely shaped – one valve was a *wavy* cylinder and the other – articulate – was a cap shaped like a mushroom.[291] On average, rudists were twenty centimeters wide, but the biggest rudists were a meter. And during the Cretaceous, they were so *prevalent and common* that they built more reefs than corals!

And it happened that ammonoids streamlined their shells. And with such shells, they moved through ocean waters *faster*, sweeping up plankton and invertebrates to eat. And they developed jaws for crushing prey. Their numbers increased enormously. And so Earth's seas were full of *many* swimming shells.

And with snake-like undulations of their tails, two swimming creatures sped through the ocean sea. And *like unto* dolphins, they had long round, narrow bodies and small flippers. But they were not dolphins; nor were they fish, for they had stubby web-like feet and snake-like skin. These swimming lizard-reptiles were two *mosasaurs.* Now one of them spied an ammonoid, sped after it, opened up its mouth and cracked it open with its jaws. The shell drifted down, while the soft body of the ammonoid wiggled in the water for several seconds until it was consumed. And so it came to be that in the coastal waters of the oceans dwelt the mosasaurs; sometimes playing like the dolphins; sometimes killing like the sharks.

Thus at this time in geo-history, the *rulers* of Earth's oceans were the great reptile predators, such as plesiosaurs, ichthyosaurs and mosasaurs. And they were joined by giant bony fish, such as xiphactinus, and by the sharks.

Now during the Mesozoic Era, seabeds became a *battle field* among life forms. Fish and swimming reptiles with shell-crushing jaws surveyed the ocean floors. Some mollusks had muscles strong enough to open clams, while sea stars with suction-tipped tube feet were able to accomplish the same feat. And crustaceans with shell-drilling claws prowled around in search of food. And Nature's prey reacted by *defen-*

---

[291] This design made a rudist look roughly like a covered basket.

*sive measures*: Sea urchins grew sharp spines; bottom dwelling bivalves and mollusks often burrowed into mud; crawling creatures such as crabs ran faster; gastropods developed thicker shells; *and so on*. But brachiopods developed few defensive measures. And their numbers did decline.

And the "hand of evolution" touched the bird. And birds became a little *lighter*. And their feathers became more well developed and complex, while their wings became more *flexible*. And so it came to be that birds *effortlessly* flew from tree to tree. And they glided in the wind and soared off hilly cliffs.

And somewhere, a newborn bird opened up its mouth as a mother bird approached. And the mother bird placed a worm within the young bird's mouth.

And in shallow waters, large, long-legged birds walked gingerly *as if* on stilts. And the ones with webbed feet and long arched necks were primitive flamingos. And the ones without webbed feet were proto-storks and proto-herons.

## Chapter III: Early Cretaceous Dinosaurs

And evolution produced new breeds of ornithischian dinosaurs. And hypsilophodonts and iguanodonts diversified, while nodosaurs appeared.

A *nodosaur* – about five meters long – inched forward on its four short and stubby legs and disappeared among a patch of ferns. And from time to time, the ferns did shake. And fifteen minutes later did it emerge, with strands of plants dangling from its beak-like mouth. Now this nodosaur looked *like unto* an armadillo, for it was covered with studded bony *plates* of different shapes and sizes. And on each of its two sides, a row of spikes stuck out. As its jaws slowly circulated in masticating plants, it sluggishly walked across an open stretch of land. Then it opened up its mouth; and deep inside, beyond a green mash of vegetation were several loosely spaced, small leaf-shaped teeth. And it came to pass that a pack of relatively large coelurosaurs came by. And the nodosaur tucked its limbs *beneath* its body and sat motionless *like unto* a bony rock. And the coelurosaurs clawed the plates, trying to make the nodosaur react. But the nodosaur *budged not*. And after several minutes, the coelurosaurs ran off.

And in proto-North-America and proto-Europe, other nodosaurs slowly moved about, feeding on low-lying plants and ferns.

And in proto-China, a two-meter-long psittacosaur[292] walked on all four limbs toward a cycad. And leaning *back* on its hind legs and letting its tail lie on the ground for balance and support, it placed its

---

[292] The name psittacosaur is derived from the Greek word "psittakos," meaning parrot: The head of this dinosaur resembled a parrot. Psittacosaurs are members of the *ceratopians*, a suborder of dinosaurs that include the protoceratops and the ceratops.

four-fingered hands upon the plant. And its toothless beak bit at the seed. And it fed for several minutes until it felt the rumbling of a heavy nearby dinosaur. And psittacosaur sped off, running swiftly *on* its two hind legs.

And while the "golden age" for sauropods had just peaked and was beginning to decline, new species of theropods appeared. And new kinds of carnosaurs joined allosaurs. And some new coelurosaurs arose, such as the *dreaded* deinonychosaurs.

In proto-North-America, a one-ton, seven-meter-long hypsilophodont stretched its neck to feed on the lower leaves of *a tall conifer*. Now nearby, below, a dozen *deinonychosaurs* crept slowly through thick vegetation; each had a tail like a salamander, a body *like unto* a greyhound dog, and a head *like unto* a lizard which was arched up like a horse. And on the second finger of each foot was a pointed "sickle" claw twelve centimeters long; the other fingers on the feet and hands were *also clawed*. And on two feet, the deinonychosaurs methodically and delicately stepped forward until they were within three dozen meters of the feeding hypsilophodont. *Suddenly*, the pack surged forward. The startled hypsilophodont tried to run. Moving at *forty-five kilometers per hour*, the deinonychosaurs threw themselves upon the giant creature and attacked it so – each one pounced and latched onto the prey with its four sets of claws. Through quick slashing strokes, the sickle "terror" claws *sliced up* the giant creature's skin – they attacked the way piranhas would but used the claws instead of teeth. Blood was everywhere. The hypsilophodont swung its tail and struck and killed one of the attacking predators. Then it fell over onto another four, crushing all their bones and organs. Like piranhas, the remaining seven sliced up the mighty prey. Mouths opened up; jaws clamped shut; *sharp and pointed teeth* bit into flesh. And when the deinonychosaurs were done, scavengers moved in. And in the end, nothing but the bones were left.

## Chapter IV: A Bouquet for Earth

It was one-hundred-and-thirty-million years ago. And one special magnolia-like plant populated the semi-isolated region of a mountain slope. And it possessed a tiny stalk with *pollen* on the end. And *this* was called a stamen. And a flying insect ate the pollen of the plant. *But not all* the pollen was consumed; some stuck to the insect's legs and body. And this insect flew to another magnolia-like plant to eat. And there it landed near a tiny *sticky* stem of oval modules. And *this* was called a pistil. And the pollen on the insect's body brushed the pistil of the plant. *Plant pollination* by insect-aided fertilization had occurred.[293] No longer did Earth's vegetation need to *depend* so much on water and on wind to reproduce.

---

[293] Insect pollination had taken place previously in the Mesozoic Era for some plants,

And plants with pistils were designated female. And plants with stamen were designated male. As millions of years went by, plants developed *colors, scents and sweet secretions* to attract the flying insects. And plants grew colored petals to protect the pollen from the wind. These *plants* were flowers. Thus Nature, the great artist of the Universe, *gave Earth its first few flowers.*[294]

And implicitly, flowers and flying insects "signed a pact" and "formed a partnership." And this symbiosis would last for tens of millions of years and through *unto this day.*

## Chapter V: A Great Underwater Magma Outflow

And it came to pass that a *giant super-plume* approached Earth's upper mantle in southwestern Panthalassa. As it expanded to a two-thousand-kilometer-sized mushroom-shaped bubble, it melted into molten rock beneath the ocean crust. And millions of years went by. And magma poured through crust, as Earth *bled* at the bottom of the ocean. Magnesium-rich lava flowed over an underwater area two-thirds the size of modern Australia. And for three-million years did magma flow out so. One-third of the Panthalassa Ocean was *black* with minerals and tiny basaltic bits. And aquatic life within the region died. Such *enormous* quantities of lava did pour forth that sea level rose ten meters![295] The lava solidified into *forty-million* cubic kilometers of basaltic rock, while building giant underwater plateaus with volcanos and with mountain ridges. And the Ontong Java Plateau was the name given to the biggest underwater elevated region. And it covered two-million square kilometers. It *would* survive *unto this day.*

And for tens of millions of years thereafter, smaller sporadic magma outbursts would occur.[296] And some volcanos would remain *above the ocean.* And these would be volcanic islands. And others would be flattened by erosion. And coral would build reefs around some such eroded islands. And *these* would be called atolls. And by these means, the islands and the *atolls* of the South Pacific would be built.

## Chapter VI: Activity in the South Atlantic

And it came to pass that a southern region of Gondwana *split apart.* And a *new* sea formed with a mid-sea ridge. There, ocean crust

---

but it was at this stage of geo-history that it began to be fully exploited.

[294] Flowering plants are called *angiosperms*, meaning "seeds borne in a vessel." The earliest angiosperms were trees and small shrubs. Today angiosperms include almost all plants, grasses, shrubs and trees.

[295] So much lava poured out that it would have buried the entire modern continental United States in a five-kilometer-deep layer.

[296] It was fortunate for life that magma bleeding had occurred beneath the sea, for had it occurred on land, the toxic carbonic and sulfuric gases would have suffocated those that breathed air, dramatic climatic changes would have taken place, and the eco-systems of the world would have been in disarray.

spread as the continents were drawn apart. Thus proto-Antarctica edged farther south while the continent containing proto-Africa and proto-South-America moved north. And during millions of years and bit by bit, *like unto* a zipper being pulled apart, the crack between proto-Africa and proto-South-America did open up. And a rift, extending into northern proto-Brazil and proto-Nigeria, gouged the continent.

And as millions of years went by, the rift between the northern halves of proto-South-America and proto-Africa opened up until a *giant sea* emerged between the two. And *this* was the beginning of the South Atlantic Ocean.

And so Gondwana now was gone, having split into *three* continents: South America, Africa, and the continent containing proto-Australia-Antarctica. As the plates containing South America and Africa did drift apart, a *mid-ocean ridge* in the South Atlantic did emerge. And magma flowing from *it* made *new ocean crust*, which spread outward from the ridge. Thus in the South Atlantic, ocean crust *west of the ridge* moved *west*, while ocean crust *east of the ridge* moved *east*. And as South America inched westward, *collisions* with island arcs and *subduction* of the ocean plate along its coast with Panthalassa *produced* the Andes Mountains.

Now the Walvis Hot Spot in the mid-ocean ridge of the South Atlantic produced enormous flows of underwater lava. And this hot spot *uplifted ocean crust*, thereby creating the island of Tristan da Cunha. Now as the ocean floor spread from the ridge, the uplifted crust moved with it. And *this* produced *a trail of underwater mountains* from Tristan da Cunha, both to the east and to the west of it. And this process would continue for the *next one-hundred-million years*. The Rio Grande Rise would be the underwater mountain chain between Tristan da Cunha and South America. And the chain between Tristan da Cunha and Africa *would* be called the Walvis Ridge.

And volcanic and mid-ocean-ridge emissions of carbonic and sulfuric gases made the temperature of Earth increase.[297] And everywhere, from pole to pole, the air was *warm or hot*. And the waters of the oceans also warmed. The hottest climate of the Phanerozoic Eon descended like a burning blanket over Earth. And so it came to pass that the temperature in Celsius on average was *fifteen* degrees above the temperature of modern times. And the tropics extended over more than half the surface of thy planet Earth.

> *The peak temperature and heat*
> *had so been reached.*
> *Henceforth, the temperature would bit by bit decline.*

---

[297] At this time, carbon dioxide levels in air had risen to more than six times those of the Holocene.

## Chapter VII: A Flooded World

*Waters shall rise up out of the north,*
*and there shall be an overflowing flood,*
*and it shall overflow the land and all that is therein.*
*And it was so.*

Now the *temperature difference* between the water at the tropics and the water at the poles *powered* deep sea currents, as it had always done. But compared with other times, the temperature difference between the two was not so great, for Earth was blanketed in greenhouse gas. Thus the deep sea Cretaceous currents were *relatively weak*. And since little oxygen in surface water was transported to the deep, aquatic deep-sea life did suffer from asphyxiation. And many deep-sea organisms disappeared. Thus at the bottom of Earth's seas, white calcium carbonate was relatively rare. Instead, *black carbon-rich* sediments lacking oxygen settled on the ocean floor. And they later lithified and formed black shale. And so it came about that the greatest Phanerozoic deposits of black shale were made.

And it came to pass that the new oceans of the world, the Indian and the Atlantic, grew wider and grew larger, while the ancient ocean of the world, the Panthalassa, *shrank in size*. Now the new oceans were *relatively shallow*, while Panthalassa was *relatively deep*. Thus deep waters were replaced by shallow waters. And this caused water to displace and enter land. And sea level *rose dramatically*, reaching its highest level of the Phanerozoic Eon – Earth's waters were *two-hundred meters higher* than in modern times. And waterways of giant finger-like protrusions did invade the land. And *flooded* were the continents of Earth. And it was so that half of all continental crust was underwater. Water covered more than four-fifths of Earth. And seas *invaded* northern Africa, eastern proto-Australia, the mid-west of proto-North-America and parts of India and South America.

Now ocean currents flowed from the Arctic Circle southward through a trough along the Urals of proto-Russia into the Tethys Sea. And the currents continued westward through the Tethys Sea and then northward through proto-Europe past eastern proto-Greenland to the Arctic Circle. And so these currents formed a *giant circulating flow of water*.

And as the seas eroded land, *much sand* was made. And some sand hardened into sandstone. And for example, the Tethys Sea deposited salt, shale and sandstone in northern Africa. And millions of years later, when the seas retreated, the sandstone rocks would dry and be subjected to erosion by Earth's winds and other forces. And sandstone *would return to sand*: The Sahara Desert would emerge.

Now vegetation grew thick in the *extensive steamy* tropics. And the waters of the flooded lands, as well as marshes, lakes and ponds, did sometimes rise and sometimes did decline. And when waters retreated, vegetation advanced and occupied the land. And when waters advanced, the vegetation drowned, died and decomposed. And the back-and-forth battle of vegetation with aquatic elements produced in places enormous quantities of dead organic matter. And later, some organic matter lithified. Thus *coal* was created in proto-Siberia, proto-Australia, proto-New-Zealand, proto-Mexico and western proto-North-America. And later some of the organic matter was buried, pressurized, lithified and liquefied. And *petroleum* was so produced.[298] And oil in the earth appeared in the Gulf of Mexico, Venezuela, Libya and the proto-Persian-Gulf.

## Chapter VIII: Flowering Plants Branch Out

*Let the Earth bring forth herb.*
*Let the fruit tree yield fruit.*
*And it was so.*
*And this happened on the third day*
*of the first month of a long lost year.*

And the symbiotic partnership of flowering plants and flying insects brought forth fruit. And flowers *spread over land* and into meadows, forests, hills and plains. And there were proto-magnolias and trees with flowers and proto-elms and proto-walnut-trees. And there were proto-figs and plants producing proto-grapes and trees with fruit. Thus Nature gave thy Earth the *World's first fruit*. And there were primitive forms of sycamores, poplars, willows, maples, birches, beeches, plants with berries, oaks and water lilies. And there was sacred vegetation like proto-laurels, proto-jujubes and proto-olive-trees.

And angiosperms spread everywhere. And although the Earth possessed low lying vegetation, there was *no grass*. Now plants survived by all conceivable ways and means. Those that did *drop* their leaves in fall were called deciduous. Those that did *retain* their leaves through winter *were* called evergreens.

Now the new flowering plants provided food for other forms of life. And flying insects, such as bees and moths, proliferated. And herbivorous dinosaurs adapted, acquiring the means to digest the new vegetation.

It would not be until the Cenozoic Era that the grape vine would appear. And one day, its fruit would be compressed, and of its juices *wine be made*. And eventually would come the pomegranate and the fig, the orange and the apple, the pear and the banana. And in the Pleistocene and Holocene, man would come to pick and *eat these fruits*.

And eventually, in many millions of years, the fields of the Earth would contain *grain-producing* crops. And there would be barley, wheat

---

[298] In the Cretaceous, more than half of the Earth's petroleum was created. In the twentieth century, this oil would provide humanity with a relatively cheap energy source.

and corn. And in the Holocene would man make foods and cereals of grains. And someday, the Earth would be full of trees that would be given a particular significance, such as the palm, mulberry, fir, willow, cedar, olive, algum,[299] sycamore and fig. And in the Pleistocene and Holocene, man would walk *among these trees*.

And high above Earth's vegetation, the flying reptiles of the air did battle to survive. And so it came to pass that some pterosaurs grew large.

And in proto-Texas, on one sunny day did a fifteen-meter-wide shadow pass swiftly over land. And suddenly, a small animal did *find itself in shade*. And it went scurrying and disappeared into a hole in earth. And above, in the air did fly a giant pterosaur. And elsewhere on the Earth were giant gliding pterosaurs, which *cast shadows* upon the land, sending tiny creatures running out of fear.

And it came to pass that the toothless *pteranodon* appeared. This pterodacyl had a head *like unto* a crested pelican, wings *like unto* an albatross, and a body *like unto* a bird. Now when it was cold, the metabolism of crawling creatures slowed, and they became lethargic, for such creatures were cold blooded. And slow-moving lizards and large insects were easy prey for pterodacyls. And pterodacyls thrived.

Now it happened that a ceratopian was *eating of* a fern. And the ceratopian *uprooted it* and walked away, dragging it along the ground. Suddenly a coleurosaur with its outstretched claws appeared before the ceratopian. And the startled ceratopian ran off, and *left* the fern *behind*; it lay there on the ground with roots exposed. And weeks went by. And it came to pass that, as the roots took earth, the fern began to grow. And it grew into a *healthy fern*. And at other times, elsewhere on Earth, plants and trees were so replanted. Thus some trees and plants did spread *not* by seeds but chance.

## Chapter IX: Mid-Cretaceaous Ammonoids

And mosasaurs and other ocean reptiles crushed the shells of ammonoids and ate the cephalopods inside. And ammonoids with *weak* shells disappeared. And in the struggle of the fittest, only those that had exotic shells with intriguing shapes and spikes survived. And they became *crown jewels* of the seas – Nature had been their royal architect. Now some ammonoids were long and thin and shaped like needles, while other were shaped like a U, a J, a spiral, or a worm. Still others looked *like unto* corkscrews, hairpins, cones or rods. Thus the seas were full of countless *ornamental* shells. But the ruthless rulers of the seas, the mosasaurs, despite the spikes, did sometimes find a way to crush the shells and eat the fleshy ammonoids inside.

---

[299] Sandalwood.

## Chapter X: Much Continental Drift

And tens of millions of years went by. And it came to pass that Africa was drifting *north and east*. And the western part of the Tethys Sea was getting narrower. The Tethys Sea became a *waterway*.

And it came to be that a piece of western India broke off. And this piece was Madagascar. As India drifted north, Madagascar *would remain behind*. Thus Madagascar stayed off the coast of eastern Africa. And the Mozambique Channel was the name given to the waterway between the two.

And it *happened* that western proto-Australia passed over a hot spot in the Earth's asthenosphere. And for millions of years, the hot spot, *like unto* a blowtorch, carved off a giant piece of land. And several million years went by. And the giant piece of land moved out to sea — it was an island. *New Zealand* was its name.

And proto-North-America edged west. And proto-Eurasia drifted north and east. And proto-Greenland in between was pulled from *both* the east and west. And something had to give. And so it happened that proto-North-America and proto-Greenland *rifted*. And magma flowed between the two. And with time, the rift became a little wider, and water from the North Atlantic Sea *invaded* the western coast of proto-Greenland: The Labrador Sea was made. And the North Atlantic Sea became the North Atlantic Ocean.

And as proto-North-America drifted west, ocean crust created in Panthalassa was subducted and was thrust *under* western proto-North-America, thereby lifting vast amounts of land. And so, *height was added* to the Rocky Mountains from proto-Alaska all the way to proto-Mexico.

And it came to pass that the northwestern shelf of proto-North-America touched the northeastern shelf of proto-Siberia. And the northernmost part of Panthalassa was *closed off*. And a giant water region, centered at the northern pole, was thus created. It was the Arctic Ocean.

And the Panthalassa Ocean, which during the last fifty-million years had shrunk considerably, was now renamed. And the *Pacific Ocean* was its name. And all the modern oceans of the World were there on Earth: the Indian, Atlantic, Arctic and Pacific oceans.

## Chapter XI: Cretaceous Chalk

And coccolithophores flourished in the seas. The oceans seemed overpopulated with these floating bits of algae. And when they died, their fine *limestone casings* settled on the ocean floor, and *chalk* was made. Each year for millions of years in certain places on the Earth, chalk layer after layer was laid down. And thick chalk beds emerged in western proto-Australia, proto-Europe, eastern proto-Russia, southern proto-North-America and southern proto-Scandinavia.

And tens of millions of years later, when seas retreated, some chalk would be *exposed to air* and it would dry. And white cliffs in Calais, France and Dover, England would appear.

## Chapter XII: Late-Cretaceous Dinosaurs

And Earth's new flowering vegetation provided new food for certain dinosaurs. And these plant-eating dinosaurs did flourish. And *these herbivores* became the food for theropods. And so the number of theropods did also grow.

And during many million years, psittacosaur-like ornithischians evolved, some growing round and fat and falling forward on all fours. And such dinosaurs eventually *transformed* into two-meter-long, four-hundred-pound protoceratops and leptoceratops.

Now in proto-Mongolia, a group of *protoceratops* were browsing on some plants and trees – they ate with beak-like mouths, which acted as large pincers, clipping twigs and leaves. Each had a short bone plate around its thick enormous neck. Emerging from each forehead was a *large shield plate*; such plates protected the reptiles' necks and *mammoth heads* – their heads were one-fourth of their body length. Now the *leptoceratops*, the distant cousins of the protoceratops, had somewhat smaller forehead plates, and they dwelt in proto-North-America.

Now like all dinosaurs, protoceratops laid eggs which at birth cracked open into baby dinosaurs. But by chance some eggs remained *unhatched*. And a few such unhatched eggs along with those from other dinosaurs were embedded in the earth. And some petrified and survived the destructive elements of Nature *for sixty-five-million years or more*. And so these unhatched relics remained *unto this day*. And in modern times, they looked *like unto* oval stones in shell chips in the Gobi desert sand and in the dirt at other places on the Earth.

And it came to pass that a few *new* sauropods, such as *titanosaurs*,[300] appeared. And save that their vertebrae were *solid* instead of hollowed out, these heavy giant herbivores were similar to diplodocuses, camarasaurs and "brontosaurs."

And it so happened that, in central proto-Asia, iguanodont-like ornithopods evolved into the *hadrosaurs*, the "duck-billed" dinosaurs. And soon the hadrosaurs diversified and spread to all the corners of thy planet Earth.

In proto-Montana, a *herd* of maiasaura[301] hadrosaurs were browsing. The adults were about nine meters long and must have weighed four tons. With powerful *circular* motions of the upper jaws, their beak-like mouths ground *into a pulp* flowering plants, pine nee-

---

[300] One titanosaur, saltasaurus of South America, was a rare example of a sauropod with bony studs upon its back.

[301] Maiasaura means "good mother lizard."

dles, branches, shrubs and fruits. And one among the herd did yawn. In the rear of the mouth, beyond a pulp of vegetation, were several hundred closely packed enamelled teeth. And in the lower jaw, one tooth was *missing*. And in upper jaw, one tooth was *growing in*. Now using her forearms, one female in the herd scraped the earth into a mound one meter wide and half-a-meter high. And after she had dug some dirt out of the middle of the pile, she moved some twigs and leaves there. Then she sat *upon* the mound. And several other nearby female hadrosaurs were also sitting on round piles of dirt. And beneath one such dinosaur were eggs. Like beads upon a bracelet, the eggs were spaced *evenly* around a circle. And this maiasaura then sat up, and with her hands she spread some leaves and twigs upon the eggs until they *hardly could be seen*. And on all four limbs she walked off to eat some bushes and some plants.

And in proto-Canada another hadrosaur, whose name was ed-montosaurus, had a *thousand* diamond-shaped sharp teeth inside its mouth. And this hadrosaur and others like it used the battery of tightly packed enamel teeth to shred plant matter.

Now evolution "provided" some ornithischians with *strange head shapes*. And for example, some duck-billed dinosaurs grew crests upon their crowns: corythosaurus, hypacrosaurus and lambeosaurus had vertical flat disks, while parasaurolophus had a long curved tube pro-truding backward from its head. Now the crests contained no brain – they were simply chambers filled with fluids and with gas. And when these creatures uttered sounds, the sounds resonated in their crowns, and *foghorn-like notes* among the members of a herd were heard.

Now in proto-Canada there was a group of pachycephalosaurs, most of whom were feeding on the leaves and fruit of forest trees. Each was about three meters long and had a *dome* upon its head made out of bone. And it happened that two males within a group squared off, threatening to bang their heads. The other pachycephalosaurs moved away, as the two males engaged and butted heads.

And it came to pass that nodosaurs evolved – some grew larger; they had spread to all the northern continents and even some had headed south. As in the Early Cretaceous, they were *clothed in bony plates*. And their tail was a bony club with many horns. Now some di-nosaurs acquired stronger plates with spikes and a *ball of bone* at tail's end: These were *ankylosaurids* – another branch in the evolution-ary tree of dinosaurs. And they were tank-like herbivores, which, like the nodosaurs, crawled slowly on all fours. They had bones above their eyes, like ossified eyebrows. And when threatened by a predator, they swung their tail as a club.

And it came to pass that *ceratops* appeared in proto-North-America. They were horned bird-hipped dinosaurs, with heads as the rhinoceroses' and bodies as the elephants'. Centrosaurus, triceratops and torosaurus were examples. *Triceratops*, which had *three horns* upon its face, was the biggest of this group — nine meters long, ten tons; most ceratops were two-thirds this size. Now ceratops *had* large forehead shields and pointed facial horns, of which the biggest could be a meter long.[302] And their huge heads, the largest of any land-living creature, contained beak-like mouths, which were toothless in the front but full of teeth in back.[303]

Now some ceratops were *feeding* on some flowering shrub-like plants similar to modern magnolias, while others were eating the numerous fibrous leaves which had fallen off some palms and other trees. These horned dinosaurs were *robust, round and plump*. They had toes in hoofs, fat legs, tough hide, and strong thick necks. And they crawled along the ground with heads held *low* so that, from the front, only shields and horns were seen. And like knights in armor with lances pointing forward, they advanced.

Now in proto-Mongolia, a female protoceratops was standing near a nest containing eggs. And when it *happened* that a pack of toothless theropods approached and started jumping wildly, she lowered her head and *charged forward* like a bull. Like matadors, the theropods did leap aside. And as *swiftly* as a roadrunner, each raced around the protoceratops and grabbed an egg. And she turned around and charged toward the nest. But the theropods, each with egg in hand, sped off and disappeared into a grove of palms.[304]

And with the passage of time, *new* coelurosaurs evolved. And dromaeosaurs with sickle claws similar to deinonychosaurs appeared in the northern hemisphere.[305] And *it came to be* that one of the most intelligent of dinosaurs emerged: Stenonychosaurus[306] with its *enormous eyes* came out to hunt small animals and reptiles in evening and at night.

And in a vast plain, a group of *ornithomimosaurs* pecked the earth with beaks. But these long-necked, toothless, *ostrich-looking* theropods were not eating seeds — their beaks were picking up squirming crickets, bugs and beetles. Now it happened that one among the ornithomimosaurs spied a tiny animal running quickly like a rat. And this ornithomimosaur sped off and chased the fleeing prey. And running at *fifty-five kilometers per hour*, it overcame the animal and stabbed it with its beak repeatedly until it died. The others then ran over, joined the "feast," and *pecked* the prey to pieces — each

---

[302] Through the battle to survive and reproduce, species of ceratops acquired *horns of many types* and developed different kinds of forehead shields.

[303] Many ornithischians had teeth only in the rear of their mouths.

[304] The name of one dinosaur, oviraptor, means "egg thief." Oviraptor was a toothless coelurosaur similar in shape to deinonychosaur but half its size and without its sickle claw. The first oviraptor specimen uncovered was found clutching an egg.

[305] The dromaeosaurs of the Late Cretaceous were smaller than deinonychosaurs.

[306] Based on brain to body size, it is believed that stenonychosaurus was as intelligent as the modern opossum.

ornithomimosaur raised its small head up and let a piece of meat slide down its throat.

And it happened that a carnosaur evolved, grew larger, dropped a claw[307] and became the *biggest predator* to ever live on Earth. It was *tyrannosaurus rex*, the king of carnivores. And it was fifteen meters long, five meters tall and weighed eight tons.

Now hidden in a dense growth of palms and hardwood trees, a tyrannosaurus was waiting. And its *dangling tiny arms* did hardly budge, nor did it move its partly opened mouth; inside were backward curving pointed teeth, each serrated on the rear side and about the size of railroad bolts. Now it *happened* that a hadrosaur passed by. And the tyrannosaurus *suddenly* lunged out. But the hadrosaur was quick. On its two hind legs it ran away unharmed. Now nearby on the forest floor, insects fed on a mix of flesh, dried blood and bones, for just one week before, the teeth of this self-same tyrannosaurus had bitten into the neck of a parasaurolophus. And so, with their *powerful enormous jaws*, tyrannosaurs attacked any dinosaur regardless of its size. Even giants, such as the "brontosaurs," fell victim to tyrannosaurs.[308]

And ceratops, tyrannosaurs and hadrosaurs were just some of the *many kinds* of dinosaurs that thundered as they walked the Late-Cretaceous lands of Earth.

## Chapter XIII: The Hot Spot Pele

And it came to pass that there was a *hot spot* in the upper mantle of the northwest Pacific Ocean. And the hot spot was called *Pele*, after the fiery-eyed goddess of volcanos. And during thousands of years, Pele melted mantle thereby creating magma. And the magma *pushed up through* the crust and made an underwater mountain, which then rose above the ocean as an island. And the island was called Meiji. And millions of years went by. And the ocean crust in the Pacific moved mostly north and somewhat to the west. And eruptions from the Pele hot spot suddenly occurred *again*. And another Pacific island rose above the sea. And during the next ten-million years, Pele, *like unto* a blowtorch, scorched the ocean crust. And a ridge of islands formed.

---

[307] During the Mesozoic Era, there was a slight evolutionary tendency for some groups of dinosaurs to drop digits. The proto-coelurosaurs had *four or five fingers*, but by the Middle Jurassic the hands of coelurosaurs had *three claws*, although the chicken-sized campsognathus had only two. Among the carnosaurs, most had *three claws* on a hand. Exceptions were ceratosaurus and a few early megalosaurs that had four and the tyrannosaurs, which appeared in the Late Cretaceous – they had *two*. The ancestry stock of ornithopods had *five toes*. By the Jurassic Period, their feet had only *four*, and the inner toe was short. In the Cretaceous, most had *three toes* on their hind feet and some had only two. The evolutionary pattern of losing digits would be repeated in the Cenozoic Era with the ungulate mammals.

[308] Tyrannosaurus was the most ferocious predatory to ever terrify the Earth – it made the shark look like a swan; it made the lion look like a lamb. No other predator would be more powerful.

# Chapter XIV: The Deccan Traps

*And there arose a smoke out of the pit,
as the smoke of a great furnace,
and the air and the Sun were darkened
by reason of the smoke in the pit.*

Now the Cretaceous was coming to an end. And India was still in the southern hemisphere but heading north. And it so happened that India passed over a *hot spot* in the lithosphere, below which, there was a mantle plume. And magma pushed up through the lithosphere. And lava did flow lavishly *over* western-central India.

And during the next few hundred-thousand years, lava flows erupted *on and off*. Now the first lava flow formed one basaltic layer of rock. And the next burst poured *upon the first*, creating one more layer. And as tens of thousands of years went by, the lava flows occurred *repeatedly*. Each flow spread out upon one-hundred-thousand square kilometers of land; each produced several thousand cubic kilometers of rock; and each burst built a layer that was tens-of-meters thick. And *layer upon layer* of lava did solidify. And in the end, the lava covered two-million square kilometers of land and occupied two-million cubic kilometers of space. In places, the basaltic rock was more than two-thousand meters thick. And this rock formation was provided with a name. And the name was *Deccan Traps*, which means the "southern staircase."

Now when the Deccan Traps erupted, dust and ash rose up and formed dark clouds, which engulfed the Earth and blocked the Sun. And a *darkness* was upon the face of Earth. And the temperature of Earth did drop by five degrees.

And enormous quantities of toxic gases were released into the atmosphere.[309] And for hundreds of thousands of years, haze surrounded Earth.

And iron bits in lava aligned themselves with Earth's magnetic fields. And the lava froze and fixed the iron filings *firm in place*. But sometimes the currents in the liquid core of Earth reversed so that the north magnetic pole became the south magnetic pole, while the south became the north. And this was a *polarity reversal* of Earth's magnetic field. And this has happened ever since thy planet Earth has had magnetic fields. This has happened quite irregularly. But at seventy-million years BC, roughly every million years, the polarity reversed. And like magnetic tape, the lava in the Deccan Traps made a *record* of reversals.[310]

---

[309] The emissions from eruptions gave off *sixty-trillion* kilograms of chlorine and of fluorine, *six-thousand-trillion* kilograms of sulfur compounds and *thirty-thousand-trillion* kilograms of $CO_2$ into the lower atmosphere.

[310] In modern times, geologists would inspect basaltic rock and would see the *message* that had been recorded of Earth's magnetic field. Doing this for the Deccan Traps, they

And the Deccan Traps created *chaos* for the ecosystems of the Earth. And bad air, poor sunlight and fluctuating temperatures made it *difficult* for life. But life went on.

## Chapter XV: Late-Cretaceous Life

It had once been a proto-loon. Now it had grown so large and awkward that it failed to fly. It was *hesperornis*. And on a shallow marsh in proto-Kansas, it was paddling with its large webbed feet. The two-meter-long creature used its *feathers* to *float* instead of fly. Suddenly it darted forward and plunged its head into the water. Flapping its feet, it dived below the surface. And deep below, it bit a fish with its sharp, backward-oriented teeth.

And as time advanced, some huge hesperornises evolved, of which the largest was *five meters long*. And there appeared another water fowl, which could not fly and mainly fed on fish. One smaller one was named baptornis.

And it came to pass that floating on the waters of Earth's offshore seas were birds that looked like modern gulls. And unlike baptornis and hesperornis, these birds could fly as well as float.

Now the earliest mammals, the tricondonts had perished. They had been replaced by *plant-eating* squirrel-like and mouse-like animals. Their incisor teeth were able to slice open fruit and seeds. Now most *egg-laying* mammals would by the end of the Eocene die out. However, some species would survive *unto this day*. And they would be the spiny anteater and the duck-billed platypus.

Now among mammals, a revolution in reproduction had occurred: *giving birth to live offspring*. And *marsupials* in proto-North-America, which looked like small opossums, produced their young in relatively *undeveloped states*. And with much care, a mother kept them in a body pouch till *they* were ready for the wild. And during millions of years, marsupials spread from proto-North-America to South America.

And in proto-Asia, a shrew-like mammal with a bulging belly was sniffing in some vegetation with her upturned nose. Then her large eyes spied a worm. And she lashed out at it and caught it with her long incisor teeth.

Fifteen minutes later, she burrowed into some weed-like vegetation and gave birth. She licked away the mucus from the newborn and then suckled it. And *she* was a *placental*:[311] Her newborn, which had

---

would know when lava flowed. And they would read the rock for *other* lava flows of other times in geo-history, as well as for the magma emerging from mid-ocean ridges. And by these means, geologists would know when lavas flowed. Now when lava poured out at the *equator*, the iron filings oriented *horizontally*. On the other hand, when lava poured out at a north pole or a south pole, the iron filings oriented *vertically*. Thus the *angle* of the iron filings indicated *latitude*. And by these means, geologists would know the latitude of lava flows.

[311] In the Cenozoic Era, the placentals – animals reproducing with a uterus – would make up the majority of mammals, including man.

developed in her *womb*, was just like her but smaller as far as body features were concerned.

And another shrew-like placental mammal dwelt in trees and ate the insects there. Its brain was relatively large. And in the forests, rodent-like mammals scavenged seeds and nuts. And they were joined by *insectivores*, such as proto-shrews and proto-moles. Elsewhere, a few mammals had developed hoofs on toes.

And so small populations of egg-laying, placental and marsupial mammals were everywhere on Earth. And thus it came to pass that the World began to have a mix of *different* types of mammals.

And snakes slithered through fields, climbed trees and swam *like unto* eels in marshes, ponds and lakes. And amphibious turtles paddled in the seas and waddled on reed-ridden sandy shores.

And the world was full of life.[312] Evolution had designed it all. Nature had been the *master architect*. But forces in the cosmos would soon take most of it away.

*(And a voice spake, saying,*
*"He built his house upon the sand.*
*And the rain descended, and the floods came,*
*and the wind blew and beat upon the house,*
*till it so fell.")*

## Chapter XVI: Nature's Holocaust

*A star shall fall from Heaven.*

There was a star glowing in the heavens *brighter* than the planet Venus. But it was *not* a star of hope. Indeed, it was not a star at all.

And it came to pass that a ten-kilometer-sized asteroid sped through the wilderness of outer space near *thy planet Earth*. And the asteroid was *drawn* to it by the strong pull of gravity. And it was *as if* the hand of Nature led it so. The asteroid pierced Earth's upper atmosphere. And it grew hot and *glowed*. And from the ground on Earth, animals looked up and saw a midnight sun moving through the sky at night. And the giant object descended through the atmosphere at *twenty-five-kilometers per second* and blew a hole in it. And air burned and made nitrous oxide from oxygen and nitrogen. The animals of Earth heard a sissing sound – it was the sirens of the heavens. And it was *as if* the Judgement Day had come.

And the midnight sun grew bigger and grew brighter.

And a segment of the asteroid broke off. That piece smashed proto-Manson, Iowa. The main part struck the western Gulf of Mexico near proto-Yucatán. And there was a fireball explosion of *one-hundred-*

---

[312] The creatures mentioned in this Book of *The Cretaceous* are just a fraction of the countless creatures that dwelt on Earth at that time.

*million megatons.*[313] And when the asteroid struck the ocean floor, crust melted into molten rock, and an upheaval of magma, vapor, rock debris and water shot up. *Eight-kilometer-tall* waves sped out. And the ground *shook so violently* in proto-North-America and South America that trees were uprooted and plants were tossed into the air. And dinosaurs, reptiles and large land creatures lost their footing and fell over. And small animals flew through the air and landed on their backs.

Now at the impact, a cloud of water vapor, dust and ash shot up. And some of it sped out beyond the upper atmosphere and into outer space. The rest remained and made a *giant cloud*. Shocked quartz was sprayed all over the Americas. And little basaltic balls like bullets *rained down on Earth*. And below the cloud and rain of pellets, lava flowed lavishly over parts of proto-Mexico.

A crater two-hundred-kilometers in diameter had been created in the crust underneath the sea and in the Gulf of Mexico.

And no living organism, no microbe within five-hundred kilometers of the impact was alive – all life within this region had been instantly *incinerated* by the blast. The flesh of all the animals had turned to crisp and ash – this was *Nature's holocaust*.

And shock waves travelled through the mantle of the Earth and bounced off the outer and the inner core. Earthquakes occurred around the globe. And the Deccan Traps on the other side of Earth ignited and they *spit out flames*.

*The wrath of Nature was upon the face of Earth.*

And red ashes and bits of glowing rock rained down on proto-Mexico. They ignited plants and trees. And *angry fires* raged in proto-Mexico. And vegetation fueled the flames which flickered *like unto* huge red tongues reaching for the heavens. And one-million-square kilometers of plains and forests burned. Then the fires *spread* to proto-Texas, proto-Belize and proto-Guatemala. Behind the flames were charred wood, charred leaves and charcoal.

And there was panic among Earth's creatures in the region. The slower animals were *overrun by flames* and instantly cremated. The fastest creatures fled the flames, but found themselves surrounded soon by fire and by heat. And air was *full of smoke*. And all animals, small and large, slow and fast, which did not die by burning, choked. The animals fell over, struggled on the ground for several minutes and then were *motionless*.

And several kilometer-sized waves travelled seven times around the globe. And for seven days, the oceans rose and fell. And continents were *flooded* and were *drained*. And ocean life was tossed about *like unto* salad in a bowl. And many shellfish, marine reptiles, sponges,

---

[313] This is equivalent to ten-thousand times the explosive power of the world's stockpile of nuclear warheads at the time of the 1980's.

plankton, algae, fish and ocean organisms found themselves on land and died.

And magma spurted from the Deccan Traps in India. And a *cloud* of ash and gas two-thousand kilometers in size did hover there. And lava flowed on top of lava. And lava ignited forests to the north and east. And as in proto-Central-America, a *ring of fire* ranged outward, burning vegetation in its path. And flames spread rapidly *as if* transported by horses and by chariots. And heat incinerated creatures living on the continent of India. The flames raised their heads and hands to heaven and *quivered* with the fear of hell.

Now the air in southern proto-North-America and in northern South America was *black* and full of particles. Visibility was half a meter. And as living creatures breathed in soot, they coughed and choked, and their lungs *filled up* with dirt and smoke. They toppled to the ground and died.

And ants and other insects had a feast feeding on the dead.

And clouds of dust, meteorite debris, water vapor, smoke and ash spread *around the globe*. And asteroid dust and ash relatively rich in iridium settled on the Earth. And the atmosphere was full of particles and soot. And all around the world, the largest creatures suffocated so. And Earth's environment was ruined. And as for creatures, being big was suddenly a big big disadvantage.

And large pieces of atmospheric fallout rubbed against the molecules of air, became incandescent and *caught fire*. It was *as if* fireworks were everywhere around the globe. And incandescent pieces landed in the trees, setting them *ablaze*. And half the forests of the world were trees of flames. And hell was *upon the face of Earth*. And smoke added to the black of an already black black atmosphere.

And soon the Sun was no longer visible from Earth – a *curtain of darkness* had descended on thy Earth. And during the next day, it was night. And during the day after, it *was* still night. Indeed, for the next nine months, it would be night. And being robbed of light, plants *no longer* photosynthesized. And many plants thus died. And bacteria and microorganisms *multiplied profusely* in decaying bio-matter.

On the surface of the oceans and the seas, algae succumbed and formed a scum. Oceans stank. And inland, swamps and marshes turned *green, then brown*. And they too gave off a putrid stink. And plankton-feeding fish and water-life feasted on the dead remains. But for many, it *was* but their last supper.

And the surviving small herbivores on land ate decaying plants and trees. And these creatures feasted *as if* without a worry.

And nitrous oxide in the atmosphere mixed with water and made nitric acid. Then clouds let loose their rain. And it rained an *acid rain*. And although the rain washed away some smoke and soot, when it landed on the leaves of plants and trees, the acid ate into organic matter. And leaves of plants and trees had *holes*. And when rain landed on the shellfish on the sandy beaches, the shells dissolved and disappeared. And the worm-like creatures living in the shells were *exposed* to Nature's elements and to hungry seashore birds.

And a month went by. And still darkness reigned on Earth. And weed-like plants turned *yellow*. And withered were the leaves of trees. And plants grew weak and stems bent over, *as if to pray*.

In the tropics, the temperature went down. And in the polar regions, the temperature went up somewhat. But overall, the Earth began to cool. And several months went by. And trees in forests *fell*. And in Earth's seas, bacteria and microorganisms consumed the dead remains of photosynthetic plankton. And plankton-feeding fish and shellfish died. *Dead fish* floated on the surface of the oceans and the seas. And marine predators fed on the dead. And they feasted *as if* without a worry. But for many, it *was* but their last supper.

And some dead fish and shellfish washed up *onto* sandy shores. And small amphibians, reptiles and mammals, which had survived the first wave of Nature's holocaust, *feasted on the dead*.

And the living ate the dead until the dead were gone. And then the living starved. And some of them grew weak and passed away. And those that did survive ate those that had just died.

Thus the four elements – fire, water, air and earth – inflicted death upon the living of the Earth. And summer came. But summer was *without the Sun* – it was as cold as in December. And two years of winter would so follow. And emissions from the Deccan Traps raged on and filled the air with sulfur compounds, carbon monoxide, carbon dioxide and other *toxic* gases. And the gases combined with water vapor in the atmosphere and formed sulfuric and carbonic acids. And when it rained, it rained an *acid* rain.

And several months went by. And the temperature in the tropics *dropped*. And on the continents, cold-blooded creatures such as insects, reptiles, worms, amphibians and other animals became *lethargic*, for their metabolism dropped. And beetles crawled more *slowly*. And worms *barely budged* in earth. And lizards, snakes, frogs and salamanders *seemed asleep*. But warm-blooded creatures, such as birds and mammals, were more active. And they ate slowly moving bugs and worms. Some placentals fed on small lethargic frogs and snakes. And on reptiles such as baby lizards, other mammals ate.

And from the heavens fell the acid rains and washed away some soot. And the rain collected in the ponds and lakes. And the *waters* of some pools became acidic. And the acid *burned* the skin of fish and other water life. And some fish bled. Some turned blue and red and white. And in small ponds, many fish were dead.

And *darkness* was upon the face of Earth. And the temperature of air declined. And water in the lakes in non-tropic regions turned to *ice*. And salamanders, small aquatic reptiles, frogs and fish froze in ice. And animals north of the tropic of Cancer and south of the tropic of

Capricorn were cold. And both warm- and cold-blooded creatures *succumbed to cold* and died.

At first, it had seemed as if the world were going to end in fire. Now it seemed as if the world would end in ice. And it was a nightmare for all life, as night lasted for nine months.

And rain fell steadily for another month, washing away the atmospheric particles and dust. And behold, in one cloud appeared a hole. Through it did *sunbeams stream* – they looked like the light from heaven streaming through a window in a church.

Now the death toll was enormous – *four-fifths* of the species of pre-existing plants and animals had gone extinct. And in a layer of earth, the dead were buried so.[314]

> *Another mass extinction had come and gone so fast.*
> *Another group of creatures had perished in the past.*

## Chapter XVII: The Survivors

And although all ammonoids had died, a few nautiloids *survived*. And amphibians, using both water and land to their advantage, faired relatively well. And so did snakes and turtles. And some freshwater life in large lakes did survive. And *deep-sea* ocean organisms mostly were *unscathed*. And the *small* did better than the big. And this was true from the giant reptiles to the tiny protozoa. And for example, the protozoa, which lived on, were one-tenth the size of Jurassic protozoa. And no land animal more than twenty-five kilograms survived.

## Chapter XVIII: On Catastrophes and Evolution

Now most of bio-history had been *without catastrophes*. In such times, evolution had responded well to regular, continuous and slowly changing situations. The creatures of the world had played the game of life; they had *obeyed* the rules of evolution; and they had *followed* the laws of Nature. They had been rewarded so. The rules *had* for years been fixed, or so it seemed.

---

[314] The death list read as follows.
(i) Dinosaurs: all dead – just bones, fossils and charred remains.
(ii) Nature's earliest flying machine, the pterosaurs: all extinct.
(iii) One-fifth of lizard species: gone.
(iv) Marine reptiles, such as ichthyosaurs, mosasaurs and plesiosaurs: forgotten pages in books on natural history.
(v) One-forth of crocodiles: dead; a few would end up as paleontologists' cabinet pieces.
(vi) Ninety percent of plankton species: extinguished from the face of Earth.
(vii) Ninety-nine percent of foraminiferan protozoa: disappeared.
(viii) Chalk-producing coccolithophore algae: decimated.
(ix) All reef-making rudists: gone forever.
(x) Many bivalve mollusks: extinct.
(xi) Shallow-marine sea life such as bryozoans, gastropods and echinoderms: decimated.
(xii) One-fifth of the coral species: decaying defunct treasures.
(xiii) Ammonoids, the sea clocks of the oceans: all relics of the past.
(xiv) The belemnites, the swimming shells containing squid-like cephalopods: all dead.

And then at random instances in geo-history, the *mighty* force of Nature's hand came pounding down on Earth. Roughly every fifty-million years, a catastrophe *struck Earth* – an asteroid, a sudden change in temperature, a burst of widespread vulcanism, a sudden rise or drop in ocean level, or a ruthless, selfish, cruel and dominating creature. At such *cataclysmic* periods, the game board was knocked off the table. And the pieces were scattered on the floor. And Earth's creatures had to play on, even without pieces, boards or rules. And during such tormented times, the game was not a game of strategy, action and re-action as in chess – the game became a game of chance, *like dice*. And even rule-abiding creatures with well-established niches went extinct. And it was as if Evolution cast lots to decide who would *live* and who would *die* and who would *rule*. So catastrophes, though rare and random, had a *haphazard* consequence for evolution.

And after such events, the pieces were picked up. New players were called in. The game began anew.

## Chapter XIX: Dinosaurs and Man

### *Can these bones live?*

The Cretaceous Period was over. The story of the living dinosaur had ended. And all that was left of dinosaurs were *bones*. And some bones survived the next sixty-five-million years of burial, erosion and uplift. And for example, the Morrison Formation in the western proto-United-States would contain seventy species of dinosaur remains. And many bones would be buried in Dinosaur Provincial Park of Alberta, Canada and in the Gobi Desert of Mongolia and China. And many of the remains and bones would survive *unto this day*. And they would be uncovered in digs by paleontologists. So tyrannosaurus, triceratops, stegosaurus and apatosaurus would survive – not as living creatures but as famous museum pieces.[315]

### *The resurrection of dry bones.*

---

[315] Man's fascination with the dinosaurs would go beyond paleontological digs. In modern times, movies would be made about dinosaurs. A few parks with bones and footprints would be set apart. Museums of natural history would be filled with all types of giant skeletons. Visitors would come and stare in awe.

Man in modern times would be fascinated by the dinosaur, a creature that dominated Earth for one-hundred-million years and more. In contrast, man to date has dominated Earth for just ten-thousand years. But man's search for understanding of the dinosaur goes beyond mere curiosity, for the story of the dinosaur raises important questions for mankind – questions such as, Will the human race, like the dinosaurs, be erased? Will there be another collision with an asteroid that will wipe out all higher forms of life? Or will it be a new disease, climatic change or war? If not, will humans be successful like the dinosaur and live a hundred-million years or more?

In modern times, evolutionists and philosophers would come to realize that bigger was not always better. And most numerous was not necessarily best. So maybe smarter is not better either. And evolutionists and philosophers would question which biological assets have true lasting value. Will Nature's experiment in creatures with intelligence bear fruit? Or will it be that the human being is too intelligent for its well-being?

*The third tome of the trilogy of geo-history, called*

# The Cenozoic Era

*And new rulers came to rule.*

## Introduction

*And they were given a plot of land –
it was the lot of their inheritance.*

It was sixty-five-million years ago. The dinosaurs were gone. And the Cenozoic Era, which means "recent life," began. And the Cenozoic would last to modern times. And thy planet Earth, like a middle-aged adult, matured.

And the Cenozoic would be divided into *three* periods: the Paleogene, the Neogene and the Quaternary. Now the Paleogene would take place between sixty-five-million years BC and twenty-four-million years BC. The Neogene would span the period from twenty-four-million years BC to one-million-and-six-hundred-thousand years BC. And the Quaternary would be the most recent and the rest. Together the Paleogene and Neogene would be called the Tertiary Period. And the Paleogene would have three epochs: the Paleocene, the Eocene and the Oligocene, lasting respectively for eight, twenty and thirteen million years. Now the Neogene would have two epochs: the Miocene and Pliocene. And they would last respectively for nineteen and four million years. And the Quaternary would have two epochs: the Pleistocene and Holocene. The Pleistocene would be the first epoch of the Quaternary, while the *Holocene* would constitute the last ten-thousand years of history *and* include the present. And the Holocene would have another name: the *Recent*.

Now Earth's collision with the asteroid was logged in a *layer of earth*, a page of a paleontologist's record book. This layer was called the *KT boundary*, for KT stood for Cretaceous-Tertiary.

And one year went by. And rains *washed away* atmospheric dust, debris and smoke. And days were mostly *overcast*, but the Sun sometimes did shine. And the temperature of Earth began to climb. And greenhouse gases, such as water vapor and carbon dioxide, in the higher atmosphere did trap Earth's heat beneath.

And a dozen years went by. The temperature of Earth had *risen*. And the ice on ponds and lakes in the upper northern hemisphere and in the lower southern hemisphere *returned to water*. And steam rose in the tropics, as that region got quite hot.

*The "real estate" of Earth was left in ruins
but was there for the taking.*

And life began to *rebound*. Unburnt seeds of flowering plants produced green shoots. And new small trees shot up among the charred remains of forests. And ground hugging vegetation began to paint the earth *a green* again. And some lizards, snakes and crocodiles crawled through the ashes and the newly forming proto-grasses.[316] And mammals, all of whom were small, did multiply. Birds made nests in old dead wood. And fish and other forms of water life begot new generations, which then spread into unpopulated waters of the oceans, seas and lakes.

*The meek had inherited the Earth.*

And so Life's vertebrates began to take control of habitats. Amphibians, reptiles, mammals, birds and fish – all relatively small in size – had become the heirs of Earth. And there were *fowls* in the heavens, *fishes* in the seas and *animals* on land.

Now the Deccan Traps continued pouring forth red lava. And *sulfuric and carbonic gases* escaped from "bloody cracks" in India. And such emissions kept the Earth supplied with greenhouse gas. And Earth grew very *warm* – on average, the temperature in Celsius was twelve degrees above the temperature of modern times.

Now it would take two-hundred-thousand years for temperatures to "normalize." But even then, it would be ten degrees hotter than in the Holocene, for normal temperatures in the Paleocene were high.

And the level of the sea was *two-hundred meters higher* than in the Holocene. And during the Cenozoic Era, Earth's waters would recede. And on average, sea level would go *down*.

Now the few foraminifera, which had survived the catastrophic asteroid collision, multiplied. And foraminiferan protozoa made a remarkably recovery, increasing *enormously in number and in kind*.

And flowers flourished, for flying insects were abundant and dead plants made good soil. Seeds caught the winds and travelled to *new territory*. And flowering plants and trees did spread around the World, becoming the *most abundant form* of plants on land.

And it came to pass that bony fish did multiply in number and *diversify in kind*, many obtaining the shapes and forms of fish today. These bony fish prevailed among aquatic vertebrates.

And coral made a *comeback* from the asteroid catastrophe. And new types appeared, and the construction of large reefs resumed. So coral started making *great majestic structures* once again. And these underwater architects would work relentlessly *unto this day*. The modern oceans of thy World would thus abound with colored reefs. And the most renowned, the thousand-seven-hundred-kilometer-long Great Barrier Reef in the Coral Sea off Australia's northeast coast, would be built, beginning in the Paleocene. And this *multicolored temple* would survive *unto this day*.

---

[316] Here, "proto-grass" means low growth vegetation.

*The first book of the Cenozoic, called*

# The Paleocene

## Chapter I: Mammals Multiply

*And it was commanded that*
*the female should give birth in travail*
*and feed her young from her own breast.*

It was sixty-five-million years ago. The Paleocene began. And it came to pass that mammals diversified into *many different* species. Some mammals ate of other forms of food, such as insects, eggs and fruits. Some ate the meat of smaller mammals, birds, and lizards. And these carnivores had furry elongated bodies of the form of modern weasels. And in the trees of tropical swamp forests, from branch to branch they scampered, much as modern squirrels do. On four short legs they sometimes crawled to outer limbs, while their bushy tails did trail behind and the branches of the trees waved *up and down.*

And it happened that a marsupial gave birth to tiny newborn offspring. And the mother placed the weak and undeveloped infants in her *body pouch.* There, they sipped the warm milk of her breasts. And it was *as if* the infants were still fetuses, for they continued to develop as if her pouch was an *external second womb.* And for many months, the mother nurtured them. And elsewhere in the fields and woods of the Americas did marsupials give birth. And as millions of year went by, their numbers multiplied.

And in South America, there were *flesh-eating marsupials*, which looked *like unto* wolves, *except* that they were smaller. And many marsupials dwelt in the continent of proto-Antarctica-Australia. Now during the Oligocene, their numbers would increase dramatically. And there would be forms like the present-day squirrel, fox, rat, hare, mole, mouse and bear. And tens of millions of years thereafter, these creatures would become kangaroos, wallabies, Tasmanian devils, koalas and opossums. And they would survive *unto this day.*

And some mammalian insectivores of the Late Cretaceous *achieved* large eyes and cone-like snouts. And their bodies *were like* those of small modern squirrels. And they were *the first tree shrews.* They dwelt in trees and fed on bits of fruit, on caterpillars and on beetles. Now another group of the insectivores grew needle fur. And these hedgehog-like animals hid during day, when there was light. And they came *out at night* to feed on worms, beetles, bugs and crawling insects and on small lizards, frogs and mice.

And in proto-North-America, a primitive primate dwelt. And its name was purgatorius. And one day, it was struck by a random falling rock and died. And it left behind a molar tooth, which happened to survive *unto this day*.[317]

And at this time in geo-history, Earth had many egg-laying mammals, most of whom were rodent-like. And for example, ptilodus, which looked like a squirrel with a lengthy tail, scampered among the trees in search of nuts and seeds, which it cracked open with its two pairs of large and blade-like teeth.

And the ancestors of the *ungulates* emerged.[318] They were the *condylarths*. And at this time in geo-history, they dwelt in proto-North-America and looked like furry dogs with long prehensile tails. When predators drew near, they could escape by climbing trees. They sniffed the earth for insects, small animals or fruit. Other "archaic ungulates" assumed the forms of small hyenas, wolves or bears. And most were omnivores.

## Chapter II: Birds Evolve

*Let the fowl multiply. And it was so.*
*And this happened on the fifth day*
*of the first month of a long lost year.*

And it came to pass that proto-flamingos, proto-storks and proto-herons became flamingos, storks and herons. And primitive versions of birds of prey, such as falcons, vultures, condors, secretary birds and hawks, appeared. And these birds were just some of the *countless birds* that flew the skies of Earth.

Now the *largest* Paleocene bird was diatryma, a predator that lived in the continents of the northern hemisphere. And diatryma had a strong hooked beak, stood two meters tall but could not fly.

And it happened that a small mammal died. And in an open field, its carcass lay. And half-a-dozen primitive forms of vultures soon descended. They clawed and pecked the flesh. And when they flew off, only *bones* were left.

And primitive pelicans and gulls occupied the coastal lands. And offshore, a pelican did dive into the ocean waters and did catch a small fish in its *basket beak*. And other pelicans dove and did the same. And meanwhile, gulls pecked at shrimp and small shellfish which had washed up on the beach.

## Chapter III: The Late Paleocene

And mammals continued to evolve. And one new creature grew a membrane of thick skin between its neck and hands. And in a cypress forest, it leaped from tree to tree. Once airborne, it spread its

---

[317] In Montana during modern times, a paleontologist picked up the tooth and realized it was from a primate. Purgatorius was probably the first primate.

[318] Ungulate means "hoofed animal."

arms and glided through the air. And elsewhere among Earth's trees did primitive forms of *flying lemurs* dwell.

Now some furry mammals in proto-Mongolia *developed* large ears, short tails and two pairs of upper-jaw incisor teeth. And these small creatures were primitive forms of rabbits, hares and pikas.[319] And on strong hind legs, they *hopped about* among the bushes and the trees.

And some archaic mammals in South America and proto-North-America grew as *big* as modern rhinos – they were the largest mammals at this time, and they were ungulates. The *uintatheres* were saber-toothed and had small horns upon their head, while the coryphodonts dwelt in swamps and marshes where they fed by uprooting plants with their small tusks.

Now in proto-France, a primate emerged that looked like a larger version of a modern squirrel. And its long toes and fingers, which happened to be clawed, curled around the branches of a tree. It moved about almost the way that modern monkeys do. And plesiadapis, as it was known, was not alone: Earth had many primates of this kind, dwelling in the trees of proto North America and Europe.

And it happened that the first *edentates* came about. In modern times, their descendants would include the anteater, sloth and armadillo. But at this time in geo-history, they looked like small foxes with elongated snouts. And they had *lost all their teeth* except the canines *in the front*, but *in the back* they had horny pads instead. They clawed the earth in search of insects buried in the soil. And to avoid Earth's predators, they spent endless hours hiding underground in burrows.

And edentates, proto-flying-lemurs, primates, proto-hares, marsupials, insectivores, uintatheres and condylarths were just some of the *many mammals* that occupied the lands of Earth.[320]

And it had come to pass that the first few blades of grass had just appeared. Finally had Earth its *first green grass*. And the wind blew through the blades *as though* someone there were blowing them.

Now the Paleocene was coming to its end. And it came to pass that as proto-Greenland began to edge *away* from proto-Europe, the continental crust between the two did *crack*. And a hot spot in the mantle fed magma to the region. And great amounts of lava flowed, as Earth was *ripped apart*. And volcanos popped up northwest of proto-Norway, on the eastern coast of proto-Greenland in the proto-British-Isles. From now until the Early Eocene, two-million cubic kilometers of

---

[319] And pikas are small-eared mouse-like rabbits without tails.

[320] In modern times, paleontologists would classify extinct mammals from their teeth in fossils. From this information, paleontologists would realize that in the Paleocene there were rodent-like plant-eating *taeniodonts* and meter-sized bear-like *tillodonts* and even larger more ancient flesh-eating creatures called *creodonts*. The suffix "dont" is used in the names because "dont" means tooth in Greek.

lava would solidify on top of land. And another eight-million cubic kilometers would flow inside the Earth and cool into basaltic rock.[321]

And during millions of years, it came to pass that proto-Australia drifted north and pulled *away* from proto-Antarctica, leaving it behind. Thus *two* new continents were formed from one: Between the Indian and Pacific oceans was Australia; in the Antarctic Circle was Antarctica.

And *currents* in the Tethys Seaway freely flowed from east to west. They started in the West Pacific Ocean and passed between India and southern proto-Asia till they reached the northern Indian Ocean. Then the currents continued westward, flowing between southern proto-Europe and northern proto-Africa, and finally spilling into the East Atlantic Ocean.

And waters *flowed* back and forth between the Atlantic and Pacific oceans through the Panamanian Seaway, for proto-North-America and South America were *separated*. And throughout most of the Tertiary Period, this would be the case: South America would be a giant island continent in the southern hemisphere. And as for proto-Panama, it *would* be underwater.

---

[321] In all, so much basaltic rock was made that, if it were placed uniformly over the United States, it would have covered it to a thickness of a thousand meters.

*The second book of the Cenozoic, called*

# The Eocene

*And so the kingdom of the mammals was established.*

## Chapter I: Mammals Evolve

It was fifty-seven-million years ago. The Eocene began. And it came to pass that certain *archaic* mammals died. And *new* species took their place. And mammals multiplied. And a great diversity of forms appeared. And many had *increased in size*. And the mammal became the dominant land animal – the *golden age for mammals* had arrived.

And beneath the shadow of a tree, three rodents gnawed relentlessly. And one gnawed tree bark, one gnawed a bone, and one gnawed some nuts. They were doing this to wear down teeth, for their incisors grew continuously. And one rodent opened up its mouth. And its incisor teeth – one pair on the lower jaw and one pair on top – indeed were *long and sharp*. Now nearby, a mammalian carnivore, which was hiding in an underbrush, inched forward. And the three rodents heard a sound and scurried into burrows. And inside one such burrow was a litter of screeching baby rodents.

And in proto-North-America and proto-Europe, the number of *different* types of rodents increased enormously. And in these lands did dwell primitive versions of squirrels, beavers, mice and rats.

And through environmental pressures and the survival of the fittest did one mammal, named icaronycteris, develop *webs* for wings. And it was *Earth's first bat*. Eventually, its descendants would fly better than most birds. And soon it came to pass that many like icaronycteris did fly the skies of Earth. And they had heads *like unto* rats, foxes, bulldogs, donkeys, pigs and cats, except their heads were small. And during day, they slept together in communities in trees and caves and in the crevices of cliffs. And during night, they flew frantically about and fed on flying insects. And eventually, to navigate, they would learn to echo ultra-sounds off objects.

And in shallow seas, some mammals waded through *Earth's waters* trying to catch fish. And although several were quite bulky, buoyancy did help support their heavy frames. And during millions of years, their limbs became more flipper-like.

And it came about that archaic forms of ungulates evolved. And Earth had artiodactyls, perissodactyls and notoungulates. Now at this time, ungulates had *five-toed hoofs*, and they ate leaves of small plants and bushes but not the blades of grass, for grass was rare, having just appeared on Earth. Many ungulates had tails, which could be seen swinging back and forth.

Now *notoungulates* dwelt in South America. The smaller ones were similar to rabbits but had hoofs, while the larger ones were horse-like or were hog-like but had *fur* like that of modern bears. In the Oligocene, notoungulates would flourish, with rhinoceros-like and bear-like forms appearing. And they would still be quite abundant in the Miocene, but thereafter, their numbers *would* diminish. And after the Great American Mammal Battle of the Pliocene, they would perish in the Pleistocene.

Now perissodactyl means "odd finger." Eventually, perissodactyls would lose two or four toes on their hind feet while the middle toe would lengthen and get wider. Thus *perissodactyls* would be the mammals with one, or three, toed hoofs. They would live in Africa, Asia, North America and Europe, eventually *evolving* into tapirs, zebras, asses, horses and rhinoceroses. And others, such as the chalicotheres and the titanotheres, would go *extinct*. Now titanotheres, also known as brontotheres, were hairy, heavy animals two meters tall, three meters long. And it happened that in the forests of proto-Asia, a group of these rhinoceros-like creatures were browsing on the leaves of trees and bushes. And above their noses, they had *horns*, like the bony knobs of modern-day giraffes. And although the horn of one of them was shield-like and flat, the others had roundish Y-shaped horns. And nibbling leaves nearby these browsing brontotheres were chalicotheres. Their shape was *like unto* the modern horse, but their legs were massive like the bear's, *and* their feet were clawed.

Now *artiodactyls* would later lose one toe or three toes to become the *even-toed hoofed* animals. And many would grow horns and antlers. They would populate all continents except Australia. And eventually they would develop into sheep, pigs, pronghorns, buffalo, giraffes, gazelles, gnus, bison, hippopotamuses, goats, impalas, cattle, camels, llamas, deer and antelopes.

Now during the Tertiary, perissodactyls would *prevail* over artiodactyls. But in the Recent, this would be *reversed*: Artiodactyls would become more numerous.

And it came to pass that a series of genetic changes during millions of years caused an insectivore of the Paleocene to evolve into a hedgehog. And besides insects, it fed on frogs, tiny lizards, rodents, baby birds and worms. And through its offspring did this creature multiply its numbers. And soon, many "balls of bristles" were crawling through the vegetation of the Earth at night. And these were *Nature's first hedgehogs*.

And below a half-crescent moon, a furry mammal, which looked like mouse, twitched back and forth its cone-shaped snout – it must have been sniffing for a worm, an insect or a small invertebrate. Now early in the morning before the Sun had lit the sky, this creature burrowed to make *a hole in earth* its home. And twelve hours later, when the black of night descended, it again came out. And in the manner of a domesticated modern cat, it stroked its fur with its forefeet; and with its tongue, it licked its fur. Now *throughout* the northern hemisphere, many such mouse-like-looking mammals hid in burrows during day and lived nocturnal lives. The ones with rat-like bodies were the *moles*. And the ones with delicate bodies were the *shrews*. Now some shrews were very small, weighing no more than a penny. And Nature's moles were superb diggers of the earth, capable of constructing elaborate concentric rings of tunnels.

And in a dense forest of proto-Wyoming, a hairy lemur-like creature sat upon a tree limb, blinking its large round eyes in its bear-like head. *Notharctus* was its name. And it sat up. And with its large rabbit-like hind legs, it walked along, grabbing the tree limb with its thumb and fingers as it went. Its long furry tail lagged behind, providing balance *like unto* a tightrope-artist's pole. Then it paused, and its hand reached up and grabbed a pear. And *of this fruit* it ate. Then its tail curled around a tree limb *as if* for safety's sake.

And elsewhere, in proto-western-Europe and in the black of night, an Eocene tarsier clung to a tree trunk with its feet and hands, whose digits were equipped with *gripping pads*. And instead of having claws like most other animals, it had almost human-looking fingernails. Now overall, this tarsier looked like notharctus, but its tail was thinner and more bare. And its legs were longer than its arms. And from time to time, its large, bat-like ears *wiggled* as if to listen for the movements of nocturnal predators. And its *marble-like* enormous eyes scrutinized the leaves for caterpillars and for crawling bugs. And suddenly it spied a beetle in another tree. It sprang forth, leaped and landed in the other tree. And it grabbed the beetle and placed it in its mouth. Then its small sharp teeth bit through the beetle's shell. In seconds was the insect so consumed.

Now during the next fifty-million years, many mammals would evolve and *change dramatically*. But tarsiers would not. Thus the tarsiers of the Eocene would look like the tarsiers of the Recent, which would live in the Philippines and the surrounding islands.[322] Thus like modern tarsiers, the hands of ancient tarsiers had four bony fingers and a thumb.

Now the notharctus and the tarsier were *not* the only primates of the Eocene, for throughout the northern hemisphere, small creatures with *brains* that were relatively large did dwell in trees. And their hands had fingers and a thumb, while their feet had one big toe.[323] And they crawled up trunks, walked on bough limbs, grabbed branches and did swing about. And they used their tails for balance, and they used their *hands* to grip. And they fed on insects, fruits, nuts, seeds and leaves. And these primates were the lemurs, proto-monkeys and tree-shrew-like mammals.

---

[322] To see a living tarsier nowadays is like seeing a mammal that is fifty-million years old.

[323] Man would eventually inherit these features.

And in northern India, one pig-sized mammal spent much time in pools and ponds. Often the water reached its neck. And so it held its head up high to breathe. And as millions of years went by, this species obtained an elongated snout with nostrils at the end.

Now *mammals* fed their young at birth with *milk*. And this made mammals *different* from other animals. And through their *warm* bodies, red blood did circulate, *pumped* by four-chambered hearts. And to support their rapid metabolic processes, mammals breathed in *oxygen in air*. Now all land-living forms *had* some kind of *hair* – long thick hair was fur. And mammals had backbones, skeletons and skulls to maintain structure. And muscles let these creatures move about, while sweat glands helped to keep their bodies cool. And a few, like skunks, when threatened, secreted from a gland a foul odor to fend off a predator. Now the body chamber of a mammal was divided into *two* – the divider was the diaphragm. The lower part contained digestive organs, while the upper part contained the lungs and heart.

And at this time and henceforth, Earth had *many types* of mammals. The mammals were Earth's children, having *inherited the World*. And everywhere were condylarths, uintatheres, artiodactyls, creodonts, perissodactyls, primates and notoungulates – the beasts of Earth were *everywhere*.

## Chapter II: The Continents Continue Drifting

And it came to pass that proto-Eurasia and proto-Greenland *separated*. And the Greenland and Norwegian seas were made. And the Arctic and Atlantic oceans were connected. And proto-Greenland now was Greenland, and proto-North-America *turned into* North America.[324] And proto-Eurasia was Eurasia, that is, Europe joined with Asia.

And during thousands of years, the mantle hot spot in the Norwegian Sea pushed earth and some volcanos *up above the sea*. And the Great Faeroe Island formed.

And land animals in Europe could *no longer pass* so easily to Canada and North America. And likewise, land animals in North America could *no longer pass* so easily to Europe. In the Early Eocene and hitherto, animals had migrated back and forth along a lush green route near to the Arctic Circle.[325] Now the separation of the continents

---

[324] There is no definite moment when a land body such as *proto*-North-America "turns into" its modern form because the process is gradual, lasting millions of years. What is clear, however, is that in the Cretaceous Period when the eastern part of proto-North-America was attached to proto-Greenland and to proto-Europe, and the western part was flooded, it was not so easy to identify North America on a world map. By the end of the Eocene, this had changed; although its outline was somewhat different from today, North America was recognizable. The same statement holds concerning the other geological structures, such as mountains, seas and oceans.

[325] Not only were there no polar caps on Earth at this time but temperatures were sufficiently high to support much vegetation and wild life within both the Arctic and Antarc-

would eventually lead to a separation of the corresponding faunal evolutionary paths.

And India drifted north and was very near to southern Asia. And India left behind the magma hot spot that had made the Deccan Traps. But the hot spot continued to make lava flows and seamounts *underneath the sea*. And as the Indian-Australian tectonic plate edged north, the hot spot forged a line of underwater plateaus, mountains and volcanos. During the next fifty-million years, the underwater Laccadive-Chagos Ridge, the Saya de Malha Bank, the Mascarene Plateau and the Seychelles would be made. And some seamounts would rise *up above the sea*. And these islands would be the Maldives, the Chagos Archipelagos, the Seychelles and the Mascarenes. And in the Recent, the hot spot would sit underneath Réunion, a volcanic island five-hundred kilometers east of Madagascar.

Now the riftings of Australia from Antarctica and of North America from Greenland had been accompanied by vulcanism which had produced much *greenhouse gas*. And in addition, cold deep-ocean currents were *not being circulated* to the surface as efficiently as in the Paleocene. And during several million years, Earth's mean global temperature rose by three degrees, reaching the maximum it would achieve within the Cenozoic Period. In Celsius, the World was on average fourteen degrees warmer than in modern times. But during the rest of the Eocene, the Earth would *cool dramatically*, dropping ten degrees. Then starting at the beginning the Oligocene, *temperatures* would be approximately steady till the middle of the Miocene, when *they* would drop again.

## Chapter III: Mammals Continue to Develop

And the development of mammals so *continued*. And some edentates in South America grew a tougher skin. And when at night they rummaged earth in search of food, they sometimes were attacked by predators. And those edentates with *tougher* skin survived *more* often, while those with *softer* skin survived *less* often. And since edentates passed their traits to offspring, eventually these animals acquired coats of *armored skin*. And those edentates that could roll themselves into a ball were *armadillos*. And those with turtle-shell-like armor were the *glyptodonts*.

Now some archaic ungulates spent much time in *ocean water* seeking fish to eat. And they used their paws to paddle and to swim. And mammals with poorer paws for swimming *caught fewer fish*. And those with fat flat digits on their hands and feet swam better and consequently *caught more*. And it was *these mammals* that lived longer and survived more often. And so eventually it came to pass that feet

---

tic circles. In the Early Eocene, palms and cycads were growing as far north as 60 degrees latitude, and alligators and tortoises were dwelling above 75 degrees latitude!

and hands *evolved to fins*. Likewise, tails turned into *flat* fins that could flap. And these species became *Earth's mammals of the sea*. So swimming in the ocean seas were small-whale-like creatures, such as the archaeocetes and sea cows. Now archaeocetes had sharp and pointed teeth, which were loosely packed. About three meters long but less than half-a-meter wide, they *were* as sleek as seals. Now the *sea cows* were shorter but were heavy boned and bulkier. Millions of years of evolution had changed their bodies for survival in the seas – *no longer could* they live on land. And sea cows would endure for forty-five-million years of geo-history to become the modern manatee and dugong.

And it came to pass that *hyracotherium, the first horse*, also known as eohippus, did appear in North America and Eurasia. And this perissodactyl was no bigger than a little dog: about two dozen centimeters tall and sixty centimeters long. And the hoofs in back had three toes, while the hoofs in front had four. And hyracotherium ate whatever it could find – plants, small animals or fruit, which it chewed up with low-crowned teeth.

And elsewhere on the Earth, a heavy pig-like perissodactyl fed on shrubs and trees, often pulling at the twigs and leaves. And a primitive *tapir* was this creature. It was covered with short bristly hair, and it had an elongated head and snout. And like others of its kind, it lived near lakes and ponds in wooded lands.

And it came to pass that certain small Eurasian animals began to spread to other lands. And rabbits, rodents and small mammals *made their way* to North America from Asia by an Arctic route.

## Chapter IV: Birds Develop Further

*And the heavens were full of flying fowl.*

And birds evolved. And *almost every form* of modern bird was present on the Earth. Flying through the air and nesting in the trees and bushes were tropic birds, swifts, cuckoos, pigeons, songbirds, albatrosses, bustards, birds of prey and cranes. And owls were the prevailing predators at night. And web-footed waterfowl paddled in the marshes, ponds and lakes. These fowls were primitive forms of swans and geese and ducks.

*And the World also had its first* living *hummingbirds.*

## Chapter V: Asia Is Complete

And several million years went by. And India touched Asia, and the continent of Asia *was* complete. And the westward flowing currents of the eastern Tethys Seaway thus were blocked. But still the currents of the Tethys flowed *from east to west*, but the flow started in the northwest Indian Ocean. From there, it passed between Africa and Europe, and ended then in the Atlantic Ocean.

And although India had met with Asia, India *continued moving north*, drifting ten centimeters every year.

## Chapter VI: The Emperor's Islands

And it came to pass that Meiji, the island of the northwest Pacific Ocean which was created in the Cretaceous, sank *below the sea*. And it sank because of gravity. And the Meiji Island thus became the Meiji Seamount. Now the hot spot Pele, which had made Meiji, was two thousand kilometers away and mostly to the south and somewhat to the east of it. And there was a *line* of volcanic islands between Pele and the seamount Meiji.[326] And these islands were provided with a name: the Emperor Islands. Now it *came* to pass that the Pacific Plate began to drift *more* toward the west. And Pele torched the Earth and made the Abbott Island and the beginning of another island chain.

## Chapter VII: Nummulites and Mummies

Now it came to pass that certain forms of foraminiferan protozoa and algae formed a symbiotic creature. And these foraminiferans were *nummulites*. Now the nummulites provided homes for algae, while the algae provided nummulites with nourishment. And so on the sea-bed of the shallow waters of the Tethys Seaway, microscopic organisms secreted shells built of many tiny *chambers* in a spiral *labyrinth*. And they constructed, what was for them, a *giant object* of the size of a flat coin. And it came to pass that the algae-protozoa partnership did flourish. And so the nummulites verily multiplied their numbers. And they came to dominate the Tethys Seaway life. Now when they *died*, they *rested* on the seabed floor. And year after year for millions of years did nummulitic "coins" heap up. Now eventually these shells would be compressed and lithified to limestone. And forty-million years thereafter would Egyptians mine the limestone, cut it into *giant blocks* and put the blocks together. And great pyramids would be constructed in sands around the Nile, with labyrinthine passages to *chambers* where *dead* pharaohs *lay*.[327]

## Chapter VIII: New Ungulates Appear

And during millions of years, through genetic changes induced by efforts to escape Earth's predators, a primitive three-toed tapir grew into a *larger* form with slender legs. And this creature which could run quite fast was named the running rhino. And tapir-like perissodactyls

---

[326] The word "Meiji" also happens to refer to the late-nineteenth and early-twentieth century reign of Emperor Mutsuhito of Japan.

[327] The Egyptians might have constructed the pyramids but the microscopic nummulites built the stones. At this time, nummulites were so common that the Eocene is sometimes called the "Nummulitic Epoch."

with thicker legs also did appear – and the *first "proto-rhinoceroses"* roamed the Earth.

And in crossing a mountain range some artiodactyls became *separated* from their brethren. And during millions of years, they evolved into a *different* species group. They would become the mammals that would evolve into the pigs. And through a similar geographic separation, new artiodactyls with four-toed hoofs appeared in North America. And they were named *protylopus*. Although they had body forms like those of deer and were the size of rabbits, *they* were *the first camels*.

## Chapter IX: Around the Pacific Ocean, Mountains Are Made

Now it came to pass that the relatively rapid subduction of the Juan de Fuca tectonic plate ruptured the upper mantle *off the northwest coast* of the United States. And *Earth* bled magma, and volcanos popped up in Oregon and Washington, including the progenitor of Mount Saint Helens. And a chain of mountains rose *up* toward the sky. They were the Cascade Mountains.

And during the Cenozoic, the Nazca Plate subducted *off of western South America* as South America crept west. And magma from the asthenosphere fed volcanos in the Andes. And as the crust below the Andes was squeezed by the eastward-moving Nazca Plate and westward-moving Argentina and Brazil, the Andes *grew in height*.

And similar tectonic processes were proceeding on the other side of the Pacific Ocean. Subduction provided a *foundation* of support for Japan, Taiwan, the peninsula of Kamchatka and the Philippines. And magma from the asthenosphere fueled the volcanos of Pacific Basin islands. Along the Pacific Rim were rows of pillars of ascending smoke.

## Chapter X: The Himalayas

And it came to pass that India pushed into southern Asia with *tremendous* force and inconceivable momentum, for although the speed was low – ten centimeters did it move per year – the mass of India was *huge*. And India was buoyant, strong and solid. And so when India "struck" Asia, the crust in southern Asia buckled, creating waves of *giant* anticlines and synclines in the Earth. And crust and rocks did strain, compress and squeeze. And ordinary rock turned into metamorphic rock.

And it was like pushing a shovel over dirt: Dirt accumulated in a pile. But the shovel blade was not thirty centimeters wide – the blade was India, which was *three-thousand kilometers* across. And the pile of dirt was not just several centimeters tall – the pile was the proto-Himalayan Mountains, which were several thousand meters high.

And during the next two-million years, India pushed one-hundred kilometers *inland into Asia*. And Asian crust was squeezed. And something had to give. And so the proto-Himalayas *rose*.

And during the next ten-million years, northern India would try to thrust *beneath* the southern part of Asia. But the crust of India would be too buoyant, so that only the underside of India *would* be able to slide under. And the proto-Himalayan Mountains *would* be lifted up, grow taller and become the Himalayas. And crust farther north in Asia would be squeezed and shortened. And to shorten, the crust would have to *thicken*. Thus an elevated plateau would come about. And this would be the *beginning* of Tibet.

And as northern India inched forward, its upper crust would be subjected to great forces *and* break *off*. And only the deepest part of northern India would be subducted. And a horizontal slip fault would be forced to form. *Strong and frequent* earthquakes would so shake these lands. And the upper crust would pile up, making the Lesser Himalayan Range and adding mountains to the region.

Now the partial subduction of India would activate great magma flows. And *volcanos* would funnel up in southern proto-Tibet and in the Himalayas.

And the movement of India into Asia would further raise the Himalayas, making them the *highest* peaks on Earth. And new folds in Earth would form. And new ranges would be added to the Himalayas. And the Himalayas would remain as majestic monuments *unto this day*. And north of them, Earth's crust would be compressed, shortened and then thickened, and proto-Tibet would grow taller, and get bigger *and* become Tibet. Tibet would exist as an elevated plateau five-thousand meters high above sea level.

Now the stress created by the continental collision would be felt as far away as Central Asia: Asia would *crack open* in the middle. And the crustal crack would fill with water to make in South Siberia a lake. And *Lake Baikal would* the lake be called. And it would be the *deepest* lake on Earth. In the Recent, it would house one-fifth of the species of the World's freshwater fish.

Now the Himalayas would *weigh down* on the northern part of India, causing it to sink somewhat. And a relatively low-land region would appear. Then erosion would wash sediments into this land. And the Granges Plain would form.

And by the Holocene, India would push two-thousand kilometers inland into Asia, causing the *Tibetan crust* to double. And erosion *there* would wear away loose sediments, leaving *rugged* rocks exposed. And in places, remnants of the Tethys Ocean floor would then be visible! And nearby, the Himalayan Mountains would be the greatest and most rugged mountains on the Earth.[328]

---

[328] Even in the twentieth century, India is still moving north at several centimeters per

## Chapter XI: The Faeroe Islands

And as the Eurasian tectonic plate drifted to the east, it carried forth the Great Faeroe Island into *the* Norwegian Sea. And since the hot spot, which had made the island, stayed behind, the island *lost support* from upward flowing heat. And during the next several dozen million years, the Great Faeroe Island sank below the sea. But the *highest peaks* remained exposed to air. And they became the *Faeroe Islands*.

## Chapter XII: The Alps and Other Mountains in Southern Europe

Now proto-Italy[329] and other islands protruding off the coast of Africa in the Tethys Seaway moved *northward* with the drifting Africa. And these islands struck the southern European coast. And it was *as if* Europe had been "booted in the stomach." And these islands stuck to southern Europe. And during millions of years, they pushed the earth, made it fold and forged some rugged mountains: the Pindus in Greece, the Dinaric Alps in Yugoslavia, the Carpathians in eastern Europe, and the Alps in Austria and Switzerland. And Italy continued thrusting forward and made the Alps the *tallest peaks in Europe*.

## Chapter XIII: Development of Life in the Late Eocene

*It was a wondrous time,*
*a time when foxes had holes*
*and birds of the air had nests.*

And the temperature of Earth continued to decline. And one bird *adapted* to the colder waters near the southern pole. It grew a thicker layer of fat, and it evolved short feathers that could insulate like fur. And as webs emerged between its toes, and wings developed into fins, it became a skillful swimmer. And in the Antarctic, there were others just like it. They were Earth's *first penguins*, playful birds that lived in groups and socialized. And as for food, they swam for fish.

And a new fork in the evolutionary tree arose. And mammalian carnivores split into the doglike and the catlike types. Now the *catlike carnivores* had claws that *could retract into the skin*. And this was done while walking or while running. And the claws came out to climb a tree or claw a prey, such as a small lizard, bird or mammal. But the proto-mongooses and the proto-civets often fed on eggs, fish, insects, worms, nuts and roots instead. Now the *doglike animals* had claws that could *not* retract into the skin. And during the Late Eocene, there were the

---

year. It will take tens of millions of years more before retarding forces cause India to cease its "runaway behavior" and bring it to a stop. At that point far in the future, part of India will be underneath South Asia – the rest will be on top.

[329] At this stage, Italy was an island between Africa and Europe.

primitive raccoons, dogs, foxes, jackals, ferrets, weasels, badgers, skunks and otters. And doglike carnivores had a splendid *sense of smell*. In contrast, the catlike creatures had outstanding hearing and uncanny sight, for they hunted often in the evening and at night. Eventually, many carnivores would acquire spots and stripes for camouflage to help them in their hunting.

And wading through a shallow swamp of northern Africa was moeritherium, a mammal slightly larger than a pig with a body round and heavy like a hippopotamus. For *semi-aquatic life* had this creature been "designed" – four thick legs permitted it to move through vegetation in the water; its *nose*, which resembled a short hose, and its *eyes* and *ears* were positioned high up on its head, so that it could *breathe* and *see* and *hear* when entering deep pools; even its neck muscles had grown large and strong from holding up its head. Now moeritherium was a primitive version of an elephant. Later, its descendants would evolve a *longer nose*; and this would be a *trunk*. The trunk would be able to lift up vegetation and place it in its mouth. Likewise, moeritherium's *two large teeth*, which stuck down from its upper jaw, would lengthen into *tusks*. Such tusks would be effective in uprooting vegetation and in stripping bark from trees. And they would also be for defense and display.

And it came to pass that, in North America, the descendants of hyracotherium evolved to larger forms: first orohippus and then *epihippus*. But these horses were still small – about the size of dogs.

And the mammals that had taken to the ocean seas to feed on fish evolved to *large beasts* with fish-like hairless bodies and powerful tails of two flat flukes. Upon their heads were *holes*, which were used for breathing. And these mammals were predators of prey – primitive versions of dolphins, porpoises and small-sized whales. But one among them, basilosaurus, was a giant. It was the *largest mammal* of the Eocene: narrow, round and twenty meters long – Nature's sea-serpent *verily it was*.[330]

And it came to pass that land in central Russia lifted up. And the waters of the Ural Trough did *drain* and disappear – no longer was a barrier of water there. And animals from Asia migrated into Europe. And animals from Europe migrated to Siberia and China. And the animals from each continent *for land and food* did fight. And the "better" species won. And the condylarths, uintatheres and creodonts lost battles, and their diversity declined. But certain other mammals "profited." And Eurasian faunal evolution underwent a major change.

Now elsewhere in the World, life was evolving in geographically well separated regions: South America, Africa, Antarctica and Australia *were* all "island continents." And North America was connected to

---

[330] The remains of this creature were discovered in the early 1830's. It created quite a stir when it was put on display as a sea-serpent monster.

Asia only by a northern narrow strip of land. And as animals evolved in "their separated universes," divergent groups of species came to dwell in different parts of Earth. And for example, placentals were prevailing in the northern continents, while marsupials were dominating in Australia and in Antarctica. And notoungulates were dwelling only in the land of South America, while horses were confined to northern continents. And the same *divergent evolution* was happening on smaller lands: Madagascar had its set of unique faunal species. And New Zealand had no snakes, having separated from Gondwana before this reptile had evolved. And many lands had *their* own flightless bird: the ostrich in Africa, the rhea in South America, the emu and cassowary in Australia; and the kiwi in New Zealand. And during much of the remaining Tertiary Period, animals in their respective "isolated worlds" would *continue to diverge*. And exotic forms of faunal would emerge. But environmental pressures would *also* lead to animals of *similar body forms* in distant lands. And for example, corresponding to the placental wolves, cats, anteaters, rabbits, mice and flying squirrels would be Australian marsupials resembling wolves, cats, anteaters, and so on. And this would be *convergent evolution*.

## Chapter XIV: Geological Changes in Western United States

And it came to pass that the Pacific Ocean tectonic plate stopped moving east and started drifting to the *north and west*. And subduction of this plate off western North America *turned off*. And so a transform strike-slip boundary replaced a convergent boundary of plates. And a *new fault system* thus was born – the San Andreas Faults. Now the Pacific Plate transported western California with it. So western California started slowly sliding north. And although volcanic eruptions occurred less frequently, *earthquakes* struck quite often: Whenever Californian crust slipped *suddenly* against and past the North American continental plate, *then* the Earth did shake.

And since the Pacific Plate no longer pushed against the western part of North America, the compression of the continent *relaxed*. And the uplift of the Rocky Mountains ceased. And during the next thirty-five-million years, the crust in and around Nevada stretched. And in doing so, it sank and made a *basin*: the Great Basin.

*The third book of the Cenozoic, called*

# The Oligocene

*And death was upon the face of Earth.*
*And from the dust emerged new life.*

## Chapter I: A Mass Extinction

It was thirty-seven-million years ago. The Oligocene began. And it came to pass that the temperature of Earth in Celsius declined by five degrees. And water turned to *ice* in West Antarctica. And for the first time since the Early Triassic Period, Earth had a southern polar cap. And within the Antarctic Circle, *icebergs* floated in the seas.

And the *drop in temperature* was a shock for many forms of ocean life. And countless mollusks, plankton, deep-sea organisms, proto-whales and snails *died out*. But the deep-sea life that did manage to survive was more robust and learned to cope with cold. And these would be the deep-sea fauna of the Holocene.

Now since it was *ocean* water that made the Antarctic ice, sea level dropped. And shallow off-shore habitats *dried up*. And some sea life moved out to deeper seas.

And cooler air caused the jungles and thick vegetation of the tropics to grow thin. And open forests formed where jungles once had been. And the cold made life for animals more difficult. And certain mammals suffered, and their numbers dropped. And many creatures that had appeared at the dawn of the Cenozoic Era *went extinct*, including taeniodonts, tillodonts, condylarths and almost all the creodonts. And archaic forms of flying lemurs died. And numerous primates, such as notharctus, could not cope with cold and so did *not survive*. And there were hardly any primates left in North America. And many perissodactyls did succumb to cold and die.

But smaller animals were less susceptible to cold. And new smaller mammals multiplied and took control of Earth.

And squirrel-like creatures of the Eocene evolved to chipmunks, marmots, squirrels and related mammals. And modern forms of rats and mice appeared. And a few rodents grew, instead of fur, a coat of spines. And these were *Earth's first porcupines*. And other rodents developed *webs* between their toes. And they used the webs and long hind legs to swim. And they collected branches, twigs and logs, and piled them in a stream or pond. And these structures were their homes. These creatures were thy *Earth's first beavers*.

And rodents bred rapidly, and they produced large litters. And their numbers increased enormously. And soon *one-third* of the mammals of the Earth were small rodents, such as squirrels, chipmunks, mice and rats.

## Chapter II: New Waterways

And it came to pass that the gap between Canada and Greenland, which had started in the Late Cretaceous, *widened*. And the Davis Strait and Baffin Bay were born.

And it happened that a *rift* appeared in northeast Africa. And many million years went by. And the rift grew longer. And when waters from the Indian Ocean entered it, the Gulf of Aden formed. And the Arabian Peninsula began to break from Africa. And many million years went by. And as the Arabian Peninsula moved north, a *new* sea opened up. It was the Red Sea of the Middle East.

## Chapter III: Ungulates Continue to Evolve

And in North America it came to pass that the descendants of protylopus grew larger and evolved into *poëbrotherium*, a goat-sized camel. And as for other artiodactyls, evolutionary progress *was* made too. And archaic forms of pigs gradually changed *into* pigs, but with giant heads, tiny brains, and bony flanges that protruded sidewise just beneath their eyes. And it also came to pass that a new grazing animal arose. It bit off leaves on trees and pulled up grass, then crushed the vegetation with its teeth. And when the cellulose was swallowed, microbes in its stomach went to work in decomposing it. But since the cellulose was *not so easy* to break down, it was *regurgitated* to the creature's mouth and further chewed with much saliva added. And several times did the plant matter pass between its mouth and stomach, until it was finally digested. Now there were others like this mammal that did crew the cud – they were the *ruminants*. Cellulose was so difficult to process that ruminants and other artiodactyls possessed sophisticated stomachs with *four chambers*, each with a particular digestive function. And this gave these creatures their extensive sagging abdomens. The same would be true for their descendants: In the Holocene, the bellies of the cows, goats, giraffes, pigs, deer, antelopes and hippopotamuses would be round and big.

Now when epihippus had trotted, it had done so on its *central* toes. And with time had its side toes consequently shrunk. And it eventually did come to pass that one toe of the fore foot of the horse did altogether disappear. And this new three-toed horse was *mesohippus* – it was larger than its predecessors – slightly smaller than a modern sheep. And as open spaces replaced dense jungles and thick woods, running speed became a valued asset for an animal. And horses so adapted, gradually becoming bigger, stronger, faster. And a new horse somewhat larger than mesohippus did emerge. It was *miohippus*. And it ran and trotted in the lands where forests bordered open fields.

## Chapter IV: New Mammals Appear

For the rest of the Cenozoic Era, several developments would affect the evolution of land life. And among them was the cooler climate. Not only would animals have to *respond* by acquiring more insulating mechanisms such as thicker fur or skin, but some would have to *move* to warmer places on the Earth. And the decline of certain jungles and thick forests would lead to open areas where running speed and eyesight would play more important roles. And the newly forming grass areas would profit only those that took advantage of them; some herbivores would gain the means to digest grass;[331] grass-grazing animals would be a new food source for predators. And as the ecological niches of the World were more densely populated, competition would affect the evolution of land mammals; like the dinosaurs, a battle to be bigger was already happening. And while amphibians, reptiles and fish were only slowly changing, mammals were still undergoing an explosive radiation.

And it *came about* that the tough skin of one edentate developed into thick and overlapping leaf-shaped *scales*. And this mammal had three-toed claws in front and five-toed claws in back, and its head was long and thin. Its tongue lashed out, grabbing ants and drawing them into its mouth. And with its tail, it sometimes hung from trees. And it could also roll into a ball. And on Earth were others like this animal; *they* were the pangolins. And they would fight in evolutionary battles and survive *unto this day*.

And elephants *evolved to* several species among which were phiomia and palaeomastodon. These creatures' heads were elongated and were funnel-shaped. And their tusks, which numbered four, *and* their trunks were short compared with modern elephants. Now the three-meter-tall *palaeomastodon* had a body *like unto* a hippopotamus's. And the tusks of the upper jaw curved *down*, while those of the lower jaw curved *up* and were farther forward. Now *phiomia* was donkey-sized and lived in Egypt and in India. And its upper tusks were pointed cylinders, while its lower ones were *flat and shovel-shaped*.

And millions of years went by and were recorded in a layer of rock.

And proto-*pinnipeds* appeared. And they had *webs* between the fingers of the hands and tails *that* were fingered fins instead of feet. And these seal-like creatures mainly fed on fish in seas. When on land, they waddled when they moved. But when in water, their streamlined bodies swam with ease.

And the *first dogs* emerged on Earth: Cynodictis and hesperocyon looked like short-leggèd weasels but in fact were dogs.[332] These sharp-

---

[331] Grass has siliceous grit in its tissues that makes it especially difficult to digest.

[332] Scientists know these creatures were dogs from the structure of their ear bones and from their teeth.

tooth creatures had strong and well-developed legs and feet. And they *sniffed along the ground* to find their prey. And after finding such a prey, they chased it with extraordinary speed. Now it happened that larger, stronger, sluggish forms of dog-like animals arose on Earth. And they were primitive forms of pandas and of bears. These highly furry creatures ate nuts, ants, seeds, fish, rodents, honey, bamboo shoots, small animals and cabbage roots.

And primitive antelopes, deer, horses, camels, cats and dogs formed herds and packs that roamed the prairies, woods and plains of Earth.

### Chapter V: Some Mammals Become Big

And five-million years went by. The Oligocene was coming to its end. And many mammals grew to *larger* forms. And there were big pigs, cats and wolf-like dogs. And the descendants of phiomia and palaeomastodon *evolved to* elephants and mastodons. And mastodons moved into Asia. And the modern-looking rhinoceros arose. And there were many different species: *Paraceratherium*,[333] a giant rhinoceros without a horn, was eight meters long, six meters tall and weighed more than twenty tons. And among the mammals that have ever lived on land, paraceratherium was the largest of them all.

And rhinoceroses cooled off within the *shade* of trees or in the *water* of a pool or pond. And their bulky bodies were covered with a thick and nearly hairless skin – such skin was hide. And many species were about four meters long, two meters tall and weighed a ton – their size was their protection from Earth's predators. And a *horn* sticking upward just above their broad square muzzles made them looked like mammal versions of the ceratops.

It was a sunny day in the Late Oligocene. And in an open field, one rhino nibbled on short grass. And nearby, some dung was drying out. And when the dung was dry, the rhino kicked it with its foot. And in the field lay many piles of dung, which were well separated and spread out. Now it happened that another rhino ventured to the field. And its nose began to twitch. Then it trotted off to find another spot to graze. And elsewhere, other rhinos scattered dung to *claim* their grazing turfs.

And a changing World of cooling weather and of shrinking forests induced Earth's species to adapt. And some edentates evolved to furry bear-like creatures. And they were *ground sloths*. And they fed on fresh or fallen leaves.

And it seemed *as if* the hand of Nature *touched* a certain group of primates. And some *came down from trees* and occupied the land. And it came to pass that monkeys evolved into their modern forms and that

---

[333] Paraceratherium conjures up the image of the Trojan horse. It is also known as indricotherium and baluchitherium.

the progenitors of apes emerged. And some monkeys during day did hide, only coming out to eat in evening and at night. And primates used their *eyes* to find their food, to avoid their predators, to grab for branches and to walk about. For them, *sense of smell* gave way to *sense of sight.*

*The fourth book of the Cenozoic, called*

# The Miocene

*It was a land which flowed with milk and honey.*

## Chapter I: Migrations

*As moved the clouds above,
so moved the herds below.*

It was twenty-four-million years ago. The Miocene arrived. The continents assumed their present-day positions. And Earth's topography, vegetation, climate and geography took on a modern form.

And a great animal *migration* did begin. And it would proceed for *several million years*. And primitive weasels, dogs, rhinoceroses, bears and deer of Europe spread in all directions. And some headed *east* to Asia. And it was *as if* these creatures were searching for a promised land. And they continued travelling, sometimes to the north or south but mostly to east until the West Pacific Ocean *blocked their way*. And there their journey stopped. And several hundred thousand years went by. Then the "chosen creatures" headed up and down the West Pacific coast. And some arrived in East Siberia. There, they *crossed* the narrow Bering-Strait land bridge to Canada. And it was *as if* they were marching forward in a procession *like unto* the one when animals went up the ramp and entered Noah's Ark. And these animals migrated south and spread through North America. And North America became their *home.*

And elsewhere in the World, Earth's mammals *moved about*. And around the globe, rodents multiplied, went rampant and ran wild, occupying the fertile niches of the earth. They filled the fields and forests of the World. And among them were guinea pigs, mice, rats, woodchucks, chipmunks, beavers, hamsters, gophers, gerbils, porcupines and squirrels.

And even in the Recent, rodents would remain the *most prolific* of the mammals. In modern times, man would accidently carry them in boats to other lands. And rats from *Europe* and from *Asia* would end up on the *other* continents. And even exotic isolated islands, which had *no* rodents in the Pleistocene, *would* have pesty creatures running rampant in the Holocene.[334]

---

[334] In the Middle Ages, rats would spread bubonic plague through Europe. And twenty-

## Chapter II: Miocene Aquatic Mammals

*And so the seas were given whales.*
*And this happened on the fifth day*
*of the first month of a long lost year.*

And it came to pass that dolphins, whales and porpoises evolved
into their modern forms. And their *hearing* was outstanding – for
them, sound was a means for navigating and for finding food; *sound
was sight.* And they contorted their bodies, flapped their tails, made
splashes and they dove. They dove to swim and eat. And each swam
by fanning up and down a flat tail fin. And when one surfaced, it exhaled through a *blowhole* on its upper body, spraying white water out
and up. And their bellies sometimes surged above the sea and landed
back in water with a *splash.* And they swam with *others in a school.*

And the modern pinnipeds appeared: Earth's seas were *full* of
sea lions, seals and walruses, smooth-skinned mammals sporting
"mustache whiskers" and darting through the ocean waters. And walruses had *tusks,* which pointed down. And except for the earless seals,
pinniped males mated with a *harem* of pinniped females, often barking
and fighting for them. And pinnipeds fed on fish, crabs, octopi and
shrimp. And seals played with partners in playful water games.

## Chapter III: Miocene Land Mammals

And it came to pass that mammalian land carnivores underwent a
dramatic evolutionary transformation into *many different forms.*
Now the primitive dogs of the Oligocene evolved to foxes, jackals and
other *doglike creatures.* The ones that built their dens in trees and
looked like bandits were raccoons. The ones that scurried, stopped,
stood up and looked around and then ran off were badgers, prairie
dogs and weasels. The ones that stank when threatened by a predator
were skunks. The ones with velvet fur were wolverines and minks. And
the ones that adapted to the water were the otters. Now *fresh-water* otters fed on bird eggs, fish, amphibians, small animals and snails,
while *ocean species* fed on fish, seaweed, crabs and clams. They sometimes cracked clam shells with rocks while swimming on their backs.[335]

And there were many types of modern-looking dogs. Their brains
were relatively large compared with other mammals. In packs did *they*
run swiftly after prey. And they cared for newborns of a litter *in a den*
constructed in a tree trunk, in the ground, in a log or in a cave.

And *bears* ate huge amounts of food before the winter season and
*slept away* the colder months in dens. Now most bears were brown or
black, but those living in the polar zones were white.[336] And the big-

---

five-million Europeans would die. See the New Testament Book of *Catastrophes.*
[335] Man excluded, this is one of the rare examples of an animal using a tool.
[336] Evolution selected the color of the fur to aid in camouflage.

gest were the grizzlies weighing *seven-hundred kilograms*, while the smallest were the sun bears weighing less than thirty kilograms. And the quite playful pandas dwelt among Earth's bamboo trees and often ate their leaves.

And *catlike* carnivores evolved. Civets and mongooses did emerge. And some cats grew into larger forms. And Earth had bobcats, jaguars and hyenas; the hyenas were brown, striped or *spotted*. And the spotted ones were called the laughing hyenas because of the *hideous howls* that they made at night.

And it happened that a cat was walking in some woods. And its whiskers brushed a bush. And so the cat leaped to the side. And other cats did also use their *whiskers* for guidance and for feeling. Now elsewhere, a cat was walking in the night. And its eyes *were as* a pair of marbles, blinking as they searched for prey. And when the cat did spy a rat, instantly it *froze in place*. Its body lowered *as if* to hug the ground. And stealthily it took a few steps forward. Then it stopped again. And half-a-dozen seconds passed. And it crawled forward a few steps, then paused again. And it gathered strength and made a *short quick dash*. The rat began to run. And the cat clasped the rat in its front claws and bit it *at its neck* with teeth and jaws. The cat pounced upon it several times until the rat lay still. And then the cat scraped away the skin with its front paws. And its tongue, as rough as harsh sandpaper, licked away a layer of under-skin. And when the cat had finished eating, it raked and scratched the bark of an oak tree; and when it walked away, its claws were somewhat cleaner and were sharper than before. And lions, tigers, leopards, cheetahs, sabertooths and other bigger cats killed prey in much the *same* way as this cat. And if a large animal were killed, some vultures and some jackals soon drove the wild cat away and ate whatever meat remained. Then hyenas would come in and scare away the vultures and the jackals and would eat their fill, which was often only bones and skin. Thus typically, many creatures ate a kill.

Now a great fork in the evolutionary tree for horses had occurred. Horses had separated into those that fed on *leaves* and those that fed on *grass*. And like almost every group of mammals, horses would have an intricate phylogeny.

The *leaf-eating* lineage of horses, the anchitherines, would continue evolving in the Miocene: Their evolutionary tree would have many branches as several species would appear. And although not growing larger than a sheep, they would be "successful" for a while. They would *spread* from North America to Asia through the Bering-Strait land bridge. And they would even go as far as Europe. But in the end would they become "dead ends" on Life's evolutionary tree, as changing vegetation, mammal competition, and small size did take their toll: By the end of the Miocene, the last anchitherines – sinohippus in Asia and megahippus in North America – would *perish*.

Now the other lineage of horses arose as follows: miohippus from the Oligocene had evolved into the *larger* parahippus; this pony-sized horse had acquire a *cement-like coating* on its teeth, enabling it to feed on both leaves and grass in North America. Then parahippus evolved into the *equines* and the hipparionines, horses that grazed *exclusively on grass*. And they had *manes* like modern horses; their feet possessed a central hoof with two adjacent tiny toes; and they had rigid legs, well suited for swift running. Now the hipparionines would repeat the history of the anchitherines: They would evolve into many species, become "successful" and spread throughout the world – first to Asia, then to Europe and to Africa. But in the Pleistocene would they succumb to competition and cold temperatures. Now the equines would remain in North America throughout the Miocene, branching into many species and eventually become the modern horse, the equus.

And in North America, poëbrotherium evolved from one species to the next and eventually to camelus, the modern camel, and into lama. And eventually camels would *cross* the Bering-Strait land bridge to Asia. And twenty-million years later, the lama would migrate *south* through Panama to South America. And it would evolve into the guanaco, the alpaca and the llama of the Pleistocene and Holocene.

And the battle to survive encouraged mammals to get *bigger*. And this is what happened to the elephants: They developed longer trunks, larger ears and bigger tusks. Now the largest *mastodons* were three meters tall and weighed four tons. Most had no lower tusks, while their upper tusks were one to two meters long and slightly curved and often S-shaped. Now *amebelodon*, a descendant of phiomia, had short round upper tusks, while the lower ones were flat and used to shovel and uproot Earth's vegetation. And the heads of stegolophodons were less funnel-shaped than heads of mastodons. The stegolophodons *dwelt* in China and in India, but later they would spread to Africa and Europe.

And these giant mammals ate *two-hundred kilograms* of vegetation daily. And their trunks pulled tall grass from the ground, or broke off the lower leaves and branches of the forest trees. Thus elephants ate not with hands or paws but with their *trunks*. And they also drank with *them*, using them like straws to draw up water. And sometimes they sprayed the water in the air to cool themselves. And their tails often waved back and forth to brush away the flies.

And some sloths began to live in trees. And they became the *tree sloths*. And others developed long noses and long tongues. And these toothless creatures were called anteaters, for they fed on termites and on ants.

*And an aardvark "stepped off an ark" and onto land.*

And advanced primates *appeared* in Europe and East Africa. And ancient forms of gibbons, gorillas, chimpanzees and other apes walked on hind feet, often using the knuckles of their hands as crutches. And other primates, using one arm then the other, swung from limb to limb and tree to tree.[337]

And the above-mentioned mammals were just some of the *many* types of mammals that in the Miocene inhabited thy Earth.

## Chapter IV: Africa Joins Southwest Asia

Now the northward drift of Africa drove the Arabian Peninsula into southwest Asia. And the Tethys Sea was *severed*. And so the ancient Tethys Sea was gone – the Indian Ocean had consumed the eastern part. The only waters that remained were those between North Africa and Europe. And these became the waters of the proto-Mediterranean-Sea.

And as Arabia continued to penetrate southwestern Asia, earth *buckled up* and formed great folds of crust. And the Taurus and Zagros Mountains in Turkey and Iran were made. And among them was Mount Elbrus, the highest Caucasus peak. And among them was Mount Ararat, the site where Noah's ark is reported to have settled when the biblical great flood subsided.

And so for the first time in the Cenozoic, Africa and Asia were *connected*. And many African animals migrated across the Arabian Peninsula and entered India and Europe. And among them were the elephants and mastodons. And during the next several million years, mastodons continued on to Central Asia, Siberia, Canada and other parts of North America.

And it *happened* that some primitive apes followed the migrations of the animals out of Africa and into Asia. Henceforth, the African and Asian apes would lead *separate evolutionary paths*. And the Asian apes would develop into the modern gibbon and orangutan, while the African apes would evolve into gorillas, chimpanzees and man.

## Chapter V: Hot Spots

And the mantle hot spot which had forged the Faeroe Islands forged *another island* at the Mid-Atlantic Ridge. And it was Iceland. And Iceland was full of mountains, volcanos *and* hot steamy springs, for the land of Iceland was not cold – deep down the earth was *hot*.

And it was about sixteen-million years BC. And *magma* from a mantle hot spot broke through the lithosphere in the northwestern part of the United States. And this was the first of *many lava bursts*. And during the next one-million years, one-thousand eruptions of gigantic *lava flows* occurred. Each flow produced a thousand cubic kilometers of lava and basaltic rock. And each gave off *three-trillion kilograms* of sulfur gases and *sixteen-trillion kilograms* of $CO_2$. And these toxic fumes

---

[337] This is known as brachiating.

seeped into the atmosphere and disrupted the global climate and environment, causing some destruction of Earth's life. And in all, a *million
cubic kilometers* of magma poured out and onto land, thereby making a
plateau the size of New York State. And these lava flows created the
Columbia River flood basalts.

And in the coming years, North America would drift toward the
*west*. And the position of the hot spot over land would thus move to the
*east*. And in modern times, the hot spot would diminish in its strength
and be centered *under* Yellowstone National Park, at the junction of
Idaho, Wyoming and Montana. And its heat would make Old Faithful
give off steam.

## Chapter VI: The Temperature of Earth
## Takes a Sudden Drop

One thousand years had passed since the last flow of lava from the
Columbia River flood basalts. And the atmosphere of Earth had
*ample greenhouse gases*. And the weather *warmed* somewhat. And a
million years went by. And repeated rains did wash away the extra
$CO_2$. And the temperature of Earth began to drop again, declining
three degrees during the next eight-hundred-thousand years. And the
southern polar cap enlarged: All of Antarctica was covered in a layer of
*ice*.

And the deep sea waters of the oceans, which had been so warm
in the Cretaceous, *also started cooling*. And ocean temperature in Celsius would on average drop by eight degrees during the next ten-million
years.

And cooling waters began *killing ocean life*. And many mollusks
and plankton species disappeared. And the dying would continue for
many hundred-thousand years, as Earth's temperature declined.

And three-million years went by – it was twelve-million years BC.
And the cold conditions brought some ice to regions of the Arctic. And
*glaciers* grew in Alaska and the northern parts of Canada, Siberia and
Greenland. And some *icebergs* floated in the Arctic Ocean. And for the
first time in more than two-hundred-million years, Earth had a northern polar cap, albeit very small and piecemeal.

## Chapter VII: Primates Continue to Evolve

And it *happened* that the first ground-dwelling monkeys did appear,
living on land instead of in the trees. And some primitive Miocene
apes *evolved* to pliopithecus, sivapithecus, proconsul, ramapithecus and
dryopithecus. And these Middle-Miocene primates were proto-hominids.
Now ramapithecus *dwelt* in Kenya, Pakistan and India. And sivapithecus, which was quite similar to ramapithecus, occupied the Middle

East, North Africa and southern Asia.[338] Eventually the sivapithecines would *evolve into* orangutans. Now the gibbon-like pliopithecus lived in Europe and East Africa. And dryopithecus did dwell in Europe and in China. It had chimpanzee-like limbs but its body was gorilla-like. And in Africa, proconsuls lived in forest trees and fed on fruit; the males were somewhat larger than the females, but both were of the sizes of baboons. And they had feet, shoulders and elbows like chimpanzees, but their wrists were monkey-like. At *different rates* were body parts evolving.[339] Now it would happen that an ape-like "neighbor" of sivapithecus, named gigantopithecus, would grow into a towering "gorilla" almost three meters tall. Verily would it be the "King Kong" of the proto-hominids.

.     .     .     .     .     .     .

And a chimpanzee broke a twig off a short cedar tree, *removed the leaves* and stripped away the smaller stems. And she poked the denuded twig into a termite nest and moved it in and out. In a frenzy ran the termites. And the chimpanzee pulled out the stick. And she licked and ate the termites that were crawling on it.

And in the past, vultures had used rocks to break a hard ostrich egg, and otters had used stones to crack a clam or oyster shell, but this was *the first time* that an animal had *made a tool*.

## Chapter VIII: The Mediterranean Sea

*And the sea was blown back by a strong east wind.*
*And so the sea was made into dry land.*

And several million years went by – it was six-million years ago. And northern Africa *touched* southern Europe. And the proto-Mediterranean-Sea was severed from the East Atlantic Ocean. And one-hundred-thousand years went by. And a cooler climate made the polar caps expand. And when ocean water was converted into ice on land, sea level fell. And the proto-Mediterranean-Sea went *dry*. And all fish and marine life in the region ended up on land and died. And animals from Africa came and *ate* the dead fish and dead shrimp. And animals from Europe came and *ate* the dead shrimp and dead fish. And some African animals crossed into Europe through the proto-Mediterranean, which was not a sea but *land*. And some European animals did the same; they entered Africa. And evaporites, in the form

---

[338] Both ramapithecus and sivapithecus are named after Hindu gods: Siva, "the Destroyer," is one of the three chief Hindu deities and is often considered the creative and reproductive force. The other two are Brahma and Vishnu. Brahma, "the Creator," is the pervading soul of the Universe. Vishnu, "the Preserver," has made nine appearances on Earth. The tenth and remaining visit is still to come. Rama, one of these incarnations of Vishnu, is the Hindu god of chivalry and virtue. Siva is also know as "Lord of the Beasts."

[339] This is often true in general: When one animal evolves into another, some changes may occur early and some may occur late.

of salts and minerals, made a thirty-meter layer. And the land *was as* the desert of Death Valley, California.

And thirty-thousand years went by. And sea level rose somewhat. And water from the Atlantic Ocean filled the lowlands between Africa and Europe. And the proto-Mediterranean became a sea *again*. And thirty-thousand years went by. And sea level dropped a bit. And the waters of the proto-Mediterranean were *drained* again, and another layer of salt and sand was laid.

And during the next one-million years, fluctuations in sea level, climate and geography *drained and filled* the proto-Mediterranean-Sea *three dozen times*.[340]

And finally northeastern Africa and southeastern Europe permanently separated. And the Strait of Gibraltar opened up. And waters filled for good the lowlands between Africa and Europe. And the modern Mediterranean Sea came into being. And *unto this day* and henceforth would it *be*.

## Chapter IX: Canyons

And it came to pass that, beneath Southwest United States, the mantle *warmed*. And the heat made continental crust *expand*. And Colorado, Arizona, Utah and the Rocky Mountains in that region lifted up, and the Colorado Plateau, which was an elevated plain, was built. And rivers in the region flowed down steep slopes. And during the next few million years, the rivers *cut their way* through sediments and rock and forged deep river valleys and great canyons. Among them was Grand Canyon.

## Chapter X: Horns and Antlers

Now the Miocene was coming to an end. And it *happened* that four-toed ruminants evolved to two-toed forms. And chevrotains, which were relatively short and primitive ruminants, *appeared*. They had no horns, but males had two saber-tooth-like tusks. And during several million years, giraffes, which fed on trees, had developed *longer necks* to reach the leaves. And around this time in geo-history, the first deer evolved solid bony outgrowths on their heads. And "soon," others, such as pronghorns, cattle, cows and antelope, had horns. The horns were often used to fend off predators. And some horned ruminants took part in *butting*: Two animals squared off, drove forward at each other and then rammed the horns. And other creatures *wrestled*: first engaging antlers, then trying to push and pull or swing the other to the ground. And this was done to strengthen horns and antlers. And this was done

---

[340] The repeated evaporations and refillings of the proto-Mediterranean-Sea deposited enormous quantities of ocean solvents and produced a kilometer-thick layer of minerals, sand and salts. In all, one-twentieth of the salt in Earth's oceans was removed and put in the basin of the proto-Mediterranean-Sea.

to determine who was dominant. And this was done by males in their quest females. And the ruminants with bigger antlers reproduced more often. And with time, deer and antelope developed elaborate and branch-like horns.

## Chapter XI: Savannas Everywhere

And Nature, the great architect, had "*designed*" vast grassland habitats. And animals did occupy these lands and did adapt. Many mammals developed grinding teeth for grazing stubborn straw-like grass. And for example, horses evolved long molars with cement-like covered crowns. And the legs of many grazing mammals had become long and thin while still remaining strong: They were "designed" for running speed. And indeed, *speed* was needed in the open fields when predators approached. And it came to be that *new forms* of artiodactyls, carnivores and elephants appeared. And wild animal kingdoms populated the savannas of the World. And communities of big game, similar to those of East Africa today, were *everywhere*. And the forests of the Earth were full of foxes, tree sloths, pigs, dogs, deer, antelope, anteaters, tapirs, monkeys, pandas, wolves, mice, weasels, squirrels, armadillos, small cats, wild cats, boars and rats. And from river to winding river, from mountain to towering mountain, from plain to windy plain, everywhere were mammals. Nature's majestic animals were *everywhere* on Earth.

*The fifth book of the Cenozoic, called*

# The Pliocene

*And sheep gathered in a flock.*

## Chapter I: The Hawaiian Islands

It was five-million years ago. It was the Pliocene. And the temperature of Earth continued to go slowly down. And *glaciers* grew in southern Argentina. And icebergs floated in the oceans near Antarctica. And as water turned to ice on land, sea level *dropped*. And it was falling ten meters every million years.

And it came to pass that the Emperor Islands sank *beneath the sea* – they had descended due to *their own weight*. And this chain of submerged islands was renamed the *Emperor Seamount*. And Pele, the hot spot in the mantle, which initially had made the chain, was in the mid-Pacific-Ocean three-thousand kilometers away. Meanwhile, Pele had built *another seamount-island chain*. And the island of Midway was midway along the chain. And Abbott, the island farthest to the west, did sink below the sea. And now the *Abbott Seamount* was its name.

And as magma from Pele burst through the ocean crust, *another volcanic island* formed. And it was provided with a name. And the name was Kauai. And two-million years went by. And the Pacific Tectonic Plate transported Kauai to the north and west. And Pele torched the Earth once more, and the island of Oahu rose. And one-and-a-half-million years passed by. And the hot spot made Maui. And a million years went by, and the island of Hawaii rose. Thus Pele *made* the Hawaiian Islands, the Emperor Seamount and a seamount-island chain northwest of Honolulu. And in the Holocene, Pele would occupy the crater Kilauea. And Loihi, a submerged active volcano, would be off the south coast of Hawaii. And Loihi would be waiting for the moment *to rise up* and make a new Hawaiian island.

Now the Hawaiian Islands provided a habitat, which was *isolated* from the continents. There, floral life and faunal life *pursued* a special path of evolution. And for example, the only mammals living there were bats. And toads, lizards, frogs and snakes were absent. And in the isolated islands, *special forms* of life evolved. And so it came to pass that the Hawaiian Islands were blessed with fifteen-hundred types of flowering plants. And these flowers were not found in *any other land*. And many different types of mosses, algae, fungi, ferns and trees did flourish in volcanic ash and earth. And one-thousand types of snails did crawl on grass and soil. And in the jungle, fruit flies lived and multiplied.[341] And exotic insects, birds and plants made Hawaii an exotic land.

---

[341] One-fourth of the world's fruit-fly species are indigenous to Hawaii.

Now Hawaii would remain a natural and exotic kingdom up to modern times. But around four-hundred years AD, the first humans *would* arrive. And in one-thousand years AD, Polynesians would come in boats and populate the islands. And they would *bring* fruit-bearing trees and other plants. And in the year one-thousand-seven-hundred-seventy-eight, the first Europeans would set foot upon the sandy shores. And humans would eventually bring mammals such as cattle, cats, goats, deer, dogs, pigs and rats. Now some of these animals would be brought for food. But others would be brought by accident. Likewise, lizards, quail, pheasants, partridges and turkeys would arrive in boats. And years later would they crawl and fly in fields and forests. And cattle, goats, deer and pigs would go wild and then eat the vegetation. And exotic forms of plants would *disappear*. And cats and dogs would battle small Hawaiian animals. And frogs, lizards, toads and European birds would eat exotic insects. And unique Hawaiian wildlife would thus decline. And although by the beginning of the third millennium the Hawaiian Islands would still be rich with distinctive forms of life, certain wildlife species would have disappeared and *gone extinct*.[342]

Now during the Cenozoic Era, *other* mantle hot spots had made island chains and seamounts in all the oceans of the World. But such activity in the West Pacific was particularly widespread. And examples were the Tuamotu Archipelago and the Line Islands, as well as the Marshall and the Gilbert and the Austral islands. And in the Indian Ocean, it happened that the Ninetyeast Ridge was created by a *hot spot* during the period of geo-history from eighty-million years BC to thirty-million years BC. And it stretched *five-thousand kilometers* in length: from the Andaman Islands in the Bay of Bengal south along the ninety-degree east longitude to the Broken Ridge Plateau at thirty degrees south latitude. And the hot spot which forged the Ninetyeast Ridge went on to build the Great Kerguelen Island near Antarctica. And millions of years of erosion wore the island down. And in the Recent most of it would disappear *beneath the sea*. And it would become the Kerguelen Plateau, an elevated underwater plain. But some volcanic peaks would still remain exposed to air, and islands would they be.

## Chapter II: Artiodactyls Prosper

And evolution took one step forward. And a series of slow changes produced the ape-man from the ape. And the *hand* of evolution was working everywhere. The artiodactyls did diversify. And there were *many* forms of deer, sheep, pigs, camels, cattle, goats and antelopes. And as artiodactyls multiplied, their numbers increased enormously.

---

[342] The transportation by humans of remote life to other isolated island ecosystems would happen frequently in the Holocene.

And territoriality came into play, as each individual or herd *claimed* a plot of land sufficient for its needs. And when threatened by an invader of its kind, the artiodactyl or the herd fought almost to the death to save its land.

And the equines of the Late Miocene evolved to many forms. And for example, there were hipparion and *pliohippus*. And species such as pliohippus evolved into the zebra, ass and modern horse. And these three creatures *crossed* from North America to Asia along the Bering-Strait land bridge.

And it happened that in Africa a pig-like mammal from the Miocene evolved into a giant creature with thick columnar legs to support its three-ton body. And this heavy artiodactyl was the *Earth's first hippopotamus.*

And some animals did move in *flocks*. And these included oxen, cattle, rams, goats, cows and sheep. It was three-million years ago or so. And it would not be long before *shepherds* led such flocks. And it would not be long before man rode the backs of horses, camels, mules and other animals of transportation. And from the palm, the lamb, and vine, man would "soon" be making oil, wool and wine.

## Chapter III: North and South America Are Joined

*And a great whirlwind shall be raised up
from the coasts of Earth.*

And out of the sea did the Isthmus of Panama rise up. And the equatorial *flow* of water between the Atlantic and Pacific oceans *stopped*. And the currents of the Gulf Stream up the eastern coast of the United States flowed *stronger* and attained full force. And the Panamanian Seaway was no more. Instead, there was the strip of land called Panama. And North and South America "joined hands" – the Americas were now *united*. And sea life in the eastern Pacific just west of Panama was cut off from sea life in the Caribbean just east of Panama. And during the next three-million years, sea life on each side would follow *separate* evolutionary paths.

Thus the Pacific and Atlantic oceans were divided by a strip of land. And this division would remain *unto this day*. But in modern times, man *would* connect the two by a canal. And near Panama, Pacific waters then would flow into Atlantic waters. Likewise would Atlantic waters flow into Pacific waters.

And with two Americas connected, animals from South America did migrate *north*. And animals from North America did migrate *south*. And the Great American Animal Interchange took place. And South American ground sloths, porcupines and armadillos appeared in California, Texas, Florida and other southern parts of the United States. And North American wolves, raccoons, dogs, horses, tapirs, llamas, cats and mastodons invaded South America. And the Great American

Mammal Battle started. And the North did "win the war," although there are mostly losers in such wars. And hundreds of South American mammal species *went extinct*. And for example, almost all hoofed animals, marsupials and edentates of South America did disappear. And rhinoceroses departed from the face of North America.

Now the currents of the Gulf Stream brought warm waters to the Labrador Sea and the northwest Atlantic Ocean. And there did warm and *moist* air rise. And clouds were made. Thus clouds floated over eastern Canada and Greenland almost every day. And almost every afternoon, the clouds let loose their moisture, as falling water drops. And through the cold air mass above the Earth, the water droplets passed. And tiny *crystals* formed. And so it snowed. And for hundreds of thousands of years in this region did it snow. And eastern Canada turned *white* with snow and ice. And Greenland changed from brownish green to *white*. And glaciers grew in eastern Canada and Greenland. And another part was added to the northern polar cap.

## Chapter IV: The Earth Grows Very Cold

And the temperature of Earth continued to decline. And *snow and ice* were added to the southern polar cap. And the northern polar cap expanded into other places. And ice *entered* northern Europe. And ice spread *southward* to the northern parts of North America and Russia.

Thus the water from the oceans had been placed in ice and snow on northern Europe, Canada, Antarctica, Siberia and Greenland. And sea level consequently dropped.

It was two-and-a-half-million years ago. Alaska had just pulled away from Asia. There was now a *gap* between the two. And water did invade the land between Alaska and Siberia. And for the first time in *a long time*, the Bering Strait was *verily* a strait. And so the Arctic and Pacific oceans were connected by a waterway. Thus the land bridge between Alaska and Siberia had disappeared as if it had collapsed. And migrations of land animals between America and Asia *ceased*.

And as ice accumulated in northern Europe, Canada, Antarctica, Siberia and Greenland, giant glaciers formed. And ice blocks filled the Arctic Ocean. And Earth had sizeable, thick polar caps.

Now the large temperature differences between the tropics and the poles fueled the currents of the oceans. And *swift* deep-sea currents flowed from the poles to the equator, while swift surface currents flowed from the equator to the poles. And so the deep waters of the seas and oceans everywhere on Earth were cold – in Celsius were they but just a few degrees.

And compared with other epochs of the past, the Earth was very cold: The Ice Age had begun.

*The sixth book of the Cenozoic, called*

# The Pleistocene

*And a deep cold descended on the Earth.*

## Chapter I: Mammals Adapt to a Cold Climate

It was one-million-and-six-hundred-thousand years ago. The Quaternary Period began. And it would last to modern times. And at one-point-six-million years ago, the first epoch of the Quaternary, the Pleistocene, began. And the Pleistocene was also called the *Great Ice Age*, although the Earth was already in the midst of an ice age.

And evolution took one step forward. And ape-men spent more time on land than in the trees. And homo erectus, the upright-walking proto-man, emerged on Earth about this time.[343]

And it happened that some birds evolved to giant forms. Certain condors were the largest *flying* birds on Earth. But even larger were some *flightless* birds, such as the elephant bird of Madagascar: It was about three meters tall and weighed nearly *half a ton*. Even its eggs were huge: ten kilograms. And in Australia, New Guinea and adjacent islands ran birds a meter to two meters long. And the brown ones were the emus, while the black ones with the colored heads were cassowaries. But the *tallest bird* to ever be was dinornis maximus: In New Zealand did this three-and-a-half-meter flightless moa dwell. And the elephant bird and dinornis maximus lived *almost* unto this day: But in the second half of the second millennium AD, *after man arrived* in Madagascar and New Zealand, these two giant birds did go extinct.

And in North America, the descendants of pliohippus, which were the zebra, ass and modern horse, *all died and disappeared*. But these three did survive in Africa and in Eurasia. And in the second millennium AD, Spaniards traversing the Atlantic Ocean would *reintroduce* the horse to North and South America.

And many mammals grew *thicker fur* to fight the colder climate. And the pigs with dense hair were the peccaries. And there appeared one type of *woolly* elephant with a pair of enormous[344] curving, heavy tusks. And four meters tall, this creature was a *mammoth*. And mammoths lived in northern Asia, North America and Europe. And in Eurasia there emerged rhinoceroses with *heavy coats of fur*. And later, a Stone Age artist would etch images of these woolly creatures on a wall inside a cave. Then twenty years thereafter would the caveman die. And much later in the Pleistocene would the woolly rhinoceroses go extinct. But in the cave the illustrations would live on. And in modern times, archaeologists would discover the woolly rhinos *and* the art.

---

[343] For the evolution of man, see the New Testament Book of *Homogenesis*.

[344] The length of the tusk was almost four meters.

And in South America dwelt macrauchenia, the bio-freak of mammals: It had the neck of a giraffe, a truck like that of a small elephant, the body of a camel and the legs of a rhinoceros. And this animal was huge – three meters long, three meters tall.

And some edentates evolved to giant forms. And crawling over land were turtle-like glyptodons with shells *four meters* wide. And some giant ground sloths grew six meters long and weighed *three tons*. And they were larger than most elephants.

And *large mammals* also occupied the more temperate regions of the Earth. And there were bison, giant wild hogs, ground sloths, giant beavers, hippopotamuses, elephants and mastodons. And mammal evolution seemed to follow the path of reptile evolution of the Mesozoic – again *bigger* seemed equivalent to "better."

## Chapter II: A Glacial Maximum

*And in those days
they shall seek death and shall not find it.
And they shall desire to die,
but death shall flee from them.*

Now the gravitational interplay of Earth and Sun and Moon has *perturbed* the motion of the Earth throughout all time. And at this point in geo-history, this disturbance had made the orbit of the Earth a bit *more circular*. And when near the perihelion, the Earth received *less light* from Sun. And the Earth cooled down a bit. And so the northern and the southern polar caps grew larger. And the larger caps, being white, reflected well the sunlight. And the *reflected light* went into heat in air, which rose up through the atmosphere and into outer space. Thus Earth retained less heat. And Earth cooled down some more. And the polar caps grew larger.

And since the polar snow and ice kept the Arctic and Antarctic regions cold, a large temperature difference existed between the tropics and the poles. And this created *swift air currents*. And the rain cycle thus sped up. In the polar regions, it snowed instead of rained, and snow accumulated quickly. And falling rains elsewhere washed great quantities of $CO_2$ out of the atmosphere. And the amount of carbon-dioxide gas decreased. And with less greenhouse gas, Earth *retained less heat*. And the temperature of Earth descended even more.[345]

And *snow and ice* did pile up. And white mountains of the snow and ice were made. And the "ice-snow mountains" grew to heights of several thousand meters in Canada, northern Russia, northern Europe, Greenland and Antarctica. And because air was colder at the higher elevations, the snow melted very little during summer. And the polar caps grew even *thicker*.

---

[345] The temperature was five degrees Celsius cooler than in modern times.

And in many places on the Earth, snow accumulated in the mountains. And for example, the Rockies, Alps, Andes and many other ranges did fill up with *snow*, which persisted through the summers. And even mountains in China, Central America, New Zealand, Mexico, Tasmania and southern Africa had *glaciers* all year round.

And in winter in the northern hemisphere, glaciers grew and headed *south*. And in the United States, they reached Pennsylvania, New Jersey, Iowa, New York, Ohio, South Dakota, Illinois, Wyoming, Oregon and Idaho. And in Eurasia, glaciers covered Germany, England, Poland, northern Russia and Siberia. And the southern tip of South America was also *under ice*.

And so it came to pass that glaciers covered *forty-five-million square kilometers* of land — one-third the land of Earth. And five per cent of Earth's water was in ice. And the oceans were one-hundred meters *lower* than in modern times. And ice piled up so much that continental crust below the ice sank *several hundred meters*.

A glacial maximum in the *Great Ice Age* was taking place.

And it happened to be springtime. And by a *haphazard act* of Nature, winter ice high in a mountain trough had made a *dam* — above the ice there lay a lake. And in effect, the icé was holding back the waters of the lake. And a month went by. And when ice in the ice dam melted some, the ice dam grew too thin and broke. And water from the lake rushed down the mountain side — it was an avalanche *not* of snow but ordinary water. And the water poured into the valley down below. And suddenly the valley was a lake. And another month went by. And the flooded valley drained and once again was dry.

And elsewhere on the Earth, the springtime melting of the snow and ice *unleashed great floods*.

And glaciers in the mountains retreated during summer. And glaciers during winter grew and slid down mountain slopes. And they grew down along the *paths of least resistance*, descending as white arms of snow from peaks. At lower elevations, the white arms spread to long white fingers. And as the ice and snow descended, the sides of mountains wore away. And valley regions in the mountains got deeper and got rounder. Thus geo-processes carved *U-shaped valleys* in the sides of mountains.

And in the northern hemisphere, glaciers continued spreading south. And ice by rubbing stones did *polish* them. And some rocks became embedded in the ice. And as the ice advanced, the rocks in ice moved forth. And some rocks were transported lengthy distances. At the same time, rocks embedded in the underside of glaciers scratched the rocks in earth. Thus *scratches* in Earth's rocks told stories of the glaciers' motions.

And glaciers wore away the surfaces of rocks and stones. And pieces broke. And clay, grains, chips and pebbles were mixed with bits of rock and boulders. And these were *till*, the debris from ice erosion.

And conglomerate rock, which formed from till when it was pressed together, was provided with a name. And *tillite* was its name. Thus till and tillite were the telltale signs of glaciation.

And in many places, vegetation froze and subsequently died in ice. And the advancing ice *drove* animals *away* from favored habitats, forcing them to migrate to the milder climatic regions of the Earth. And for the *good land* that remained, the animals did battle. And life verily did suffer. And the number of animals on Earth declined.

And when summer came, ice melted and made water. And the water rushed down the slopes of mountains, sometimes passing over ledges. Earth's mountains were *full of lakes and waterfalls*.

And sediments were deposited each summer in the glacial lakes. And each winter did the lakes freeze over. And a series of yearly sedimentary layers were made. And these were *varves*.

Now water, or $H_2O$, consists of two hydrogen atoms and one oxygen atom. And know thee and all around thee that water can be *heavy* or be *light*. *Heavy water* contains a heavy oxygen-eighteen nucleus, an isotope of oxygen. And *light water*, which is normal water, contains a normal oxygen-sixteen nucleus.[346] Now most ocean water is normal water. But *small quantities* of ocean water are of the heavy type. And because the molecules of heavy water verily are heavier, they move more slowly. And because they move more slowly, their evaporation rate is *lower*. Thus when ocean water evaporates, it is mostly normal water that does enter air. And since it is the water vapor in the air that snows down upon the polar caps, the polar caps – being predominantly normal ice – have very little heavy ice. Now since normal water more readily evaporates, *more heavy water is left behind in oceans*. So *during this glacial maximum*, water in the ocean had more heavy $H_2O$. And to make their shells, shellfish processed the oxygen in ocean water, combining it with calcium and carbon. Thus during this glacial maximum, the shells weighed *slightly* more, for they contained more oxygen-eighteen. And when the shellfish died, their shells settled on the ocean floor and made a layer of sediments, which later turned to limestone. Thus during the glacial maximum, the limestone of the Earth was heavier, for it contained more oxygen-eighteen.

## Chapter III: A Glacial Minimum

And eighty-thousand years went by. Now it had come to pass that the motion of the planets and the Moon had *perturbed* the orbit of the Earth around the Sun, making it a tiny bit *less circular*. And when near the perihelion, the Earth received *more light* from Sun. And during this time, the northern and the southern polar caps did shrink somewhat. And the brown earth around the melted regions did absorb sun-

---

[346] In other words, the heavy water molecule weighs more because it has two extra neutrons in the oxygen-atom's nucleus.

light. Thus Earth retained more heat. And so the Earth did *warm a little* – the temperature of Earth increased one-half degree. And the polar caps got even smaller.

And with less snow and ice at polar regions, the temperature difference between the tropics and the poles decreased. And air currents in the atmosphere *blew a little slower*. And since warm moist air was being uplifted not as often as before, it rained a *little less*. And carbon-dioxide-gas removal by Earth's rain proceeded at a slower pace. And the amount of atmospheric $CO_2$ increased, thereby helping Earth *retain its heat*. And Earth's temperature inched up a little more.

And as ice and snow melted in the higher elevations, the height of ice-snow mountains dropped. And since air was warmer at the lower elevations, the next layer of ice and snow melted *even* quicker.

And in the temperate zones, the amount of snow declined in mountain ranges. And snow was also *disappearing* from the mountains in the equatorial regions of the Earth. And in summer in the northern hemisphere, the glaciers did retreat. And brown land appeared where *white* snow once had been. And it seemed *as if* brown ground were moving north. And soon grass occupied that wet brown earth. Brown regions turned to green. And small bushes, plants and trees shot up. And animals moved in, inhabiting the land.

And after twenty-thousand years, the glaciers retreated to the Arctic Circle. And only the Arctic Ocean, Greenland and the northern part of Canada were under ice.

And the average temperature of Earth attained a local maximum – it was a few degrees *warmer* than in modern times.

A glacial minimum in the *Great Ice Age* was taking place.

And the water *from melted snow* made rivers overflow. And continents were flooded for a while, but eventually they drained. And this water was *recycled to the oceans*. Now because this continental water was mainly normal water, the heavy water in the oceans was diluted. And the percentage of oxygen-eighteen in the seas *went down*. Likewise the fraction of oxygen-eighteen in shells and ocean sediments *went down*.

And after ice had melted, turned to water and drained away, a heavy weight was taken off the chests of continental crust. And the crust in Canada, northern Europe and Siberia rose *several hundred meters*.

## Chapter IV: The Variations in Glaciations

And more or less *each* one-hundred-thousand years would Earth's orbit vary from an almost perfect circle. Thus glacial maximums would happen roughly every hundred-thousand years. Thus glacial minimums would happen roughly every hundred-thousand years. Now of these *one-hundred-thousand years*, extensive glaciations would endure for eighty-thousand years, while "warm" interglacial periods would occupy the remaining twenty-thousand years, during which green grass would spread in northern regions of the Earth. And furthermore, *Earth's spinning axis* would precess with time, and its angle to the solar-system plane would change. And these variations would affect the climate, causing additional small changes in Earth's temperature. And these changes would combine with those created by the variations of Earth's orbit shape. And so, some glaciations *would* be more intense than others. And between two-million years BC and the Holocene, Earth would undergo twenty major glaciations and a dozen minor ones.

Now in Central China *during glacial maximums*, it was relatively cold and dry. And strong winds blew the Gobi-Desert dust and sand, some of which had originated from erosion by the glaciers; the name for such windblown dust was *loess*. And plateaus of loess formed. And some loess settled on surrounding hills. Now Central China *during glacial minimums* was relatively warm and wet. And *ordinary soil* was piled onto loess. Thus the variations in the glaciations created alternating layers of soil and loess. And a *record* of the times was made in earth in hills in Central China.

And during glacial minimums, sea level rose one-hundred meters. And during glacial maximums, sea level dropped one-hundred meters. And the *fluctuations* in the level of the sea played havoc with Earth's ocean life. And cnidarians, coral reefs, mollusks, bryozoans and crustaceans sometimes ended up on land or deep below the sea, and subsequently died.

Now in modern times, scientists would drill the sea floors, remove some *cores* of ocean crust and analyze them. And the levels of oxygen-eighteen in shells and limestone would be measured. And scientists would drill into the polar caps of northern Canada, Antarctica and Greenland. And *columns of ice* would be removed. And the ice would be *examined* for its dust content, for its oxygen-eighteen levels, for its composition, for its ice-snow patterns, and for other indicators of Earth's past. And *air bubbles* trapped in ice would be time capsules: They would be examined for their carbon-dioxide content and for percentages of certain other molecules. And the *sedimentary rocks* of Earth would be inspected. And ancient pollen, loess, varves and tillite would be found. And transported boulders, scratched rocks and polished stones would also be discovered. And from all this information, the variations in Earth's climate for the Pleistocene and Holocene *would be deduced*.

Now it came to pass that *vast glaciers* entered lowlands in the central part of North America, where weak rocks lay. And ice pushed away the rock and sediments, thereby carving out *enormous basins* in the Earth. And for innumerous millenniums, the ice lay frozen there. And when the ice did finally retreat, it left the basins bare. And water from runoff *and* from rain did fill the lowland region. And several lakes were made. They were Lake Ontario, Lake Huron, Lake Superior, Lake Erie and Lake Michigan.

And elsewhere around the World did glaciers carve out basins. And from these basins, *other lakes were made.*

Now *giant mammals* found it difficult adapting to the fluctuating climate. And glyptodonts died out. And the number of ground sloths, giraffes, wild hogs, rhinoceroses, giant beavers, bison, hippopotamuses, elephants and mastodons declined – from time to time, a frigid mass of air *swept over Earth* and left a herd of mammals dead. And other creatures also died.

Now at this time, it came to pass that homo erectus evolved into the homo sapiens, the species now called man.[347] And so man emerged and dwelt in the land of the living. And man *multiplied his numbers,* spreading to all four corners of the World. And man went out to *dominate the land.*

## Chapter V: The Earth Gets a Little Warmer

It was sixteen-thousand years BC. The last great glaciation climaxed: From this point on, the Earth would *warm.* Now since the sea was one-hundred meters lower than the level of today, the continents were larger – more margins were exposed to air and dry. And during the next eight-thousand years, glaciers would *disappear* from northern parts of the United States. And several thousand years thereafter, *glaciation* in the southern half of Canada would *cease.* And in north Eurasia, ice would similarly retreat.

## Chapter VI: Massive Growth and the Last Mass Extinction

*And man increased exceedingly
and had much cattle and camels and asses.*

And in the warmer weather, man felt comfortable – life was *no longer* cruel, harsh and cold. And man began to multiply *more rapidly.* And homo sapiens numbered in the millions.

And to feed himself, man hunted mammals, birds and other creatures. And man learned to hunt *efficiently.* And for example, pits were dug in earth and covered with branches, leaves and parts of trees. And unsuspecting animals fell in. Or near a cliff, a long line of men raised their weapons high and hollered at a herd of grazing buffalos. And instantly, the animals were *panic stricken,* darting off in one direction as a group – they fled in a stampede. And they ran and ran, until suddenly, the plateau was no more. And the first row of buffalos did see the cliff and *try to stop.* But the buffalos behind them would not stop. And bodies tumbled head over heels into the depths below. And

---

[347] This began the moment at which an almost paradoxical situation arose, in which a life form, namely man, would attempt to understand itself. Man's brain would be the path to the understanding of himself and of the Universe.

hours later did men skin the beasts. And they would use the hides for clothes and tents. And men would also eat the meat.

Now mostly, man hunted *out of hunger* – he had to feed himself. And under "natural law," there is no sin in this. But some men hunted for sadistic *pleasure*, killing because they liked to kill.[348] And in the providence of Nature, these men were *committing sin*.[349]

And homo sapiens could not control themselves – they copulated frequently. And they did so because Nature instilled in them the *great desire* to do so. And man procreated man, multiplying his numbers *manyfold*. And man went out in all directions seeking habitats in all of Earth. And the four corners of the compass did he occupy.

*(And a voice spake, saying,*
*"By being less, ye shall be more.")*
*But no one heard these words.*

And with his newly acquired hunting skills, man could kill the biggest of Earth's creatures. With man around, being bigger was not better, for the biggest animals were often easiest to kill. And they were the most desired, for they had more meat and hide. And with a weapon in his hand, man felt invincible, *like unto a god*. But man was not a god, for in the eyes of Nature, *some* men were committing sin.

*Thus man trespassed against his faunal kin.*

And the ground sloths *went extinct*. But those that lived in trees were beyond the reach of hands and spears; they survived. And many species of mammoths, mastodons and giant beavers disappeared *forever from the Earth*. And dozens of other large majestic mammals went extinct.

*And the silent voice of Nature*
*cried out in words of grief.*
*Her voice was not heard.*
*A silent voice cannot be heard.*

And to kill for food and meat is *one* thing. But to kill and to destroy for pleasure is another. And to kill and destroy something that can never be again is the *greatest sin of all*.

And man continued the wanton executions. And Nature's "children," the animals, were killed in hordes.

And so the final mass-extinction episode in geo-history began.

*(And a voice spake, saying,*
*"Woe unto them that join house to house,*
*that lay field to field,*

---

[348] And at the same time, there were others who used wooden staffs and watched over flocks of sheep.

[349] Since Nature is basically neutral, the concept of sin in this context technically does not make sense. However, if one imposes man's moral view of things, the idea of sin in the natural world does have meaning.

> *till there be no place,*
> *that they may be placed alone*
> *in the midst of the Earth.")*

And in the Late Pleistocene, man *cultivated* plants, vegetables and trees in organized arrangements in the earth. And this was farming. And man made "slaves" of animals: This was called *domestication.* And pigs were put in sties. And cows were put in barns. And cattle were contained on ranches with barb wire. And sheep and goats were similarly roped off. And cats and dogs were taken in as pets. And camels, mules and donkeys found crates and boxes on their backs. And horses were employed for riding. And oxen were employed for pulling. And so on.

> *(And a voice spake, saying,*
> *"Are ye not thy mammals' keepers?")*

And the number of homo sapiens increased. Now the situation was like an unrestrained explosive growth of cells. The homo sapiens *were as* malignant cells; the host was Earth.[350] It was a cancer in its early stage. And like a living organism, Earth at this stage possessed a tumor which was small and hardly could be felt. But when unchecked, such a malignancy can grow and grow. And eventually, it can consume its host.

Henceforth, human growth would go *unchecked.* And the density of human beings would sky rocket. And people would battle over land. And people would *claim all land.* And except in Antarctica, which was desolate and under snow, by the twentieth century, every foot of land would be owned by an individual, a government or an institution.

> *(And a voice spake, saying,*
> *"For what shall it profit man*
> *if he shall gain the world*
> *and lose his own soul?")*

And the extinction of the mammals by man would continue in the first two millenniums AD, as *witnessed* in the following:

The last small North African elephants would be *killed* by man in the second century AD. And the last American mastodon would be *exterminated* in the fourth century AD. And the last *large African bush* elephant would *die* at the hand of man in the twentieth century AD.[351]

And some men in hunting for fun and sport would overkill. And for example, in modern times, deer in Europe *would* be decimated.

And buffalo and bison would be butchered.

---

[350] With the exception of size, cells being much smaller than human beings, the analogy with a cancer is almost perfect: In a typical dictionary, a cancer is defined as an uncontrolled harmful growth in an otherwise healthy body.

[351] Of the three-hundred known species of the proboscideans, only two exist today: elephas maximus and loxodonta africana. Of the extinct species, dozens have disappeared because of man.

*(And a voice spake, saying,*
*"He that killeth an ox is as if he slew a man.")*

And man would even battle man. And this *also* would be sin. And wars often would be fought for land – the history books would list accounts of countless senseless *wars*. Europeans would fight Europeans. Asians would fight Asians. And the Europeans and the Asians would engage each other in some wars. And Europeans would set sail and come to North America. And they would bring diseases, guns and horses. And native American Indians would become sick and often die. And with tomahawks and bows and arrows, the Indians would fight the battles and be *killed*. And almost all the Indians would die. And there would be more wars – World-War-One and World-War-Two and post-World-War-Two-type wars.

Thus *animals* would man kill. Thus *mammals* would man kill. Thus *humans* would man kill.

And in modern times, the extinctions would continue: And in the year one-thousand-seven-hundred-forty-one AD, the Steller's sea cow would be *discovered* near some islands in the Bering Sea. And these ten-meter-giant creatures would be among the most mild-mannered mammals. And unfortunately for them, they would be *not* afraid of man. And when hunters came, the inoffensive creatures would not flee. And *they* would be an easy prey. And so the sea cows would be killed by greedy Russian sealers for their food, their meat being especially tasty to the palate. And for seventeen years, they would be slaughtered unremittingly. And in the year one-thousand-seven-hundred-sixty-eight, the killing would *finally* be stopped. But it would stop not because man realized what he was doing or that the sea cows were in pain – it would stop because the *last* Steller's sea cow would be slain.

And the tarpan, the gray wild horse of southern Russia, would perish in the nineteenth century AD. And the Przewalski's horse, a small reddish-brown wild horse, would *last be seen* on the border of Mongolia and China in the year nineteen-sixty-eight – later, it would be unknown whether it *was* alive or dead.

And the enumeration of victims could go on and on. The list is very long.[352]

And in the twentieth century, man would attack pests with pesticides. And man would attack trees through deforestation. And man would attack insects with insecticides. And man would man attack. And when this happened systematically to a culture or a race, it would be genocide.

---

[352] It has been estimated that the number of species that have gone extinct because of man is in the thousands. Most of these extinctions were not deliberate; they resulted because of the spread of humans throughout the world, occupying the majority of the fertile habitats. The human-induced extinction rate at the onset of the third millennium is about one species per year.

And in the near future, the extermination of *Earth's children* will go on, for man cannot stop it. Man knows that a problem does exist, but his *numbers* are too great. With billions of humans on the Earth, it is too late.

And the Great Eye observed the Earth *from far away* and saw disease. Earth, the living creature, had a cancer, an uncontrollable growth of parasitic cells. At the death of Christ, the Great Eye saw a *two-hundred-million* cells. At a thousand years AD, the Great Eye saw *three-hundred-million* cells. In eighteen-hundred-fifty, the cell-count reached a *billion*. At the onset of the third millennium, it was *six-billion*. The cancer cell was man; the host was Earth. And so Earth had billions of inhabitants *consuming* what it had to give. And the Great Eye saw that the surface of the Earth was scarred with man-made buildings, roads, plowed lands, airports and countless other structures. *Disfigured* was the face of Earth.

The cancer has put *great demands* on Earth.[353] It has weakened and has started to consume the Earth. And like all cancers which are not arrested it will destroy its host unless measures are employed. Both the cancer and the body are at stake.

And what can Nature do? Nature cannot stop the killing. Nature instilled in man the *instincts* that make man act the way he does. In this sense, *it* is Nature's fault. In this sense, Nature indirectly is responsible: Nature and evolution through survival principles made the *desires* and the *wants*. And now the rules cannot be changed. Homo sapiens are creatures copulating *uncontrollably*, producing offspring at *enormous rates*. The laws of evolution thus must run their course.[354]

## Chapter VII: The End of the Pleistocene

It was eight-thousand years BC. The Pleistocene was over. The Holocene began. In geological terms, the time was *almost now*. The Earth was still alive. The next ten-thousand years would constitute the *Recent*. What happened in the Recent *is well known*.

And a line in time was drawn. And it was declared that *that* which was before the line was old. And *that* which was beyond the line was new. And *that* which was old was written in a book. And that book was named *The Old Testament*.

---

[353] Since the beginning of the industrial revolution in the middle of the nineteenth century, man and his machines have poured enough carbon dioxide into the air to increase atmospheric carbon-dioxide levels by twenty-five per cent. The temperature of Earth has gone up one-half degree Celsius. By tinkering with the atmosphere, man has begun to twiddle Earth's thermostat in an unpredictable and potentially dangerous way.

[354] One can only wait until the climax of the crisis finally is reached. Perhaps the quality of life will drop so dramatically that rigorous self-imposed population controls will be put in place. Or perhaps man will turn on man, and kill himself in mass destruction. This would be a final holocaust. And it would terminate the mass extinction caused by man. And then perhaps in the aftermath, one male and one female will remain and will be waiting for the ark. And this will give humanity another start.

*The Last Two Books*

*of the New Testament*

# Prophets

*I will go and see before I die.*

## Chapter I: A King's Last Wish

Now it happened that a twentieth-century king was lying sick in bed. And he called for his twelve prophets. And when they came, he spoke to them. "Behold now, I am old. I know not the day of my death, but it is *soon*. And my body and my mind are weak. But my curiosity is still strong and I want to behold the future before I die. I know what is written: 'The Sun shall be darkened and the Moon shall not give her light.' But *more* I want to know."

## Chapter II: Hosea

And the king asked the first prophet, whose name was Hosea, "What will happen within a hundred years from now?" And Hosea answered, saying, "Particle physicists will have determined what causes electroweak symmetry breaking and so man *will know* what makes mass. Biologists will understand the genetic code of DNA. The amount of carbon dioxide in the atmosphere will increase by fifty per cent, and the Earth will be warmer by two degrees. Astronomers will tell us the composition of *dark matter*."

## Chapter III: Joel

And the king asked the second prophet, whose name was Joel, "What will happen within a thousand years from now?" And Joel answered, saying, "Scientists will construct *entire but primitive* life forms. Astronomers will measure the mass of the Universe sufficiently well as to know its ultimate fate. We will know whether infinitesimal strings govern the behavior of all matter. Physicists will *begin* to understand the Uni-Law in its basic form."

## Chapter IV: Amos

And the king asked the third prophet, whose name was Amos, "What will happen within ten-thousand years from now?" And Amos responded, saying, "Polaris, the present north pole star in the Little Dipper, will *no longer* be the north pole star, for the spin-axis of the Earth will have precessed and will point elsewhere. Vega in the constellation Lyra will be the new pole star. Ye shall look for Vega to find north. The Earth will be cooling and beginning a *new ice age*. Concerning man, man will fabricate sophisticated life forms such as the mammals that existed in the twentieth century, and man will construct new life forms that *never have existed* on the Earth. Humans will occupy and live on other planets of the solar system. Scientists will build an instrument to detect the cosmic relic neutrinos. And the neutrinos will sing a *beautiful* song. And the song they sing will be the song they sang one second after the Big Bang, but they will sing it *softer*. And man will listen to the song and behold the Universe as it was when it was one second old."

## Chapter V: Obadiah

And the king asked the fourth prophet, whose name was Obadiah, "What will happen within one-hundred-thousand years from now?" And Obadiah answered, saying, "The Earth will have reached the final stages of another ice age. Glaciers will have advanced into northern Europe, Asia and the United States. *One-third of the land* on Earth will be *under ice*. Sea level will be one-hundred meters lower than today. But in another twenty-thousand years, the Earth will warm, and an interglacial period, similar to the present, will occur. Science will reach such a sophisticated level of understanding that I cannot explain the advances to thee, except for one: Man will build an instrument to detect the cosmic relic gravitons. And the gravitons will sing a *beautiful* song. And the song they sing will be the song they sang at the Planck time during the Big Bang, but they will sing it *softer*. And man will listen to the song and behold the Universe as it was when it was just created, when it was one tenth of one millionth of one trillionth of one trillionth of one trillionth of a second old."

## Chapter VI: Jonah

And the king asked the fifth prophet, whose name was Jonah, "What will happen within a million years from now?" And Jonah said, "It shall come to pass that life forms which originated on Earth will occupy planets in other stellar systems." And the prophet paused and then added, "Experiments in a test tube will be performed which *reproduce in miniature* the Big Bang. The pieces of the Uni-Law will be partially reassembled. It will be like a broken ancient Egyptian urn which is glued back together. And with the exceptions of some scratches and some tiny holes, it *will* be *whole*. And the perfect sphere of Ultra-Super-Symmetry will be deduced and understood."

## Chapter VII: Micah

And the king asked the sixth prophet, whose name was Micah, "What will happen within ten-million years from now?" And Micah answered, saying, "It shall come to pass that life forms which originated on Earth will engage in battles with life forms which originated elsewhere in a war called the Galactic War of Diverse Origins." The king was amazed. And the prophet added, "And it shall come to pass that on Earth, the continents of North and South America will *stop moving away* from the continents of Africa and Europe. And Africa will have separated from Arabia. And a piece of eastern Africa will have broken off and made an island three-times the size of Madagascar. And the Hawaiian Islands will be *beneath the sea*. And they will be called the Old Hawaiian Seamounts. And to the southeast will be new islands. And these will be called the New Hawaiian Islands. And Baja California and a slither of southwestern California will have *drifted* north and be a long island off the west coast of the United States. And Los Angeles will be west of Sacramento. And Tijuana, Mexico, will be west of Fresno, California."

## Chapter VIII: Nahum

*Tombstones – what be they but monuments*
*to those already dead?*

A nd the king asked the seventh prophet, whose name was Nahum, "What will happen within a hundred-million years from now?" And Nahum answered, saying, "It shall come to pass that Baja California and Los Angeles will have slid into the Aleutian trench south of Alaska. And they will be drawn into the lower crust and *disappear*. And Baja California and Los Angeles will be *lost*. And above them will be mountains. And the mountains will be *like unto* tombstones – testimony of their demise. And elsewhere in the world, the Americas will be approaching Africa and Europe. And the Atlantic Ocean will be *half* its present size. And Australia and New Guinea will have drifted north. And they will be off the coast of Vietnam. And I am sorry to say that a twenty-kilometer-sized comet will have struck the Earth and *caused a mass destruction*. And ninety percent of the life forms on Earth will have been extinguished."

## Chapter IX: Habakkuk

A nd the king asked the eighth prophet, whose name was Habak-kuk, "What will happen within a billion years from now?" And Habakkuk responded, saying, "It shall come to pass that the nearby Sagittarius dwarf galaxy will *crash* into our galaxy, the Milky Way. And it will be a collision of two galaxies. And it will be *like unto* a battle of two armies; the stars will be the soldiers. And destruction on a galactic scale will ensue. And star wars will be real."

## Chapter X: Zephaniah

*The Sun shall be no more thy light by day;*
*neither shall the Moon give thee its light.*

A nd the king asked the ninth prophet, whose name was Zephaniah, "What will happen within ten-billion years from now?" And Zephaniah answered, "It shall come to pass that the Sun will *exhaust its hydrogen fuel.* And its core will contract, and helium will ignite, and an explosion will occur. And the explosion will blow off the outer part of Sun, and the envelope will grow to *engulf* Mercury, Venus and the Earth. And the evening before the helium flash will be the *"last supper" for those on Earth* – the next day all life on Earth will be *no more.* And the Sun will become a red giant star. And the Sun will burn helium as its principal source of energy. And let me mention a few things that will transpire after. It shall come to pass that the Sun will contract over the next few billion years. And the Sun will become a white dwarf with a size *one-hundred* times smaller than its current size. And eventually it will exhaust its nuclear fuels. And the Sun will grow dim and then be *black.* And the Sun will be a brown dwarf – a dense, small, dark body. And the fire in the hearth will be *no more.* And *no longer* will *be* the Sun a star."

## Chapter XI: Haggai

And the king asked the tenth prophet, whose name was Haggai, "What will happen one-hundred-billion years from now?" And Haggai answered, saying, "It shall come to pass that *small black holes* in the Universe will *evaporate and disappear.*"

## Chapter XII: Zechariah

*And the stars of heaven fell unto the Earth,*
*even as a fig tree casteth its untimely figs,*
*when it is shaken by a mighty wind.*
*And the heavens departed*
*as a scroll when it is rolled together.*

And the king asked the eleventh prophet, whose name was Zechariah, "What will happen within a trillion years from now?" And Zechariah answered, saying, "*It shall come to pass* that the Etamitlu[355] Event will have taken place. And the king asked, "What is the Etamitlu Event?" And the prophet replied, "I can tell thee only what is written: 'The stars of heaven shall fall, and the powers that are in heaven shall be shaken.' It will be *Nature's Judgement Day.* And it will *end* the night that began three-hundred-thousand years after the Big Bang. And it is something that twentieth century man cannot understand – small is the mind of man."

## Chapter XIII: Malachi

And the king asked the twelfth and last prophet, whose name was Malachi, "What will happen within ten-trillion years from now?"

---

[355] Pronounced "ee-TAM-mit-lu."

And Malachi responded, saying, "It is strange. I see *nothing*. I don't know why." And the prophet paused and then added, "My king, in ten days thou will die."

And the king was both pleased and disappointed. And in ten days did he die.

## Chapter XIV: Postscript

A nd in the future, man will better understand the Universe of ancient times. And the *point at which man's understanding starts* will sooner start. Thus as man in time moves forward, he *shall* look *further* back.

*In walking forward, he shall walk back.*

And in the future, man will become an artist and creator of life itself. And he will capture the *spirit of Nature* that instilled into complex molecules the *spirit of life*.

And in the end, Heaven and Earth shall pass away. And all things, *which are material and physical*, shall disappear. But the Uni-Law shall still remain.

# The Last Commandment

*Ask and it shall be given.*
*Seek and ye shall find.*
*Knock and it shall be opened.*

*This is the* last commandment.
*the final Word.*

## Chapter I: "So"

*Speak to the Earth and it shall teach thee.*

So thou shall recognize thy destiny – so thou shall know it well. So thou shall take thy ship and steer it in a *just path*. Put desire behind motivation and be driven.

So let curiosity be thy guide. Seek truth in Heaven as on Earth.

Do not let the *water* slip between the fingers of thy hands.

So thou shall take the pledge to *seek* the truth, the whole truth, and nothing but the truth, so help ye God.

So dare to do what thou might not dare *to do*. So go to where thou might not dare *to go*.

And pick a path among the paths. Pick it wisely. Pick it justly. Act thus so.

So be *consumed* by knowledge. So be *consumed* by creativity.

So contemplate the *sacred letters*, from Aleph to Tau. They are Aleph, Beth, Gimel, Daleth, He, Vau, Zain, Cheth, Teth, Jod, Caph, Lamed, Mem, Nun, Samech, Ain, Pe, Tzaddi, Koph, Resh, Schin and Tau.

So thou shall understand the law. So thou shall see it. So thou shall thus obey the law. So be it.

## Chapter II: "Know"

*And when thou seest the Sun, and the Moon, and the stars,*
*even all the hosts of Heaven,*
*shouldest then thou be driven to worship them.*

And *know* the Universe from large to small. Know the Universe from Z to A. Know the laws of Nature from tau to aleph. Know the history of the World *from alpha to omega*. Know this, know more, know all.

And know the *natural* history: the beginning and the Big Bang. Know the transitions of the past from electroweak breaking to Recombination. Know the destruction. Know star formation. Know these and know them well. And know *the light*.

Know *it*. Know what *it* is. And know that *it* be written in the rock and that *it* be embedded in a cell.

And know the elements. *Know* how they be made. And know the almighty alchemists: the early Universe, the supernovas and the stars.

The *foundation for biology* has been laid. Build there thyself a temple. And when thy temple has been built, know that ye shall find *great riches* there.

And know the difference between plant and animal. Know the difference between animal and mammal. And know the *origin* of thy origins. Know the ape, the monkey and the chimpanzee. Know the *metamorphosis* of the monarch butterfly. Know what was, what is and what will be.

And know *thy place* on Earth. And know where be the Earth among the planets. And where be the Sun within the Milky Way. And where be the Milky Way within the Universe. And know the vastness of the Universe. Thus know *thy place* within the Universe.

Try to hold truth in thy hand. It shall *be like unto* water. The water in thy hand shall try to slip through thy fingers to the sand. Know that thou shall need to *press together firmly* the fingers of thy hand.

Turn to the skies and stare. Heaven, stars, planets and the Universe are there.

> *Know thy constellations.*
> *Know that Cygnus be a swan*
> *and that she fly so.*
> *And know that Aries be a ram*
> *and that he wander so.*
> *Know that Pisces be the fishes.*
> *Know that Taurus be a bull.*
> *And recognize that Andromeda, the princess,*
> *rides the back of Pegasus, the flying horse.*
> *Know that the constellations have an influence.*
> *Know that Gemini be twins.*
> *Know that Libra be the balance.*
> *Know that Hercules be the strong son of Zeus*
> *and that Perseus be the heroic son of Zeus.*
> *Recognize the half-man half-horse archer in the sky –*
> *he be Sagittarius.*
> *Know that Aquarius pours its waters on the Earth.*
> *Know Canis Major, the greater dog.*
> *And know Canis Minor, the lesser dog.*
> *And know Aquila, the eagle.*
> *Know that Boötes be the guardian of bears,*
> *that the horned goat be Capricorn*
> *and that Cepheus be a king of Ethiopia.*
> *Know that Cassiopeia be an "M" in winter and a "W" in summer.*
> *Know that the largest constellation in the sky be Hydra,*
> *the water monster.*
> *Recognize Orion – he be the hunter.*
> *Know that the big dipper be Ursa Major, the greater bear*
> *And that the little dipper be Ursa Minor, the lesser bear.*

> *Know that Corona Borealis be the northern crown.*
> *Know that Lepus be the hare,*
> *And that Lyra be the lyre.*
> *And know that Scorpio be the scorpion,*
> *that Sextans be the sextant,*
> *that Draco be the dragon*
> *and that Serpens be the serpent.*
> *And know that Delphinus be the dolphin,*
> *that Cancer be the crab,*
> *that Virgo be the virgin*
> *and that Leo be the lion.*

The microworlds contain *great riches*. The skies contain *salvation*. Know that these are so.

> *Have faith in thyself and in thy science.*
> *Study Nature and make of it a science and an art.*
> *Take science and make of it a doctrine.*
> *Thou shall be consumed by it.*
> *It shall be like blood in thy own heart.*
> *Knowledge shall be the sacred crown.*
> *Wear it upon thy head.*
> *Nature, knowledge, science and thou –*
> *till death do thee part.*

Know that thy beats be *measured*.

## Chapter III: "Go"

> *Go, let us build a tower,*
> *whose top may reach to Heaven.*

*N*ature has spoken. Here are *Her* words. Go my children. Be curious and learn. When thou see a rainbow, know that it be the refraction of *a little light*. When thou see a face in a mirror, know that it be thy face – know thy *reflection*.

Go, my children, and build thyselves a microscope. And when thou see a fuzzy gel, know *that it be a cell*. And when thou see *some motion*, know that it be a protozoon or amoeba. And try to understand. And try to understand the accident of *life*.

Go, my children, and find the *Holy Way*. Know the breath of life. Know the body. Know the cell. Know the organelle. Go and decipher the secret code, the code of life, the code of DNA.

Go, my children, and build thyselves a telescope. And with thy eye and telescope go scrutinize the sky. Peer at the Universe. It shall be *music* to thine eyes – thine eyes shall be like ears which hear a little verse. When thou see the Moon, know that it be made of rock. And when thou see the four small lights near Jupiter, know that they be its Galilean moons. And go observe the planets and know them. Know

Pluto and Uranus. Know Mercury and Mars. Know Neptune, Saturn, Jupiter and Venus. And go *explore* the stars. See Antares, Betelgeuse, Capella, Deneb, Regulus, Vega, Spica, Rigel and Arcturus. And know that Alpha Centuri be the *nearest star*. And know that Sirius be the *brightest star*. And know Polaris be the north, *at least for now*. And know that Algol winks at thee. And go and explore the heavens. And when thou see the fuzzy glow in Hercules, know that it be a sphere of a *hundred-thousand stars*. And when thou see the ring in Lyra, know that it be a nebula. Reach to the heavens and try to slip it on thy finger. And the fuzzy glow in Orion, know that it be not a star but a cloud of gas – the Great Nebula is it. And in Taurus see the seven sisters, the Pleiades, and know they be an open cluster. Know that the seventh star is faint, for she is Merope and *ashamed* to show her face. And go and see the haze in the great constellation of Andromeda, and know that it be our nearest spiral galaxy. And the *milky incandescent white* which sweeps through Cygnus on the clearest blackest night, know that it be rays of light from our own galaxy, the Milky Way.

Go, my children. Obey and know the laws. Let us pray for them. Pray for the four forces. Pray for the pull of gravity beneath thy feet. Go and *feel* the gravity beneath thy feet. Know the neutron and its weak decay. Know that in a proton be there three quarks held together by *the strong force*. Know the needle of a compass and the current in a wire. Know that these forces are the forces of desire.

Go, my children, and stare at the starry black. And when thou see a shooting star, know that it be but just a grain of dust that burns.

Go, observe, and *weigh thy Universe*. To know its weight shall be to know its fate, for if its weight be *less* than critical, thy Universe *forever* is – it will expand forever. But even if it be forever, it will, just like a living creature, age. And in old age will it be cold. And in coldness will it die a *slow steady death*. A death from entropy will so prevail. But if its weight be *more* than critical, thy Universe is *not forever* – it will collapse like a giant star before its supernova burst. And this will be the *Second Coming* – the Big Crunch; the Big Bang will occur again but in reverse. And the World will reheat, shrink in size, die and disappear. So go and weigh thy Universe.[356]

And go and build a satellite. And go and build a cyclotron. And try to see. And try to hear. And try to feel. And *try to understand*.

Go cultivate thy curiosity. Go stimulate the "forces" in thee far. Go *grow thy knowledge* far. Go reap thy inspiration. And go and do what John Donne has done: *Go and catch a falling star*.

---

[356] The twentieth century poet Robert Frost would have the insight to see that the world must end in one of these two fates in his poem *Fire and Ice*: If the mass is more than critical, then the world will end in fire. But if the mass is less than critical, then the world will end in ice.

## Chapter IV (Psalm VIII):
## What Be a Man Who Knoweth Nature?

And this is the psalm for the eighth day, which is the last day of the leap week. And when the leap week and eighth day come, *ye* shall *know* it.

*What be a man who knoweth Nature?*
*A man among the few who cannot lose his way,*
*for all around him Nature hath provided signs and clues.*
*And the Sun warmeth him at day; and the Moon cooleth him at night –*
*So day be pleasant; so night be pleasant too.*
*But when a night be cold, useth he a fire and flame for heat,*
*the same old flame and fire which giveth light.*
*And when he walketh, it be a moist kind soil beneath his feet.*
*And the Moon and stars be always there to light the night.*
*The man, who knoweth Nature, understandeth the meanings*
*of Earth's rivers, winds and rocks.*
*And he appreciateth that the World should be a land*
*in which the lion and the lamb can live together.*
*And so he be a shepherd of the flocks,*
*hitherto, for now, forever.*
*And when shouteth he for help –*
*it be his inner voice and wisdom which do answer.*
*And in every tree there be a bird that sings to him.*
*There even be for him* meaning *in the sound of wind;*
*for he be a man whose knowledge be well rooted.*
*What be a man who knoweth Nature?*
*A man whose every footstep be sure-footed.*

*He doth sit beneath the fig tree and doth meditate.*
*And a strange mist doth swirl about his head.*
*And of the World around him doth he contemplate.*
*And he be at peace within himself and with the Universe.*
*Now night for him be normal and be natural, as natural as day itself,*
*for night be part of day and candles light the way.*
*And knoweth he what be on river's other side – and he not be afraid.*
*He knoweth where all bridges be.*
*And with Nature doth he live in harmony.*
*And when the day be hot, in a cool cave doth he dwell.*
*Seeth he a good path through the desert*
*and where there be a water well.*
*For him, even a dry desert holdeth pleasures:*
*Lizards, snakes and creeping creatures be some of Nature's masterpieces.*
*In every land on Earth there be great treasures.*
*The man who knoweth never thirsteth for a rain;*
*yet he always hungereth to know.*

*To him, paths in wooded lands present a pleasant set of possibilities.*
*And knoweth he which way to go.*
*What be a man who understandeth Nature's universal laws?*
*A man who ageth but doth not get old,*
*for he learneth in the morning, for he learneth in the evening,*
*as he learneth all his life.*
*He be a man whose soul cannot be sold.*
*To him, all things have meanings.*
*And Nature's plants and animals do bring him happiness.*
*What be a man who knoweth these Great Things?*
*A being blessed in blissfulness.*

## Chapter V: The Final Word

*Thy faith hath saved thee: go in peace.*

So know the Universe as it be now. And know that it be *vast and black*. And know that it be *cold and almost endless*. And know that it be full of *countless* galaxies but that *most* of it be void. So the galaxies *be* filled with a hundred-billion stars. So the stars do shed their *little light*. And from this little light *ye see*. So take with thee the light of Nature and go forth.

# Index/Glossary

The italicized words in this index are defined in context in *The Bible According to Einstein*.